Manual de gramática

2nd EDITION

Eleanor Dozier

Zulma Iguina

CORNELL UNIVERSITY

HH **HEINLE & HEINLE PUBLISHERS, INC.**
BOSTON, MASSACHUSETTS 02116 U.S.A.

I(T)P® **AN INTERNATIONAL THOMSON PUBLISHING COMPANY**

Boston • New York • London • Bonn • Detroit • Madrid • Melbourne • Mexico City •
Paris • San Francisco • Singapore • Tokyo • Toronto • Washington • Albany NY •
Belmont CA • Cincinnati OH

The publication of **Manual de gramática, Second Edition,** was directed by the members of the Heinle & Heinle College Foreign Language Publishing Team:

Wendy Nelson, Editorial Director
Tracie Edwards, Market Development Director
Gabrielle B. McDonald, Production Services Coordinator
Stephen Frail, Developmental Editor

Also participating in the publication of this program were:
Publisher: Vincent Duggan
Project Manager: Christine E. Wilson, IBC
Associate Market Development Director: Kristen Murphy
Production Assistant: Lisa LaFortune
Manufacturing Coordinator: Wendy Kilborn
Compositor: Christine E. Wilson, IBC
Cover Design: Design Five and Ha Nguyen
Interior Design: Design Five

Clip art from Macromedia Freehand was used in the production of this ancillary.

Second edition ISBN: 0-8384-9832-9
10 9 8 7 6 5 4 3 2

Contents

Chapter 2 Nouns and Noun Determiners 25

Chapter 3 Pronouns 53

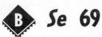

Chapter 4 Prepositions, Adverbs, and Conjunctions ... 101

 Prepositions 102

Chapter 5 Verbs: Formation ... 147

A Indicative Mood 148

Chapter 6 Verbs: Usage 175

Chapter 7 Ser, Estar, Haber, Hacer, and Tener ... 257

Preface

The place of grammar in the foreign language curriculum has changed. Language textbooks contain mostly abbreviated segments on grammatical points and lexical difficulties, dispersed throughout the text in proximity to situations, themes, functions, or tasks where they may be of use. The positive significance of this primary focus on the intent and content of the message rather than on the accuracy of form *per se* is undeniable. However, when the student has to write a paper, and needs to look up a form or a usage, the context-oriented textbook is inadequate.

Accordingly, we have constructed what we consider to be a useful tool for the intermediate level student who needs a clear and simple reference to grammar. Our intention has been to provide the student with a means to understand the sometimes complex and subtle conceptual distinctions between English and Spanish, and, when there is no graspable concept involved, to clearly perceive particular differences between the two.

NOTES ON THE SECOND EDITION

Our goals in preparing this second edition were the following: to correct and clarify the explanations wherever we were aware of the need, to prepare a more balanced and varied set of exercises, and, last but not least, to provide clear cross-references between related chapters and between chapters and their respective exercises.

We are grateful to Heinle and Heinle, and the numerous anonymous reviewers who have helped us in this effort to improve the *Manual*. In addition, we are immensely grateful to Margarita Suñer for her support and guidance, and to our colleagues at Cornell and elsewhere who help us make this a better tool: David Cruz de Jesús, Luis Morató Peña, Judith Némethy, Miriam Rice, Jeannine Routier Pucci, and Amalía Stratakos Tió. We owe special thanks to both Carmen Sualdea, a reviewer, and to Ana V. Ras, copyeditor and native reader, for their very helpful suggestions with specific references. Although we have not been able to implement all of the suggestions, they have all served a most positive function. We are also grateful to Gabrielle McDonald for assigning this project to Christine E. Wilson of IBC. In her role as project manager and compositor, she proved to be as precise as any author could hope for in her critiques of this work. We would also like to thank the proofreaders, Patrice Titterington and Margaret Hines, whose attention to detail has helped make this textbook as accurate as possible. Most of all, we are in debt to our students, who have helped us through their dialogue with us to see what helps and what does not when it comes to illustrating clearly the workings of this language for them to be able to better understand and use it.

We consider that this text is just one step in an ongoing process requiring the full involvement of motivated students and teachers in a dialogue that should focus not on the learning of rules for the sake of learning rules, but rather on helping to clarify the content of the message the individual wishes to comprehend or to communicate.

We would appreciate any feedback from users of this edition, students and instructors alike, to help us further improve it. Send us your comments to the Department of Modern Languages, 203 Morrill Hall, Cornell University, Ithaca, NY 14853, or e-mail us at ed15@cornell.edu or zi10@cornell.edu.

Eleanor Dozier and Zulma Iguina

REVIEWERS

Peter R. Alfieri, Salve Regina University
Tamara Al-Kasey, Carnegie Mellon University
Dennis Perri, Grinnel College
Suzanne Tierney Gula, University of Delaware
Richard Curry, Texas A&M University
Michael Morris, Northern Illinois University
Judith Némethy, New York University
John D. Nesbitt, Eastern Wyoming College
Teresa Smotherman, University of Georgia
Dan Adams, Snow College
Oswaldo A. López, Miami Dade Community College
Tina Lopez Snideman, Sante Fe Community College
Deborah Baldini, University of Missouri, St. Louis
Guadeloupe Gomez, University of Texas, El Paso
Kathleen Wheatley, University of Wisconsin, Madison
Timothy Murad, University of Vermont
Barbara Gonzalez-Pino, University of Texas, San Antonio
Graciela Crvalan, Webster University
Lucrecia Artalejo, Northeastern Illinois University
Gerardo Lorenzino, Yale University

SOME LANGUAGE CHOICES

For reasons of personal preference in some cases, and to avoid confusion in other instances, we have made the following choices.

1. We have chosen to use the accent on *sólo* as an adverb and on non-neutral demonstrative pronouns (*ése, éste, aquél,* etc.), even where there is no ambiguity.

2. We have opted for the use of *lo* as direct object, human or not, and of *le* in the case of human direct objects with the impersonal *se.* We have tried to avoid situations where other dialects may be in conflict.

3. We have used the verb tense and mood nomenclature closest to the English, so it is more recognizable for the students. Students wishing to become familiar with the standard terminology used in texts in the Spanish-speaking world may wish to take note of the following differences.

English Terminology	*Manual* Terminology	Spanish Terminology
Imperfect	Imperfecto	Pretérito Imperfecto
Preterite	Pretérito	Pretérito Indefinido
Pluperfect	Pluscuamperfecto	Pretérito Pluscuamperfecto
Present Perfect	Presente Perfecto	Pretérito Perfecto
Conditional	Condicional	Potencial
Conditional Present	Condicional Presente	Potencial Simple
Conditional Perfect	Condicional Perfecto	Potencial Compuesto

REFERENCES

Following is an intentionally skeletal bibliography of those published texts that we consider indispensable reference tools. To this list needs to be added that of the articles published continually in professional journals, which contribute to our evolving perspective of the field, as well as the unpublished dialogue with other human beings, professional and not, which informs our thinking on the subject of communication in different languages.

Alarcos Llorach, E. et al. *Lengua española.* Madrid: Santillana, 1981.

Bello, A. *Gramática.* Caracas: Ediciones del Ministerio de Educación, 1972.

Bull, W. *Spanish for Teachers.* Ronald, 1965.

Campos, H. *De la oración simple a la oración compuesta.* Georgetown University Press, 1993.

de Bruyne, J. *A Comprehensive Spanish Grammar.* Blackwell, 1995.

Gili Gaya, S. *Curso superior de sintaxis española.* Barcelona: Vox, 1964.

King, L. D. and Suñer, M. *Gramática española: Análisis y práctica.* McGraw-Hill. Forthcoming.

Lázaro, F. *Curso de lengua española.* Madrid: Ediciones Anaya, 1983.

Real Academia Española. *Gramática de la lengua española.* Madrid: Espasa-Calpe, 1931.

Real Academia Española. *Esbozo de una nueva gramática de la lengua española.* Madrid: Espasa-Calpe, 1991.

Seco, R. *Diccionario de dudas y dificultades de la lengua castellana.* Madrid: Espasa-Calpe, 1986.

Seco, R. *Manual de gramática española.* Aguilar, 1988.

CHANGES IN THE SECOND EDITION

Those who are familiar with the first edition will find the following changes.

Chapter 1

- Nominal clause definition—corrected (we owe this to Carmen Sualdea and her reference to F. Lázaro)
- Accent rules for *sólo* and *éste* (we owe these to Ana Ras and her reference to R. Seco)

Chapter 2

- Nominalized words and phrases—expanded
- Personal *a*—expanded
- Definite articles—expansion on the absence of the article and word order
- Adjectives that commonly precede the noun—expanded list *(primer, segundo, tercer,* etc.; *algún, varios; ambos; mucho, poco; tanto; otro)*
- Descriptive adjectives that change meaning depending upon placement—expanded list *(bueno, diferente, medio, puro, único)*

Chapter 3

- Transitive and intransitive distinction—expanded and corrected (the correction we owe to Carmen Sualdea and her reference to F. Lázaro)
- Differences between *usted* and *tú*—expanded
- Subject pronoun absence in Spanish—expanded
- Stressed and unstressed object pronouns—expanded
- Impersonal *se*—expanded explanation of the contrast between passives in English and in Spanish (we owe this to Jeannine Routier-Pucci)
- Possessive pronouns—added specificity of *de usted, de él,* etc.
- Interrogatives—clarification of *¿qué?* vs. *¿cuál?* (we owe this to Miriam Rice)
- Word order with direct and indirect interrogation—added
- Relative pronouns—correction of *cuyo* information (we owe this to Carmen Sualdea and her reference to E. Alarcos)

Chapter 4

- Adverbs—addition

Chapter 5

- Change of numbering system from 1,2,3 to A,B,C
- Cross references to Usage of these verb forms in Chapter 6

Chapter 6

- Change of numbering system from 1,2,3 to A,B,C
- Cross references to Formation in Chapter 5
- Special note on different uses and translations of "would"—addition
- Verbs of state or nonaction—expanded clarification
- Table "More about the Imperfect"—relocated to go just after segment on verbs of state
- Pluperfect—added after preterite and imperfect

- Modal auxiliaries—added at the end of Compound tenses
- Future vs. progressive—expanded
- Subjunctive: nonuse of subjunctive in nominal clauses—added (this we owe to Jeannine Routier-Pucci)
- Subjunctive: word order in adjectival clauses—added
- Subjunctive: graphic on sequence of tenses—explained
- *Gustar* word order—added
- Indirect discourse word order—added

Chapter 7

- *Ser* vs. *Estar;* explanation—added (we owe this to Margarita Suñer and her reference to W. Bull)
- *Estar* vs. *Haber*—added
- Passive: special note on differences between English and Spanish (we owe this to Jeannine Routier-Pucci)

Chapter 8

- In the first edition, this was Appendix 1
- Used numbers instead of letters to list separate items
- Sorted alphabetically
- Apply—added *aplicación, solicitud*
- Ask—added *pedido, cuestión*
- At—several additions
- Attend—several additions
- Because—added *gracias a*
- But—added *sin embargo*
- Learn—added *averiguar*
- Meet—expanded
- Put—expanded

END MATTER

The order of the end matter material has been altered in this edition. The first section now contains the exercises, while the second one contains the verb tables. The Answer Key now appears at the end of the book in a perforated section, for those instructors who prefer to have students remove it.

The first edition had an imbalance in the number of exercises provided for each chapter, and for parts of chapters. For this edition, we have corrected this imbalance, as well as prepared a greater variety of formats of exercises. We have added review exercises and essay topics for those who wish to assign them.

The most practical change we have made in the exercises may be the numbering system. In this second edition, each exercise has a distinct number, starting with the number of the chapter it relates to, and followed by a number from one to the total number of exercises for that chapter. This improved numbering system and cross-referencing will make navigation from chapter to exercise to answer key and back much easier. (Within chapters, we have added references [inside brackets] to exercises relating to the specific chapter segment.) The icon used to denote references to the *Ejercicios* section is as follows:

DESCRIPTION OF USES OF THIS *Manual*

For those who are considering adopting this text for the first time, we offer the following suggestions for use.

Students at the intermediate level use this *Manual:*

- as assigned by the instructor, or by self-diagnosed need, to review grammar or lexical points
- as assigned by the instructor, or by self-diagnosed need, to practice grammar and lexical points with self-correcting exercises to determine the level of comprehension attained, and consequent possible need for further clarification or practice
- as directed by instructor as pre-reading or pre-listening focus on form, to review grammar or lexical points used in high frequency in materials to be covered
- as self-diagnosed need when outside materials present an obstacle in a grammar or lexical point, as a reference tool for clarification of usage
- as directed by instructor feedback or self-diagnosed need, as a reference tool to improve accuracy in oral or written production
- as a verb form check when writing the language (Verb Tables, pages 427–463)

Instructors of the intermediate level make use of this *Manual* in different manners as well.

- One way is to assign grammar or lexical points to review or to study. The order in which they make their assignments depends upon the type of syllabus they create. If their course offers a grammar review and is centered on communication in typical conversational contexts, the instructor might create a syllabus assigning a grammar point or two per week that is related to the content of the topic of the week. An example of such a set of weekly assignments follows.

  Week 1: Sentence components and verb structure (Chapter 1.A and B); Interrogatives (Chapter 3.D); Exclamatives (Chapter 3.E)

Week 2: Accents (Chapter 1.D); Lexical Variations (Chapter 8)

Week 3: Past tenses form and usage (Chapter 5.A.2; Chapter 6.B)

Week 4: *Ser / Estar,* etc. (Chapter 7); *Gustar* (Chapter 6.I)

Week 5: Personal Pronouns: subject; direct, indirect, and prepositional object (Chapter 3.A)

Week 6: Nouns and noun determiners: Articles: definite and indefinite; personal *a* (Chapter 2.A, B.1)

Week 7: Adjectives (Chapter 2.B.2)

Week 8: Prepositions (Chapter 4.A)

Week 9: *Se* (Chapter 3.B)

Week 10: Conditional form and usage (Chapter 5.B; Chapter 6.E and G.6)

Week 11: Relative Pronouns (Chapter 3.G)

Week 12: Subjunctive form and usage (Chapter 5.C, Chapter 6.G)

Instructors who use the *Manual* this way have students use the exercises in the book for practice, and then give them homework exercises, which incorporate what they have reviewed in grammar with the rest of the material they are covering in class. These exercises created by instructors are most often related to the topic being discussed in class, and with the readings. A variety of formats may be used, from analysis of relevant lexical or grammatical aspects of the text being read to essays, and going through the gamut of exercise formats we are all familiar with, such as fill-in-the-blank, substitution, question-answer, transformation, translation, etc. The format and quantity of exercises offered by the instructor vary with the focus of the course and the time allotted for correction of the material.

• The *Manual* is also used for courses that are structured around individualized work, to guide each student in review of specific areas of need, in the feedback provided for written work or oral work, for example. If a given student has particular difficulty with accents or the forms of the preterite, (s)he can be directed to review the appropriate pages in the *Manual* and practice with the self-correcting exercises; some instructors have students explain why certain mistakes they make are in fact wrong, using the *Manual* as guidance for the explanation. Under this type of format no syllabus is used, but rather each student is guided based on his or her particular needs. Students might be asked to analyze their own corrected assignments and determine the frequency of their errors, so as to become more aware of their own needs and be more motivated to seek the guidance of the *Manual.* Instructors using this format might grade for progress, and in so doing, give students more of an incentive to understand and to improve.

- Another use of this *Manual* is as a self-help tool for students who are working outside of a classroom structure, or in a course where language is not the focus. We often have students who want to brush up their Spanish before going abroad to work, and who want to review their grammar; they don't want to take classes, either because they don't have time or the funds, but would like to practice with self-correcting exercises. The students who have used the *Manual* for this purpose have indicated to us that it is very useful to them, and that they continue to use it once they are "in the field." Other students who have used the *Manual* as a self-help tool are those who take literature classes, or classes in any area abroad, and need to write papers in Spanish for these courses. Many students with a Spanish major have told us that they have found this text to be very useful as a reference tool in their advanced courses.

- The *Manual* also serves to provide instructors in training with a greater clarity in their analytic knowledge of the language. This is not an advanced grammar text, and yet its simple and clear explanations are useful in that they provide a focus on the contrastive presentation of grammar points designed for the English-speaking student, as well as a focus on dialectal variety. Even experienced instructors reach for the *Manual* to refresh their memory as to certain rules, or to make a point in a discussion on grammar; native speakers of the language find in it the diversity of dialects other than their own, as well as a focus on the contrasting English usage.

Chapter 1

Overview

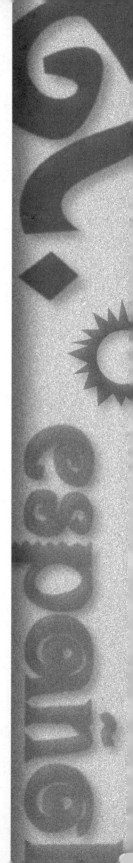

1

◆A Sentence Components

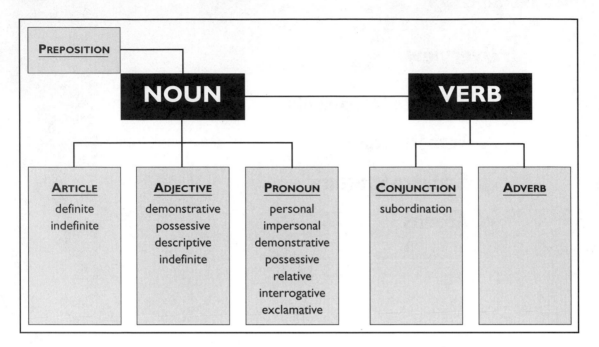

A sentence is a self-contained unit of communication that may be formed with combinations of the following eight types of words: nouns, verbs, prepositions, articles, adjectives, pronouns, conjunctions, and adverbs. Each of these types of words has its own particular function to perform in a sentence.

NOUN: may serve as the subject of a verb, its direct or indirect object, or the object of a preposition. In Spanish, equivalents of nouns (i.e., words or groupings of words that may have the same grammatical functions as a noun) are pronouns, infinitives, and nominalized words or groups of words.

VERB: the grammatical core of a sentence; expresses an action or state. Its form changes in agreement with subject, tense, mood, aspect, and voice.

ARTICLE: accompanies and modifies as to specificity a noun or its equivalent.

ADJECTIVE: accompanies and modifies a noun or its equivalent.

ADVERB: modifies a verb, an adjective, another adverb, or a sentence.

PRONOUN: is used to avoid repeating a noun whose reference is clear.

PREPOSITION: relates a noun or its equivalent to another noun, to the verb, or to the rest of the sentence.

CONJUNCTION: joins two parts of a sentence. Conjunctions of subordination introduce subordinate clauses.

The following table enlarges on what we have just covered and gives the Spanish terms.

WORD TYPE	TIPO DE PALABRA	SUBCATEGORÍAS Y EJEMPLOS	GRAMMATICAL FUNCTION	FUNCIÓN GRAMATICAL
Noun	Nombre o sustantivo	Propio (España...)	Subject; direct/indirect object; prepositional object	Sujeto; objeto directo/indirecto; objeto de preposición
		Común (libro...)		
Pronoun	Pronombre	Personal (yo, me, mí...)	Same as the noun	Igual que el nombre
		Impersonal (se, uno...)		
		Demostrativo (eso, esto...)		
		Posesivo (el mío, el tuyo...)		
		Interrogativo (¿qué?, ¿quién?...)		
		Exclamativo (¡qué!, ¡quién!...)		
		Indefinido (alguien, algo...)		
		Relativo (que, el que, cuyo...)	Replaces the noun and introduces a relative clause. Subject or object of verb in the subordinate clause, or prepositional object	Reemplaza el nombre e introduce una cláusula relativa. Sujeto u objeto del verbo de la cláusula subordinada, u objeto de preposición
Article	Artículo	Definido (el, la; los, las)	Accompanies and modifies the noun or its equivalent	Acompaña y modifica el nombre o su equivalente
		Indefinido (un, una; unos, unas)		

WORD TYPE	TIPO DE PALABRA	SUBCATEGORÍAS Y EJEMPLOS	GRAMMATICAL FUNCTION	FUNCIÓN GRAMATICAL
Adjective	Adjetivo	Calificativo (*verde, grande...*)	Accompanies and modifies the noun or its equivalent	Acompaña y modifica el nombre o su equivalente
		Demostrativo (*ese, esta...*)		
		Posesivo (*mi, tu, su...*)		
		Indefinido (*algún, ningún...*)		
Preposition	Preposición	(*a, de, en, por, para, con, desde...*)	Introduces the noun or its equivalent	Introduce el nombre o su equivalente
Verb	Verbo	Transitivo/ Intransitivo	Provides action or description; is the core of the sentence	Proporciona acción o descripción; es el núcleo de la frase
		1ª, 2ª, 3ª conjugación		
Adverb	Adverbio	(*rápidamente, bien, mal, muy...*)	Modifies a verb, an adjective, another adverb, or a sentence	Modifica un verbo, un adjetivo, otro adverbio o una frase
Conjunction	Conjunción	De coordinación (*y, o, pero, sino...*)	Links two parts of speech or clauses	Une dos palabras o grupos de palabras
		De subordinación (*que, aunque...*)	Introduces a subordinate clause	Introduce una cláusula subordinada

Ejercicios 1.1–1.2, página 304

Verb Structure

MODO	MOOD	TIEMPO Y ASPECTO	EJEMPLO	EXAMPLE
Infinitivo	*Infinitive*	Presente	**estudiar**	to study
		Perfecto	**haber estudiado**	to have studied
Participio	*Participle*	Presente	**estudiando**	studying
		Pasado	**estudiado**	studied
Indicativo	*Indicative*	Presente	**estudio**[1]	I study
		Presente perfecto	**he estudiado**	I have studied
		Futuro	**estudiaré**	I will study
		Futuro perfecto	**habré estudiado**	I will have studied
		Pretérito	**estudié**	I studied
		Imperfecto	**estudiaba**	I studied, would study, was studying
		Pluscuamperfecto	**había estudiado**	I had studied
Condicional[2]	*Conditional*	Presente	**estudiaría**	I would study
		Perfecto	**habría estudiado**	I would have studied
Subjuntivo	*Subjunctive*	Presente	**estudie**	
		Presente perfecto	**haya estudiado**	
		Imperfecto	**estudiara**	
		Pluscuamperfecto	**hubiera estudiado**	
Imperativo	*Imperative*	(sólo una forma)	**¡Estudien!**	Study!

PRÁCTICA

Ejercicio 1.3, páginas 304–305

---

1. The examples for the indicative, conditional, and subjunctive are given in the first-person singular *(yo)*. The example for the imperative is given in the *ustedes* form.

◆ Sentence Structure

A sentence may be composed of one or many clauses. These clauses can be identified by the fact that they have a verb that is conjugated (not in the infinitive or participle form).

Ejercicio 1.4, página 305

I. INDEPENDENT CLAUSES

Independent clauses are not dependent upon another, nor do they have other clauses depending upon them. They may be found alone …

> **Conocimos a Juan en la fiesta.**
> *We met John at the party.*

or they may be attached to one another by means of conjunctions of coordination.

> **Conocimos a Juan en la fiesta y hablamos con él sobre la universidad.**
> *We met John at the party and spoke with him about the university.*

2. MAIN OR PRINCIPAL CLAUSES

A main clause is a clause that could be independent by its meaning, but that has one or more clauses that are its dependents.

> <u>**Vamos a quedarnos en un hotel**</u> **para que nuestros amigos no se incomoden.**
> *We are going to stay in a hotel so that our friends are not inconvenienced.*

3. DEPENDENT OR SUBORDINATE CLAUSES

In Spanish, a subordinate or dependent clause is introduced by a subordinating conjunction or adverbial phrase *(que, porque, cuando, tan pronto como…)* or by a relative pronoun *(que, el que, lo que, cuyo…)*. Dependent clauses **depend** upon a main clause. The relationship of the dependent clause to the main clause varies according to the type of dependent clause: nominal, adverbial, or adjectival.

---

2. Some grammarians consider the conditional to be a tense of the indicative mood, not a mood in itself. Because it is used for contexts that are modally different from those in which other moods are used, and because it has two tenses itself, we have chosen to consider it a mood. The only situation where it could be considered a tense of the indicative is when it is used as a future of the past.

A **nominal** clause is one that behaves like a noun and can serve the function of subject, direct object of the verb of the main clause, or object of a preposition.

> **Quiero pan.**   *I want bread.*
>
> **Quiero que me ayudes.**   *I want you to help me.*

Both *pan* and *que me ayudes* function in these sentences as the direct object of the main verb *Quiero*.

An **adverbial** clause is one that behaves like an adverb and modifies the verb of the main clause by indicating manner (how?), purpose (what for?), reason (why?), time (when?), condition (under what condition?), etc.

> **Salió rápidamente.**   *She left quickly.*
>
> **Salió tan pronto como pudo.**   *She left as soon as she could.*

Both *rápidamente* and *tan pronto como pudo* modify the main verb *Salió* by indicating how the action took place.

An **adjectival** clause behaves like an adjective and modifies a noun. Adjectival clauses are also called relative clauses because they always begin with a relative pronoun, which replaces a noun in the main clause (its antecedent) and introduces the subordinate clause that modifies the antecedent.

> **Quiero leer una novela divertida.**
> *I want to read a fun novel.*
>
> **Quiero leer una novela que me haga reír.**
> *I want to read a novel that will make me laugh.*

Both *divertida* and *que me haga reír* modify the noun *novela*.

English/Spanish Terminology

ENGLISH	SPANISH
sentence	*frase, oración*
phrase	*expresión*
clause	*cláusula*
main clause	*cláusula principal*
subordinate or dependent clause	*cláusula subordinada*
independent clause	*cláusula independiente*
relative clause	*cláusula relativa*

TYPE OF CLAUSE	SUBCATEGORY	INTRODUCED BY	FUNCTION
Independent		(Nothing)	(Exists on its own)
Main clause		(Nothing)	(Could exist on its own)
Subordinate	Nominal	Conjunction of subordination	Subject or direct object of verb of main clause
	Adverbial	Conjunction of subordination or adverbial phrase	Modifies the verb of the main clause, by describing manner, purpose, reason, time, condition, etc.
	Adjectival	Relative pronoun	Modifies the antecedent of the relative pronoun

The following chart gives examples of main and dependent or subordinate clauses.

MAIN CLAUSE	SUBORDINATE CLAUSE
	Introduced by
	CONJUNCTION [NOMINAL CLAUSE]
Le dije a Elsa *I told Elsa*	**que me gustaba la universidad.** *(that)[3] I liked the university.*
	CONJUNCTION [ADVERBIAL CLAUSE]
Nos fuimos *We left*	**porque hacía mucho frío.** *because it was very cold.*
	RELATIVE PRONOUN [ADJECTIVAL or RELATIVE CLAUSE]
Fuimos a una fiesta *We went to a party*	**que dieron nuestros amigos.** *(that)[4] our friends gave.*

---

3. In English, the conjunction may be omitted. This is impossible in Spanish, where all conjunctions must be stated.
4. In English, the relative pronoun may be omitted within certain contexts. In Spanish, the relative pronoun is always stated.

In some complex sentences, one clause may be broken into two parts with another subordinate inserted in between.

> **El libro que leí ayer fue muy interesante.**
> *The book I read yesterday was very interesting.*

Main clause: **El libro (...) fue muy interesante.**
Subordinate clause: **que leí ayer** [relative clause]

In some complex sentences, a subordinate clause may serve as a main clause to yet another subordinate (sub-subordinate) clause.

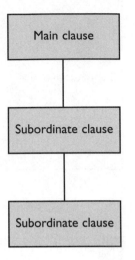

> **La clase de español que me recomendaste que tomara me ha interesado mucho.**
> *The Spanish class (that) you recommended (to me) (that) I take has interested me a lot.*

Main clause: **La clase de español (...) me ha interesado mucho.**
Subordinate clause #1: **que me recomendaste** [relative or adjectival clause]
Subordinate clause #2 (subordinate clause #1 serves as its main clause): **que tomara** [nominal clause]

One main clause may have two subordinates of equal value connected with a conjunction of coordination *(y, o, pero, sino)*.

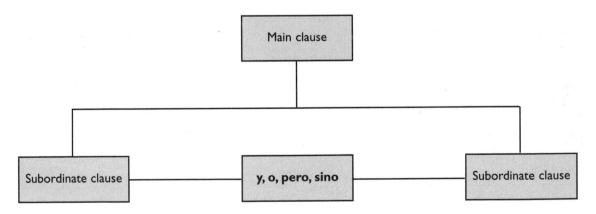

> **Me dijo que lo haría y que[5] me lo daría.**
> *She told me (that) she would make it and (that she would) give it to me.*

Main clause: **Me dijo**
Subordinate clause #1: **que lo haría** [nominal]
Subordinate clause #2: **que me lo daría** [nominal]
Conjunction of coordination: **y**

Yo sabía que Juan lo había hecho o que había ayudado a sus amigos a hacerlo.
I knew that Juan had done it, or that he had helped his friends do it.

Main clause: **Yo sabía**
Subordinate clause #1: **que Juan lo había hecho** [nominal]
Subordinate clause #2: **que había ayudado a sus amigos a hacerlo** [nominal]
Conjunction of coordination: **o**

Me dijo que vendría, pero que llegaría tarde.
He told me that he would come, but that he would arrive late.

Main clause: **Me dijo**
Subordinate clause #1: **que vendría** [nominal]
Subordinate clause #2: **que llegaría tarde** [nominal]
Conjunction of coordination: **pero**

No le dije que viniera, sino que me llamara.
I did not tell her to come, but rather to call me.

Main clause: **No le dije**
Subordinate clause #1: **que viniera** [nominal]
Subordinate clause #2: **que me llamara** [nominal]
Conjunction of coordination: **sino**

One sentence may have two main clauses connected with conjunctions of coordination, each main clause having its subordinate clause(s).

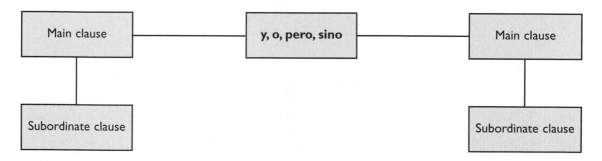

---

5. This conjunction may be omitted because it is a repetition of the previous one: *Me dijo que lo haría y me lo daría.*

Lamento que no puedas venir, pero estoy contento de que tus amigos te hayan invitado a cenar.
I am sorry you cannot come, but I am glad (that) your friends invited you to dinner.

Main clause #1: **Lamento**
Subordinate clause #1: **que no puedas venir** [nominal]
Main clause #2: **estoy contento de**
Subordinate clause #2: **que tus amigos te hayan invitado a cenar** [nominal]
Conjunction of coordination: **pero**

Me dijo que necesitábamos boletos y luego llamó para que nos reservaran dos.
She told me that we needed tickets, and then she called so that they would reserve two for us.

Main clause #1: **Me dijo**
Subordinate clause #1: **que necesitábamos boletos** [nominal]
Main clause #2: **luego llamó**
Subordinate clause #2: **para que nos reservaran dos** [adverbial]
Conjunction of coordination: **y**

The complexity of a sentence is practically limitless. The following diagram is an example of a sentence with one main clause and four subordinates, three of which are subordinated to the first subordinate clause.

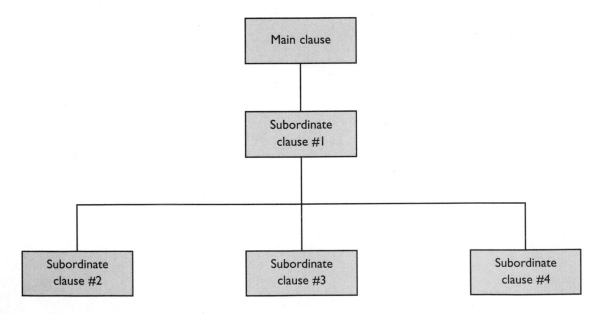

Mis amigos me habían dicho que cuando regresaran para las vacaciones me llamarían para que pudiéramos salir juntos a pesar de que tuviéramos poco tiempo.

My friends had told me that when they returned for vacation they would call me so that we could go out together, in spite of the fact that we might have little time.

Main clause: **Mis amigos me habían dicho**
Subordinate Clause #1: **que me llamarían** [nominal]
Subordinate Clause #2: **cuando regresaran para las vacaciones** [adverbial]
Subordinate Clause #3: **para que pudiéramos salir juntos** [adverbial]
Subordinate Clause #4: **a pesar de que tuviéramos poco tiempo** [adverbial]

PRÁCTICA

Ejercicios 1.5–1.10, páginas 305–307

◆ Accents

I. SYLLABIFICATION

The division of a word into syllables aids in the application of rules on accents.

a. Consonants (*Consonantes*)

Single intervocalic consonants: one consonant between two vowels joins the following vowel to form a syllable. (Remember that in Spanish *ch*, *ll*, and *rr* represent one consonant.)

ta/**z**a	me/**s**a	mi/**s**a	ma/**c**e/ta
ca/la/**b**a/za	ta/**ll**a	me/**ch**a	ba/**rr**o
fe/**rr**o/ca/**rr**i/**l**e/ro			

Ejercicio 1.11, página 307

Two intervocalic consonants: these are separated (except *ch*, *ll*, and *rr*).

lá**m**/**p**a/ra	pa**n**/**t**a/lla	a**n**/**g**us/tia	co**m**/**p**u/ta/do/ra
pe**r**/**s**o/na	e**n**/**c**ar	di**c**/**c**io/na/rio	

Do not separate the consonants *b*, *c*, *f*, *g*, and *p*, followed by *l* or *r*, or the combinations *dr* and *tr*.

ta/**bl**a	fe/**br**e/ro	te/**cl**a	re/**cr**e/o
a/**fl**o/jar	a/**fr**en/ta	re/**gl**a	a/**gr**io
re/**pl**e/to	de/**pr**i/mir	po/**dr**i/do	re/**tr**a/to

Ejercicio 1.12, página 307

Three or more intervocalic consonants: with three or more consonants between vowels, only the last consonant joins the next vowel (unless it is *l* or *r*).

cons/ta   ins/**pi**/ra   ins/**t**an/te   in/**gl**és

com/**pr**ar

Ejercicio 1.13, página 307

b. Vowels *(Vocales)*

STRONG VOWELS	WEAK VOWELS	VOWEL COMBINATIONS
a	i	**Hiato:** two vowels forming two syllables
e	u	**Diptongo:** two vowels forming one syllable
o		**Triptongo:** three vowels forming one syllable

Hiatus *(Hiato):* two vowels of equal strength represent two syllables. Each strong vowel represents one syllable; when combined with another strong vowel, they are separated.

ca/**e**/mos   le/**e**n   em/ple/**o**   em/ple/**a**/do

If a weak vowel before or after a strong vowel is stressed, there is a separation; a stressed weak vowel in combination with a strong vowel will always have an accent mark.

ca/**í**/da   re/**í**/mos   ma/**ú**/lla   gra/d**ú**/en

tí/os   sa/l**í**/an   rí/en   gr**ú**/a

re/**ú**/no

Ejercicio 1.14, página 307

Diphthong *(Diptongo)*: a combination into one syllable of two weak vowels or one strong and one weak represents a diphthong and is not separated.

I/ta/**lia**	**bai**/le	**vie**/nen	**rei**/no
re/me/**dio**	**vio**/lín	**cuan**/do	**au**/la
rue/da	**deu**/da	**rui**/do	**ciu**/dad
cuo/ta	es/ta/**dou**/ni/den/se		

Stressed strong vowel: the same is true even when there is an accent on the strong vowel of the diphthong.

di**á**/fa/no	tam/b**ié**n	na/c**ió**	gu**á**r/da/lo
fu**é**/ra/mos	qu**ó**/rum[6]	bai/l**á**is	die/ci/s**éi**s
ói/ga/me	c**áu**/sa/me	**Éu**/fra/tes	

Ejercicio 1.15, página 308

Triphthong *(Triptongo)*: a triphthong is one syllable formed by three vowels.

a/ve/ri/g**uái**s	lim/p**iéi**s

More than one syllable occurs if there is more than one strong vowel or a stressed weak vowel in the combination.

se/**ái**s	ca/**í**/an	re/**í**/a/mos

Ejercicio 1.16, página 308

---

6. Words imported from other languages follow the same accentuation rules as other Spanish words.

The *h* in Spanish is not pronounced; if it is enclosed between two vowels, these two vowels will interact as if they were next to each other.

No accent required:

a/ho/rrar	re/**ha**/cer	re/**ho**/gar	**ahi**/ja/do
re**hi**/lar	re**hun**/dir		

Accent required:

pro/**hí**/bo	**bú**/ho

PRÁCTICA

Ejercicio 1.17, página 308; Ejercicio de repaso 1.18, página 308

2. STRESS

Every word with more than one syllable in Spanish has one syllable with more stress than the rest. Depending on the type of word it is, or where the stress falls, the word may or may not require a written accent.

a. Categorization of Words by Stress

In Spanish, words with more than one syllable are categorized as follows.

TYPE	SYLLABLE WHERE STRESS FALLS	EXAMPLE
Aguda	*Last* (última)	ca / mi / **né**
Llana	*Next-to-last* (penúltima)	**lá** / piz
Esdrújula	*Third-to-last* (antepenúltima)	**quí** / mi / ca
Sobresdrújula	*Fourth-to-last* (anteantepenúltima)	**cóm** / pre / me / lo

b. Rules for Written Accents

Agudas: this type of word only needs a written accent when the word ends in a vowel or *n* or *s*.

Accent required:

      a<u>mó</u>   vi<u>ví</u>   vi<u>vís</u>   fran<u>cés</u>

      cai<u>mán</u>

No accent required:

      a<u>mar</u>   vi<u>vir</u>   espa<u>ñol</u>   ciu<u>dad</u>

      J<u>e</u><u>rez</u>

Llanas: this type of word only needs a written accent when the word ends in a consonant other than *n* or *s*.

Accent required:

      ca<u>rác</u>ter   imb<u>éc</u>il   <u>lá</u>piz   <u>tú</u>nel

      ver<u>sá</u>til

No accent required:

      <u>ha</u>blo   a<u>cen</u>to   nece<u>si</u>ta   conso<u>nante</u>

      fran<u>ce</u>ses   <u>mar</u>gen   <u>lu</u>nes   ex<u>a</u>men

      estu<u>dia</u>ron   <u>bai</u>las

Esdrújulas and *sobresdrújulas:* these types of words always require an accent mark.

Esdrújulas:

      ca<u>rá</u>tula   est<u>ú</u>pido   lu<u>cié</u>rnaga

Sobresdrújulas:

      vend<u>á</u>moselo   <u>dé</u>moselas   pong<u>á</u>monoslas

PRÁCTICA

Ejercicios 1.19–1.22, páginas 308–309

c. Special Cases

(1) ADVERBS ENDING IN -MENTE

Adverbs formed from an adjective + *mente* require an accent only when their original adjective had one.

rápido	is the adjective form of the adverb	**rápidamente**
fácil	is the adjective form of the adverb	**fácilmente**
lento	is the adjective form of the adverb	**lentamente**

Ejercicio 1.23, página 309

(2) MONOSYLLABLES

Monosyllables (words consisting of only one syllable) must be left **without** a written accent mark. There is only one part of the word that can be stressed, thus no accent is needed.

a al ti la le lo di da me fui fue dio Dios

Some monosyllables are homonyms (words with the same spelling or pronunciation but with different meanings). One of the two will have an accent mark to distinguish it from the other.

el *the*		**mas** *but*		**se** [pron.]		**te** *you, yourself*	
él *he*		**más** *more*		**sé** *I know*		**té** *tea*	

de *of, from*		**mi** *my*		**tu** *your*		**si** *if*	
dé[7] *give*		**mí** *me*		**tú** *you*		**sí** *yes, itself, oneself*	

Me preguntó <u>el</u> nombre <u>de mi</u> profesora.	*She asked me the name of my professor.*
—¿A ti[8] <u>te</u> lo dijo?	*"Did she tell you?"*
—<u>Sí</u>, a <u>mí</u> me lo dijo.	*"Yes, she told me."*

---

7. When the verb *dar* is conjugated in the imperative and has a pronoun attached, it loses the accent: *dele*. It is no longer a homonym of the preposition in this situation. Of course, it regains the accent when a second pronoun is added, due to the fact that we must maintain the stress on the verb and the new word is an *esdrújula: démelo.*

8. Beware of the temptation to place an accent over *ti*, just because *mí* has one: *ti* is not a homonym, as is *mí*.

¿<u>Tú</u> también necesitas que te <u>dé</u> la llave?	*Do you also need me to give you the key?*
No <u>sé</u> <u>si</u> <u>él</u> quiere <u>más</u> <u>té</u>.	*I don't know if he wants more tea.*
El problema en <u>sí</u> no es tan grave.	*The problem in itself isn't so serious.*

PRÁCTICA

Ejercicio 1.24, página 309

(3) NON-MONOSYLLABIC HOMONYMS

Although they are not monosyllables, the following words are homonyms also. One of the two will have an accent mark to distinguish it from the other.

(a) *Aun*[9] vs. *Aún*
(b) *Solo* vs. *Sólo*
(c) Demonstrative Pronouns
(d) Exclamative and Interrogative Adjectives, Pronouns, or Adverbs

(a) *Aun* vs. *Aún*

The word *aún* requires an accent when it means "still" *(todavía)*; however, when it means "even," it has no accent mark *(aun)*.

| <u>Aun</u> de día hace frío. | *Even during the day it is cold.* |
| <u>Aún</u> no hemos llegado. | *We still have not arrived.* |

(b) *Solo* vs. *Sólo*

The word *solo* may be an adjective ("alone") or an adverb ("only"). An accent is used on the adverb to distinguish it from the adjective. This accent is optional, except in cases of possible confusion between the two uses.

| Vivo <u>solo</u>. | *I live alone.* |
| Mi hermana <u>sólo</u> come fruta. | *My sister only eats fruit.* |

Here, the accent on *sólo* is optional, because it cannot be confused with "alone," which would have to be *sola*.

---

9. Although *aun* is a monosyllable, we have placed it outside of the category because when it takes an accent, *aún,* it is not a monosyllable.

Mi tío viaja <u>solo</u> en tren.	*My uncle travels alone by train.*
Mi tío viaja <u>sólo</u> en tren.	*My uncle travels only by train.*

Here, the accent on *sólo* is required to avoid confusion with "alone."

(c) Demonstrative Pronouns

The words *ese, esa, esos, esas; este, esta, estos, estas; aquel, aquella, aquellos, aquellas* may be adjectives or pronouns. An accent is used on the pronoun to distinguish it from the adjective. This accent is optional, except in cases of possible confusion between the two uses.

Mira <u>ese</u> perro. [adj.]	*Look at that dog.*
<u>Éste</u> es mío. [pron.]	*This one is mine.*

The accent on *éste* in this last example is optional.

En <u>este</u> país todos tienen animales domésticos: <u>éstos</u> perros, <u>aquéllos</u> gatos.	*In this country, everybody has pets: some have dogs, others cats.* (literally: these, dogs, those, cats)

The accent on *éstos* and *aquéllos* in this last example is required to indicate their use as pronouns referring back to people [*todos*]; without the accent, they would be adjectives accompanying dogs and cats.

The neutral form of the pronouns *eso, esto,* and *aquello* have no adjective equivalent and thus do not require an accent.

Mira <u>eso</u>. [neutral pron.]	*Look at that.*

(d) Exclamative and Interrogative Adjectives, Pronouns, or Adverbs

Exclamative and interrogative adjectives, pronouns, or adverbs take an accent. In exclamations and interrogations, there is not always an interrogative or exclamative pronoun or adverb. You might, for example, ask: *¿Me dijiste la verdad?* or exclaim: *¡Bien dicho!* None of these words has an accent. You might also exclaim: *¡Que te vaya bien!* Here the *que* is a conjunction, not a pronoun or adjective, and has no accent.

Some examples of exclamative pronouns and adverbs are as follows.

¡<u>Qué</u> día!	*What a day!*
¡<u>Cómo</u> trabajas!	*How you work!*
¡<u>Cuánto</u> comes!	*How much you eat! (i.e., You eat a lot!)*

Some examples of interrogative adjectives, pronouns, and adverbs are in the chart below.

INTERROGATIVE[10] (ACCENT MARK)		NONINTERROGATIVE (NO ACCENT MARK)
Direct Discourse[11]	Indirect Discourse	
¿Qué? = *What?*		**Que** = *That, which, who*
¿Qué quieres? *What do you want?*	**No sabía qué** hacer. *I did not know what to do.*	**Quiero que estudies.** *I want you to study.* (literally: *I want that you study.*) [conjunction] **El libro que quiero es azul.** *The book that I want is blue.* [relative pronoun]
¿Por qué? = *Why?*		**Porque** = *Because*
¿Por qué llamaste? *Why did you call?*	**No sé por qué** llamó. *I do not know why he called.*	**Llamé porque** quise. *I called because I wanted to.*
¿Cómo? = *How?*		**Como** = *Like*
¿Cómo llegó? *How did she get here?*	**No sé cómo** llegó. *I do not know how she got here.*	**Trabaja como** yo. *He works like me.*
¿Cuánto? = *How much/many?*		**Cuanto** = *As much/many as*
¿Cuántos libros tienes? *How many books do you have?*	**No sé cuántos** tengo. *I do not know how many I have.*	**Te di cuantos** pude. *I gave you as many as I could.*
¿Dónde? = *Where?*		**Donde** = *Where, in which*
¿Dónde está? *Where is it?*	**Me dijo dónde** estaba. *He told me where it was.*	**Es la casa donde** me crié. *It is the house in which I grew up.*
¿Cuándo? = *When?*		**Cuando** = *When*
¿Cuándo llega? *When does it arrive?*	**Me dijo cuándo** venía. *She told me when she was coming.*	**Lo vi cuando** entró. *I saw him when he came in.*
¿Quién? = *Who(m)?*		**Quien** = *Who(m), he who*
¿Quién es? *Who is it?*	**Me dijo quién** era. *He told me who it was.*	**Ése es el hombre con quien llegó.** *That is the man with whom she arrived.*

---

10. **Interrogative vs. noninterrogative.** This distinguishes words that are used in questions, whether directly stated or indirectly related, from words that are not interrogative at all, such as conjunctions, relative pronouns, and adverbial phrases.

QUE

Please note that the "noninterrogative" column for *Que* contains conjunctions and relative pronouns that frequently have no translation into English, whereas the columns to the left, "interrogative," contain interrogative words that will always be stated in English. Notice the translation of the following sentences.

Quiero <u>que</u> estudies.	*I want you to study.*
El libro <u>que</u> quiero es azul.	*The book (that) I want is blue.*

POR QUÉ VS. *PORQUE* • *CÓMO* VS. *COMO* • *CUÁNTO* VS. *CUANTO*

It is not difficult to remember when these words require an accent mark because of the difference in meaning of the two.

por qué = *why*	**cómo** = *how*	**cuánto** = *how much/many*
porque = *because*	**como** = *as, like*	**cuanto** = *as much/many*

DÓNDE VS. *DONDE*

Whereas in most cases you can see that the translations of the accented and unaccented words are different, in the case of *dónde* and *donde* there is not always a difference. It would help perhaps to think of the unaccented word as a relative pronoun that requires an antecedent, or a noun prior to it and to which it refers.

Es la <u>casa donde</u> me crié.	*It is the <u>house in which</u> I grew up.* OR: *It is the <u>house</u> I grew up in.*

The interrogative *dónde,* whether in direct or in indirect discourse, never has an antecedent.

—¿<u>Dónde</u> está?	*"<u>Where</u> is she?"*
—No sé <u>dónde</u> está.	*"I do not know <u>where</u> she is."*

---

11. **Direct vs. indirect discourse.** This distinguishes questions that are asked directly (e.g., What is your name?) from reported questions (e.g., He asked me what my name was.).

Cuándo vs. cuando

With these two words, the distinction is perhaps even harder to make; for there to be an accent mark, there must be an explicit or implicit question involved. The non-interrogative "when" might be replaced by "at the time" without much change in meaning, whereas the interrogative could be replaced by "at what time." Compare the following sentences.

No sé cuándo se fue.	*I do not know when (at what time) she left.*
Lloramos cuando se fue.	*We cried when (at the time) she left.*

Frequently in indirect discourse in English, there is a greater stress on the word when it is interrogative in nature than when it is not; compare the following, reading them out loud.

Te vi <u>cuando</u> entraste.	*I saw you <u>when</u> you came in.*
No sé <u>cuándo</u> entraste.	*I don't know <u>when</u> you came in.*

Quién vs. quien

Quién with an accent mark is used whenever there is a question, explicit or implicit. *Quien* without an accent mark is not interrogative. It is a relative pronoun, usually preceded by a noun (which is its antecedent). It may also be used with no antecedent at the beginning of a sentence. In such cases, it means "He who … " or "Whoever …".

¿<u>Quién</u> eres?	*<u>Who</u> are you?*
No sé <u>quién</u> eres.	*I don't know <u>who</u> you are.*
El hombre con <u>quien</u> habla es espía.	*The man with <u>whom</u> she is talking is a spy.*
<u>Quien</u> busca encuentra.	*<u>He who</u> seeks shall find.*

PRÁCTICA

Ejercicios 1.25–1.32, páginas 309–311; Ejercicios de repaso 1.33–1.34, página 311

Chapter 2

Nouns and Noun Determiners

A Nouns and Their Equivalents

B Noun Determiners

Nouns and Their Equivalents

I. INTRODUCTION

a. Definition

Nouns: words that can take on the grammatical function of the subject of a verb.

> **Esa <u>estudiante</u> sabe mucho de gramática.**
> *That student knows a lot about grammar.*

PRÁCTICA

Ejercicio 2.1, página 312

b. Noun Equivalents

Other words that can have the basic function of the subject of a verb are pronouns, infinitives, and any nominalized word (word converted into a noun).

Pronouns: words that replace nouns but have the same gender and number as the noun to which they refer.

<u>Ellas</u> me lo dijeron.	*They told me.*
¿<u>Cuál</u> es el mío?	*Which one is mine?*
<u>El mío</u> habla mejor que el tuyo.	*Mine speaks better than yours.*
<u>El que</u> vino ayer fue Juan.	*The one who came yesterday was Juan.*
Esa casa es <u>mía</u>.	*That house is mine.*

Infinitives (see Chapter 6.H, pages 231–235, on the use of the infinitives and the present participles):

<u>Caminar</u> es bueno para la salud.	*To walk (Walking) is good for one's health.*
Me gusta <u>cantar</u>.	*I like to sing. (Singing is pleasing to me.)*

Nominalized words and phrases:

> **<u>El azul</u> del Mediterráneo siempre me sorprende.**
> *<u>The blue</u> of the Mediterranean always surprises me.*

Note that often in the case of nominalized adjectives in Spanish the person or object being referred to is included in the meaning of the adjective. In English this reference is stated, often in the form of man, woman, people, or when the reference is more specific, as the pronoun "one."

> **<u>El ciego</u> llegó temprano hoy.**
> *<u>The blind **man**</u> arrived early today.*

> **<u>Esa rubia</u> es la que solicitó el puesto.**
> *<u>That blonde **woman**</u> is the one who applied for the job.*

> **<u>Unos jóvenes</u> limpiaron la casa.**
> *<u>Some young **people**</u> cleaned the house.*

> **Este jabón no sirve. Tengo que encontrar <u>el bueno</u>.**
> *This soap is no good. I have to find <u>the good **one**</u>.*

Any adjective can be nominalized. Remember this when you want to write something equivalent to the above contexts, where "one" or "people," or other equivalents, are involved in English.

> **<u>El primero</u> en terminar gana.**
> *<u>The first **one**</u> to finish wins.*

> **<u>El último</u> en irse cierra las ventanas.**
> *<u>The last **one**</u> to leave closes the windows.*

> **Deberíamos respetar a <u>los mayores</u>.**
> *We should respect <u>older **people**</u>.*

> **Es una batalla entre <u>los buenos y los malos</u>.**
> *It's a battle between <u>the good **guys** and the bad **guys**</u>.*

The placement of the neuter *lo* in front of a nominalized adjective is also frequently used in Spanish, and alters the meaning of the adjective to make it a generalization or a characteristic.

> **<u>Lo interesante</u> es el silencio.**
> *<u>What is interesting</u> is the silence.*

> **<u>Lo mejor</u> de ese lugar es el calor que hace.**
> *<u>The best thing</u> about that place is the heat.*

Lo bueno y **lo malo** no se mezclan.
Good and *evil* do not mix.

Eso es **lo absurdo** de la situación.
That is the absurdity of the situation.

Lo verde de este lugar siempre me sorprende.
The greenness of this place always surprises me. (OR: *It always surprises me how green this place is.*)

Me encanta **lo dulce** combinado con **lo agrio**.
I love the combination of sweet (foods, things, flavors …) and sour (foods, things, flavors …).

Notice the different uses of the nominalized adjective *extranjero*.

El extranjero llegó ayer.	*The foreigner arrived yesterday.*
Viajarán al extranjero.	*They will travel abroad.*
Evita **lo extranjero.**	*He avoids what is foreign.*

Nominalized phrases are also frequent in Spanish.

El de la corbata roja es el presidente.
The man with the red tie is the president.

La de azul es mi hermana.
The one in blue is my sister.

Los de al lado siempre hacen ruido.
The people next door always make noise.

Me caen bien **los que cumplen sus promesas**.
I like people who fulfill their promises.

PRÁCTICA

Ejercicio 2.2, página 312

c.   Noun Companions

Articles and adjectives are words that accompany and modify nouns. They agree with the noun they modify.

la casa blanca, **las** casas rojas	*the white house, the red houses*
el árbol, **los** árboles	*the tree, the trees*

una mesa, **un** libro	*a table, a book*
esa casa, **esas** casas	*that house, those houses*
este libro, **estos** libros	*this book, these books*
nuestra casa, **vuestras** ideas	*our house, your ideas*
mis libros, **tus** cuadernos	*my books, your notebooks*
una niña **bonita**	*a pretty girl*

Prepositions are words that relate a noun or its equivalent to another noun, to the verb, or to the rest of the sentence.

Estoy **en** mi oficina.	*I am in my office.*
Llegó una carta **para** ella.	*A letter arrived for her.*
Después **de** estudiar, saldremos **a** cenar.	*After studying, we will go out to eat dinner.*

2. NOUNS: GENDER AND NUMBER

a. Gender *(Género)*

All Spanish nouns are either masculine or feminine.

Most nouns ending in **-o, -l,** and *-r* are **masculine.**

el libro *book*	**el barril** *barrel*	**el actor** *actor*

EXCEPTIONS:

la foto *photo*	**la capital** *capital*	**la moral** *morale, morals*
la mano *hand*	**la cárcel** *jail*	**la piel** *skin*
la moto *motorcycle*	**la catedral** *cathedral*	**la sal** *salt*
la radio *radio*	**la miel** *honey*	**la señal** *sign, signal*

Most nouns ending in *-a, -d, -ción, -sión, -umbre,* and *-z* are **feminine.**

la casa *house*	**la libertad** *liberty*
la costumbre *custom, habit*	**la luz** *light*
la condición *condition*	**la decisión** *decision*

EXCEPTIONS:

el día *day*	**el clima** *climate*
el tranvía *streetcar*	**el crucigrama** *crossword puzzle*
	el drama *drama*
el ataúd *coffin*	**el fantasma** *ghost*
el césped *lawn*	**el idioma** *language*
el huésped *guest*	**el panorama** *panorama*
	el poema *poem*
el arroz *rice*	**el problema** *problem*
el lápiz *pencil*	**el programa** *program*
el maíz *corn*	**el sistema** *system*
el matiz *shade of color*	**el telegrama** *telegram*
el pez *fish*	**el tema** *theme, topic*

el mapa *map*

el planeta *planet*

el poeta *poet*

Languages, days of the week, mountains, rivers, and oceans are **masculine.**

el español *Spanish*	**el lunes** *Monday*	**los Pirineos** *Pyrenees*

Letters of the alphabet are **feminine.**

la a *a*	**la hache** *h*	**la ere** *r*

Infinitives are **masculine** when nominalized.

el amanecer *dawn*	**el poder** *power*

Many Spanish nouns referring to humans and animals occur in pairs, sometimes similar in form, sometimes not, but gender is always distinguished.

el hombre *man*	**la mujer** *woman*
el actor *actor*	**la actriz** *actress*
el rey *king*	**la reina** *queen*
el toro *bull*	**la vaca** *cow*

Some Spanish nouns referring to humans are identical in form—only the modifier shows the gender.

el/la estudiante *student*	**el/la demócrata** *democrat*
el/la joven *young man/woman*	**el/la ciclista** *cyclist*
el/la modelo *model*	**el/la comunista** *communist*
el/la turista *tourist*	**el/la pianista** *pianist*
el/la atleta *athlete*	**el/la guía** *guide*

Some nouns can change meaning with a change in gender.

el policía *policeman*	BUT:	**la policía** *policewoman/the police*
el guía *guide (e.g., tour guide)*	BUT:	**la guía** *guide (woman)/guidebook*
el papa *pope*	BUT:	**la papa** *potato*
el cura *priest*	BUT:	**la cura** *cure*

Some nouns exist only in one gender, but serve for both sexes. The following examples can refer to women as well as to men.

Mi tía es <u>un ángel</u>.	*My aunt is an angel.*
Esa niña es <u>un amor</u>.	*That little girl is a sweetheart.*

These examples can refer to men as well as to women.

Mi padre es <u>una persona</u> encantadora.	*My father is a charming person.*
Ese hombre fue <u>una víctima</u> de la sociedad.	*That man was a victim of society.*

PRÁCTICA

Ejercicios 2.3–2.5, páginas 312–313

b. Number *(Número)*

Nouns ending in a vowel add *-s* to form the plural.

casa *house* $\rightarrow$ **casas** *houses*

Nouns ending in a consonant, in *-y,* and some ending in a stressed vowel add *-es* to form the plural.

amor *love* $\rightarrow$ **amores** *loves*

ley *law* $\rightarrow$ **leyes** *laws*

rubí *ruby* $\rightarrow$ **rubíes** *rubies*

francés *Frenchman* $\rightarrow$ **franceses**[1] *Frenchmen*

el examen *exam* $\rightarrow$ **los exámenes**[1] *exams*

Nouns ending in *-z* have plurals in *-ces.*

lápiz $\rightarrow$ **lápices**

Nouns ending in an unstressed vowel with final *-s* do not change for the plural.

el lunes $\rightarrow$ **los lunes**

el tocadiscos $\rightarrow$ **los tocadiscos**

la crisis $\rightarrow$ **las crisis**

3. PERSONAL *A*

In Spanish, direct object nouns referring to human beings are preceded by the personal *a.* The reason for the addition of the personal *a* is a combination of factors regarding the subject that might otherwise cause confusion: first, the subject of a verb might not be present, since subject pronouns in Spanish are most frequently omitted because the verb ending is considered to contain adequate reference whenever there is no ambiguity in the context; second, there is flexibility of word order in Spanish, and the subject may precede or follow a verb. Compare the following examples.

Comprendió. *He understood.*

Mi hermano comprendió. *My brother understood.*
(OR: **Comprendió mi hermano.**)

---

1. Notice the accent on *francés* and *exámenes.* A plural may acquire or lose a written accent, so that the stress may remain on the same syllable as in the singular.

If you want to form a sentence with [he + understands + my brother], in Spanish you could not simply say [*él* + *comprende* + *mi hermano*], since either *él* or *mi hermano* could be subject of the verb *comprende,* and such an ambiguous construction would be grammatically incorrect. To form the sentence correctly in Spanish, add the personal *a* (and omit the personal pronoun if the context is otherwise unambiguous).

Comprendió a mi hermano.	*He understood my brother.*

The use of the personal *a* with human direct objects extends to all contexts, no matter what the subject of the verb may be. The personal *a* is used with persons, as its name indicates, and not with things.

Vi el libro en tu casa.	*I saw the book in your house.*
Vi a Carmen en la clase.	*I saw Carmen in class.*
Conocemos ese barrio.	*We are familiar with that neighborhood.*
Conocemos al tío de Juan.	*We know Juan's uncle.*

If the persons referred to are not specific, and are thus dehumanized to the point of being perceived for all practical purposes as objects, omit the personal *a.*

Buscan secretarios bilingües.	*They are looking for bilingual secretaries.*
Busco a mi secretaria.	*I am looking for my secretary.*

Conversely, if the nonhuman direct object could act as subject of the verb, it is considered equivalent to human, and is preceded by the personal *a.* This is the case for animals and impersonated concepts.

El cazador mató al león.	*The hunter killed the lion.*
El científico vio a la Muerte.	*The scientist saw Death.*

In both sentences, the direct object could act as subject: the lion could kill the hunter, and Death could see the scientist.

With the verb *tener,* do not use the personal *a* if *tener* means "to have" or "to possess."

Tengo cuatro tíos.	*I have four uncles.*

However, if *tener* means "to keep" or "to hold," use the personal *a.*

Tenemos a mi padre en el hospital.	*We have my father in the hospital.*

Because the pronouns *alguien, nadie,* and *quien* refer to persons, they are preceded by the personal *a* when they function as direct objects.

Oí <u>a</u> alguien llorando.	*I heard someone crying.*
No conozco <u>a</u> nadie aquí.	*I do not know anyone here.*
¿<u>A</u> quién viste?	*Whom did you see?*

Direct object pronouns *(lo, la, los,* and *las)* are never accompanied by the personal *a* although they may refer to persons. The pronoun form used would be the stressed form.

Lo vi <u>a él</u> ayer.	*I saw him yesterday.*
La llamé <u>a ella</u> anoche.	*I called her last night.*
<u>A ellos</u> no los entiendo nunca.	*I never understand them.*
Las regañé <u>a ellas</u> ayer.	*I scolded them yesterday.*

(Notice that these are examples of repetitive object pronouns, used for emphasis or clarification. If there is no doubt as to reference, the only required pronoun in the four sentences above is the unstressed *lo, la, los,* or *las.*)

PRÁCTICA

Ejercicios 2.6–2.8, páginas 313–315

B Noun Determiners

Noun determiners are the words that accompany and modify nouns.

I. ARTICLES

a. Definite Articles

DEFINITE ARTICLES		
	Singular	**Plural**
Masculine	el	los
Feminine	la	las

Definite articles agree with the noun they accompany.

el hombre *(the) man*   **la mujer** *(the) woman*

los libros *(the) books*   **las clases** *(the) classes*

Definite articles are also used in the case of nominalization of words or expressions, such as adjectives, infinitives, expressions with *de* used for characteristics and pronouns.

Me gusta el azul.	*I like blue.*
El alto es mi padre.	*The tall one is my father.*
La rubia ganó.	*The blond woman won.*
Los ricos no entienden.	*Rich people do not understand.*
Todo se olvida con el correr del tiempo.	*Everything is forgotten with the passing of time.*
La de sombrero es mi hermana.	*The one with a hat is my sister.*
Ya llegaron los míos.	*Mine already arrived.*

Notice that *la* is changed to *el* when a feminine noun starts with a stressed *a* or *ha*.

el agua *water*   **el aula** *classroom*

el alma *soul*   **el ave** *bird*

el ama de casa *housewife*   **el hacha** *axe*

el águila *eagle*   **el hambre** *hunger*

In the plural, this is no longer necessary, since there is no hiatus.

las aguas, las almas, las amas de casa, etc.

Feminine nouns beginning with an unstressed *a* or *ha* use *la*.

la abeja *bee*   **la harina** *flour*

PRÁCTICA

Ejercicio 2.9, página 315

Definite articles have two functions in Spanish—they may refer to a **specific** item or a group of **specific** items.

> **La conferencia le gustó al público.**   *The audience liked the speech.*

They may refer to a **generalized** concept (English uses no article here).

> **Las conferencias de ese tipo son muy buenas para la gente, porque aumentan los conocimientos humanos.**
> *Speeches of that type are very good for people, because they increase human knowledge.*

(1) SUBJECTS

As a rule, sentences in Spanish do not begin with unaccompanied subject nouns, as they might in English.

> **La gente es así.** OR: **Así es la gente.**   *People are like that.*
>
> **El amor es eterno.**   *Love is eternal.*

In the above examples, the noun being used as subject also happens to be a generalized concept (all people, all love), and therefore it is natural in Spanish to add the definite article. However, in cases where generalization does not apply (not all people, but some people), you may choose to alter the word order in Spanish, and place the subject after the verb.

> **Venía gente a verlo.**   *People came to see him.*
>
> **Llegaron noticias de Juan esta mañana.**   *News from John arrived this morning.*

NOTE: It would be an error (an anglicism) to say ~~Gente venía...~~ , ~~Noticias llegaron...~~ .

In some contexts you can work around this type of difficulty of translation by altering the context and adding "there were," thus converting the subject into an object of a new clause.

> **Había gente que venía a verlo.**   *There were people who came to see him.*

With "people" in particular, when it is not a generalized concept, you can omit the subject entirely, and let a plural of the verb serve as impersonal subject "they."

> **Venían a verlo.**   *They came to see him.*

(2) TITLES

Use the definite article when speaking **about,** not **to,** someone you address with a title *(señor, señora, señorita, profesor, profesora, doctor, doctora).*

> **La** señora Gómez le explicó a **la** profesora Ruiz por qué su hijo había faltado.
> *Mrs. Gómez explained to Professor Ruiz why her son had missed class.*

EXCEPTIONS: *don, doña, san, santo, santa*

> **Don** Jesús Gamboa es un ranchero muy conocido de esta región.
> *Don Jesús Gamboa is a very well-known rancher of this region.*

When addressing someone directly, no article is used.

> —**Profesora Ruiz, perdone la ausencia de mi hijo: estuvo enfermo.**
> *"Professor Ruiz, forgive my son's absence: he was ill."*

> —**No se preocupe, Señora Gómez, le ayudaré a repasar.**
> *"Do not worry, Mrs. Gómez, I will help him review."*

(3) LANGUAGES

The definite article is used before the names of languages, except when the name of the language follows *en* or the verb *hablar.*

Escribe el español con facilidad.	*She writes Spanish easily.*
Hablo español.	*I speak Spanish.*
Me lo dijo en español.	*She told me that in Spanish.*

Omit the article after *de* when two nouns are used, one to modify the other.

mi profesora de español	*my Spanish professor*
el libro de ruso	*the Russian book*

With *aprender, entender, comprender, enseñar, leer,* and other verbs relating to activities with language, the article is optional.

Aprendí (el) español a los seis años.	*I learned Spanish when I was six.*
Mi madre enseña (el) inglés.	*My mother teaches English.*

The article is necessary if an adverb is used between the verb and the name of the language.

Aprendí fácilmente el español cuando tenía seis años.	*I learned Spanish easily when I was six.*

(4) POSSESSIVES VS. ARTICLES

With parts of the body, articles of clothing, and anything that pertains to the person in situations where there could be no ambiguity, the possessive is not necessary; a definite article is most frequently used.

El estudiante levantó <u>la</u> mano.	*The student raised his hand.*

In sentences where the part of the body, article of clothing, etc., is the direct object of the verb, and the indirect object indicates the possessor, an article is used instead of a possessive.

El dentista me sacó <u>el</u> diente.	*The dentist extracted my tooth.*
Nos admiró <u>el</u> uniforme.	*He admired our uniform.*

With reflexive verbs, the definite article is used with parts of the body and articles of clothing.

Me lavé <u>las</u> manos.	*I washed my hands.*
Se quitaron <u>el</u> abrigo.	*They took off their coats.*

In most cases, the definite article accompanies a prepositional object.

Lo llevaron <u>a la cárcel</u>.	*They took him to jail.*
Salimos <u>de la iglesia</u> a esa hora.	*We left the church at that time.*
Estaban <u>en el salón</u>.	*They were in the room.*

When *casa, clase,* or *misa* are objects of *a, de,* or *en,* omit the article.

Voy <u>a clase</u> a las ocho.	*I go to class at eight.*
Saldremos <u>de misa</u> a las once.	*We will leave church at eleven.*
No está <u>en casa</u> ahora.	*She is not at home now.*

With days of the week, always use the article, even after *hasta* and *para*.

<u>El lunes</u> tenemos una prueba.	*On Monday we have a test.*
¡<u>Hasta el lunes</u>!	*See you on Monday!*
Esta tarea es <u>para el viernes</u>.	*This assignment is for Friday.*

The definite article is not used after *ser,* except when the sentence translates into English with **on.**

Hoy <u>es</u> miércoles.	*Today is Wednesday.*
La prueba <u>es el</u> lunes.	*The test is <u>on</u> Monday.*

PRÁCTICA

Ejercicios 2.10 2.11, página 315

b. Indefinite Articles

INDEFINITE ARTICLES		
	Singular	**Plural**
Masculine	un	unos
Feminine	una	unas

Indefinite articles agree with the noun they accompany. The same exception applies for feminine indefinite articles as for definite articles. *Una* is changed to *un* when a feminine noun starts with a stressed *a* or *ha.*

¡Tengo <u>un</u> h<u>a</u>mbre!	*I am so hungry!*
	(I have such a hunger!)

The indefinite article is used much more in English than in Spanish, where, in most cases, it has more the meaning of the number "one." In the plural, *unos* and *unas* mean "some."

Omit the indefinite article after *ser* when an unmodified noun referring to profession, religion, nationality, or marital status is used.

Es estudiante.	*She is a student.*	**Es mexicana.**	*She is (a) Mexican.*
Soy católico.	*I am (a) Catholic.*	**Eres soltero.**	*You are a bachelor.*

If the noun is modified, use the article.

Es <u>una</u> estudiante muy aplicada.	*She is a very hardworking student.*
Es <u>un</u> dentista joven.	*He is a young dentist.*
Es <u>una</u> mexicana famosa.	*She is a famous Mexican.*

Omit the indefinite article before or after *cierto, cien, mil, otro, medio, semejante, tal,* and *¡qué…!* .

Había <u>cierta</u> duda en su voz.	*There was a certain (some) doubt in her voice.*
Hay <u>cien</u> invitados.	*There are a hundred guests.*
Necesito <u>mil</u> dólares.	*I need a thousand dollars.*
¿Puede darme <u>otro</u> ejemplo?	*Can you give me another example?*
Pesa cinco kilos y <u>medio</u>.	*It weighs five and a half kilos.*
¿Puedes creer <u>semejante</u> mentira?	*Can you believe such a lie?*
Nunca dije <u>tal</u> cosa.	*I never said such a thing.*
<u>¡Qué</u> problema!	*What a problem!*

Omit the indefinite article in negative sentences after *haber* used impersonally and *tener.*

<u>No hay</u> respuesta.	*There is no answer.*
<u>No tiene</u> coche.	*He has no car.*

If you use the singular article, it has the meaning of the number "one."

No tiene <u>un</u> coche —tiene dos.	*He does not have one car—he has two.*
No tengo ni <u>un</u> centavo.	*I do not have a single cent.*

Omit the indefinite article after *sin.*

Salió <u>sin</u> abrigo.	*She went out without a coat.*

Omit the indefinite article after *con* when the object is being referred to as a type of object.

Escriban <u>con</u> pluma, por favor.	*Please write with a pen.*

If the object is specific or the number "one" is present, use the article.

Pudo hacerlo con <u>una</u> mano.	*He was able to do it with one hand.*

PRÁCTICA

Ejercicios 2.12–2.13, página 316

2. ADJECTIVES

a. Demonstrative Adjectives

DEMONSTRATIVE ADJECTIVES[2]	Singular	Plural
Masculine	este	estos
Feminine	esta	estas
Masculine	ese	esos
Feminine	esa	esas
Masculine	aquel	aquellos
Feminine	aquella	aquellas

este = *this,* **ese** = *that* (near you),
aquel = *that* (over there, far from you)

These adjectives precede the noun and agree with it. Remember that in their adjective form they have no accent, whereas in their pronoun form they may, in cases of ambiguity. (See the section on demonstrative pronouns, page 21, for more on the use of the accent.) If it is difficult for you to remember which is which, it might help to remember that the adjective is always accompanied by a noun, but the pronoun is never accompanied by a noun. (The pronoun subsumes the noun, replacing it.)

Este libro es mío, y ése [pron.] **es tuyo.** (The accent on *ése* is optional here.)	*This book is mine, and that one is yours.*
Dame esa libreta, por favor.	*Give me that notebook, please.*
¿Recuerdas aquellos días?	*Do you remember those days?*

PRÁCTICA

Ejercicios 2.14–2.15, página 316

---

2. See Chapter 3.C.1, pages 80–81, on demonstrative pronouns (*éste, ése, esto, eso,* etc.).

b. Possessive Adjectives [3]

"SHORT" POSSESSIVE ADJECTIVES		
	Singular	**Plural**
1st-person singular	mi	mis
2nd-person singular	tu	tus
3rd-person singular	su	sus
1st-person plural	nuestro, nuestra	nuestros, nuestras
2nd-person plural	vuestro, vuestra	vuestros, vuestras
3rd-person plural	su	sus

Possessive adjectives agree in gender and in number with the thing possessed, **not** with the possessor.

No tengo <u>mis</u> libros hoy.	*I do not have my books today.*
Me gustan <u>vuestras</u> ideas.	*I like your ideas.*
<u>Sus</u> manos siempre están limpias.	*His hands are always clean.*
Ellos me regalaron <u>su</u> coche.	*They gave me their car.*

"LONG" POSSESSIVE ADJECTIVES		
	Singular	**Plural**
1st-person singular	mío, mía	míos, mías
2nd-person singular	tuyo, tuya	tuyos, tuyas
3rd-person singular	suyo, suya	suyos, suyas
1st-person plural	nuestro, nuestra	nuestros, nuestras
2nd-person plural	vuestro, vuestra	vuestros, vuestras
3rd-person plural	suyo, suya	suyos, suyas

---

3. See Chapter 3.C.2, pages 81–82, on possessive pronouns (*el mío, el tuyo,* etc.).

Long possessive adjectives are used when the possessive follows the noun, where the English would use "of … ".

Es una amiga <u>mía</u>.	*She is a friend of mine.*

They are also used after the verb *ser*.

Este libro es <u>mío</u>.	*This book is mine.*
Esta caja es <u>mía</u>.	*This box is mine.*

Suyo in certain contexts may cause ambiguity, since it can refer to "his," "hers," "yours," or "theirs." In such a case, it is best to use *de él, de ella, de usted, de ellos, de ellas, de ustedes* instead.

Aquí están sus cosas: creo que esta bufanda es <u>de él</u>; este abrigo es <u>de ella</u>; este sombrero es <u>de usted</u>. ¿No es así?
Here are your things: I think this scarf is <u>his</u>; this coat is <u>hers</u>; this hat is <u>yours</u>. Am I right?

PRÁCTICA

Ejercicios 2.16–2.17, página 317

c. Forms of Descriptive Adjectives

Descriptive adjectives are those that modify nouns, such as *rojo, viejo*, etc.

(1) COMMON ADJECTIVE ENDINGS

Adjectives ending in *-o* change to *-a* for the feminine.

un libro viej<u>o</u>	*an old book*
una casa viej<u>a</u>	*an old house*

Adjectives ending in a consonant, *-e*, or *-ista* do not generally change for gender.

un hombre <u>joven</u>, una mujer <u>joven</u>	*a young man, a young woman*
un final <u>triste</u>, una mirada <u>triste</u>	*a sad ending, a sad look*
un vestido <u>azul</u>, una camisa <u>azul</u>	*a blue dress, a blue shirt*
un país <u>comunista</u>, una idea <u>comunista</u>	*a Communist country, a Communist idea*

EXCEPTIONS: Adjectives referring to nationality ending in a consonant **do** change for gender.

español, española, españoles, españolas	*Spanish*
alemán, alemana, alemanes, alemanas	*German*
francés, francesa, franceses, francesas	*French*
inglés, inglesa, ingleses, inglesas	*English*

(2) ADJECTIVES WITH SHORT AND LONG FORMS

Bueno and *malo* drop the final *-o* before a singular masculine noun.

un buen libro/un libro bueno	*a good book*
el mal tiempo/el niño malo	*the bad weather / the bad child*

Grande becomes *gran* before a singular noun of either gender.

un gran evento	*a great event*
una gran amiga	*a great friend*

Santo becomes *San* before any masculine name, unless it begins with *To-* or *Do-*.

San Juan de la Cruz	**Santo Tomás**
San Nicolás	**Santo Domingo**

Adjectives ending in a consonant add *-es* for the plural, and accents may be added or deleted to maintain the stress on the same syllable as the singular.

joven, jóvenes	*young*

PRÁCTICA

Ejercicio 2.18, página 317

d. Position of Descriptive Adjectives

There are a few adjectives, principally quantitative in nature, that always precede the noun; to this group belong all ordinal numbers such as *primer, segundo, tercer,* etc.; *algún, varios; ambos; mucho, poco; tanto; otro.*

Era mi *primer viaje* a México.	*It was my first trip to Mexico.*
***Algún* día volveré.**	*Some day I'll go back.*

Tengo *varios* <u>amigos</u> **aquí.**	*I have several friends here.*
Sueño en *ambas* <u>lenguas</u>**.**	*I dream in both languages.*
Muchas <u>gracias</u>**.**	*Thank you very much. Many thanks.*
Tiene *poca* <u>paciencia</u>**.**	*He has little patience.*
No necesito *tanto* <u>dinero</u>**.**	*I don't need so much money.*
Quiero *otro* <u>café</u>**.**	*I want another coffee.*

Nonquantitative descriptive adjectives in Spanish usually **follow** the noun they modify; as a rule, they serve the purpose of restricting which person, thing, or place is being referred to.

Viene a hablarnos un profesor <u>famoso</u>**.**	*A famous professor is coming to talk to us.*
Me gusta la casa <u>verde</u>**.**	*I like the green house.*

In the sentences above, a contrast is being established between the mentioned nouns and others that do not have the same quality indicated in the adjective: A famous professor is coming, not an unknown one; I like the green house, not the white one or the others.

Descriptive adjectives will **precede** the noun if this noun indicates someone or something that is already identified, known, or otherwise restricted. When adjectives precede the noun, their function is explicative, not restrictive. They add to the already identified thing or person, describe it, color it, decorate it, or define it, with innate or inherent characteristics or traits. Often, the adjective itself is already associated with the noun.

This is the case, for example, with proper nouns, but also with nouns describing things or relations of which we only have one (a nose, a navel; a mother, a father, a husband, a wife, etc.).

el <u>extravagante</u> **Dalí**   *the extravagant Dalí*
[Salvador Dalí was extravagant by definition]

el <u>elegante</u> **Museo del Prado**   *the elegant Prado Museum*
[elegance is an inherent quality of the museum]

la <u>conocida</u> **profesora Sainz**   *the famous Professor Sainz*
[her fame precedes her]

la <u>simbólica</u> **torta de manzanas**   *the symbolic apple pie*
[apple pie is symbolic in the United States]

tu <u>pequeño</u> **ombligo**   *your small navel*
[smallness is an inherent quality of your navel]

su <u>gigantesca</u> nariz[4]   *his gigantic nose*
[gigantic is a characteristic of his nose]

mi <u>hermosa</u> madre   *my beautiful mother*
[my mother is innately beautiful]

A common noun that refers to a specific person, place, or thing would also fit in the category described above.

nuestra <u>adorada</u> maestra
our adored teacher [we know her name]

el <u>utilísimo</u> manual
the very useful manual [we know it by title]

los <u>impresionantes</u> avances de la tecnología moderna
the impressive advances of modern technology [*de la tecnología moderna* clearly specifies the progress to which we are referring]

If an identified or proper noun is followed by an adjective, the implication is that there are two or more such things or people.

el Museo del Prado <u>moderno</u>
the modern Museo del Prado [either the museum was renovated, or there are two parts to the museum, one modern, one not]

el vaso <u>lleno</u>
the full glass [not the others, which are not full]

When an adjective is used to describe an inherent quality of something, it may have poetic or oratorial overtones, especially when it is universally redundant.

La <u>blanca</u> nieve cubría los montes…
The white snow covered the hills … [snow is inherently white; this construction is poetic]

Adjectives of nationality **always follow** the noun.

Esa novela es de un autor <u>argentino</u>.
That novel is by an Argentine author.

Fifteen common descriptive adjectives change meaning depending on their location. Examples of these fifteen adjectives can be found in the chart on the next page.

---

4. If you want to describe something already identified as big or large, avoid using *gran,* which, when placed before the noun, means "great"; other possibilities: *gigantesco, enorme, voluminoso,* etc.

ADJECTIVE	BEFORE THE NOUN	AFTER THE NOUN
ALTO	el <u>alto</u> funcionario *the high official*	el funcionario <u>alto</u> *the tall official*
ANTIGUO	el <u>antiguo</u> contrato *the old [former, not current]* *contract*	la mesa <u>antigua</u> *the old [not new]* *table*
BUENO	un <u>buen</u> estudiante *a good student [studious]*	un hombre <u>bueno</u> *a good man [moral]*
CIERTO	<u>cierto</u> tono *certain tone [indeterminate]*	una declaración <u>cierta</u> *a true statement*
DIFERENTE	<u>diferentes</u> lugares *various or several places*	lugares <u>diferentes</u> *different or distinct places*
GRANDE	un <u>gran</u> hombre *a great man*	un hombre <u>grande</u> *a big man*
MEDIO	<u>medio</u> litro *half a litre*	la clase <u>media</u> *the middle class* temperatura <u>media</u> *average temperature*
NUEVO	el <u>nuevo</u> contrato *the new [latest] contract*	un coche <u>nuevo</u> *a [brand-] new car*
POBRE	el <u>pobre</u> hombre *the poor [unfortunate] man*	un hombre <u>pobre</u> *a poor [not rich] man*
PURO	<u>pura</u> suerte *sheer luck, just luck*	agua <u>pura</u> *pure [uncontaminated] water*
RARO	la <u>rara</u> habilidad *the rare ability*	una voz <u>rara</u> *a strange voice*
SIMPLE	un <u>simple</u> adiós *just a simple good-bye* *[nothing more]*	un hombre <u>simple</u> *a simpleton*
TRISTE	una <u>triste</u> manzana *just one humble,* *insignificant apple*	una empleada <u>triste</u> *a sad employee*
ÚNICO	mi <u>único</u> problema *my only problem*	un problema <u>único</u> *a unique problem*
VIEJO	un <u>viejo</u> amigo *an old [longtime] friend*	un amigo <u>viejo</u> *an old [aged] friend*

When these special adjectives are used with nouns referring to specific, already identified people, things, or places, they lose some of their variety of meaning.

mi <u>viejo</u> padre
my old father [obviously not former or longtime]

las <u>pobres</u> obreras de esa fábrica
the poor workers of that factory [they may be pitiful or penniless, or both]

Some adjectives are fixed in certain expressions by sheer usage.

idea <u>fija</u> *set idea*	**la <u>pura</u> verdad** *the basic truth*
sentido <u>común</u> *common sense*	**<u>libre</u> albedrío** *free will*
Semana <u>Santa</u> *Holy Week*	**<u>alta</u> fidelidad** *high fidelity*

Bueno and *malo* are two special adjectives that follow the general rules, but because of the possible ambiguities of "goodness" and "badness," there are probably more subtleties regarding placement than with other adjectives. In many cases, these adjectives exist in ready-made expressions.

<u>buena</u> suerte *good luck*	**<u>mala</u> suerte** *bad luck*
un <u>buen</u> día *one day, unexpectedly*	**<u>mal</u> dormir** *sleeplessness*
de <u>buena</u> familia *from a good family*	**<u>malos</u> pensamientos** *evil thoughts*
¡<u>Buenos</u> días! *Good morning!*	

Some nouns have been formed incorporating the adjective.

la hierbabuena *spearmint*	**el malhumor** *ill temper*
la buenaventura *good fortune*	**el malparto** *miscarriage*

Ultimately, the dictionary is the best place to check special usage of common adjectives.

PRÁCTICA

Ejercicios 2.19–2.21, páginas 317–318

e. Comparisons

(1) COMPARISONS OF INEQUALITY

(a) With Adverbs, Adjectives, and Nouns

"a"	más/menos	adverb adjective noun	que	"b"

Marta comprende <u>más</u> fácilmente <u>que</u> yo.
Marta understands more easily than I.

Esa novela es <u>más</u> larga <u>que</u> ésta.
That novel is longer than this one. (The accent on *ésta* is optional.)

José tiene <u>menos</u> dinero <u>que</u> yo.
José has less money than I do.

(b) With a Numerical Expression, Use *De* Instead of *Que*

Hay <u>más de diez</u> sillas aquí.
There are more than ten chairs here.

Nos quedan <u>menos de veinte</u> minutos.
We have less than twenty minutes left.

Te di <u>más de la mitad</u>.
I gave you more than half.

Conocí a <u>menos de diez</u> personas nuevas.
I met fewer than ten new people.

No invitó a <u>más de treinta</u> personas.
He did not invite more than thirty people.

SPECIAL USE OF *MÁS QUE*

In negative sentences, *más que* is the equivalent of "only" in English, or some other exclusive type expression, and is not comparative in meaning.

No tengo <u>más que</u> tres pesos.
I have <u>only</u> three dollars.

No invitó <u>más que</u> a tres personas.
She invited <u>only</u> three people.

Nunca come <u>más que</u> fruta.
He eats <u>only</u> fruit. [He never eats anything but fruit, anything other than fruit.]

Nunca viaja <u>más que</u> a España.
She only travels to Spain. [She never travels to any other place than Spain, nowhere but to Spain.]

IRREGULAR COMPARATIVES

mejor(es)	*better, best*	**mayor(es)**	*older, oldest*
peor(es)	*worse, worst*	**menor(es)**	*younger, youngest*

(*Más bueno* and *más malo* are used only occasionally, when the emphasis is on character traits of people, especially in idiomatic expressions. *Más viejo* and *más joven* are often interchangeable with *mayor* and *menor.*)

Mi clase es <u>mejor que</u> la tuya.
My class is better than yours.

Yo canto <u>peor que</u> tú.
I sing worse than you do.

Yo soy <u>mayor que</u> tú. Yo soy <u>más viejo que</u> tú.
I am older than you.

Tú eres <u>menor que</u> yo. Tú eres <u>más joven que</u> yo.
You are younger than I.

(c)   With a Verb or Clause as Second Part of Comparison

With a noun in the first part:

más/menos	noun [masc. sing.] noun [fem. sing.] noun [masc. pl.] noun [fem. pl.]	del que de la que de los que de las que	clause

Planté más <u>maíz</u> <u>del que</u> coseché.
I planted more corn than I harvested.

Hay menos <u>nieve</u> <u>de la que</u> esperábamos.
There is less snow than we expected.

Recibió más <u>regalos</u> <u>de los que</u> dio.
He received more gifts than he gave.

Vendió menos <u>flores</u> <u>de las que</u> había comprado.
She sold fewer flowers than she had bought.

Without a noun in the first part of the comparison, use the neuter form *de lo que*.

Nevó más <u>de lo que</u> esperábamos.
It snowed more than we expected.

Fue más interesante <u>de lo que</u> creíamos.
It was more interesting than we thought.

(2) COMPARISONS OF EQUALITY

(a) *Tanto(-a, -os, -as)... como*

With a noun, use the variable *tanto(-a, -os, -as)... como,* in agreement with the noun.

Tengo <u>tantos problemas como</u> tú.
I have as many problems as you do.

(b) *Tanto como*

Alone as an adverb, use the invariable *tanto como*.

Ella no come <u>tanto como</u> yo.
She does not eat as much as I do.

(c) *Tan... como*

With an adverb or an adjective, use *tan... como*.

Ese coche está <u>tan brillante como</u> el nuestro.
That car is as shiny as ours.

Ellos hablan <u>tan bien como</u> tú.
They speak as well as you do.

f. Superlatives

The superlative in Spanish is formed with an **article** + *más/menos* + *de* (if a group is being indicated).

Iris es <u>la más lista de</u> la clase.
Iris is the smartest of the class.

Esas flores son <u>las más rojas de</u> todas.
Those flowers are the reddest of all.

Mi tío es <u>el menos presumido de</u> todos.
My uncle is the least conceited of all.

Julio es <u>el más alto</u>.
Julio is the tallest.

Este coche es <u>el menos caro</u>.
This car is the least expensive.

El más grande and *el más pequeño* become *el mayor* and *el menor* when referring to age.

Jorge es <u>el mayor</u> y Juan es <u>el menor</u>.
Jorge is the oldest and Juan is the youngest.

PRÁCTICA

Ejercicios 2.22–2.23, páginas 318–319; Ejercicios de repaso 2.24–2.25, páginas 319–320

Chapter 3

Pronouns

A Personal Pronouns

B Se

C Demonstrative and Possessive Pronouns

D Interrogatives

E Exclamatives

F Indefinites and Negatives

G Relative Pronouns

◆ Personal Pronouns

The usage of pronouns is linked to the type of verb with which they are used. The following distinctions between verb types are presented to help you determine the pronouns you will need in Spanish.

I. DEFINITIONS

a. Intransitive Verbs

Intransitive verbs have only a subject.[1] They have no direct object.

Llegué. *I arrived.*   **Salieron.** *They went out.*

When these verbs have complements, they are complements of place, of destination, of origin, of time, etc., but **never** object complements.

Llegué a casa temprano.	*I got home early.*
Voy a clase a las ocho.	*I go to class at eight.*
Volvimos del museo a las cuatro.	*We returned from the museum at four.*
Llegaron por la avenida.	*They arrived by the avenue.*

b. Transitive Verbs

Transitive verbs can have a subject and a direct and/or indirect object.

(1) WITH SUBJECT AND DIRECT OBJECT

Estudié la lección.
[subj.: **yo**; d.o.: **la lección**]   *I studied the lesson.*

Vimos la película.
[subj.: **nosotros**; d.o.: **la película**]   *We saw the movie.*

Vi a[2] tu hermana.
[subj.: **yo**; d.o.: **tu hermana**]   *I saw your sister.*

(2) WITH SUBJECT, DIRECT OBJECT, AND INDIRECT OBJECT

Le regalamos las flores a[3] mi mamá.
We gave the flowers to my mother.
[subj.: **nosotros**; d.o.: **las flores**; i.o.: **mi mamá**]

---

1. The subject pronoun in Spanish is used mostly for emphasis or clarification.
2. Personal *a* used with a human or personified direct object.

¿Le diste la carta al cartero?
Did you give the letter to the mailman?
[subj.: **tú**; d.o.: **la carta**; i.o.: **el cartero**]

Les dio la niña[4] a los padres adoptivos.
She gave the child to the adoptive parents.
[subj.: **ella**; d.o.: **la niña**; i.o: **los padres**]

(3) WITH SUBJECT AND INDIRECT OBJECT ONLY

There are special verbs in Spanish that are sometimes called "flip" verbs because they are most frequently the opposite of English in construction, the subject in English being the indirect object in Spanish, and the object in English being the subject in Spanish. The verb *gustar* is used generally as a model of this type of verb. (See Chapter 6.I, pages 236–239, on *gustar*-type verbs.)

Me gusta esta clase.	*I like this class.*
Spanish—subj.: **esta clase;** i.o.: **a mí**	English—subj.: *I;* d.o.: *this class*
Le caes bien a mi hermano.	*My brother likes you.*
Spanish—subj.: **tú;** i.o.: **a mi hermano**	English—subj.: *My brother;* d.o.: *you*
Nos encanta Madrid.	*We love Madrid.*
Spanish—subj.: **Madrid;** i.o.: **a nosotros**	English—subj.: *We;* d.o.: *Madrid*

It is essential to notice that there can be significant differences between English and Spanish regarding verbs and their transitive or intransitive nature; these are principally lexical distinctions that directly affect the choice of pronouns. It takes a lot of practice and experience dealing with the language to dominate these differences, and the dictionary is not always the best friend. Some students find that it helps to maintain a booklet of lists of intransitive and transitive verbs they use, verbs that have multiple uses, and differences between English and Spanish verb usage. Such a list should be based on direct use you have made of the language, and more specifically, points of difficulty you have encountered in your writing, where your instructor has corrected you, for example, or details you note as you study. Such a booklet of lists might be subdivided into the following five categories.

1. Intransitive: *ir, venir, llegar…*

---

3. Preposition *a* used to introduce an indirect object.

4. In case of possible ambiguity, the personal *a*, usually required before the human direct object *la niña,* is eliminated. Here, there is an indirect object *(los padres)* introduced by the preposition *a*. If the personal *a* were used before *la niña,* it wouldn't be clear who is being given to whom.

2. Transitive with direct object (indirect object possible): *aprender, comer, beber, estudiar, ver, querer…* [NOTE: Most of these verbs can be used intransitively as well, without an object.] In these sentences, no object is stated: **what** I ate or **what** we learn is not at issue.

Ya comí hoy.	*I already ate today.*
Todos aprendemos.	*We all learn.*

3. Transitive with indirect object (direct object possible): *dar, regalar, enviar; decir, comunicar, gritar, escribir…* (Most verbs of communication fit here, as well as verbs related to giving or sending.)

4. Transitive with indirect object (direct object **impossible**): *gustar, caer bien…*

5. Problem verbs:

- RETURN: In English, the verb "to return" can be transitive or intransitive, but in Spanish it is translated by two different verbs.

Volví ayer.	*I <u>returned</u> yesterday.*
Devolví el libro.	*I <u>returned</u> the book.*

- LOOK AT: In Spanish this translates into *mirar,* which is transitive.

Miro el libro.	*I <u>look at</u> the book.*

- LOOK FOR: In Spanish this translates into *buscar,* which is transitive.

Busco el libro.	*I <u>look for</u> the book.*

PRÁCTICA

Ejercicio 3.1, página 321

2. SUBJECT PRONOUNS

SUBJECT PRONOUNS		
Person	**Singular**	**Plural**
1st	yo	nosotros
2nd	tú	vosotros
3rd	él/ella/usted*	ellos/ellas/ustedes*

*_Usted_ is used to address someone else, and is therefore a second person rather than a third (first person is the speaker, second person is the one addressed, third person is the one talked about or referred to). However, the forms of object pronouns and of verbs that correspond to _usted_ are all in the third person, and for that reason, in this table and all of the following related tables on object pronouns, forms relating to _usted_ are placed under third person.

*_Ustedes_ is the plural of _tú_ or _usted_ in Latin America, but in Spain, it is only the plural of _usted; vosotros_ is the plural of _tú._

*_Usted_ and _ustedes_ are often seen in the abbreviated forms _Ud._ and _Uds._

*_Usted_ is used to varying degrees in different dialects. As a general rule, you will notice that it is more common in Latin America than it is in Spain. It is used to mark difference of some sort, either of age or of status. For example, an adolescent would address an adult of equal or higher status with _usted;_ the parents of a household would possibly address the servants with _tú,_ but the servants would use _usted_ to address them. In some families, _usted_ is used between parents and children; in others, _tú_ is more common, but at times you might hear a scolding parent switch to _usted_ as form of address for a son or daughter from whom (s)he wishes to establish greater distance to be effective in the scolding.

As for deciding which form of address to use in any given situation, _usted_ or _tú,_ the local use should help determine your choice, but while you wait to hear what others do, the following rule of thumb might serve: at places of business or government offices, it would be safest to use _usted_ as a general rule; in social contexts, it is generally safe to use _tú_ with anyone your age or younger; it would be safest to use _usted_ with anyone else.

The subject pronoun in Spanish is most frequently absent. Normally, the reference to the subject is contained in the verb ending itself, and the context often clarifies sufficiently for there to be no need to use a subject pronoun. This is true even for the third person, as long as the context is not ambiguous.

Juan se levantó y caminó a la ventana. Miró afuera y suspiró: "Otro día de nieve".
Juan got up and walked to the window. He looked outside and sighed: "Another day of snow."

Notice in the above series of sentences that _caminó, miró,_ and _suspiró_ do not require the use of _él_ because it is understood that all verbs following the first one with Juan as subject will also have him as subject unless it is otherwise indicated. Such absolute clarity is not really required in Spanish, however; you will frequently run across narratives that start with no specificity as to the subject, and clarify it only later in the context.

Se levantó y caminó a la ventana. Miró afuera y suspiró: "Otro día de nieve". Entonces oyó la voz de su compañero de cuarto que le gritaba: ";Juan!"

If you try to translate this, you must read on to the end before you can begin the English, because you can't really know if the subject of the verbs is "she" or "he" until you get to the name "Juan."

There are essentially four reasons to use the subject pronoun: focus, contrast, change of subject, and with *usted*.

Focus: The subject pronoun is not used when the subject is not being focused upon. Compare the two following brief dialogues.

—¿Cuántos hermanos tienes?	*"How many brothers do you have?"*
—Tengo tres hermanos.	*"I have three brothers."*
—¿Quién hizo esto?	*"Who did this?"*
—Lo hice <u>yo</u>.	*"<u>I</u> did it."*

In the first situation, what is being asked relates to the object of the verb, the brothers, and not to the subject of the verb. Given that *tienes* and *tengo* indicate without a doubt who the subject is, there is no reason to add *tú* or *yo*. However, in the second situation, the question asks for the subject of the verb, and for that reason, the subject must be stated in the response, either as a noun or as a pronoun.

Contrast: The subject pronoun is used to mark a contrast between two different subjects.

<u>Nosotros</u> llevamos la ensalada, y <u>tú</u> el pan.
<u>We</u> will take the salad, and <u>you</u> the bread.

Change of subject: In paragraphs where you change from one subject to another, you must use the new subject either in pronoun or in noun form.

Caminaron juntos hasta el borde del lago. <u>Él</u> la abrazó, y le dijo que la quería. <u>Ella</u> se quedó callada.
They walked together to the edge of the lake. He put his arms around her and told her he loved her. She remained quiet.

In the above series of sentences the subject changes from "they" to "he" to "she." Notice, however, that you would not need to add the subject if there were no change of subject.

Héctor caminó con ella hasta el borde del lago. La abrazó y le dijo que la quería. Esperó una respuesta, pero no oyó nada.
Hector walked with her to the edge of the lake. He put his arms around her and told her that he loved her. He waited for an answer, but heard nothing.

With *usted*: Use of *usted* as a subject pronoun conveys an idea of formality or courtesy.

¿Desea usted algo más?	*Would you like something else?*
Usted conoce a mi prima, ¿verdad?	*You know my cousin, don't you?*

The third person subject pronouns *él, ella, ellos,* and *ellas*[5] refer only to persons, never to things. There is no subject pronoun for "it" (or its plural "they") in Spanish.

Esa mesa es de madera.	*That table is made of wood.*
Es de madera.	*It is made of wood.*
Me gusta[6] **esa película.**	*I like that movie.*
Me gusta mucho.	*I like it a lot.*
Se venden[7] **muchos autos ahora.**	*Many cars are sold now.*
Se venden rápido.	*They are sold quickly.*

Ejercicios 3.2–3.4, página 321

3. DIRECT OBJECT PRONOUNS

a. Formation and Usage

DIRECT OBJECT PRONOUNS		
Person	**Singular**	**Plural**
1st	me	nos
2nd	te	os
3rd	lo/la*	los/las*

*Note that object pronouns that correspond to *usted* are listed under 3rd person because they are the same form.

---

5. These pronouns cannot be used as subjects when they refer to things; however, they can be used as prepositional objects referring to things: **¿Y esos tomates? ¿Qué vas a preparar con ellos?** *And those tomatoes? What are you going to prepare with them?*

6. For *gustar* and similar verbs, the subject in English is the indirect object in Spanish, and the object in English is the subject in Spanish.

7. With the impersonal *se* construction with inanimate objects, the inanimate object functions as the subject of the verb. This translates frequently as the passive voice in English.

Direct object pronouns receive the direct action of the verb.

Me ven.	*They see <u>me</u>.*
Te conocen.	*They know <u>you</u>.*
Nos escuchan.	*They listen to <u>us</u>.*
Os entiendo.	*I understand <u>you</u>.*
Lo vi ayer.	*I saw <u>him</u>/<u>you</u> (usted) yesterday.*
Las conozco bien.	*I know <u>them</u>/<u>you</u> (ustedes) well.*

In most of Spain, but not in most of Latin America, *le(s)* is used instead of *lo(s)* for male human beings.

No <u>lo</u> conozco. (Latin America)	*I do not know him.*
No <u>le</u> conozco. (Spain)	*I do not know him.*

The use of *le* for human direct object is called *leísmo,* and the users of this are *leístas.* Learners of Spanish should adopt this use of *le* only when they adopt the rest of the dialectal traits of the region, which include the use of *vosotros.*

Os is used only in Spain, for the plural of *te.*

	Latin America *(I saw you.)*	Spain *(I saw you.)*
Singular	Te vi.	Te vi.
Plural	Los vi (a ustedes).	Os vi.

The direct object pronoun replacing an inanimate object will reflect the gender and number of the noun it replaces.

Miro la televisión. ¿Tú <u>la</u> miras?	*I watch television. Do you watch it?*

b. Stressed and Unstressed Object Pronouns (Direct and Indirect Object)

It is important to note the difference between the unstressed pronoun forms *me, te, lo, la, le, se, nos, os, los, las, les,* and the stressed forms *a mí, a ti, a él, a ella, a usted, a sí, a nosotros, a vosotros, a ellos, a ellas, a ustedes.* The first set of unstressed pronouns are the ones that are used in most standard reference conditions, and the second set are added to the first if special focus is given, or additional stress is required, or clarification that is needed in the case of the third person. Consider the following contexts.

Focus: To answer questions asking specifically for the object.

—¿A quién llamó?	*"Whom did he call?"*
—A mí. (OR: Me llamó a mí.)	*"Me."*

Stress: English marks the stress by pronouncing pronouns (or other words) more emphatically, where Spanish cannot. In Spanish we add words to indicate stress. In the example below, capitalized words are pronounced emphatically. Notice the Spanish need for additional words. In this case, the additional words (which are underlined in the following examples) are the stressed forms of the pronouns.

No te escribió a ti, me escribió a mí, así que me quiere a mí y no a ti.
He didn't write YOU, he wrote ME, so he loves ME and not YOU.

Clarification: When the third-person pronoun is used, and ambiguity of reference exists, the stressed form is added to clarify.

—¿Viste a Ricardo y a Luisa?
—Sí, los vi. Pero la vi a ella primero, y no lo vi a él hasta después. No estaban juntos. Quería preguntarles por qué, pero no me atreví.
"Did you see Ricardo and Luisa?"
"Yes, I saw THEM. But I saw HER first, and did not see HIM until later. They were not together. I wanted to ask them why, but didn't dare."

A frequent mistake made by English-speaking learners of Spanish is to use the stressed form instead of the unstressed form of the pronouns in full sentences: [~~Vi a ella. Quería preguntar a ellos~~.] The stressed form can only exist alone when there is no verb present, and in such cases, the unstressed form cannot be used: it cannot stand alone.

c. *Lo:* The Neuter (Invariable) Pronoun

The neuter *lo* refers to an idea or situation that is not specific enough to be either masculine or feminine.

—Nos queda poco tiempo.	*"We have little time left."*
—Sí, ya lo sé.	*"Yes, I know it."*

Lo is used as a complement to replace adjectives, pronouns, or nouns with *ser, estar,* and *parecer;* notice that in English the equivalent of *lo* in most cases is merely represented by emphasis on the verb when spoken.

—Creo que ella es muy lista.	*"I think she is very clever."*
—Yo no creo que lo sea.	*"I do not think she is."*

—Esa mujer es la tía de Juan.	*"That woman is Juan's aunt."*
—Sé que no lo es porque conozco a su tía.	*"I know she is not because I know his aunt."*
—¿Estas llaves son tuyas?	*"Are these keys yours?"*
—No, no lo son.	*"No, they are not."*
—¿Estás frustrada?	*"Are you frustrated?"*
—Sí, lo estoy.	*"Yes, I am."*
—Pareces loca.	*"You are acting crazy."*
—Quizá lo parezca, pero no lo estoy.	*"Maybe I look that way, but I am not."*

PRÁCTICA

Ejercicios 3.5–3.8, página 322

4. INDIRECT OBJECT PRONOUNS

INDIRECT OBJECT PRONOUNS		
Person	**Singular**	**Plural**
1st	me	nos
2nd	te	os
3rd	le*	les*

* When combined with *lo(s)* or *la(s)*, *le(s)* becomes *se*.

NOTE: Object pronouns that correspond to *usted* are listed under 3rd person because they are the same form.

Le dio la manzana a la maestra. → **Se la dio.**
He gave the apple to the teacher. *He gave it to her.*

Les regaló el coche. → **Se lo regaló.**
She gave them the car. *She gave it to them.*

The indirect object is used to indicate the person(s) receiving the direct object or to indicate the person or thing that is affected in some way by the action of the verb.

Me regaló sus guantes.	*He gave me his gloves.*
¿**Te** dijo su secreto?	*Did she tell you her secret?*
Les mandó la carta.	*She sent them the letter.*

There are many possible translations into English of indirect objects in Spanish, with a variety of prepositions used in the English version.

Le hiciste la tarea.	*You did the homework <u>for</u> him.*
Les quitó la llave.	*He took the key <u>away from</u> them.*
Nos pidió ese favor.	*He asked that favor <u>of</u> us.*

Verbs commonly used with indirect objects may be flip verbs (see Chapter 6.I, pages 236–239, on verbs like *gustar*) or other verbs that may change meaning if used with a direct object.

No le creo.	**No lo creo.**
I do not believe him (or her).	*I do not believe it.* (what he is saying)
i.e., he is lying.	[He may be telling what he believes to be the truth, but I think the truth is different: i.e., he is not lying.]
¿**Le** pagaste?	¿**La** pagaste?
Did you pay him (or her)?	*Did you pay it?* (e.g., **la cuenta**)
Le gané.	**Lo** gané.
I beat him (or her) [at a game].	*I won it.*
Le pegué duro.	**Lo** pegamos.
I hit him (or her) hard.	*We glued it.*
Le di en la cara.	**Me lo** dio.
I hit him (or her) in the face.	*He gave it to me.*
Le robaron.	**Lo** robaron.
They robbed him (or her).	*They stole it.*
Le extraña que hagas eso.	**Lo** extraña mucho.
It surprises him (her) that you do that.	*She misses him a lot.*

PRÁCTICA

Ejercicios 3.9–3.12, páginas 323–324

5. REQUIRED REPETITIVE OBJECT PRONOUNS

The following object pronouns must be used, however redundant it may sound.

a. Direct Object Pronouns

Direct object pronouns must be used when the object noun precedes rather than follows the verb.

<u>La salida</u> *la* **encontrará a su derecha.**   *You will find the exit to the right.*

<u>A todos los niños</u> *los* **felicitó.**   *He congratulated all of the children.*

<u>A ella</u> **no** *la* **vi.**   *I did not see her.*

Direct object pronouns must also be used whenever the pronoun *todo (toda, todos, todas)* is used as a direct object.

Lo **vendieron** <u>todo</u>.   *They sold it all.*

La **cantaron** <u>toda</u>. **(la canción)**   *They sang it all.*

Nos **invitaron a** <u>todos</u>.   *They invited all of us.*

b. Indirect Object Pronouns

These are almost always used redundantly even though their referent appears in the clause.

Le **dije** <u>a Maira</u> **que venías.**   *I told Maira you were coming.*

Les **regalé eso** <u>a los niños</u>.   *I gave that to the children.*

Le **caes bien** <u>a mi hermano</u>.   *My brother likes you.*

Le **caes bien** <u>a él</u>.   *He likes you.*

Le **caes bien.**   *He likes you.*

Les **hace falta** <u>a sus padres</u>.   *Her parents miss her.*

Les **hace falta** <u>a ellos</u>.   *They miss her.*

Les **hace falta.**   *They miss her.*

Ejercicio 3.13, página 324

6. ORDER OF OBJECT PRONOUNS WHEN COMBINED

ORDER OF OBJECT PRONOUNS WHEN COMBINED			
#1	#2	#3	#4
se	2nd-person	1st-person	3rd-person
se	te os	me nos	lo(s) la(s) le(s)

Examples:

Se te cayeron los libros.	*You dropped your books.*
Se os dirá cuando sea tiempo.	*You will be told when it is time.*
Se me dijo la verdad.	*I was told the truth.*
Se nos acabaron las ideas.	*We ran out of ideas.*
Se lo expliqué.	*I explained it to him/her.*
Se los regalé.	*I gave them to him/her.*
Se la mandaron.	*They sent it to them.*
Se le olvidó.	*He/She forgot it.*
Te lo dije.	*I told you (so/it).*
Te la regalé.	*I gave it to you.*
Me lo dijeron.	*They told me (so/it).*
Me la enseñaron.	*They showed it to me.*
Nos lo contaste.	*You told us (so/it).*
Nos la enseñaron.	*They showed it to us.*

PRÁCTICA

Ejercicio 3.14, página 325

7. POSITION OF OBJECT PRONOUNS

Direct and indirect object pronouns must be placed before or after their related verb, depending upon the form of the verb itself. There is no choice as to position after the verb with the affirmative command. There is no choice as to position before the verb with every other form except the infinitive and the present participle; with these last two, pronouns may be placed before or after the verb phrase, as long as all pronouns relating to the same verb are placed in the same position.

VERB FORM	POSITION OF PRONOUN(S)	EXAMPLES
conjugated verb	before	**<u>La</u> vi ayer.** *I saw her yesterday.*
compound tense	before auxiliary *(haber)*	**Nunca <u>la</u> he visto.** *I have never seen her.*
infinitive	before auxiliary or after infinitive	**<u>Me la</u> quiero comprar.** **Quiero comprár<u>mela</u>.** *I want to buy it (for myself).*
present participle	before auxiliary or after present participle[8]	**<u>Lo</u> estaba mirando.** **Estaba mirándo<u>lo</u>.** *I was looking at it.*
affirmative command	after[8]	**Míra<u>la</u>. Cómpra<u>telos</u>.** *Look at it. Buy them (for yourself).*
negative command	before	**No <u>la</u> mires.** **No <u>te los</u> compres.** *Do not look at it. Do not buy them.*

The only time there is a choice as to pronoun position is in a verb phrase containing a conjugated verb and an infinitive or present participle. There are some circumstances, however, where this flexibility is lost; in the following cases, the pronoun must always be placed after the infinitive or present participle.

If the infinitive follows a preposition:

> **Viajaremos para conseguir<u>lo</u>.**   *We will travel to get it.*

---

8. When pronouns are attached to the end of an infinitive, a present participle, or a command, an accent may be needed to maintain the original stress on the verb: *vender—venderlos—vendérselos; vendiendo—vendiéndolos; vende—véndelos.*

If a present participle is used adverbially:

Salieron persiguiéndo<u>la</u>. *They left pursuing her.*

If an infinitive or present participle follows a command:

Vaya a comprar<u>lo</u>. *Go and buy it.*

Sigue estudiándo<u>lo</u>. *Continue studying it.*

Ejercicio 3.15, página 325

8. PREPOSITIONAL OBJECT PRONOUNS

PREPOSITIONAL OBJECT PRONOUNS		
Person	**Singular**	**Plural**
1st	mí	nosotros
2nd	ti	vosotros
3rd	él/ella	ellos/ellas
formal	usted	ustedes
reflexive	sí	sí

Prepositional object pronouns are used after prepositions.

Lo hizo <u>por</u> _mí_. *She did it because of me.*

Puedes contar <u>con</u> _nosotros_. *You can count on us.*

Se fue <u>sin</u> _ella_. *He left without her.*

Lo guardó <u>para</u> _sí_. *He kept it for himself.*

Lo guardó <u>para</u> _él_. *She kept it for him.*

Estaba sentado <u>frente a</u> _vosotros_. *He was sitting in front of you.*

Corrió <u>tras</u> _ella_. *He ran after her.*

Estaba <u>cerca de</u> _ti_. *He was close to you.*

No encuentro mi diccionario; ayer trabajé <u>con</u> *él*.	*I cannot find my dictionary; yesterday I worked with it.*
La gorra de Roberto es parte de él; nunca sale <u>sin</u> *ella*.	*Roberto's cap is a part of him; he never leaves without it.*

The following prepositions take the subject pronoun form for *yo* and *tú*.

entre:

Estaba sentado <u>entre</u> *<u>tú</u>* y *<u>yo</u>*.	*He was sitting between you and me.*

según:

<u>Según</u> *<u>tú</u>*, esto es incorrecto.	*According to you, this is incorrect.*

Como, excepto, and *menos* take *yo* and *tú*, unless they are followed by another preposition. Use the pronoun that goes with the last preposition.

como:

Mis amigos piensan <u>como</u> <u>*yo*</u>.	*My friends think like me.*
<u>A</u> mí no me duele <u>como</u> <u>a</u> *<u>ti</u>*.	*It does not hurt me the way it does you.*

excepto:

Todos lo vieron <u>excepto</u> <u>*yo*</u>.	*They all saw it except me.*
Les dieron <u>a</u> todos <u>excepto</u> <u>a</u> *<u>mí</u>*.	*They gave to everyone but me.*
Se lleva bien <u>con</u> todos <u>excepto</u> <u>con</u>*migo*.	*He gets along with everyone but me.*

menos:

Todos <u>menos</u> *<u>tú</u>* comieron postre.	*They all ate dessert except you.*
Hubo carta <u>para</u> todos <u>menos</u> <u>para</u> *<u>ti</u>*.	*There was a letter for everyone but you.*

The preposition *con* with *mí, ti,* and *sí* becomes *conmigo, contigo,* and *consigo.*

Ven <u>con</u>*migo*.	*Come with me.*
Pensé que estaba <u>con</u>*tigo*.	*I thought he was with you.*
Se lo llevó <u>con</u>*sigo*.	*He took it along (with himself).*

Consigo is used when the subject of the verb is the same as the object of *con,* as in the previous example. In situations where the subject is different from the object of *con,* use the standard third-person prepositional pronoun.

> **Fuimos al cine con Juan. Fuimos al cine <u>con</u> *él*.**
> *We went to the movies with Juan. We went with him.*
>
> **Quiero bailar con María. Quiero bailar <u>con</u> *ella*.**
> *I want to dance with Maria. I want to dance with her.*
>
> **Me gusta hablar con mis vecinos. Me gusta hablar <u>con</u> *ellos*.**
> *I like to talk with my neighbors. I like to talk with them.*
>
> **Nunca he ido al cine con mis hermanitas. Nunca he ido al cine <u>con</u> *ellas*.**
> *I have never gone to the movies with my little sisters. I have never gone to the movies with them.*

Ejercicio 3.16, página 325; Ejercicio de repaso 3.17, páginas 325–326

 Se

I. INTRODUCTION

The pronoun *se* in Spanish can have different usages, depending upon the context in which it is used:

- The indirect object pronouns *le* and *les,* when followed by a direct object pronoun such as *lo* or *la,* are transformed into *se*. (See Chapter 3.A.4, page 62.)
- *Se* is also the third-person singular and plural form of the reflexive pronoun.
- In its function as a reflexive pronoun, *se* can be used in constructions with a thing as a subject and a person as an indirect object to describe an accidental occurrence. In *Se me olvidó la tarea,* the subject of the verb is *tarea* and the person is the indirect object. In this type of sentence the thing is doing the action to itself (thus the reflexive), and the person appears as an innocent bystander or victim, indirectly affected by the event.
- The impersonal usage of *se* is where the action is being done with no subject mentioned—clearly someone is doing it, but it is irrelevant to the context. When you read *Se habla español* on the door of a store, it indicates that Spanish is spoken in that store in case of need. It is irrelevant to state who speaks the language.

OVERVIEW OF USES OF *SE*

1. *Le* or *les* transformed before *lo(s)* or *la(s)*
   Le di la flor. → **Se la di.**
   I gave her the flower. → *I gave it to her.*

2. Third-person reflexive
   Ella se levanta temprano. *She wakes up early.*

   Third-person reciprocal
   Ellos se odian. *They hate each other.*

3. Irresponsible or accidental
   Se me cayó el libro. *I dropped the book.*

4. Impersonal
   Se habla español. *Spanish is spoken.*

2. REFLEXIVE PRONOUNS

a. Reflexives

REFLEXIVE PRONOUNS

Person	Singular	Plural
1st	me	nos
2nd	te	os
3rd	se	se

A reflexive construction occurs when the subject and the object of a verb are the same person. In some cases, the object of the verb is direct.

Me lavo.   *I wash myself.*

In other cases, the object of the verb is indirect.

Se escribían todos los días.   *They wrote (to) each other every day.*

Certain verbs that refer to daily personal habits are most frequently used in the reflexive construction (see Chapter 6.J, pages 241–249, on reflexive verbs).

bañarse *to bathe (oneself)*   **lavarse** *to wash (oneself)*

despertarse *to wake (oneself) up*   **levantarse** *to get (oneself) up*

These verbs can be used nonreflexively, in a standard transitive construction, with the object different from the subject.

La madre bañó a su bebé. → **Lo bañó.**
The mother bathed her baby.   *She bathed him.*

Ella se bañó a las seis. → **Se bañó.**
She bathed (herself) at six.   *She bathed (took a bath).*

Possessives change to definite articles with parts of the body or articles of clothing.

Me lavé <u>las</u> **manos.**   *I washed my hands.*

Me puse <u>el</u> **abrigo.**   *I put on my coat.*

To stress or emphasize the reflexive pronouns, the following reflexive prepositional or stressed object pronouns are used.

REFLEXIVE PREPOSITIONAL OBJECT PRONOUNS		
Person	**Singular**	**Plural**
1st	mí	nosotros
2nd	ti	vosotros
3rd	sí	sí

These pronouns are used to mark a stressed pronoun after prepositions, and sometimes in constructions where the verb itself is not reflexive, but the action is.

Es muy codicioso. Se guarda todo <u>para sí (mismo)</u> y no deja nada para los demás.   *He is very greedy. He keeps everything for himself and leaves nothing for the rest.*

Lo hago <u>por mí</u>.   *I do it for myself.*

Lo compró <u>para sí</u>.   *She bought it for herself.*

Trajo el paraguas <u>consigo</u>.   *She brought the umbrella (with her).*

b. Reciprocals

The plural pronouns can be used for reciprocal actions as well.

Ellos <u>se</u> conocen bien. *They know each other well.*

In case of ambiguity, the following may be added.

RECIPROCAL	= *each other*	
	Singular	**Plural**
Masculine	el uno al otro	unos a otros
Feminine	la una a la otra	unas a otras

REFLEXIVE	= *myself, yourself,* etc.	
Person	**Singular**	**Plural**
1st	a mí mismo(a)	a nosotros(as) mismos(as)
2nd	a ti mismo(a)	a vosotros(as) mismos(as)
3rd	a sí mismo(a)	a sí mismos(as)

<u>Nos</u> conocemos <u>el uno al otro</u>.
We know each other. (Reciprocal)

<u>Nos</u> conocemos <u>a nosotros mismos</u>.
We know ourselves. (Reflexive—each one of us knows him- or herself.)

Ejercicios 3.18–3.20, páginas 326–327

3. *SE ME* CONSTRUCTION: ACCIDENTAL OR IRRESPONSIBLE *SE*

In Spanish there is a structure that is very commonly used when dealing with accidental, chance, or unplanned situations, where something happens that was not intended. This is often the case with such actions as forgetting, dropping, burning, breaking, etc. In these situations, the thing involved in the accident becomes the subject of the verb, and the verb is used in a reflexive format. The person, or victim of the accident, becomes the indirect object of the verb. Therefore, it might appear misleading to name this *se* differently from any other reflexive *se*—the only reason it is invariable is because things are always third-person singular or plural, never first- or second-person, forms that are reserved for humans.

Examples:

Se rompieron mis lentes. [subj.: **mis lentes;** d.o.: none]	*My glasses broke.*
Se rompió tu regla. [subj.: **tu regla;** d.o.: none]	*Your ruler broke.*
<u>**Se me**</u> **rompieron los lentes.**[9] [subj.: **los lentes**; i.o.: **a mí**)	*I (accidentally) broke*[10] *my glasses.* [subj.: *I*; d.o.: *my glasses*]
<u>**Se me**</u> **rompió tu regla.** [subj.: **tu regla;** d.o.: none]	*I (accidentally) broke your ruler.*

In English, as in Spanish, there are a number of verbs that can be used in such a way that the thing to which the accident occurred is the subject of the verb: things break, fall, tear, close, open, go out (light), wrinkle, get dirty, get wet, go bad, etc.

The difference in structure in Spanish is that to this accidental occurrence can be added the person to whom it happened. Notice that the possessive changes to a definite article when referring to a part of the body or an article of clothing or personal possession.

<u>**Se me**</u> **rompieron los lentes.**	*My glasses broke.*
<u>**Se te**</u> **rompieron los lentes.**	*Your* (tú) *glasses broke.*
<u>**Se le**</u> **rompieron los lentes.**	*His/Her/Your* (Ud.) *glasses broke.*
<u>**Se nos**</u> **rompieron los lentes.**	*Our glasses broke.*
<u>**Se os**</u> **rompieron los lentes.**	*Your* (Vosotros) *glasses broke.*
<u>**Se les**</u> **rompieron los lentes.**	*Their/Your* (Uds.) *glasses broke.*

---

9. The nouns in these sentences that function as subject or indirect object may be placed before or after the verb.

Se me rompieron los lentes. = Los lentes se me rompieron.

10. If the action of breaking was done on purpose, the verb and pronouns behave "normally" in Spanish, with the person being the subject of the verb.

Ese chico me puso tan furioso que le rompí los lentes. (subj.: **yo**; d.o.: **lentes**)
That kid made me so angry that I broke his glasses.

Notice that *rompieron* is third-person plural because the subject of the verb is plural: *los lentes*. If the subject were singular, the verb would be singular too.

> **Se te rompió el lente.** *Your lens broke.*

If you wish to state the person to whom the accident happened, remember that the grammatical function of the person is the indirect object, introduced with the preposition *a*.

> **Se le olvidó la cita al paciente.** *The patient forgot the appointment.*
>
> **A Quico se le perdieron los boletos.** *Quico lost the tickets.*
>
> **Se le rompió el paraguas a Carmelita.** *Carmelita's umbrella broke.*

If the subject of this type of sentence need not be stated because it has already been mentioned before in the context, remember the basic rule that in Spanish there is no subject pronoun equivalent to "it" in English (or "they" when it is the plural of "it").

> —**¿Qué pasó con tu lente?** *"What happened to your lens?"*
> —**Se me rompió.** *"It broke."*

The following verbs can be used with this construction.

quemársele a uno *to burn*

On purpose: **Quemaron los libros.** *They burned the books.*
Accidental (no victim): **Los libros se quemaron.** *The books burned (up).*
Accidental (with victim): **Se nos quemaron los libros.** *Our books burned (up).*

caérsele a uno *to drop; to fall* (**Dejar caer** is used for the purposeful action, and means, literally, *to let fall*.)

On purpose: **Dejó caer el vaso.** *He dropped the glass.*
Accidental (no victim): **El vaso se cayó.** *The glass fell.*
Accidental (with victim): **Se le cayó el vaso.** *He dropped the glass.*

olvidársele a uno *to forget*

On purpose: **Olvidemos nuestros problemas.** *Let's forget our problems.*
Accidental (no victim): impossible in Spanish.
Accidental (with victim): **Se nos olvidó el libro.** *We forgot the book.*

In Spanish, a variety of unfortunate accidental occurrences can be described with this construction.

> **Se me cerró la puerta en la mano.** *The door closed on my hand.*
>
> **Se nos apagó el fuego.** *The fire went out (on us).*

Se nos fue la luz.	*The light (electricity) went out (on us).*
Los temblores no se me van.	*My shaking will not go away.*
Se te arrugó la falda.	*Your skirt got wrinkled.*
Se les ensuciaron los pantalones.	*Their pants got dirty.*
Se me cierran los ojos.	*My eyes are closing.*
El frío no se te va a quitar si no te pones los calcetines.	*The cold you feel is not going to go away if you do not put on your socks. (You will not warm up …)*
Siempre se te ocurren las ideas más raras.	*You always come up with the strangest ideas. (They come to your mind unexpectedly.)*
Se nos pasó la hora; ya son las nueve.	*We are running late; it is already nine. (The hour went by us … We forgot the time …)*
Se me quedaron los libros en casa.	*I left my books at home. (They stayed at home.)*
Se te paró el reloj.	*Your watch stopped.*
Se me pararon los pelos.	*I got goose bumps.*
Se le dobló la foto.	*She accidentally folded the picture. (Her picture got folded.)*

Notice that this construction cannot be used with every accident or involuntary action, even if the word "accidentally" or some similar indication of accident is added.

Me robaron el coche.	*They stole my car.*
Leímos el libro equivocado.	*We read the wrong book.*
Me caí.	*I fell down.*
Lo vi sin querer.	*I saw it by accident (unintentionally).*
Chocamos.	*We crashed (had a car accident).*

PRÁCTICA

Ejercicios 3.21–3.25, páginas 327–328; Ejercicio de repaso 3.26, páginas 328–329

4. IMPERSONAL *SE*

a. Introduction

The impersonal *se* is used for actions with no specific subject. These sentences correspond to the English passive voice or the impersonal "they," "you," "people," or "one."

En algunas regiones de México <u>se habla</u> maya.
In some regions of Mexico, they speak Maya.

No entiendo por qué <u>se dicen</u> tantas mentiras.
I do not understand why people tell so many lies.

No <u>se debe</u> llevar mucho cuando <u>se viaja</u>.
One should not take much when one travels.

There are other ways of expressing impersonal sentences in Spanish.

En España usan el "vosotros" como plural de "tú".
In Spain they use "vosotros" as the plural of "tú."

En época de sequía la gente come lo que haya.
In times of drought, people eat whatever there is.

Uno nunca sabe lo que el futuro puede traer.
One never knows what the future might bring.

In English the passive is used much more than in Spanish, where it is found mostly in literary contexts; the passive voice in Spanish can be seen in increasing frequency in journalistic prose, but this is considered to be the result of literal translation from English. For those who have not yet reached expertise in the language, it is best to avoid the passive voice in Spanish; instead, if the action of the verb has a subject or agent, use the active voice, and if there is no subject, use an impersonal structure. The stronger the degree of impersonality, the more Spanish would tend to use the impersonal *se*.

(1) AGENT PRESENT

Agent present → Spanish: active
She was awakened by the dog. → **El perro la despertó.**

In such a context as the one above, where the agent (dog) is stated, the active voice is preferred in Spanish. Although it would not be grammatically incorrect, there would be no reason to use a passive construction here in Spanish because there is an agent, or subject for the action of the verb (the dog). However, it would be grammatically incorrect to use the impersonal *se* to render this sentence into Spanish, given the presence of an agent.

(2) NO AGENT: IMPERSONAL

No agent: impersonal	→	Spanish: impersonal *se*
Spanish is spoken.	→	**Se habla español.**

The impersonal *se* is ideal for a context such as the one above, where there is no agent, and if you were to try to think about the implied subject of the verb you would see that it is impersonal, in that it could be replaced with "people," and not a specific individual.

(3) NO AGENT: NOT IMPERSONAL

No agent: not impersonal	→	Spanish active: nonspecific subject
She was found.	→	**La encontraron. Alguien la encontró.**

In the above context the subject is omitted, either because it is not the focus of the sentence, or because it is unknown, but notice that it does not have the same degree of impersonality as the implied subject of the previous sentence. If you tried to visualize the doer of the action of finding, you could imagine a specific individual or individuals rather than a generalized "people." The most common translation into Spanish would be the active with a nonspecific subject such as "they" or "somebody."

b. Impersonal *Se* with Inanimate Objects

When referring to inanimate objects, the inanimate object functions grammatically as the subject of the verb (i.e., the verb agrees in number with the inanimate object[s]).

Se habla español.	*Spanish is spoken.*
Se hablan muchas lenguas en Suiza.	*Many languages are spoken in Switzerland.*

If the subject of the verb has been stated previously in the context, and you wish to replace it with a pronoun, remember that there is no subject pronoun for inanimate objects (it/they).

Se habla.	*It is spoken.*
Se hablan.	*They are spoken.*
¿Cómo se dice eso?	*How do you say that?*
¿Cómo se dice?	*How do you say it?*
¿Cómo se prepara ese platillo?	*How do you prepare that dish?*
Se prepara con huevos y leche.	*You prepare it with eggs and milk.*

c. Impersonal *Se* with Persons

When an impersonal *se* structure refering to a sentence talks about a human being and not an inanimate object, the grammatical function of the person is that of the **direct object** of the verb, and there is no agreement; the personal *a* is used to differentiate from the reflexive. The verb remains invariable in person and number.

Se castigó <u>al</u> criminal.	*The criminal was punished.*

NOTE: If you were to use *el* instead of *al,* the structure would be reflexive: *The criminal punished himself.*

If the human direct object is plural, the verb is not affected.

Se torturaba a los disidentes.	*The dissidents were tortured.*

The person may be replaced by an indirect object[11] pronoun, although its function remains that of a direct object.

Se <u>le</u> castigó.	*He was punished.*
Se <u>les</u> torturaba.	*They were tortured.*

This construction avoids the confusion with reflexive constructions.

Reflexive:

Se castigaron.	*They punished themselves (or each other).*
Se mataron.	*They killed themselves (or each other).*

Impersonal:

Se <u>les</u> castigó.	*They were punished.*
Se <u>les</u> mató.	*They were killed.*

In rare cases where the persons are being perceived as a category, and not as specific individuals, they are treated in this construction as if they were things.

Se buscan empleados.	*Help needed. Now hiring.* (Literally: *Employees are being sought.*)

Notice that no article is used with *empleados,* since they are nonspecific.

---

11. In some dialects, the direct object is always used, *lo(s)* or *la(s),* whether animal or human. The examples would then be *se lo torturó (al hombre); se la bañó (a la gata).*

d.   Impersonal *Se* with Both Human and Inanimate Objects

In sentences with impersonal *se* and both human and inanimate objects, the person is the **indirect object** of the verb, and the inanimate object continues to function as the grammatical subject of the verb.

No se me dio una copia.	*I was not given a copy.*
No se nos anunciaron los cambios.	*The changes were not announced to us.*
Se les envió una invitación a los padres.	*The parents were sent an invitation. (OR: An invitation was sent to the parents.)*

Notice that in the third example, *les* is a repetitive indirect object pronoun referring to *los padres.*

e.   Impersonal Reflexive Construction—*Uno*

It is not possible to use both the reflexive and the impersonal *se* together. Use *se* as a reflexive pronoun and *uno* as an impersonal pronoun. Notice the variations of position in the following sentences.

Uno se levanta temprano en el ejército.
Se levanta uno temprano en el ejército.
One gets up early in the army.

Uno se broncea rápido con ese sol.
Con ese sol se broncea uno rápido.
With that sun, one tans quickly.

Ejercicios 3.27–3.30, páginas 329–330

Demonstrative and Possessive Pronouns

1. DEMONSTRATIVE PRONOUNS

In their form, these are identical to demonstrative adjectives (see page 41), except that, to distinguish them, an accent is added on the stressed syllable. (See page 21 for the use of the accent.)

DEMONSTRATIVE PRONOUNS		
	Singular	**Plural**
Masculine	éste	éstos
Feminine	ésta	éstas
Masculine	ése	ésos
Feminine	ésa	ésas
Masculine	aquél	aquéllos
Feminine	aquélla	aquéllas

éste = *this one;* **ése** = *that one* (near you);
aquél = *that one* (over there, far from you)

Examples:

Esta mesa es más grande que <u>ésa</u>.	*This table is larger than that one.*
—¿Qué asiento prefieres?	*"Which seat do you prefer?"*
—Me gusta más <u>éste</u>.	*"I like this one better."*
—¿Desea Ud. este pastel?	*"Do you want this cake?"*
—No, deme <u>aquél</u>, el de chocolate.	*"No, give me that one, the chocolate one."*

When there is no noun as referent for the pronoun, the neutral pronoun is used. Since there is no equivalent in adjective form, there is no need for the accent.

NEUTRAL DEMONSTRATIVE PRONOUNS	
esto	*this*
eso	*that*
aquello	*that*

Examples:

Esto es riquísimo.	*This is delicious.*
¿De quién es **eso**?	*Whose is that?*
Aquello fue aburrido.	*That was boring.*

2. POSSESSIVE PRONOUNS

Possessive pronouns are formed with the "long" form of the adjective (see page 42), with an added definite article that agrees with the possessed item, not with the possessor.

POSSESSIVE PRONOUNS	
mine	**el mío, la mía, los míos, las mías**
yours *(tú)*	**el tuyo, la tuya, los tuyos, las tuyas**
ours	**el nuestro, la nuestra, los nuestros, las nuestras**
yours *(vosotros)*	**el vuestro, la vuestra, los vuestros, las vuestras**
yours *(Ud./Uds.)* his hers its theirs	**el suyo, la suya, los suyos, las suyas**

Examples:

Mi mochila pesa más que <u>la tuya</u>.	*My knapsack weighs more than yours.*
—¿Cuál es mi café?	*"Which is my coffee?"*
—Éste es <u>el suyo</u>.	*"This one is yours."*
—Mis abuelos están en Florida.	*"My grandparents are in Florida."*
—¿Y <u>los vuestros</u>?	*"And yours?"*
—<u>Los nuestros</u> están en California.	*"Ours are in California."*

With *ser* the article is omitted.

Esa llave es <u>mía</u>.	*That key is mine.*

The article is used when there is a choice between items.

—¿Cuáles son tus llaves?	*"Which are your keys?"*
—Éstas son <u>las mías</u> y ésas son <u>las tuyas</u>.	*"These are mine and those are yours."*

Wherever there may be ambiguity regarding the reference of *suyo,* you can clarify the context by specifying with *de él, de ella, de usted, de ellos, de ellas, de ustedes.*

—¿**Cuál es mi café?**	*"Which is my coffee?"*
—**Éste es el <u>de usted</u>, este otro es el <u>de él</u>, ése es el <u>de ella</u>, y aquél es el <u>de ustedes</u>.**	*"This one is yours, this other one is his, that one is hers, and that one over there is yours."* (plural in Latin America, formal plural in Spain)

When the possessed item is not specific, but general (my things, my part, etc.), the neutral form *lo* is used instead of the article.

Quiero <u>lo mío</u> y nada más.	*I want what is mine, and nothing else.*

Ejercicio 3.31, página 330

◆ **D** Interrogatives

¿Qué?	*What? (before a noun—Which?)*
¿Cuál?	*Which? (before **ser**—What?)*
¿Cuánto(a)(s)?	*How much? How many?*
¿Quién?	*Who?*
¿Dónde?	*Where?*
¿Cómo?	*How?*
¿Por qué?	*Why?*
¿Cuándo?	*When?*

I. *¿QUÉ?*

This interrogative can be used either before a verb, or before a noun.

¿Qué quieres?	*What do you want?*
¿Qué es esto?	*What is this?*
¿Qué película prefieres ver?	*Which movie do you prefer to see?*

2. ¿CUÁL?

This interrogative too can be used before a verb, before *de* and a noun phrase, but not before a noun.

¿Cuál prefieres?	*Which one do you prefer?*
¿Cuál de estos libros es tuyo?	*Which one of these books is yours?*
¿Cuál es el tuyo?	*Which one is yours?*

3. ¿QUÉ? VS. ¿CUÁL? WITH SER

¿Qué? + *ser* asks for a definition, or the meaning of words.

¿Cuál? + *ser* asks for a pinpointing or specification.

We present here a few sets of dialogues for you to compare.

—¿Qué es "la bamba"?	*"What is 'La Bamba'?"*
—Es un baile folklórico mexicano.	*"It is a Mexican folkloric dance."*
—¿Cuál es "La Bamba"?	*"Which one is 'La Bamba'?"*
—Es la que están tocando ahora.	*"It's the one they are playing now."*

In these two dialogues, the context is completely different. The first person asking a question might have heard the two words "la bamba" for the first time, and is asking for the other person to explain what they mean. In the second dialogue, the person asking the question knows what "La Bamba" is, but cannot identify it when it is being played, and thus asks the other person to let him or her know when it is played.

—¿Cuál es tu apellido?	*"What is your last name?"*
—Gómez.	*"Gómez."*
—¿Cuál es tu apellido?	*"Which one is your last name?"*
—Es éste.	*"It's this one."*

Such a question with *¿Qué?* would be one inquiring about the meaning of the two words *tu* and *apellido,* or about the origin of the name.

—¿Qué es "tu apellido"?	*"What is 'tu apellido'?"*
—Es mi nombre de familia.	*"It's my family name."*
—¿Qué es tu apellido?	*"What is your last name?"*
—Es italiano.	*"It's Italian."*

If you want to ask about the difference between two things, you would ask the following.

¿Cuál es la diferencia?	*What is the difference?*

A child wanting to know what the word "difference" means would use *¿Qué?* for this question.

¿Qué es "diferencia"?	*What is "difference"?*

¿Cuál es? is used when you have in front of you a set of items out of which you want someone to select a specific one.

—¿Cuál es el tuyo?	*"Which one is yours?"*
—Éste.	*"This one."*

Following are some more examples of the use of *¿Cuál es?*. Think about the implications these same questions would have if they were asked with *¿Qué es?*.

¿Cuál fue el problema?	*What was the problem?*
¿Cuál era la fecha?	*What was the date?*
¿Cuál es tu número de teléfono?	*What is your phone number?*

When a noun follows the interrogative instead of the verb, *qué* is preferred.

¿Qué color te gusta más?	*What color do you prefer?*
¿Cuál es tu color favorito?	*Which is your favorite color?*

Who has a singular and a plural form in Spanish: *¿Quién? ¿Quiénes?*.

¿Quién te dijo eso?	*Who told you that?*
¿Quiénes fueron a la fiesta?	*Who (all) went to the party?*

Whose is translated with the preposition *de* preceding *¿quién(es)?*.

¿De quién es esto?	*Whose is this?*

In Spanish, the preposition must always precede the interrogative.

¿De dónde eres?	*Where are you from?*
¿Para qué sirve esto?	*What is this for?*
¿Con cuál lo escribiste?	*Which one did you write it with?*

4. "How?"

The translation into Spanish of questions starting with "How?" will vary depending upon whether a verb or an adjective or adverb follows the interrogative.

a. "How" + Verb = ¿*Cómo*?

¿<u>Cómo</u> estás?	*How are you?*
¿<u>Cómo</u> lo hiciste?	*How did you do it?*
¿<u>Cómo</u> llegaron?	*How did they get here?*

Be aware of the following questions.

¿<u>Cómo</u> te llamas?	*What is your name?*
¿<u>Cómo</u> es?	*What is he/she/it like?*

b. "How" + Adjective or Adverb

Never use ¿*cómo*? to translate "how?" followed by an adjective or adverb.

HOW + Adjective or Adverb QUESTION	NOUN EQUIVALENT	SPANISH QUESTION	LITERAL MEANING
How tall is he?	height = **estatura**	¿Qué estatura tiene?	What height does he have?
		¿Cuánto mide de estatura?	What does he measure in height?
How important is it?	importance = **importancia**	¿Qué importancia tiene?	What importance does it have?
		¿Cuál es su importancia?	What is its importance?
How far is it?	distance = **distancia**	¿A qué distancia queda?	At what distance is it?
How big is it?	size = **tamaño**	¿De qué tamaño es?	What size is it?
How old is she?	age = **edad**	¿Qué edad tiene?	What age does she have?
How fast do you run?	speed = **velocidad**	¿A qué velocidad corres?	At what speed do you run?
How often do you see him?	frequency = **frecuencia**	¿Con qué frecuencia lo ves?	With what frequency do you see him?

In Mexico, "How tall is he?" is translated as *¿Qué tan alto es?*, and in the Caribbean as *¿Cuán alto es?*, but in many other Spanish-speaking countries, neither of these forms is used. This type of question must be reformulated using a noun instead of the adjective or adverb by saying, for example, "What is his height?". If you learn the last type of reformulated question, you'll be best equipped for communicating this question in any Spanish-speaking country.

These questions may also be asked as follows.

¿Es muy alto? ¿Cómo es de alto?   **¿Es de nuestra edad?**

¿Es muy importante?   **¿Corres muy rápido?**

¿Queda muy lejos?   **¿Lo ves a menudo/frecuentemente?**

¿Es muy grande? ¿Cómo es de grande?

"How much/many?" = *¿Cuánto(a)(s)... ?*

¿<u>Cuánto</u> dinero tienes?   *How much money do you have?*

¿<u>Cuántos</u> huevos compraste?   *How many eggs did you buy?*

5. WORD ORDER

In questions beginning with interrogative words the standard word order is inverted: the verb precedes the subject.

¿<u>Qué</u> vio Rafael?   *What did Rafael see?*

¿<u>Cuándo</u> salió Silvana?   *When did Silvana leave?*

¿<u>Por qué</u> gritaron los niños?   *Why did the children yell?*

This rule applies in indirect discourse as well. (Notice the difference in English.)

No sé <u>qué</u> vio Rafael.   *I don't know what Rafael saw.*

No sé <u>cuándo</u> salió Silvana.   *I don't know when Silvana left.*

No sé <u>por qué</u> gritaron los niños.   *I don't know why the children yelled.*

Ejercicios 3.32–3.34, páginas 330–331

♦ E ♦ Exclamatives

¡Qué! + noun, adjective, or adverb	*What (a)(an) … ! How … !*
¡Cómo! + verb	*(How) … !*
¡Cuánto! + verb or noun	*How much … !*
¡Cuántos(as)! + noun	*How many … !*
¡Quién! + verb	*Who … !*

I. ¡QUÉ! + NOUN

Please notice in the following examples that Spanish does not use an article in this construction as English does when the noun is singular.

¡Qué alivio!	*What a relief!*
¡Qué problema!	*What a problem!*
¡Qué lío!	*What a mess!*
¡Qué nubes!	*What clouds!*

In some cases, the Spanish noun translates into an adjective in English, with a variety of constructions.

¡Qué asco!	*Ugh! Gross! How revolting!*
¡Qué calor (hace)!	*It is so hot!*
¡Qué frío (hace)!	*It is so cold!*
¡Qué cansancio (tengo)!	*I am so tired!*
¡Qué hambre (tengo)!	*I am so hungry!*

2. ¡QUÉ! + MODIFIED NOUN

Examples of the adjective preceding the noun:

¡Qué buena idea!	*What a good idea!*
¡Qué lindos ojos!	*What beautiful eyes!*

If the adjective follows the noun, it must be preceded by *más* or *tan*.

¡Qué libro más (tan) interesante!	*What an interesting book!*
¡Qué final más (tan) sorprendente!	*What a surprising end!*

3. ¡QUÉ! + ADJECTIVE

¡Qué interesante!	*How interesting!*

Some of these exclamations are very idiomatic, geographically or historically marked, and translate very differently depending upon the context or the period.

¡Qué rico!

This exclamation can be used in many situations. Essentially, it is a positive comment on practically anything, and means something like "How nice!". If referring to food, it could mean "Mmm! Delicious!".

Other similar expressions are as follows.

¡Qué bueno!	*Good! Great!*
¡Qué chévere!,[12] **¡Qué padre!,**[13] **¡Qué guay!,**[14] **¡Qué bestial!**[15]	*Wow!* (other equivalents: *Cool! Excellent! Awesome! Rad!*)

4. ¡QUÉ! + ADVERB

¡Qué rápido acabaste!	*You finished so fast! How quickly you finished! That was fast!*
¡Qué bien bailas!	*How well you dance! You dance so well! You are such a good dancer!*
¡Qué mal me siento!	*I feel so poorly!*

5. ¡CÓMO! + VERB

¡Cómo gritan!	*How they scream!*
¡Cómo te miraban!	*How they looked at you!*

---

12. The adjective *chévere* is used in Puerto Rico and other Caribbean countries.

13. The adjective *padre* is used in Mexico.

14. The adjective *guay* is used in Spain.

15. The adjective *bestial* is used in Bolivia, Ecuador, and other Spanish-speaking countries.

6.   ¡*CUÁNTO!* + VERB

¡Cuánto lo siento!

I am so sorry!

¡Cuánto me gusta este pan!

I like this bread so much!

¡Cuánto gastan!

They spend so much!

¡Cuánto quisiera ser así!

How I wish I could be like that!

7.   ¡*CUÁNTO(A)!* + NOUN

¡Cuánta paciencia tienes!

How patient you are! You are so patient!

¡Cuánto vino producen!

They produce so much wine!

8.   ¡*CUÁNTOS(AS)!* + NOUN

¡Cuántos amigos tienes!

You have so many friends!

¡Cuántas islas hay en el Caribe!

There are so many islands in the Caribbean!

9.   ¡*QUIÉN!* + VERB

¡Quién pudiera bailar como ella!

If only I could dance the way she does!

Ejercicios 3.35–3.36, página 331

F Indefinites and Negatives

INDEFINITE PRONOUNS	
Affirmative	**Negative**
alguien *someone*	**nadie** *nobody, no one, not anyone*
alguno(a) *someone, anyone, one*	**ninguno(a)** *no one, none, neither (of two)*
algunos *some* **unos** *some*	**ninguno** *nobody, no one, none, not any, not anyone*
algo *something*	**nada** *nothing, not anything*
cualquiera *anybody, any*	**nadie** *nobody, no one, not anyone*

Examples:

<u>Alguien</u> te llamó.	*Someone called you.*
No conozco a <u>nadie</u> aquí.	*I do not know anyone here.*
—¿Quieres <u>algo</u> de beber?	*"Do you want something to drink?"*
—No, no quiero <u>nada</u>, gracias.	*"No, I do not want anything, thank you."*
—No sé de dónde es.	*"I do not know where he is from."*
—¿Lo sabrá <u>alguno</u> de tus abuelos?	*"Would one of your grandparents know?"*
—No, <u>ninguno</u> de ellos lo sabe.	*"No, none of them knows."*
<u>Cualquiera</u> podría cantar mejor.	*Anybody could sing better.*

INDEFINITE ADJECTIVES	
Affirmative	**Negative**
algún *some* **todo** *all of*	**ningún*** *not any, no*

*Ningún is never plural.

Examples:

Algún libro tendrá eso.	*Some book will have that.*
Algunas manzanas son agrias.	*Some apples are bitter.*
Aquí no hay **ningún** niño.	*There is no little boy here.*
Toda la clase aplaudió.	*All of the class applauded.*
(NOTE: Do not use *de* after *todos*.)	
No regó **ninguna** flor.	*He did not water any flowers.*

INDEFINITE ADVERBIALS	
Affirmative	**Negative**
también *also*	**tampoco** *neither, not … either*
en alguna parte *somewhere*	**en ninguna parte** *nowhere, not anywhere*
de algún modo *somehow*	**de ningún modo** *no way, by no means*
alguna vez *ever, at some (any) time* **algunas veces** *sometimes* **una vez** *once* **algún día** *some day, ever* **siempre** *always*	**nunca** *never, not … ever*

Examples:

—Tú **también** lo hiciste.	*"You did it too."*
—Yo no lo hice. ¿Y tú?	*"I did not do it. Did you?"*
—Yo **tampoco** lo hice.	*"I did not do it either."*
—¿Dónde estará mi libro? No lo encuentro **en ninguna parte**.	*"Where is my book? I cannot find it anywhere."*
—Tiene que estar **en alguna parte**.	*"It has to be somewhere."*
—No puedo convencerlo **de ningún modo**.	*"I cannot convince him at all."*
—**De algún modo** lo convencerás.	*"Somehow you will convince him."*
—Cantó **una vez** en Buenos Aires.	*"She sang in Buenos Aires once."*
—Yo **nunca** la oí cantar.	*"I never heard her sing."*
—**Algún día** comprenderás.	*"Some day you will understand."*
—No comprenderé **nunca**.	*"I will never understand."*

| —<u>Siempre</u> cometes el mismo error. | *"You always make the same mistake."* |
| —Y tú <u>nunca</u> cometes errores... | *"And you never make mistakes ... ."* |

In questions, *alguna vez* and *algún día* mean "ever," the first for the standard meaning of "ever," the second for a distant future.

—¿Has ido a España <u>alguna vez</u>?	*"Have you ever been to Spain?"*
—No, <u>nunca</u> he ido a España.	*"No, I have never been to Spain."*
—¿Irás a España <u>algún día</u>?	*"Will you ever go to Spain?"*

If the negative precedes the verb, it is used alone; if it follows the verb, *no* or *ni* must precede the verb.

| <u>Nadie</u> te llamó. | *No one called you.* |
| <u>No</u> te llamó <u>nadie</u>. | |

| <u>Nada</u> le gusta. | *He does not like anything.* |
| <u>No</u> le gusta <u>nada</u>. | |

| <u>Nunca</u> lo vi. | *I never saw it.* |
| <u>No</u> lo vi <u>nunca</u>. | |

| <u>Tampoco</u> lo vi. | *I did not see it either.* |
| <u>No</u> lo vi <u>tampoco</u>. | |

Multiple negatives are frequent in Spanish.

| <u>Nunca</u> entiendes <u>nada</u>. | *You never understand anything.* |

| <u>Nunca</u> le digas <u>nada</u> a <u>nadie</u>. | *Never tell anything to anyone.* |

Ningún (Ninguna) is used for emphatic negatives.

| No tengo interés. | *I have no interest. I am not interested.* |

| No tengo <u>ningún</u> interés. | *I have no interest whatsoever. I am not interested at all.* |

NOTE: "Any," "anything," and "anyone" in English can be either negative or indefinite and translate differently into Spanish depending upon the usage.

NEGATIVE	INDEFINITE
No veo <u>ninguno</u>. *I do not see <u>any</u>.*	**Podríamos usar <u>cualquiera</u>.** *We could use <u>any</u>.*
No quiero <u>nada</u>. *I do not want <u>anything</u>.*	**<u>Cualquier cosa</u> serviría.** *<u>Anything</u> would work.*
No traigas a <u>nadie</u>. *Do not bring <u>anyone</u>.*	**<u>Cualquiera</u> podría hacer eso.** *<u>Anyone</u> could do that.*

Ejercicio 5.37, páginas 331–332

 Relative Pronouns

I. FORMATION AND USAGE

RELATIVE PRONOUNS
que *(invariable)*
el que (los que, la que, las que)
el cual (los cuales, la cual, las cuales)
lo que *(invariable)*
lo cual *(invariable)*
quien (quienes)
cuyo (cuyos, cuya, cuyas)
donde *(invariable)*

A relative pronoun refers to a noun (its antecedent) from the main clause and introduces a subordinate clause: a relative or adjectival clause. It joins two references to the same noun. (See Chapter 6.G.3, pages 211–212, on the use of the subjunctive in adjectival clauses.)

1. **El estudiante se especializa en español.**
   The student is a Spanish major.
2. **El estudiante vino a verme.**
   The student came to see me.
1 + 2. **El estudiante <u>que</u> vino a verme se especializa en español.**
   The student who came to see me is a Spanish major.

In English, the relative pronoun is often not expressed.

> *The house we saw yesterday is too big.*

In Spanish, however, the relative pronoun cannot be omitted.

> **La casa <u>que</u> vimos ayer es demasiado grande.**

The relative pronoun follows its antecedent immediately; only a few structures, such as prepositions, can come between them.

> **Se quemó la <u>casa frente a la cual</u> me había estacionado.**
> *The house in front of which I had parked burned down.*

The antecedent *(casa)* and its relative pronoun *(la cual)* are separated by the preposition *frente a.*

A relative pronoun may hold the same variety of grammatical functions in a sentence that a noun can; it can thus be the subject, direct object, or indirect object of the verb of the relative clause or the object of the preposition that precedes it.

> **La autora <u>que</u> nos habló ayer es famosa en Chile.**
> *The author who spoke to us yesterday is famous in Chile.*
> Function of **<u>que</u>:** subject of **habló**

> **El perro <u>que</u> vimos es de los vecinos.**
> *The dog (that) we saw is the neighbors'.*
> Function of **<u>que</u>:** direct object of **vimos**

> **El hombre <u>al que</u> le preguntamos no sabía la respuesta.**
> *The man (whom) we asked did not know the answer.*
> Function of **<u>al que</u>:** indirect object of **preguntamos**

> **La ventana al lado de <u>la cual</u> trabajo no cierra bien.**
> *The window next to which I work does not close well.*
> Function of **<u>la cual</u>:** object of the preposition **al lado de**

There is often a variety of pronouns you may use depending upon the grammatical structure of the sentence. To simplify your task in learning to use these pronouns, we will be presenting here a reduced set of options that are always grammatically correct.

ANTECEDENT = ONE NOUN	NO PREPOSITION	PREPOSITION*
	que	el cual/el que**
ANTECEDENT = CLAUSE	lo que/lo cual	
the one ...	el que	
what	lo que	
whose	cuyo	

*A, de, en, and con may take que alone when the antecedent is an inanimate object.

**El/La que and el/la cual agree with their antecedent; cuyo agrees with the noun that follows it.

2. RELATIVE PRONOUNS WITHOUT A PREPOSITION

Que can always be used, whether the antecedent is an inanimate object or a human being. (Quien is <u>never</u> correct in this type of sentence.)

La casa <u>que</u> tengo en Ithaca es vieja. (a thing)
The house (that) I have in Ithaca is old.

El amigo <u>que</u> vive en Ithaca es viejo. (a person)
The friend who lives in Ithaca is old.

3. RELATIVE PRONOUNS WITH A PREPOSITION

a. El cual / el que[16]

The forms *el/la cual*, *los/las cuales*, *el/la que*, and *los/las que* can always be used. (NOTE: Always place the preposition before the relative pronoun.)

La compañía para <u>la cual/la que</u> trabajo es japonesa.
The company for which I work (I work for) is Japanese.

La mujer para <u>la cual/la que</u> trabajo es puertorriqueña.
The woman for whom I work (I work for) is Puerto Rican.

---

16. There is dialectal variation; in many areas, *el que* is preferred to *el cual*.

b. Exceptional Prepositions

The following prepositions[17] may be used with *que* alone when the antecedent is an inanimate object (not human): *a, de, en, con.*

> **La iglesia <u>a que</u> voy está en el centro.**
> *The church I go to is downtown.*

> **El libro <u>de que</u> me habló parece interesante.**
> *The book he talked to me about seems interesting.*

> **La silla <u>en que</u> me senté estaba pegajosa.**
> *The chair in which I sat was sticky.*

> **El lápiz <u>con que</u> escribo se me rompió.**
> *The pencil with which I write broke.*

4. ADDITIONAL USES

a. *Lo que / lo cual* (invariable)

If the antecedent is an entire clause, both *lo que* and *lo cual* are possible.

> **El examen fue difícil, <u>lo que/lo cual</u> nos sorprendió.**
> *The exam was hard, which surprised us.*

b. *El que*[18]

When used with *ser,* this pronoun means "the one," "the one who," "the one (that)," "the one (which)."

> **Margarita es <u>la que</u> me regaló estas flores.**
> *Margarita is the one who gave me these flowers.*

> **Ese libro es <u>el que</u> me gusta.**
> *That book is the one (that) I like.*

> **Esas mujeres, <u>las que</u> están vestidas de traje (y no las otras), son abogadas.[19]**
> *Those women, the ones wearing suits (not the other ones), are lawyers.*

---

17. They can also be used with *el que* or *el cual.*

18. *El que* followed by the subjunctive means "whoever" or "whomever."
    Regálaselo al que quieras. *Give it to whomever you want.*
    La que le gane a Sánchez se hará famosa. *Whoever beats Sánchez will become famous.*

19. If you were to use *la que* instead of *que* in the following sentence, it would translate as "the one who" and would sound absurd—in most cases.
    Mi madre, <u>que</u> vive en México, nunca viaja. *My mother, who lives in Mexico, never travels.*

Mi coche, <u>el que</u> está en el garaje, es un Ford.
My car, the one that is in the garage, is a Ford. (I have another one.)

<u>La que</u> me gustó fue la verde.
The one (table) I liked was the green one.

<u>Los que</u> no tenían eran los azules.
The ones they did not have were the blue ones.

<u>La que</u> me cae bien es Nilda.
The one I like is Nilda.

In structures such as these, *quien* is only required if the sentence is a proverb.

<u>Quien</u> bien te quiera te hará llorar.
Whoever loves you a lot will make you cry.

c. *Lo que*

When used without an antecedent at the beginning of a sentence, *lo que* means "what."

<u>Lo que</u> no entiendo es por qué lo hicieron. Eso es <u>lo que</u> me molesta.
What I do not understand is why they did it. That is what bothers me.

<u>Lo que</u> dijiste no es verdad.
What you said is not true.

<u>Lo que</u> me gustó fue la mesa.
What I liked was the table.

NOTE: *Lo que* followed by the subjunctive means "whatever."

Haré <u>lo que</u> digas.
I will do whatever you say.

d. *Cuyo*

This is a word that joins the attributes of a relative and a possessive: it means "whose." It functions like an adjective, and agrees with the noun referring to the possessed element, not with the possessor.

Tenemos un perro <u>cuyos</u> ojos siempre parecen tristes.
We have a dog whose eyes always seem sad.

NOTE: The interrogative "Whose?" is translated into Spanish with *¿De quién(es)?* (notice the accent mark).

> **¿De quién es este libro?** (direct discourse)
> *Whose book is this?*

> **No me dijo de quién era el libro.** (indirect discourse)
> *He did not tell me whose book it was.*

e. *Donde*

Donde means "where" and is invariable.

> **Prefiero las oficinas <u>donde</u> entra mucha luz del día.**
> *I prefer offices where there is a lot of daylight.*

NOTE: The interrogative "Where?" is translated into Spanish with *¿Dónde?*, with an accent mark.

> **¿Dónde están los niños?**
> *Where are the children?*

Remember that the interrogative in indirect discourse can be distinguished from the relative pronoun because of the absence of an antecedent.

> **Quería saber dónde estabas.**
> *He wanted to know where you were.*

f. "Who"

"Who" in a question translates as *quién*, but in a relative clause it is *que*.

(1) INTERROGATIVE PRONOUN: ¿QUIÉN?

> <u>**¿Quién**</u> **te dio eso?** (direct discourse)
> <u>*Who*</u> *gave you that?*

> **No sé <u>quién</u> lo hizo.** (indirect discourse)
> *I do not know <u>who</u> did it.*

(2) RELATIVE PRONOUN: QUE

Please be aware of the danger of translating "who" with *quien* in relative clauses, especially when there is no preposition before it. *Quien* is **never required** to translate the relative "who" or "whom."

Que translates as "who" when there is no preposition.

> **El candidato <u>que</u> copie perderá.** (**Never** use *quien* here.)
> *The candidate <u>who</u> copies will lose.*

(3) E<small>L CUAL</small> / <small>EL QUE</small>

El cual or *el que* are always possible with prepositions.

> **La estudiante con <u>la cual</u> llegaste es nueva.** (also: **con <u>la que</u>, con <u>quien</u>**)
> *The student with <u>whom</u> you arrived is new.*

g. "What"

"What" in a question translates as *qué,* but in a relative clause it is *lo que.*

Questions:

> **¿Qué dijo?** (direct discourse)
> *<u>What</u> did he say?*

> **No sé <u>qué</u> hacer.** (indirect discourse)
> *I do not know <u>what</u> to do.*

Relative clause:

> **Eso es <u>lo que</u> me gusta.**
> *That is <u>what</u> I like.*
> (antecedent = *that*)

> **<u>Lo que</u> hizo fue horrible.**
> *<u>What</u> he did was horrible.*
> (relative clause without an antecedent)

PRÁCTICA

Ejercicios 3.38–3.40, página 332; Ejercicios de repaso 3.41–3.42, páginas 333–335

Chapter 4

Prepositions, Adverbs, and Conjunctions

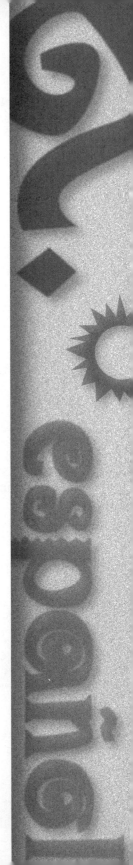

A Prepositions

B Adverbs

C Conjunctions

D Transitions

◆ Prepositions

I. FUNCTION OF PREPOSITIONS

A preposition relates a noun or its equivalent to another noun, to the verb, or to the rest of the sentence.

With nouns:

Salí <u>con Ana</u>.	*I went out with Ana.*
Esta comida es <u>para mi perro</u>.	*This food is for my dog.*

With pronouns:

Vete <u>con ellos</u>.	*Go with them.*
Entremos <u>en ésta</u>.	*Let's go into this one.* (e.g., **tienda**)
Vamos <u>en el mío</u>.	*Let's go in mine.* (e.g., **coche**)
¿Esta tortilla es <u>para alguien</u>?	*Is this tortilla for someone?*
No, no es <u>para nadie</u>.	*No, it is not for anyone.*
¿<u>Con quién</u> saliste?	*Whom did you go out with?*
Ése es el hombre <u>con el cual</u> llegó.	*That is the man she arrived with.*

With infinitives:

Terminé rápido <u>para salir</u>.	*I finished quickly so as to go out.*

When used in combination, prepositions may be grouped with adverbs or with other prepositions to form a single prepositional expression.

debajo de	**Se escondió <u>debajo de</u> la mesa.** *He hid under the table.*
delante de	**Ella se sienta <u>delante de</u> mí.** *She sits in front of me.*
dentro de	**La pluma está <u>dentro de</u> mi chequera.** *The pen is inside of my checkbook.*
detrás de	**Yo me siento <u>detrás de</u> ella.** *I sit behind her.*

encima de	**Pon las llaves <u>encima de</u> mi mochila.** *Put the keys on top of my knapsack.*
enfrente de	**Está <u>enfrente de</u> usted.** *It is in front of you.*
frente a	**Me senté <u>frente a</u> la estatua.** *I sat in front of the statue.*
fuera de	**Eso está <u>fuera de</u> mi alcance.** *That is out of my reach.*
para con	**Su actitud <u>para con</u>migo ha cambiado.** *His attitude toward me has changed.*
por delante de	**El desfile pasa <u>por delante de</u> la casa.** *The parade passes in front of the house.*
por encima de	**El avión voló <u>por encima de</u> mi casa.** *The plane flew over my house.*

PRÁCTICA

Ejercicio 4.1, página 336

2. VERBS USED WITHOUT PREPOSITIONS

The following verbs are transitive in Spanish, whereas in English they are not. The difference is that in Spanish, the thing or person you are waiting for, looking for, etc., is the direct object of the verb.

agradecer *to be grateful for*	**Te agradezco la ayuda.** *I am grateful to you **for** your help.*
buscar *to look for*	**—¿Qué buscas?** **—Estoy buscando mis llaves, pero no las encuentro.** *"What are you looking **for**?"* *"I am looking **for** my keys, but I cannot find them."*

esperar *to wait for*	**Esos niños siempre esperan el autobús en la esquina.** *Those children always wait **for** the bus on the corner.*
pedir + thing *to ask for* (something)	**Siempre me piden dinero cuando no tengo.** *They always ask me **for** money when I do not have any.* (See also *preguntar por* + person.)
pensar + inf. *to plan on*	**Pensamos ir a Sudamérica el verano entrante.** *We are planning **on** going to South America next summer.* (See also *pensar en* and *pensar de.*)

3. INDIVIDUAL PREPOSITIONS

a. *A*

(1) USAGE

A	
Usage	**Examples**
To introduce the indirect object	**Se lo dio <u>a</u> Jorge.** *He gave it to Jorge.*
To indicate direction toward something or some place, after a verb of movement **(ir, venir, bajar, subir, dirigirse, acercarse...)**	**Fueron <u>a</u> la cabaña.** *They went to the cabin.* **Subieron <u>al</u> tren.** *They got onto the train.*
To indicate the time at which something happens	**Me levanté <u>a</u> las ocho.** *I got up at eight.*
To indicate the period of time after which something happened	**Se divorciaron <u>a</u> los dos años.** *They divorced after two years.*
To indicate the distance at which something is	**Mi auto está <u>a</u> una cuadra.** *My car is one block away.*
Al + infinitive: To indicate simultaneous actions	**<u>Al</u> entrar, lo vi.** *When I went in, I saw it.*

(2) PERSONAL A

PERSONAL A	
Usage	**Examples**
To introduce a human or personified direct object	**Veo <u>a</u> Juan.** *I see Juan.* **Veo <u>a</u> mi perro.** *I see my dog.*
With indefinite pronouns **alguien, nadie, alguno, ninguno, cualquiera,** when referring to humans	**No veo <u>a</u> nadie.** *I do not see anyone.*
Omission	**Examples**
After **tener**	**Tengo una hermana.** *I have a sister.*
With indefinite direct objects	**Buscan secretarias.** *They are looking for secretaries.*

(See Chapter 2.A.3, pages 32–34, for more on the personal *a*.)

(3) EXPRESSIONS WITH A

a caballo

> **Llegaron <u>a caballo</u>.**
> *They arrived on horseback.*

a causa de

> **No pudimos ir <u>a causa de</u> la tormenta.**
> *We were unable to go because of the storm.*
>
> *because* + conjugated verb = **porque:**
> **No pudimos ir <u>porque</u> había una tormenta.**
> *We were unable to go because there was a storm.*

a eso de

> **Llegaron <u>a eso de</u> las tres.**
> *They arrived at about (around) three.*
> (NOTE: *A eso de* is used only with time, not with space: *It is about two miles away.* = **Está a unas dos millas.**)

a fondo

> **Quiero que estudies esto más <u>a fondo</u>.**
> *I want you to study this more in depth.*

a fuerza de	**A fuerza de trabajar día y noche, lo terminé.** *By (dint of) working day and night, I finished it.*
a la vez	**No puedo hacer dos cosas a la vez.** *I cannot do two things at the same time.*
al menos	**Nos quedan al menos dos horas.** *We have at least two hours left.*
a lo mejor	**¿Qué es eso? No sé; a lo mejor es el viento.** *What is that? I do not know; maybe it is the wind.*
a mano	**Lo hice a mano.** *I did it by hand.*
a menudo	**Visito a mi abuela a menudo.** *I visit my grandmother frequently (often).*
a ojo	**No tengo cinta métrica; tendré que calcular la distancia a ojo.** *I do not have a measuring tape; I will have to calculate the distance by eye (roughly, guessing).*
a pesar de	**Me gusta jugar en la nieve a pesar del frío.** *I like to play in the snow in spite of the cold.*
a pie	**Prefiero ir a pie por el ejercicio.** *I would rather go on foot (walking) for the exercise.*
a tiempo	**¡Por fin llegaste a tiempo!** *You finally arrived on time!*
a veces	**A veces no sé qué decir.** *Sometimes I do not know what to say.*

(4) Verbs with *A*[1]

acostumbrarse a + inf.
Me acostumbré a levantarme temprano.
I got used to getting up early.

aprender a + inf.
Quiero aprender a patinar.
I want to learn how to skate.

apresurarse a + inf.
Se apresuró a esconder el regalo.
She hurried to hide the present.

asistir a + noun
(not inf.)
Asistieron a clase ayer.
They attended class yesterday.

atreverse a + inf.
Se atrevió a hablar.
He dared to speak.

ayudar a + inf.
Me ayudaron a pintar la casa.
They helped me paint the house.

comenzar a + inf.
Comencé a estudiar inglés a los cinco años.
I began to study English at the age of five.

detenerse a + inf.
Los turistas se detuvieron a admirar la estatua.
The tourists stopped to admire the statue.

empezar a + inf.
Los pájaros empiezan a cantar al amanecer.
The birds begin to sing at dawn.

enseñar a + inf.
¿Quién te enseñó a cantar así?
Who taught you to sing like that?

invitar a + inf.
Te invito a ir al cine.
I invite you to go to the movies.

ir a + inf.
Vamos a comer a las ocho.
We are going to eat at eight.

---

1. Some verbs, like *aprender,* use *a* only to link to a following infinitive; others, like *acostumbrarse,* use *a* with any object including an infinitive; still others, like *asistir,* govern *a,* but do not take infinitives.

negarse a + inf.	**La víctima se negó a identificar al criminal.** *The victim refused to identify the criminal.*
ponerse a + inf.	**De repente, se puso a gritar.** *Suddenly, he began to scream.*
resignarse a + inf.	**Tendrás que resignarte a ganar menos dinero.** *You will have to resign yourself to earning less money.*
volver a + inf.	**Tu amigo volvió a llamar.** *Your friend called again.*

b. *Con*

(1) USAGE

CON	
Usage	**Examples**
To express accompaniment	**Vengan <u>con</u> nosotros al cine.** *Come with us to the movies.*
Followed by a noun in adverbial expressions	**Lo visitamos <u>con</u> frecuencia.** *We visit him frequently.*
To indicate adherence, content, possession	**El hombre <u>con</u> la guitarra se llama José.** *The man with the guitar is named José.*
Followed by an instrument or tool	**Tendremos que cortarlo <u>con</u> el serrucho.** *We will have to cut it with the saw.*
To indicate relation	**Habló <u>con</u> su novia.** *He spoke with his girlfriend.*
To indicate concession	**<u>Con</u> todo el dinero que tiene, más vale que no se queje.** *With all the money he has, he'd better not complain.*

(2) Expressions with Con

con respecto a	No sé qué hacer <u>con respecto a</u> mi abuela. *I do not know what to do regarding my grandmother.*
con tal (de) que	Te ayudaré <u>con tal (de) que</u> me pagues. *I will help you provided that you pay me.*

(3) Verbs with Con

casarse con	Se casó con su novio en Las Vegas. *She married her fiancé in Las Vegas.*
encontrarse con	Me encontré con mis amigos en el centro. *I met my friends downtown.*
enojarse con	Creo que se enojó conmigo. *I think she got mad at me.*
meterse con	No te metas con esa pandilla. *Do not get involved (mixed up) with that gang.*
quedarse con	Se quedó con mi libro. *She kept my book.*
soñar con	Anoche soñé contigo. *Last night I dreamed about you.*

c. *De*

(1) Usage

DE	
Usage	**Examples**
Possession	**El suéter <u>de</u> María es lindo.** *María's sweater is pretty.*
Origin, nationality	**Jorge es <u>de</u> Colombia.** *Jorge is from Colombia.*
Material something is made of	**La mesa es <u>de</u> madera.** *The table is (made of) wood.*
With noun complements functioning as adjectives	**Me encanta la clase <u>de</u> español.** *I love Spanish class.*
Followed by a noun, to describe condition or state	**<u>De</u> niña, me dormía fácilmente.** *As a child, I fell asleep easily.*
With **estar** to signify "acting as"	**Están <u>de</u> directoras este semestre.** *They are working (acting) as directors this semester.*
With **estar** in typical expressions: **de pie, de rodillas, de luto, de acuerdo con, de buen humor, de mal humor, a favor de, en contra de, de huelga, de vacaciones, de viaje, de visita, de vuelta, de regreso**	**No estoy <u>de</u> acuerdo contigo.** *I do not agree with you.* **Los obreros están <u>de</u> huelga.** *The workers are on strike.*
To indicate the place of something or someone	**La farmacia <u>de</u> la esquina cerró.** *The corner drugstore closed.* **Conozco a la gente <u>del</u> barrio.** *I know the people of the neighborhood.*
To describe people by something physical or worn	**El hombre <u>del</u> bigote.** *The man with the mustache.* **La mujer <u>de</u> ojos azules.** *The woman with blue eyes.*

(2) Expressions with De

(See Chapter 7.D, page 272, for expressions with *estar + de*.)

de buena/mala gana	Lo hizo <u>de buena gana</u>. *He did it willingly.*
de esta manera	Mira, se hace <u>de esta manera</u>. *Look, this is the way you do it.*
de modo que	Habló rápido <u>de modo que</u> no la interrumpieran. *She spoke quickly so that they would not interrupt her.* <u>De modo que</u> no me vas a decir tu secreto, ¿eh? *So, you are not going to tell me your secret, are you?*
de nuevo	El vecino se estacionó <u>de nuevo</u> en nuestra entrada. *The neighbor parked in our entrance again.*
de pie	He estado <u>de pie</u> todo el día. *I have been standing all day long.*
de repente	<u>De repente</u> empezó a llover a cántaros. *Suddenly it started pouring.*
de veras	<u>De veras</u> que no sé la respuesta. *I really do not know the answer.*
de vez en cuando	<u>De vez en cuando</u> me gusta viajar. *Once in a while I like to travel.*

(3) Verbs with De

acabar de + inf.	Acabo de comer. *I just ate.* Acababa de comer. *I had just eaten.* Acabé de comer. *I finished eating.*
acordarse de	Me acordé de ponerme el reloj. *I remembered to put on my watch.*
alegrarse de	Me alegro de verte. *I am glad to see you.*

arrepentirse de	**Se arrepintió de haberse burlado de ella.** *He regretted having made fun of her.*
avergonzarse de	**Me avergüenzo de mis estupideces.** *I am ashamed of my stupidities.*
burlarse de	**¡No se burlen de él!** *Do not make fun of him!*
darse cuenta de	**Me di cuenta de mi error.** *I realized my mistake.*
dejar de	**Dejen de molestar al perro.** *Stop bothering the dog.*
depender de	**—¿Cuál es la verdad?** **—Depende de quién habla.** *"Which is the truth?"* *"It depends on who is speaking."*
despedirse de	**Nos despedimos de nuestros padres en el aeropuerto.** *We said good-bye to our parents at the airport.*
enamorarse de	**Se enamoró de ella.** *He fell in love with her.*
enterarse de	**¿Te enteraste de las noticias?** *Did you hear (find out about) the news?*
estar enamorado(a) de	**Estamos enamorados de la misma chica.** *We are in love with the same girl.*
irse de + place	**Se fueron de la universidad ayer.** *They left the university yesterday.*
olvidarse de	**No te olvides de sacar la basura.** *Do not forget to take out the garbage.*
pensar de	**¿Qué piensas de este libro?** *What do you think about this book?* (i.e., Do you like it?)
quejarse de	**Se quejaron del trabajo.** *They complained about the work.*

reírse de	**Nunca se ríen de mis chistes.** *They never laugh at my jokes.*
terminar de + inf.	**Terminé de preparar la cena.** *I finished preparing dinner.*
tratar de + inf.	**Trataron de ayudarme, pero no pudieron.** *They tried to help me, but could not.*
tratarse de	**—Me gustó esa película.** **—¿De qué se trata?** **—Se trata de una familia durante la Segunda Guerra Mundial.** *"I liked that movie."* *"What is it about?"* *"It is about a family during the Second World War."*

d. *En*

(1) USAGE

EN	
Usage	**Examples**
To indicate where something takes place or is located	**Estábamos <u>en</u> la playa.** *We were at the beach.*
Signifiying "in, inside"	**Ese cuaderno está <u>en</u> mi mochila.** *That notebook is in my knapsack.*
Signifing "on, on top of"	**Tu libro está <u>en</u> mi escritorio.** *Your book is on my desk.*
With time expressions—months, years, and other expressions of time (but not days of the week: **Lo haré el lunes.** *I will do it on Monday.*)	**La visité <u>en</u> enero.** *I visited her in January.* **No quería verlo <u>en</u> ese momento.** *I did not want to see him at that moment.*
With ordinal numbers followed by the infinitive	**Fue el primero <u>en</u> irse.** *He was the first to leave.*

(2) EXPRESSIONS WITH *EN*

en cambio
    Yo no hablaba su idioma; ellos, en cambio, sí hablaban inglés.
    I did not speak their language; they, however, did speak English.

en cuanto
    Llámame en cuanto llegues a casa, por favor.
    Call me as soon as you get home, please.

en cuanto a
    En cuanto a la comida india, no sé mucho.
    In regard to Indian food, I do not know much.

en frente de
    Se sentó en frente de mí en el cine.
    She sat in front of me at the movies.

en seguida
    Vendrá en seguida (OR: enseguida).
    He will come right away (immediately).

en vez de
    En vez de llorar, deberíamos reír.
    Instead of crying, we should laugh.

(3) VERBS WITH *EN*

Some of these may take the infinitive, others not.

consentir en
    Ella nunca consentirá en casarse contigo.
    She will never consent to marrying you.

consistir en
    ¿En qué consiste este programa?
    What does this program consist of?

convenir en
    Convinimos en encontrarnos a las diez.
    We agreed to meet at ten.

convertirse en
    Estas semillas pronto se convertirán en plantitas.
    These seeds will soon become little plants.

empeñarse en	**Se empeñó en pagarme lo que me debía.**
	He insisted on paying me what he owed me.
entrar en	**Entró en la clase corriendo.**
	He entered the classroom running.
especializarse en	**Ella se especializa en ingeniería.**
	She is majoring in engineering.
fijarse en	**No me había fijado en sus ojos.**
	I had not noticed his eyes.
influir en	**La enseñanza influye en nuestras decisiones.**
	Education influences our decisions.
insistir en	**Insistimos en pagar.**
	We insist on paying.
pensar en	**Pienso en ti a menudo.**
	I often think of you.
tardar en	**Tardaron mucho en contestar.**
	They took a long time to answer.

PRÁCTICA

Ejercicios 4.2–4.7, páginas 336–338

e. *Para*

(1) USAGE

PARA	
Usage	**Examples**
Destination	**Lo escribí para la profesora de historia.** *I wrote it for the history professor.*
Purpose	**Lo hice para ti.** *I did it for you. (e.g., to give it to you)* **Fue a la tienda para comprar pan.** *He went to the store to (so as to) buy bread.* **¿Para qué sirve esto?** *What is this for?* **Es un buen libro para leer.** *It is a good book to read.* **Necesita una mesa para estudiar.** *He needs a table to study.*
Destination in time, deadline	**Lo terminaré para las diez.** *I will finish it by ten.*
Destination in space	**Salimos para Europa.** *We left for Europe.* **Ven para acá.** *Come over here.*
Comparison with the "norm"	**Para extranjero, habla muy bien.** *For (Considering he is) a foreigner, he speaks very well.*
To indicate the employer	**Ella trabaja para el gobierno.** *She works for the government.*
With **estar**, meaning "to be about to" (in Spain)	**¿Estabais para salir?** *Were you about to leave?*

(2) EXPRESSIONS WITH *PARA*

no estar para bromas

No estoy para bromas hoy.
I am not in the mood for jokes today.

no ser para tanto

¡No llores! No es para tanto.
Do not cry! It is not that bad.

para siempre

Pensé que la conferencia duraría para siempre.
I thought the lecture would last forever.

f. *Por*

(1) Usage

POR	
Usage	**Examples**
To introduce the agent of the passive voice	**Esa novela fue escrita <u>por</u> Cervantes.** *That novel was written by Cervantes.*
Reason	**Lo hice <u>por</u> ti.** *I did it because of you.*
Cause	**<u>Por</u> comer tanto, le dio dolor de estómago.** *He got a stomachache from eating so much.* **No fuimos <u>por</u> la lluvia.** *We did not go because of the rain.*
Through time	**Trabajó <u>por</u> dos horas.** *She worked for two hours.*
Through space	**Pasamos <u>por</u> el parque.** *We went through the park.* **Los vi <u>por</u> aquí.** *I saw them somewhere around here.*
Means of communication	**Te llamaron <u>por</u> teléfono.** *They called you on the phone.*
Means of transportation	**Lo mandaron <u>por</u> avión.** *They sent it airmail.*
Exchange	**Te daré un dólar <u>por</u> tu ayuda.** *I will give you a dollar (in exchange) for your help.*
Indicating substitution (instead of)	**Ella trabajó <u>por</u> mí porque estaba enfermo.** *She worked for (instead of) me, because I was ill.*
With verbs of movement, introducing a noun, signifying "to get" or "to fetch"	**Fue a la tienda <u>por</u> pan.** *He went to the store for (to fetch) bread.*
With **estar,** meaning "to be about to" (in Latin America) or "to be in favor of"	**Estamos <u>por</u> salir.** *We are about to leave.* **Yo estoy <u>por</u> la libertad de expresión.** *I am in favor of freedom of speech.*
With **quedar,** followed by the infinitive, meaning "(yet) to be done"	**Me quedan dos tareas <u>por</u> hacer.** *I have two assignments (yet) to be done.*

(2) Expressions with *Por*

por eso	**Llueve. <u>Por eso</u> llevo el paraguas.** *It is raining. That is why I am taking my umbrella.*
por fin	**<u>Por fin</u> me dieron trabajo.** *They finally gave me work.*
por lo general	**<u>Por lo general</u> estudio de noche.** *As a rule, I study at night.*
por lo menos	**Me dijo que tardaría <u>por lo menos</u> una hora.** *He told me that it would take him at least an hour.*
por otra parte	**No me gusta el clima aquí. <u>Por otra parte</u>, sí me gusta el pueblo.** *I do not like the climate here. On the other hand, I do like the town.*
por poco	**¡<u>Por poco</u> me caí!** *I almost fell!*
por... que + subjunctive	**<u>Por más que</u> trate, no puedo alzarlo.** *However much I try, I cannot lift it.* **<u>Por más</u> sed <u>que</u> tenga, no bebe.** *However thirsty she may be, she will not drink.* **<u>Por</u> alto <u>que</u> sea, no alcanzo el techo.** *However tall I may be, I cannot reach the roof.*
por supuesto	**—¿Te gustaría ir al cine conmigo?** **—¡<u>Por supuesto</u>!** *"Would you like to go to the movies with me?"* *"Of course!"*

(3) Verbs with *Por*

esforzarse por

> **Ella se esfuerza por darles lo mejor a sus hijos.**
> *She makes an effort to give her children the best.*

interesarse por

> **Me intereso por tu futuro.**
> *I am interested in your future.*

preguntar por + person

> **Llamó Carlos y preguntó por ti.**
> *Carlos called and asked for you.*

preocuparse por

> **No te preocupes por mí.**
> *Do not worry about me.*

tomar por

> **Lo tomaron por idiota.**
> *They took him for an idiot.*

PRÁCTICA

Ejercicios 4.8–4.10, página 338

4. LIST OF EXPRESSIONS WITH PREPOSITIONS (ENGLISH–SPANISH)

EXPRESSIONS WITH PREPOSITIONS			
English	**Spanish**	**English**	**Spanish**
again	de nuevo	not to exaggerate	no ser para tanto
almost	por poco	of course	por supuesto
as soon as	en cuanto	often	a menudo
at about, around (time)	a eso de	on foot	a pie
at least	al menos, por lo menos	on horseback	a caballo
at the same time	a la vez	on the other hand	por otra parte
because of	a causa de	on time	a tiempo
because of that	por eso	once in a while	de vez en cuando
by dint of	a fuerza de	provided that	con tal (de) que
conversely, however	en cambio	really	de veras
finally	por fin	regarding	con respecto a
forever	para siempre	sometimes	a veces
however much . . .	por... que... + subj.	standing	de pie
immediately	en seguida; enseguida	suddenly	de repente
in depth	a fondo	that is why	por eso
in front of	en frente de	to agree to	convenir en
in general, as a rule	por lo general	to ask a question	hacer una pregunta
in regard to	en cuanto a	to ask for someone	preguntar por alguien
in spite of	a pesar de	to ask for something	pedir algo
in such a way that	de modo que	to be about, deal with (e.g., a story)	tratarse de
in that way	de esa manera	to be ashamed of	estar avergonzado de
instead of	en vez de	to be glad that	alegrarse de
maybe	a lo mejor	to be in love with	estar enamorado de
not to be up for jokes	no estar para bromas	to get used to	acostumbrarse a

EXPRESSIONS WITH PREPOSITIONS

English	Spanish	English	Spanish
to begin to	comenzar a, empezar a, ponerse a	to laugh at	reírse de
to complain about	quejarse de	to learn to	aprender a
to consent to	consentir en	to look for	buscar (no prep.)
to consist of	consistir en	to major (specialize) in	especializarse en
to dare to	atreverse a	to make an effort to	esforzarse por
to delay in doing	tardar en	to make fun of	burlarse de
to depend on	depender de	to marry, get married to	casarse con
to do again	volver a	to meet	conocer, encontrarse con
to fall in love with	enamorarse de	to notice	fijarse en
to feel ashamed of	avergonzarse de	to plan (to do something)	pensar + inf. (no prep.)
to find out about	enterarse de	to realize	darse cuenta de
to finish	terminar de	to refuse to	negarse a
to fire someone	despedir a alguien	to remember	acordarse de
to forget about	olvidarse de, olvidar (no prep.), olvidársele a uno	to repent, regret	arrepentirse de
to get angry with	enojarse con	to say good-bye to	despedirse de
to have just (done)	acabar de	to stop to (do something)	detenerse a
to help to	ayudar a	to take for	tomar por
to hurry to	apresurarse a	to teach to	enseñar a
to influence	influir en	to thank (someone) for	agradecer (no prep.)
to insist on	empeñarse en, insistir en	to think about	pensar en, pensar de
to intend to (do something)	pensar + inf. (no prep.)	to try to	tratar de
to interest oneself in, become interested in	interesarse por	to wait for	esperar + noun (no prep.)
to invite to	invitar a	to worry about	preocuparse por
to keep	quedarse con	willingly/unwillingly	de buena/mala gana

5. REVIEW OF EXPRESSIONS WITH PREPOSITIONS

por	(más) + *adj./adv.* + que	a	lo mejor	de	pie
de	buena/mala gana	por	lo menos	por	poco
en	cambio	al	menos	de	repente
en	cuanto	por	más + *noun* + que	en	seguida
por	eso	por	más que	para	siempre
de	esta manera	a	menudo	por	supuesto
por	fin	de	modo que	con	tal (de) que
a	fondo	de	nuevo	a	tiempo
a	la vez	por	otra parte	a	veces
por	lo general	a	pie	de	veras

no estar	**para**	bromas
no ser	**para**	tanto

de	vez	**en**	cuando

a	causa	de
a	eso	de
a	fuerza	de
a	pesar	de
con	respecto	a
en	cuanto	a
en	frente	de
en	vez	de

acabar (+ inf.)	de	depender	de	olvidar	Ø
acordarse	de	despedirse	de	olvidarse	de
acostumbrarse	a	detenerse (+ inf.)	a	pedir (+ thing)	Ø
agradecer	Ø	empeñarse	en	pensar	en
alegrarse	de	empezar (+ inf.)	a	pensar (+ inf.)	Ø
aprender (+ inf.)	a	enamorarse	de	pensar (opinion)	de
apresurarse (+ inf)	a	encontrarse	con	ponerse (+ inf.)	a
arrepentirse	de	enojarse	con	preguntar (+ person)	por
atreverse (+ inf.)	a	enseñar (+ inf.)	a	preocuparse	por
avergonzarse	de	enterarse	de	quedar (+ inf.)	por
ayudar (+ inf.)	a	esforzarse	por	quedarse	con
burlarse	de	especializarse	en	quejarse	de
buscar (+ thing)	Ø	esperar	Ø	reírse	de
casarse	con	estar enamorado	de	resignarse	a
comenzar (+ inf.)	a	fijarse	en	soñar	con
consentir	en	influir	en	tardar	en
consistir	en	insistir	en	terminar	de
convenir	en	interesarse	por	tomar	por
convertirse	en	invitar (+ inf.)	a	tratar (+ inf.)	de
darse cuenta	de	irse	de	tratarse	de
dejar (to let, leave)	Ø	meterse	con	volver (+ inf.)	a
dejar (to stop) (+ inf.)	de	negarse (+ inf.)	a		

PRÁCTICA

Ejercicios 4.11–4.21, páginas 338–342

B. Adverbs

I. DEFINITION

An adverb is a word that modifies a verb, an adjective, another adverb, or a sentence. The following are examples of adverbs.

Habla <u>bien</u>.	*She speaks well.*
El pasto está <u>muy</u> alto.	*The grass is very tall.*
Camina <u>muy lentamente</u>.	*He walks very slowly.*

2. ADVERBS ENDING IN -MENTE

Adverbs ending in *-mente* are formed with the feminine of the adjective.

Adjective	→	**Feminine**	→	**+ -mente**
lento	→	lenta	→	lentamente

Adjectives that do not have a different feminine form will be formed with the base of the adjective.

Adjective	→	**Adverb**
alegre	→	alegremente
vil	→	vilmente

Adjectives with an accent maintain the accent when transformed into adverbs.

Adjective	→	**Adverb**
fácil	→	fácilmente

When placed in a series, adverbs ending in *-mente* drop the ending except for the last of the series.

El presidente habló discreta, elegante y apasionadamente.
The president spoke discreetly, elegantly, and passionately.

This rule may be ignored if the effect desired is one of monotony.

El profesor presentaba sus explicaciones detalladamente, pausadamente, aburridamente.
The professor presented his explanations in detail, slowly, boringly.

Note that one adverb ending in -*mente* may not modify another adverb ending in -*mente*. It would be incorrect to say:

~~Lo presentó sorprendentemente claramente~~.
He presented it surprisingly clearly.

You would have to say:

Lo presentó muy claramente. OR: **...con una claridad sorprendente.**

3. WORD ORDER

In Spanish the adverb is best placed close to the word it modifies. Notice the difference in English.

Raúl entró <u>silenciosamente</u> al cuarto.	*Raúl entered the room quietly.*
Habla <u>bien</u> el español.	*She speaks Spanish well.*

4. MULTIPLE-FUNCTION WORDS

There are words that serve as adjectives, as pronouns, or as adverbs depending upon their function in the sentence: *mucho, poco, bastante, tanto, cuanto, algo, nada,* etc. Compare the following sentences.

a. Comen <u>mucho</u> pan.	*They eat a lot of bread.*
b. Comen <u>mucho</u>.	*They eat a lot.*
c. Corren <u>mucho</u>.	*They run a lot.*

In sentence **a.** above, *mucho* modifies *pan,* and is an adjective. Notice that this is confirmed by the fact that if you changed *pan* to a plural, the adjective would also change. This is one distinction between adjectives and adverbs: adverbs are invariable, whereas adjectives change according to the noun they modify, as the following sentence illustrates.

d. Comen <u>muchas</u> frituras.	*They eat a lot of fried foods.*

In sentence **b.,** *mucho* can be a pronoun, which incorporates *pan*, or it could be an adverb, which is invariable and modifies the verb *comen*, and does not relate to any particular food. Similarly, if you wanted *mucho* to refer to a previously mentioned *frituras*, you would say *Comen <u>muchas</u>*. If you are dealing with a transitive verb such as *comer*, only context can determine whether or not an object is being referred to.

In sentence **c.,** the verb is intransitive, and therefore *mucho* is an adverb.

Some adjectives are frequently used as adverbs.

Habla <u>claro</u>.	*Speak clearly.*
Caminen <u>derecho</u>.	*Walk straight ahead.*
Lo pronuncian <u>distinto</u>.	*They pronounce it differently.*
Pégale <u>duro</u>.	*Hit it hard.*
Respira <u>hondo</u>.	*Breathe deep. (Take a deep breath.)*
Lo hice <u>igual</u>.	*I did it the same way.*
Juega <u>limpio</u>.	*Play fairly, cleanly. (Don't cheat.)*
Corro <u>rápido</u>.	*I run fast.*
Hablan <u>raro</u>.	*They speak in a strange fashion.*

In some cases, there can be different meanings for the same word, depending upon whether it is used as an adjective or as an adverb, or whether it ends in -*mente* or not. Consider the following differences.

Es un hombre <u>alto/bajo</u>.	*He is a tall/short man.* (adjective)
Ella habla <u>alto/bajo</u>.	*She speaks loudly/quietly.* (adverb)
Es un hombre <u>altamente</u> moral.	*He is a very moral man.*
Lo hizo <u>bajamente</u>.	*He did it meanly.*

PRÁCTICA

Ejercicio 4.22, página 342

5. ADVERBS OF PLACE

abajo	*below*
acá	*(over) here*
adelante	*ahead, in front*
adentro	*inside*
adonde	*where (to)*
¿adónde?	*where? (to)*
afuera	*outside*

ahí	*there (=* **allí***)*
allá	*(over) there*
allí	*there*
aquí	*here*
arriba	*up, above*
atrás	*back, behind*
cerca	*nearby*
debajo	*underneath, beneath, under*
delante	*ahead, in front*
dentro	*inside*
detrás	*back, behind*
donde	*where*
¿dónde?	*where?*
encima	*on top*
fuera	*outside*
lejos	*far*

a. *Acá / allá; aquí / allí*

Acá and *allá* are generally used with verbs of movement, whereas *aquí* and *allí* are used with verbs of state.

> **Vengan <u>acá</u> primero y luego vayan <u>allá</u>.**
> *Come here first and then go there.*

> **Están <u>aquí</u> ahora.**
> *They are here now.*

Aquí and *allí* refer to a more specific spot or location, whereas *acá* and *allá* refer to a general area close to or far from the speaker.

> —**No sé dónde puse mis libros. Pensé que estaban aquí.**
> —**Creo que los vi allá, en el otro cuarto. Ah, no, mira: allí están, en el estante cerca de ti.**
> *"I don't know where I put my books. I thought they were here."*
> *"I think I saw them over there, in the other room. Oh, no, look: there they are, on the shelf next to you."*

b. *Arriba, encima; abajo, debajo; bajo*

Arriba and *abajo* refer to a location above and below a reference point, whereas *encima* and *debajo* have more specificity, and mean "on top of" or "underneath," and there might be contact with the top or bottom surface.

Compare the following sentences.

No entiendo por qué mis lentes están debajo de la mesa, cuando yo los había puesto encima.	*I don't understand why my glasses are under the table, when I had put them on top.*
Ellos viven arriba.	*They live above (upstairs).*

The adverbs *debajo de* and *bajo* have a similar distinction. Notice the difference in literal vs. abstract meaning of the following sentences.

Las raíces están debajo del árbol.	*The roots are underneath the tree.*
Almorzaron bajo el árbol.	*They ate lunch under the tree.*
Trabajo bajo su supervisión.	*I work under her supervision.*

PRÁCTICA

Ejercicio 4.23, páginas 342–343

6. ADVERBS OF TIME

ahora	*now*
anoche	*last night*
anteayer	*the day before yesterday*
antes	*before(hand)*
aún	*still, yet*
ayer	*yesterday*
cuando	*when*
¿cuándo?	*when?*
después	*after(wards)*
entonces	*then, so then*

hoy	*today*
jamás	*never*
luego	*then*
mañana	*tomorrow*
mientras	*while*
nunca	*never*
pronto	*soon*
reclén	*recently, just, newly*
siempre	*always*
tarde	*late*
temprano	*early*
todavía	*still, yet*
ya	*already*

a. *Aun, aún*

Aún with an accent is a synonym of *todavía*. Without an accent it is a synonym of *incluso*.

Aún no la he visto.	*I have not seen it yet.*
Aun de adulto se me antojan.	*Even as an adult I crave them.*

b. *Nunca, jamás*

Jamás is stronger than *nunca*. The two can be combined for an even stronger negative.

Nunca volveré.	*I shall never return.*
Jamás volveré.	*I shall <u>never</u> return.*
Nunca jamás volveré.	*I shall never, ever return.*

c. *Tarde, temprano*

Tarde and *temprano* can be used with the verb *ser* only in the very limited context of the impersonal expression of time of day, "it is late" or "it is early," where "it" does not refer to anything specific, but is an impersonal subject similar to "it" in "it is three o'clock."

Es tarde.	*It is late. (time of day)*
Es temprano.	*It is early.*

If the subject of "to be" is not impersonal, or if "it" refers to something specific, you cannot use *ser* in Spanish. The most common way of stating these sentences is with the verb *llegar*.

<u>Llegó</u> tarde.	<u>It</u> is late. (the package)
<u>Llegué</u> tarde.	<u>I</u> am late.
<u>Llegaste</u> temprano.	<u>You</u> are early.

Tarde and *temprano* are commonly used with action verbs.

Comen tarde en España.	They eat <u>late</u> in Spain.
Me levanto temprano.	I get up <u>early</u>.

Tarde o temprano means "sooner or later."

Tarde o temprano ganaremos.	We'll win sooner or later.

d. *Ya, ya no, todavía, todavía no*

Beware of these expressions: they are very useful if you learn their meaning, but they tend to cause confusion. Compare the following pairs of sentences.

<u>Ya</u> comí.	I <u>already</u> ate.
<u>Todavía no</u> he comido.	I have <u>not</u> eaten <u>yet</u>.
<u>Todavía</u> anda en triciclo.	He <u>still</u> rides a tricycle.
<u>Ya no</u> anda en triciclo.	He <u>no longer</u> rides a tricycle.

Ya can also be used emphatically; English would emphasize the pronunciation of specific words to indicate the same emphasis, and some dialects in English might use "already."

¡Ya voy!	I am <u>coming</u>! (already, or right away)
Ya sé.	I <u>know</u> (already).

e. Examples of Adverbs of Time

Ahora son las tres.	It's now three o'clock.
Anoche soñé contigo.	I dreamt about you last night.
Llegaron anteayer.	They arrived the day before yesterday.
Lo cociné antes.	I cooked it beforehand.
Ayer limpié mi cuarto.	Yesterday I cleaned my room.
Habla cuando quiere.	He speaks when he wants to.

Iremos después.	*We shall go afterwards.*
Entonces lo vi.	*Then I saw it.*
Hoy es lunes.	*Today is Monday.*
Luego la felicitaron.	*Then they congratulated her.*
Mañana será otro día.	*Tomorrow is (will be) another day.*
Lo hice mientras dormías.	*I did it while you were sleeping.*
Nunca he bailado tanto.	*I have never danced so much.*
Pronto llegaremos.	*We will soon arrive.*
Son recién casados.	*They are newlyweds.*
Siempre te querré.	*I shall always love you.*

PRÁCTICA

Ejercicios 4.24–4.25, páginas 343–344

7. ADVERBS OF MANNER

así	*like this, like that, such, thus, so*
bien	*well, very; thoroughly*
como	*like*
¿cómo?	*how?*
mal	*badly*
según	*accordingly, it depends*

a. *Así*

Así is used to signify "like this" or "like that"; English-speaking students often add "como" before it, which is a mistake. Consider the following sentences.

—**¿Cómo lo hiciste?**	*"How did you do it?"*
—**<u>Así</u>.**	*"<u>Like this</u>."*

Así can also be used as an adjective to modify a noun.

Estudiamos los adverbios, y cosas <u>así</u>.	*We studied the adverbs, and things <u>like that</u>.*

b. *Bien*

Bien can have two meanings: when it modifies a verb it means "well"; when it modifies another adverb or an adjective, it intensifies it, and means "really" or "very."

Cocinas <u>bien</u>.	*You cook <u>well</u>.*
Está <u>bien</u> lindo el día.	*The day is <u>really</u> beautiful.*

With *estar* there can be a difference to the meaning of *bien*.

—¿Cuál quieres?	*"Which one do you want?"*
—El rojo está <u>bien</u>.	*"The red one is <u>okay</u> (or <u>good</u>)."*
Su hija está <u>bien</u> ahora.	*Your daughter is <u>well</u> now.*

Bien can also be used as an adjective.

Viene de una familia <u>bien</u>.	*He is from a <u>well-to-do</u> family.*

Ejercicio 4.26, página 344

8. ADVERBS OF QUANTITY

algo	*somewhat, rather, a bit*
apenas	*barely, scarcely*
bastante	*enough, really, rather*
casi	*almost*
cuanto	*as much*
¿cuánto?	*how much?*
demasiado	*too much*
más	*more*
medio	*half*
menos	*less*
mucho, muy	*very*
nada	*not at all*

poco	*little*
sólo	*only*
tanto	*so much*

a. *Demasiado, mucho, muy*

Demasiado is not used as frequently as "too" or "too much" is in English. The indication of excess can be in the context of the sentence, or in words such as *mucho* or *muy*, rather than in *demasiado*.

Es temprano para que vuelva.	*It is too early for him to be back.*
Ya es tarde para ti.	*It is too late for you.*
Es muy joven para beber.	*He is too young to drink.*
Hace mucho calor para salir.	*It is too hot to go out.*

If there is any ambiguity as to the indication of excess, *demasiado* would be used.

Hablas demasiado.	*You talk too much.*

Beware of the common mistake of combining *demasiado* and *mucho*.

b. Examples of Adverbs of Quantity

Estoy <u>algo</u> incómoda.	*I am slightly uncomfortable.*
<u>Apenas</u> llegamos.	*We just made it.*
<u>Apenas si</u> me habló.	*He barely spoke to me.*
No comes <u>bastante</u>.	*You don't eat enough.*
Es <u>bastante</u> tarde.	*It is quite late.*
<u>Casi</u> lo compré.	*I almost bought it.*
Come <u>cuanto</u> quiere.	*She eats as much as she wants.*
Gritan <u>demasiado</u>.	*They scream too much.*
Trabajas <u>mucho</u>.	*You work a lot (too much).*
Es <u>muy</u> fuerte.	*It is very strong.*
No estoy <u>nada</u> seguro.	*I am not at all sure.*
Se ejercita <u>poco</u>.	*He exercises little.*

<u>Sólo</u> lee.	*She only reads.*
¡Nieva <u>tanto</u>!	*It snows so much!*

Ejercicio 4.27, página 344

9. ADVERBS OF CONFIRMATION, DOUBT, OR NEGATION

acaso	*perhaps, maybe, by chance*
bueno	*okay, yes*
no	*no, not*
¿no?	*no?, not?, right?, isn't it?*
quizá(s)	*perhaps*
sí	*yes, certainly, definitely*
¿sí?	*yes?*
tal vez	*perhaps*
también	*also, as well*
tampoco	*neither*
ya	*yes, alright, sure, indeed, of course*

a. *Acaso / quizá / tal vez*

These three words all have a similar meaning of doubt, but have uses that are slightly different. The use of the subjunctive adds to the doubt of the context, or indicates future action. Consider the following examples.

¿<u>Acaso</u> dudas de mí?	*Perhaps you doubt me?*
<u>Quizá</u> es Roberto.	*Maybe it is Roberto.*
<u>Quizá</u> sea Roberto.	*Maybe it might be Roberto.*
<u>Tal vez</u> era de noche.	*Maybe it was nighttime.*
<u>Tal vez</u> salgamos.	*Maybe we'll go out.*

b. *Bueno*

You are familiar with the word *bueno* as an adjective. When used adverbially, it is used in dialogues to indicate acceptance, and means something like "okay."

—¿**Te llamo mañana?**	*"Shall I call you tomorrow?"*
—**Bueno.**	*"Okay."*

It can also be used as a pause or a transition between instances of speech, similar to "well . . . " in English.

...**Bueno... y ahora... ¿qué hacemos?**	*Well ... and now ... what shall we do?*

In Mexico, *¿bueno?* is used to answer the telephone. Other Spanish-speaking countries would say *¿diga?* or *¿aló?*

c. *No*

No must precede the verb it modifies.

No puedo comer.	*I cannot eat.*
Puedo no comer.	*I can go without eating.*
No puedo no comer.	*I cannot go without eating.*

No is often used in the interrogative *"¿no?"* after a sentence to mean "right?" or something similar; a frequent mistake is to use *"¿sí?"* instead.

Fueron al cine, ¿<u>no</u>?	*They went to the movies, right?*

d. *Sí*

Sí is often used to emphasize the affirmative.

—**Yo no quiero ir al cine.**	*"I don't want to go to the movies."*
—**Pues yo <u>sí</u> (quiero).**	*"Well, I do."*
Ahora <u>sí</u> que vamos a gozar.	*Now we really are going to have fun.*
Ah, no, ¡eso <u>sí</u> que no!	*Oh, no. No way! (Not a chance!)*

e. *También / tampoco*

Tampoco is the negative of *también*.

—Tengo hambre.	*"I'm hungry."*
—Yo <u>también</u>.	*"Me too."*
—Pero no quiero comer tacos.	*"But I don't want to eat tacos."*
—Yo <u>tampoco</u>.	*"Me neither."*

f. *Ya*

Ya is used as an affirmative response.

—¿Terminaste tu trabajo?	*"Did you finish your work?"*
—Ya.	*"Yes."*

PRÁCTICA

Ejercicio 4.28, página 345

10. ADVERBIAL PHRASES

Notice that we have seen some of these expressions listed under the prepositions that are included in them.

a gusto	*at ease, comfortably*
a medias	*half, halfway*
a menudo	*often*
al final	*at the end*
alguna vez	*some time, ever*
en alguna parte	*somewhere*
en fin	*finally, in the long run*
en resumen	*in summary, all in all*
no... hasta	*not until*
por cierto	*certainly; by the way; as a matter of fact*
por fin	*finally*
por poco	*almost*

Examples:

Viven muy <u>a gusto</u> aquí.	*They live very comfortably here.*
No lo hagas <u>a medias</u>.	*Don't do it halfway.*
Viajan <u>a menudo</u>.	*They travel often.*
<u>Al final</u> de la película, lo vi.	*At the end of the movie, I saw him.*
¿Lo has visto <u>alguna vez</u>?	*Have you ever seen it?*
Lo vi <u>en alguna parte</u>.	*I saw it somewhere.*
<u>En fin</u>, así fue.	*Well, that's how it was.*
<u>En resumen</u>, me divertí.	*In summary, I had fun.*
<u>No</u> iré <u>hasta</u> enero.	*I won't go until January.*
<u>Por fin</u> llegamos.	*We finally arrived.*
<u>Por cierto</u>, nevó.	*By the way, it snowed.*
<u>Por poco</u> me caigo.	*I almost fell down.*

(Notice the special use with this phrase of the present tense in Spanish to refer to the past.)

PRÁCTICA

Ejercicio 4.29, página 345

11. RELATED ADVERBS AND PREPOSITIONS

Compare the sentences in the chart on the next page, and notice the addition of *de* for certain prepositional structures.

RELATED ADVERBS AND PREPOSITIONS

Adverb	Example	Preposition	Example
abajo *below, downstairs*	**Los niños están <u>abajo</u>, en la cocina.** *The children are downstairs, in the kitchen.*	**bajo** *below, under (not physically underneath)*	**Nos sentamos <u>bajo</u> los árboles.** *We sat under the trees. (not underneath their roots, however)*
(a)delante *in front, ahead*	**Sigan <u>adelante</u>.** *Continue ahead.*	**delante de** *in front of, ahead of*	**Ella se sienta <u>delante de</u> mí.** *She sits in front of me.*
(a)dentro *inside*	**Prefiero trabajar <u>adentro</u>.** *I prefer to work inside.*	**dentro de** *inside*	**Mi cuaderno está <u>dentro de</u> la gaveta.** *My notebook is inside the drawer.*
(a)fuera *outside*	**Vamos <u>afuera</u> a jugar.** *Let's go outside to play.*	**fuera de** *out(side) of*	**Estaba <u>fuera de</u> nuestro alcance.** *It was out of our reach.*
alrededor *around*	**Miraron <u>alrededor</u>, pero no vieron nada.** *They looked around, but did not see anything.*	**alrededor de** *around*	**Corrimos <u>alrededor de</u> la casa.** *We ran around the house.*
atrás *behind, back*	**¿Dónde están los niños? Están <u>atrás</u>, jugando a la pelota.** *Where are the children? They are in the back, playing ball.*	**detrás de, tras** *behind, after*	**Venían <u>detrás de</u> nosotros.** *They were coming behind us.* **Venían <u>tras</u> nosotros.** *They were coming after (pursuing) us.*
cerca *near, nearby*	**Viven <u>cerca</u>.** *They live nearby.*	**cerca de** *near, close to*	**Ese árbol está muy <u>cerca de</u> la casa.** *That tree is very close to the house.*
debajo *below, underneath*	**Lo pusieron <u>debajo</u>.** *They put it underneath.*	**debajo de** *below, under(neath)*	**El perro duerme <u>debajo de</u> la casa.** *The dog sleeps underneath the house.*
encima *on top*	**Cayó <u>encima</u>.** *It fell on top.*	**encima de** *on top of, above*	**Ponga la fruta <u>encima de</u> las latas de conserva.** *Put the fruit on top of the cans of preserves.*
enfrente *facing, in front, across the street*	**La casa de <u>enfrente</u> es linda.** *The house across the street is pretty.*	**enfrente de, frente a** *in front of, facing*	**Hay tres árboles <u>frente a</u> la casa.** *There are three trees in front of the house.*
lejos *far away*	**¿Vives <u>lejos</u>?** *Do you live far away?*	**lejos de** *far from*	**No está muy <u>lejos de</u> la casa.** *It is not very far from the house.*

Ejercicio 4.30, página 346

Conjunctions

I. USAGE

A conjunction is a word that is used to join two parts of speech. This union may be of equal parts, or the second half of the union may be subordinated to the first. If the union is one of two equal parts, conjunctions of coordination are used; if the second part is subordinated to the first, conjunctions of subordination are used.

2. CONJUNCTIONS OF COORDINATION

Conjunctions of coordination join any two parts of speech: nouns, adjectives, adverbs, pronouns, etc., or two clauses of equal value.

CONJUNCTIONS	
Spanish	English
y/e	and
o/u	or
pero	but
sino	but rather
ni... ni	neither . . . nor

Y becomes *e* before words beginning with *i* or *hi.*

> **España e Italia se encuentran en el sur de Europa.**
> *Spain and Italy are in the south of Europe.*

O becomes *u* before words beginning with *o* or *ho.*

> **No importa que sea mujer u hombre.**
> *It does not matter whether it is a man or a woman.*

Pero is used to indicate something contrary to what precedes it.

> **Sé que hace frío, <u>pero</u> yo tengo calor.**
> *I know it is cold, but I am hot.*

> **No hace calor, <u>pero</u> yo estoy sudando.**
> *It is not hot, but I am sweating.*

Sino is used after a negative to indicate alternate (rather, instead).

> **No fue Marta sino Juana la que me lo dijo.**
> *It was not Marta, but (rather) Juana who told me.*

Sino becomes the conjunction *sino que* before a conjugated verb.

> **No me lo vendió <u>sino que</u> me lo regaló.**
> *She did not sell it to me, but rather gave it to me.*

No sólo... sino también is translated as *not only … but also.*

> **<u>No sólo</u> trajeron flores, <u>sino también</u> una botella de vino.**
> *They not only brought flowers, but also a bottle of wine.*

Ejercicios 4.31–4.33, páginas 346–347

3. CONJUNCTIONS OF SUBORDINATION

Conjunctions of subordination introduce a subordinate clause. *Que* is the most common conjunction of subordination.

> **Veo <u>que</u> estás cansada.**   *I see (that) you are tired.*

In English, the conjunction "that" may be omitted, but in Spanish it must be stated.

> **Dice <u>que</u> viene.**   *He says he is coming.*

Most prepositions combined with *que* become conjunctions to introduce clauses instead of nouns or their equivalent. This is usually the case when the subject of the main verb and the subject of the subordinate are different.

> **Te llamé <u>para</u> darte las últimas noticias.** (infinitive equal to noun)
> *I called you to give you the latest news.*

> **Te llamé <u>para que</u> supieras que estoy pensando en ti.**
> *I called you so (that) you would know (that) I am thinking about you.*

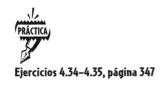

Ejercicios 4.34–4.35, página 347

◆ Transitions

The following are words that may be useful in writing; some of these are prepositions, others are adverbs and conjunctions.

regarding, concerning	**con respecto a** **en cuanto a** **en lo tocante a** **por lo que se refiere a**

> **Con respecto a** su pedido, enviaré el libro esta tarde.
> *Regarding your order, I will send the book this afternoon.*

> **En cuanto al** precio, le cobraré luego.
> *As for the price, I shall charge you later.*

> **En lo tocante al** diccionario que pide, no lo tenemos.
> *Concerning the dictionary you ask for, we do not have it.*

> **Por lo que se refiere a** lo demás, me comunicaré con los interesados.
> *As for the rest, I will get in touch with the interested parties.*

according to	**según**

> **Según** el patrón, no hay fondos.
> *According to the boss, there are no funds.*

in general, as a rule	**por lo general**

> **Por lo general**, yo gano.
> *In general, I win.*

in the first place; secondly …	**en primer lugar; en segundo lugar...**

> **En primer lugar**, no tengo tiempo. **En segundo lugar**, no quiero.
> *In the first place, I don't have time. Secondly, I don't want to.*

for example	**por ejemplo**
almost always	**casi siempre**
almost (n)ever	**casi nunca**
for the most part	**en gran parte**

Por ejemplo, casi siempre comen arroz blanco.
For example, they almost always eat white rice.

more and more	**cada vez más** **de más en más**
less and less	**cada vez menos** **de menos en menos**

Hay cada vez más guerras y cada vez menos humanidad.
There are more and more wars and less and less humanity.

by chance, perhaps, maybe	**acaso**
maybe, perhaps	**a lo mejor** **quizás** **tal vez**

¿Acaso no ves que lo hago por tu bien? Quizás algún día comprendas; a lo mejor cuando te cases, o tal vez cuando seas madre.
Don't you see I am doing this for your own good? Maybe someday you will understand; possibly when you get married, or perhaps when you are a mother.

luckily, fortunately	**por suerte**
unfortunately	**por desgracia**

Por desgracia, tuvo un accidente. Por suerte, nadie se hizo daño.
Unfortunately, he had an accident. Luckily, nobody got hurt.

in turn	**a su vez** **por su parte**
on the other hand	**por otro lado**

Mi padre, por su parte, nos llevaba al cine los sábados.
My father, in turn, would take us to the movies on Saturday.

Por otro lado, era mi madre la que luchaba con nuestros problemas cotidianos.
On the other hand, it was my mother who struggled with our daily problems.

thus, therefore, then	**entonces**
	por consiguiente
	por lo tanto
for that reason	**por eso**
	por ese motivo
	por esa razón
as a result	**como consecuencia**
	como resultado

Estaba harto del gobierno. <u>Por consiguiente</u>, decidió mudarse con la familia a otro país. <u>Por eso</u> terminamos viviendo en México, y <u>como resultado</u>, todos hablamos español.

He was fed up with the government. Therefore, he decided to move to another country. For that reason we ended up living in Mexico, and as a result, we all speak Spanish.

in fact, as a matter of fact	**de hecho**
actually	**en realidad**
nowadays	**actualmente**
	hoy en día

<u>En realidad</u>, no sé cuándo empezó todo. <u>Actualmente</u> no quedan rasgos de la lucha. <u>De hecho</u>, tenemos muy pocos datos.

Actually, I don't know when everything began. Nowadays there are no traces left of the struggle. As a matter of fact, we have very little data.

(Notice that *actualmente* and "actually" are false cognates.)

nevertheless, yet, however	**sin embargo**
	no obstante
in spite of	**a pesar de**

Somos pobres. <u>No obstante</u>, venceremos <u>a pesar de</u> todo.
We are poor. Nevertheless, we shall prevail in spite of it all.

since (time)	**desde**
since (because)	**como**

<u>Desde</u> el día en que llegué aquí, la vida ha sido más fácil.
Since the day I came here, life has been easier.

<u>Como</u> tenía hambre, comí.
Since I was hungry, I ate.

Certain expressions are used as a transition between related thoughts in the same sentence.

... *but* ...	**...pero / sino...**
... *and* ...	**...y / e...**
... *also* ...	**...también...**
... *because* ...	**...porque...**

To introduce a less closely connected thought, often at the beginning of a new sentence, the following expressions may be used.

However, ... But, ... Yet, ...	**Sin embargo,**
In addition, ... Also, ...	**Además,**
Since ... , Because ...	**Como** **Puesto que** **Ya que** **Debido a que**

A frequent error is the use of *Pero* at the beginning of a sentence, followed by a comma. When a comma is used to separate it from what follows, the emphasis on the meaning of *pero* is such that it would be better to replace it with the stronger *Sin embargo*. The same is true for *también,* which is awkward when followed by a comma: the best term in such a context would be *Además*.

Consider the following informal statement:

Ayer llamé a Luisa. <u>Como</u> ella no me llamaba, la llamé yo. <u>Pero</u> no le dije por qué llamaba <u>porque</u> no quería que supiera lo que siento. <u>Sin embargo</u>, sí quería oír su voz, y <u>también</u> contarle de la visita de mis padres. <u>Además</u>, no quería dejar pasar más tiempo sin comunicarme con ella.
Yesterday I called Luisa. <u>Since</u> she wouldn't call me, I called her. <u>But</u> I didn't tell her why I was calling <u>because</u> I didn't want her to know what I feel. <u>However</u>, I did want to hear her voice and <u>also</u> to tell her about my parents' visit. <u>Besides</u>, I didn't want to let more time go by without communicating with her.

(Notice that the third sentence begins with *pero,* but if you look closely, it is different from the fourth sentence. The third sentence is a continuation of the second one, not a new thought, and could equally have been placed after a comma instead of a period. The fourth sentence, on the other hand, does have a different focus.)

For concluding, the following might be useful.

in conclusion	**en conclusión**

En conclusión, es mejor tratar de vivir bien.
In conclusion, it is best to try to live well.

in short, to summarize	**para resumir**
	en resumen
	en resumidas cuentas

En resumen, es un cuento de amor tradicional.
In short, it's a traditional love story.
Para resumir, diría que es un cuento de amor tradicional.
To summarize, I would say it is a traditional love story.

from the above, it can be concluded that	**de lo anterior, se puede concluir que**

De lo anterior, se puede concluir que no todo lo que reluce es de oro.
From the above, it can be concluded that not all that shines is made of gold.

anyway	**de todos modos**
in any case	**en todo caso**
after all	**después de todo**
in the end, all in all	**a fin de cuentas**

De todos modos, siguieron siendo amigos. En todo caso, nadie se mudó. Después de todo, se conocían desde la primaria. A fin de cuentas, todos salieron ganando.
Anyway, they continued being friends. In any case, nobody moved. After all, they knew each other since primary school. In the end, everyone ended up winning.

PRÁCTICA

Ejercicios 4.36–4.37, páginas 348–349; Ejercicios de repaso 4.38–4.39, páginas 349–351

Chapter 5

Verbs: Formation

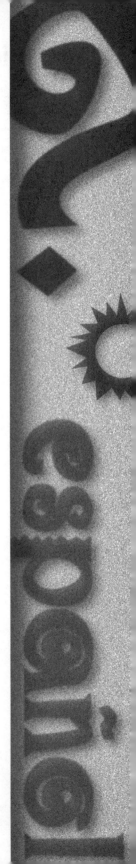

- **A** Indicative Mood
- **B** Conditional Mood
- **C** Subjunctive Mood
- **D** Imperative Mood
- **E** Infinitive
- **F** Participle

Indicative Mood

I. PRESENT INDICATIVE

[For contextualized usage of the present indicative, see Chapter 6.A: Present Indicative, pages 176–177.]

a. Regular Verbs

	-ar	*-er*	*-ir*
	Hablar	**Comer**	**Vivir**
yo	habl**o**	com**o**	viv**o**
tú	habl**as**	com**es**	viv**es**
él, ella, usted	habl**a**	com**e**	viv**e**
nosotros	habl**amos**	com**emos**	viv**imos**
vosotros	habl**áis**	com**éis**	viv**ís**
ellos, ellas, ustedes	habl**an**	com**en**	viv**en**

b. Stem-Changing Verbs

e → i

	-ar	*-er*	*-ir*
	Cerrar	**Perder**	**Sentir**
	c**i**erro	p**i**erdo	s**i**ento
	c**i**erras	p**i**erdes	s**i**entes
	c**i**erra	p**i**erde	s**i**ente
	cerramos	perdemos	sentimos
	cerráis	perdéis	sentís
	c**i**erran	p**i**erden	s**i**enten

Other verbs with this change:

-ar	*-er*	*-ir*
comenzar	defender	mentir
empezar	encender	preferir
negar	entender	
pensar	querer	

e → i		

Pedir

pido
pides
pide
pedimos
pedís
piden

Other verbs with this change: *conseguir, impedir, seguir, elegir, repetir, servir*

o → ue	*-ar*	*-er*	*-ir*

Contar	Volver	Dormir
cuento	vuelvo	duermo
cuentas	vuelves	duermes
cuenta	vuelve	duerme
contamos	volvemos	dormimos
contáis	volvéis	dormís
cuentan	vuelven	duermen

Other verbs with this change:

-ar	*-er*	*-ir*
costar	devolver	morir
encontrar	llover	
mostrar	mover	
probar	poder	
recordar		

Other verbs with this change, with some variation:

Oler	Jugar
huelo	juego
hueles	juegas
huele	juega
olemos	jugamos
oléis	jugáis
huelen	juegan

c. Spelling-Changing Verbs

Spelling changes are made with the purpose of maintaining the same sound throughout the verb; for example, a verb with an infinitive ending in *-ger* or *-gir* (not the "hard" *g* of "go") will have a *j* in the conjugation in front of an *a* or an *o*. If the *g* were maintained, the sound would become hard.

Escoger
escojo
escoges
escoge
escogemos
escogéis
escogen

Other verbs with this change:

-er	*-ir*
coger	corregir
proteger	dirigir
elegir	
exigir	
fingir	

gu → g

Distinguir
distingo
distingues
distingue
distinguimos
distinguís
distinguen

Other verbs with this change: *seguir, conseguir*

c → zc

Before **o:** **Parecer**
parezco
pareces
parece
parecemos
parecéis
parecen

Other verbs with this change:

-er	-ir
agradecer	conducir
aparecer	introducir
conocer	producir
merecer	traducir
obedecer	
ofrecer	
permanecer	
reconocer	

$c \rightarrow z$

Before **o:**

Convencer

convenzo
convences
convence
convencemos
convencéis
convencen

Other verbs with this change: *vencer, torcer, ejercer, mecer*

d. Classified Irregular Verbs

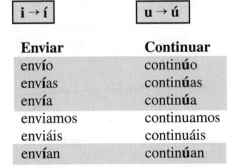

$i \rightarrow í$	$u \rightarrow ú$
Enviar	**Continuar**
envío	continúo
envías	continúas
envía	continúa
enviamos	continuamos
enviáis	continuáis
envían	continúan

Other verbs with this change:

-iar	-uar
confiar	acentuar
criar	actuar
guiar	graduar

Reunir is similar:

Reunir
reúno
reúnes
reúne
reunimos
reunís
reúnen

$$\boxed{\text{ui} \rightarrow \text{uy}}$$

Concluir
concluyo
concluyes
concluye
concluimos
concluís
concluyen

Other verbs with this change: *construir, distribuir, contribuir, huir, destruir, incluir*

e. Other Irregular Verbs

Caer	Hacer	Poner*	Salir	Traer°	Valer
caigo	hago	pongo	salgo	traigo	valgo
caes	haces	pones	sales	traes	vales
cae	hace	pone	sale	trae	vale
caemos	hacemos	ponemos	salimos	traemos	valemos
caéis	hacéis	ponéis	salís	traéis	valéis
caen	hacen	ponen	salen	traen	valen

*Like *poner: componer, disponer, proponer, suponer*
°Like *traer: atraer, distraer*

Decir	Tener	Venir
digo	tengo	vengo
dices	tienes	vienes
dice	tiene	viene
decimos	tenemos	venimos
decís	tenéis	venís
dicen	tienen	vienen

Like *decir: desdecir, maldecir*
Like *tener: atenerse, contener, detener, mantener, obtener, sostener*
Like *venir: convenir, prevenir*

Dar	Estar	Haber*	Ir
doy	estoy	he	voy
das	estás	has	vas
da	está	ha	va
damos	estamos	hemos	vamos
dais	estáis	habéis	vais
dan	están	han	van

Oír	Saber	Ser	Ver
oigo	sé	soy	veo
oyes	sabes	eres	ves
oye	sabe	es	ve
oímos	sabemos	somos	vemos
oís	sabéis	sois	veis
oyen	saben	son	ven

Haber has a special third-person singular form: *hay* for "there is, there are."

PRÁCTICA

Ejercicios 5.1–5.8, páginas 352–356

2. PAST TENSES OF THE INDICATIVE

[For contextualized usage of the past indicative, see Chapter 6.B: Past Indicative Tenses: Preterite vs. Imperfect vs. Pluperfect, pages 177–189.]

a. Imperfect Indicative

Regular:

-ar	*-er*	*-ir*
Hablar	**Comer**	**Vivir**
hablaba	comía	vivía
hablabas	comías	vivías
hablaba	comía	vivía
hablábamos	comíamos	vivíamos
hablabais	comíais	vivíais
hablaban	comían	vivían

Irregular:

Ir	Ser	Ver
iba	era	veía
ibas	eras	veías
iba	era	veía
íbamos	éramos	veíamos
ibais	erais	veíais
iban	eran	veían

PRÁCTICA

Ejercicios 5.9–5.12, páginas 356–358

b. Preterite

Regular:

-ar	*-er*	*-ir*
Hablar	**Comer**	**Vivir**
hablé	comí	viví
hablaste	comiste	viviste
habló	comió	vivió
hablamos	comimos	vivimos
hablasteis	comisteis	vivisteis
hablaron	comieron	vivieron

PRETERITE TENSE (Irregular Stems with "u")		
Infinitive	**Stem**	**Endings**
andar	anduv-	
caber	cup-	-e
estar	estuv-	-iste
haber	hub-	-o
poder	pud-	-imos
poner	pus-	-isteis
saber	sup-	-ieron
tener	tuv-	

PRETERITE TENSE (Irregular Stems with "i")	
Infinitive	**Stem**
hacer*	hic-
querer	quis-
venir	vin-

Hacer has a third-person singular spelling change to *hizo*.

Dar has -*ir* endings.

di
diste
dio
dimos
disteis
dieron

Ir and *ser* are identical in the preterite.

fui
fuiste
fue
fuimos
fuisteis
fueron

Irregular: stem change in *j* (including all verbs in -*ducir*):

Decir	**Producir**	**Traer**
dije	produje	traje
dijiste	produjiste	trajiste
dijo	produjo	trajo
dijimos	produjimos	trajimos
dijisteis	produjisteis	trajisteis
dijeron	produjeron	trajeron

All -*ir* verbs with stem changes in the present show a stem change in the third-person singular and plural of the preterite.

e → i

Pedir	Reír	Sentir
pedí	reí	sentí
pediste	reíste	sentiste
pidió	rió	sintió
pedimos	reímos	sentimos
pedisteis	reísteis	sentisteis
pidieron	rieron	sintieron

o → u

Dormir
dormí
dormiste
durmió
dormimos
dormisteis
durmieron

Spelling changes:

i → y

Caer	Creer	Leer	Oír	Concluir*
caí	creí	leí	oí	concluí
caíste	creíste	leíste	oíste	concluiste
cayó	creyó	leyó	oyó	concluyó
caímos	creímos	leímos	oímos	concluimos
caísteis	creísteis	leísteis	oísteis	concluisteis
cayeron	creyeron	leyeron	oyeron	concluyeron

*Applies to verbs ending in -*uir* with the same spelling change in the present tense.

c → qu   g → gu   z → c

Buscar	Llegar	Alcanzar
busqué	llegué	alcancé
buscaste	llegaste	alcanzaste
buscó	llegó	alcanzó
buscamos	llegamos	alcanzamos
buscasteis	llegasteis	alcanzasteis
buscaron	llegaron	alcanzaron

Other verbs with this change:

-*car*	-*gar*	-*zar*
explicar	apagar	almorzar
sacar	colgar	comenzar
tocar	entregar	empezar
	jugar	
	negar	
	pagar	

Ejercicios 5.13–5.17, páginas 358–361

c. Present Perfect Indicative

[For contextualized usage of the present perfect indicative, see Chapter 6.C.2.a, page 191; more on probability under Chapter 6.F, pages 200–201.]

The present perfect indicative is formed with the present indicative of the auxiliar *haber* + a past participle always ending in -*o*.

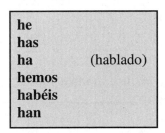

he	
has	
ha	(hablado)
hemos	
habéis	
han	

Ejercicio 5.18, páginas 361–362

d. Pluperfect Indicative

[For contextualized usage of the pluperfect indicative, see Chapter 6.B.5, pages 188–189, and Chapter 6.C.2.c, page 192.]

The pluperfect indicative is formed with the imperfect indicative of the auxiliary *haber* + a past participle always ending in *-o*.

había	
habías	
había	(hablado)
habíamos	
habíais	
habían	

PRÁCTICA

Ejercicio 5.19, página 362

3. FUTURE

[For contextualized usage of the future, see Chapter 6.C.2.b, page 191, 6.D, pages 197–198, and 6.F, pages 200–201.]

a. Simple Future

The future tense is formed with the infinitive plus endings that are identical for all verbs.

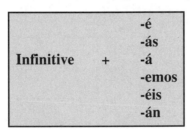

Infinitive +	**-é**
	-ás
	-á
	-emos
	-éis
	-án

-ar	*-er*	*-ir*
Hablar	**Comer**	**Vivir**
hablar**é**	comer**é**	vivir**é**
hablar**ás**	comer**ás**	vivir**ás**
hablar**á**	comer**á**	vivir**á**
hablar**emos**	comer**emos**	vivir**emos**
hablar**éis**	comer**éis**	vivir**éis**
hablar**án**	comer**án**	vivir**án**

FUTURE TENSE (IRREGULAR STEMS)			
Infinitive	Stem	Infinitive	Stem
caber	cabr-	querer	querr-
decir	dir-	saber	sabr-
haber	habr-	salir	saldr-
hacer	har-	tener	tendr-
poder	podr-	valer	valdr-
poner	pondr-	venir	vendr-

Verbs derived from these have the same irregularity: *desdecir, deshacer, suponer, mantener,* etc.

PRÁCTICA

Ejercicios 5.20–5.22, páginas 362–363

b. Future Perfect

The future perfect tense is formed with the future of the auxiliary *haber* + a past participle always ending in *-o*.

habré	
habrá	
habra	(hablado)
habremos	
habréais	
habrán	

PRÁCTICA

Ejercicio 5.23, página 363

Conditional Mood

[For contextualized usage of the conditional, see Chapter 6.E, pages 198–200, and Chapter 6.G.6, pages 226–227.]

1. PRESENT CONDITIONAL

The present conditional is formed with the infinitive plus endings that are identical for all verbs.

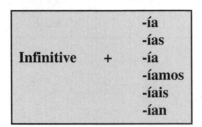

Infinitive	+	-ía -ías -ía -íamos -íais -ían

-ar	-er	-ir
Hablar	**Comer**	**Vivir**
hablaría	comería	viviría
hablarías	comerías	vivirías
hablaría	comería	viviría
hablaríamos	comeríamos	viviríamos
hablaríais	comeríais	viviríais
hablarían	comerían	vivirían

CONDITIONAL TENSE (IRREGULAR STEMS)			
caber	cabr-	**querer**	querr-
decir	dir-	**saber**	sabr-
haber	habr-	**salir**	saldr-
hacer	har-	**tener**	tendr-
poder	podr-	**valer**	valdr-
poner	pondr-	**venir**	vendr-

Verbs derived from these have the same irregularity: *desdecir, deshacer, suponer, mantener,* etc.

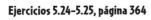
PRÁCTICA

Ejercicios 5.24–5.25, página 364

2. CONDITIONAL PERFECT

The conditional perfect is formed with the present conditional of the auxiliary *haber* + a past participle always ending in *-o*.

habría	
habrías	
habría	(hablado)
habríamos	
habríais	
habrían	

Ejercicio 5.26, páginas 364–365; Ejercicio de repaso 5.27, página 365

Subjunctive Mood

[For contextualized usage of the subjunctive, see Chapter 6.G, pages 202–230.]

1. PRESENT SUBJUNCTIVE

a. Regular Verbs

The present subjunctive is formed by dropping the *o* of the first-person singular present indicative and adding the "opposite" vowel endings: *e* for *-ar* verbs and *a* for *-ir/-er* verbs.

	-ar	*-er*	*-ir*
	Hablar	**Comer**	**Vivir**
yo	hable	coma	viva
tú	hables	comas	vivas
él, ella, usted	hable	coma	viva
nosotros	hablemos	comamos	vivamos
vosotros	habléis	comáis	viváis
ellos, ellas, ustedes	hablen	coman	vivan

b. Stem-Changing Verbs

If the verb is stem-changing in the present indicative, the present subjunctive will show the same changes.

Cerrar	Perder	Contar	Volver
cierre	pierda	cuente	vuelva
cierres	pierdas	cuentes	vuelvas
cierre	pierda	cuente	vuelva
cerremos	perdamos	contemos	volvamos
cerréis	perdáis	contéis	volváis
cierren	pierdan	cuenten	vuelvan

Exceptions: In the first- and second-person plural forms of stem-changing -ir verbs, the e of the stem changes to i, and the o of the stem changes to u.

Pedir	Sentir	Dormir
pida	sienta	duerma
pidas	sientas	duermas
pida	sienta	duerma
pidamos	sintamos	durmamos
pidáis	sintáis	durmáis
pidan	sientan	duerman

c. Irregular Verbs

If the verb is irregular in the present indicative, the present subjunctive will show the same irregularities.

Decir	Oír	Tener
diga	oiga	tenga
digas	oigas	tengas
diga	oiga	tenga
digamos	oigamos	tengamos
digáis	oigáis	tengáis
digan	oigan	tengan

Enviar	Continuar	Reunir
envíe	continúe	reúna
envíes	continúes	reúnas
envíe	continúe	reúna
enviemos	continuemos	reunamos
enviéis	continuéis	reunáis
envíen	continúen	reúnan

Parecer	Conducir	Concluir
parezca	conduzca	concluya
parezcas	conduzcas	concluyas
parezca	conduzca	concluya
parezcamos	conduzcamos	concluyamos
parezcáis	conduzcáis	concluyáis
parezcan	conduzcan	concluyan

The following verbs also maintain the irregularity throughout all persons:

PRESENT SUBJUNCTIVE (IRREGULAR STEMS)			
Infinitive	1st Person	Infinitive	1st Person
caber	quepa	salir	salga
caer	caiga	traer	traiga
hacer	haga	valer	valga
poner	ponga	venir	venga

Even *dar, estar, haber, ir, saber,* and *ser,* all of which have a first-person singular present indicative that does not end with -*o,* remain regular in their endings.

Dar[1]	Estar	Haber
dé	esté	haya
des	estés	hayas
dé	esté	haya
demos	estemos	hayamos
deis	cstéis	hayáis
den	estén	hayan

Ir	Saber	Ser
vaya	sepa	sea
vayas	sepas	seas
vaya	sepa	sea
vayamos	sepamos	seamos
vayáis	sepáis	seáis
vayan	sepan	sean

---

1. The first- and third-person singular forms of *dar* have an accent to differentiate them from the preposition *de.*

If the verb has spelling changes in the present indicative, the present subjunctive will show the same irregularities.

g → j		**gu → g**

Escoger	**Dirigir**	**Distinguir**
escoja	dirija	distinga
escojas	dirijas	distingas
escoja	dirija	distinga
escojamos	dirijamos	distingamos
escojáis	dirijáis	distingáis
escojan	dirijan	distingan

c → z	**c → qu**	**g → gu**	**z → c**

Convencer	**Buscar**	**Llegar**	**Alcanzar**
convenza	busque	llegue	alcance
convenzas	busques	llegues	alcances
convenza	busque	llegue	alcance
convenzamos	busquemos	lleguemos	alcancemos
convenzáis	busquéis	lleguéis	alcancéis
convenzan	busquen	lleguen	alcancen

All verbs ending in:

    -ger are like *escoger (g → j)*   *-car* are like *buscar (c → qu)*

    -gir are like *dirigir (g → j)*   *-gar* are like *llegar (g → gu)*

    -guir are like *distinguir (gu → g)*   *-zar* are like *alcanzar (z → c)*

Most verbs ending in *-cer* and *-cir* and all verbs ending in *-ducir* are like *parecer (c → z)*.

Ejercicios 5.28–5.33, páginas 365–367

2. IMPERFECT SUBJUNCTIVE

The imperfect tense of all verbs without exception is formed by dropping *-ron* from the third-person plural preterite and adding *-ra, -ras, -ra, ´-ramos, -rais, -ran* or *-se, -ses, -se, ´-semos, -seis, -sen.* In most of Latin America, the *-ra* forms predominate.

	-ar	-er	-ir
	Hablar	**Comer**	**Vivir**
yo	habla**ra**	comie**ra**	vivie**ra**
tú	habla**ras**	comie**ras**	vivie**ras**
él, ella, usted	habla**ra**	comie**ra**	vivie**ra**
nosotros	hablá**ramos**	comié**ramos**	vivié**ramos**
vosotros	habla**rais**	comie**rais**	vivie**rais**
ellos, ellas, ustedes	habla**ran**	comie**ran**	vivie**ran**

OR:	yo	habla**se**	comie**se**	vivie**se**
	tú	habla**ses**	comie**ses**	vivie**ses**
	él, ella, usted	habla**se**	comie**se**	vivie**se**
	nosotros	hablá**semos**	comié**semos**	vivié**semos**
	vosotros	habla**seis**	comie**seis**	vivie**seis**
	ellos, ellas, ustedes	habla**sen**	comie**sen**	vivie**sen**

All verbs irregular in the preterite show the same irregularities in the imperfect subjunctive.

IMPERFECT SUBJUNCTIVE (IRREGULAR STEMS)			
Infinitive	**1st Person**	**Infinitive**	**1st Person**
andar	anduviera	**poder**	pudiera
caber	cupiera	**poner**	pusiera
caer	cayera	**poseer**	poseyera
concluir	concluyera	**preferir**	prefiriera
conducir	condujera	**producir**	produjera
dar	diera	**querer**	quisiera
decir	dijera	**reír**	riera
dormir	durmiera	**saber**	supiera
estar	estuviera	**seguir**	siguiera
haber	hubiera	**sentir**	sintiera
ir	fuera	**ser**	fuera
leer	leyera	**tener**	tuviera
oír	oyera	**traer**	trajera
pedir	pidiera	**venir**	viniera

PRÁCTICA

Ejercicios 5.34–5.35, páginas 367–369

3. PRESENT PERFECT SUBJUNCTIVE

The present perfect subjunctive is formed with the present subjunctive of the auxiliary *haber* + a past participle always ending in *-o*.

> **haya**
> **hayas**
> **haya**   (hablado)
> **hayamos**
> **hayáis**
> **hayan**

Ejercicio 5.36, página 369

4. PLUPERFECT SUBJUNCTIVE

The pluperfect subjunctive is formed with the imperfect subjunctive of the auxiliary *haber* + a past participle always ending in *-o*.

> **hubiera**
> **hubieras**
> **hubiera**   (hablado)
> **hubiéramos**
> **hubierais**
> **hubieran**

OR:

> **hubiese**
> **hubieses**
> **hubiese**   (hablado)
> **hubiésemos**
> **hubieseis**
> **hubiesen**

Ejercicio 5.37, páginas 369–370; Ejercicio de repaso 5.38, página 370

◆ Imperative Mood

I. DIRECT COMMANDS

a. *Tú*

Affirmative commands are formed with the third-person singular of the present indicative.

> Examples: **habla, come, vive, cierra, abre**

Eight exceptions:

TÚ IMPERATIVE (IRREGULAR AFFIRMATIVE FORMS)			
Infinitive	Form	Infinitive	Form
decir	di	salir	sal
hacer	haz	ser	sé
ir	ve	tener	ten
poner	pon	venir	ven

Object pronouns are attached to the ending of the affirmative imperative, and a written accent is added when it is necessary to maintain stress on the same syllable of the stem.

Háblame.	*Talk to me.*
Ciérrala.	*Close it.* (**la = la puerta**)
Ábrelo.	*Open it.* (**lo = el sobre**)
Dímelo.	*Tell it to me.* (**lo = el secreto**)
Hazlo.	*Do it.* (**lo = el trabajo**)
Vete.	*Go away.* (**irse** is reflexive)
Póntelo.	*Put it on.* (**lo = el abrigo; ponerse** is reflexive)

Negative commands are formed with the second-person singular of the present subjunctive.

> Examples: **no hables, no comas, no vivas, no cierres, no abras**

Those irregular in the affirmative are regular in the negative.

TÚ IMPERATIVE (NEGATIVE FORMS)			
Infinitive	Form	Infinitive	Form
decir	no digas	salir	no salgas
hacer	no hagas	ser	no seas
ir	no vayas	tener	no tengas
poner	no pongas	venir	no vengas

Pronouns are placed before the imperative in the negative.

No me hables.	*Do not talk to me.*
No la cierres.	*Do not close it.*
No lo abras.	*Do not open it.*
No me lo digas.	*Do not tell it to me.*
No lo hagas.	*Do not do it.*
No te vayas.	*Do not go away.*
No te lo pongas.	*Do not put it on.*

Ejercicios 5.39–5.42, páginas 370–371

b. *Usted/Ustedes*

The imperative of *usted/ustedes* is formed with the third-person singular and plural of the present subjunctive, for both the affirmative and the negative.

hable	**coma**	**viva**	**cierre**	**abra**
hablen	**coman**	**vivan**	**cierren**	**abran**
no hable	**no hablen**			

The command may be followed by the pronoun to be more formal and polite.

Hable usted con la gerencia.　　　*Speak with the management.*

Pidan ustedes lo que deseen.　　　*Order whatever you wish.*

Examples of affirmative *usted*/*ustedes* imperatives with pronouns:

USTED(ES) IMPERATIVES (AFFIRMATIVE FORMS)		
Usted	*Ustedes*	**Translation**
hábleme	háblenme	*talk to me*
ciérrela	ciérrenla	*close it*
ábralo	ábranlo	*open it*
dígamelo	díganmelo	*tell it to me*
hágalo	háganlo	*do it*
váyase	váyanse	*go away*
póngaselo	pónganselo	*put it on*

Examples of negative *usted*/*ustedes* imperatives with pronouns:

USTED(ES) IMPERATIVES (NEGATIVE FORMS)		
Usted	*Ustedes*	**Translation**
no me hable	no me hablen	*do not talk to me*
no la cierre	no la cierren	*do not close it*
no lo abra	no lo abran	*do not open it*
no me lo diga	no me lo digan	*do not tell it to me*
no lo haga	no lo hagan	*do not do it*
no se vaya	no se vayan	*do not go away*
no se lo ponga	no se lo pongan	*do not put it on*

PRÁCTICA

Ejercicio 5.43, páginas 371–372

c. *Vosotros*

The affirmative is formed with the infinitive, minus the *r,* plus *d.*

hablad	**decid**
cerrad	**haced**
abrid	**id**

Examples of affirmative *vosotros* imperatives with pronouns:

Habladme.	*Talk to me.*
Cerradla.	*Close it.*
Abridlo.	*Open it.*
Decídmelo.	*Tell it to me.*

With the reflexive pronoun *os,* the *d* of the ending is dropped. (The only exception is *ir: idos.*)

Levantaos.	*Get up.*
Callaos.	*Be quiet.*
Laváoslas.	*Wash them.* (**las = las manos**)
Ponéoslo.	*Put it on.* (**lo = el abrigo**)

The negative *vosotros* imperative is formed with the second-person plural of the present subjunctive.

No me habléis.	*Do not talk to me.*
No la cerréis.	*Do not close it.*
No me lo digáis.	*Do not tell it to me.*
No lo hagáis.	*Do not do it.*
No os vayáis.	*Do not go away.*
No os lo pongáis.	*Do not put it on.*

PRÁCTICA

Ejercicios 5.44–5.47, páginas 372–373

d. *Nosotros*

Affirmative commands are formed with the first-person plural of the present subjunctive.

hablemos	**digamos**
comamos	**hagamos**
abramos	**pongamos**

Exception: *Ir* and *irse* in the affirmative imperative become *vamos* and *vámonos*.

With pronouns:

Hablémosle.	*Let's talk to him.*
Cerrémosla.	*Let's close it.* (**la = la puerta**)
Abrámoslo.	*Let's open it.* (**lo = el sobre**)
Hagámoslo.	*Let's do it.* (**lo = el trabajo**)

With *nos* and *se,* drop the final *s* of the verb.

Digámoselo.	*Let's tell it to him.* (**lo = el secreto**)
Levantémonos.	*Let's get up.*
Callémonos.	*Let's be quiet.*
Lavémonoslas.	*Let's wash them.* (**las = las manos**)
Pongámonoslo.	*Let's put it on.* (**lo = el abrigo**)

In the negative imperative, pronouns precede the verb.

No le hablemos.	*Let's not talk to him.*
No la cerremos.	*Let's not close it.*
No lo hagamos.	*Let's not do it.*
No nos levantemos.	*Let's not get up.*
No nos las lavemos.	*Let's not wash them.*

PRÁCTICA

Ejercicios 5.48–5.49, página 373

2. INDIRECT COMMANDS

When a command is being given to one person, but meant to be carried out by another, *que* + the present subjunctive third-person singular or plural is used.

Que venga.	*Let him come. Have him come. Tell him to come.*
Que lo haga Regina.	*Let Regina do it. Have her do it. Tell her to do it.*
Que pague Elena.	*Let Elena pay. Have her pay. Tell her to pay.*

Ejercicio 5.50, página 373; Ejercicios de repaso 5.51–5.55, página 374

E Infinitive

1. PRESENT INFINITIVE

This is the standard form used as identification of any verb.

hablar   *to speak*
comer   *to eat*
vivir   *to live*

2. PERFECT INFINITIVE

This is formed with the infinitive of the auxiliary *haber* + the past participle of the verb.

haber hablado   *to have spoken*
haber comido   *to have eaten*
haber vivido   *to have lived*

Participle

[For contextualized usage of the participle, see Chapter 6.H, pages 234–235.]

1. PRESENT PARTICIPLE OR GERUND

Regular present participles are formed with *-ando* and *-iendo*.

> **hablar: hablando**
>
> **comer: comiendo**
>
> **vivir: viviendo**

Stem-changing verbs ending in *-ir* have stem changes: $e \rightarrow i$, $o \rightarrow u$.

> **sentir: sintiendo**
>
> **pedir: pidiendo**
>
> **dormir: durmiendo**

The ending *-iendo* becomes *-yendo* when added to a stem that ends in a vowel.

> **concluir: concluyendo**   **leer: leyendo**
>
> **caer: cayendo**   **oír: oyendo**

Other irregular present participles:

> **decir: diciendo**   **poder: pudiendo**
>
> **ir: yendo**   **venir: viniendo**

PRÁCTICA

Ejercicios 5.56–5.58, página 375

2. PAST PARTICIPLE

Regular past participles are formed by adding *-ado* and *-ido* to the stem of the infinitive.

> **hablar: hablado**
>
> **comer: comido**
>
> **vivir: vivido**

IRREGULAR PAST PARTICIPLES

Infinitive	Past Participle	Infinitive	Past Participle
abrir	abierto	**morir**	muerto
cubrir	cubierto	**poner**	puesto
decir	dicho	**resolver**	resuelto
escribir	escrito	**volver**	vuelto
hacer	hecho		

Verbs derived from the above infinitives have the same irregularity: *descubrir, devolver,* and *suponer* are examples. There are many more such verbs, such as *recubrir, encubrir, desdecir, envolver, revolver, reescribir, rehacer, deshacer, posponer, anteponer, deponer, reponer,* etc.

Some verbs have two past participles: one regular used in compound tenses with *haber* and one irregular used as an adjective.

he bendecido	*I have blessed*
bendito (un lugar bendito)	*holy, blessed (a holy place)*
he freído	*I have fried*
frito (papas fritas)	*fried (french fries)*
he maldecido	*I have cursed*
maldito (maldito examen)	*awful, accursed (accursed exam)*
he prendido	*I have arrested*
preso (un hombre preso)	*prisoner (a male prisoner)*
he soltado	*I have released*
suelto (pelo suelto)	*loose (flowing hair)*
he imprimido	*I have printed*
impreso (la palabra impresa)	*printed (the printed word)*

PRÁCTICA

Ejercicios 5.59–5.61, página 376

Chapter 6

Verbs: Usage

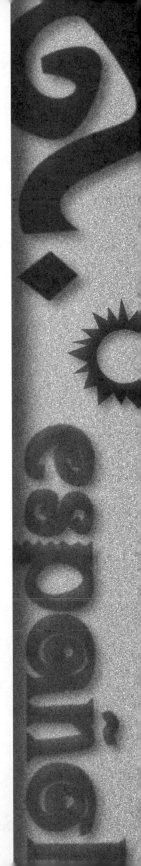

A Present Indicative

B Past Indicative Tenses: Preterite vs. Imperfect vs. Pluperfect

C Compound Tenses

D Ways of Expressing the Future

E Conditional

F Probability

G Subjunctive

H Infinitives and Present Participles

I Verbs Like *Gustar*

J Reflexive Verbs

K Indirect Discourse

◆A Present Indicative

[To review the formation of the present indicative, see Chapter 5.A.1, pages 148–153.]

The present indicative in Spanish is equivalent to the present or present progressive in English.

Hablo español.	*I speak Spanish.*
Viven en España.	*They are living in Spain.*

In the interrogative, it is equivalent to the English "do" or "does" + a verb.

¿Hablas español?	*Do you speak Spanish?*

In addition to this, it can be translated as:

¿Lo compro?	*Shall I buy it? Should I buy it?*

With *si* meaning "if":

Si lo hace Iris, le pago.	*If Iris does it, I will pay her.*

With *si* meaning "whether," the future is used in Spanish.

No sé si lloverá.	*I do not know if (whether) it will rain.*

For polite commands:

Nos da la cuenta, por favor.	*Give us the check, please.*

Acabar + *de* in the present means "to have just."

Acabo de comer.	*I just ate.*

The present progressive in Spanish, formed with the present indicative of *estar* + a present participle, is used to express ongoing actions in the present, as in English.

Estamos estudiando.	*We are studying.*

Never use the present progressive in Spanish to refer to the future.

Josefina se va mañana a las diez.	*Josefina is leaving tomorrow at ten.*

Other auxiliary verbs used occasionally in the progressive are *andar, ir,* and *seguir.*

Anda buscando a su perro.	*He is looking for his dog. He is going around looking for his dog.*

| Poco a poco vamos comprendiendo. | *We are understanding little by little.* |
| Siguen durmiendo. | *They are still sleeping. They continue sleeping.* |

Ejercicios 6.1–6.3, páginas 377–379

Past Indicative Tenses: Preterite vs. Imperfect vs. Pluperfect

[To review the formation of the imperfect indicative, see Chapter 5.A.2.a, pages 153–154; preterite indicative, Chapter 5.A.2.b, pages 154–157; pluperfect indicative, Chapter 5.A.2.d, page 158.]

I. INTRODUCTION

The preterite and the imperfect are two aspects of the past tense of the indicative; each one is used following specific criteria. Any verb can be conjugated in either of the two, and it depends on the **context** in which the verb is used whether you use one or the other. If the context demands the imperfect and you use the preterite instead, at best you may be creating a very funny sentence. It is wise to try to reduce the chances of making such mistakes. There are several ways of explaining the difference between the two aspects. These are three of the most popular.

- Action vs. state
- Beginning–middle–end
- Diachronic vs. synchronic

2. ACTION VS. STATE

a. Definitions

A verb of **action** may be best defined as one that denotes movement or change, such as *caminar, correr,* and *viajar.* Even *quedarse* (to stay) must be considered a verb of action because it is the contrary of a verb of action—*irse* (to leave).

A verb of **state** is one that denotes no movement or change, such as *ser, estar, parecer,* and *querer.*

b. Verbs of Action: Preterite Is the Rule, Imperfect Is the Exception

Once you have determined that you are dealing with a verb of action, you must visualize the perspective or focus given the verb within its specific context. If the action is being perceived as **beginning** or **ending** at a specified point, or as a **completed** act within the context, you must use the preterite.

If the speaker or narrator is focusing on the **middle** of the action, seeing it as **habitual, interrupted, descriptive/photographic,** or **"future,"** you must put it in the imperfect.

Many times in English this difference can be seen as the one between "walked" and "was walking" or "used to walk," but this is not always the case.

Compare the following sentences.

1. Celia <u>caminó</u> toda la tarde.   *Celia walked all afternoon.*

In sentence #1, the act of walking is perceived as **complete,** with no reference to habit, interruption by another act, or presence of any other simultaneous acts. **However long it may have lasted,** it must be in the preterite.

2. Celia <u>caminaba</u> todas las tardes por una hora.   *Celia used to walk (OR: would walk) in the afternoons for one hour.* (habitual)

In sentence #2, the act of walking is perceived as **habitual** and must be in the imperfect. However, if there were in the sentence an indication of the number of times the act was done, this would no longer be considered as habitual, but **repetitive.** Repetitive actions take the preterite: *Caminé tres veces hasta la tienda.* If there is an indication in the sentence of **how long the habit lasted,** this specification of limits of time takes precedence over the habitual aspect, and the verb must be in the preterite: *Por tres años acompañé a Celia a la escuela todos los días.*

3. Cuando la vi, Celia <u>caminaba</u> hacia su casa.   *When I saw her, Celia was walking towards her house.* (interrupted)

In sentence #3, the act of walking is perceived in the **middle,** giving the reader no visualization of a beginning or an end, only the point at which the act of "seeing" *(vi)* made contact with the act of walking, or **interrupted** it. Notice that when we say "interrupted" it does not mean that the act stopped, only that another action intervened when the first one was in progress. For **interrupted** actions, you must use the imperfect.

4. Cuando la vi, Celia <u>caminaba</u> con su perro y su amiga. El perro <u>corría</u> de un lado a otro y <u>olía</u> todo lo que estaba en el camino. La amiga <u>platicaba</u> incesantemente mientras Celia <u>escuchaba</u>, distante. *When I saw her, Celia was walking with her dog and her friend. The dog was running here and there and smelling everything along the way. The friend was chatting incessantly while Celia listened, lost in thought.* (descriptive, simultaneous, photographic acts)

In sentence #4, the various acts of Celia, the dog, and the friend are seen as occurring **simultaneously.** At the moment when the eyes of the narrator catch the scene, these acts are taking place all at once. These acts are called **descriptive** in many grammar books. They may also be seen as **photographic** in the sense that the onlooker could have taken a picture at the instant his eyes caught the scene, and the photograph would have shown all of the actions taking place at once: Celia taking a stride forward, the dog running to the side with his nose to the ground, the friend with her mouth open, speaking, and Celia's gaze blank, distant. This type of action takes the imperfect. In other words, imagine a snapshot of a scene where a number of actions are caught in mid-action by the camera: each of these actions in progress would be in the imperfect.

5. Me sentía triste porque mi mejor amiga se <u>casaba</u> ese fin de semana. *I felt sad because my best friend was getting married that weekend.* (The friend had not yet gotten married when this feeling was expressed—future in relation to the rest of the narration in the past.)

In sentence #5, the action of getting married has not yet occurred in relation to the context in the past. The imperfect serves as future in the past here.

In indirect discourse (see Chapter 6.K, pages 249–255), the imperfect is used to shift the present to the past.

DIRECT DISCOURSE	INDIRECT DISCOURSE
Me caso mañana. *I am getting married tomorrow.*	**Marta me dijo que se <u>casaba</u> el día siguiente.** *Marta told me that she was getting married the following day.*

The same logic applies to the near future form *ir a* + an infinitive. When shifted to the past, this expression is always in the imperfect.

PRESENT	PAST
Esta noche voy a cenar con mis amigos. *Tonight I am going to have dinner with my friends.*	**Esa noche <u>iba</u> a cenar con mis amigos.** *That night I was going to have dinner with my friends.*

(1) Special Note on "Would"

In English, habitual actions can be expressed by using the auxiliaries "used to" or "would" before the verb, or simply the verb in the past: all of these can be translated by the imperfect in Spanish.

Cuando era niño, mis padres me <u>llevaban</u> al cine una vez por semana.
When I was a kid, my parents <u>would take</u> me (OR: used to take me, took me) to the movies once a week.

It must be noted that "would" has other uses in English for which the imperfect in Spanish cannot be used: one of them is the conditional, for which Spanish also uses the conditional.

Si fuera rico, me <u>compraría</u> una isla.
If I were rich, I <u>would buy</u> an island.

A third use of "would" is in the negative, to indicate refusal. For this, Spanish could use the preterite of *querer.*

<u>No quiso</u> decirme el secreto, por más que yo insistiera.
He <u>would not</u> tell me the secret, no matter how much I insisted.

This is not to be confused with a negative of a habit (the context will indicate whether it was a habit or a refusal at one particular moment).

Mi hermano <u>no me decía</u> nunca nada triste.
My brother <u>would not tell me</u> anything sad ever.

(2) Action vs. State Review Elimination Checklist

With a verb of **action,** follow the steps indicated below, so as to decide, by process of elimination, which tense to use.

> 1. Be certain that you are dealing with a verb of action.
>
> 2. Ask yourself if the action is one of the following:
>   a) habitual?
>   b) interrupted?
>   c) photographic?
>   d) future in the past?
>
> If the answer is "yes" to any of the above, use the imperfect.
>
> If the answer is "no" to all of the above, use the preterite.

c. Verbs of State: Imperfect Is the Rule, Preterite Is the Exception

If the verb you are dealing with is a **verb of state** *(ser, estar, haber, tener, parecer, etc.)*, you will follow a different set of rules to determine whether to use imperfect or preterite.

At times, the identification of a verb of state is rendered easiest by asking the question "Is this an action?" and if the answer is negative, you are probably dealing with a verb of state. A nonaction verb, in essence, is what we are calling a verb of state here. Thus, for example, "to have" or "to be" are not actions, and they belong to this category. But "to jump," "to walk," "to talk," are actions, and do not belong to this category. In some cases, a verb could fit either category, depending on how it is perceived in the context. The verb "to think," for example, can be an action when it is perceived as a single act of thinking; or it can be perceived as a nonaction (or state) when it refers to holding an opinion: in the first case, it would be preterite, in the second it would be imperfect. Another contrast would be between the two uses of *ir* as verb of action versus auxiliary for the future; in the first case, it would follow the standard rules of a verb of action, but in the second case it belongs to verbs of nonaction. Compare the following sentences.

> **<u>Pensé</u> que estabas dormido.**
> *I thought you were asleep.*

> **En esa época <u>pensaban</u> que el mundo era plano.**
> *At that time they thought the world was flat.*

When the verb is a nonaction verb, or verb of state, use the imperfect as a rule.

> **Yo <u>tenía</u> quince años en esta foto.**
> *I was fifteen years old in this picture.*

> **En ese entonces, mi padre <u>estaba</u> en México.**
> *At that time, my father was in Mexico.*

> **A mí me <u>gustaba</u> la vida allá.**
> *I liked life there.*

> **<u>Iba</u> a llover.**
> *It was going to rain.*

When a nonaction verb, or verb of state, is affected by the context to show a change or a reaction, or a time limitation, the preterite is used.

Nonaction or state:

> **<u>Estaba</u> en una fiesta cuando llamaste.**
> *I was at a party when you called.*

Time limitation:

> **<u>Estuvimos</u> en esa fiesta unas tres horas.**
> *We were at that party for about three hours.*

Nonaction or state:

> **Mi madre <u>tenía</u> cuatro hijos en esa época.**
> *My mother had four sons at that time.*

Action:

> **Mi madre <u>tuvo</u> su tercer hijo en este hospital.**
> *My mother had her third child in this hospital. (childbirth)*

Nonaction or state:

> **Me <u>gustaban</u> las películas de horror cuando era adolescente.**
> *I liked horror movies when I was a teenager.*

Reaction:

> **Me <u>gustó</u> la película que vimos anoche.**
> *I liked the move we saw last night.*

As a basic rule, use the imperfect every time you have a **verb of state,** with the exception of contexts where there is a clear indication of **change, reaction,** or **implied action,** or if there is a **specified limitation of time,** in which cases you must use the preterite.

IMPERFECT	PRETERITE
No implication of change, reaction or action, or time limitation	**To indicate a sudden change, a reaction, or time limitation**
Eran las dos de la tarde. *It was two o'clock.*	**De repente, fueron** las dos de la tarde. *Suddenly, it was two o'clock in the afternoon.* (Here, the expression **de repente** is altering the standard way of seeing time.)
Jorge **tenía** catorce años. *Jorge was fourteen years old.*	Jorge **cumplió** catorce años ese día. *Jorge turned fourteen that day.* (NOTE: You do not use **tener** here.)
Mi madre **creía** en Dios. *My mother believed in God.*	En ese instante **creyó** en Dios. *In that instant, he believed in God.* (Sudden conversion)
Hacía mucho frío ayer. *It was very cold yesterday.*	Todo ese invierno **hizo** mucho frío. *All that winter it was very cold.* (This sentence is almost identical to the one to the left. The only difference is in the way the narrator wishes to perceive the cold, as in progress or lasting a specific amount of time.)
Había diez sillas en la clase. *There were ten chairs in the classroom.* (NOTE: These are objects, not events.)	**Hubo** una tormenta, una huelga, una pelea, un incendio, etc. *There was a storm, a strike, a fight, a fire, etc.* (Events or actions)
Estaba en España cuando oí la noticia. *I was in Spain when I heard the news.*	**Estuve** en España por dos años. *I was in Spain for two years.* (Time limit: **dos años**)

PRÁCTICA

Ejercicio 6.4, página 380

There are some verbs that actually change meaning when used in the preterite: *saber, conocer, poder, querer, tener que, acabar de.* Consider the following differences.

SABER

Imperfect—to know

Sabía español cuando era niño.　　　*He knew Spanish as a child.*

Preterite—to find out, or become informed, or realize

Supo que ella había muerto.　　　*He found out that she had died.*

CONOCER

Imperfect—to know

Conocíamos a los Gómez.   *We knew the Gomezes.*

Preterite—to meet (for the first time, as in being introduced)

Conocí a Marta en la fiesta.   *I met Marta at the party.*

(NOTE: To say "to meet" for someone you know already, when it means to get together with that person, use *encontrarse con*. See Chapter 8.B.16, page 291.)

PODER

Imperfect—to be able, can

Podían trabajar juntos.   *They could work together.*

Preterite—affirmative: to succeed, be able, manage; negative: to fail

Después de mucho esfuerzo, pudieron abrir la ventana.   *After a lot of effort, they succeeded in opening the window.*

No pudieron salir.   *They could not (failed to) get out.*

QUERER

Imperfect—to want

Queríamos viajar.   *We wanted to travel.*

Preterite—affirmative: to attempt, try; negative: to refuse to

Quiso escapar, pero no pudo.   *He tried to escape, but failed.*

No quiso ayudarme.   *He would not help me.* (He refused to.)

Note carefully this use of "would" in English, which is different from the habitual and the conditional.

TENER QUE

Imperfect—obligation not necessarily fulfilled

Tenía que trabajar, pero fui al cine.   *I had to work, but went to the movies.*

Preterite—fulfilled obligation

Tuve que trabajar anoche.   *I had to work last night (and did).*

ACABAR DE (more on this verb in Chapter 8.B.1, pages 278–279)

Imperfect—to have just done something

> **Acababa** de comer cuando llegaste.   *I had just eaten when you arrived.*

Preterite—to finish

> **Acabé** de comer y me fui.   *I finished eating and left.*

The verb *ser* is a special case when used in the following type of sentence.

> *ser* + time expression + relative pronoun + verb

> **Fue** la última vez que lo **vi**.   *It was the last time I saw him.*

> **Era** la primera vez que lo **veía**.   *It was the first time I saw him.*

What determines the tense of the verb *ser* in these examples above is the tense of the second verb.

The sentence in the imperfect would in most likelihood be found at the **beginning** or in the **middle** of a context describing that first time of seeing someone, when the description of the encounter is still in progress. The sentence in the preterite would be at the **end** of the narrative, closing the description of the first encounter.

3. BEGINNING–MIDDLE–END

Another way of perceiving the preterite and the imperfect is by means of the three concepts of **beginning, middle,** and **end.** The preterite would be used for actions seen at their origin or at their end, or as begun and ended in the past; the imperfect is used for actions perceived in the middle, or in process, with no vision of beginning or end.

a.   Preterite: Beginning and/or End

> Beginning |———————— - - - - - -

> **Empecé** a trabajar a las tres.   *I started to work at three.*

> End - - - - - - ——————————|

> **Trabajé** hasta las cuatro de la tarde.   *I worked until four in the afternoon.*

> **Estuve** en México hasta la edad de veinte años.   *I was in Mexico until the age of twenty.*

```
┌─────────────────────────────────────────────┐
│ Beginning and end ├─────────────────┤        │
└─────────────────────────────────────────────┘
```

Trabajé desde las tres hasta las cuatro.   *I worked from three to four.*

Estuve en España por dos meses.   *I was in Spain for two months.*

There are times when the distance between beginning and end is reduced to the extent that it is invisible. All that can be perceived is a point in time at which something occurred. The act is not seen as in process.

Ayer comí en un restaurante mexicano.
Yesterday I ate in a Mexican restaurant.

Me levanté, me vestí y me fui a clase.
I got up, got dressed, and left for class.

b.   Imperfect: Middle

```
┌─────────────────────────────────────────────┐
│ Middle - - - - - - ─────────── - - - - -      │
└─────────────────────────────────────────────┘
```

Cuando entré, las dos hablaban de sus clases.
When I entered, both were speaking about their classes.
(I don't know when they began speaking; they were in the process of speaking when I entered.)

Tenía veinticinco años cuando fui a Barcelona.
I was twenty-five years old when I went to Barcelona.
(It is not stated when I began to be twenty-five, only that it was during that year in which I was twenty-five.)

In summary, since the imperfect is used only to refer to the middle of events, with no concern as to their beginning or end, and the preterite is used to focus specifically on the beginning or end of an event, or to encompass the entirety of the occurrence of the event from beginning to end, we can safely state the following general rule: **Use the preterite every time except to refer to the middle of events.**

There is a certain parallelism between the imperfect tense and the present tense. Remember that the **present** tense is used for the following:

1. To refer to something that is happening at the present moment, at the moment of speaking
    Lee una novela. *He reads (is reading) a novel.*

2. To refer to a customary event
    Siempre me despierto al amanecer. *I always wake up at dawn.*

3. To indicate futurity
    Dice que sale en una hora. *He says he is leaving in an hour.*

The **imperfect** is used for these three types of reference, recalling them from the past:

1. What was happening in the past
    Leía una novela. *He read (was reading) a novel.*

2. What was customary in the past
    Siempre me <u>despertaba</u> al amanecer. *I always woke up* (OR: *used to wake up, would wake up*) *at dawn.*

3. What was going to happen
    Dijo que <u>salía</u> en una hora. *He said he was leaving in an hour.*

4. DIACHRONIC VS. SYNCHRONIC

Yet another way of perceiving the difference between the preterite and the imperfect is one that relates to narration. If we were to say that a story is basically formed by actions that advance the plot and descriptions that add color, we could visualize the diagram of a story with two sets of lines: one horizontal, along which the actions that advance the plot successively, one after the other, are located (diachronic); and along it, vertical lines along which descriptive portions are formed, not advancing in time, but immobile, forming a sort of painting or visual framework in which the other actions will occur (synchronic). Depending upon the type of novel or story, you may have a mostly horizontal line, or a short horizontal line, indicating that little really happened in the plot, but many vertical lines, indicating a great deal of description. Thus, a summary of a story would be **preterite**; a typical love story could be seen like this: "They met, they fell in love, he met her parents, he gave her an engagement ring, they got married, they had children, they lived happily ever after." On the other hand, the weather when they met, or what the scenery was when he gave her the engagement ring, or what everyone was doing in church while she walked up the aisle would be in the **imperfect.**

The diagram on the next page plots out the verbs of the paragraph below it. Notice that the <u>horizontals</u> are in the **preterite** (diachronic) and the <u>verticals</u> are in the **imperfect** (synchronic); numbers identify the preterite, letters the imperfect.

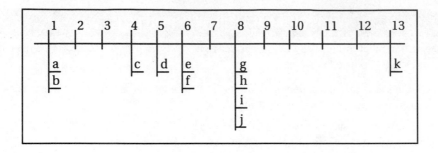

Esta mañana cuando me <u>desperté</u> [1], el sol <u>brillaba</u> [a] y los pájaros <u>cantaban</u> [b]. Me <u>levanté</u> [2] y me <u>bañé</u> [3]. <u>Fui</u> [4] a la cocina donde ya <u>comían</u> [c] mis hermanos y me <u>preparé</u> [5] el desayuno. <u>Parecía</u> [d] un día normal.

En camino al trabajo, <u>ocurrió</u> [6] algo muy extraño. En la carretera, que a esa hora de la mañana por lo general <u>estaba</u> [e] vacía, <u>había</u> [f] una fila de carros larguísima. Cuando <u>llegué</u> [7] por fin hasta el frente de la fila, <u>pude</u> [8] ver que un carro de policía <u>estaba</u> [g] estacionado al lado de la carretera, y que dos policías <u>paraban</u> [h] y <u>miraban</u> [i] dentro de cada carro, como buscando a alguien o algo. Un motociclista <u>iba</u> [j] delante de mí, y cuando le <u>tocó</u> [9] a él pasar la inspección, el policía le <u>pidió</u> [10] que se quitara el casco para mostrarle la cara. Al llegar yo, me <u>quité</u> [11] las gafas de sol, y <u>pasé</u> [12] sin problema. Pero me <u>asusté</u> [13] mucho al ver que uno de los policías <u>tenía</u> [k] un rifle.

This morning when I woke up, the sun was shining and the birds were singing. I got up and bathed. I went to the kitchen where my brothers were already eating and prepared myself breakfast. It seemed to be a normal day.

On the way to work, something very strange happened. On the road, which at that time in the morning was usually empty, there was a very long line of cars. When I finally arrived at the front of the line, I was able to see that a police car was parked on the side of the road, and that two police officers were stopping and looking inside each car, as if they were looking for someone or something. A motorcyclist was (going) ahead of me, and when it was his turn to pass inspection, the police officer asked him to take off his helmet to show him his face. When I arrived, I took off my sunglasses, and passed with no problem. But I became very frightened when I saw that one of the police officers had a rifle.

PRÁCTICA

Ejercicios 6.5–6.12, páginas 380–383

5. PLUPERFECT

[To review the formation of the pluperfect indicative, see Chapter 5.A.2.d, page 158.]

When narrating or reporting something from the past, it often happens that one of the actions precedes the others. In such a case, the pluperfect is used. Pluperfect comes from "plus" which means "more," and "perfect" which means "completed." This is a tense that is used to report actions that ended before the basic past timeline that the narrator is using.

An extreme example of this would be to say that if a historian is telling the story of the Second World War, and during that narration wants to refer back to events in the First World War, (s)he would use the pluperfect. However, the distance between the two pasts does not have to be so great. It could be a matter of minutes; as long as there is a reference back to an action completed prior to the basic past timeline, the pluperfect would be used.

The use of the pluperfect exists in English as well, but is not as frequently used as it is in Spanish. Consider the following sentences.

> **El príncipe vio que a Cenicienta se le <u>había caído</u> un zapato al huir.**
> *The prince saw that Cinderella had lost a shoe while running away.*

The basic timeline here is the moment when the prince appeared on the scene outside the palace, after midnight. He ran outside and looked for Cinderella, saw that she was gone, and noticed her shoe on the steps. He immediately assumed that while she was running away, she had lost the shoe. The loss of her shoe occurred prior to the prince seeing the shoe. Note that if we were narrating this in the present, you would have the following set of verbs (notice the tenses): the prince runs out, looks for Cinderella, sees she is gone, notices her shoe on the steps, assumes she *lost* it while running away. The only past tense is this series is "lost." Roughly speaking, you could say that the pluperfect is to the past what the past is to the present.

Note that if the story is told from a different perspective, the tenses may change.

> **Mientras corría escaleras abajo, se le cayó un zapato. Después el príncipe lo encontró y lo usó para encontrar a la misteriosa desconocida.**
> *While she ran, one of her shoes fell off. Later the prince found it and used it to find the mysterious stranger.*

The point of view for the above narration is different. Here, it is Cinderella first who is being observed while she runs, and the loss of her shoe is perceived in the process of her descent down the stairs. The prince comes in afterwards, following the timeline in a logical way: there is no referring back to prior events. There is no pluperfect.

PRÁCTICA

Ejercicio 6.13, página 383; Ejercicios de repaso 6.14–6.19, páginas 383–386

Compound Tenses

I. INTRODUCTION

In the table that follows, the verbs in bold are what we call "compound tenses," because they are formed of more than one part. Notice that for the progressive form, *estar* is used with the **present participle.** For the perfect forms, *haber* is used as auxiliary with the **past participle.** Progressive perfect forms combine *estar* in the perfect form (auxiliary *haber* + the past participle of *estar*) and the present participle of the verb being conjugated.

	MOOD	TENSE	NONPROGRESSIVE	PROGRESSIVE
S	Indicative	Present	camino	**estoy caminando**
I	Indicative	Future	caminaré	**estaré caminando**
M	Indicative	Imperfect	caminaba	**estaba caminando**
P	Indicative	Preterite	caminé	**estuve caminando**
L	Conditional	Present	caminaría	**estaría caminando**
E	Subjunctive	Present	camine	**esté caminando**
	Subjunctive	Imperfect	caminara	**estuviera caminando**
P				
E	Indicative	Present Perfect	**he caminado**	**he estado caminando**
R	Indicative	Future Perfect	**habré caminado**	**habré estado caminando**
F	Indicative	Pluperfect	**había caminado**	**había estado caminando**
E	Conditional	Perfect	**habría caminado**	**habría estado caminando**
C	Subjunctive	Present Perfect	**haya caminado**	**haya estado caminando**
T	Subjunctive	Pluperfect	**hubiera caminado**	**hubiera estado caminando**

2. PERFECT TENSES

As a rule, perfect tenses are used to focus on the completion of an action in relation to a moment, present or past.

PERFECT TENSES			
Formation	Auxiliary Haber	+	Past Participle
Example	Hemos		llegado.
Translation	We have		arrived.

a. Present Perfect Indicative

[To review the formation of the present perfect indicative, see Chapter 5.A.2.c, page 157.]

This tense refers to completed events in relation to the present.

Hemos regresado del museo.	*We have returned from the museum.*
Todavía no he terminado el libro.	*I still have not finished the book.*

b. Future Perfect

[To review the formation of the future perfect, see Chapter 5.A.3.b, page 159.]

This tense refers to a future event that will have been completed by a specific time or after another event in the future.

Habremos terminado para las cinco.	*We will have finished by five.*

The future perfect can also be found in contexts expressing probability, for probably completed actions in the past.

¿Adónde crees que fue Roberto?	*Where do you think Roberto went?*
No sé. Habrá ido a la tienda.	*I do not know. I guess he went to the store.*

c. Past Perfect (Pluperfect) Indicative

[To review the formation of the pluperfect indicative, see Chapter 5.A.2.d, page 158.]

This tense refers to an event prior to another one in the past.

> **Ya había terminado de comer cuando llamaste.**
> *I had already finished eating when you called.*

d. Conditional Perfect

[To review the formation of the conditional perfect, see Chapter 5.B.2, page 161.]

This tense refers to an event that is the future in relation to another event in the past.

> **Me dijeron que <u>habrían terminado</u> para el viernes pasado.**
> *They told me they would have finished by last Friday.*

This form can also be found in probability structures, referring to an action in the past prior to another one in the past.

> **¿Por qué piensas que esa estudiante se aburría en clase el semestre pasado?**
> *Why do you think that student was bored in class last semester?*

> **No sé. Ya <u>habría leído</u> los mismos libros para otra clase.**
> *I do not know. Maybe she had already read the same books for another class.*

e. Present Perfect Subjunctive

[To review the formation of the present perfect subjunctive, see Chapter 5.C.3, page 166.]

This tense describes an event that is completed in relation to the present.

> **Me sorprende que <u>haya llegado</u> tarde.**
> *It surprises me that he arrived late.*

f. Pluperfect Subjunctive

[To review the formation of the pluperfect subjunctive, see Chapter 5.C.4, page 166.]

This tense describes an event that was completed before another in the past.

> **Nos sorprendió que <u>hubiera cenado</u> antes de venir.**
> *It surprised us that he had eaten before coming.*

3. SIMPLE PROGRESSIVE TENSES

a. Introduction

The progressive is used to express an ongoing action.

PROGRESSIVE TENSES			
Formation	Auxiliary Estar	+	Present Participle
Example	Estamos		estudiando.
Translation	We are		studying.

Exception: *Ir* and *venir* are **never** used in the progressive in Spanish.

Vamos a España.	*We are going to Spain.*
Viene a cenar.	*She is coming to dinner.*

In Spanish, the progressive is **never** used for states or conditions.

Llevaba una chaqueta de cuero.	*She was wearing a leather jacket.*
Tengo zapatos puestos.	*I am wearing shoes.*
Estoy sentado.	*I am sitting.* (position)
Faltaban dos sillas.	*Two chairs were missing.*
Se te ve la camiseta.	*Your undershirt is showing.*

b. Present Progressive

This tense is formed with the present of *estar* and refers to ongoing actions in the present.

<u>Estoy trabajando</u> en este momento y no podré ayudarte.	*I am working at this moment and will not be able to help you.*
Pronto comeremos; <u>están preparando</u> la cena.	*We will eat soon; they are preparing dinner.*

The present progressive is **never** used in Spanish to refer to the future, as it often is in English.

Lo vamos a hacer mañana.	*We are doing it tomorrow.*

c. Future Progressive

This tense is formed with the future of *estar* and refers to ongoing actions in the future.

> **Mañana, domingo, a las siete de la tarde, Asunción estará cenando. Lo sé porque siempre hace lo mismo.**
> *Tomorrow, Sunday, at seven in the evening, Asunción will be eating dinner. I know it because she always does the same thing.*

The future progressive is also used to express probability in the present.

> —¿Qué hace Regina?
> —No lo sé. **Estará estudiando.**
> *"What is Regina doing?"*
> *"I do not know. She must be studying."*

d. Past Progressive

This tense is formed with the imperfect or preterite of *estar* and refers to an ongoing or finished action in the past.

> **Estaba trabajando cuando me llamaste.**
> *I was working when you called.*

> **Estuve trabajando toda la mañana.**
> *I was working all morning.*

The past progressive can **never** be used to refer to a future of the past.

> **Iba a llover.**
> *It was going to rain.*

e. Conditional Present Progressive

This tense, formed with the present conditional of *estar,* refers to an ongoing action that is future in the past, a backshift from the section on future progresssive (above).

> **Cecilia me dijo que el día siguiente, domingo, a las siete de la tarde, Susana estaría cenando. Añadió que lo sabía porque siempre hacía lo mismo.**
> *Cecilia told me that the next day, Sunday, at seven in the evening, Susana would be eating dinner. She added that she knew it because she always did the same thing.*

The conditional progressive is also used to express probability for an ongoing action in the past.

> —¿Por qué no vino Georgina a clase ayer?
> —Quién sabe. **Estaría durmiendo.**
> *"Why did Georgina not come to class yesterday?"*
> *"Who knows. Maybe she was sleeping."*

f. Subjunctive Present Progressive

This tense is formed with the present subjunctive of *estar* and refers to an ongoing action in the present, colored by the subjunctive.

> **Dudo que mis hijos <u>estén comiendo</u> lo suficiente.**
> *I doubt that my children are eating enough.*

g. Subjunctive Imperfect Progressive

This tense is formed with the imperfect subjunctive of *estar* and refers to an ongoing action in the past, colored by the subjunctive.

> **No podía creer que <u>estuvieran peleando</u> todavía.**
> *I could not believe they were still fighting.*

4. PERFECT PROGRESSIVE TENSES

a. Introduction

This combination serves to focus on the completion of an ongoing action in relation to another moment, present, past, or future.

PERFECT PROGRESSIVE TENSES				
Formation	Auxiliary **Haber**	+	Past Participle **Estar**	+	Present Participle Main Verb
Example	**Hemos**		estado		**corriendo.**
Translation	*We have*		*been*		*running.*

b. Indicative Present Perfect Progressive

> **Mi madre <u>ha estado llamándome</u> todos los días.**
> *My mother has been calling me every day.*

c. Indicative Future Perfect Progressive

> **Para cuando llegue, <u>habré estado manejando</u> durante doce horas sin parar.**
> *By the time I get there, I will have been driving for twelve hours nonstop.*

This form can also serve for probability, when referring to a completed ongoing action in the past.

> —¿Por qué está tan cansada Zelmira?
> —No sé. **Habrá estado trabajando** toda la noche.
> *"Why is Zelmira so tired?"*
> *"I do not know. She was probably working all night."*

d. Indicative Pluperfect Progressive

> Cuando por fin me dejaron entrar, <u>había estado esperando</u> tres horas.
> *When they finally let me in, I had been waiting for three hours.*

e. Conditional Perfect Progressive

> La policía <u>habría estado vigilando</u> la casa si se lo hubieras pedido.
> *The police would have been watching the house if you had asked them.*

This form can also be used for probability, when referring to a completed ongoing action in the past prior to another.

> —¿Por qué crees que tardó tanto en abrir la puerta?
> —<u>Habría estado escondiendo</u> las pruebas.
> *"Why do you think he took so long to open the door?"*
> *"He must have been hiding the evidence."*

f. Subjunctive Present Perfect Progressive

Use in subordinate clauses when the main verb is in the present set and to refer to a completed ongoing action in the past.

> Dudo que <u>haya estado haciendo</u> lo que decía.
> *I doubt that he was doing what he said.*

g. Subjunctive Pluperfect Progressive

Use in subordinate clauses to refer to a completed ongoing action in a moment in the past prior to another one also in the past.

> Me sorprendió que <u>hubiera estado haciendo</u> planes sin decirme nada.
> *It surprised me that he had been making plans without telling me anything.*

5. MODAL AUXILIARIES

It should be noted that there are other auxiliaries in addition to *haber* and *estar,* which are used with a main verb and alter its value in one way or another. These are called modal auxiliaries. Each of these can exist as the main verb of a sentence and have a different meaning or weight. Among modal auxiliaries the following are used with the present participle: *ir, venir;* the following are used with the infinitive: *ir a, tener que, poder, haber de, deber.* Some examples follow.

<u>Vamos</u> preparándonos poco a poco.
We are preparing ourselves little by little.

<u>Vengo</u> planeando esto desde hace ya varios años.
I have been planning this for several years now.

<u>Van a</u> darme la respuesta mañana.
They are going to give me the answer tomorrow.

Ustedes <u>tienen que</u> decirnos la verdad.
You have to tell us the truth.

No <u>podemos</u> nadar.
We cannot swim.

<u>Han de</u> saber la verdad.
They must know the truth. (*probability)*

<u>Deberías</u> comer más.
You should eat more.

Ejercicios 6.20–6.21, página 386

Ways of Expressing the Future

[To review the formation of the future, see Chapter 5.A.3, pages 158–159.]

The future in Spanish can be expressed with the simple future.

Mañana <u>iremos</u> al cine.   *Tomorrow we will go to the movies.*

It can also be expressed with the present of *ir* + *a* + an infinitive.

Mañana <u>vamos a ir</u> al cine.   *Tomorrow we are going to go to the movies.*

It can also be expressed with the present tense.

Mañana <u>vamos</u> al cine.   *Tomorrow we are going to the movies.*

NOTE: The future CANNOT be expressed in Spanish with the progressive, as it can in English. This is a very common error, which should be avoided. Note carefully in the following sentence how the progressive future in English is translated into Spanish.

Esta tarde <u>vamos a comer</u>   *This afternoon we <u>are eating</u> here.*
(OR: <u>comemos</u>) aquí.

Remember that the progressive in Spanish can only be used for actions that are occurring at the moment. *Estamos comiendo* can only refer to the ongoing action of eating, now, in the present. Notice that the following context is not future, and for that reason, can be translated with the progressive.

No puede venir al teléfono   *He cannot come to the phone now: he*
ahora: <u>está comiendo</u>.   *is eating.*

Ejercicios 6.22–6.23, página 387

 # Conditional

[To review the formation of the conditional, see Chapter 5.B, page 160.]

I. INTRODUCTION

The conditional is used to express the following:

- Courtesy with conditional of modal auxiliaries
- Hypothetical situations with or without condition expressed with *si*
- Future of the past
- Probability in the past

2. COURTESY WITH CONDITIONAL OF MODAL AUXILIARIES

This is merely a softening of the indicative, as in English; the difference between "can you" and "could you," "must not" and "should not," "I want" and "I would like," etc.

¿**Podría** Ud. ayudarme, por favor?   *Could you help me, please?*

No **deberías** decir eso.   *You should not say that.*

The verb *querer* can be used in the same fashion, but is most frequently used in the imperfect subjunctive to express courtesy.

Quisiera que me ayudaras.   *I would like you to help me.*

Ejercicio 6.24, página 387

3. HYPOTHETICAL SITUATIONS WITH OR WITHOUT CONDITION EXPRESSED WITH *SI*

[See Chapter 6.G.6, pages 226–227, on *si* ("if") clauses.]

En esa situación, yo **tendría** mucho miedo.
In that situation, I would be very frightened.

Yo en tu lugar no le **pagaría** por grosero.
In your place, I would not pay him, because he was rude.

Si pudiera, me **compraría** ese coche.
If I could, I would buy that car.

4. FUTURE OF THE PAST

[See Chapter 6.K, pages 249–255, on indirect discourse.]

Dijo que **irían** al cine hoy.   *He said they would go to the movies today.*

Ejercicio 6.25, página 387

5. PROBABILITY IN THE PAST

(See Chapter 6.F, pages 200–201, on probability.)

¿Dónde <u>estaría</u> Juan?	*I wonder where Juan was.*
¿Adónde <u>habría</u> ido?	*I wonder where he had gone.*

Ejercicio de repaso 6.26, página 388

Probability

[To review the formation of the tenses in this section, see Chapter 5.A.3, pages 158–160, on simple future and future perfect, and Chapter 5B, pages 160–161, on present conditional and conditional perfect.]

English has many ways of expressing probability. Here is a list of some of the many possibilities of expressing doubt with the question "Who is it?".

I wonder who it is.	*Who do you suppose it is?*
Who can it be?	*Who do you think it is?*
Who in the world is it?	

Spanish uses a variety of tenses to express probability.

The **future** is used to express probability in the present.

> **¿Quién <u>será</u>?**
> (All of the variations of the English above would be translated like this.)

The **future progressive** form is frequently used with verbs of action.

¿Qué <u>estarán haciendo</u>?	*I wonder what they are doing.*

The **future perfect** is used to express the preterite or the present perfect.

<u>Habrá ido</u> al cine.	*He probably went to the movies.* *I guess he went to the movies.* *He has probably gone to the movies.* *I suppose he went … etc.*

The **conditional present** is used to express the imperfect aspect of the past.

<u>Estaría</u> en el cine. *He probably was at the movies.*
  He must have been at the movies.
  I guess he was … etc.

The **conditional progressive** form is used for verbs of action.

<u>Estaría bañándose</u>. *He was probably bathing.*

The **conditional perfect** is used to express the pluperfect.

<u>Habría salido</u> temprano. *He probably had gone out early.*
  He must have gone out early.
  I guess he went out … etc.

The following parallel columns show how probability is expressed in Spanish. On the left, the sentences are formed with the adverb *probablemente* and the standard form of the verb, whereas the column to the right gives you the altered verb tense that expresses probability without the need for the adverb.

STANDARD	PROBABILITY	TRANSLATION
Probablemente **está** en casa.	**Estará** en casa.	*He must be home.*
Probablemente **está bañándose.**	**Estará bañándose.**	*He must be bathing.*
Probablemente **estaba** en casa.	**Estaría** en casa.	*He must have been home.*
Probablemente **estaba comiendo.**	**Estaría comiendo.**	*He must have been eating.*
Probablemente **murió.**	**Habrá muerto.**	*He must have died.*
Probablemente lo **ha visto.**	Lo **habrá visto.**	*He must have seen it.*
Probablemente **había regresado.**	**Habría regresado.**	*He must have returned.*

In English, the first sentence above could also be: "He's probably at home," "I guess he's at home," "I suppose he's at home," etc. Each sentence in the chart above could thus have a variety of translations in English.

PRÁCTICA

Ejercicios 6.27–6.28, página 388

G. Subjunctive

[To review the formation of the tenses of the subjunctive, see Chapter 5.C, pages 161–166.]

1. INTRODUCTION

The subjunctive is used mainly in subordinate clauses and in some independent clauses introduced by *ojalá, quizá(s),* and *tal vez.*

There are three types of subordinate clauses in which the subjunctive might be necessary.

- Nominal
- Adjectival
- Adverbial

Each type of clause will have its own set of rules to determine whether or not you need to use the subjunctive. It is therefore necessary to be able to recognize the three types.

2. NOMINAL CLAUSES

a. Definition and Usage

Definition: A nominal clause is one that has the same function as a noun would (i.e., it may be the subject of the main verb or its direct object).

Quiero <u>pan</u>.	*I want bread.*
Quiero <u>que me ayudes</u>.	*I want you to help me.*

Both *pan* and *que me ayudes* have the same function in the sentence, that of direct object of the main verb; *que me ayudes* is called a **nominal clause** because it behaves like a noun. In the sentence *Me gusta que canten* the subordinate clause is the subject of the main verb.

Use of the subjunctive: What determines whether or not you need to use the subjunctive in the nominal clause is the **verb** of the main clause. If this verb indicates fact or truth, the subordinate clause will be in the indicative. This would be the case for such verbs as to see, to notice, to observe, to be clear, obvious, true.

Es obvio que no me entiendes.	*It is obvious that you do not understand me.*
Es cierto que viajé a Rusia.	*It is true that I traveled to Russia.*
Veo que tienes bastante dinero.	*I see you have enough money.*
Me fijé que era hora de irnos.	*I noticed it was time to leave.*

However, if the verb of the main clause indicates anything other than a mere statement of fact, such as emotion, doubt, desire, approval, feeling, volition, influence, etc., the verb of the nominal clause will have to be in the subjunctive.

Me encanta que <u>vengan</u>.	*I am delighted that they are coming.*
Dudo que ellos <u>puedan</u> hacerlo.	*I doubt that they can do it.*
Quiero que me <u>des</u> pan.	*I want you to give me bread.*
Me gusta que <u>participen</u> tanto.	*I like them to participate so much.*

Parecer, creer, and *pensar* in the negative or interrogative take the subjunctive only when there is doubt in the mind of the speaker. Also, *parecer* followed by an adjective takes the subjunctive.

Parece que <u>va</u> a llover.	*It seems it is going to rain.*
<u>No</u> parece que <u>vaya</u> a llover.	*It does not seem that it is going to rain.*
Parece <u>increíble</u> que <u>hagan</u> eso.	*It seems incredible that they do that.*
Creo que <u>puede</u> hacerlo.	*I believe he can do it.*
<u>No</u> creo que <u>pueda</u> hacerlo.	*I do not believe he can do it.*
Pienso que <u>vendrá</u>.	*I think he will come.*
<u>No</u> pienso que <u>venga</u>.	*I do not think he will come.*

Sentir will change meaning if followed by the subjunctive.

Siento que <u>voy</u> a estornudar.	*I feel I am going to sneeze.*
Siento que <u>estés</u> enferma.	*I am sorry that you are ill.*

PRÁCTICA

Ejercicios 6.29–6.32, páginas 389–390

b. Subjunctive after Expressions of Emotion

If the main clause contains a verb or an expression of emotion, this affects the verb of the subordinate clause; whether it is true or not that the action of the subordinate occurred or will occur, the subjunctive must be used.

<u>Estás</u> aquí.	*You are here.*
Sé que <u>estás</u> aquí.	*I know you are here.*
Me alegro de que <u>estés</u> aquí.	*I am glad you are here.*

Following is a list of commonly used verbs of emotion.

esperar
to hope

Espero que puedas venir.
I hope you can come.

lamentar
to regret

Lamento que esté enferma.
I regret that she is ill.

sentir
to be sorry, regret

Siento que no puedas ir.
I am sorry you cannot go.

temer
to fear

Temo que sea muy tarde.
I fear it is too late.

tener miedo
to be afraid

Tengo miedo de que haya una tormenta.
I am afraid there will be a storm.

Reflexive verbs:

alegrarse de
to be happy, glad

Me alegro de que se encuentre mejor.
I am glad he is feeling better.

avergonzarse de
to be ashamed

Se avergüenza de que su padre beba.
He is ashamed that his father drinks.

Flip verbs:

encantarle a uno
to delight, "love" (not romantic)

Me encanta que jueguen.
I am delighted that they play.

Nos encantaría que vinieran.
We would love you to come.

enojarle a uno
to anger, to make angry, be angry

Nos enoja que nos griten.
It angers us that they yell at us.
We are angry that they yell at us.

gustarle a uno
to please, like

Le gusta que ganen.
It pleases him that they win.
He likes them to win.

molestarle a uno
to annoy, be annoyed

¿Te molesta que haga ruido?
Does it annoy you that I make noise?

sorprenderle a uno
to surprise, be surprised

Les sorprende que podamos hacerlo.
They are surprised that we can do it.

Use of the infinitive in the subordinate clause: For verbs of emotion, if the subject is the same in both clauses, use an **infinitive** in the subordinate clause.

Sentimos no <u>poder</u> ir a la fiesta.	*We are sorry we cannot go to the party.*
Quiero <u>darte</u> un regalo.	*I want to give you a present.*
Me encantó <u>bailar</u> contigo.	*I loved dancing with you.*
Me gustó <u>visitar</u> a mis abuelos.	*I enjoyed visiting my grandparents.*

PRÁCTICA

Ejercicio 6.33, página 390

c.   Subjunctive after Expressions of Volition and Influence

If the main clause contains a verb or an expression of volition or influence, the subjunctive must be used in the subordinate clause.

Quiero que <u>cantes</u> conmigo.	*I want you to sing with me.*

Commonly used verbs of volition:

desear *to want*	**¿Desea que le traiga algo de beber?** *Do you want me to bring you something to drink?*
empeñarse en *to insist*	**Se empeña en que la respeten.** *She insists that they respect her.*
insistir en *to insist on*	**Insistieron en que les pagáramos.** *They insisted on our paying them.*
necesitar *to need*	**Necesito que me escuches.** *I need you to listen to me.*
oponerse a *to object to*	**Se oponía a que le abrieran la maleta.** *He objected to their opening his suitcase.*
preferir *to prefer*	**Prefiero que me hables en español.** *I prefer that you speak to me in Spanish.*
querer *to want*	**Queremos que llegue la primavera.** *We want spring to arrive.*

Use of the infinitive in the subordinate clause: For verbs of volition, if the subject is the same in both clauses, use an **infinitive** in the subordinate clause.

Deseamos <u>ir</u> solos.	*We want to go alone.*
Se empeña en <u>gritar</u>.	*He insists on yelling.*
Insisto en <u>llamar</u> primero.	*I insist on calling first.*
Necesitas <u>estudiar</u>.	*You need to study.*
Me opongo a <u>votar</u> por él.	*I refuse (object) to vote for him.*
Prefieren <u>viajar</u> en barco.	*They prefer to travel by ship.*
Quiero <u>darte</u> un regalo.	*I want to give you a present.*

Verbs of communication such as *decir, escribir,* and *telefonear* may be followed by the indicative or the subjunctive; if they are used with the subjunctive, they imply a command.

Dijo que quería irse.	*He said he wanted to leave.*
Me dijo que me fuera.	*He told me to leave.*

Commonly used verbs of influence with a direct object:

dejar*	**Dejé que él pagara.**
to let, allow	*I let him pay.*
hacer*	**Hizo que limpiaran su cuarto.**
to make	*He made them clean their room.*
invitar a*	**La invito a que cene con nosotros.**
to invite	*I invite you to eat dinner with us.*
obligar a*	**Los obliga a que bailen.**
to force	*He forces them to dance.*

Commonly used verbs of influence with an indirect object:

aconsejar	**Le aconsejo que se calle.**
to advise	*I advise you to be quiet.*
advertir	**Les advierto que estudien.**
to warn	*I warn you to study.*
convencer	**¿Te convencieron que hablaras?**
to convince	*Did they convince you to speak?*
exigir	**Exigen que cerremos la puerta.**
to demand	*They demand that we close the door.*

impedir *	**Impidieron que fuera al baile.**
to prevent	*They prevented her from going to the dance.*
mandar *	**Mandó que te callaras.**
to order	*He ordered you to be quiet.*
pedir	**Nos pide que lleguemos temprano.**
to ask	*He asks us to arrive early.*
permitir *	**Le permiten que regrese tarde.**
to allow	*They allow him to return late.*
persuadir a	**Me persuadieron a que cantara.**
to persuade	*They persuaded me to sing.*
prohibir *	**Te prohíbo que salgas con ellos.**
to forbid	*I forbid you from going out with them.*
recomendar *	**Nos recomiendan que tomemos aspirina.**
to recommend	*They recommend that we take aspirin.*
rogar	**Le ruego que me disculpe.**
to beg	*I beg you to forgive me.*
sugerir	**Sugieren que comamos aquí.**
to suggest	*They suggest that we eat here.*

Dejar, hacer, invitar a, obligar a, exigir, impedir, prohibir, recomendar, mandar, and *permitir* are commonly used with the infinitive, even if there is a change of subject, and with a direct or indirect object pronoun: **Le dejé pagar. Las hizo limpiar su cuarto. Te mandó callarte. Le permiten regresar tarde.** (See Chapter 6.H, pages 231–233, on the infinitive.)

Impersonal expressions:

bastar	**Basta que me lo pidas.**
to be enough	*It is enough that you ask me for it.*
convenir	**Conviene que lleguen temprano.**
to be suitable, a good idea	*It is a good idea that you arrive early.*
importar	**No importa que no tengas dinero.**
to matter	*It does not matter that you do not have money.*
más valer	**Más vale que me pague pronto.**
to be better	*He had better pay me soon.*

PRÁCTICA

Ejercicio 6.34, página 390

d. Subjunctive after Expressions of Doubt and Negation of Reality

If the main clause contains a verb or an expression of doubt, or a negation of reality, the subjunctive must be used in the subordinate clause.

Dudo que pueda hacerlo.	*I doubt that he can do it.*
Niega que él lo haya visto.	*She denies that he saw it.*

Commonly used verbs of doubt and negation of reality:

dudar *to doubt*	**Dudo que venga esta noche.** *I doubt that he will come tonight.*
negar *to deny*	**Negó que fuera verdad.** *He denied that it was true.*
puede ser *it may be*	**Puede ser que llueva hoy.** *It may be that it will rain today.*
no creer *not to believe*	**No creo que sepa la verdad.** *I do not believe that he knows the truth.*
no decir *not to say*	**No digo que seas culpable.** *I do not say that you are guilty.*
no pensar *not to think*	**No piensa que tú le creas.** *He does not think you believe him.*
no ser *not to be*	**No es que no quiera, es que no puedo.** *It is not that I do not want to, it is that I cannot.*
no significar *not to mean*	**Eso no significa que no te quiera.** *That does not mean that he does not love you.*

PRÁCTICA

Ejercicio 6.35, páginas 390–391

e. Subjunctive after Impersonal Expressions with *Ser*

If the main clause contains an impersonal expression with *ser* + an adjective or a noun, and the adjective or noun denotes anything but truth or certainty, the subjunctive must be used in the subordinate clause.

Indicative:

<u>Es verdad</u> que se <u>fue</u> temprano.   *It is true that he left early.*

<u>Es cierto</u> que <u>hace</u> frío.   *It is true that it is cold.*

Subjunctive:

<u>Es posible</u> que <u>pueda</u> hacerlo.   *It is possible that he can do it.*

<u>No es cierto</u> que lo <u>haya visto</u>.   *It is not true that he saw it.*

Commonly used impersonal expressions taking the subjunctive:

(ser) bueno *(to be) good*	**Es bueno que sepas hacerlo sola.** *It is good you know how to do it alone.*
malo *bad*	**Fue malo que se lo dijeras.** *It was bad for you to tell him.*
mejor *better*	**Es mejor que nos vayamos temprano.** *It is better that we leave early.*
curioso *curious, odd*	**Es curioso que no haya correo.** *It is odd that there is no mail.*
extraño *strange*	**Fue extraño que no me saludara.** *It was strange that he did not greet me.*
fantástico *fantastic*	**Es fantástico que puedas venir.** *It is fantastic that you can come.*
raro *strange, odd*	**Es raro que no haga frío.** *It is strange that it is not cold.*
triste *sad*	**Es triste que se vayan.** *It is sad that you are leaving.*
deseable *desirable*	**Es deseable que pague al contado.** *It is desirable that you pay cash.*

importante *important*	**Es importante que lo aprendan.** *It is important that they learn it.*
necesario *necessary*	**Es necesario que estudies más.** *It is necessary that you study more.*
difícil *unlikely*	**Es difícil que haga calor en invierno.** *It is unlikely to be (that it be) hot in winter.*
fácil *likely*	**Es fácil que venga hoy.** *It is likely that he will come today.*
imposible *impossible*	**Es imposible que se lo haya dicho.** *It is impossible that she told him.*
posible *possible*	**Es posible que se hayan ido.** *It is possible that they left.*
probable *probable*	**Es probable que no lo sepa.** *It is probable that he does not know it.*
(una) lástima *a pity*	**Es una lástima que esté lloviendo.** *It is a pity that it is raining.*
(una) maravilla *a wonder*	**Es una maravilla que comprenda.** *It is a wonder that he understands.*
(una) pena *a pity*	**Es una pena que no puedas venir.** *It is a pity that you cannot come.*

Notice that these expressions parallel the categories of verbs of emotion, volition, influence, and doubt or uncertainty. All impersonal expressions take the subjunctive, except those that denote absolute certainty.

Es evidente, obvio, cierto, claro, etc.

Ejercicio 6.36, página 391; Ejercicio de repaso 6.37, página 391

3. ADJECTIVAL CLAUSES

a. Definition

An adjectival clause is one that modifies a noun as an adjective would.

> **Quiero leer una novela <u>divertida</u>.**
> *I want to read a fun novel.*

> **Quiero leer la novela <u>que me regalaste</u>.**
> *I want to read the novel you gave me.*

> **Quiero leer una novela <u>que me haga reír</u>.**
> *I want to read a novel that will make me laugh.*

b. Usage

Notice that *que* in this sentence is a **relative pronoun** (see Chapter 3.G, pages 93–99) and not a conjunction, as is the case in nominal clauses. The **antecedent** of the relative pronoun in this sentence is *novela*. To determine whether or not to use the subjunctive in an adjectival or relative clause, you must find the antecedent and see whether, within the context of the main clause, it is existent or not. You will only use the subjunctive if the antecedent is nonexistent, or if its existence is unknown or uncertain.

> **Tengo una casa que <u>tiene</u> dos pisos.**
> *I have a house that has two floors.*

> **Quiero una casa que <u>tenga</u> dos pisos.**
> *I want a house that has two floors.*

Notice that in the first sentence, the fact that I have the house means that the house exists, and thus you must use the **indicative** in the subordinate clause, but in the second sentence, the house I want has not been found, and I do not know if it exists. For this reason, the verb of the subordinate must be in the **subjunctive.** Compare the following sentences.

> **Conozco a una mujer que <u>es</u> ingeniera.**
> *I know a woman who is an engineer.* (existent)

> **No conozco a nadie que <u>sea</u> brasileño.**
> *I do not know anyone who is Brazilian.* (existence unknown)

> **Hay alguien aquí que <u>está fumando</u> una pipa.**
> *There is someone here who is smoking a pipe.* (existent)

> **¿Hay alguien aquí que <u>sea</u> doctor?**
> *Is there someone here who is a doctor?* (existence unknown)

Lo que is followed by the subjunctive when the implied antecedent is totally unknown and the implication is "whatever it might be." If the antecedent is known by the speaker, the indicative is used.

> **Haré lo que me digas.**
> *I shall do what (whatever) you tell me to do.*

> **Haré lo que me dijiste.**
> *I shall do (specifically) what you told me to do.*

NOTE: When a long adjectival clause complements the subject of the main verb, English places the subject plus its clause first, but Spanish would tend to place it last.

> **Esta mañana llamó [el reportero <u>al que querías entrevistar sobre el artículo</u>].**
> *[The reporter (whom) <u>you wanted to interview about the article</u>] called this morning.*

In the above sentence, the reporter is the subject of the main verb "called."

PRÁCTICA

Ejercicios 6.38–6.39, página 392

4. ADVERBIAL CLAUSES

a. Definition

An adverbial clause is one that modifies the verb in the main clause in the same manner as an adverb would, by indicating how, when, for what purposes, and under what circumstances the action of the main clause takes place.

Salió <u>rápidamente</u>.	*He left quickly.*
Salió <u>tan pronto como pudo</u>.	*He left as soon as he could.*

b. Usage

Use of the subjunctive: If the action of the subordinate clause has not been accomplished at the time indicated in the main verb, the subjunctive is used. This rule permits us to subdivide conjunctions into two categories, according to the meaning of the conjunction; some conjunctions, such as *para que* and *antes de que,* will always introduce an action that has not yet taken place at the time of the main clause.

Lo hago para que tú no tengas que hacerlo.
I am doing it so that you will not have to.

Vino antes de que lo llamáramos.
He came before we called him.

Other conjunctions, such as *cuando,* can refer to situations that already occurred or that have not yet occurred. If they refer to a situation that already took place, the verb of the subordinate will be in the indicative; if not, it will be in the subjunctive.

Mi perro viene cuando lo llamo.
My dog comes when I call him.

Mi perro vendrá cuando lo llame.
My dog will come when I call him.

Some conjunctions take the indicative and not the subjunctive because they generally refer to situations that already occurred: some examples are **así que, porque, desde que.**

La obra me aburrió, así que me fui temprano.
The play bored me, so I left early.

Se lo regalé a Luis porque él me lo pidió.
I gave it to Luis because he asked me for it.

No lo he visto desde que se graduó.
I have not seen him ever since he graduated.

Following is a table of conjunctions that take the subjunctive, either always or occasionally.

ALWAYS SUBJUNCTIVE	OCCASIONALLY SUBJUNCTIVE
para que	cuando
a fin de que	apenas
a menos que	en cuanto
salvo que	tan pronto como
a no ser que	aunque
antes de que	a pesar de que
con tal de que	después de que
sin que	mientras
en caso de que	hasta que

When the subject of the main verb is the same as the subject of the subordinate verb, some of these conjunctions change into prepositions.

Obligatory change:

antes de que → **antes de**	**Antes de salir, me puse el abrigo.** *Before going out, I put on my coat.*
para que → **para**	**Para preparar esto, necesitas dos huevos.** *To prepare this, you need two eggs.*
sin que → **sin**	**Se fue sin despedirse.** *He left without saying good-bye.*
después de que → **después de**	**Después de cenar, jugaron a la baraja.** *After eating dinner, they played cards.*

Optional change:

hasta que → **hasta**	**No se irá hasta haberse acabado la comida.** OR: **No se irá hasta que se acabe la comida.** *He will not leave until he has finished his food.*

The conjunctions in the chart on the next page **always** take the subjunctive, or the infinitive if the subject is the same for both the main verb and the subordinate; they would **never** be followed by an indicative, however.

CONJUNCTION	MEANING	EXAMPLES

para que
a fin de que
	so that	Subjunctive:
		Preparé la comida para que la <u>comieras</u>. *I prepared the food so that you would eat it.*
		
		Infinitive (same subject for both verbs):
		    para que → para
		    a fin de que → a fin de
		Se vistió para <u>salir</u>. *He got dressed to go out.*
		Estudia a fin de <u>mejorarte</u>. *Study to improve yourself.*

a menos que **salvo que** **a no ser que**	*unless*	Subjunctive: **Iremos al parque a menos que <u>llueva</u>.** *We will go to the park unless it rains.*
antes de que	*before*	Subjunctive: **Lo preparé todo antes de que <u>llegaran</u> los invitados.** *I prepared everything before the guests arrived.* Infinitive: **antes de que → antes de** **Se despidió antes de <u>irse</u>.** *He said good-bye before leaving.*
con tal que **con tal de que**	*provided (that)*	Subjunctive: **Prepararé la comida con tal de que tú <u>laves</u> los platos.** *I will prepare the food provided you wash the dishes.* Infinitive: **con tal de que → con tal de** **Iré al cine con tal de <u>poder</u> ir con ustedes.** *I will go to the movies provided I can go with you.*
sin que	*without*	Subjunctive: **Salí sin que ellos me <u>oyeran</u>.** *I left without their hearing me.* Infinitive: **sin que → sin** **Salí sin <u>hacer</u> ruido.** *I left without making any noise.*
en caso de que	*in case (that)*	Subjunctive: **Traje abrigo en caso de que <u>hiciera</u> frío.** *I brought a coat in case it was cold.*

The conjunctions in the chart on the next page only take the subjunctive when the situation referred to has not been experienced or if there is an implication of futurity in the main clause.

CONJUNCTION	MEANING	EXAMPLES
cuando	*when*	Subjunctive: **Vendré cuando <u>pueda</u>.** *I will come when I can. (whenever that might be)* Indicative: **Vino cuando <u>pudo</u>.** *He came when he could.*
apenas **en cuanto** **tan pronto como**	*as soon as*	Subjunctive: **Vendré en cuanto <u>pueda</u>.** *I will come as soon as I can.* Indicative: **Vino en cuanto <u>pudo</u>.** *He came as soon as he could.*
aunque **a pesar de que** **aun cuando**	*even if* (subj.) *although* (indic.)	Subjunctive: **Vendrá aunque no lo <u>invites</u>.** *He will come even if you do not invite him.* Indicative: **Vino aunque no lo <u>invitaste</u>.** *He came although you did not invite him.*
después de que	*after*	Subjunctive: **Llegaré después de que tú te <u>hayas ido</u>.** *I will arrive after you have left.* Indicative: **Llegó después de que tú te <u>fuiste</u>.** *He arrived after you had left.* Infinitive: **Llamó después de <u>irse</u>.** *He called after leaving.*
mientras	*provided (that), as long as* (subj.) *while,* (indic.)	Subjunctive: **Mientras no <u>digas</u> la verdad, no te escucharé.** *As long as you do not tell the truth, I will not listen to you.* Indicative: **Yo miraba la televisión mientras ella <u>trabajaba</u>.** *I watched TV while she worked.*
hasta que	*until*	Subjunctive: **No me iré hasta que me <u>digas</u> tu secreto.** *I will not leave until you tell me your secret.* Indicative: **No me fui hasta que me <u>dijo</u> su secreto.** *I did not leave until he told me his secret.* Infinitive: **No me iré hasta <u>saber</u> la verdad.** *I will not leave until I know the truth.*

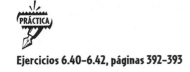

Ejercicios 6.40–6.42, páginas 392–393

5. SEQUENCE OF TENSES

a. Introduction

The relationship between the action of the main clause and that of the subordinate clause will determine which tenses you may use. We will present three perspectives, the first more generally applicable than the other two, which relate to specific formats only.

- Chronological relativity
- Aspect relativity
- Tense relativity from indicative to subjunctive

b. Chronological Relativity

The first perspective we will present is the one that uses one basic concept for all combinations: the relativity of occurrence of the actions in the sentence.

The first question would be: What is the tense of the verb of the main clause? There are two general subdivisions of tenses for the verb of the main clause:

- The **present set** (present, present perfect, future, or imperative)
- The **past set** (imperfect, preterite, pluperfect, conditional present, or conditional perfect)

The next question is: When did the action of the subordinate clause occur in relation to the action of the verb of the main clause? After it? At the same time? Before it? Before another action in the past? We will call the four relationships as follows:

- Subsequent
- Simultaneous
- Prior
- Prior to prior

The last question is: Which tense of the subjunctive must be used? There are four tenses of the subjunctive:

- Present
- Present perfect
- Imperfect
- Pluperfect

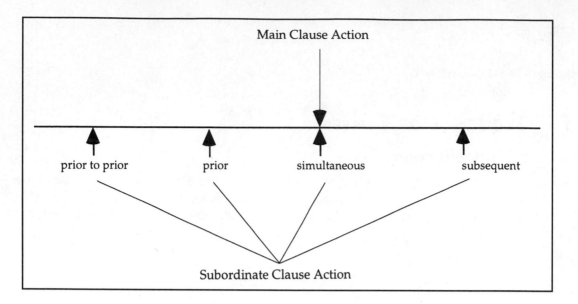

For the above graphic, where the main clause action is simultaneous with the subordinate clause action, the following sentences might serve as examples.

Both actions present:

No <u>creo</u> que <u>esté</u> lloviendo en este momento.
I do not think it is raining at this moment.

Both actions past:

Me <u>molestaba</u> que me <u>mirara</u> de esa manera.
It bothered me that he should look at me that way.

The chart on the next page indicates which tense could be used for each situation.

MAIN VERB TENSE	CHRONOLOGICAL RELATIVITY OF SUBORDINATE TO MAIN	SUBORDINATE CLAUSE: TENSES OF THE SUBJUNCTIVE	EXAMPLES	REF. #
Present set	1. Subsequent OR 2. Simultaneous	a. Present	Dudo que llueva mañana.	1a
			Dudo que esté enfermo.	2a
	3. Prior	b. Present perfect	Dudo que ya haya comido.	3b
		c. Imperfect	Dudo que estuviera verde.	3c
	4. Prior to another prior action	d. Pluperfect	Me sorprende que no hubiera llamado antes de venir.	4d
Past set	1. Subsequent OR 2. Simultaneous	c. Imperfect	Dudaba que se acabara pronto la conferencia.	1c
			Dudaba que estuviera enfermo.	2c
	3. Prior	d. Pluperfect	Dudaba que hubiera dicho esa mentira.	3d

Please note that the present and present perfect subjunctive cannot be used in sentences where the main clause is in the past set.

Explanation and further contextualization of the examples in the table:

1a. **Dudo que <u>llueva</u> mañana.**
I doubt (now) that it <u>will rain</u> tomorrow.
The act of raining is subsequent to the moment of doubt; my doubt is formulating itself now, the rain has not yet occurred.

2a. **Dudo que <u>esté</u> enfermo.**
I doubt (now) that he <u>is</u> ill (now).
The illness is simultaneous to the moment of doubt.

3b. **Dudo que ya <u>haya comido</u>.**
I doubt (now) that he <u>has eaten</u> (or ate) already.
My doubt relates to his having eaten already. Has he already eaten? Did he eat already? I doubt it.

3c. **Dudo que <u>estuviera</u> verde.**
I doubt (now) that it <u>was</u> green (yesterday).
I was just told that the apple I ate yesterday was green and that is what caused my stomach trouble. I doubt now that the apple was green (or unripe). I think my stomach trouble was due to something else.

4d. **Me sorprende que no <u>hubiera llamado</u> antes de venir.**
I am surprised that he <u>had not called</u> before he came.
Yesterday, David came to visit me. He did not call before coming. Now that I think about it, it surprises me that he had not called before coming yesterday.

1c. **Dudaba que se <u>acabara</u> pronto la conferencia.**
I doubted that the lecture <u>would end</u> soon.
The end of the lecture is subsequent to my doubt. I was doubting about the eventual ending of the lecture happening soon.

2c. **Dudaba que <u>estuviera</u> enfermo.**
I doubted that he <u>was</u> ill.
I was at a party, and a friend of mine arrived and told me that my roommate could not come because he was sick. I doubted at that moment that my roommate was sick at that moment. The two actions are simultaneous.

3d. **Dudaba que <u>hubiera dicho</u> esa mentira.**
I doubted that he <u>had told</u> that lie.
I was told yesterday that my younger brother had lied about his age a few days before. When I was told this, I doubted it. His alleged lie was prior to my doubt.

More examples:

1a. Subsequent to a main verb in the present set:

No quiero que <u>vayas</u> al cine.
I do not want you to go to the movies.

Dile a Natalia que me <u>llame</u>.
Tell Natalia to call me.

Nunca te lo he dicho para que no te <u>enojes</u>.
I have never told you so you would not get angry.

2a. Simultaneous to a main verb in the present set:

Me sorprende que la manzana ya <u>esté</u> madura.
I am surprised the apple is already ripe.

Encontraré una casa que <u>tenga</u> invernadero.
I will find a house that will have a greenhouse.

3b. Prior to a main verb in the present set:

¿Conoces a alguien que <u>haya viajado</u> a Chile?
Do you know someone who has traveled to Chile?

Me iré cuando <u>haya terminado</u>.
I shall leave when I have finished.

Llámala, a menos que ya lo <u>hayas hecho</u>.
Call her, unless you have already done so.

3c. Prior to a main verb in the present set:

Es extraño que no <u>supiera</u>.
It is strange that she did not know.

Me sorprende que no <u>pudiera</u> hacerlo.
It surprises me that he was not able to do it.

4d. Prior to another action prior to a main verb in the present set:

Carlota vino a cenar a casa anoche.
Carlota came to dinner last night.

Antes de venir, había llamado para averiguar si podía traer algo.
Before coming, she had called to find out whether she could bring something.

Me sorprende que <u>hubiera llamado</u> antes de venir ayer.
It surprises me that she had called before coming yesterday.

Los empleados se quejan de que los patrones nunca les <u>hubieran pedido</u> su opinión antes de cambiar esa regla.
The employees complain that the bosses never asked their opinion before changing that rule.

Lamentamos que no <u>hubieran recibido</u> nuestro mensaje antes de salir de viaje.
We are sorry that they had not received our message before they left on their trip.

La adivina sabe el pasado de Raúl sin que nadie se lo <u>hubiera contado</u> antes.
The soothsayer knows Raúl's past without anyone having told her before.

1c. Subsequent to a main clause in the past set:

Dudaba que mi hermana <u>viniera</u> a visitarme para Navidad.
I doubted that my sister would come to visit me for Christmas.

Mi hermana me lo dio en caso de que lo <u>necesitara</u> más tarde.
My sister gave it to me in case I needed it later.

Querían una compañía de seguros que <u>cumpliera</u> en caso de accidente.
They wanted an insurance company that would pay its part in case of an accident.

Preferiría que te <u>fueras</u>.
I would prefer that you leave.

2c. Simultaneous to a main clause in the past set:

Me encantó que <u>llegaran</u> a tiempo.
I was delighted that they arrived on time.

La artista lo pintó sin que nadie la <u>viera</u>.
The artist painted it without anyone seeing her.

No había nada allí que le <u>gustara</u>.
There was nothing there that she liked.

3d. Prior to a main verb in the past set:

Dudaba que Miguel <u>hubiera dicho</u> esa mentira.
I doubted that Miguel had told that lie.
(I doubted, yesterday when I was told, that he had told the lie the week before.)

Salió corriendo en caso de que no le <u>hubieran quitado</u> la pistola al ladrón.
He ran out in case they had not taken the gun away from the thief.

Buscaban una casa a la que ya le <u>hubieran hecho</u> todas las reparaciones necesarias.
They were looking for a house that would have already had all the necessary repairs.

Se habían hablado sin que nadie los <u>hubiera presentado</u>.
They had talked to each other without anyone having introduced them.

Los bomberos habrían llegado antes de que la casa se <u>hubiera quemado</u> si ese accidente no hubiera ocurrido en la carretera.
The firemen would have arrived before the house had burned down if that accident had not happened on the highway.

c. Aspect Relativity

The second perspective we will present elaborates on the distinction between the use of the imperfect and present perfect subjunctive when the main clause is in the **present set** (3b and 3c from the preceding table).

Aspect: Perfective (completed) and inchoative (beginning) vs. ongoing and habitual[1]

Use the **present perfect subjunctive** when the action of the verb of the subordinate clause is **perfective** or **inchoative** in aspect; this means that the action is perceived as completed (perfected, in grammatical terms) or beginning (inchoative) in the past. In many cases, it is the meaning of the verb itself that will determine the aspect ("to begin" is often inchoative, though it can be perceived as progressive or ongoing in "I was beginning … ").

Perfective:

> **Es extraño que Luis no <u>haya venido</u> a clase.**
> *It is strange that Luis did not come to class.*

> **¿Has conocido a alguien que <u>haya viajado</u> a Chile?**
> *Have you met anyone who has traveled to Chile?*

> **Me iré cuando <u>haya terminado</u>.**
> *I shall leave when I have finished.*

> **Llámala, a menos que ya lo <u>hayas hecho</u>.**
> *Call her, unless you have already done so.*

Inchoative:

> **Dudo que el vuelo <u>haya salido</u> a tiempo.**
> *I doubt that the flight left on time.* (focus on the beginning of the flight)

> **Me sorprende que todavía no <u>hayan empezado</u> a leer la novela.**
> *I am surprised that you still have not begun to read the novel.*

Use the **imperfect subjunctive** when the action of the verb of the subordinate clause is **imperfective** in aspect; this means that the action is perceived as ongoing or stative in the past, or habitual.

Ongoing or stative:

> **Jorge dice que <u>era</u> gordo de niño. Dudo que <u>fuera</u> gordo.**
> *Jorge says he used to be fat as a child. I doubt that he was fat.*

---

1. This is the same difference that applies to preterite and imperfect in the indicative. (See Chapter 6.B: "Past Indicative Tenses: Preterite vs. Imperfect vs. Pluperfect," pages 177–189.)

Estaban jugando cuando entré. Me sorprende que <u>estuvieran</u> jugando.
They were playing when I entered. It suprises me that they were playing.

Habitual:

Nunca he conocido a nadie que <u>cantara</u> así de niño.
I have never met anyone who could sing that way as a child.

Se avergüenza de que sus padres nunca <u>pagaran</u> impuestos.
She is ashamed that her parents never used to pay taxes.

d. Tense Relativity from Indicative to Subjunctive

This explanation runs parallel to the previous two explanations, but might be more palatable to some.

1. MAIN CLAUSE IN THE PRESENT SET

Notice the conversion of each of the tenses of the indicative in the sentences on the left of the chart below, through the filter of the main clause *Dudo...*, for example, into the appropriate subjunctive in the new subordinate clause.

INDICATIVE	MAIN CLAUSE	SUBJUNCTIVE
Irá al cine.	Dudo	que vaya al cine.
Va al cine.	Dudo	que vaya al cine.
Iba al cine.	Dudo	que fuera al cine.
Fue al cine.	Dudo	que haya ido/fuera al cine.
Ha ido al cine.	Dudo	que haya ido al cine.
Habrá ido al cine.	Dudo	que haya ido al cine.
Había ido al cine.	Dudo	que hubiera ido al cine.

The above sentences translate as follows:

I doubt that he	*will go*	*to the movies.*
	goes/is going	
	used to go/was going	
	went	
	has gone	
	will have gone	
	had gone	

Table of tense conversions with *dudo:*

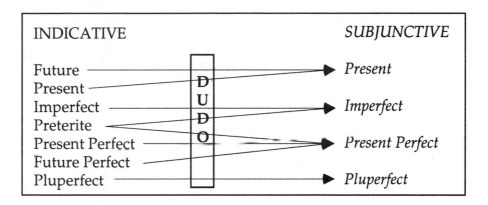

2. MAIN CLAUSE IN THE PAST SET

INDICATIVE	MAIN CLAUSE	SUBJUNCTIVE
Irá al cine.		
Va al cine.	Dudaba	que fuera al cine.
Iba al cine.		
Fue al cine.		
Fue al cine.		
Ha ido al cine.	Dudaba	que hubiera ido al cine.
Habrá ido al cine.		
Había ido al cine.		

The above sentences translate as follows:

I doubted that he	would go	to the movies.
	went/was going	
	used to go	
	went	

I doubted that he	went/had gone	to the movies.
	had gone	
	would have gone	
	had gone	

Table of tense conversions with *dudaba:*

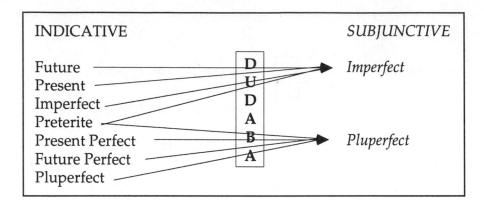

Ejercicios 6.43–6.51, páginas 393–396

6. IF (SI) CLAUSES

a. Sequence of Tenses

In Spanish, sentences that contain a clause with *si* (if) or the implication of a condition follow a rigid construction pattern that must always be followed. Memorize the following three types of sentences and remember that they are essentially unchanging, as long as the time frame is the same for both clauses (if both refer to the past, for example).

SI CLAUSE		MAIN CLAUSE
1. Indicative	↔	Indicative or Imperative
2. Imperfect Subjunctive	↔	Present Conditional
3. Pluperfect Subjunctive	↔	Past (Perfect) Conditional or Pluperfect Subjunctive

Sentence type #1 refers to situations that are possible. For example, one could say:

    1a. **Si llueve, me llevo el paraguas.** *If it rains, I take my umbrella.*

    1b. **Si llueve, llévate el paraguas.** *If it rains, take your umbrella.*

    1c. **Si llovía, me llevaba el paraguas.** *If it rained, I used to take my umbrella.*

Notice that in each case we are speaking about the possibility of it raining. Just about any tense of the indicative can be used, and usually the same tense is used for both clauses. In the main clause (the one that does not begin with *si*), you can also find the imperative (sentence type 1b).

The future does not occur in conditional "if" clauses; it does occur when *si* means "whether."

> **No sé si lloverá o no.**   *I don't know if (whether) it will rain or not.*

Sentence types 2 and 3 refer to situations that are contrary to the truth. Type 2 refers to a situation contrary to the present truth. For example:

2a. **Si estuviera lloviendo, no saldría.**
    If it were raining (now), I would not go out.

2b. **Si fuera rico, me compraría un coche deportivo**.
    If I were rich (now), I would buy myself a sports car.

Sentence type 3 refers to a situation contrary to past reality:

3a. **Si hubiera estudiado más, habría/hubiera pasado el examen.**
    If I had studied more (last week), I would have passed the exam.

There exist exceptions to the rule, as can be seen when a situation in the past affects the present.

> **Si no hubiera llovido anoche, hoy todo estaría seco.**
> *If it had not rained last night, everything would be dry today.*

All of these sentences can be inverted in order of clauses, beginning with the main clause instead of the *si* clause.

b. *Como si* (As If)

The expression *como si* is always followed by the past subjunctive—either the imperfect subjunctive to speak of an action simultaneous with the main verb, or the pluperfect subjunctive to speak of an action prior to the main verb.

> **Habla como si te <u>conociera</u>.**
> *He speaks as if he knew you.*

> **Te saluda como si te <u>hubiera visto</u> antes.**
> *He greets you as if he had seen you before.*

Ejercicios 6.52–6.54, página 396

7. OJALÁ

Sentences with *ojalá* can be translated into English as either "I hope" or "I wish." When you **hope (for)** something, it is because you do not know what the reality of the situation is. Consider the following sentences:

1. *I hope that it will not rain tomorrow.* (hope for the future)

2. *I hope that it is not raining.* (hope for the present)

3. *I hope that our team won.* (hope for the past)

In these sentences, the speaker does not know: 1. whether it will rain, 2. whether it is raining, or 3. whether the team won or lost.

On the other hand, when you **wish (for)** something, it is contrary to the actual reality. Consider the following sentences.

4. *I wish it were not raining.* (It is in fact raining; wish for the present)

5. *I wish our team had won.* (Actually, they lost; wish for the past)

To translate this difference in Spanish, you use *ojalá* with different tenses of the subjunctive.

Present subjunctive—hope for the future and the present:

Ojalá que no llueva mañana.	*I hope it will not rain tomorrow.*
Ojalá que no esté lloviendo.	*I hope it is not raining.*

Present perfect subjunctive—hope for the past:

Ojalá que nuestro equipo haya ganado.	*I hope our team won.*

Imperfect subjunctive—wish for the present and the future:

Ojalá que no estuviera lloviendo.	*I wish it were not raining.*
Ojalá que pudiera venir mañana.	*I wish he could come tomorrow.*

Pluperfect subjunctive—wish for the past:

Ojalá que nuestro equipo hubiera ganado.	*I wish our team had won.*

PRÁCTICA

Ejercicios 6.55–6.56, página 397

8. EXPRESSIONS OF LEAVE-TAKING

In English, when saying good-bye to someone, the imperative is often used in expressions of well-wishing: "Have a good day," "Have a good time," "Have fun," "Get well," etc. In Spanish, it is not the custom to always express such feelings unless you know the person well, and even then, a simple *adiós, chau, nos vemos,* and *hasta luego* are more common in most cases. However, if you do wish to express any of the following, you cannot use the imperative for them in Spanish. For someone whom you address as:

Tú:

Que² te vaya bien.	*May it go well for you.*
Que pases buen día.	*Have a good day.*
Que pases un buen fin de semana.	*Have a good weekend.*
Que la/lo pases bien.	*Have a good one.*
Que te diviertas.	*Have fun.*
Que te alivies.	*Get well.*
Que te mejores.	*Get better (Get well).*
Que Dios te acompañe.	*May God accompany you.* (for someone leaving on a trip)

Usted:

Que le vaya bien.

Que pase buen día.

Que pase un buen fin de semana.

Que la/lo pase bien.

Que se divierta.

Que se alivie.

Que se mejore.

Que Dios lo/la acompañe.

Ustedes:

Que les vaya bien.

Que pasen buen día.

Que pasen un buen fin de semana.

Que la/lo pasen bien.

Que se diviertan.

Que se alivien.

Que se mejoren.

Que Dios los/las acompañe.

---

2. Notice that this *que* does not have an accent mark, even if you choose to place the expression in an exclamation. This is because it is not an exclamative *que,* but the conjunction.

Notice that these verbs are of different constructions.

In a standard construction, with a subject and a direct object, the verb agrees with the person being addressed.

Verb	Direct object	Example
pasar	buen día	**Que <u>pasen</u> buen día.** *May <u>you</u> have a good day.*
	un buen fin de semana	**Que <u>pases</u> un buen fin de semana.** *May <u>you</u> have a good weekend.*
	lo/la bien	**Que lo <u>paséis</u> bien.** *May <u>you</u> have a good one.*

With reflexive verbs, when the same word serves as both subject and object, the verb agrees with the person being addressed.

Verb	Reflexive pronoun	Example
divertir	te, se, os	**Que <u>te diviertas</u>.** *Have fun.*
aliviar	te, se, os	**Que <u>os aliviéis</u>.** *Get well.*
mejorar	te, se, os	**Que <u>se mejoren</u>.** *May <u>they</u> get well.*

With flip verbs, with a subject and an indirect object, the verb itself remains invariable, because the subject is impersonal: *irle bien a uno*.

Verb	Indirect object	Example
ir	te, le, les, os	**Que <u>te vaya</u> bien.** *May <u>it</u> go well for <u>you</u>.*

With *Dios* as the subject and the person being addressed as the direct object:

Verb	Indirect object	Example
acompañar	te, lo(s), la(s), os	**Que Dios <u>los acompañe</u>.** *May <u>He</u> (God) accompany <u>them</u> (los).*

PRÁCTICA

Ejercicios 6.57–6.60, páginas 397–398

Infinitives and Present Participles

I. INFINITIVES

a. Present Infinitive

The **infinitive** functions like a **noun** in Spanish, and like a noun, it can be the subject or object of a verb, or object of a preposition. In English, the present participle is frequently used in these roles.

The infinitive as a subject (sometimes preceded by the article *el*):

<u>Caminar</u> es bueno para la salud.	*Walking is healthy.*
Me gusta <u>comer</u> helado.	*I like eating (to eat) ice cream.*
Nos encanta <u>ver</u> esas películas.	*We love seeing those movies.*
El <u>trabajar</u> tanto en la computadora le dañó los ojos.	*Working so much on the computer harmed his eyes.*

The infinitive as a direct object:

Quiero <u>aprender</u> el español.	*I want to learn Spanish.*
No sé <u>hacer</u> eso.	*I do not know how to do that.*
Pienso <u>comprar</u> ese coche.	*I am planning on buying that car.*
Debemos <u>estudiar</u> la lección.	*We must study the lesson.*
Decidimos <u>ir</u> al cine.	*We decided to go to the movies.*
¿Desea <u>comprar</u> algo?	*Do you wish to buy something?*
Logré <u>convencerla</u>.	*I succeeded in convincing her.*
Parece <u>estar</u> triste.	*He seems to be sad.*

Verbs used with a direct object pronoun and the infinitive (*dejar, hacer*):

No *lo* dejan <u>jugar</u>.	*They do not let him play.*
Lo hizo <u>recitar</u> el poema.	*She made him recite the poem.*

Verbs used with an indirect object pronoun and the infinitive (*permitir, aconsejar, impedir, prohibir, recomendar, rogar*):

No *le* permiten <u>salir</u>.	*They do not let him go out.*
Les aconsejo <u>llegar</u> temprano.	*I advise you to arrive early.*
Le impidieron <u>hablar</u>.	*They prevented him from speaking.*
Les prohíbe <u>beber</u> cerveza.	*He forbids them to drink beer.*
Le recomiendo <u>ver</u> esa película.	*I recommend that you see that movie.*
Les ruego <u>escucharme</u>.	*I beg you to listen to me.*

Verbs of perception are used with a direct object and an infinitive (*ver, oír*):

La *vi* <u>llegar</u> hace una hora.	*I saw her arrive an hour ago.*
Los *oí* <u>cantar</u> anoche.	*I heard them sing (singing) last night.*

The infinitive as an object of a preposition:

Se fue *sin* <u>despedirse</u>.	*He left without saying good-bye.*
Lo hice *para* <u>ayudarte</u>.	*I did it to help you.*
Eso te pasa *por* <u>comer</u> tanto.	*That happens to you for eating so much.*
Antes de <u>salir</u>, siempre desayuna.	*Before going out, he always eats breakfast.*
Estoy cansada *de* <u>estudiar</u>.	*I am tired of studying.*

The infinitive after *que* (*hay que, tener que, algo que, nada que, poco que*):

Hay que <u>tener</u> confianza.	*It is necessary to have confidence.*
Tienes que <u>venir</u> conmigo.	*You have to come with me.*
No tiene *nada que* <u>hacer</u>.	*He does not have anything to do.*
Tenemos *poco que* <u>hacer</u>.	*We have little to do.*

The infinitive after *de* with *fácil, difícil, posible,* and *imposible*:

Ese sonido es difícil *de* <u>pronunciar</u>.	*That sound is difficult to pronounce.*

In the above sentence, the subject of the verb *ser* is *sonido*. However, if the infinitive itself is to be the subject of *ser,* the preposition *de* must be omitted.

Es difícil <u>pronunciar</u> ese sonido.	*It is difficult to pronounce that sound.*

The same construction is used with *fácil, posible,* and *imposible*.

The construction *al* + **infinitive** is used for an action that occurs at the same time as the main verb.

Al <u>entrar</u>, los saludaron a todos.	*When they entered (Upon entering), they greeted everyone.*
Al <u>verlos</u>, los saludé.	*When I saw them, I greeted them.*

The infinitive in advertising, signs, commands, questions:

No <u>fumar</u>.	*No smoking.*
Prohibido <u>tirar</u> basura.	*No littering.*
¿Por qué <u>engordar</u>? Con nuestro sistema puede usted adelgazar sin ningún esfuerzo.	*Why get fat? With our system, you can lose weight effortlessly.*

The infinitive with a passive meaning after *oír, ver, mirar, escuchar, dejar, mandar, hacer*:

Lo he oído decir.	*I have heard it (being) said.*
Hice copiar las pruebas.	*I had the tests copied.*
Mandé comprar sellos.	*I ordered stamps to be bought.*

b.   Perfect Infinitive

The perfect infinitive (formed with the auxiliary *haber* in the infinitive, plus the past participle of the main verb) is used to express an action that occurred before the action of the main verb, when the subject is the same for both.

Debes de <u>haberlos dejado</u> en el coche.	*You must have left them in the car.*
Creo <u>habérselo dicho</u>.	*I think I told him that.*
Se fue sin <u>haber comido</u> nada.	*He left without having eaten anything.*
Se cansó de la película después de <u>haberla visto</u> tres veces.	*He got tired of the movie after having seen it three times.*

2. PRESENT PARTICIPLES

[To review the formation of the present participle, see Chapter 5.F.1, page 173.]

The **present participle,** when not used with auxiliaries such as *estar*, functions in Spanish like an **adverb** and refers to an action occurring at the same time as or prior to the main action, indicating manner, cause, or condition. In this usage, it is also a "gerund."

Manner:

> **Entró <u>gritando</u>.**
> *He entered yelling.*

Cause:

> **<u>Siendo</u> persona sencilla, nunca pensó que otros no fueran honrados.**
> *Being a simple person, he never thought that others would not be honest.*

Condition:

> **<u>Estando</u> los padres en casa, él no llamará.**
> *With the parents at home, he will not call.*

In Spanish, the present participle may be used to indicate simultaneity of two actions.

> **Preparó la cena <u>escuchando</u> el radio.**
> *He prepared dinner while he listened to the radio.*

As a rule, the present participle follows the main verb. However, in cases where it describes a cause or condition related to the main verb, it may be placed before.

> **<u>Explicándoselo</u> claramente de antemano, no habrá ambigüedad.**
> *By explaining it clearly to them in advance, there will be no ambiguity.*

In English the present participle can be used as an adjective. In these cases, Spanish uses:

1. an adjective (**not** formed with the present participle form):

una persona <u>interesante</u>	*an <u>interesting</u> person*
un interés <u>creciente</u>	*a <u>growing</u> interest*
los problemas <u>existentes</u>	*the <u>existing</u> problems*

2. *de* + noun or infinitive:

      papel <u>de escribir</u>   *<u>writing</u> paper*
      dolores <u>de crecimiento</u>   *<u>growing</u> pains*

3. a clause:

      Vio un pájaro <u>que cantaba</u>.   *She saw a bird <u>singing</u>.*
      Es una niña <u>que está creciendo</u>. *She's a <u>growing</u> child.*

4. a preposition:

      el libro <u>con</u> fotos de   *the book <u>containing</u> pictures*
      España   *of Spain*

      lo <u>de</u> ella   *those things <u>belonging</u> to her*

5. a past participle for postures and other conditions:

parado	*standing*	**aburrido**	*boring*
sentado	*sitting*	**divertido**	*amusing*
acostado	*lying down*	**entretenido**	*entertaining*

In idiomatic expressions, the present participle of some verbs of motion indicates location.

      Mi cuarto se encuentra <u>entrando</u> *My room is to the left of the entrance.*
      a la izquierda.

      Esa tienda está <u>pasando</u> el museo. *That store is beyond the museum.*

In summary, never use the present participle form in Spanish as if it were a **noun** (i.e., as subject, object, or object of preposition) or as an **adjective.** In Spanish, it only functions as an **adverb.**

PRÁCTICA

Ejercicios 6.61–6.69, páginas 398–400

◆ Verbs Like *Gustar*

I. FORMATION

The verb *gustar* ("to like") behaves differently in Spanish than it does in English. What in English is the subject of the verb, in Spanish is the **indirect object,** and the direct object of the English sentence is the **subject** of the Spanish sentence.

> **Me gustan las películas mexicanas.**   *I like Mexican movies.*

In the Spanish sentence, *me* is the **indirect object** of the verb, and *las películas mexicanas* is the **subject.** (Notice the agreement of the verb with the plural of its subject.) To illustrate more clearly the fact that *me* is the indirect object, notice that if you wished to give emphasis to the person, you would add *a mí* to the basic sentence (and **not** *yo*).

> **A mí me gustan las películas**   *I like Mexican movies.*
> **mexicanas.**

For further emphasis on this structure, look at the **subject,** *películas mexicanas.* If you wished to replace the subject with a pronoun, it would be impossible. The rule is that **a thing that is a subject cannot be replaced by a pronoun,** because subject pronouns always refer to people. If you do not wish to repeat the noun, because, for example, you already mentioned it in the context preceding the sentence, you would simply omit it.

> **Me gustan.**   *I like them.*

One last means of emphasizing this construction is to see what happens when the question is asked: "Who likes Mexican movies?" In English, the answer is "I (do)." Observe what happens in Spanish.

> **—¿A quién le gustan las películas**   *"Who likes Mexican movies?"*
> **mexicanas?**
> **—A mí.**   *"I do."*

You would **never** answer *yo* to this question, because the person is the indirect object, not the subject of the verb. (See page 55 for more on pronouns with these verbs.)

2. WORD ORDER

For verbs like *gustar,* the subject, when it is a noun or other nominalized form, is most commonly placed after the verb. In the following sentences, the subject is underlined (note in the translation the subject is different in English).

> **Te gustaban <u>las películas de misterio</u>.**   *You used to like mystery movies.*
>
> **Me encantó <u>bailar</u> contigo.**   *I loved dancing with you.*

A Beto le hacen falta <u>sus padres</u>.	*Beto misses his parents.*
Te caerá bien <u>Juanita</u>.	*You will like Juanita.*

With *faltar, sobrar,* and *quedar,* **always** place the subject **after** the verb.

Te falta <u>un ejercicio</u>.	*You are missing an exercise.*
Nos sobró <u>comida</u>.	*We had food left over.*

3. VERBS SIMILAR TO *GUSTAR*

There is a group of verbs that behave the same way *gustar* does.

caer bien/mal	*to like/to dislike*
encantar	*to "love"* (as on bumper stickers)
faltar	*to lack*
hacer falta	*to miss; to need*
quedar	*to have remaining, left*
sobrar	*to have in excess, left over*

Some of these verbs have other uses and meanings, for example, *caer* and *caerse* mean "to fall, fall down," and *faltar* can mean "to be absent." Also, the verb *quedarse* used reflexively means "to stay, remain." Thus, depending upon the grammatical construction you give the sentence, its meaning can change dramatically.

Caer bien/mal   *to like/to dislike (a person)*

Mis amigos me caen bien.	*I like my friends.*
Creo que <u>les caigo bien</u> a tus padres.[3]	*I think your parents like me.*
El novio de mi hermana <u>me cae mal</u>. OR: El novio de mi hermana no <u>me cae bien</u>.	*I do not like my sister's boyfriend.*

---

3. The majority of these verbs is used exclusively in the third-person singular or plural, but those that may have a person as subject can be used in any person. The two most common verbs of this category are *caer bien* and *hacer falta.*

Me haces falta.	*I miss you.*
Le caigo bien.	*She likes me.*

Given the meaning of *gustar* in certain dialects, it is best to avoid using it with human beings as the subject of the verb, or to make certain it is being used with its true meaning.

Gustar is used with things or with people perceived as professionals, such as professors, presidents, etc. When you use *gustar* with these, you mean that you respect their work, not necessarily that you like them personally.

Me <u>gusta</u> mi profesor de historia. Es excelente, y siempre viene preparado.	*I like my history professor. He is excellent and he always comes prepared.*
Me <u>cae bien</u> mi profesor de historia. Es muy simpático.	*I like my history professor. He is very nice.*

If you use the verb *gustar* with an individual whose relationship to you is other than professional, the implication is that you are attracted to that person.

Me gusta Silvia.	*I am attracted to Silvia.*

Caer bien/mal with food:

Le <u>cayó</u> muy <u>mal</u> la cena.	*Dinner disagreed with her.*

Encantar   *to love* (as in "I love New York.")

Bumper-sticker "love" is different from sentimental love. Once you understand its meaning, you can use it, as bumper stickers do, with almost anything **except sentimental love.**

Me <u>encanta</u> Nueva York, me encantan los perros, los bebés, etc.	*I (just) love New York, dogs, babies, etc. (I ❤ NY)*

Sentimental love is expressed with *querer.*

Te quiero. Te quiero mucho.	*I love you. I love you a lot.*

(Te amo is more literary, more poetic than *te quiero.)*

Quiero mucho a mis padres, a mi perro...	*I love my parents, my dog …*

Faltar   *to lack*

A esta baraja le faltan dos cartas.	*This deck of cards lacks (is missing) two cards.*

Hacer falta   *to miss (a person), to need (a thing)*

Me haces falta.	*I miss you.*
Te hace falta un abrigo.	*You need a coat.*

Quedar *to have left*

    Nos quedan cinco minutos.   *We have five minutes left.*

Sobrar *to have left over, in excess*

    Les sobró mucha comida.   *They had a lot of food left over.*

There are other verbs that are used in the same type of construction, but these behave essentially the way the English does, and are not used in exactly the opposite type of construction. These other verbs are:

bastarle a uno *to be sufficient*	**parecerle a uno** *to seem*
convenirle a uno *to be convenient*	**pasarle a uno** *to happen*
dolerle a uno[4] *to hurt*	**sentarle bien a uno** *to suit*
importarle a uno *to matter*	**sucederle a uno** *to happen*
interesarle a uno *to interest*	**tocarle a uno** *to be one's turn*

Examples:

Me <u>bastan</u> cinco minutos.	*Five minutes are sufficient for me.*
No nos <u>conviene</u> esa hora.	*That time is not convenient for us.*
¿Te <u>duele</u> la pierna?	*Does your leg hurt?*
No nos <u>importa</u> si llueve.	*It does not matter to us if it rains.*
Me <u>interesaría</u> participar.	*It would interest me to participate.*
Me <u>parece</u> increíble.	*It seems incredible to me.*
Siempre me <u>pasan</u> cosas así.	*Things like that always happen to me.*
Te <u>sienta</u> bien el azul.	*Blue suits you.*
¿Qué te <u>sucedió</u>?	*What happened to you?*
A mí me <u>toca</u> jugar.	*It is my turn to play.*

---

4. The subject of *doler* can only be a body part.

    Me duele la pierna.   *My leg hurts.*

If you want to say "That shoe hurts," you need the verb *lastimar*.

    Ese zapato me lastima.

The translation of "hurt" with animate objects is *hacer daño*.

    ¿Te hizo daño?   *Did he hurt you?*

4. ARTICLES

Remember to use the definite article in Spanish with *gustar, caer bien,* and *encantar* when their subject is general in nature. (See Chapter 2.B, page 36.)

Me gusta <u>el</u> chocolate semiamargo.	*I like semisweet chocolate.*
Me caen bien <u>los</u> hijos de Juana.	*I like Juana's sons.*
Me encantan <u>las</u> playas.	*I love beaches.*

5. CHANGES IN MEANING

Some verbs can have other meanings if used in different grammatical constructions.

convenir en *to agree to*	<u>Convinimos</u> **en encontrarnos en la plaza a las dos.** *We agreed to meet in the plaza at two o'clock.*
importar + d.o. *to import*	**Los EE.UU. <u>importan</u> automóviles del Japón.** *The U.S. imports cars from Japan.*
interesarse por/en *to be interested in*	**Ella <u>se interesa</u> en la política.** *She is interested in politics.*
parecerse a *to look like*	**Tú <u>te pareces a</u> tu mamá.** *You look like your mother.*
pasar + d.o. *to pass*	**Pasa la sal, por favor.** *Pass the salt, please.*
sentar/sentarse *to seat/to sit*	**La mamá <u>sentó</u> al niño en la silla.** *The mother sat the child on the chair.* <u>Te sentaste</u> **en mi silla.** *You sat on my chair.*
tocar *to touch* OR: *to play* (a musical instrument)	**Los turistas lo <u>tocaban</u> todo.** *The tourists touched everything.* <u>Tocamos</u> **la guitarra.** *We play the guitar.*

PRÁCTICA

Ejercicios 6.70–6.75, páginas 400–401

◆ Reflexive Verbs

Grammatically speaking, the reflexive construction implies that the subject of the verb receives the action of the verb as well. In other words, the subject and the object are the same. (See Chapter 3.B.2, pages 70–72, on reflexive pronouns.)

Nonreflexive:

Miro el cielo.	*I look at the sky.*
subject = **yo**; object = **el cielo**	

Reflexive:

Me **miro** en el espejo.	*I look at myself in the mirror.*
subject = object = **yo**	

In many cases Spanish uses a reflexive when no evident reflexivity appears to exist in the English translation. This is why we perceive this lesson as a lexical rather than grammatical one, and offer a list that may serve as a memory aid.

Notice that in Spanish, the reflexive almost always indicates a change of state or the beginning of an action. Consider the differences between the following sentences.

Me **dormí** a las siete.	*I fell asleep at seven.*
Dormí siete horas.	*I slept seven hours.*
Estaba dormido.	*I was asleep.*
Me **estaba durmiendo** cuando llamaste.	*I was falling asleep when you called.*
Se **sentó** frente a nosotros.	*He sat down in front of us.*
Está sentado frente a nosotros.	*He is sitting in front of us.*
Me **enamoré** de él.	*I fell in love with him.*
Estoy enamorada de él.	*I am in love with him.*

Change of emotional state, or emotional reaction to something:

aburrirse *to get bored*	**divertirse** *to have fun*
alegrarse *to rejoice, be glad*	**enojarse** *to become or be angry*
asustarse *to become or be frightened*	**enorgullecerse** *to feel or be proud*
avergonzarse *to be ashamed, embarrassed*	**entristecerse** *to become or be sad*
calmarse *to calm down*	**preocuparse** *to worry*

Change of physical state:

acostarse *to lie down*	**moverse** *to move* (physically)
despertarse *to wake up*	**mudarse** *to move* (residences)
dormirse *to fall asleep*	**secarse** *to dry off, dry out*
levantarse *to get up*	**sentarse** *to sit down*
mojarse *to get wet*	**volverse** *to turn around*

Change of mental state or level of consciousness or memory:

acordarse *to remember*	**equivocarse** *to be mistaken*
darse cuenta *to realize*	**fijarse** *to notice*
enterarse *to find out*	**olvidarse** *to forget*

Verbs with more than one usage: Some verbs may be used in the reflexive construction or not. The basic meaning of the verb may change depending upon the construction used.

Los soldados <u>marcharon</u> por una hora.	*The soldiers marched for an hour.*
Los invitados *se* <u>marcharon</u>.	*The guests left.*

Other verbs of this type are:

bajar *to go down*	**bajarse** *to get down from, get off*
caer *to fall*	**caerse** *to fall down*
despedir *to fire* (a person)	**despedirse de** *to say good-bye to*
dormir *to sleep*	**dormirse** *to fall asleep*
ir *to go* (somewhere)	**irse** *to leave*

Reflexive pronouns are also used in situations where the subject is somehow affected by the action of the verb; with verbs of consumption, such as eating and drinking, the implication in the reflexive is one of enjoyment or thoroughness of the consumption.

<u>Comí</u> a las cuatro.   *I ate at four.*

¿*Te* <u>comiste</u> todo el desayuno?   *Did you eat all of your breakfast?*

Other verbs of this type:

aprender *to learn*	**aprenderse** *to learn (thoroughly, by heart)*
beber *to drink*	**beberse** *to drink (up, totally)*
saber *to know*	**saberse** *to know (thoroughly, by heart)*
tomar *to drink, eat, take*	**tomarse** *to drink, eat (up, totally)*

The verbs in the nonreflexive form are used with a more general meaning, while in the reflexive they are used with more specific information.

Aprender es fácil.   *It is easy to learn.*

Aprenderse el vocabulario es difícil.   *Learning vocabulary is difficult.*

Obligatory reflexives: These verbs exist exclusively in the reflexive form.

acordarse *to remember*	**jactarse** *to brag, boast*
arrepentirse *to regret, repent*	**quejarse** *to complain*
atreverse *to dare*	**rebelarse** *to rebel*
equivocarse *to make a mistake*	**suicidarse** *to commit suicide*

On the following pages are lists of verbs that are frequently or always used in the reflexive construction.

REFLEXIVE VERBS (ENGLISH–SPANISH)			
English	**Spanish**	**English**	**Spanish**
address someone	**dirigirse <u>a</u> alguien**	*commit suicide*	**suicidarse**
approach something, get near something or someone	**acercarse <u>a</u> algo o alguien**	*complain about something*	**quejarse <u>de</u> algo**
be angry with someone	**enojarse <u>con</u> alguien**	*dare to do something*	**atreverse <u>a</u> hacer algo**
be ashamed of something	**avergonzarse <u>de</u> algo**	*die*	**morirse**
be called, named	**llamarse**	*dry off, dry out*	**secarse**
be frightened of something	**asustarse <u>de</u> algo**	*face/confront something or someone*	**encararse <u>con</u>/ enfrentarse <u>a</u> algo o alguien**
be interested in something	**interesarse <u>por</u> algo**	*fall asleep*	**dormirse**
be mistaken, make a mistake	**equivocarse**	*fall behind, be late*	**atrasarse**
be proud	**enorgullecerse**	*fall down*	**caerse**
be quiet, shut up	**callarse**	*fall in love with someone*	**enamorarse <u>de</u> alguien**
become (by physical or metaphysical transformation)	**convertirse <u>en</u> algo**	*feel*	**sentirse**
become (describing mood)	**ponerse** (+ adj.)	*fight with someone*	**pelearse <u>con</u> alguien**
become (describing undesired state [blind, crazy…])	**volverse** (+ adj.)	*find out about something*	**enterarse <u>de</u> algo**
become (through one's efforts [a lawyer, doctor…])	**hacerse** (+ noun)	*forget something*	**olvidarse <u>de</u> algo**
become sad	**entristecerse**	*get ahead*	**adelantarse**
begin to do something	**ponerse <u>a</u> hacer algo**	*get along (not get along) with someone*	**llevarse bien (mal) <u>con</u> alguien**
brush (one's teeth, hair…)	**cepillarse**	*get bored*	**aburrirse**
calm down	**calmarse, tranquilizarse**	*get divorced*	**divorciarse**
comb (one's hair)	**peinarse (el pelo)**	*get down from something, get off (bus, train, tree…)*	**bajarse <u>de</u> algo**

REFLEXIVE VERBS (ENGLISH–SPANISH)

English	Spanish	English	Spanish
get lost	perderse	make an appointment/a date with someone	citarse con alguien
get married to someone	casarse con alguien	make an effort to do something	esforzarse por hacer algo
get onto something, get on (bus, train…)	subirse a algo	make fun of someone	burlarse de alguien
get rid of something	deshacerse de algo	make up one's mind to do something	decidirse a hacer algo
get sick, become ill	enfermarse	meet someone (not for the first time)	encontrarse con alguien
get up	levantarse	miss out on something	perderse algo
get used to something	acostumbrarse a algo	move away from something	alejarse de algo
get well	aliviarse, curarse	move (change residences)	mudarse
get wet	mojarse	move (one's body, objects)	moverse
get worse	empeorarse	notice something	fijarse en algo
graduate	graduarse	object to something	oponerse a algo
have fun	divertirse	prepare to do something	disponerse a hacer algo
improve (one's condition)	mejorarse	put on something (article of clothing)	ponerse algo
insist on doing something	empeñarse en hacer algo	realize something	darse cuenta de algo
interfere with someone	meterse con alguien	rebel	rebelarse
keep something	quedarse con algo	refer to something	referirse a algo
laugh at something or someone	reírse de algo o alguien	refuse to do something	negarse a hacer algo
leave	marcharse, irse	rejoice/be glad about something	alegrarse de algo
lie down, go to bed	acostarse	remember something	acordarse de algo
look like someone or something	parecerse a alguien o algo	repent (about) something	arrepentirse de algo

REFLEXIVE VERBS (ENGLISH–SPANISH)

English	Spanish	English	Spanish
resign oneself to	**resignarse <u>a</u> algo**	*stay*	**quedarse**
rub (up against)	**frotarse**	*take off/remove something*	**quitarse algo**
say good-bye to someone	**despedirse <u>de</u> alguien**	*take something away/with oneself*	**llevarse algo**
scratch oneself	**rascarse**	*trust someone*	**fiarse <u>de</u> alguien**
sit down	**sentarse**	*wake up*	**despertarse**
specialize/major in something	**especializarse <u>en</u> algo**	*worry about something*	**preocuparse <u>por</u> algo**

REFLEXIVE VERBS (SPANISH–ENGLISH)

Spanish	English	Spanish	English
aburrirse	*get bored*	**atreverse a hacer algo**	*dare to do something*
acercarse a algo o alguien	*approach something, get near something or someone*	**avergonzarse de algo**	*be ashamed of something*
acordarse de algo	*remember something*	**bajarse de algo**	*get down from something, get off (bus, train, tree…)*
acostarse	*lie down, go to bed*	**burlarse de alguien**	*make fun of someone*
acostumbrarse a algo	*get used to something*	**caerse**	*fall down*
adelantarse	*get ahead*	**callarse**	*be quiet, shut up*
alegrarse de algo	*rejoice/be glad about something*	**calmarse**	*calm down*
alejarse de algo	*move away from something*	**casarse con alguien**	*get married to someone*
aliviarse	*get well*	**cepillarse**	*brush (one's teeth, hair…)*
arrepentirse de algo	*repent (about) something*	**citarse con alguien**	*make an appointment/a date with someone*
asustarse de algo	*be frightened of something*	**convertirse en algo**	*become (by physical or metaphysical transformation)*
atrasarse	*fall behind, be late*	**curarse**	*get well*

REFLEXIVE VERBS (SPANISH–ENGLISH)

Spanish	English	Spanish	English
darse cuenta de algo	realize something	enterarse de algo	find out about something
decidirse a hacer algo	make up one's mind to do something	entristecerse	become sad
deshacerse de algo	get rid of something	equivocarse	be mistaken, make a mistake
despedirse de alguien	say good-bye to someone	esforzarse por hacer algo	make an effort to do something
despertarse	wake up	especializarse en algo	specialize/major in something
dirigirse a alguien	address someone	fiarse de alguien	trust someone
disponerse a hacer algo	prepare to do something	fijarse en algo	notice something
divertirse	have fun	frotarse	rub (up against)
divorciarse	get divorced	graduarse	graduate
dormirse	fall asleep	hacerse (+ noun)	become (through one's efforts [a lawyer, doctor...])
empeñarse en hacer algo	insist on doing something	interesarse por algo	be interested in something
empeorarse	get worse	irse	leave
enamorarse de alguien	fall in love with someone	lavarse	wash or bathe oneself (or a part of oneself)
encararse con algo o alguien	face/confront something or someone	levantarse	get up
encontrarse con alguien	meet someone (not for the first time)	llamarse	be called, named
enfermarse	get sick, become ill	llevarse algo	take something away/with oneself
enfrentarse a algo o alguien	face/confront something or someone	llevarse bien (mal) con alguien	get along well (not get along) with someone
enojarse con alguien	be angry with someone	marcharse	leave
enorgullecerse	be proud	mejorarse	improve (one's condition)

REFLEXIVE VERBS (SPANISH–ENGLISH)			
Spanish	**English**	**Spanish**	**English**
meterse con alguien	interfere with someone	**quedarse**	stay
mojarse	get wet	**quedarse con algo**	keep something
morirse	die	**quejarse de algo**	complain about something
moverse	move (one's body, objects)	**quitarse algo**	take off/remove something
mudarse	move (change residences)	**rascarse**	scratch oneself
negarse a hacer algo	refuse to do something	**rebelarse**	rebel
olvidarse de algo	forget something	**referirse a algo**	refer to something
oponerse a algo	object to something	**reírse de algo o alguien**	laugh at something or someone
parecerse a alguien o algo	look like someone or something	**resignarse a algo**	resign oneself to
peinarse (el pelo)	comb (one's hair)	**secarse**	dry off, dry out
pelearse con alguien	fight with someone	**sentarse**	sit down
perderse	get lost	**sentirse**	feel
perderse algo	miss out on something	**subirse a algo**	get onto something, get on (bus, train…)
ponerse (+ adj.)	become (describing mood)	**suicidarse**	commit suicide
ponerse a hacer algo	begin to do something	**tranquilizarse**	calm down
ponerse algo	put on something (article of clothing)	**volverse** (+ adj.)	become (describing undesired state [blind, crazy…])
preocuparse por algo	worry about something		

REFLEXIVE VERBS WITH CHARACTERISTIC PREPOSITIONS				
a	**con**	**de**	**en**	**por**
acercarse a	casarse con	acordarse de	convertirse en	esforzarse por
acostumbrarse a	citarse con	alegrarse de	empeñarse en	interesarse por
atreverse a	encararse con	alejarse de	especializarse en	preocuparse por
decidirse a	encontrarse con	arrepentirse de	fijarse en	
dirigirse a	enojarse con	asustarse de		
disponerse a	llevarse bien con	avergonzarse de		
enfrentarse a	meterse con	bajarse de		
negarse a	pelearse con	burlarse de		
oponerse a	quedarse con	darse cuenta de		
parecerse a		deshacerse de		
ponerse a		despedirse de		
referirse a		enamorarse de		
		enterarse de		
		fiarse de		
		olvidarse de		
		quejarse de		
		reírse de		

Ejercicios 6.76–6.78, páginas 401–402

Ⓚ Indirect Discourse

I. INTRODUCTION

Indirect discourse is the relating of oral statements without quoting them directly.

DIRECT DISCOURSE	INDIRECT DISCOURSE	
	Present	**Past**
—Te llamaré mañana. *"I will call you tomorrow."*	**Dice que me llamará mañana.** *He says that he will call me tomorrow.*	**Dijo que me llamaría al día siguiente.** *He said that he would call me the following day.*

Notice the three possible types of changes in indirect discourse:

- Verb [will → would]
- Person [I → He; you → me]
- Time reference [tomorrow → the following day]

As logic indicates, these changes do not always occur, or only some of them might occur. For example, if I am quoting what I just said today about today, there will be no change ("It is cold today." "I am saying it is cold today."). However, when there is a change of person or of time reference between the direct quote and the indirect quote, there will be changes, as in English. If the communication verb is in the past, there is a change in most tenses.

2. VERB-TENSE CHANGES

Present Indicative → **Imperfect Indicative**

Lo <u>hago</u>.
I do it.

Dijo que lo <u>hacía</u>.
He said he did it.

Present Subjunctive → **Imperfect Subjunctive**

Quiere que <u>vaya</u>.
He wants me to go.

Dijo que quería que <u>fuera</u>.
He said he wanted me to go.

Present Perfect Indicative → **Pluperfect Indicative**

Nos <u>han visto</u>.
They have seen us.

Dijeron que nos <u>habían visto</u>.
They said they had seen us.

Present Perfect Subjunctive → **Pluperfect Subjunctive**

Dudo que lo <u>hayan visto</u>.
I doubt that they saw it.

Dijo que dudaba que lo <u>hubieran visto</u>.
He said that he doubted they had seen it.

Preterite → **Pluperfect Indicative**

Lo <u>vi</u>.
I saw it.

Dijo que lo <u>había visto</u>.
He said he had seen it.

Future	→	Present Conditional

Future → **Present Conditional**

<u>Iré</u> mañana.
I will go tomorrow.

Dijo que <u>iría</u> al día siguiente.
He said he would go the next day.

Future Perfect → **Perfect Conditional**

Para el lunes <u>habré acabado</u>.
By Monday I will have finished.

Dijo que para el lunes <u>habría acabado</u>.
He said that by Monday he would have finished.

Imperative → **Imperfect Subjunctive**

<u>Cómete</u> la fruta.
Eat your fruit.

Me dijo que me <u>comiera</u> la fruta.
She told me to eat my fruit.

3. NO VERB-TENSE CHANGES

The following verb tenses never change in indirect discourse, even if the communication verb is in the past (notice, however, changes in **pronouns**).

- Imperfect indicative or subjunctive
- Pluperfect indicative or subjunctive
- Conditional present or perfect

<u>Íbamos</u> a comer.
We were going to eat.
→
Dijeron que <u>iban</u> a comer.
They said they were going to eat.

Ya <u>habíamos comido</u>.
We had already eaten.
→
Contesté que ya <u>habíamos comido</u>.
I answered that we had already eaten.

<u>Dudo</u> que me <u>estuvieras</u> mintiendo.
I doubt that you were lying to me.
→
Me dijo que <u>dudaba</u> que le <u>estuviera</u> mintiendo.
He told me that he doubted that I was lying to him.

Si <u>fuera</u> rico, me lo <u>compraría</u>.
If I were rich, I would buy it.
→
Pensó que si <u>fuera</u> rico, se lo <u>compraría</u>.
He thought that if he were rich, he would buy it.

Verb changes in a nutshell (when communication verb is in the past):

Present*	→	Imperfect
Preterite	→	Pluperfect
Future°	→	Conditional
Imperative	→	Imperfect Subjunctive

* Present indicative becomes imperfect indicative, present subjunctive becomes imperfect subjunctive, present perfect indicative becomes pluperfect indicative (i.e., present of auxiliary becomes imperfect of auxiliary), present perfect subjunctive becomes pluperfect subjunctive (i.e., present of auxiliary becomes imperfect of auxiliary).

° Future becomes conditional present, future perfect becomes conditional perfect (i.e., future of auxiliary becomes conditional of auxiliary).

4. PERSON CHANGES

Logic rules here, just as it does in English. Any reference to an individual that is altered by a change of a point of view will affect all references to the individual. Read the following transformations carefully.

Direct discourse:

Vamos a visitar a <u>nuestros</u> padres.   *<u>We</u> are going to visit <u>our</u> parents.*

Indirect discourse:

Dijeron que iban a visitar a <u>sus</u> padres.   *They said <u>they</u> were going to visit <u>their</u> parents.*

Direct discourse:

<u>Te</u> di <u>tu</u> libro.   *I gave <u>you</u> <u>your</u> book.*

Indirect discourse:

Ella le dijo que <u>le</u> había dado <u>su</u> libro.   *She told him <u>she</u> had given <u>him</u> <u>his</u> book.*

Direct discourse:

No voy con<u>tigo</u>.   *I am not going with <u>you</u>.*

Indirect discourse:

Ella me dijo que no iba con<u>migo</u>.

She told me <u>she</u> was not going with <u>me</u>.

5. TIME CHANGES

In indirect discourse in the past, time expressions will change unless the relation of the statement occurs within the same day. (If I say something today about tomorrow, and you repeat my words before the day is up, there is no change; the same logic applies here as in English.) If the relation of the direct statement is done on a day other than the one on which the statement was made, "yesterday" becomes "the day before" and "tomorrow" becomes "the next day." In Spanish, some common changes are:

ahora → **entonces**

<u>Ahora</u> sí puedo.
Now I can.

Dijo que <u>entonces</u> sí podía.
He said that he could then.

ayer → **el día anterior**

Lo hice <u>ayer</u>.
I did it yesterday.

Confesó que lo había hecho <u>el día anterior</u>.
He confessed that he had done it the day before.

anoche → **la noche anterior**

La vi <u>anoche</u>.
(La = la película)
I saw it last night.

Dijo que la había visto <u>la noche anterior</u>.
He said that he had seen it the night before.

mañana → **al día siguiente**

Iré <u>mañana</u>.
I will go tomorrow.

Anunció que iría <u>al día siguiente</u>.
He announced that he would go the following day.

la semana pasada → **la semana anterior**

La vi <u>la semana pasada</u>.
I saw her last week.

Admitió que la había visto <u>la semana anterior</u>.
He admitted that he had seen her the week before.

| la semana entrante | → | la próxima semana |

Te llamaré <u>la semana entrante</u>.
I will call you next week.

Me prometió que me llamaría <u>la próxima semana</u>.
He promised me he would call me the following week.

6. OTHER CHANGES

a. Connectives

When the quotations are for questions requiring a yes/no type **answer,** connect them with *si* ("whether, if"). When the quotations are for "yes" and "no" **responses,** use *que* before *sí* or *no*.

Example:

DIRECT DISCOURSE	INDIRECT DISCOURSE
—¿Quieres ir al cine conmigo? **—No.** *"Do you want to go to the movies with me?"* *"No."*	**Me preguntó si quería ir al cine con él.** **Yo le contesté que no.** *He asked me if I wanted to go to the movies with him.* *I said "no."*

b. This, That, and the Other

When the speaker changes locations from the moment of direct speech to the moment of reported speech, other things change referentially as well.

—¿Quieres <u>esto</u>? → **Me preguntó si quería <u>eso</u>.**
"Do you want <u>this</u>?" → *He asked me if I wanted <u>that</u>.*

c. Verbs of Communication

- For questions: *preguntar*
- For statements: *exclamar, agregar, contestar, responder, insistir, confesar, admitir,* etc.
- For requests or commands: *rogar, pedir, suplicar, decir, insistir,* etc.

d. A Note on Word Order with Indirect Interrogatives

In English you would say:

> *I do not know what Rafael saw.*

In the combination of what + Rafael + saw, notice that Rafael is placed before the verb. The word order of these elements in Spanish is different. The subject is placed after the verb when dealing with an indirect interrogative.

> **No sé qué vio Rafael.**

The same applies to any indirect question.

> **Me pregunto cuándo vienen los invitados.**
> *I wonder when the guests are coming.*

> **No puedo imaginar dónde están mis llaves.**
> *I cannot imagine where my keys are.*

Ejercicios 6.79–6.80, páginas 402–403; Ejercicios de repaso 6.81–6.82, páginas 403–406

Chapter 7

Ser, Estar, Haber, Hacer, and Tener

- **A** Overview
- **B** *Ser* vs. *Estar*
- **C** *Estar* vs. *Haber*
- **D** Expressions with *Estar* and *Tener*
- **E** Time Expressions

◆ Overview

The verb "to be" in English can be translated into Spanish in different ways, depending upon the context. The study of the different translations of "to be" is broken down into categories of verbs and expressions: *ser* vs. *estar;* idiomatic expressions with *estar* and *tener;* passive voice with *ser* vs. resultant condition with *estar; hacer* with time expressions, etc.

Examples of *ser, tener,* and *haber* ("there is/are") with nouns and pronouns:

Ángela **es** mi amiga.	*Angela is my friend.*
Éste es Javier.	*This is Javier.*
Carmen **es** profesora.	*Carmen is a professor.*
Es católica.	*She is a Catholic.*
Es soltero.	*He is a bachelor.*
Ese libro **es** mío.	*That book is mine.*
Fue Gema la que lo hizo.	*It was Gema who did it.*
Tengo veinte años.	*I am twenty years old.*
La niña **tiene** sed, calor, hambre, etc.	*The little girl is thirsty, hot, hungry, etc.*
Hay un lápiz en la mesa.	*There is a pencil on the table.*
Hay dos sillas en el corredor.	*There are two chairs in the hallway.*

Examples of *hacer* + noun and *estar* + adjective or present participle in descriptions of the weather:

Hace calor hoy.	*It is hot today.*
Hace frío hoy.	*It is cold today.*
Hace viento.	*It is windy.*
Hace buen tiempo.	*The weather is good. (We are having good weather.)*
Hace mal tiempo.	*The weather is bad. (We are having bad weather.)*
Está nublado.	*It is cloudy.*
Está lloviendo, nevando.	*It is raining, snowing.*

Examples of *ser* (characteristic) and *estar* (subject to change) with adjectives:

Jorge <u>es</u> peruano.	*Jorge is Peruvian.*
<u>Es</u> alto, delgado.	*He is tall, slender.*
Rosa <u>está</u> emocionada.	*Rosa is excited.*
Berta <u>está</u> triste.	*Berta is sad.*

Examples of *ser* and *estar* with prepositions:

<u>Soy</u> de Guatemala.	*I am from Guatemala.*
<u>Estoy</u> de pie, de rodillas, de luto, etc.	*I am standing, kneeling, in mourning, etc.*
<u>Estoy</u> por salir.	*I am about to go out.*

Example of *estar* with present participle:

<u>Están</u> *leyendo, cantando.*	*They are reading, singing.*

Examples of *ser, estar,* and *haber* with past participles:

Passive—*ser*

Esa novela <u>fue</u> *escrita* por Cervantes.	*That novel was written by Cervantes.*

Resultant condition—*estar* (past participle = adjective):

La novela <u>está</u> *escrita.*	*The novel is written.*

Perfect tenses—*haber* (to have as an auxiliary verb):

<u>He</u> *escrito,* <u>había</u> *escrito...*	*I have written, I had written …*

◆B Ser vs. Estar

We have broken down the uses of these two verbs based on the type of word that follows or precedes the verb: in some cases only one of the two can be used, in other cases there are choices.

I. WITH EQUAL ELEMENTS: *SER*

The verb *ser* is used when the verb "to be" serves to make an equation between two grammatically similar elements, such as two nouns, pronouns, adverbs, or clauses, or two noun equivalents, such as a noun and a relative clause, or a pronoun and a noun, or a noun or pronoun and an infinitive, etc.

> **El hombre es un animal.** (noun = noun)
> *Man is an animal.*

> **Esto es mío.** (pronoun = pronoun)
> *This is mine.*

> **Aquí es donde vamos a comer.** (adverb = adverb clause)
> *Here is where we are going to eat.*

> **Trabajar así es volverse loco.** (infinitive = infinitive)
> *To work like that is to go mad.*

> **Lo que yo digo es lo que vale.** (clause = clause)
> *What I say is what counts.*

> **Héctor es el alto.** (noun = pronoun)
> *Hector is the tall one.*

> **Esa mujer es la que te presenté ayer.** (noun = clause)
> *That woman is the one I introduced to you yesterday.*

> **Eso es vivir.** (pronoun = infinitive)
> *That is living.*

The verb *ser* is also used for telling time.

> —¿Qué hora **es**?   *"What time is it?"*
> —**Es** la una. **Son** las tres y media.   *"It is one o'clock. It is three thirty."*

2. WITH ADJECTIVES

a. Predicate Adjectives

The contrast between the norm vs. change of norm is the one we find most useful to understand the different uses of *ser* and *estar* with adjectives.

When the adjective describes an aspect of the subject that is considered to be the norm universally, the verb *ser* is used.

> **El hielo es frío.**   *Ice is cold.*

For an object that is not by definition cold, the verb *estar* would be used.

La superficie <u>está</u> fría.   *The surface is cold.*

The concept of "norm" is one that can vary depending upon the speaker; the following sentence was spoken by a loving son.

Mi madre <u>es</u> maravillosa. <u>Es</u>   *My mother is marvelous. She is very*
bellísima, joven y muy simpática.   *beautiful, young, and very nice.*

The same woman, perceived by someone else, might be thought of differently. To give an extreme example, if the woman were particularly modest or self-deprecating, she might see herself very differently.

<u>Soy</u> vieja, fea y antipática.   *I am old, ugly, and not nice.*

Any change in the norm, or subjective reaction, would take the verb *estar*.

<u>Está</u> pálida hoy porque   *She is pale today, because she has*
<u>ha estado</u> enferma.   *been sick.*

Over time, the norm might change as well. Imagine you have just met someone, and you perceive him as being fat. You describe him as follows:

<u>Es</u> gordo.   *He is fat.*

Yet, someone who knew him before knew him as slim, and perceives his current weight as a change from the norm.

Siempre <u>fue</u> delgado. Ahora   *He was always thin. Now he is fat.*
<u>está</u> gordo.

As you see, there is a choice between the two verbs based on the perception of norm or change, a choice that could mean a lot depending upon the context. If you want to tell someone how beautiful he/she is, in Spanish you must decide whether you want to make a statement about the beauty of the person always, or the beauty of the person at the moment.

¡Qué bella <u>eres</u>!

¡Qué bella <u>estás</u>!

In English, the first would be: "You are so beautiful!" The second might best be translated: "You look so beautiful!" The implications of this difference are the same in the two languages.

If you are describing an object to someone who does not know about it, and want to paint a picture that you would consider a standard for the object, you would use *ser*.

Los girasoles <u>son</u> grandes.	*Sunflowers are big.*

If you are growing sunflowers, and observing their daily changes, or if you find something to be different from what you expected, you would use *estar*.

Este girasol <u>está</u> grandísimo.	*This sunflower is very large.*
¡Qué grandes <u>están</u> los girasoles este año!	*The sunflowers are so big this year!*

Certain adjectives tend to indicate conditions rather than standard attributes, and would therefore tend to be used mostly with *estar*. This would be the case of adjectives indicating illness, reactions such as joy or sadness, changes in weight, size, or other aspects. *Enfermo, contento, harto,* and *bien* are most always used with *estar*.

Mi padre <u>está</u> *enfermo*.	*My father is sick.*
<u>Estoy</u> *contenta* de verte.	*I am happy to see you.*
<u>Estamos</u> *hartos* de tanto trabajo.	*We are tired of (fed up with) so much work.*
¿<u>Estás</u> *bien*?	*Are you okay?*

Other adjectives may vary in their meaning depending upon which verb is used. Some of the more dramatically altering adjectives follow.

(1) *Aburrido* (boring vs. bored)

Esa película <u>fue</u> aburrida.	*That movie was boring.*
El público <u>estaba</u> aburrido.	*The audience was bored.*

(2) *Bueno* (good vs. in good health, tasty)

La fruta <u>es</u> buena para la salud.	*Fruit is good for your health.*
¡Qué buena <u>está</u> esta manzana!	*This apple is so good (tasty)!*

NOTE: To avoid ridicule, it may be best to avoid the combination of *estar* and *bueno* when describing people. In some countries, such as Mexico, some *piropos* (compliments men pay women on the streets) allude to how good a woman *está;* a typical one would be: *"¡Qué buena estás!"* Culturally, this does not translate; it is a comment on physical attraction. In other countries, *"Estoy bueno."* only means "I am feeling okay now." If you want to refer to health, you can always use expressions such as *sentirse bien, sentirse mejor, estar bien, estar mejor*.

(3) CALLADO (QUIET BY NATURE VS. SILENT NOW)

Francisco <u>es</u> muy callado.	*Francisco is very quiet (by nature).*
Ustedes que siempre hablan tanto, ¿por qué <u>están</u> tan callados ahora?	*You who always talk so much, why are you so quiet now?*

(4) CIEGO (BLIND VS. BLINDED FIGURATIVELY OR MOMENTARILY)

Ese limosnero <u>es</u> ciego.	*That beggar is blind.*
¡<u>Estoy</u> ciega!	*I am blind!* (Context: suddenly I can't see a thing, although my eyesight is normal.)

NOTE: *Mudo* (mute) and *sordo* (deaf) behave similarly.

(5) CÓMODO (COMFORTABLE OBJECT VS. COMFORTABLE PERSON)

Esta silla <u>es</u> cómoda.	*This chair is comfortable.*
<u>Estoy</u> cómodo.	*I am comfortable.*

(6) FRÍO (COLD AS NORM OR NOT, USED WITH OBJECTS)

El invierno <u>es</u> frío.	*Winter is cold.*
Tu mano <u>está</u> fría.	*Your hand is cold.*

NOTE: Remember the uses of *tener* and *hacer* with nouns for temperatures. Note that *frío* can be an adjective or a noun, whereas *caliente* is the adjective for the noun *calor*. *Tener* is used with people, *hacer* is used impersonally for weather.

<u>Tengo</u> frío (calor).	*I am cold, hot.*
<u>Hace</u> frío (calor) afuera.	*It is cold (hot) out.*

(7) LISTO (CLEVER [PERSON OR ANIMAL] VS. READY)

Mi hermana <u>es</u> muy lista.	*My sister is very clever.*
¿Ya <u>están</u> listos?	*Are you ready?*

NOTE: To speak of a clever idea or concept, you could use the adjective *inteligente* or *genial* (stronger).

(8) Maduro (mature vs. ripe)

Ese niño <u>es</u> muy maduro.   *That boy is very mature.*

El aguacate <u>está</u> maduro.   *The avocado is ripe.*

(9) Rico (wealthy vs. delicious)

Mi tío <u>es</u> rico.   *My uncle is rich.*

La comida <u>estuvo</u> rica.   *The meal was delicious.*

(10) Verde (green vs. unripe)

Los aguacates <u>son</u> verdes.   *Avocadoes are green.*

El aguacate <u>está</u> verde.   *The avocado is unripe.*

(11) Vivo (smart, bright person vs. alive)

<u>Son</u> muy vivos tus hermanos.   *Your brothers are very bright.*

Mi abuela todavía <u>está</u> viva.   *My grandmother is still alive.*

NOTE: In parallel with this use of *estar* is its use with *muerto*. For example: *Mi abuelo está muerto.* However permanent death may be, it is viewed more as a change from the state of living. Also, to speak of bright ideas, you could use *inteligente* or *genial* (stronger).

b. Expressions with "To Be"

Some frequent errors occur with the following expressions with "to be." Note the correct translation.

I am cold.	**Tengo frío.**
It is cold.	**Hace frío.** [weather] **Es / Está frío.** [something is cold; norm / not norm]
I am dead.	**Estoy muerto(a) (de cansancio).** **Estoy agotado.**
I am done.	**Terminé.** **He terminado.** **Ya acabé.** (etc.)
It is done.	**Está terminado.** **Ya está.** (etc.)

I am excited.	**Estoy emocionado.**
I am finished.	**Terminé.** **He terminado.** **Ya acabé.** (etc.)
It is finished.	**Está terminado / hecho.** **Se terminó.** **Ya está.** (etc.)
I am glad.	**Me alegro.**
I am happy.	**Estoy contento.** [reaction] **Soy feliz.** [in my life]

(NOTE: *Alegre* is closer to "joyful," an outer expression of joy, than to "happiness," an inner feeling, which may be unseen.)

I am hot.	**Tengo calor.**
It is hot.	**Hace calor.** [weather] **Está caliente.** [the soup, for example] (This can also mean "in heat" for animals.)
I am hungry.	**Tengo hambre.**
I am interested.	**Me interesa.**
I am late.	**Llegué tarde.**
It is late.	**Es tarde.**
I am sad to hear that.	**Me apena mucho oír eso.** **Me da mucha pena...**
I am short. [not tall]	**Soy bajo.**
I am short (of money).	**No tengo suficiente dinero.**
It is short. [the line]	**Es / Está corta.**
I am sitting.	**Estoy sentado.**
I am sorry.	**Lo siento.**

It is working.	**Está funcionando.**
I was born.	**Nací.**
That is the problem.	**He allí el problema, etc.**

(NOTE: This expression is used when pointing to or presenting something. *He* is invariable and serves as an demonstrative adverb. Other English renderings: "There's the rub." **He allí la dificultad.** "Here's the situation: ... " **He aquí la situación: ... .**)

c. Impersonal Expressions

Generally impersonal expressions are formed with *ser*.

Es bueno dormir mucho.	*It is good to sleep a lot.*
Es interesante viajar.	*It is interesting to travel.*
Fue maravilloso estar allí.	*It was marvelous to be there.*

Use *estar* with *bien* and *claro*.

Está bien que vengan tus amigos.	*It is okay for your friends to come.*
Está claro que ya no me quieres.	*It is clear that you do not love me any more.*

3. WITH PREPOSITIONS AND ADVERBS

a. *De*

Use *ser* to indicate origin, the material something is made of, or possession.

Soy de México.	*I am from Mexico.*
El edificio era de ladrillo.	*The building was made of bricks.*
Este paraguas es de María.	*This umbrella is María's.*

Use *estar* with set expressions, which indicate opinion, temporary condition or position, or change of location (see table under "Expressions with *estar* and *tener*"), such as *estar de acuerdo, estar de buen humor, estar de luto, de pie, de rodillas, de viaje, de vuelta.*

Estoy *de acuerdo* contigo.	*I agree with you.*
Mis padres están *de buen humor* hoy.	*My parents are in a good mood today.*

Estoy <u>*de luto*</u> **por la muerte de mi padre.**	*I am in mourning for the death of my father.*
Los niños <u>estuvieron</u> <u>*de pie*</u> **todo el día.**	*The boys were standing all day long.*
La mujer <u>estaba</u> <u>*de rodillas*</u>, **rezando.**	*The woman was kneeling, praying.*
La familia <u>está</u> <u>*de viaje*</u>.	*The family is away (on a trip).*
¿Cuándo <u>estarán</u> <u>*de vuelta*</u>?	*When will they be back?*

b.   Time and Place

To indicate location or time of an event, use *ser.* To indicate location of an object or a person, use *estar.*

La conferencia <u>es</u> **a las diez en el auditorio.**	*The lecture is at ten in the auditorium.*
El profesor <u>está</u> **en su oficina.**	*The professor is in his office.*
La sal <u>está</u> **en la mesa.**	*The salt is on the table.*

Note that some words can signify either an event or an object: for example, an exam can be the paper itself or the event; a movie can be a videocassette or reel or the showing of it.

El examen <u>es</u> **esta noche en Morrill Hall.**	*The exam is tonight in Morrill Hall.*
El examen <u>está</u> **debajo del libro en la gaveta del centro.**	*The exam is under the book in the middle drawer.*
La película <u>es</u> **arriba.**	*The movie is (being shown) upstairs.*
La película <u>está</u> **al lado del televisor.**	*The movie is next to the TV set.*

Adverbs of time and place and adverbial clauses function similarly.

La conferencia <u>es</u> **cuando te dije.**	*The lecture is when I told you.*
El libro no <u>está</u> **donde lo dejé.**	*The book is not where I left it.*

PRÁCTICA

Ejercicios 7.1–7.7, páginas 407–408

4. WITH PAST AND PRESENT PARTICIPLES

a. With Present Participles

With the present participle, *estar* is used to indicate the progressive.

> **Estoy** estudiando.   *I am studying.*

b. With Past Participles: Passive Voice and Resultant Condition

With past participles, *ser* would be used to indicate the passive voice, and *estar* to indicate a condition resulting from a completed action.

Passive voice:

> **Las ventanas _fueron_ abiertas a las ocho.**
> *The windows were opened at eight.* (Somebody opened them.)

> **Los edificios _son_ construidos por ingenieros.**
> *Buildings are built by engineers.*

Resultant condition:

> **Las ventanas _están_ abiertas.**
> *The windows are open.* (It does not matter who did it.)

If what is being focused upon is not the action or who did it, but the result of the action, the verb *estar* is used with the past participle functioning as an adjective.

> **El edificio _está_ terminado.**   *The building is finished.*

(1) FORMATION OF THE PASSIVE VOICE

The passive voice in Spanish is formed essentially in the same way as in English.

ACTIVE VS. PASSIVE VOICE				
Active	**La tormenta**	**destruyó**		**la casa.**
	subject	verb		direct object
	The storm	*destroyed*		*the house.*
Passive	**La casa**	**fue destruida**	**por**	**la tormenta.**
	subject	verb		agent
	The house	*was destroyed*	*by*	*the storm.*

To change from active to passive voice:

- The subject of the active sentence becomes the agent (preceded by *por*) of the passive.
- The direct object of the active sentence becomes the subject of the passive sentence.
- The verb of the active sentence undergoes the following transformation: the verb itself becomes a past participle (variable in gender and number with its new subject) and is preceded by the verb *ser* in the same tense and mood of the verb of the original active sentence.

Examples:

ACTIVE	PASSIVE
Isabel Allende escribió esa novela. → *Isabel Allende wrote that novel.*	**Esa novela fue escrita por Isabel Allende.** *That novel was written by Isabel Allende.*
Heinle & Heinle publicará el libro. → *Heinle & Heinle will publish the book.*	**El libro será publicado por Heinle & Heinle.** *The book will be published by Heinle & Heinle.*
Ella había corregido las tareas. → *She had corrected the homework.*	**Las tareas habían sido corregidas por ella.** *The homework had been corrected by her.*

(2) A NOTE ON THE PASSIVE VOICE

The passive voice, very common in English, is rarely used in Spanish. It can be seen more and more in journalism, which is translated directly from the English, often on the World Wide Web, for example, but this is not the standard use. If there is a subject, or an agent, or someone who does the action, whether present in the sentence or implied, Spanish prefers the active voice, and if there is no agent implied, the impersonal *se* is used instead.

Subject of the action	Spanish preference	English preference
Stated	ACTIVE	ACTIVE or PASSIVE
Absent but implied	ACTIVE	ACTIVE or PASSIVE
Absent and irrelevant	Impersonal *se*	PASSIVE

Stated subject:

Los meseros sirvieron la cena.   *The waiters served dinner.*

Los meseros sirvieron la cena.   *Dinner was served by the waiters.*

Although the second sentence in English is passive, and there could be an equivalent passive constructed in Spanish, it would not be the choice of Spanish speakers, who would tend to use the active whenever the doer of the action is stated.

Absent but implied subject:

Sirvieron la cena a las diez.   *Dinner was served at ten. (when I was at my neighbors' house last night)*

Here, the neighbors are the ones who served dinner at ten, but they are not mentioned in the English sentence: they are implied, however, and their role in the serving is relevant. For this reason, Spanish would use the active structure.

Absent and irrelevant subject:

Se habla español.   *Spanish (is) spoken.*

When the doer of the action is not a part of the statement, not present, or even relevant to the focus of the sentence, Spanish uses the impersonal *se*.

NOTE: For more on the impersonal *se,* see Chapter 3.B.4, pages 76–79. When the grammatical subject of the English passive is an indirect object of the verb, it is impossible to use the passive in Spanish: such structures can be translated with the impersonal *se* or other impersonal structures.

No se me dijo la verdad.   *I was not told the truth.*
OR: **No me dijeron la verdad.**

In the above sentence, "I" is the grammatical subject of the English passive sentence, but strictly speaking it is the person **to whom** the truth was not told: it is the indirect object of the verb to tell.

PRÁCTICA

Ejercicio 7.8, página 409

◆ *Estar* vs. *Haber*

When indicating the existence or presence of people or things, *estar* and *haber* have different uses.

Estar means "to be," and has a specific subject.

Los libros <u>están</u> en la mesa.	*The books are on the table.*

In the above sentence whoever hears the sentence knows which books are being referred to: they are specific books.

Haber (*hay, había,* etc.) means "there is, there are, there were, etc.," and has no subject: it is impersonal.

<u>Hay</u> libros en la mesa.	*There are books on the table.*

In the above sentence, what is being focused upon is not the location of specific books, but the mere existence of unspecified books on the table.

Note that *hay* is invariable in number: it does not change to plural. When it is used in any tense or mood, it remains invariable in number.

<u>Había</u> cuarenta estudiantes en el salón.	*There were forty students in the room.*
<u>Hubo</u> varios accidentes en esa esquina.	*There were several accidents on that corner.*
No creo que <u>haya</u> suficientes horas en el día.	*I don't think there are enough hours in the day.*

PRÁCTICA

Ejercicio 7.9, página 409

D Expressions with *Estar* and *Tener*

1. Expressions with *Estar*

EXPRESSIONS WITH *ESTAR*			
estar a favor de	*to be for, in favor of*	**estar de regreso**	*to be back*
estar ausente[1]	*to be absent*	**estar de rodillas**	*to be kneeling*
estar contento[2]	*to be glad, pleased, happy*	**estar de vacaciones**	*to be on vacation*
estar de acuerdo con	*to agree with*	**estar de viaje**	*to be traveling*
estar de buen (mal) humor	*to be in a good (bad) mood*	**estar de visita**	*to be visiting*
estar de huelga	*to be on strike*	**estar de vuelta**	*to be back*
estar de luto	*to be in mourning*	**estar en contra de**	*to be against*
estar de pie[3]	*to be standing*		

2. Expressions with *Tener*

Notice that *tener frío* and *tener calor* are used exclusively for people or animals. If you wish to say that an **object** is hot or cold, use *ser* or *estar*.

EXPRESSIONS WITH *TENER*			
tener _____ años	*to be _____ years old*	**tener la culpa**	*to be guilty*
tener calor	*to be hot*	**tener lugar**	*to take place*
tener cuidado	*to be careful*	**tener miedo**	*to be afraid*
tener en cuenta que	*to bear in mind that*	**tener prisa**	*to be in a hurry*[4]
tener éxito	*to be successful, succeed*	**tener razón**	*to be right*[5]
tener frío	*to be cold*	**tener sed**	*to be thirsty*
tener ganas de	*to feel like, desire*	**tener sueño**	*to be sleepy*[6]
tener hambre	*to be hungry*	**tener vergüenza**	*to be ashamed*

1. This expression may only be used with *estar;* "to be late" = *llegar tarde;* "to be on time" = *llegar a tiempo.*
2. This expression may only be used with *estar.*

PRÁCTICA

Ejercicios 7.10–7.11, páginas 409–410; Ejercicios de repaso 7.12–7.14, página 410

Time Expressions

I. INTRODUCTION

a. Counting Forward

In Spanish, as in English, time can be perceived in various ways: we can narrate a story from beginning to end, with a series of preterites and imperfects.

Me levanté, me bañé y desayuné.	*I got up, I bathed, and I had breakfast.*
Mientras desayunaba, sonó el teléfono.	*While I was eating breakfast, the phone rang.*

We can state the duration of an action in a variety of ways.

Estudié por cuatro horas.	*I studied for four hours.*
Viví en España por seis meses.	*I lived in Spain for six months.*

b. Counting Backward

However, if we want to say how long something has lasted counting back, as we do in English with "I have been studying for four hours" (counting back from the present) or "I had been studying for four hours when you called" (counting back from a moment in the past—when you called), in Spanish we most frequently use expressions with *hacer que* and *llevar*.

---

3. The expression used for "to be sitting" is *estar sentado,* whereas *sentarse* means "to sit down" (the process of changing from the standing to the sitting position).

4. "to hurry up" = *apurarse*

5. "to be wrong" = *estar equivocado*

6. "to have a dream" = *tener un sueño*

2. DURATION

a. Counting Back from the Present

EXPRESSION (INVARIABLE)	AMOUNT OF TIME	EXPRESSION	ACTION VERB FORM (VARIABLE)
Hace (invariable)		**que**	Present tense (**yo, tú,** etc. ...)

EXPRESSION (VARIABLE)	AMOUNT OF TIME	ACTION VERB FORM (INVARIABLE)
Llevo (Llevas, Lleva, etc. ...)		1. Affirmative: present participle
		2. **Estar**: Ø (no verb)
		3. Negative: **sin** + infinitive

Affirmative: The sentence "I have been studying for three hours" (implication: and continue to do so) could be translated as:

> <u>Hace</u> tres horas <u>que estudio</u>.
> OR: <u>Llevo</u> tres horas <u>estudiando</u>.

Notice where the person is expressed in these two sentences: with *hace… que* the person doing the action is perceived in the second verb (*estudio* [*yo*]), whereas with *llevar* the person is seen in the verb *llevar* itself (*Llevo* [*yo*]) and not in the action verb *estudiando*.

With *estar*: If the main "action" verb is *estar,* the expression with *llevar* would **not** state the verb.

> <u>Hace</u> tres horas <u>que estamos</u> aquí.
> OR: <u>Llevamos</u> tres horas aquí.

Never use *estando* in sentences like *Llevamos tres horas aquí.*

Negative: the sentence "We have not slept for two nights" (i.e., the last two nights) could be translated as:

> <u>Hace</u> dos noches <u>que no dormimos</u>.
> OR: <u>Llevamos</u> dos noches <u>sin dormir</u>.

In the negative, the sentence with *llevar* does not take the present participle for its second verb, but the **infinitive** preceded by *sin*.

b. Counting Back from a Moment in the Past

EXPRESSION (INVARIABLE)	AMOUNT OF TIME	EXPRESSION	ACTION VERB FORM (VARIABLE)
Hacía (invariable)		**que**	Imperfect tense (**yo, tú,** etc. ...)

EXPRESSION (VARIABLE)	AMOUNT OF TIME	ACTION VERB FORM (INVARIABLE)
Llevaba (Llevabas, etc. ...)		1. Affirmative: present participle
		2. **Estar**: Ø (no verb)
		3. Negative: **sin** + infinitive

Affirmative: the sentence "I had been studying for three hours" (implication: when something interrupted my work), would be translated as:

> **Hacía** tres horas <u>que estudiaba</u>.
> OR: <u>Llevaba</u> tres horas <u>estudiando</u>.

Here, *hacer* and *llevar* are in the **imperfect,** as is the main verb of the first sentence. In the second sentence, the main verb is still in the **present participle.**

With *estar*: apply the same rule as for *estar* counting back from the present. (See page 274.)

> **Hacía** tres horas <u>que estábamos</u> allá.
> OR: <u>Llevábamos</u> tres horas allá.

Negative: the sentence "We had not gone to the movies for a long time" would translate as follows:

> **Hacía** mucho tiempo <u>que no íbamos</u> al cine.
> OR: <u>Llevábamos</u> mucho tiempo <u>sin ir</u> al cine.

As you see, the same rules apply for the negative in the past as did in the present. The only difference is that the verbs must be kept in the imperfect (all but the infinitive, of course).

3. AGO

Another type of sentence that counts time in reverse relates to finished actions in the past, as opposed to actions that have been going on and continue to go on (duration). In English, this reverse counting uses the expression "ago," as in the example "I did that two hours ago." (as opposed to "I did it at three o'clock."). To translate sentences with "ago," you cannot use *llevar,* only *hace* [present] … *que* + preterite.

> **Hace** tres años **que** se fue. *He left three years ago.*
> OR: Se fue **hace** tres años.

This same situation shifted into a past context would use the following structure:

> **Hacía** tres años **que** se había ido. *He had left three years before.*

We can also refer to things that "were happening" some time ago. For these actions, Spanish uses the imperfect of the main verb, usually with the progressive form for verbs of action, and nonprogressive for verbs of state.

> **¿Qué estabas haciendo <u>hace</u> dos horas?** *What were you doing two hours <u>ago</u>?*

> **Me estaba bañando <u>hace</u> dos horas.** *I was bathing two hours <u>ago</u>.*
> OR: **Hace dos horas, me estaba bañando.**[7]

> **¿Dónde estaba usted <u>hace</u> treinta minutos?** *Where were you thirty minutes <u>ago</u>?*

Ejercicios 7.15–7.16, página 411; Ejercicios de repaso 7.17–7.18, páginas 411–412

---

7. Notice the absence of *que* from the expression.

Chapter 8

Lexical Variations

A Introduction

B Terms and Expressions

A Introduction

The contents of this chapter are not technically grammatical in nature: they are lexical. Then again, some of the most commonly covered grammatical points are more a focus on lexical differences, and for this reason we are not concerned that this chapter may be out of place in a grammar manual. On the contrary, we include this list of terms here because they represent some of the most common areas of difficulties for students, and we consider a focused practice of them to be useful to improve accuracy of expression.

In some cases, the terms have been covered under grammatical chapters, and are being consolidated and reviewed in this chapter from the point of view of vocabulary. *Acabar* was covered under preterite and imperfect, and then under accidental *se;* "what" is covered previously under interrogatives, and under relative pronouns; what we do here is consolidate the two for a brief focused review. Some of these points have been touched upon under reflexives, such as "become or get"; what we do here is bring the more common terms to the front, and present them more thoroughly by filling out some of the subtle lexical distinctions surrounding them. Other expressions in this list are shown for the first time here, and may be false cognates (apply, attend, exit, realize), or differences in perception (e.g. movement: coming and going, bringing and taking).

B Terms and Expressions

We have arranged these terms in alphabetical order rather than in conceptual or other types of groupings to help locate them more easily for quick reference.

1. ACABAR

acabar = *to finish*

> **Acabé la tarea.**   *I finished the homework.*

acabar de (+ inf.) = *to finish doing something*

The meaning of this expression changes depending upon the context in which it is used.

> **Acabé de *poner* la mesa.**   *I finished setting the table.*
>
> **Cuando acabes de *lavar* los platos, sécalos y guárdalos.**   *When you finish washing the dishes, dry them and put them away.*

When used in the present and imperfect indicative, it may mean "to have just" (done something):

Present Indicative:

> **Acabo de** *comer.*   *I just ate.*

Imperfect Indicative:

> **Acabábamos de** *terminar.*   *We had just finished.*

acabarse = *to end, finish, use up, or eat up* [reflexive]; *to be no more, run out of* (accidental **se**)

Me acabé el pan.	*I ate up all the bread.*
Se acabó el azúcar.	*There is no more sugar.*
Se acabaron los limones.	*There are no more lemons.*
Se nos acabó la leche.	*We have no more (ran out of) milk.*
Se nos acabaron los cacahuates.	*We have no more (ran out of) peanuts.*

Ejercicios 8.1–8.2, página 413

2. APPLY

aplicar = *to apply* (e.g., an ointment)

> **Instrucciones: aplicar la crema sobre la herida cuatro veces al día.**
> *Instructions: apply the cream to the injury four times a day.*

aplicación *(f.)* = *application* (of a theory, of one's efforts, of a medication, etc.)

> **Estudia con aplicación.**
> *S(he) studies with application (diligence).*

solicitar = *to apply* (for job, loan, fellowship, university acceptance, etc.)

> **Solicité el puesto de subgerente.**
> *I applied for the job of assistant manager.*

> **Le dieron la beca que solicitó.**
> *They gave him the fellowship (s)he applied for.*

<u>Solicitaré</u> entrada a cuatro universidades.
I shall apply to four universities.

solicitud *(f.)* = *application* (form to fill out for a job, university, loan, etc.)

    Envié la <u>solicitud</u> a tiempo.   *I sent the application on time.*

Ejercicios 8.3–8.4, páginas 413–414

3. ASK

pedir algo (without a preposition) = *to ask for something*

    Me <u>pidieron</u> dinero.   *They asked me for money.*

pedir que = *to ask to*

    Le <u>pedí</u> que me despertara.   *I asked him to wake me up.*

preguntar: "¿...?" = *to ask: "... ?"*

    Me <u>preguntó</u>, "¿Qué hora es?"   *He asked me, "What time is it?"*

preguntar si..., qué..., cuándo..., (etc.) = *to ask if ... , what ... , when ... , (etc.)*

    Le <u>preguntaré</u> si tiene un mapa.   *I will ask him if he has a map.*

    Nos <u>preguntaron</u> qué queríamos.   *They asked us what we wanted.*

hacer una pregunta = *to ask a question*

    ¿Me permite <u>hacerle una pregunta</u>?   *May I ask you a question?*

pedido *(m.)* = *request, order*

    ¿Cuál es el número de su <u>pedido</u>?   *What is your order number?*

cuestión *(f.)* = *matter, question*

    Es una <u>cuestión</u> de estética.   *It's a matter (question) of aesthetics.*

Ejercicios 8.5–8.6, página 414

4. AT

En is the usual equivalent of "at" referring to **static** location in space.

Estoy <u>en</u> casa.	*I am <u>at</u> home.*
Estoy <u>en</u> la casa de mi hermano.	*I am <u>at</u> my brother's house.*
Me quedé <u>en</u> su apartamento.	*I stayed <u>at</u> his apartment.*

This could extend to actions that take place within the confines of a certain location.

Comimos <u>en</u> ese restaurante.	*We ate at that restaurant.*

A would be used for **movement** "to" a destination.

Vamos <u>a</u> casa.	*We are going home.*
Viajamos <u>a</u> Puerto Rico. (for travel within the island, you would use *en* or *por*)	*We traveled to Puerto Rico.*

A is the usual equivalent of "at" referring to time of day.

La clase es <u>a</u> las diez.	*Class is <u>at</u> ten.*

Other expressions:

<u>en</u> este momento	*<u>at</u> this moment*	**tirar <u>a</u>, lanzar <u>a</u>**	*to throw <u>at</u>*
<u>a</u> veces	*<u>at</u> times*	**vender <u>a</u> un precio**	*to sell <u>at</u> a price*
<u>a</u> la puerta	*<u>at</u> (outside) the door*	**estar <u>a</u> la mesa**	*to be <u>at</u> the table*
BUT: **<u>en</u> la puerta**	*<u>at</u> (inside) the door*	**<u>a</u> mi lado**	*<u>at</u> my side*

Ejercicios 8.7–8.8, página 414

5. ATTEND

asistir a = *to attend* (a class, formal meeting, conference, etc.)

<u>Asistimos</u> a una reunión esta tarde.	*We attended a meeting this afternoon.*
Hoy no <u>asistí</u> a clase.	*Today I did not attend class.*

asistencia *(f.) = attendance, audience*

<table>
<tr><td>La <u>asistencia</u> a clase es un requisito.</td><td>*Attendance at class is a requirement.*</td></tr>
<tr><td>Había un desconocido en la <u>asistencia</u>.</td><td>*There was a stranger in the audience.*</td></tr>
</table>

asistencia social *(f.) = welfare*

<table>
<tr><td>Muchos reciben <u>asistencia social</u>.</td><td>*Many receive welfare.*</td></tr>
</table>

atender *= to assist, serve* (a person), *pay attention, tend to*

<table>
<tr><td>¿En qué puedo <u>atenderlo</u>?</td><td>*How may I assist you?*</td></tr>
<tr><td>Me <u>atendieron</u> de inmediato.</td><td>*They served me immediately.*</td></tr>
<tr><td><u>Atiéndanme</u>, por favor.</td><td>*Pay attention, please.*</td></tr>
<tr><td><u>Atiende</u> a tus amistades, Gregorio.</td><td>*Tend to your friends, Gregorio.*</td></tr>
</table>

atento(a) *= attentive, well-mannered, polite, kind*

<table>
<tr><td>Su marido es muy <u>**atento**</u> con ella.</td><td>*Her husband is very considerate toward her.*</td></tr>
<tr><td>Es un joven muy <u>**atento**</u>.</td><td>*He is a very polite young man.*</td></tr>
</table>

(See also Chapter 8.B.23, page 297.)

PRÁCTICA

Ejercicios 8.9–8.10, página 415

6. BECAUSE

Por and *a causa de* mean "because of" and are used with **nouns**. (*Por* can also have other meanings, such as "on account of," "instead of," etc. Context should indicate the meaning.)

<table>
<tr><td>Lo hice <u>por</u> mi hermano.</td><td>*I did it because of (on account of, instead of) my brother.*</td></tr>
<tr><td>No salimos <u>a causa de</u> la tormenta.</td><td>*We did not go out because of the storm.*</td></tr>
</table>

Por is used with **pronouns**.

<table>
<tr><td>Dejó su carrera <u>por</u> ella.</td><td>*He gave up his career because of her.*</td></tr>
<tr><td>Vendrán temprano <u>por</u> eso.</td><td>*They will come early because of that.*</td></tr>
</table>

Por can also be used with an **infinitive** [same subject], whereas *a causa de* **cannot.**

Me enfermé <u>por</u> comer tanto.	*I got sick because I ate so much.*

Porque is used **only** with a **conjugated verb.**

No salí <u>porque</u> estaba lloviendo.	*I did not go out because it was raining.*

Gracias a is used when there is a positive force involved.

Salí pronto del hospital <u>gracias a</u> tu ayuda.	*I got out of the hospital quickly because of (thanks to) your help.*

PRÁCTICA

Ejercicios 8.11–8.12, página 415

7. BECOME OR GET

alegrarse = *to become happy, be glad*

<u>**Me alegro**</u> **de que puedas venir.**	*I am glad you can come.*

callarse = *to become quiet, keep silent, shut up*

¡<u>Cállate</u>!	*Be quiet!*

calmarse = *to become calm, calm down*

Al ver a su madre, <u>se calmó</u>.	*When he saw his mother, he calmed down.*

cansarse = *to get tired*

<u>**Me cansé**</u> **de trabajar.**	*I got tired of working.*

empobrecerse = *to become poor*

<u>**Se fueron empobreciendo**</u> **poco a poco.**	*They became poor little by little.*

enfermarse = *to get sick*

<u>**Te**</u> **vas a <u>enfermar</u> si sales así.**	*You are going to get sick if you go out like that.*

enfurecerse = *to become furious*

> **Su padre se enfureció al oír las noticias.**
>
> *Her father became furious when he heard the news.*

enloquecerse = *to go mad, become crazy*

> **Al perderla, se enloqueció.**
>
> *When he lost her, he went crazy.*

enojarse = *to get angry*

> **No te enojes conmigo.**
>
> *Do not get angry with me.*

enriquecerse = *to become rich*

> **Pensaban enriquecerse con eso.**
>
> *They thought they could get rich with that.*

entristecerse = *to become sad*

> **Se entristecieron sus hijos más que él.**
>
> *His children became sadder than he did.*

envejecerse = *to become old*

> **Con este producto, nadie se envejece.**
>
> *With this product, nobody gets old.*

mejorarse = *to get better, improve*

> **¡Que te mejores pronto!**
>
> *I hope you get better soon!*

tranquilizarse = *to become calm, calm down*

> **Con esa música, se tranquilizaron.**
>
> *With that music, they calmed down.*

ponerse (+ **serio, pálido, triste,** and other underlined adjectives of involuntary and passing psychological or physical states) = *to become* (serious, pale, sad …)

> **Se puso** *triste* **al oír las noticias.**
>
> *He became sad upon hearing the news.*

hacerse (+ **abogado, médico,** and other nouns of profession) = *to become* (a lawyer, doctor …)

> **Mi hermana se hizo** *abogada.*
>
> *My sister became a lawyer.*

llegar a ser (+ <u>nouns or adjectives</u> expressing importance or high personal status) = *to become* (rich, famous …)

> **Llegó a ser** *famoso.*   *He became famous.*

convertirse en = *to become or turn into* (by physical transformation)

> **El vino se convirtió en vinagre.**   *The wine became (turned into) vinegar.*

Ejercicios 8.13–8.14, página 416; Ejercicio de repaso 8.15, página 416

8. BUT

pero = *but* (nevertheless)

> **Tengo suficiente dinero, pero no quiero ir.**
> *I have enough money, but I do not want to go.*

> **No tengo suficiente dinero, pero voy a ir.**
> *I do not have enough money, but I am going to go.*

> **El nuevo gerente es eficaz, pero antipático.**
> *The new manager is efficient, but disagreeable.*

sino = *but* (but rather, but instead—when contrasting with a negative in the first part)

> **No es antipático, sino serio.**
> *He is not disagreeable, but (rather) serious.*

> **No fue a la tienda, sino al banco.**
> *He did not go to the store, but (instead) to the bank.*

sino que = **sino** followed by a conjugated verb

> **No se lo vendí, sino que se lo *regalé*.**
> *I did not sell it to him, but gave it to him (instead).*

NOTE: A common mistake in intermediate-level essay papers is to use *pero* at the beginning of a sentence, followed by a comma. This emphasis on *pero* is incorrect in Spanish: to translate an emphatic initial "but," it would be best to use *Sin embargo*.

Ejercicio 8.16, páginas 416–417

9. COME AND GO

venir = *to come* (towards the speaker)

Decidieron <u>venir</u> a vernos.	*They decided to come see us.*
¡<u>Ven</u> acá!	*Come here!*

ir = *to go* (away from the speaker)

NOTE: In English this is frequently translated as "to come."

<u>Voy</u> a tu casa esta tarde.	*I will go to your house this afternoon.*
¡<u>Voy</u>!	*I am coming!* (literally, in Spanish, "I am going.")

llegar = *to arrive, to get someplace*
llegar tarde, temprano = *to be late, early*

Los huéspedes <u>llegaron</u> esta mañana.	*The guests arrived (got here) this morning.*
<u>Llegamos</u> al hotel a las tres.	*We got to the hotel at three.*
<u>Llegaste temprano</u>.	*You are early. (You arrived early.)*
<u>Llegué tarde</u> al trabajo.	*I was late to work.*
Lamento <u>haber llegado tarde</u>.	*I am sorry I am late.*

PRÁCTICA

Ejercicios 8.17–8.18, página 417

10. DESPEDIR

despedir = *to fire, dismiss*

Esa empresa <u>despidió</u> a veinte empleados.   *That firm fired twenty employees.*

despedirse = *to say good-bye*

<u>Nos despedimos</u> en el aeropuerto.   *We said good-bye at the airport.*

Ejercicios 8.19–8.20, páginas 417–418

11. EXIT AND SUCCESS

éxito = *success*

El <u>éxito</u> del hotel depende de la calidad del servicio.
The success of the hotel depends upon the quality of service.

tener éxito = *to be successful*

Si se esmeran, <u>tendrán éxito</u>.
If you make an effort, you will be successful.

salida = *exit*

¿Dónde se encuentra la <u>salida</u> de emergencia?
Where is the emergency exit?

suceso = *event*

Fue un <u>suceso</u> de tal importancia que vinieron los reporteros.
It was such an important event that the reporters came.

Ejercicios 8.21–8.22, página 418

12. Go and Leave

ir = *to go* (<u>towards</u> a specific destination)

Ayer <u>fuimos</u> al museo.	*Yesterday we went to the museum.*

irse = **marcharse** = *to leave* (direction <u>away from</u> some understood location)

El señor Cárdenas ya <u>se fue</u>.	*Mr. Cárdenas already left.*
El gerente <u>se va</u> a las cinco.	*The manager leaves at five.*
No está; <u>se marchó</u>.	*He is not in; he left.*

salir = *to go out*

Los niños <u>salieron</u> a jugar.	*The children went out to play.*
Los huéspedes <u>salieron</u> a la playa.	*The guests went out to the beach.*
<u>Saldremos</u> esta noche a las siete.	*We will go out tonight at seven.*

salir vs. *irse* (intransitive) = *to leave*

Salir is used as a synonym for *irse* when the person leaving is also leaving an enclosed area, such as a building. *Irse* is more permanent than *salir,* for example, when a person is at home or in the office and leaves expecting to return, *salir* is used more frequently. At the end of the day, when a person leaves the office until the next day, *irse* would be more common. (Notice that these verbs are intransitive in Spanish, and do not take direct objects in the same manner as in English.)

In the following sentences *salir* would be preferable.

Elena <u>salió</u> *de* casa hace una hora.	*Elena left home an hour ago.*
La secretaria <u>salió</u> *a* almorzar.	*The secretary went out to lunch.*

In sentences like the following you could only use *irse*.

Estábamos en la playa platicando cuando de repente Luis se levantó y <u>se fue</u>.	*We were on the beach chatting when suddenly Luis got up and left.*
Lo siento, pero el gerente ya <u>se fue</u>.	*I am sorry, but the manager has already left.*

Salir is commonly used with travel and with means of transportation. The logic here is that the enclosure from which the traveler departs is his or her country, and for trains, buses, planes, and ships, the enclosure is the station, airport, or port.

Saldremos para España la semana entrante.	*We will leave for Spain next week.*
El tren **sale** a las nueve.	*The train leaves at nine.*
Su vuelo **sale** de Madrid esta tarde.	*Your flight leaves Madrid this afternoon.*

NOTE: The parallel term *salida* is used to indicate the **departure** of a person, flight, etc.

La **salida** del vuelo es a las cinco.	*The flight leaves at five.*

dejar (+ noun or pronoun) (transitive) = *to leave* (something or someone)

Dejé *las maletas* en el taxi.	*I left the suitcases in the taxicab.*
Su hermano *la* **dejó** en el aeropuerto.	*Her brother left her at the airport.*

dejar (+ inf.) = *to let*

No me **dejó** *pagar* nada.	*She did not let me pay for anything.*

dejar de (+ inf.) = *to stop*

De repente **dejaron de** *hablar.*	*Suddenly, they stopped talking.*

Ejercicios 8.23–8.24, páginas 418–419

13. GUIDE

el guía = *guide* (person)

El guía habló de la estatua.	*The guide spoke about the statue.*

la guía = *guide* (booklet or female guide)

Está explicado en **la guía**.	*It is explained in the guidebook.*
La guía hablaba catalán.	*The guide (fem.) spoke Catalan.*

Ejercicios 8.25–8.26, página 419: Ejercicio de repaso 8.27, página 419

14. KNOW

conocer = *to know* (someone); *to meet* (someone) *for the first time* (make someone's acquaintance) [preterite]

> <u>**Conozco**</u> a Luis.   *I know Luis.*
>
> Ayer <u>**conocí**</u> a Luis.   *Yesterday I met Luis.*

(See Section B.16 on "to meet," page 291.)

conocer = *to be familiar with* (something)

> No <u>**conozco**</u> la ciudad.   *I do not know the city.*

saber = *to know* (something)

> <u>**Saben**</u> nuestra dirección.   *They know our address.*

saber (+ inf.) = *to know how* (to do something)

> Ella <u>**sabe**</u> hablar español.   *She knows how to speak Spanish.*

saber que..., qué..., si..., cuándo... = *to know that ... , what ... , if ... , when ...*

> <u>**Sabíamos**</u> que hacía calor.   *We knew that it was hot.*
>
> No <u>**sé**</u> qué hacer.   *I do not know what to do.*
>
> ¿<u>**Sabes**</u> si llamó?   *Do you know if he called?*

Ejercicios 8.28–8.29, páginas 419–420

15. LEARN

aprender = *to acquire knowledge* (by study or intentionally)

> <u>**Aprendí**</u> el español.   *I learned Spanish.*

enterarse de = *to find out, discover* (something) *accidentally or intentionally*

> <u>**Se enteró de**</u> que nos íbamos.   *He found out we were leaving.*
>
> <u>**Se enteraron de**</u> la verdad.   *They discovered the truth.*

averiguar = *to find out* (information by investigation)

> Tengo que <u>**averiguar**</u> dónde está.   *I have to find out where it is.*

saber [preterite] = *to find out, learn about* (something) *by chance*

      Supe que estabas enfermo.   *I found out (heard) you were sick.*

Ejercicios 8.30–8.31, página 420

16. Meet

conocer [preterite] = *to meet, make* (someone's) *acquaintance*

      Lo conocí en la fiesta.   *I met him at the party.*

NOTE: When the verb *conocer* is conjugated in other tenses, it means "to know" someone or "to be familiar with" something.

encontrarse (con) = *to meet* (by appointment, by chance)

      Me encontré con ella para almorzar.   *I met her for lunch.*

      Me encontré con él en el tren.   *I ran into him on the train.*

      Nos encontraremos en el restaurante.   *We shall meet at the restaurant.*

encontrar = *to find*

      Encontré cien pesos en la calle.   *I found a hundred pesos on the street.*

      Encontraron a la niña perdida.   *They found the lost child.*

toparse con = *to meet* (run into, meet by chance)

      Se topó con mi primo en la tienda.   *He met (ran into, met by chance) my cousin at the store.*

tropezar con = *to meet* (run into, run across, stumble upon)

      Tropezó con ellos cn el cine.   *He ran into them at the movies.*

NOTE: In other contexts, *tropezar* or *tropezarse* means "to trip" or "to stumble" literally, not figuratively.

      Me tropecé y me caí.   *I tripped and fell.*

(See also Chapter 8.B.19, pages 294–295.)

Ejercicios 8.32–8.33, página 420

17. ORDER

el orden = *order, organization, neatness*

> **Es esencial que preparen este postre en el <u>orden</u> indicado.**
> *It is essential that you prepare this dessert in the order indicated.*

> **Por favor archíveme estos folletos en <u>orden</u> alfabético.**
> *Please file these brochures in alphabetical order for me.*

la orden = *order, request*

> **Recibirá sus <u>órdenes</u> del supervisor.**
> *You will receive your orders from the supervisor.*

> **¿Puedo tomarles la <u>orden</u> (el <u>pedido</u>)?**
> *May I take your order?*

> **Juan Rodríguez, a sus <u>órdenes</u>.**
> *Juan Rodríguez, at your service.*

PRÁCTICA

Ejercicios 8.34–8.35, página 421

18. PENSAR

pensar en = *to think about* (someone or something)

> **Siempre <u>pienso en</u> mi hermano cuando veo ese cuadro.**
> *I always think of my brother when I see that painting.*

> **<u>¿En</u> qué <u>piensas</u>?**
> *What are you thinking about?*

pensar de = *to think* (something [opinion]) *about* (someone or something)—it is only used in direct or indirect interrogatives

> **¿Qué <u>piensas de</u> este hotel?**
> *What do you think about this hotel?*

> **No quiso decirme lo que <u>pensaba de</u> mi comida.**
> *He did not want to tell me what he thought about my food.*

pensar (+ inf.) = *to think about, plan on* (doing something)

　　—¿Qué <u>piensas</u> *hacer* este verano?
　　—<u>Pienso</u> *trabajar* en un restaurante.
　　"What are you planning on doing this summer?"
　　"I am planning on working in a restaurant."

PRÁCTICA

Ejercicios 8.36–8.37, página 421

19. PEOPLE VS. MACHINES

PEOPLE VS. MACHINES		
	People	**Mechanical Devices**
to run	**correr**	**andar/funcionar**
	Jorge corre. *Jorge runs.*	**Mi coche anda.** *My car runs.*
	People	**Machines and Systems**
to work	**trabajar**	**andar/funcionar**
	Jorge trabaja. *Jorge works.*	**El reloj no funciona.** *The clock is not working.* **Este método funciona.** *This method works.*
	People and Events	**Motors**
to start	**comenzar/empezar**	**poner en marcha/arrancar**
	Empiezo a trabajar a las 7. *I start work at 7 o'clock.* **Comienza a las 8.** *It starts at 8 o'clock.*	**Puse el auto en marcha.** *I started the car.* **Mi coche no arranca.** *My car will not start.*
	People	**Things**
to run out	**salir corriendo**	**acabársele a uno**
	Jorge salió corriendo. *Jorge ran out.*	**Se nos acabó el tiempo.** *We ran out of time.*
	People	**Lights**
to go out	**salir**	**apagarse**
	Jorge salió. *Jorge went out.*	**Se apagó la luz.** *The light went out.*

As a general rule, remember to think about the meaning of the English expression when you have a verb used with a preposition. The following are some other prepositional usages.

To work out:

- as in a person doing exercises: **hacer ejercicio**

Hago ejercicio al levantarme por la mañana.	*I work out when I get up in the morning.*

- a problem: **resolver un problema**

No pudieron resolver el problema.	*They were unable to work out the problem.*

To run across:

- something: **dar con, tropezar con**

La busqué por todos lados hasta que al fin di con ella en la biblioteca.	*I looked for her everywhere until at last I ran across her in the library.*

- literally, a room, a place: **atravesar corriendo**

Atravesó el cuarto corriendo.	*He ran across the room.*

To run down:

- as in a liquid running down a surface: **escurrir, gotear**

El sudor le goteaba por la cara.	*The sweat ran down his face.*

- with batteries: **descargarse**

La batería se descargó durante el invierno.	*The battery ran down during the winter.*

- with watches: **acabarse la cuerda**

Se le acabó la cuerda al reloj y paró.	*The watch ran down and stopped.*

- the stairs: **bajar corriendo**

Bajamos las escaleras corriendo para recibirla.	*We ran down the stairs to greet her.*

To run into:

- e.g., a tree with your car: **chocar con**

    <u>Choqué con</u> el árbol.   *I ran into the tree.*

- a person by chance: **tropezar con, toparse con, encontrarse con**

    <u>Tropezamos con</u> / <u>Nos topamos con</u> / <u>Nos encontramos con</u> ella en la biblioteca.
    We ran into her at the library.

To turn out:

- a light: **apagar**

    <u>Apaga</u> la luz.   *Turn out the light.*

- things turn out right, wrong, etc.: **las cosas salen bien, mal, etc.**

    —¿Cómo <u>salió</u> todo?   *"How did everything turn out?"*
    —**Bien.**   *"Okay."*

(See also Chapter 8.B.16, page 291.)

Ejercicios 8.38–8.39, páginas 421–422

20. PLAY

jugar = *to play* (a game)

    Me gusta <u>jugar</u> al ajedrez.   *I like to play chess.*

tocar = *to play* (an instrument)

    Ella <u>toca</u> el piano.   *She plays the piano.*

a play = **una obra (de teatro)** [theater play], **una jugada** [sports, games]

a game = **un juego** [board game, card game, etc.], **un partido** [team sport, unit], **una partida** [game unit, round]

Ejercicios 8.40–8.41, página 422; Ejercicio de repaso 8.42, páginas 422–423

21. PUT

poner = *to put; to set* (table)

<u>Pusimos</u> la llave sobre la mesa.	*We put the key on the table.*
<u>Pongan</u> la mesa.	*Set the table.*

guardar, ahorrar = *to put away*

<u>Guarden</u> los platos.	*Put the plates away.*
Necesito <u>ahorrar</u> algo de dinero.	*I need to put some money away.*

NOTE: There are many other uses of this expression in English: check the dictionary when you want to use it.

meter = *to put in*

¿<u>Metiste</u> el coche en el garaje?	*Did you put the car in the garage?*
El niño <u>se metió</u> el dedo en la boca.	*The boy put his finger in his mouth.*

ponerse = *to put on; to become* (when used with an adjective)

<u>Me puse</u> el abrigo.	*I put my coat on.*
<u>Se puso</u> azul.	*He became blue.*

aguantar, soportar = *to put up with, to stand*

Tengo que <u>aguantar</u> todas tus quejas.	*I have to put up with all of your complaints.*
¡Ya no <u>aguanto</u> el calor!	*I can't stand the heat any more!*
No sé cómo me <u>soporta</u>.	*I don't know how (s)he puts up with me.*

NOTE: "To support" someone morally is *apoyar;* financially it is *mantener.*

PRÁCTICA

Ejercicios 8.43–8.44, página 423

22. REALIZE

darse cuenta de = *to realize*

> **No <u>me di cuenta de</u> la hora que era.**
> *I did not realize what time it was.*

> **No <u>te das cuenta de</u> las implicaciones de tus actos.**
> *You do not realize the implications of your actions.*

realizar = *to come true, to carry out*

> **Ahora sí que se me <u>realizará</u> el sueño de viajar a Sudamérica.**
> *Now my dream to travel to South America will really (**sí**) come true.*

> **Ese empleado <u>realiza</u> sus funciones con mucha eficacia.**
> *That employee carries out his duties very efficiently.*

Ejercicios 8.45–8.46, páginas 423–424

23. SERVE

servirle = *to serve* (a person); *to help*

¿Le <u>sirvo</u> más vino?	*Shall I serve you more wine?*
¿Le <u>serviste</u> agua a esa persona?	*Did you serve that person water?*
¿En qué puedo <u>servirle</u>?	*How may I help you?*

servirlo, servirla, servir algo = *to serve something*

—**Ya es hora de <u>servir</u> la comida.**	*"It is time to serve the meal."*
—**¿Dónde está la ensalada?**	*"Where is the salad?"*
—**Ya la <u>serví</u>.**	*"I already served it."*

(See also Chapter 8.B.5, pages 281–282.)

Ejercicios 8.47–8.48, página 424

24. SPEND

gastar = *to spend* (money)

> **<u>Gastamos</u> mucho en ese viaje.**   *We spent a lot on that trip.*

pasar = *to spend* (time)

> **<u>Pasamos</u> tres semanas allá.**   *We spent three weeks there.*

desperdiciar = *to waste*

> **No <u>desperdicies</u> dinero.**   *Do not waste money.*

> **No <u>desperdicien</u> mi tiempo.**   *Do not waste my time.*

Ejercicios 8.49–8.50, páginas 424–425

25. TAKE

tomar = *to take*
llevar = *to take* (away, in a specified direction)
llevarse = *to take* (away, no specified direction)

tomar = *to take* (something [a bus, etc.], drink)

> **<u>Tomó</u> la llave sin decir nada.**   *He took the key without saying anything.*

> **Quiero <u>tomar</u> una cerveza bien fría.**   *I want to drink a very cold beer.*

> **<u>Tome</u> el autobús.**   *Take the bus.*

> **¿Cuánto tiempo <u>tomará</u>?**   *How long will it take?*

Toma (Tome usted) is used when you hand someone something ("Here.").

> —**¿Tienes un lápiz?**   *"Do you have a pencil?"*
> —**Sí. <u>Toma.</u>** (*handing out the pencil*)   *"Yes. Here."*
> —**Gracias.**   *"Thanks."*

llevar = *to take* (someone or something [somewhere]) (English also uses "bring" for this. Spanish distinguishes between movement **away from** the speaker's place [*llevar*] versus **to** the speaker's place [*traer*].)

Llevamos a mis padres al aeropuerto.	*We took my parents to the airport.*
Llevaremos toallas a la playa.	*We will take towels to the beach.*

llevarse = *to take* (something away, with oneself)

El mesero **se llevó** mi tenedor.	*The waiter took my fork away.*

apuntar / bajar = *to take down*

La operadora **apuntó** el mensaje.	*The operator took down the message.*
El botones **bajará** su equipaje.	*The bellboy will take (bring) your luggage down.*

subir = *to take up*

El botones **subirá** el equipaje.	*The bellboy will take the luggage up.*

admitir / alojar = *to take in*

Esa casa de huéspedes sólo **admite** adultos.	*That guesthouse only takes in adults.*

sacar = *to take out*

Sacaron a los niños a pasear.	*They took the children out for a stroll.*

quitarse = *to take off*

Se quitó la ropa para bañarse.	*He took off his clothes to bathe.*

tener lugar = *to take place*

El concierto **tendrá lugar** esta noche.	*The concert will take place tonight.*

traer = *to bring* (toward the speaker only)

El mesero nos **trajo** la comida muy rápido.	*The waiter brought us the food very quickly.*

PRÁCTICA

Ejercicios 8.51–8.52, página 425

26. TIME

tiempo = *time; weather*

No tengo <u>tiempo</u> para ayudarte hoy.	*I do not have time to help you today.*
Hace buen <u>tiempo</u> hoy.	*The weather is nice today.*

vez = *time* (countable)

Toma café cuatro <u>veces</u> al día.	*He drinks coffee four times a day.*
Esta <u>vez</u> yo pago.	*This time, I will pay.*

hora = *time* (chronological)

—**¿Qué <u>hora</u> es?**	*"What time is it?"*
—**Es <u>hora</u> de irnos.**	*"It is time to leave."*

rato = *time, while*
ratito = *a little while*

Hace <u>rato</u> (ratito) que estoy esperando.	*I have been waiting for some time (a [little] while).*

divertirse = *to have a good time*

<u>Nos divertimos</u> mucho en la fiesta ayer.	*We had a very good time at the party yesterday.*
BUT: **Ayer tuvimos buen tiempo.**	*Yesterday we had good weather.*

Ejercicios 8.53–8.54, páginas 425–426

27. WHAT

¿Qué es... ? = *What is ... ?* (asking for a definition)

<u>¿Qué es</u> un "cántaro"?	*What is a "cántaro"?*

¿Cuál es... ? = *What is ... ?* (asking for identification or specification)

<u>¿Cuál es</u> la diferencia entre los dos?	*What is the difference between the two?*

¿Qué (+ noun) ... ? = *What, Which* (+ noun) ... ?

¿Qué *libro* **leíste anoche?**	*What (Which) book did you read last night?*
¿Qué *ciudades* **visitaste en Sudamérica?**	*What cities did you visit in South America?*
¿Qué (*comida*) **vamos a comer?**	*What are we going to eat?*
¿Qué (*ropa*) **te vas a poner esta nochc?**	*What are you going to wear tonight?*

¿Cómo? = *Excuse me?*

NOTE: *¿Cómo?* is more polite in Spanish than *¿Qué?* for "What?" when asking for someone to repeat what they just said.

¿Cómo? OR: **¿Cómo dijo?**

Lo que = *What* (relative pronoun, not used in interrogatives)

Lo que me gusta de la película es el misterio.	*What I like about the movie is the mystery.*
No me dijo **lo que** quería.	*He did not tell me what he wanted.*

PRÁCTICA

Ejercicios 8.55–8.56, página 426; Ejercicio de repaso 8.57, página 426

Ejercicios

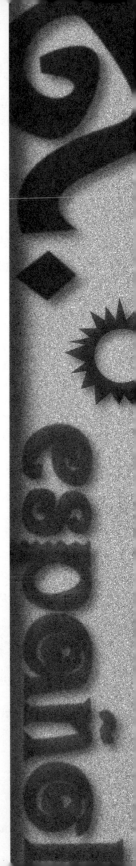

Chapter 1   Overview

The following exercises are designed for self-correcting. The answer key section begins on page 473.

 Sentence Components

[Chapter 1.A, pages 2–5]

Ejercicio 1.1   *Identifique las palabras en negrilla* (boldfaced) *en las frases siguientes.*

Modelo: Me gusta **el** café **negro.**

   *el: artículo definido; **negro:** adjetivo calificativo*

1. Después **de** trabajar varias horas **en** la computadora, **se** me cansan los ojos.
2. Cuando estudio, me gusta poner música **clásica** en el tocadiscos.   **3. Ayer** fuimos al parque **a** jugar a la pelota con unos **amigos.**   **4. Mi** mamá me llamó **por** teléfono ayer a **las** ocho de la mañana.   **5. Este** libro es más interesante que **ése.**   **6.** Me gustan **tus** zapatos más que los **míos.**   **7. Algunos** profesores son más estrictos que **otros.**   **8.** El libro **que** compré ayer me costó **mucho** dinero.   **9.** Mi hermana me dijo **que** tú eras **un** futbolista famoso.   **10.** Tengo dos dólares **y** veinte centavos, **pero** no es suficiente para ir al cine.

Ejercicio 1.2   *Haga el análisis gramatical de las siguientes oraciones.*

Modelo: Juan estudia español.

   Juan: *sustantivo propio, sujeto del verbo "estudia" ; **estudia:** verbo estudiar, 3ª persona singular del presente del indicativo; **español:** sustantivo común, masc. sing., objeto directo del verbo "estudia"*

1. Los niños cantaron una canción.   **2.** Marta me regaló este libro.   **3.** Estos ejercicios son fáciles.

 Verb Structure

[Chapter 1.B, page 6]

Ejercicio 1.3   *Identifique el modo (MAYÚSCULA) y el tiempo (minúscula) de los verbos en negrilla.*

MODELO: El niño **llegó cantando** de la escuela; **estaba** contento porque le **habían dado** un premio por **portarse** bien.

llegó: INDICATIVO pretérito; cantando: PARTICIPIO presente; estaba: INDICATIVO imperfecto; habían dado: INDICATIVO pluscuamperfecto; portarse: INFINITIVO

Estábamos todos en la cocina **preparando** la cena cuando mi hermana **anunció** que tenía buenas noticias —**se había ganado** la lotería. Mi mamá le dijo que **pensara** con mucho cuidado en lo que quería **hacer** con el dinero, porque si no, lo **gastaría** todo y luego se arrepentiría. Pero mi hermana ya lo había planeado todo. —No te **preocupes,** Mami; a ti y a Papi les **daré** la mitad para que la **pongan** en el banco, y el resto lo usaré para comprarme ropa y otras cosas que **necesito.**

 # Sentence Structure

[Chapter 1.C, pages 7–13]

Ejercicio 1.4 *Subraye los verbos conjugados en el texto siguiente.*

MODELO: Ayer mis hermanos y yo nos levantamos temprano.

Ayer mis hermanos y yo nos <u>levantamos</u> temprano.

Para las vacaciones de Navidad, mi papá, mi hermana y yo íbamos a San Blas, y nos quedábamos en un hotel en la playa. La noche de Navidad, cuando todos los demás estaban celebrando en el hotel, nos íbamos a un lugar ya seleccionado en la playa oscura y hacíamos un fuego con leña que habíamos recogido el día anterior. Llevábamos comida para cocinar en el fuego, y pasábamos la noche allí, oyendo las olas del mar y mirando las estrellas.

Ejercicio 1.5 *Divida el texto en cláusulas usando una barra (/) y cuente el total de cláusulas.*

MODELO: Tengo una hermana que vive en España.

Tengo una hermana / que vive en España. (2)

Necesito que me ayudes a preparar la cena. Tendremos cinco invitados a cenar y quiero que todo esté perfecto. ¿Podrías poner la mesa, por favor? Y cuando acabes con eso, ven a la cocina para ayudarme con la comida. Las verduras para la ensalada están lavadas; sólo hay que cortarlas y ponerlas en la ensaladera. Quiero prepararles la receta de pollo que les gustó tanto la última vez que vinieron.

Ejercicio 1.6   *Subraye todas las cláusulas independientes del texto siguiente.*

MODELO: Me desperté a las tres y bajé a hacerme café sin que nadie me oyera.

Me desperté a las tres y *bajé a hacerme café sin que nadie me oyera.*

El invierno está casi terminado. Ya no hace frío, y la nieve se ha transformado en lluvia. Pronto tendremos que empezar a preparar el jardín para que podamos plantar las hortalizas. Estoy tan contento de que la primavera esté en camino porque me gusta el calor. El invierno aquí es tan triste y gris, y me canso de la ropa pesada que tengo que ponerme.

Ejercicio 1.7   *Subraye todas las cláusulas principales del mismo texto.*

MODELO: Me desperté a las tres y bajé a hacerme café sin que nadie me oyera.

Me desperté a las tres y <u>*bajé a hacerme café*</u> *sin que nadie me oyera.*

El invierno está casi terminado. Ya no hace frío, y la nieve se ha transformado en lluvia. Pronto tendremos que empezar a preparar el jardín para que podamos plantar las hortalizas. Estoy tan contento de que la primavera esté en camino porque me gusta el calor. El invierno aquí es tan triste y gris, y me canso de la ropa pesada que tengo que ponerme.

Ejercicio 1.8   *Subraye todas las cláusulas subordinadas del mismo texto.*

MODELO: Me desperté a las tres y bajé a hacerme café sin que nadie me oyera.

Me desperté a las tres y bajé a hacerme café <u>*sin que nadie me oyera*</u>.

El invierno está casi terminado. Ya no hace frío, y la nieve se ha transformado en lluvia. Pronto tendremos que empezar a preparar el jardín para que podamos plantar las hortalizas. Estoy tan contento de que la primavera esté en camino porque me gusta el calor. El invierno aquí es tan triste y gris, y me canso de la ropa pesada que tengo que ponerme.

Ejercicio 1.9   *Haga el análisis lógico de las frases siguientes.*

MODELO: Quiero que me ayudes a preparar la cena.

Quiero: *cláusula principal;* **que me ayudes... cena:** *cláusula subordinada nominal, objeto directo de "quiero"*

1. Necesito un libro que describa la revolución mexicana.   **2.** Te prestaré dinero a condición de que me pagues mañana.   **3.** Sé que no puedes hablar ahora.

Ejercicio 1.10   *Haga el diagrama de las frases siguientes. (Use los diagramas del capítulo para inspirarse.)*

1. Quiero que veas el libro que conseguí sobre la revolución mexicana.   **2.** Es necesario que los norteamericanos comprendan que estas tierras les pertenecían a los mexicanos originalmente, y que antes eran de los indios que vivieron en ellas por siglos.   **3.** Me pidió que le comprara pan y le contesté que no tenía dinero.

Accents (Syllabification: Consonants)

[Chapter 1.D.1, pages 14–15]

En los siguientes ejercicios, divida cada palabra en sílabas.

Ejercicio 1.11   Consonantes sencillas intervocálicas.

raza	meta	visa	callo	serrano
fecha	cerro	caballo	metiche	

Ejercicio 1.12   Dos consonantes intervocálicas.

campo	pantera	ángulo	musgo	refresco
fantoche	mantilla	mercado	sincero	cencerro
vibra	hablo	autografiar	retrato	adrenalina
reflorecer	aglomerar	negro	aplastar	reprimir
declive				

Ejercicio 1.13   Tres o más consonantes intervocálicas.

anglosajón	empresario	constante	estrecho	espléndido
instituto	inspección	instrumento	embrollo	transmitir
resplandor	transcribir			

Accents (Syllabification: Vowels)

[Chapter 1.D.1, pages 15–17]

Ejercicio 1.14   Hiatos.

recaer	crear	creer	veo	sea
caos	boa	coactar	coexistir	gentío
frío	reí	vestía	etíope	ataúd
raíz	vía	mío	reúnan	continúa
rehúsa				

Ejercicio 1.15   Diptongos.

aviador	aire	bienestar	deleite	miope
oiga	resguardo	causa	fueron	endeudarse
fuimos	diurno	duodeno	Dios	hueso
cariátide	recién	comió	aguántate	acuérdense
cantáis	volvéis	óiganlos	enjáulalo	

Ejercicio 1.16   Triptongos y otras combinaciones.

veían	seáis	caíamos	esquiáis	vivíais
traían	caeríais	oíais	enviéis	creías
actuéis	adquirierais			

Ejercicio 1.17   La "h" intervocálica.

ahora	rehago	ahí	rehíce	prohíben
rehúsa	ahogar	desahogar	ahumado	cacahuate
alcahuete	cohete	rehúyen	sobrehumano	zaherir

Ejercicio 1.18   Repaso.

divida	las	siguientes	palabras	en
sílabas	luego	vea	cuando	necesitan
acentos	porque	rey	reina	voy
boina	bueno	bien		

Accents (Stress)

[Chapter 1.D.2, pages 17–24]

Ejercicio 1.19   *Indique para cada palabra si es **aguda, llana, esdrújula** o **sobresdrújula**.*

1. camino   2. caminó   3. caminaba   4. caminábamos   5. caminad   6. compra
7. compró   8. compraba   9. comprábamos   10. cómpralo   11. cómpramelo
12. español   13. españoles   14. francés   15. trances   16. encéstalo

Ejercicio 1.20   *Las siguientes palabras son **agudas**. Póngales acento a las que lo necesiten.*

1. presto   2. enterrar   3. preparad   4. desperte   5. dividir   6. farol   7. piedad
8. pedi   9. peor   10. caiman   11. cocinar   12. imparcial   13. cajon   14. finlandes
15. trajin   16. temblor   17. cristal   18. riñon

Ejercicio 1.21 *Las siguientes palabras son **llanas**. Póngales acento a las que lo necesiten.*

1. lapiz **2.** llamas **3.** llaman **4.** pluma **5.** hablaron **6.** españoles **7.** dioses
8. dia **9.** deme **10.** españolita **11.** peruano **12.** consigo **13.** traje **14.** examen
15. caracter **16.** lunes **17.** labio **18.** infertil

Ejercicio 1.22 *Las siguientes palabras son **esdrújulas** y **sobresdrújulas**; la sílaba tónica (con énfasis) de las palabras de más de una sílaba está subrayada. ¿Necesitan acento?*

1. matalo **2.** regalamelo **3.** callense **4.** estupido **5.** parpado **6.** capitulo
7. projimo **8.** bajame **9.** animo **10.** cascara **11.** decada **12.** exito **13.** pajaro
14. aspero **15.** hungaro **16.** vinculo **17.** maquina **18.** pildora

Ejercicio 1.23 *Póngales acento a los adverbios que lo necesiten. (La sílaba con énfasis en la parte del adjetivo original está subrayada.)*

1. rapidamente **2.** facilmente **3.** lentamente **4.** dificilmente **5.** piadosamente
6. brillantemente **7.** friamente **8.** despiadadamente **9.** secamente **10.** felizmente
11. fijamente **12.** calidamente **13.** cientificamente **14.** misericordiosamente
15. solamente **16.** finalmente **17.** gravemente **18.** proximamente

Ejercicio 1.24 *Las palabras siguientes son **monosílabas**; no hay nada subrayado porque el énfasis es único. Póngales acento si lo necesitan. (Las frases están traducidas por si se necesita.)*

1. A el le va bien. *(It's going well for him.)* **2.** Di que el rey te lo dio. *(Say that the king gave it to you.)* **3.** Vio a Dios. *(She saw God.)* **4.** El te no me da tos. *(Tea doesn't make me cough.)* **5.** No se si se fue. *(I don't know if he left.)* **6.** Tu no le des. *(Don't you feed her.)* **7.** Tu voz se te va. *(Your voice is going.)* **8.** Sin ti no se lo da. *(Without you she won't give it to her.)* **9.** No le de la fe. *(Don't give him your faith.)* **10.** Yo si se la di. *(I did give it to her.)* **11.** A ti te doy lo que hay. *(I give you what there is.)* **12.** No hay mas miel por mi. *(There is no more honey because of me.)*

Ejercicio 1.25 *Ponga un acento donde se necesite; la sílaba tónica (con énfasis) de las palabras de más de una sílaba está subrayada.*

1. Aun los ricos necesitan amor. **2.** Los niños aun no han comido. **3.** Estoy solo.
4. Solo me siento solo cuando ando mal acompañado. **5.** Pasame esa llave, por favor. **6.** No quiero esta fruta, prefiero esa. **7.** Por eso no quiso ir con nosotros.
8. Me gustaria comprarme ese terreno. **9.** ¡Que buena suerte tienes! **10.** ¡Como canta!

Ejercicio 1.26   *Ponga un acento sobre los **que** que lo necesiten.*

1. Prefiero **que** no llueva.   **2.** ¿**Que** dijiste?   **3.** No sé **que** dije.   **4.** Creo **que** dije **que** preferiría **que** no lloviera.   **5.** ¡**Que** locura!   **6.** Dime **que** crees.   **7.** El día **que** no llueva aquí, no sabremos **que** hacer.   **8.** Haremos lo **que** ustedes quieran.   **9.** La última vez **que** vinieron, nos costó mucho decidir **que** cuarto darles.   **10.** ¡**Que** duerman en el piso!

Ejercicio 1.27   *Llene el espacio en blanco con **porque** o **por qué**; traduzca las frases 4 y 5.*

1. Te llamé _____ tengo noticias.   **2.** ¿_____ no me llamaste antes?   **3.** No te puedo decir _____: ¡es un secreto!   **4.** El asesino no pudo explicar _____ había matado al policía.   **5.** El asesino no lo pudo explicar _____ había matado al policía.   **6.** Yo creo que lo hizo _____ tenía miedo.   **7.** ¿Tú matarías a alguien simplemente _____ tienes miedo?   **8.** ¿ _____ no?   **9.** ¡_____ no se debe matar a nadie!   **10.** No sé _____ se fue.   **11.** Se fue _____ no le hacías caso.

Ejercicio 1.28   *Póngale acento a **como** si lo necesita; traduzca las frases 4–7.*

1. Como no tengo hambre, no **como**.   **2.** ¿**Como** puedes decir eso?   **3.** Necesitas pensar **como** yo para comprenderme.   **4.** Muéstrame **como** comes con palillos.   **5.** ¡**Como** comes!   **6.** ¿**Como como**?   **7. Como como como**.   **8.** Ella se viste **como** yo.   **9.** Es un libro **como** los demás.   **10.** Si baila **como** canta, ha de ser una maravilla.

Ejercicio 1.29   *Póngale acento a **cuanto** si lo necesita.*

1. ¿**Cuanto** cuesta este cuarto?   **2.** No sé **cuanto** cuesta.   **3.** ¿**Cuantos** hermanos tienes?   **4.** Me pregunto **cuantos** años tiene esa mujer.   **5.** Nadie sabe **cuantas** veces se repetirá.   **6.** Le di **cuanto** dinero tenía al ladrón.   **7.** No sabe **cuanto** me arrepentí de darle mi dinero.   **8.** La profesora le dará **cuanta** información tenga.

Ejercicio 1.30   *Póngale acento a **donde** si lo necesita.*

1. ¿**Donde** vives?   **2.** Vivo **donde** viven mis padres.   **3.** No sé **donde** vive mi amiga.   **4.** Me dijo **donde** vivía, pero se me olvidó.   **5.** Apunté su dirección en la libreta **donde** tengo todas las direcciones.   **6.** No sé **donde** puse la libreta.   **7.** ¿No estará **donde** siempre la pones?

Ejercicio 1.31   *Póngale acento a **cuando** si lo necesita; traduzca las frases 7 y 8.*

1. Llegarán **cuando** estemos en la finca.   **2.** ¿**Cuando** llegas?   **3.** No me dijo **cuando** iban a llegar.   **4. Cuando** lleguen, les serviremos cerveza.   **5.** ¿Nos escondemos **cuando** los veamos llegar?   **6. Cuando** me gradúe, iré al Caribe.   **7.** ¿ ...**cuando** te gradúes?   **8.** ¿**Cuando** te gradúas?

Ejercicio 1.32   *Póngale acento a **quien** si lo necesita.*

1. ¿**Quien** se llevó mi paraguas?   **2.** No sé **quien** se lo llevó.   **3.** El amigo con **quien** vino Marieta tenía paraguas.   **4.** ¿Te dijo **quien** era el chico con **quien** estaba?   **5.** No me dijo con **quien** había venido.   **6.** Dime con **quien** andas y te diré **quien** eres.

Accents (Review)

Ejercicio 1.33   *Ponga un acento sobre las vocales que lo necesiten; la sílaba con énfasis está subrayada, a menos que sea monosílaba.*

ARMANDO: ¿Esta Juan?

MIGUEL: Creo que fue al cine, y no se cuando va a regresar. ¿Para que lo quieres?

ARMANDO: Quiero pedirle prestado un libro para mi clase de español.

MIGUEL: ¿Sabes que libro es?

ARMANDO: Si. Es uno que tiene la portada negra.

MIGUEL: Yo se donde lo tiene, pero no estoy seguro si te lo podria prestar.

ARMANDO: A mi me dijo que no lo necesitaba este semestre.

MIGUEL: Si tu te lo llevas, y el lo necesita, yo voy a sentirme muy mal. ¿Por que no te tomas una taza de te, y esperas a que regrese Juan?

ARMANDO: Bueno. Mientras espero, prestame el libro para mirarlo, por favor.

MIGUEL: Voy a buscarlo. [...] ¿Es este, verdad?

ARMANDO: No, ese no. Es el otro, el de gramatica. Tiene casi la misma portada, pero un titulo diferente.

MIGUEL: A ver si lo encuentro; esperame. [...] Aqui lo tienes.

ARMANDO: Gracias.

Ejercicio 1.34   Temas de ensayo.

Escriba un párrafo en el pasado sobre uno de los temas siguientes. Cada vez que escriba una palabra, piense en la pronunciación correcta de la palabra, y decida si necesita acento o no.

- un momento inolvidable
- una experiencia cómica
- una lección cultural

ATAJO

Phrases: Describing the past; Sequencing events
Vocabulary: Emotions
Grammar: Accents; Verbs: Preterite; Verbs: Imperfect

Chapter 2   Nouns and Noun Determiners

 ## Nouns and Their Equivalents (Introduction)

[Chapter 2.A.1, pages 26–29]

Ejercicio 2.1   *Conceptual questions.*

What is a noun? What type of grammatical functions can it have in a sentence? What other types of words can behave this way? What is a nominalized word? Can you think of an example?

Ejercicio 2.2   *Traduzca las oraciones siguientes, usando equivalentes de nombres para lo subrayado.* ("*lo subrayado*" = what is underlined)

1. "Which of these books is mine?" "That one is <u>yours</u>."   **2.** I prefer <u>walking</u> in the morning.   **3.** <u>Tall people</u> and <u>blonde people</u> always stand out here. (stand out = *sobresalir*)   **4.** In the Hispanic world, <u>older people</u> live with their families.
5. <u>Decent people</u> often lose.   **6.** <u>The good guy</u> and <u>the bad guy</u> in this movie look alike *(se parecen)*.   **7.** <u>Good and evil</u> are enemies.   **8.** <u>What is strange</u> is the color.
9. <u>That foreigner</u> speaks Spanish.   **10.** Sometimes <u>what is foreign</u> is frightening (*asusta*) because it's different.   **11.** In this picture, <u>the one in the grey suit</u> *(traje)* is my father, <u>the one with the hat</u> is my brother, and <u>the ones above</u> are my cousins.

Nouns and Their Equivalents (Nouns: Gender and Number)

[Chapter 2.A.2.a–b, pages 29–32]

Ejercicio 2.3   *Use un artículo definido con cada palabra para indicar si es masculina o femenina.*

Esa mañana cuando vio _____ amanecer, renació en ella brevemente _____ amor por _____ vida. Recordó _____ cena de aquella última noche, _____ sal y _____ miel que había puesto en _____ arroz exótico que había preparado para celebrar su aniversario; recordó _____ poema que su marido le había leído; y también recordó

_____ metal helado de_____ barandal en que se había recargado para no desmayarse, _____ auto, _____ barro, _____ ataúd. Y luego revivió _____ días que pasó en _____ cama, sin salir nunca de _____ casa en que habían vivido tantos años juntos; por _____ mañana recogía _____ periódico, hacía _____ crucigrama, leía sobre _____ problemas de _____ capital, _____ carril extra que iban a poner, _____ catedral y _____ cárcel que se tenían que reparar. Y miraba _____ césped que no paraba de crecer, y todas _____ ramas que se acumulaban porque había perdido _____ costumbre de cuidar _____ propiedad. Miraba _____ televisión, buscaba _____ dramas con _____ tramas más simples, _____ telenovelas, y _____ programas sensacionalistas, como el que hablaba sobre _____ hotel en que todos _____ huéspedes tenían pesadillas. Se le estaba olvidando _____ español, _____ idioma que hablaba con él. Tenía frente a ella _____ foto de su marido, y un recorte de periódico con _____ cara de_____ juez que le había dado _____ libertad a _____ asesino. Pasó _____ mano por _____ papel como para tocar de nuevo al ser que había perdido; acercó _____ imagen a _____ luz. Sintió _____ piel que le ardía por _____ rabia. _____ lunes iría a _____ corte, y llevaría _____ lápiz que había encontrado y que serviría posiblemente de prueba; les hablaría de_____ ruido que había oído que era como _____ señal de_____ radar de un coche. No podía aceptar que _____ corrupción en _____ sistema hubiera llegado a tal punto. No sabía si se atrevería a irse en _____ moto de su marido, o si tomaría en vez _____ tranvía. Miró _____ mapa de _____ ciudad para determinar _____ distancia. Era increíble _____ poder de_____ mal, y _____ imposibilidad de elevar _____ moral después de semejante lección. Después de luchar por _____ justicia, se daría _____ viaje que habían planeado darse juntos a _____ Pirineos.

Ejercicio 2.4 *Escriba el equivalente femenino de las siguientes palabras.*

el hombre, el estudiante, el joven, el actor, el modelo, el turista, el rey, el policía, el comunista, el toro

Ejercicio 2.5 *Indique en español la diferencia de significado entre el masculino y el femenino de los siguientes nombres.*

1. el policía / la policía   **2.** el papa / la papa   **3.** el guía / la guía   **4.** el cura / la cura

Nouns and Their Equivalents (Personal A)

[Chapter 2.A.3, pages 32–34]

Ejercicio 2.6 *Llene el espacio en blanco con el **a** personal si se necesita.*

1. Le gusta mirar _____ la televisión.   **2.** Vimos _____ nuestros vecinos en el centro.
3. No reconocieron _____ mi hermano.   **4.** ¿ _____ quién viste hoy?   **5.** ¿ _____ qué

viste hoy?   **6.** Estoy buscando _____ mis llaves.   **7.** Esa compañía busca _____ empleados nuevos.   **8.** El jefe buscaba _____ su secretaria.   **9.** Tienen _____ tres gatos.   **10.** Tiene _____ su hijo en una escuela privada.   **11.** _____ ellas no las vieron hasta el final.   **12.** No oímos _____ nadie.   **13.** ¿Viste _____ alguien? **14.** ¿Quieres _____ algo?

Ejercicio 2.7   *Sustituya el objeto directo en negrilla con las palabras entre parén-tesis, y añada el **a** personal cada vez que se necesite. Fíjese que los verbos **mirar** (to look at), **esperar** (to wait for, to expect) y **buscar** (to look for) en español toman un objeto directo.*

1. Miro **el libro.** (el jardín, mi hermanito, tus ojos, la pizarra, la película, los veci-nos, el periódico, el espejo) [*I look at the book, the garden, my little brother, your eyes, the blackboard, the movie, the neighbors, the newspaper, the mirror*]

2. No oye **el teléfono.** (Juan, mi gato, nadie, la tarea, el profesor, la explosión, tu voz, los niños en la calle, nada) [*He doesn't hear the telephone, Juan, my cat, nobody, the assignment, the professor, the explosion, your voice, the children in the street, nothing*]

3. Jorge tiene **un apartamento.** (un hermano, una computadora, dos coches, su abuelo en un asilo de ancianos) [*Jorge has an apartment, a brother, a computer, two cars, his grandfather in a home*]

4. Quiero **dinero.** (amigos, felicidad, amor, comida, mis padres, mi familia, vivir bien) [*I want money, friends, happiness, love, food; I love my parents, my family; I want to live well*]

5. Espera **mi llamada.** (la alarma, Luis, su respuesta, tus hermanos, tu padre, alguien, ¿Quién?, ¿Qué?) [*Wait for my call, the alarm, Luis, his answer, your brothers, your father, someone, Whom is (s)he waiting for? What is (s)he waiting for?*]

6. Vio **una casa.** (una amiga, la pantalla, el reloj, mi perro, la carta, la gente que quería, gente) [*He saw a house, a friend, the screen, the watch, my dog, the letter, the people he wanted, people*]

7. Buscaban **respuestas.** (el banco, una receta, sus hijos, empleados, algo, sus gatitos, alguien, ¿Quién?, ¿Qué?) [*They were looking for answers, the bank, a recipe, their children, employees, something, their kittens, someone, Whom were they looking for?, What were they looking for?*]

Ejercicio 2.8   *Traduzca al español, usando el **a** personal cuando se necesite.*

She looked at the mirror and then she looked at her fiancé *(novio)* out in the garden. Then, she checked *(verificó)* her make-up *(maquillaje)* and her hairdo *(peinado),* and admired her dress. She had two sisters who had gotten married before her. She had

her mother waiting outside while she spent one last moment alone. She loved
Rodolfo. She had never met anyone like him. She wanted this wedding, but she was
afraid. She didn't want to lose her childhood. She didn't want to lose her family.
Suddenly, she heard her name. She heard her mother. And she remembered her
mother and her father and their happiness. And she felt ready.

Noun Determiners (Articles: Definite Articles)

[Chapter 2.B.1.a, pages 34–39]

Ejercicio 2.9 *Póngale a cada nombre el artículo definido correcto. Todos los
nombres de la lista son femeninos, pero ¿usan **la** o **el**?*

avioneta, atracción, avenida, agua, alarma, alma, ama, águila, aguja, autonomía, aula,
avicultura, ave, habitación, habichuela, hacha, hamburguesa, hambre, hartura, aguas,
alarmas, almas, hambres

Ejercicio 2.10 *Llene el espacio en blanco con un artículo definido si se necesita.*

1. _____ vida debe disfrutarse.   2. _____ señor Ruiz dice que _____ chocolate es
malo para _____ salud, pero _____ doña Luisa sabe que él come _____ chocolate
todos los días.   3. —_____ Señorita Guzmán, ¿le gusta _____ chocolate?   4. Ayer
compramos _____ verduras, pero no tenían _____ verduras que tú pediste.   5. _____
inglés es más difícil que _____ español.   6. Hablo _____ español, pero sueño en
_____ inglés.   7. Mi clase de _____ español es la más divertida de todas.   8. Aprendí _____ español cuando tenía seis años.   9. A mi padre le costó trabajo aprender
_____ español.   10. Salieron temprano de _____ escuela y, como su padre había
salido de _____ cárcel ese día, fueron a _____ iglesia a dar gracias.   11. Salimos de
_____ clase y fuimos directamente a _____ casa porque teníamos que vestirnos para
llegar a _____ misa a tiempo.   12. _____ miércoles vamos a tener una prueba.
13. ¡Hasta _____ jueves!   14. Hoy es _____ viernes.

Ejercicio 2.11 *Traduzca, usando artículos definidos donde se necesiten.*

1. Happiness is found in love.   2. Family and friends are the basis of a good life.
3. I speak Spanish. I read French easily.   4. Let's go home.   5. See you Monday!
(Hasta…)   6. People who need people are lucky.   7. People arrived constantly.
8. News in the papers is mostly bad news.   9. Professor López, news about your
colleague Professor Gómez came today.   10. I washed my hands.   11. She raised her
hand.   12. They put him in jail.   13. On Friday there's no class.   14. The chicken is
for Tuesday.

Noun Determiners (Articles: Indefinite Articles)

[Chapter 2.B.1.b, pages 39–40]

Ejercicio 2.12 *Llene el espacio en blanco con un artículo indefinido si se necesita.*

1. Jorge es _____ arquitecto. **2.** Carlitos es _____ argentino. **3.** Rafael es _____ hombre interesante. **4.** Es _____ cantante mexicano. **5.** Georgina es _____ protestante muy severa. **6.** ¡Qué _____ dilema! **7.** ¡Qué _____ lindo día! **8.** Esa viejita acaba de cumplir _____ cien años. **9.** Vamos a discutir _____ otro tema ahora. **10.** Tomaría _____ mil años corregir el daño que se ha hecho. Lo dudo —yo creo que tomaría _____ millón. **11.** Dentro de _____ media hora nos iremos. **12.** No tengo _____ bicicleta. **13.** Ese pobre chico no tiene ni _____ amigo. **14.** Se fue sin _____ chaqueta.

Ejercicio 2.13 *Traduzca.*

Margarita was Puerto Rican. She was a student at the University of Puerto Rico. She was a hardworking student, and she had a certain style in the way she expressed herself that her professors considered original. She once won a prize of a hundred dollars for an analytic essay. She wrote one hundred words on one topic, with three and a half pages of reference. She wrote without a computer; she didn't even have a typewriter. What a writer! Nobody had ever seen such a thing. There hasn't been another writer of her quality since she graduated.

Noun Determiners (Adjectives: Demonstrative Adjectives)

[Chapter 2.B.2.a, page 41]

Ejercicio 2.14 *Llene cada espacio en blanco con todas las posibilidades.*

este, esta, estos, estas, ese, esa, esos, esas, aquel, aquella, aquellos, aquellas

1. ¿De quién es _____ automóvil? **2.** ¿Para quién son _____ mensajes? **3.** ¿Por qué viajan por _____ carreteras? **4.** ¿Te acuerdas de _____ mañana? **5.** ¿Por qué no paramos en _____ gasolinera? **6.** _____ mapa no nos sirve para nada. **7.** ¿Ves _____ montañas? No paremos hasta llegar allá.

Ejercicio 2.15 *Traduzca.*

1. Are those books new? **2.** These apples are for you *(fam. sing.)*. **3.** That class does not cover these topics. **4.** These students are very good. **5.** That man is a friend. **6.** Those days are unforgettable.

Noun Determiners (Adjectives: Possessive Adjectives)

[Chapter 2.B.2.b, pages 42–43]

Ejercicio 2.16 *Llene cada espacio en blanco con todas las posibilidades.*

> **mi, mis, mío, mía, míos, mías; tu, tus, tuyo, tuya,
> tuyos, tuyas; su, sus, suyo, suya, suyos, suyas;
> nuestro; nuestra, nuestros, nuestras;
> vuestro, vuestra, vuestros, vuestras**

1. Ésa es _____ casa. **2.** _____ coche es más económico que el mío. **3.** _____ problemas no se pueden resolver en un día. **4.** _____ manos son más grandes que las mías. **5.** ¿Tienes las llaves _____ ahí? **6.** ¿Cuántos amigos _____ vienen? **7.** Espero que _____ familia haya pasado un fin de semana fantástico.

Ejercicio 2.17 *Traduzca.*

1. My cousins are coming today. **2.** Did your brother call (*fam. sing.*)? **3.** His arm is swollen. **4.** Their books are wet. **5.** She gave me her ring. **6.** She is a friend of mine. **7.** This pen is mine.

Noun Determiners (Adjectives: Forms of Descriptive Adjectives)

[Chapter 2.B.2.c, pages 43–44]

Ejercicio 2.18 *Haga los cambios necesarios para que el adjetivo concuerde con el nombre.*

1. la casa (verde) **2.** la casa (blanco) **3.** la casa (azul) **4.** el político (respetable)
5. el político (izquierdista) **6.** el político (prometedor) **7.** la profesora (severo)
8. la maestra (comunista) **9.** los niños (feliz) **10.** los vecinos (gritón)

Noun Determiners (Adjectives: Position of Descriptive Adjectives)

[Chapter 2.B.2.d, pages 44–48]

Ejercicio 2.19 *Reescriba las frases siguientes usando el adjetivo entre paréntesis para modificar el nombre en negrilla. Luego traduzca la frase al inglés.*

1. La **vez** que fui a Madrid fue en 1992. (primera) **2.** ¡**Gracias!** (Muchas)

3. Luisito no tiene **dinero.** (tanto)   **4.** Somos **hermanos.** (medios)   **5.** Tráeme un **cuchillo,** por favor. (otro)

Ejercicio 2.20   *Reescriba las frases siguientes usando el adjetivo entre paréntesis para modificar el nombre en negrilla. Puede haber más de una posibilidad. Haga todos los cambios necesarios.*

1. Ese hombre vende **muebles.** (antiguos)   **2.** La **gente** no siempre es infeliz. (pobre)
3. A esa **millonaria** la persiguen los periodistas. (pobre)   **4.** Te presento a Guzmán, un **amigo;** hoy es su cumpleaños —cumple dieciocho años. (viejo)   **5.** Desde que construyeron el **garaje,** ya no usan el viejo. (nuevo)   **6.** Te presento a mi **vecino.** (nuevo)   **7.** Mi **esposa** está de viaje. (linda)   **8.** Cornell es una **universidad.** (grande)
9. Charlie Chaplin fue un **actor.** (grande)   **10.** En esta tina, el **agua** se abre aquí. (caliente)   **11.** Subimos a la **torre** de la biblioteca. (alta)   **12.** Está enamorado de tu **hermana.** (bella)   **13.** Cruzaron el **río** Amazonas. (ancho)   **14.** Visitaron la **catedral** de Gaudí. (impresionante)   **15.** Ésta es la **oportunidad** que tendremos. (única)
16. Me gustan las **casas.** (blancas)   **17.** Las **nubes** flotaban como algodón por el valle. (blancas)   **18.** Era un cielo extraño: abajo había **nubes (1),** y arriba **nubes (2).** [**(1)** blancas, **(2)** negras]   **19.** Esa película es de un **director.** (español)   **20.** Se le veía un **aire** de inseguridad. (cierto)   **21.** Sabían que eran **acusaciones.** (ciertas)
22. Tenía la **capacidad** de hacer que todos se sintieran a gusto. (rara)   **23.** Era un **sonido** que nadie podía identificar. (raro)   **24.** Te voy a decir la **verdad.** (pura)
25. Es un disco de **fidelidad.** (alta)   **26.** Querían estar en Sevilla para la **Semana.** (Santa)   **27.** La mejor solución es usar nuestro **sentido.** (común)

Ejercicio 2.21   *Traduzca al inglés de una manera que explique claramente la diferencia entre los dos usos del adjetivo en cada caso.*

1. Fuimos a diferentes lugares. Fuimos a lugares diferentes.   **2.** Es un buen político. Es un político bueno.   **3.** Ese auto me causó puros problemas. Busca la vida pura.
4. Tenemos raros momentos de satisfacción. Es un platillo raro.   **5.** Me tomó media hora. Eso se hacía en la Edad Media.   **6.** Es el único problema. Es un problema único.

Noun Determiners (Adjectives: Comparisons)

[Chapter 2.B.2.e, pages 49–52]

Ejercicio 2.22   *Llene el espacio en blanco con lo necesario para establecer una comparación. Cada espacio puede necesitar más de una palabra.*

1. Beto come más ruidosamente _____ nadie.   **2.** Sabina es más lista _____ Raúl.
3. Elsa gana menos dinero _____ tú.   **4.** Hay más _____ veinte árboles aquí.   **5.** Me

diste menos _____ la mitad.   **6.** Mi bicicleta es mejor _____ la tuya.   **7.** Hace más frío _____ esperaba.   **8.** Llovió menos _____ creíamos.   **9.** Nunca ganaré tanto dinero _____ Héctor.   **10.** Ese coche es _____ bello como éste.   **11.** Esa niña grita más _____ las demás.   **12.** Había menos _____ cinco jugadores en la cancha. **13.** Ese examen no fue tan fácil _____ los otros.   **14.** Compré más servilletas _____ necesitábamos.   **15.** Hay más servilletas _____ invitados.   **16.** Tengo menos trabajo _____ esperaba.   **17.** Elvira trabaja _____ como su hermano, pero no gana _____ dinero como él. Y a mí me parece que él no es _____ listo como ella.

Ejercicio 2.23   *Escriba tres comparaciones para cada serie de dos elementos, una con **más**, otra con **menos** y otra de igualdad (con **tan** o **tanto**).*

1. España y México.   **2.** Los Estados Unidos e Hispanoamérica.   **3.** Las culturas hispanas y las culturas anglosajonas.   **4.** El amor y el odio.   **5.** La televisión y el cine.   **6.** La escuela y la universidad.   **7.** Los niños y los adultos.

Chapter 2 Review

Ejercicio 2.24   *Llene los espacios en blanco con la traducción de lo que se encuentra entre paréntesis, con su selección de las opciones ofrecidas, o con lo que le parezca lógico para el contexto. Si no debe ponerse nada en el espacio en blanco, use el símbolo "Ø".*

Hace como veinte años yo fui a estudiar a _____ Estados Unidos para obtener _____ bachillerato en _____ (un/una) universidad allá. _____ primer año lo pasé con muchísimos contratiempos causados por _____ inglés *(caused by English)*, idioma que en _____ entonces *(at that time, back then)* yo casi no hablaba y mucho menos comprendía. Tuve que tomar _____ (un/una) examen para demostrar cuánto inglés sabía, y qué clases necesitaba tomar para poder comprender _____ (los/las) conferencias y hacer todos _____ (los/las) trabajos escritos durante _____ *(my)* futuros estudios en _____ *(that)* universidad. Se me hizo muy difícil comprender _____ (estas/aquellas) conferencias de biología, dadas en _____ (un/una) enorme salón con otros cientos de estudiantes que, al igual que yo, estaban en _____ *(their)* primer año. Recuerdo que casi no podíamos ver _____ *(the)* profesor si no teníamos _____ *(the)* suerte de sentarnos hacia _____ *(the)* frente del salón, cosa que yo siempre trataba de hacer pues se me facilitaba así entender mejor lo que él decía.

_____ *(Some of my)* recuerdos más gratos de _____ *(that first year)* fueron de _____ *(my new friends)* allá, por medio de los cuales pude comprender y aprender un poco sobre _____ *(the culture of that country)* donde iba a vivir durante _____ *(so much time)*. No es por nada, pero de verdad que la mía fue _____ *(a unique experience)* comparada con _____ *(the one)* de muchos que _____ *(were better prepared than I was)*. Imagínate _____ *(that type)* de estudiante que se la pasa perdiendo el tiempo, yendo a fiestas cada semana, y dejando _____ (their) trabajo para último minuto, _____ (ese/este) mismo que se queja _____ (more strongly than anyone). En realidad puedo decir que aproveché _____ (my) tiempo en Estados Unidos. El último año ya _____ (English) era parte de _____ (my daily life); podía hacer todos los trabajos _____ (without a problem) y salí _____ (as well as my friends) en todas las clases que tomé.

    ¿Qué fue _____ (the best [thing]) de haber estudiado allá? Creo que fue el haber conocido _____ (another culture) y el haber compartido _____ (mine) con _____ (many other foreign students) cuyos intereses y experiencias eran a veces diferentes y otras similares a los míos. _____ (El/Lo) bueno fue haber visto en persona _____ (the great melting pot [crisol]) de razas y culturas en un ámbito estudiantil y con todos nosotros llenos de esperanzas para _____ (a better international future). Por eso, hija mía, yo estoy contentísima de _____ (your) interés en estudiar _____ (abroad) y apoyo tu decisión.

Ejercicio 2.25   Temas de ensayo.

Prestando atención al uso de artículos y adjetivos, y a la forma, género y número de los nombres, escriba un párrafo sobre uno de los temas siguientes:

- describa a su mejor amigo
- compare a dos de sus amigos
- describa a su familia

ATAJO

Phrases: Comparing and contrasting; Describing people
Vocabulary: Body; Family members; Nationality; Personality; People
Grammar: Adjective agreement; Article; Nouns: Irregular gender

Chapter 3   Pronouns

 Personal Pronouns (Definitions)

[Chapter 3.A.1, pages 54–56]

Ejercicio 3.1   *Conceptual Questions.*

What is a pronoun? What is its relationship with a noun? What type of grammatical functions can it have in a sentence? What other types of words can behave this way? What different types of pronouns exist?

Personal Pronouns (Subject Pronouns)

[Chapter 3.A.2, pages 56–59]

Ejercicio 3.2   *Decida si se necesita pronombre sujeto o no.*

1. —¿Cuándo salieron? —[Nosotros / Ø] salimos a las siete.   **2.** —¿Quién está ahí? —Soy [yo / Ø].   **3.** —¿Qué hacen? —[Ellos / Ø] están comiendo.   **4.** Mis vecinos sacaron la basura, pero [yo / Ø] no me acordé.   **5.** ¿Tendrías [tú / Ø] tiempo de ayudarme?   **6.** —¿Por qué no está Luis? —[Él / Ø] está enfermo.

Ejercicio 3.3   *Traduzca, prestando atención al sujeto: ¿necesita pronombre en español?* (you = **tú**)

1. I bought a book.   **2.** It is in José's room.   **3.** We are going to study together this afternoon.   **4.** You have to start your assignments (*tareas*) for tomorrow.   **5.** They (your assignments) are long.   **6.** I know you studied, but I have not finished yet. **7.** María is here; she wants to talk to you.

Ejercicio 3.4   *En el próximo párrafo hay varios momentos de ambigüedad y de repetición innecesaria. Añada (Add) los pronombres que faltan y tache (cross out) los innecesarios.*

Mike y Luisa han sido novios desde hace ya cinco años. Ellos se quieren mucho y ellos se van a casar. Tiene seis años más que ella, pero parece más madura que él. Desde niña había soñado en una boda maravillosa, con toda su familia y sus amigos presentes. Pero no quiere lo mismo que ella: prefiere una boda muy privada, en que sólo estén ellos dos, y dos testigos.

Personal Pronouns (Direct Object Pronouns)

[Chapter 3.A.3, pages 59–62]

Ejercicio 3.5 *Reemplace la comida con un pronombre y reescriba la frase.*

1. Traigan la comida. *(mandato)* **2.** Quiero guardar la comida. **3.** He guardado la comida. **4.** Están cocinando la comida. **5.** Compramos la comida. **6.** No toques la comida. *(mandato)*

Ejercicio 3.6 *Reescriba la frase reemplazando el objeto directo con un pronombre.*

1. Veo a mi vecina por esta ventana. **2.** Llevé a mis hijas al banco. **3.** No conocen a la maestra. **4.** Josefina es un poco extraña; nadie entiende a Josefina. **5.** Los vecinos miraban a la muchacha mientras barría la calle. **6.** El vendedor llamó a la clienta. **7.** Oían a la niña cantar. **8.** Oían a la niña cantar la canción. **9.** Buscaron a la asesina. **10.** Encontraron a la doctora. **11.** Invitaron a Anita al baile. **12.** Extraño a mi madre.

Ejercicio 3.7 *Reescriba la frase reemplazando el objeto directo con un pronombre.*

1. Veo a mi vecino por esta ventana. **2.** Llevé a mis hijos al banco. **3.** No conocen al maestro. **4.** Roberto es un poco extraño; nadie entiende a Roberto. **5.** Los vecinos miraban al muchacho mientras barría la calle. **6.** El vendedor llamó al cliente. **7.** Oían al niño cantar. **8.** Oían al niño cantar la canción. **9.** Buscaron al asesino. **10.** Encontraron al doctor. **11.** Invitaron a Panchito al baile. **12.** Extraño a mi padre.

Ejercicio 3.8 *En el próximo párrafo hay mucha repetición innecesaria. Encuentre los nombres que son objeto directo, tache los que son innecesarios y reemplácelos con pronombres.*

Tengo la costumbre de observar a mis vecinos. Ayer vi a mis vecinos llegar en su coche: habían comprado plantas nuevas; sacaron las plantas del coche y dejaron las plantas en la tierra cerca de la casa porque no podían ponerse de acuerdo sobre dónde poner las plantas. Ella quería meter las plantas en la casa. Él le dijo que prefería las plantas afuera. Ella dijo que el frío de la noche iba a matar las plantas, y él le contestó que era necesario acostumbrar las plantas a los cambios de temperatura. La situación era típica, y terminó como siempre: ella miró mal a su marido y se fue, y él se encogió de hombros y siguió con lo que hacía como si nada. Después de una hora ella llamó a su marido para que entrara a cenar. Yo podía oír sus risas mientras platicaban durante la cena.

Personal Pronouns (Direct and Indirect Object Pronouns)

[Chapter 3.A.3–4, pages 59–63]

Ejercicio 3.9 *Junte las partes para formar frases completas. Reemplace los nombres en negrilla con el pronombre adecuado.*

1. los turistas / miraban / **a los indígenas**   **2.** el policía / dijo / **al vagabundo** / que se tenía que ir   **3.** regaló / **sus libros viejos** / al asilo   **4.** mandaron / **el paquete** / a su familia   **5.** el abuelo / contó / **el cuento** / a sus nietos   **6.** hicieron / **la cama** / a los huéspedes   **7.** el padre / quitó / **la llave** / a su hijo   **8.** mi amigo / pidió / **el dinero** / a su tía

Ejercicio 3.10 *Traduzca.*

1. I beat **him**.   **2.** I won **it** (the money = *el dinero*).   **3.** They robbed **him** (his neighbors).   **4.** They stole **it** (the money = *el dinero*).   **5.** We believe **him**.   **6.** We believe **it**.   **7.** They hit **him**.   **8.** They glued **it** (the map = *el mapa*).   **9.** I paid **her**. **10.** I paid **it** (the bill = *la cuenta*).

Ejercicio 3.11 *Continúe escribiendo sobre el tema con el contexto indicado en la primera frase, usando los elementos entre paréntesis y haciendo las transformaciones necesarias para evitar la repetición.*

MODELO: El candidato dio su presentación ayer. (observamos / al candidato mientras hablaba, / reconocimos / al candidato / como el mejor / y / dijimos / al candidato / que recomendaríamos / al candidato / para el puesto)

*El candidato dio su presentación ayer. **Lo** observamos mientras hablaba, **lo** reconocimos como el mejor y **le** dijimos que **lo** recomendaríamos para el puesto.*

1. Luisa es una amiga mía que va a estudiar a España durante un año. (conozco / a Luisa / desde hace cuatro años. / vi / a Luisa / ayer / y / hablé / a Luisa / de su año en el extranjero; prometí / a Luisa / que / escribiría / a Luisa / durante su ausencia)

2. El hijo de la señora Ruiz no llegó a su casa en toda la noche. (La señora Ruiz / llamó / a su hijo / a su teléfono celular / y / preguntó / a su hijo / por qué no / había hablado / a ella / de sus planes; / regañó / a su hijo / por su irresponsabilidad; / él / pidió / a ella / que / perdonara / a él)

3. Su adorado perrito nuevo había desaparecido. (Habían estado buscando / al perrito / desde hacía varias horas / cuando por fin oyeron / al perrito / llorando / y / encontraron / al perrito / medio enterrado en el barro; sacaron / al perrito / y / llevaron / al perrito / a casa donde / dieron / al perrito / un baño)

Ejercicio 3.12 *Reescriba el próximo párrafo usando los pronombres correctos.*

Conocí a Elena el primer día que llegué a la universidad, cuando vi (a ella) en el cuarto que íbamos a compartir como compañeras de cuarto. Saludé (a ella) y dije (a ella) que estaba contenta de conocer (a ella). Ella abrazó (a mí) y contó (a mí) con mucho entusiasmo sus planes para la universidad. Poco a poco llegué a conocer (a ella) y cada vez encontraba (a ella) más simpática. Le gustaban (a ella) las mismas cosas que (a mí), teníamos el mismo horario para todo, y nunca nos peleamos. Hasta el día en que entró en nuestra vida Julio. Yo vi (a él) primero, un día de frío intenso, en la cafetería, y me enamoré a primera vista. Conté (a ella) de mi experiencia, y lo único que ella quería era conocer (a él), supuestamente por mi bien, para animarme más. Pues no fue así: cuando ella vio (a él) por primera vez, ella quiso (a él) también, y él parecía querer (a ella) de la misma manera. Yo me quedé congelada, mirando (a ella) primero, luego (a él), en unos segundos que parecieron durar una eternidad. Después, dije (a ella) que yo había visto (a él) primero, y que ella no tenía el derecho de quitarme (a él). Como yo nunca había dicho (a él) lo que sentía, sin embargo, y ellos dos evidentemente compartían el mismo sentimiento de amor, yo ya había perdido. Y lo sabía. Ahora, después de muchos años, quiero (a ellos) a los dos, y visito (a ellos) y a su familia cada vez que puedo: están casados y tienen cuatro hijos. Yo nunca me casé, y así me gusta.

Personal Pronouns (Required Repetitive Object Pronouns)

[Chapter 3.A.5, page 64]

Ejercicio 3.13 *Llene el espacio en blanco con un pronombre repetitivo de objeto directo o indirecto si se necesita. Si no se necesita nada, use el símbolo "Ø".*

1. Ayer _____ compré el pan. **2.** El pan _____ compré ayer. **3.** Esta tarde _____ vi a Juan en la tienda. **4.** A Juan _____ vi en la tienda esta tarde. **5.** El correo _____ llegó hace media hora. **6.** Hace media hora que _____ llegó el correo. **7.** Marta _____ bañó al niño. **8.** Al niño Marta _____ bañó. **9.** Toda la gente _____ vio el globo. **10.** Anoche _____ terminé todos. **11.** Mañana _____ enviaremos el regalo a Marieta. **12.** No _____ digas a Juan el secreto. **13.** Nunca _____ cuentes todo a tus amigos. **14.** Ese día _____ regañaron a todos nosotros. **15.** Con esa lluvia _____ crecerán todas las plantas.

Personal Pronouns (Order of Object Pronouns When Combined)

[Chapter 3.A.6, page 65]

Ejercicio 3.14 *Conteste afirmativamente, reemplazando las palabras en negrilla con pronombres, y haciendo los demás cambios necesarios.*

1. ¿Te dio **los regalos**?   **2.** ¿Les enseñaste **la cosecha a los vecinos**?   **3.** ¿Te contó **la noticia**?   **4.** ¿Le dijiste **el secreto a Socorro**?   **5.** ¿Se limpiaron ustedes **las botas**?   **6.** ¿Os enviaron **la carta**?

Personal Pronouns (Position of Object Pronouns)

[Chapter 3.A.7, pages 66–67]

Ejercicio 3.15 *Conteste las preguntas siguientes en el afirmativo, reemplazando las palabras en negrilla con el pronombre adecuado si se necesita pronombre. No use los nombres en negrilla en sus respuestas. No use pronombre si no se necesita.*

1. ¿Están preparando **la cena**?   **2.** ¿Le pudieron vender **la casa a ese cliente**?   **3.** ¿Le va a hacer **los mandados a su mamá**?   **4.** ¿Le has mandado **el libro a Nilda**?   **5.** ¿**La casa** está pintada?   **6.** ¿Te gustó **el restaurante**?   **7.** ¿**Joaquín** le dio **las flores a Marina**?   **8.** ¿Se habla **español**?

Personal Pronouns (Prepositional Object Pronouns)

[Chapter 3.A.8, pages 67–69]

Ejercicio 3.16 *Traduzca al español.* (you = **tú**)

1. This is for you.   **2.** According to her, it was wrong.   **3.** They were looking at him.   **4.** They were looking for him.   **5.** This is between him and me.   **6.** Her children are like her.   **7.** I am talking about you.   **8.** Sing with me.   **9.** I will sing with him.   **10.** She took it away with her.

Personal Pronouns (Review 1)

Ejercicio 3.17 *El párrafo siguiente contiene mucha repetición: tache los pronombres repetitivos innecesarios, ya sean sujeto, objeto directo u objeto indirecto.*

Para Navidad yo siempre he querido ir a la playa, porque desde niña mi padre me acostumbró a mí a celebrar este día lejos de la sociedad materialista, en un rito de comunión con la naturaleza y el universo. Mi hermana, mi padre y yo, nosotros íbamos a quedarnos una semana en la playa, y desde el día en que nosotros llegábamos, nosotros empezábamos a juntar leña en un lugar que mi padre escogía en la playa, donde hubiera un enorme tronco para descansar. Nosotros juntábamos leña por toda la playa cada día antes de la Nochebuena, y esa noche, cuando el resto de la gente en el hotel estaba celebrando con grandes banquetes y bailes, nosotros salíamos a escondidas por detrás, nosotros íbamos en la oscuridad a encontrar nuestro sitio escogido, y allí nosotros nos instalábamos para pasar la noche en la playa. Nosotros encendíamos la hoguera con la leña que nosotros habíamos juntado, y nosotros nos recargábamos contra el tronco a mirar el cielo y el mar. En el cielo brillaban las estrellas, y en el mar se veían las luces que echaban unos pececitos minúsculos. Era un espectáculo realmente impresionante. Las olas producían un ritmo que nos calmaba a nosotros. De vez en cuando mi padre rompía el silencio, y él nos contaba a nosotros de sus experiencias como vaquero, o él nos recitaba a nosotros uno de sus poemas, o él nos cantaba a nosotros una canción y él nos pedía a nosotros que nosotros cantáramos también. Son momentos que yo jamás olvidaré. Y por eso ahora que ya yo soy mayor y que mi padre ha muerto, cada vez que llega la época de Navidad, yo me dirijo hacia una playa.

Se (Reflexive Pronouns)

[Chapter 3.B.2, pages 70–72]

Ejercicio 3.18   *Traduzca, usando verbos reflexivos.* (you = **tú**)

1. We noticed his smile.   **2.** He fell in love with her.   **3.** We worry about you.
4. They found out about the accident the next day.   **5.** I took off my clothes.   **6.** She stayed there.   **7.** We complained about the time.   **8.** He said good-bye to his family.
9. They realized it was late.   **10.** They never got used to the weather.   **11.** He does not dare knock at the door.   **12.** They look like their mother.

Ejercicio 3.19   *Reemplace el nombre objeto directo de las siguientes frases con un pronombre, y luego añada una segunda parte de la frase que sea reflexiva. Use los pronombres que necesite para marcar el énfasis.*

MODELO: Veo **a mi hermano.** (...y a mí también...)

   Lo veo a él y me veo a mí mismo también.

1. Conocemos **a Isabel.** (...pero a nosotros mejor...)   **2.** Oyes **a tus compañeros.** (...y a ti al mismo tiempo...)   **3.** Roberto respeta **a sus padres.** (...y a Roberto también)

Ejercicio 3.20 *Reescriba el párrafo siguiente llenando los espacios en blanco con el pronombre que se necesite: puede ser reflexivo o no. Si no se necesita nada, escriba el símbolo "Ø". Si el pronombre va conectado al verbo, el número precede el verbo.*

Esa mañana los pájaros (1) _____ despertaron a Marisol. Después de (2) estirar_____, (3) _____ levantó, (4) _____ cepilló los dientes, y (5) _____ bañó. Después del baño, (6) _____ secó (7) _____, (8) _____ maquilló con mucho cuidado, y (9) _____ peinó (10) _____ de la manera más sencilla. (11) _____ miró (12) _____ en el espejo por buen rato, para asegurarse (13) _____ de que todo estuviera perfecto: este día iba a tener la entrevista de trabajo más importante de su vida, y (14) _____ sentía muy nerviosa. (15) _____ conocía (16) _____ muy bien, y (17) _____ sabía que si no estaba perfectamente presentable, no estaría cómoda en la entrevista. La compañía que (18) _____ iba a entrevistar (19) _____ había llamado (20) _____ la semana anterior para hacer cita para ese día. La madre de Marisol y la dueña de la compañía (21) _____ conocían (22) _____ desde antes de que ella naciera, y fue así que Marisol consiguió la cita. Ahora tenía miedo de quedar mal con su madre, porque (23) _____ sentía que si no conseguía el trabajo, iba a (24) desilusionar_____. Ambas eran mujeres fuertes: Marisol y su madre (25) _____ conocían bien a sí mismas, pero no (26) _____ conocían (27) _____.

Se (Se Me Construction: Accidental or Irresponsible Se)

[Chapter 3.B.3, pages 72–75]

Ejercicio 3.21 *Vuelva a escribir estas frases usando el se accidental.*

1. Olvidamos nuestra cita. 2. Quemé los plátanos. 3. Perdimos nuestras llaves. 4. Mojaron su pelo. 5. Rompiste tu taza.

Ejercicio 3.22 *Traduzca las frases siguientes usando el se accidental y el verbo indicado. (you = tú)*

1. He left his book. *(quedársele a uno)* 2. Our clothes got wet. *(mojársele a uno)* 3. I ran out of coffee. *(acabársele a uno)* 4. Your papers fell. *(caérsele a uno)* 5. She forgot her notes. *(olvidársele a uno)* 6. Their plates broke. *(rompérsele a uno)*

Ejercicio 3.23 *Llene el espacio en blanco con lo que falta para completar la frase, usando el modelo como base.*

Modelo: *A Marta se le olvidó el libro.*

1. A Jorge se _____ perdió el paraguas. 2. A nosotros se _____ rompió el jarro.

3. A mí se _____ cayó el guante.   **4.** Se _____ quemaron los frijoles a ti.   **5.** A los niños se _____ cierran los ojos.

Ejercicio 3.24 *Conjugue el verbo en la forma correcta del pretérito.*

1. Se nos (olvidar) los regalos.   **2.** A ti se te (olvidar) las llaves.   **3.** A la niña se le (bajar) los calcetines.   **4.** A mí se me (romper) la silla.   **5.** A los vecinos se les (ir) la electricidad.

Ejercicio 3.25 *¿Qué pasó? Describa las situaciones siguientes usando el **se** accidental o irresponsable.*

MODELO: Ayer compraste un reloj, pero ahora no lo encuentras.

Se te perdió el reloj.

1. Ayer teníamos una cita, pero no fuimos porque no la habíamos marcado en el calendario.   **2.** El plato que compraste lo dejaste caer accidentalmente al piso y ahora está roto.   **3.** La cena que estaba preparando Beto está ahora toda negra, carbonizada.   **4.** Ayer no pude terminar mi trabajo para la clase: no había luz en mi casa.   **5.** Estabas jugando al fútbol y ahora tus zapatos están todos sucios.   **6.** No tenemos nuestros guantes: los dejamos por error en casa.

Personal Pronouns (Review 2)

Ejercicio 3.26 *(Subject, Direct Object, Indirect Object, Prepositional Object, Reflexive, Accidental* Se*) El siguiente texto está lleno de repetición excesiva: decida cuáles de las palabras subrayadas necesitan guardarse o no, o sustituirse con un pronombre.*

Yo fui estudiante de intercambio hace unos años en México, y cuando yo estuve allá, yo viví con los Rodríguez, una familia muy simpática y generosa que yo nunca olvidaré. Un día cuando yo estaba viviendo con los Rodríguez, ellos se ganaron la lotería, y la vida se puso de repente más compleja. Cada uno de los Rodríguez quería algo diferente.

Don Carlos, el padre, él quería jubilarse porque él quería poder pasar más tiempo con la familia; a él se le había ocurrido también comprar un yate para que todos pudieran divertirse paseándose por el mundo.

Doña Julia, la madre, ella nunca había trabajado más que para su familia, y en realidad ella no tenía ambiciones. Ella deseaba que no le faltara nada a ninguno de sus hijos, y ella esperaba que el dinero sirviera ese propósito. Ella prefería no gastar el dinero en nada, sino más bien depositar el dinero en el banco. En realidad, a ella no le gustaba el dinero, el dinero representaba para Doña Julia una maldición, y ella hasta le tenía un poco de miedo al dinero.

Los hijos, Carlitos, Matilde y Rosita, <u>ellos</u> tenían cada uno de ellos un plan distinto.

Carlitos, el mayor, <u>él</u> ya <u>se</u> había graduado de la universidad, y <u>él</u> estaba buscando trabajo en diferentes bufetes de abogados, pero <u>él</u> no había conseguido nada aún. <u>Él</u> seguía viviendo con la familia, y esto <u>le</u> daba <u>a él</u> algo de vergüenza porque <u>él</u> tenía novia, <u>él</u> estaba comprometido ya, pero si <u>él</u> no tenía trabajo, <u>él</u> no podía formar su propia familia. <u>Él</u> se imaginaba que el dinero <u>le</u> podría servir <u>a él</u> para abrir su propio bufete, y así <u>él</u> podría empezar a trabajar solo y ganar suficiente dinero para poder casar<u>se</u>.

Matilde estaba todavía en la universidad: <u>ella</u> estudiaba medicina. <u>Ella</u> era modesta, y <u>ella</u> no tenía ningún plan personal para el dinero, sino que veía <u>el dinero</u> como un premio para sus padres. <u>Ella</u> esperaba que con <u>este dinero</u> <u>sus padres</u> pudieran vivir más a gusto. <u>Sus padres</u> habían sacrificado tanto para <u>Matilde</u> y sus hermanos, que ahora <u>ellos</u> se merecían un descanso. <u>Ella</u> siempre había sido muy generosa, y <u>ella</u> pensaba en los problemas de otros en vez de los suyos. Por ejemplo, una vez, cuando <u>ella</u> trabajaba de voluntaria en una escuela de niños pobres, un niño no tenía bastante dinero para comprar<u>se</u> <u>a sí mismo</u> los zapatos del uniforme de la escuela, y entonces <u>ella</u> usó su propio dinero para comprar <u>los zapatos</u> <u>al niño</u>.

Rosita era la más ambiciosa de todos: para <u>Rosita</u> este dinero representaba la liberación posible de toda dependencia. <u>Ella</u> quería su parte del dinero para conseguir<u>se</u> <u>a sí misma</u> un apartamento y vivir lejos de la familia, independiente y libre. <u>Yo</u> conocía mejor <u>a Rosita</u> que a los demás, porque <u>ella</u> era compañera mía en el colegio y <u>nosotros</u> compartíamos la misma habitación en su casa. <u>Rosita</u> <u>me</u> contaba <u>a mí</u> sus planes de manera muy emocional. Cuando <u>yo</u> <u>la</u> escuchaba <u>a ella</u>, <u>yo</u> podía ver la pasión que <u>la</u> impulsaba <u>a ella</u>.

Se (Impersonal *Se*)

[Chapter 3.A.4, pages 76–79]

Ejercicio 3.27 *Traduzca usando el **se** impersonal.*

1. The house was sold. When was it sold?   **2.** One tans easily in the Caribbean.
3. The employees were fired. Why were they fired?   **4.** They were not told.   **5.** You do not say that in public.

Ejercicio 3.28 *Las frases que siguen usan la estructura impersonal; escoja la forma correcta del verbo.*

1. En algunas partes del mundo hispano se (toma / toman) una siesta por la tarde.
2. En esa tienda se (habla / hablan) español.   **3.** A los niños se les (dijo / dijeron) que no salieran de noche.   **4.** En esa época, se (mataba / mataban) a los criminales.
5. Al presidente se le (recibió / recibieron) con gran aplauso.   **6.** A los estudiantes

se les (mandó / mandaron) la información en verano.   **7.** Al gerente se le (anunció / anunciaron) los cambios hace mucho.   **8.** Se (vende / venden) libros.   **9.** Aquí no se (acepta / aceptan) cheques personales.   **10.** A la jefa ya se le (dio / dieron) las noticias.

Ejercicio 3.29   *Traduzca haciendo los cambios necesarios para usar la estructura más natural en español.*

1. He was awakened by the noise.   **2.** Naps are taken at noon.   **3.** We were brought up *(criar)* by our mother.   **4.** You were rescued *(rescatar)* by the lifeguard *(salvavidas)*.
5. I was moved by the speech.   **6.** She was sent to the hospital.   **7.** Bread was made at home in those days *(en aquel entonces)*.   **8.** The passive is hardly ever *(casi nunca)* used in Spanish.   **9.** The pizza was just delivered.   **10.** A message was left on the door.

Ejercicio 3.30   Temas de ensayo.

Un amigo le ha preguntado por correo electrónico en qué se diferencia su cultura de la cultura hispana. Escriba un párrafo describiendo algunos aspectos de su cultura, y cómo se contrasta con la hispana. Indique lo que se hace y lo que no se hace en su cultura.

Demonstrative and Possessive Pronouns

[Chapter 3.C.1–2, pages 80–82]

Ejercicio 3.31   *Traduzca.*

1. That house was more expensive than this one.   **2.** "Which house do you prefer?" "I liked that one better."   **3.** "Give me that." "What? This?"   **4.** My sister is as brave as yours.   **5.** "My parents are coming for graduation. What about yours?" (What about = ¿Y...) "Mine are not coming."   **6.** That medicine is his.   **7.** "Which towel is yours?" "This one is mine and that one is yours."   **8.** "Whose keys are these?" "These are yours (*formal sing.*), these are his, and these are hers."

Interrogatives

[Chapter 3.D, pages 82–86]

Ejercicio 3.32   *Traduzca usando los pronombres interrogativos.* (you = **tú**)

1. How did they arrive?   **2.** How much sugar do you use?   **3.** Which color do you like?   **4.** Which one do you want?   **5.** How far is the store from here?   **6.** Which one

is your name? (on a list)   **7.** What is your name?   **8.** How many books did you buy?
9. How often do you go?

Ejercicio 3.33   *Haga una pregunta para obtener como respuesta la palabra en negrilla de la frase.*

1. Es un **libro**.   **2.** Lo hice **yo**.   **3.** Tengo **veinte** años.   **4.** Vivo en **España**.   **5.** Soy de **México**.   **6.** Cerré la ventana **porque tenía frío**.   **7.** Llegamos **a las diez de la noche**.   **8.** **Éste** es el mío.   **9.** **La diferencia entre las dos películas** es que una es más vieja que la otra.   **10.** **Bien, gracias,** ¿y tú?

Ejercicio 3.34   *Transforme las preguntas directas en indirectas, empezando la frase con lo que hay entre paréntesis. No se olvide de mantener el orden correcto de verbo y sujeto.*

1. ¿De dónde son los aztecas? (Quieren saber...)   **2.** ¿Cuál es la religión? (Me pregunto...)   **3.** ¿Dónde vivían los incas? (Les interesa saber...)   **4.** ¿Cuánto dinero gana un arqueólogo? (Quieren averiguar...)   **5.** ¿Cómo conoció Romeo a Julieta? (Se le olvidó...)   **6.** ¿Quién era el actor? (No recordaba...)

Exclamatives

[Chapter 3.E, pages 87–89]

Ejercicio 3.35   *Traduzca, usando los exclamativos.*

1. What a job!   **2.** How pretty!   **3.** What an amusing game!   **4.** What good coffee!
5. How fast you run!   **6.** How the birds sing!   **7.** We loved her so much!   **8.** I am so hungry!   **9.** We visited so many cousins!   **10.** I wish I could fly the way they do!

Ejercicio 3.36   *Llene los espacios en blanco con el exclamativo correcto.*

1. ¡_____ agua más fría!   **2.** ¡_____ se ríen!   **3.** ¡_____ delicioso!   **4.** ¡_____ ojos tan verdes tienes!   **5.** ¡_____ me alegro de que puedas venir a la fiesta!   **6.** ¡_____ hermanos tienes!   **7.** ¡_____ blanca se ve la nieve!   **8.** ¡_____ buena película!
9. ¡_____ comen esos niños!   **10.** ¡_____ suerte!

Indefinites and Negatives

[Chapter 3.F, pages 90–93]

Ejercicio 3.37   *Traduzca. (you = **tú**)*

1. Something fell.   **2.** Someone spoke.   **3.** I do not see anyone.   **4.** Do you need

anything?   **5.** I do not want anything.   **6.** "Maybe one of the neighbors saw him."
"No, none of them saw him."   **7.** "I went to the movies yesterday." "I did too."
8. "John could not see." "We could not either."   **9.** "Have you ever been to Chile?"
"No, I have not ever been there. Some day I will go. My sister went there once and
liked it."   **10.** I cannot find my keys anywhere. I know they are somewhere in this
room.

Ⓖ Relative Pronouns

[Chapter 3.G, pages 93–99]

Ejercicio 3.38   *Llene el espacio en blanco con el pronombre relativo que mejor
convenga.*

1. Hay momentos en la vida _____ no se olvidarán nunca.   **2.** La mujer _____ vive
ahí es famosa.   **3.** El libro _____ nosotros compramos era caro.   **4.** _____ me atrae
de la universidad es el ambiente intelectual.   **5.** Natalia es _____ sabe bailar el
merengue.   **6.** Ésa es la casa en _____ filmaron la película.   **7.** El actor _____
aparece en esa película es muy arrogante en la vida real.   **8.** El político _____ fue
elegido no era muy popular, _____ sorprendió a muchos extranjeros.   **9.** Llegó y
apagó el radio, _____ estaba a todo volumen.   **10.** La razón por _____ hice eso fue
que sabía que no me iban a dejar en paz.   **11.** Ésta es la estatua frente a _____ nos
besamos por primera vez, ¿te acuerdas?   **12.** Ése es el pueblo _____ calles son las
más limpias.   **13.** _____ busca, encuentra.   **14.** _____ me cae bien es Roberto.
15. Esa música es _____ tocaban en la película.

Ejercicio 3.39   *Traduzca.*

1. The person who called asked for you.   **2.** What he gave you was stolen.   **3.** I do
not like what they do.   **4.** That is the bus I was waiting for.   **5.** The one who sang
that song was Rose.

Ejercicio 3.40   *Elimine todos los paréntesis, y junte la información en frases
completas, usando pronombres relativos cada vez que se necesite para evitar la
repetición.*

Un amigo mío (se llama Ernesto) me llamó de Florida. Me contó de su perrito (había
comprado el perrito hacía tres semanas) (el perrito estaba dormido a su lado). Ernesto me contó que Chico (Ernesto le dio este nombre al perrito) estaba destruyendo el
apartamento (¡Ernesto había conseguido el apartamento con tanta dificultad!) (Ernesto había gastado todo su dinero en el apartamento). Pero Ernesto no quería deshacerse de este perrito (el perrito ahora era su mejor amigo). Por eso Ernesto me pidió que
le mandara el dinero (él me había prestado el dinero hacía más de un año).

Chapter 3 Review

Ejercicio 3.41 *Reescriba el texto que sigue, llenando los espacios en blanco con pronombres personales, relativos, demostrativos, posesivos, interrogativos, negativos o indefinidos; si no necesita nada para un espacio en blanco, use el símbolo "Ø"; algunos espacios en blanco pueden tener más de una palabra. Si la palabra del espacio en blanco va conectada a la palabra anterior, el número precede la primera palabra.*

Los conquistadores llegaron a las Américas como ladrones

Al **(1)** ver_____ acercarse a sus costas, los indígenas salieron a **(2)** recibir_____ con los brazos abiertos. Nunca se imaginaron que las decoraciones que usaban para adornar sus cuerpos casi desnudos **(3)** _____ interesarían tanto a estos hombres blancos. Tampoco comprendieron por qué **(4)** _____ eran tan crueles ni qué causaba esas fiebres que **(5)** _____ daban a tantos de los suyos y que **(6)** _____ mataban eventualmente.

Bajo el manto de la virtud estos demonios blancos **(7)** _____ dijeron a los indígenas que tenían que creer en otro Dios, **(8)** _____ obligaron a escuchar toda la retórica sobre el bien y el mal que **(9)** _____ imponía la religión católica a cambio de donaciones de sus metales preciosos.

Poco a poco los conquistadores **(10)** _____ llevaron todos los tesoros **(11)** _____ encontraron en su camino, **(12)** _____ destruyeron la naturaleza y el espíritu de los indígenas; a **(13)** _____ quitaron el poder **(14)** _____ tenían, la tierra en **(15)** _____ vivían, las creencias **(16)** _____ practicaban, y muchas veces hasta la vida. **(17)** _____ dejaron sin **(18)** _____, o peor aún, **(19)** _____ impusieron otra existencia, en **(20)** _____ de reyes se transformaban en esclavos, en **(21)** _____ tenían que construir iglesias para practicar una religión diferente a **(22)** _____, murallas para proteger los nuevos gobiernos establecidos por los conquistadores para **(23)** dominar_____ a ellos, edificios en **(24)** _____ estos nuevos gobernadores controlarían el continente que antes fue **(25)** _____.

El idioma **(26)** _____ hablaban los nuevos **(27)** _____ convirtió en el idioma **(28)** _____ todos debían hablar, y poco a poco los indígenas fueron perdiendo hasta su identidad con su lengua y la pureza de su raza.

Esta historia de violencia tras violencia dejó marcado el espíritu de esta gente, **(29)** _____ se transformó de una gente saludable y fuerte con ideas claras sobre el universo en una gente **(30)** _____ único deseo era derrotar a los que **(31)** _____ habían derrotado a ellos. Los siglos fueron marcando la historia con guerras de independencia seguidas de gobiernos tiránicos **(32)** _____ imitaban al enemigo **(33)** _____ habían echado.

Hoy en día, cuando existe la posibilidad de que **(34)** _____ formen gobiernos pacíficos y tolerantes, la ambigüedad permanece muchas veces en el alma de estos pueblos (**35**) _____ nunca podrán olvidar por completo las crueldades a (**36**) _____ fueron sometidos.

En fin de cuentas, ¿(**37**) _____ somos? Algunos de nuestros antepasados fueron ya sea aztecas, o incas, o mayas, o tahínos, o de algún otro pueblo; y (**38**) _____ fueron europeos de sangre conquistadora o de otra manera criminal, presos bajo libertad condicional; y (**39**) _____ fueron africanos de sangre real convertida a la esclavitud. Ahora somos una mezcla, somos hispanos, latinos, americanos, hispanoamericanos, latinoamericanos, mestizos. Y con cada continente (**40**) _____ se añadía a la mezcla, venían sus cargas espirituales, sus tradiciones; y en la unión se formaba la multiplicidad de seres (**41**) _____ todos llevamos dentro.

Ejercicio 3.42   Temas de ensayo.

Usando pronombres personales cada vez que se necesite para evitar la repetición, escriba sobre uno de los temas siguientes.

a. Escriba un brevísimo resumen de una película que trata de relaciones entre individuos.

ATAJO

Phrases: Talking about films
Vocabulary: People
Grammar: Personal pronouns

b. Escríbale una cartita a un amigo (o amiga), contándole los chismes más recientes de un amigo (o amiga) de ambos.

ATAJO

Phrases: Writing a letter (informal)
Grammar: Personal pronouns

c. Describa su relación con su(s) compañero(s) de cuarto, o con su(s) hermano(s), o con sus amigos.

ATAJO

Phrases: Describing people

Grammar: Personal pronouns

---

d. Escriba la biografía de un personaje famoso, como por ejemplo de un conquistador, de un libertador, o de un gran revolucionario o político. Ejemplos: Cristóbal Colón, Hernán Cortés, Simón Bolívar, Che Guevara, Evita Perón.

ATAJO

Phrases: Describing people; Describing the past

Vocabulary: Cultural periods and movements; Countries; Nationality; Professions

Grammar: Personal pronouns; Verbs: Imperfect

---

e. Describa de manera paralela a dos individuos famosos. Por ejemplo, Selena y Gloria Estefan, Jon Secada y Enrique Iglesias.

ATAJO

Phrases: Comparing and contrasting

Grammar: Personal pronouns

Chapter 4 Prepositions, Adverbs, and Conjunctions

 Prepositions (Function of Prepositions)

[Chapter 4.A.1, pages 102–103]

Ejercicio 4.1 *Conceptual Questions.*

What is a preposition? Can you explain its name? What is its relationship with a noun? What is a conjunction? Can you explain its name? What is the difference between a conjunction of coordination and a conjunction of subordination?

Prepositions (Individual Prepositions)

[Chapter 4.A.3, pages 104–123]

*En los siguientes ejercicios (4.2–4.7), llene los espacios en blanco con **a, al, de, del, en, con** o **Ø** (nada), según parezca más lógico.*

Ejercicio 4.2

1. Asistiré _____ clase _____ cuanto me alivie. **2.** Comenzaron _____ cocinar ayer.
3. Creo que _____ lo mejor se encuentre _____ Margarita _____ la ciudad.
4. Decidieron caminar _____ vez de manejar; nunca llegarán _____ pie. **5.** Dudo
que puedan influir _____ su decisión. **6.** El mercado está _____ dos kilómetros.
7. El programa consiste _____ varios segmentos; en el primero, se trata _____ la
revolución mexicana. **8.** Ella me gana _____ veces, y se burla _____ mí. **9.** Este
bordado está hecho _____ mano; este otro, _____ cambio, está hecho _____ máquina. **10.** Fuimos _____ la tienda _____ el coche _____ mi padre _____ mis cuatro
hermanitos.

Ejercicio 4.3

1. Iremos al trabajo _____ pesar de la tormenta. **2.** La gente _____ barrio estaba
_____ mal humor. **3.** La mujer _____ ojos verdes trabaja _____ la tienda _____ la
esquina. **4.** Llegarán _____ eso de las cinco _____ tal de que no nieve. **5.** Lo
mediremos _____ ojo. **6.** Me acosté _____ las diez _____ coraje. **7.** Me detuve
_____ echarle gasolina al carro. **8.** Me enojé *con* ellos porque los dos estaban

hablando _a_ la vez. **9.** Me gusta montar _a_ caballo _de_ vez en cuando.
10. Me invitaron _a_ cenar _____ un restaurante que se especializa _____ comida
mexicana.

Ejercicio 4.4

1. Nadie se había fijado _en_ el cambio que ocurrió desde que se habían quejado
de/por su horario.   **2.** Necesitamos discutir esto más _a_ fondo, pero _en_ este
momento no tengo tiempo.   **3.** No veo _____ mis amigos _____ estos lentes.
4. Nos pusimos _a_ llorar cuando nos enteramos _de_ terremoto que hubo _en_ _____
Los Ángeles.   **5.** Nunca se resignará _a_ ser menos famoso.   **6.** Por favor lleguen
_a_ tiempo (*puntualmente*).   **7.** Quisiera que se rieran _de_ mis chistes, y no
_de_ mí.   **8.** _En_ cuanto empezó a ir a la escuela, Roberta aprendió _a_ _____
defenderse.   **9.** Sabemos que tardan mucho _a_ llegar a su destino.   **10.** Se casó
con ella _a_ los tres años de ser su novio.
después

Ejercicio 4.5

1. Se enamoró _de_ ella cuando le enseñó _a_ bailar el tango.   **2.** Se negó _a_
tomarse la píldora.   **3.** Se quedaron _con_ mis libros _de_ poesía.   **4.** Si esos niños
no dejan _de_ meterse _con_ mi hijo, tendré que hablar _con_ sus padres.   **5.** Soñé
con mi novia.   **6.** Su hijo le pidió _por_ dinero porque pensaba _en_ comprarle
un regalo a su madre.   **7.** Subían _a_ la montaña _con_ frecuencia.   **8.** Van _____
regalarle un libro _____ Cervantes.   **9.** Ves a tus padres _a_ menudo, y ellos
siempre se alegran _a_ verte.   **10.** Volvieron _a_ sentarse _en_ frente de mí.

Ejercicio 4.6

1. Ya empezaron _a_ salir las flores.   **2.** _En_ fuerza de hacer tanto ejercicio,
bajó de peso.   **3.** _De_ niña, se acostumbró _a_ desayunar temprano.   **4.** _De_
repente tuvieron que entrar _a_ causa de la tormenta.   **5.** _Con_ respecto a ese
asunto, parece que lo resolvieron ayer.   **6.** ¿Me podrían ayudar _a_ terminar este
trabajo?   **7.** —¿Qué haces? —Estoy buscando _Ø_ mi libreta _de_ direcciones.
8. ¿Te atreverás _a_ jugar?   **9.** Le presté el libro _a_ mi amigo _de_ buena
gana.   **10.** Estudiamos _en_ Miami.

Ejercicio 4.7

1. Iremos _____ tal de que no llueva.   **2.** —Anoche nevó. —¿_____ veras?   **3.** Mis
hijos aprenderán _____ tocar el piano desde muy jóvenes.   **4.** Pienso _____ ti _____
menudo.   **5.** ¿Qué piensan tus padres _____ mis amigos?   **6.** No te olvides _____
traerte las llaves.   **7.** Nunca dejarán _____ quererte.   **8.** Pronto se acostumbrarán
_____ la comida picante.   **9.** Decidí ir de compras _____ vez de estudiar.   **10.** _____
veces es saludable no hacer nada.   **11.** La tormenta empezó _____ repente.   **12.** ¿Tú

te atreves _____ hablarle?   **13.** No pudimos ir _____ causa de la lluvia.   **14.** Mis padres nunca consentirán _____ dejarme ir contigo.

*En los siguientes ejercicios (4.8–4.10), llene los espacios en blanco con **por, para** o Ø (nada), según parezca más lógico.*

Ejercicio 4.8

1. Fueron al centro _____ visitar el museo.   **2.** Fueron al mercado _____ verduras.
3. Toma: este regalo es _____ ti.   **4.** Viajaron _____ toda la isla.   **5.** Hay _____ lo menos quinientas personas aquí.   **6.** Prometieron que terminarían toda la construcción en el edificio _____ el semestre entrante.   **7.** Me gusta pasearme _____ la mañana.
8. Pasaremos _____ casa de tu abuelita en camino al partido.   **9.** Lo dijeron _____ que sus vecinos lo oyeran _____ que sabían que reaccionarían.   **10.** _____ fin llegó el cartero.

Ejercicio 4.9

1. Buscó _____ la carta en su bolso, pero no la encontró.   **2.** ¡Cálmate! ¡No es _____ tanto!   **3.** Necesito medicina _____ curarme.   **4.** Lo tomaron _____ idiota.
5. Iremos al mercado _____ fruta.   **6.** Fueron a la tienda _____ comprar lo necesario.
7. Te agradezco _____ la ayuda.   **8.** No pudieron salir _____ la tormenta.   **9.** La llamaremos _____ teléfono.   **10.** Saldrán _____ Madrid en la madrugada.

Ejercicio 4.10

1. —¿Quieres bailar? —¡_____ supuesto!   **2.** No estaba _____ bromas.   **3.** _____ lo general no me gusta levantarme tarde.   **4.** _____ más dinero que gane, no es feliz.
5. Tendremos que comprar _____ lo menos cuatro docenas.   **6.** Le queda un trabajo _____ escribir.   **7.** Se enfermó _____ comer tanto.   **8.** _____ llegar al museo, hay que pasar _____ el parque.   **9.** Acabo de entrar; _____ eso tengo frío.   **10.** Jorge se esfuerza _____ sacar las mejores notas de la clase.

En los siguientes ejercicios (4.11–4.14), traduzca las oraciones, prestando atención a las preposiciones. Puede ser cualquier preposición, o ninguna. (you = **tu**)

Ejercicio 4.11

1. They worry about you.   **2.** He fell in love with her.   **3.** It consists of two sections.
4. The decision depends on you.   **5.** They laughed at him.   **6.** I dream about you every night.   **7.** They said good-bye to me.   **8.** I do not want my ideas to influence your decision.   **9.** She married my brother.   **10.** He stopped drinking.

Ejercicio 4.12

1. We arrived in Madrid at two.   **2.** She opposes everything I say.   **3.** I try to help.

4. I realized my mistake.   **5.** She thanked me for the favor.   **6.** We got onto the bus.
7. Their house is five miles away.   **8.** I met my friends at the restaurant.   **9.** She studies at the university.   **10.** They will be the first to leave.

Ejercicio 4.13

1. I think about my parents every day.   **2.** Luisa's book is interesting.   **3.** I noticed the change.   **4.** I cannot help you at this moment.   **5.** They got mad at me because of my mistake.   **6.** We looked at the clock.   **7.** He saw his sister.   **8.** I asked you for money, not for advice.   **9.** I just ate.   **10.** They work for me.

Ejercicio 4.14

1. I sent it airmail.   **2.** They went to the store for bread.   **3.** I have two papers left to write.   **4.** We will have finished by ten.   **5.** For a child, he knows a lot.   **6.** They left for Guatemala yesterday.   **7.** They are looking for their keys.   **8.** They talked for three hours.   **9.** She worries about you.   **10.** What is this for?

Ejercicio 4.15   *Llene el espacio en blanco con la preposición adecuada, o con el **a** personal; si no se necesita nada, use el símbolo "Ø".*

Cuando primero llegué **(1)** _____ Guadalajara, viví **(2)** _____ un apartamento con mi esposa María y mis dos hijas. Fuimos **(3)** _____ esa ciudad porque María es
(4) _____ allí, y **(5)** _____ esta manera ella podía estar cerca **(6)** _____ su familia.
   Al principio yo daba clases **(7)** _____ el instituto cultural, pero el salario no era suficiente **(8)** _____ pagar el alquiler de una casa. **(9)** _____ eso empecé **(10)** _____ buscar **(11)** _____ otros trabajos, y después de unos años alquilé una casa, y pudimos entonces vivir más cómodamente. Unos años después nos mudamos **(12)** _____ una casa más grande, donde había un cuarto de servicio, y empleé **(13)** _____ un ama de llaves **(14)** _____ hacer todos los quehaceres domésticos.
   Mis suegros viven **(15)** _____ cuatro cuadras de nosotros, y los visitamos **(16)** _____ frecuencia. **(17)** _____ niña, María vivió en esa casa, y conoce **(18)** _____ toda la gente **(19)** _____ la región.

Ejercicio 4.16   *Llene el espacio en blanco con la expresión preposicional más apropiada para traducir lo que se encuentra entre paréntesis.*

**a caballo, a eso de, a la vez, a pesar de, a pie, de pie, a veces,
al menos, en cambio, en seguida, por lo general**

Los vecinos de nuestro rancho tenían toda clase de vehículos, y **(1)** _____ *(generally)* venían en camioneta, aunque **(2)** _____ *(sometimes)* también venían
(3) _____ *(on foot)*, **(4)** _____ *(in spite of)* la distancia; ese día, **(5)** _____ *(however)*, vinieron a visitarnos **(6)** _____ *(on horseback)*. **(7)** _____ *(Around)* las cuatro de la tarde los vimos de lejos, todos **(8)** _____ *(at once)*, y **(9)** _____ *(immediately)*

entramos a preparar algo de comer, porque así es en el campo, cuando viene alguien, hay que ofrecerle de beber y de comer, y darle la hospitalidad que se merece. **(10)** _____ *(At least)* hay que tener algo para ofrecerles. Entraron, y se sentaron en la sala. Algunos se quedaron **(11)** _____ *(standing),* pero todos estaban muy cómodos.

Ejercicio 4.17 *Llene el espacio en blanco con la expresión preposicional más apropiada para traducir lo que se encuentra entre paréntesis.*

**con tal de que, de esta manera, de vez en cuando, de modo que,
con respecto a, de nuevo, de veras, de mala gana**

(1) _____ *(Regarding)* la cuestión de los salarios, el patrón está de acuerdo que se les aumente el salario a los empleados, **(2)** _____ *(so long as)* no se pase del tres porciento, aunque en realidad tengo que decirle que el patrón aceptó esta idea **(3)** _____ *(unwillingly).* En el futuro empleará gente nueva cada año, y **(4)** _____ *(this way)* se evitará tantos aumentos que **(5)** _____ *(really)* no se puede costear. **(6)** _____ *(Once in a while)* tendrá que aumentar **(7)** _____ *(again)* el sueldo de base **(8)** _____ *(so that)* no haya quejas demasiado extremas.

Ejercicio 4.18 *Llene el espacio en blanco con la expresión preposicional más apropiada para traducir lo que se encuentra entre paréntesis.*

**a tiempo, en cuanto, en cuanto a, en frente de, en vez de,
para siempre, por eso, por fin, por lo menos, por otra parte,
por poco, por más que, por supuesto**

¡**(1)** _____ *(Almost)* nos perdemos el concierto! **(2)** _____ *(Instead of)* tomar un taxi, decidimos viajar en autobús, y **(3)** _____ *(for that reason)* no teníamos ningún control sobre el tiempo. **(4)** _____ *(On the other hand, Besides),* ninguno de nosotros había comprado boletos, **(5)** _____ *(however much)* hubiéramos discutido la necesidad de hacerlo temprano. **(6)** _____ *(In regard to, As far as . . . is concerned)* Roberto, pues **(7)** _____ *(of course)* no nos va a dejar olvidar que **(8)** _____ *(as soon as)* decidimos ir al concierto él nos dijo que consiguiéramos los boletos antes de ir porque si no tendríamos que esperar horas haciendo cola. **(9)** _____ *(Finally)* entramos justo **(10)** _____ *(on time),* y pudimos disfrutar con el concierto. Pero tuve la mala suerte de tener **(11)** _____ *(in front of)* mí a un tipo con tanto pelo que yo no podía ver nada. Pero **(12)** _____ *(at least)* pude oír la música. Éste será un recuerdo que guardaremos **(13)** _____ *(forever).*

Ejercicio 4.19 *Llene el espacio en blanco con la preposición correcta.*

Acabo **(1)** _____ acordarme **(2)** _____ mi cita con el nuevo dentista. No me acostumbro **(3)** _____ este nuevo dentista: le agradezco **(4)** _____ la ayuda que me da. Él siempre se alegra **(5)** _____ verme, y se apresura **(6)** _en_ atenderme con cuidado. El problema es que no deja **(7)** _____ hablar, y yo, claro, no puedo contestar porque tengo la boca llena de instrumentos: hasta plática conmigo en español, se avergüenza **(8)** _de_ sus errores, se burla **(9)** _de_ sí mismo porque se da cuenta **(10)** _de_ su falta de práctica. Aprendió **(11)** _a_ hablar español en la universidad, y luego se casó **(12)** _con_ una colombiana; convinieron **(13)** _en_ hablar inglés la mayor parte del tiempo porque querían que sus hijos hablaran el idioma del país, y que no se convirtieran **(14)** _en_ extranjeros en su propio país. Sin embargo, cada vez que puede, ella lo ayuda **(15)** _a_ practicar su español para que no se le olvide.

Yo lo dejo **(16)** _Ø_ hablar porque no me queda otra, pero francamente ya no puedo más. Quiero comenzar **(17)** _a_ buscar **(18)** ~~por~~ otro dentista, pero no sé si me voy a atrever **(19)** _a_ explicarle por qué me voy.

Ejercicio 4.20 _Llene el espacio en blanco con la preposición correcta._

Pensó que estaba enamorado **(1)** _____ Blanca hasta que se encontró **(2)** _____ Victoria y se enamoró **(3)** _____ ella a primera vista. Desde ese momento su vida dependía **(4)** _____ ella, y no se detuvo **(5)** _____ pensar en el efecto que tendría en Blanca el que él se despidiera **(6)** _____ ella así, sin motivo, sin siquiera enojarse **(7)** _____ ella.

Cuando Blanca supo lo que había pasado, se empeñó **(8)** _____ quedarse **(9)** _____ su novio, y empezó **(10)** _____ hacer planes de toda clase para enterarse **(11)** _____ todos los movimientos de ambos. La vida le había enseñado **(12)** _____ ser fuerte, y pensaba **(13)** _____ que si se esforzaba **(14)** _____ obtener algo, lo conseguiría. En la universidad, se había especializado **(15)** _____ sicología, y se había fijado **(16)** _____ las injusticias que podían surgir si uno no insistía **(17)** _____ conseguir lo mejor para uno mismo.

Decidió **(18)** _____ llamar **(19)** _____ Victoria y pedirle que no se metiera **(20)** _____ su novio. La invitó **(21)** _____ cenar con ella en un restaurante esa noche: llegó temprano y esperó **(22)** _____ el gran momento. Por fin, cuando hablaron, vio que Victoria se interesaba mucho **(23)** _____ su novio, y se negó **(24)** _____ dejarlo.

Pero ése no sería el final de sus esfuerzos. Pensaría **(25)** _____ otro plan.

Ejercicio 4.21 _Llene el espacio en blanco con la preposición correcta._

¿Conoces el cuento que se trata **(1)** _____ un trencito que no podía subir la cuesta? Ésta es una versión un poco modificada de la tradicional.

Había una vez un trencito que quería subir por una montaña y no podía: llegaba hasta la mitad de la cuesta y ya no podía más: tenía que volver **(2)** _____ bajar. Todos los otros trenes se burlaban **(3)** _____ él. Lo tomaban **(4)** _____ incompetente. Su mamá le decía que no se preocupara **(5)** _____ lo que los otros pensaban **(6)** _____ él, pero él no podía resignarse **(7)** _____ una vida de mediocridad. Soñaba **(8)** _____ poder subir esa cuesta y llegar hasta la cima. Un día decidió tratar **(9)** _____ llegar hasta la cima, pero sabía que necesitaría toda la suerte del mundo para lograr su sueño: por eso fue a la casa del brujo, y cuando le abrió su hija, preguntó **(10)** _____ el brujo, y ella fue a buscarlo. Cuando llegó el brujo, el trencito le pidió **(11)** _____ un favor: que le diera un talismán, o algo para ayudarlo a subir hasta la cima. El brujo se rió **(12)** _____ él, y le dijo que se olvidara **(13)** _____ talismanes, que no podría subir nunca.

El trencito se enfureció, y le gritó: "¡Sí que puedo, ya verás!" Rabiando, fue a la base de la cima, y se puso **(14)** _____ correr con todo el coraje que le había causado esta última vergüenza. Llegó hasta la mitad de la cuesta, pero esta vez no paró: olvidó **(15)** _____ su miedo, y siguió subiendo; cuando le quedaba sólo un metro **(16)** _____ llegar a la cima, se sintió sin fuerzas, pero se dijo "¡Sí que puedo! ¡Yo sé que sí puedo!", y poco a poco, usando toda su energía para cada vuelta de sus ruedas, terminó **(17)** _____ subir la cuesta.

Y así fue que el trencito logró lo que quería: convirtió la energía de su rabia en fuerza positiva.

Adverbs (Adverbs Ending in *-mente*, Word Order, Multiple-Function Words)

[Chapter 4.B.1–4, pages 124–126]

Ejercicio 4.22 *Traduzca usando la palabra más apropiada de la lista en español, y el orden correcto de palabras.*

bien, claro, derecho, distinto, duro, hondo, igual, limpio, rápido, raro

I used to get along *(llevarse)* with my neighbors well, but the other day our relationship changed. I saw that their son wasn't playing fairly: whenever my daughter won, he would hit her, and he hit her hard. After seeing that twice, I decided I had to do something fast. I went straight to my neighbors' house, and told the mother what I had seen. She took a deep breath, and looked at me in a strange way. She told me she knew this: her son was short, but highly competitive. He couldn't play the same way as the rest: he had to play differently. It was natural.

Adverbs (Adverbs of Place)

[Chapter 4.B.5, pages 126–128]

Ejercicio 4.23 *Llene el espacio en blanco con el **adverbio de lugar** correcto.*

—Nos acabamos de mudar a un edificio de apartamentos de dos pisos: hay cuatro apartamentos, dos **(1)** _____ *(below)* y dos **(2)** _____ *(above);* dos de éstos están **(3)** _____ *(in front)* y dos **(4)** _____ *(in back).* **(5)** _____ *(Outside)* hay un jardín precioso. ¿**(6)** _____ *(Where)* vives tú?

—Yo vivo **(7)** _____ *(here)*, en este edificio. Mi apartamento se encuentra **(8)** _____ *(inside)* a la derecha. ¿Quieren entrar?

—Sí, gracias.

—Pasen, pues. Déjenme enseñarles el apartamento. **(9)** _____ *(There)* está la sala, **(10)** _____ *(over here)* están las recámaras, **(11)** _____ *(over there)* está el baño.

—¡Qué lindo! Bueno, gracias por todo. Ya nos tenemos que ir.

—¿ **(12)** _____ *(Where)* van?

—Tengo una cita con el médico.

—¿Tienen que ir **(13)** _____ *(far)*? Si quieren, los llevo.

—No, muchas gracias. El consultorio del médico sólo queda a dos cuadras.

Adverbs (Adverbs of Time)

[Chapter 4.B.6, pages 128–131]

Ejercicio 4.24 *Junte las oraciones usando **adverbios de tiempo** como transición.*

(1) _____ *(Always)* he querido escribir una autobiografía, y **(2)** _____ *(the day before yesterday)* decidí que la iba a empezar. Sin embargo, **(3)** _____ *(when)* me senté a escribir, no podía decidir **(4)** _____ *(when)* debía comenzar la acción. Me preguntaba: ¿Empiezo **(5)** _____ *(now)*? ¿Empiezo en el pasado? Dieron las once de la noche y **(6)** _____ *(still not)* había escrito ni una palabra. **(7)** _____ *(So then)* decidí acostarme porque **(8)** _____ *(already)* era tarde.

(9) _____ *(Yesterday)* volví a sentarme para ver si podía inspirarme. Estuve tres horas tratando de escribir algo, pero no me gustaba nada. **(10)** _____ *(While)* escribía me sentía tonta, y sabía que **(11)** _____ *(never ever)* querría que nadie viera lo que estaba escribiendo. **(12)** _____ *(Soon)* decidí parar.

(13) _____ *(Last night)* soñé con mi autobiografía, y **(14)** _____ *(today)*, al despertarme, **(15)** _____ *(already)* estaba claro en mi mente lo que iba a escribir. **(16)** _____ *(Still not)* sabía las palabras exactas que usaría, pero sabía que escribiría sobre mis dudas. Y así fue que comencé a escribir mi autobiografía: éstas son mis primeras palabras. Me siento como un **(17)** _____ *(new-)* nacido, pero sé que **(18)** _____ *(tomorrow)*, cuando empiece a escribir de nuevo, me sentiré un poco más fuerte. Y **(19)** _____ *(then)*, poco a poco, será lo más natural del mundo, y **(20)** _____ *(no longer)* tendré vergüenza ni dudas. **(21)** _____ *(Sooner or later)* saldrá una novela de aquí.

Ejercicio 4.25 *Llene el espacio en blanco usando **ya, ya no, todavía** o **todavía no**.*

(1) _____ *(Still)* recuerdo la primera noche en que vinieron a cenar mis suegros. Me dijeron que **(2)** _____ *(already)* habían comido, y claro que **(3)** _____ *(no longer)* tenían hambre. Yo no podía creerlo; pero como **(4)** _____ *(still not)* había terminado de preparar la cena, decidí no cocinar más, y sentarme a hablar con ellos sin comer nada. Esa noche mi marido no iba a poder llegar hasta la hora del postre, así que no importaba.

Adverbs (Adverbs of Manner)

[Chapter 4.B.7, pages 131–132]

Ejercicio 4.26 *Llene el espacio en blanco con el **adverbio de modo** correcto.*

—¿Cómo se prepara una tortilla española?
—Mira, se prepara **(1)** _____ *(like this):* bates **(2)** _____ *(well)* dos huevos, los pones a cocinar en un sartén con cebollas y papas cortadas en trozos y ya **(3)** _____ *(thoroughly)* cocinadas.
—Y ¿**(4)** _____ *(how)* la volteas?
—Esto es un arte. Tienes que hacerlo bien, porque si lo haces **(5)** _____ *(badly),* la tortilla puede terminar en el piso. Necesitas algo del tamaño del sartén, **(6)** _____ *(like)* una tapa de olla.
—¿Y cuánto se cocina?
—**(7)** _____ *(It depends).* A algunos les gusta más seca que a otros.
—Suena **(8)** _____ *(really)* fácil. ¿Hacemos una ahora?
—Está **(9)** _____ *(Okay.).*

Adverbs (Adverbs of Quantity)

[Chapter 4.B.8, pages 132–134]

Ejercicio 4.27 *Llene el espacio en blanco usando el **adverbio de cantidad** correcto.*

Estoy **(1)** _____ *(rather)* cansada hoy. Dormí **(2)** _____ *(barely)* cuatro horas anoche, y no es **(3)** _____ *(enough).* **(4)** _____ *(Almost)* no tengo fuerza. Además, hace **(5)** _____ *(too)* calor para trabajar, y me duele **(6)** _____ *(so much)* la cabeza que no puedo hacer nada. Quizás si camino **(7)** _____ *(a bit)* me sienta mejor. Siempre como **(8)** _____ *(little)* para el desayuno, **(9)** _____ *(only)* pan o cereal, y por eso estoy **(10)** _____ *(half)* cansada todo el tiempo. El médico me dijo que debo ejercitarme **(11)** _____ *(more),* y tomar vitaminas. Me dijo que no debo tomar café, ni cenar **(12)** _____ *(too)* tarde. A veces creo que la salud exige **(13)** _____ *(too much),* pero en realidad, si se pudieran ver los resultados de inmediato, no sería **(14)** _____ *(so much).* ¿**(15)** _____ *(How much)* tengo que hacer para sentirme bien? Ahora mismo no estoy **(16)** _____ *(not at all)* satisfecha.

Adverbs (Adverbs of Confirmation, Doubt, or Negation)

[Chapter 4.B.9, pages 134–136]

Ejercicio 4.28 *Traduzca usando el **adverbio de confirmación, duda** o **negación** correcto.* (you = **tú**)

"You are going to pay for our tickets, **aren't you**?"
"**Yes,** but I am missing one dollar. Beto, do you **by any chance** have one you can lend me?"
"**No,** I don't have a dollar, but **I do** have 75 cents. Do you want them?"
"**Okay. Maybe** Quique or Marisol have the other 25 cents. Quique, do you have 25 cents?"
"**No.**"
"Marisol?"
"No, I don't **either.**"
"**Well,** then, **maybe** we won't go to the movies. Do you want to go for a walk in the park?"
"Oh, **no! No way!**"

Adverbs (Adverbial Phrases)

[Chapter 4.B.10, pages 136–137]

Ejercicio 4.29 *Llene el espacio en blanco usando la **locución adverbial** correcta.*

Ayer fui al cine por primera vez en años, y vi una película que me encantó. Había mucha gente, y **(1)** _____ *(often)* había partes de mucho miedo y todos gritaban. Yo descansaba muy **(2)** _____ *(comfortably)* en mi butaca, tanto que **(3)** _____ *(almost)* me duermo. Me parece que la segunda mitad de la película sólo la entendí **(4)** _____ *(halfway),* y **(5)** _____ *(as a matter of fact),* me perdí el final. Sin embargo, estoy seguro de que sé lo que pasó **(6)** _____ *(at the end),* aunque no estaré satisfecho **(7)** _____ *(until)* verificarlo con alguien. **(8)** _____ *(Oh well),* yo estoy contento porque **(9)** _____ *(finally)* fui al cine, y **(10)** _____ *(all in all),* me gustó la experiencia. Sólo quisiera encontrar **(11)** _____ *(sometime)* **(12)** _____ *(somewhere)* un cine que no fuera tan caro.

Adverbs (Related Adverbs and Prepositions)

[Chapter 4.B.11, pages 137–138)

Ejercicio 4.30 *Subraye la selección correcta para el contexto.*

Mis vecinos de (**1.** abajo / bajo / debajo de) son recién casados, y llevan una vida muy romántica, pero extraña a la vez. Los dos son estudiantes universitarios, y ella toma una clase conmigo. Siempre se sienta (**2.** adelante / delante de) mí. Ella y su marido se pasan los fines de semana (**3.** afuera / fuera de), trabajando (**4.** atrás / detrás de / tras) su garaje en motores de diferentes tipos. Es muy común verlos trabajar juntos en un mismo coche: recuerdo una mañana cuando él estaba parado (**5.** enfrente / frente a) un coche, trabajando con la cabeza metida (**6.** adentro / dentro de) el capó [*the hood*], y ella estaba acostada (**7.** abajo / bajo / debajo de) el mismo coche, haciendo algo con el aceite, creo. Yo tenía miedo que algo fuera a pasarles, pero nunca les pasa nada. A veces se pelean porque los dos quieren la misma herramienta, y terminan con carreras, en que uno corre (**8.** atrás / detrás de / tras) el otro para quitarle algo. De vez en cuando se sientan (**9.** abajo / bajo / debajo de) un árbol para descansar. El sábado pasado él salió solo; yo supuse que ella se había quedado (**10.** adentro / dentro de) porque estaría enferma, o algo así.

 # Conjunctions (Usage, Conjunctions of Coordination)

[Chapter 4.C,1–2, pages 139–140]

Ejercicio 4.31 *Llene el espacio en blanco con la conjunción de coordinación correcta:* **y, e, o, u, pero, sino, ni… ni, sino que, sino también.**

España (**1**) _____ Hispanoamérica tienen una relación ambigua: se respetan (**2**) _____ se desprecian a la vez. Su respeto mutuo se debe no sólo a que son representantes de una cultura común, (**3**) _____ al menos de culturas semejantes, (**4**) _____ a que usan el mismo idioma. Además, tienen una historia en común, (**5**) _____ eso no se puede olvidar, aunque sea una historia destructiva.

Cuando compiten entre ellos, su desprecio es equivalente a su respeto: en esas ocasiones, por una razón (**6**) _____ otra, cada uno encuentra motivo de desprecio. Un español puede despreciar a un hispanoamericano, por ejemplo, porque habla español, (**7**) _____ no lo habla como él. Un hispanoamericano puede despreciar a un español por ser descendiente de conquistadores (**8**) _____ colonizadores.

A la hora de enfrentarse al resto del mundo, lo que está muy claro es que lo más fuerte no es la división (**9**) _____ la unión de estos dos mundos. En última instancia, no son españoles (**10**) _____ hispanoamericanos, (**11**) _____ hispanos, y no les importan ya **(12)** _____ las diferencias de dialecto **(13)** _____ las diferencias culturales, **(14)** _____ los lazos que tienen en común con aquellos otros hermanos.

Ejercicio 4.32 _Traduzca, usando **pero, sino** o **sino que** para traducir_ but.

1. I was afraid but I did it.   **2.** It wasn't blue, but red.   **3.** It wasn't blue, but I bought it anyway.   **4.** I didn't buy a red car, but a blue one.   **5.** I didn't want a red car, but I bought one anyway.   **6.** I wanted a red car, but instead I bought a blue one.   **7.** I didn't buy the car, but rather I sold it.

Ejercicio 4.33 _Junte la información que sigue para formar un párrafo; use conjunciones de coordinación donde se necesiten._

Norberto me llamó. Norberto me contó de su viaje a México. Me contó de su viaje a Puerto Rico. Le gustó mucho México. Se enfermó con la comida. Le encantó Puerto Rico. Sufrió del calor. El país que más le gustó no fue México: fue Puerto Rico. Le gustó más no sólo porque tiene muchas playas; también porque es una isla. Pudo conocerla mejor en el poco tiempo que tenía.

Conjunctions (Conjunctions of Subordination)

[Chapter 4.C.3, page 140]

Ejercicio 4.34 _Llene el espacio en blanco con la conjunción de subordinación **que** cuando se necesite. Si no se necesita nada, use el símbolo "Ø"._

Yo no sabía **(1)** _____ iban a venir todos juntos a **(2)** _____ cenar. Pensé **(3)** _____ sólo venías tú, Julio, y **(4)** _____ los demás se encontrarían con nosotros en el bar para **(5)** _____ celebrar. Pero ahora **(6)** _____ están aquí, pues bienvenidos. No quiero **(7)** _____ se vayan sin **(8)** _____ comer. Creo **(9)** _____ tengo suficiente, y si no, entre todos preparamos algo. También Laura me dijo **(10)** _____ venía. Bueno, pues, déjenme **(11)** _____ servirles un vinito o algo para **(12)** _____ pueda ya empezar la fiesta.

Ejercicio 4.35 _Traduzca las oraciones siguientes usando las **conjunciones de coordinación y de subordinación** apropiadas._

You said you were going to the store to buy milk. I told you we didn't just need milk, but bread too. I see you bought neither bread nor milk, but rather that you rented a video.

◆ D Transitions

[Chapter 4.D, pages 141–145]

Ejercicio 4.36 *Llene el espacio en blanco con la **transición** correcta.*

(1) _____ *(In general),* me gusta más el teatro que el cine. **(2)** _____ *(In the first place),* el teatro es más emocionante **(3)** _____ *(because)* los actores están allí mismo frente a uno; **(4)** _____ *(secondly),* el acto de ir al teatro es un evento en sí. **(5)** _____ *(However),* me parece que además de lo divertido que es ver una obra desarrollarse, existe un suspenso especial en el teatro, que es el de la posibilidad de que alguno de los actores cometa un error. **(6)** _____ *(In fact),* a veces me pregunto si **(7)** _____ *(actually)* no vamos al teatro no tanto con el propósito de ver una obra maravillosa, sino **(8)** _____ *(perhaps)* para sentir una comunión humana con los actores que la representan. ¿**(9)** _____ *(By chance,)* no sienten otros lo que siento yo, que al escuchar cada palabra que enuncian los actores, en vez de perderme en la ilusión de la obra, me la paso esperando bajo tensión la próxima palabra, siempre con la duda de que se le vaya a olvidar, o que se vea que sólo es un acto? Cuando **(10)** _____ *(unfortunately)* un actor comete algún error, se confirma en mí la necesidad original de mi presencia allí: la de ser testigo de la humanidad que se esfuerza por alcanzar la perfección fuera de sí misma, pero que no siempre lo logra, y **(11)** _____ *(as a result)* nos recuerda nuestra propia humanidad. Si la obra tiene defectos, la aplaudo **(12)** _____ *(in spite of)* todo; aplaudo en ella el esfuerzo humano, y me siento un poco mejor, **(13)** _____ *(maybe)* por haber logrado ver estos defectos. **(14)** _____ *(On the other hand),* cuando **(15)** _____ *(fortunately)* la obra sale perfecta, aplaudo más ruidosamente, aplaudo el logro de los actores; y **(16)** _____ *(yet),* me queda una leve sensación de inferioridad, al menos hasta el momento en que pienso en la noche siguiente, cuando estos actores tendrán que volver a actuar con la misma perfección, y que existe todavía la posibilidad de que alguno de ellos tropiece.

    (17) _____ *(Regarding)* a las películas, el placer es totalmente distinto: casi siempre logran eliminar los defectos antes de mostrar la película, y **(18)** _____ *(for the most part)* lo que queda está mecánicamente perfecto. Han perfeccionado **(19)** _____ *(more and more)* la tecnología visual y el arte de manipular al público. Como público de cine, ya no somos testigos de la humanidad de los actores, sino clientes que hemos comprado dos horas de distracción. Yo al menos me pierdo en la ilusión dramática de las películas, o **(20)** _____ *(in any case)* es lo que trato de hacer. No me concentro **(21)** _____ *(almost ever)* en las palabras que enuncian los actores ni en su arte. **(22)** _____ *(In the end),* si una película no me deja disfrutarla sin distracciones, me da coraje, y no pienso para nada en la humanidad sino en el dinero que desperdicié.

    (23) _____ *(In short),* el arte dramático para mí sólo se percibe **(24)** _____ *(nowadays)* en el teatro. Lo que vemos en el cine es otra cosa.

Ejercicio 4.37 *Añada la **transición** más lógica de la lista para cada espacio en blanco.*

a pesar de, además, casi siempre, con respecto a, de hecho,
en fin de cuentas, por consiguiente, por ejemplo, por eso,
por lo tanto, por otro lado, porque, según, ya que

Mi sobrina acaba de cumplir los quince años: es muy bonita, y **(1)** _____ ha decidido tratar de hacerse modelo, **(2)** _____ los peligros que esa profesión conlleva. **(3)** _____ sus padres, es aceptable que se haga modelo, **(4)** _____ es una joven muy madura para su edad. **(5)** _____, puede reconocer la malicia de otros, y **(6)** _____ no cae en las trampas tradicionales como tantas jóvenes hoy en día.

   (7) _____ el trabajo en sí, no es tan fácil como parece. **(8)** _____, es posible que sea uno de los más agotadores. Las sesiones de fotografía, **(9)** _____, pueden tomar hasta seis horas corridas, y las modelos deben mantenerse bellas y frescas, sin ningún rasgo de cansancio ni de mal humor. **(10)** _____, deben comer con muchísimo cuidado para mantener su cutis impecable. Y, **(11)** _____ los fotógrafos pueden pedirles en una misma sesión que se vean de playa o de románticas moribundas, deben evitar el sol y todo lo que pueda afectar su color.

   (12) _____, el trabajo tiene aspectos divertidos. La modelo es el centro de atención, la visten y la maquillan para transformarla todo el día. Y **(13)** _____ tienen que viajar a diferentes partes del mundo.

   (14) _____, la experiencia tiene que ser buena.

Chapter 4 Review

Ejercicio 4.38 *Llene los espacios en blanco con preposiciones, conjunciones, adverbios o expresiones; si no necesita nada para un espacio en blanco, use el símbolo "Ø"; algunos espacios en blanco pueden tener más de una palabra.*

El debate sobre la igualdad de los hombres **(1)** _____ las mujeres nunca va **(2)** _____ terminar, y en el mundo hispanohablante es un debate que para algunos lucha contra la cultura misma **(3)** _____ manera brutal. Hay dos preguntas básicas que nunca se han contestado bien: **(4)** _____, ¿qué hay de malo con que haya diferencias? **(5)** _____, ¿cuáles son las diferencias que realmente deberían cambiar?

   (6) _____ la primera pregunta, vamos a ver qué puede haber de malo. **(7)** _____ yo, es malo que haya dominación de cualquier individuo, mujer **(8)** _____ hombre. Es malo también que haya maltrato físico **(9)** _____ mental, y que algunos tengan más derechos humanos que otros. **(10)** _____, no sé si es malo reconocer que **(11)** _____ hay ciertas diferencias puramente físicas que no se pueden cambiar: la mujer tolera el dolor mejor que el hombre, **(12)** _____ puede alzar menos peso que él; la mujer tiene más aguante que el hombre en todos los sentidos, pero el hombre es probablemente mejor **(13)** _____ la guerra **(14)** _____ su agresividad. Claro que en un mundo de paz, eso no importaría **(15)** _____ nada; **(16)** _____, uno se pregunta si habría tanta guerra si las mujeres gobernaran el mundo.

(17) _____ la segunda pregunta, **(18)** _____ empezamos a contestarla arriba: debemos insistir **(19)** _____ eliminar las diferencias que le quitan a la mujer los derechos humanos. Es fácil decir esto, **(20)** _____ las implicaciones son inmensas. En la cultura hispana, donde la mujer y el hombre tienen papeles **(21)** _____ claramente marcados en la vida cotidiana, uno pensaría **(22)** _____ un cambio de este tipo podría representar un peligro, y que habría que resignarse **(23)** _____ las diferencias con tal de no perder la base cultural que nos identifica. Algunos dicen que si la mujer se empeña **(24)** _____ ser igual al hombre en la vida profesional, y deja **(25)** _____ dedicarse al doble oficio de madre y cuidadora del hogar, **(26)** _____ la familia estadounidense, que **(27)** _____ es el centro de ese mundo, se desintegraría como lo ha hecho la familia estadounidense. Pero hemos visto que **(28)** _____ existe en el mundo hispano una liberación femenina que no sólo no ha destruido la cultura, **(29)** _____ la ha enriquecido: la mujer hispana moderna es profesional, instruida, y madre y esposa **(30)** _____. El hombre hispano moderno **(31)** _____ es profesional, instruido, y padre y marido. Ambos se esfuerzan **(32)** _____ apoyar al otro en estos cambios, y **(33)** _____ las dificultades, han logrado crear un nuevo mundo donde la cultura hispana, que **(34)** _____ de por sí era un modelo por el énfasis que le daba a la familia, se ha vuelto **(35)** _____ más poderosa internacionalmente.

(36) _____, este debate nunca se resolverá **(37)** _____ nunca se eliminarán las diferencias entre dos seres naturalmente diferentes. Lo que **(38)** _____ se puede resolver es lo que el ser humano creó como diferencias, y, **(39)** _____, eso es lo único que merece nuestra atención.

Ejercicio 4.39 Temas de ensayo.

Prestando atención al uso de preposiciones, adverbios, conjunciones y transiciones, escriba un párrafo sobre uno de los temas siguientes.

a. las aventuras de un gato que atrapa a un pájaro y lo mete en la casa de su dueño para jugar

ATAJO

Phrases: Making transitions
Vocabulary: Animals
Grammar: Prepositions; Adverbs; Conjunctions

b. las aventuras de un ratoncito que se encuentra un enorme queso suizo

ATAJO

Phrases: Making transitions
Vocabulary: Animals; Food
Grammar: Prepositions; Adverbs; Conjunctions

c. las aventuras de un niño que se pierde en el bosque

ATAJO

Phrases: Making transitions
Grammar: Prepositions; Adverbs; Conjunctions

d. Escriba una narración de una experiencia ambigua, que fue buena por ciertas razones pero mala por otras. Elabore al máximo la duplicidad de sus sentimientos.

ATAJO

Phrases: Making transitions; Weighing the evidence
Grammar: Prepositions; Adverbs; Conjunctions

Chapter 5   Verbs: Formation

◆ⒶIndicative Mood (Present Indicative)

[Chapter 5.A.1, pages 148–153]

Ejercicio 5.1   *Conjugue el verbo en la primera persona singular del presente del indicativo (yo).*

Cariño mío, te (**1.** amar). Todos los días (**2.** cantar) tu canción, y sólo (**3.** comer) lo que te gusta. Ahora (**4.** vivir) por ti; cuando (**5.** hablar) con otros, es contigo en mente; y si (**6.** caminar) por el pueblo, es contigo a mi lado. Ya no (**7.** coser) nada para mí ni para nadie. Ya no (**8.** beber) más que agua fresca, tu bebida favorita. Cuando (**9.** abrir) la puerta para salir, estás ahí. Aún cuando (**10.** imprimir) los capítulos de mi autobiografía, tu presencia me da fuerza.

Ejercicio 5.2   *Conjugue el verbo en la primera persona singular del presente del indicativo (yo).*

No sé por qué (**1.** mentir) tanto, y (**2.** seguir) mintiendo. Les (**3.** pedir) a mis amigos y a mi familia que me perdonen, pero luego (**4.** repetir) el mismo error. Siempre les (**5.** comentar) a ellos que (**6.** mezclar) la verdad con la fantasía, y así (**7.** impedir) que olviden mis mentiras. Si me critican, no (**8.** defenderse) nunca porque en realidad (**9.** querer) el castigo que me da su crítica. Cada vez que puedo, (**10.** elegir) criticarme yo mismo primero, y así (**11.** conseguir) mi propio castigo. Creo que es mejor si (**12.** revelar) mi crimen, y así me (**13.** servir) yo mismo de juez. Pero luego (**14.** cansarse) de tanto luchar conmigo mismo, y (**15.** cerrar) los ojos y (**16.** sentir) que (**17.** comenzar) a olvidarlo todo. A veces (**18.** pensar) que si (**19.** perderse) en el sueño, todo lo malo desaparecerá.

Ejercicio 5.3   *Conjugue el verbo en la tercera persona singular del presente del indicativo. (él / ella)*

Como cada día al despertarse, este día especial del año, Roberto, que es un hombre de hábitos muy establecidos, (**1.** pensar) en lo que (**2.** querer) hacer. Antes de levantarse, se (**3.** hacer) la lista de sus actividades: (**4.** recordar) que este día siempre (**5.** cortar) el pasto y (**6.** podar) las ramas largas, luego, cuando ya le (**7.** doler) el cuello, va al pueblo y (**8.** votar), porque hoy (**9.** ser) el día de las elecciones. Después (**10.** volver) a su casa, va al patio que (**11.** oler) a pasto fresco, (**12.** acostarse) en la hamaca a tomar la siesta. Después de la siesta (**13.** ir) al club y (**14.** jugar) al tenis con sus amigos.

Pero cuando (**15.** levantarse) y (**16.** mirar) por la ventana, (**17.** ver) que hoy es diferente: (**18.** llover) sin parar. Roberto apenas (**19.** dominar) su frustración lo suficiente para llamar a su mamá. Le (**20.** contar) de sus frustraciones, hasta que ella lo (**21.** interrumpir) para decirle del accidente de la noche anterior en que la tormenta destruyó el techo de su casa: ella (**22.** llorar), porque no (**23.** poder) imaginarse cómo se va a resolver su problema. Roberto (**24.** salir) corriendo a casa de su mamá, bajo la lluvia que ni siquiera (**25.** sentir), y en camino, (**26.** jurar) ya no darle tanta importancia a sus pequeños hábitos y tratar de poner las cosas en perspectiva.

Ejercicio 5.4 *Conjugue el verbo en la primera persona singular del presente del indicativo (**yo**).*

1. Siempre (proteger) a mis hijos primero.   **2.** Sé que si (seguir) trabajando sin parar, voy a terminar a tiempo.   **3.** Creo que (obedecer) demasiado a mis superiores. **4.** Cuando (traducir) del inglés al español, a veces uso anglicismos sin darme cuenta. **5.** Cada vez que patino, me (torcer) un tobillo.   **6.** Si (recoger) mi ropa todos los días, hay menos desorden.   **7.** De vez en cuando (conseguir) lo que quiero, pero no siempre.   **8.** No sabes cuánto te (agradecer) tu ayuda.   **9.** Temprano en la mañana (producir) más.   **10.** No me (convencer) de la necesidad de comprar un auto nuevo.

Ejercicio 5.5 *Conjugue el verbo en la segunda persona singular del presente del indicativo (**tú**).*

1. Si (enviar) la carta esta mañana, llegará más rapido.   **2.** Veo que (continuar) con el mismo trabajo.   **3.** Me parece que (confiar) demasiado en la gente.   **4.** ¿Siempre (reunir) a todos tus amigos en tu casa para celebrar el Año Nuevo?   **5.** Si no (criar) a tus hijos con amor, pueden tener problemas sicológicos más tarde en la vida. **6.** ¿Cuándo (graduarse / tú)?   **7.** Creo que (guiar) muy bien.   **8.** ¿En esa obra de teatro (actuar) de médico?   **9.** No siempre (concluir) lo mismo que yo.   **10.** Siempre (huir) de la verdad.

Ejercicio 5.6 *Conjugue el verbo en el presente del indicativo, primero en la primera (**yo**), luego en la tercera persona singular (**él** / **ella** / **usted** / **impersonal**) y finalmente en la primera persona plural (**nosotros**).*

1. Cuando vamos a la pista de hielo, primero (caerse) yo, luego (caerse) él, pero siempre (caerse) los dos al menos una vez antes de que se acabe el día.   **2.** No nos gusta sacar la basura: por lo general, si no lo (hacer) yo, lo (hacer) él; pero a veces no lo (hacer) para nada porque se nos olvida.   **3.** Mi hermana y yo tratamos de vestirnos de manera diferente. Yo la veo a ella vestirse y (ponerse) algo diferente de ella, o si yo me visto primero, ella (ponerse) algo distinto a lo que yo me puse. Pero a veces no nos vemos y (ponerse / nosotros) lo mismo: es un problema muy grave.   **4.** Nuestro perro tiene que salir de vez en cuando, pero siempre tiene que ir acompañado; a veces yo (salir) con él, y otras veces (salir) mi compañera de casa; es rara la vez que las dos (salir) juntas con el perro.   **5.** Cuando (traer) mi paraguas nunca llueve. A veces mi esposa (traer) el paraguas, y a veces los dos lo (traer); siempre tratamos de tener al menos uno para que no llueva.   **6.** No sé qué (valer) en mi trabajo o en mi vida. Para mí, la inspiración de otros (valer) mucho. Me imagino que todos (valer) algo para otros sin darnos cuenta.   **7.** Hoy (venir) con más hambre que nunca. Mi compañera también (venir) hambrienta hoy. Así que (venir) las dos a comer con gusto y gana.   **8.** Nunca (decir / yo) más de lo que tengo que decir; si se (decir) más de lo necesario, a veces es peor. Si sólo (decir) nosotros lo esencial, podemos mantener nuestra distancia.   **9.** No (tener / yo) suficiente dinero; si usted (tener) un par de pesos, creo que entre los dos (tener) bastante para pagar la cuenta.   **10.** Si yo les (dar) diez pesos, y usted les (dar) quince, entre los dos les (dar) el total de veinticinco.   **11.** Yo no (ir) porque (ir) Juan. Nunca (ir) los dos porque no es necesario.   **12.** Creo que (ser) responsable en cuanto a la ecología. (Ser) obvio que si todos (ser) responsables, el mundo durará más.   **13.** Yo (estar) triste porque se (estar) acabando el verano. Casi (estar / nosotros) a punto de volver a clases.   **14.** (haber / yo) de empacar las maletas para el viaje. No estoy segura pero creo que (haber) de hacer frío allá de noche. Nunca (haber / nosotros) viajado a esa parte del mundo.   **15.** A veces no (oír / yo) bien lo que anuncian en los aviones. No se (oír) nada por el ruido de los motores, creo. Si no (oír / nosotros) los anuncios, ¿será grave?   **16.** Yo (saber) hablar español, y si usted (saber) hablar francés, entre los dos (saber) quizás lo suficiente para que el viaje sea cómodo.   **17.** Es curioso que cuando yo (ver) una película y mi novio (ver) la misma película, nunca (ver) exactamente lo mismo.

Ejercicio 5.7 *Conjugue el verbo en el presente del indicativo de la persona indicada.*

1. Siempre (caminar / yo) en la madrugada.   **2.** A veces (actuar / tú) y a veces no.   **3.** Nosotros (actuar) mejor con público.   **4.** Si (adquirir / yo) esa propiedad, estaré contenta.   **5.** Siempre (adquirir / nosotros) propiedades que necesitan mejorarse.   **6.** ¿En qué (andar / vosotros)?   **7.** En la vida (aprender / nosotros) lo esencial si prestamos atención.   **8.** Cuando se asusta, mi hermanito me (tomar) de la mano.   **9.** Nunca me (avergonzar / ellos) mis padres.   **10.** Creo que a veces nosotros (avergonzar) a nuestros padres.   **11.** Si (averiguar / yo) el secreto, te lo cuento.   **12.** ¿Te (decir / yo) lo que me contaron ayer?   **13.** (decir / él) Raúl que los nuevos vecinos son muy fiesteros.   **14.** Parece que nunca les (decir / nosotros) a nuestros padres que los queremos.   **15.** ¿Qué (buscar / ellos) esos hombres?   **16.** Ya no (caber / yo) en esa sillita que usaba de niña.   **17.** Esa ropa vieja ya no me (caber).   **18.** Por suerte, no (caerse / yo) con tanta frecuencia como cuando era adolescente.   **19.** Tu hermana me (caer) bien.   **20.** ¿Siempre (cerrar / tú) la ventana de noche?   **21.** ¿No (cerrar / vosotros) la casa con llave?   **22.** Tengo un limonero en mi patio, y cada vez que quiero un limón, (escoger / yo) el más maduro.   **23.** Mis padres no siempre (escoger / ellos) los mejores regalos.   **24.** Nunca (comenzar / yo) a trabajar hasta las diez de la

noche.   **25.** Si (comenzar / nosotros) ahora, terminaremos antes de que lleguen.
26. Creo que ella (contribuir) más de lo necesario.   **27.** En verano siempre (construir / nosotros) algo nuevo, por pequeño que sea.   **28.** (Conducir / yo) mejor cuando no estoy cansada.   **29.** Es impresionante lo mucho que (producir / tú) cuando quieres.
30. Esa mujer (contar) cuentos: es una cuentera profesional.

   31. Cuando tengo un resfriado, (sonarse / yo) la nariz sin parar.   **32.** Nunca (recordar / nosotros) todo lo que tenemos que comprar si no preparamos una lista.
33. (Creer / yo) que va a hacer calor hoy.   **34.** Las brujas (poseer) poderes especiales.
35. Si les (leer / nosotros) libros a nuestros hijos, aprenderán más.   **36.** Nunca (cruzar / yo) esa calle porque es muy peligrosa.   **37.** ¿Siempre (almorzar / tú) solo?
38. Te (dar / yo) mi teléfono para que me llames.   **39.** Yo (decir) que no hace falta tanta atención.   **40.** Bueno, sí, a veces (contradecirse / yo), ¿y qué?   **41.** No siempre (elegir / yo) lo más fácil.   **42.** Me parece que (exigir / tú) demasiado de tus padres.
43. Creo que si (seguir / yo) caminando por aquí, voy a encontrar la catedral.
44. Ese niño siempre (conseguir) lo que quiere.   **45.** (Perseguir / nosotros) a los gatitos hasta que los agarramos.   **46.** Nunca (dormir / yo) bien.   **47.** ¿Y vosotros, (dormir / vosotros) bien?   **48.** Siempre (enviar / ellos) sus mensajes por correo electrónico.   **49.** A mi hermana le (enviar / nosotros) flores hoy.   **50.** (Escribir / yo) todos los días en mi diario.   **51.** (Estar / yo) muy orgullosa de ti.   **52.** Eventualmente los ladridos de mis perros me (forzar) a salir a investigar la causa de su alboroto.
53. (Hacer / yo) lo que puedo.   **54.** Estos programas (satisfacer / ellos) a los clientes, según entiendo.   **55.** (Ir / yo) al cine esta noche.   **56.** Mis amigos (ir) conmigo.
57. Mi hermanita (jugar / ella) muy bien al tenis.   **58.** Mis primos (llegar) hoy.
59. A veces un árbol (morir) por falta de agua.   **60.** Si (mover / tú) esa silla, cabremos.

   61. Las víctimas (negar / ellas) haber dado permiso.   **62.** (Oír / yo) todo lo que dicen mis vecinos.   **63.** ¿(oír / tú) la canción?   **64.** No (oír / nosotros) nada.
65. (Oler / yo) los melones antes de comprarlos.   **66.** Si los melones (oler) bien, los compro.   **67.** Dicen que (parecerse / yo) a mi madre.   **68.** Sólo te (pedir / yo) este favorcito.   **69.** ¿Cuánto (pedir) usted por esta jarra?   **70.** Siempre (perder / tú) tus lentes.   **71.** Los estudiantes (poder) entender más de lo que crees.   **72.** Si (poner / yo) la mesa ahora, lo tendré todo listo.   **73.** Mis padres (querer) visitarme.   **74.** A veces (reírse / yo) incontrolablemente.   **75.** Cuando (sonreírse) el profesor, sé que cometí un error interesante.   **76.** Siempre (reunir / ellos) suficiente dinero para los pobres.   **77.** Creo que si él le (rogar / él) un poco, ella aceptará.   **78.** ¡Qué hambre (tener / yo)!   **79.** ¿(Tener / tú) tiempo para ayudarme?   **80.** Me (torcer / yo) el tobillo.   **81.** Ese niñito (retorcerse) constantemente en su asiento.   **82.** (Traer / yo) buenas noticias.   **83.** Yo no (valer) nada.   **84.** Si (convencer / yo) a mis padres, podré ir.   **85.** Hace tiempo que (venir / yo) planeando esto.   **86.** A mi amigo le molesta cuando sus padres (intervenir) en sus asuntos.   **87.** En esa clase, (ver / nosotros) una película por semana.   **88.** Luis (vivir / él) en España.   **89.** Mi compañera (volver / ella) mañana.

Ejercicio 5.8 Temas de ensayo.

Prestando atención a las formas verbales, escriba un párrafo sobre un día típico en su vida de hoy en día; use el presente del indicativo como base para su redacción, pero no es necesariamente el único tiempo verbal que puede necesitar: use su sentido común.

ATAJO 💿

Phrases: Talking about the present; Talking about daily routines
Vocabulary: Leisure; House: Household chores
Grammar: Verbs

Indicative Mood (Past Tenses of the Indicative: Imperfect)

[Chapter 5.A.2.a, pages 153–154]

Ejercicio 5.9 *Conjugue el verbo en el imperfecto del indicativo de la persona indicada.*

1. De niña (hablar / yo) cuatro idiomas.   **2.** ¿En México (comer / tú) comida picante?
3. Creo que Carlos Fuentes (vivir) en los Estados Unidos en esa época.   **4.** Cuando estábamos en la playa, (caminar / nosotros) mucho.   **5.** ¿ (Correr / vosotros) todas las mañanas?   **6.** Las dos hermanitas se (tomar / ellas) del brazo para caminar.   **7.** En la escuela, yo (comenzar) a estudiar a las seis de la tarde.   **8.** Siempre (decir / tú) lo mismo cuando me caía.   **9.** Mi padre (ver / él) el mundo de una manera muy diferente.   **10.** (Concluir / nosotros) la ceremonia con un poema de Neruda.

Ejercicio 5.10 *Conjugue el verbo en el imperfecto del indicativo de **yo** y **nosotros**.*

1. Recuerdo que para la Navidad yo (ir) con mi familia a la playa; para la Nochebuena, (ir) todos a la playa a hacer una hoguera.   **2.** Cuando yo (ser) niño, mis dos hermanos y yo pensábamos que (ser) los tres mosqueteros.   **3.** En ese entonces no (ver / yo) que tú y yo no (ver) estas cosas de la misma manera.   **4.** Cuando trabajaba allí, nunca (pedir) favores, porque creía que si (pedir / nosotros) favores, terminábamos debiéndole demasiado a la gente.   **5.** Cuando vivía en la ciudad, siempre (cerrar) el carro con llave. De niña, en mi familia nunca (cerrar / nosotros) nada con llave.   **6.** De adolescente, (caerse / yo) todo el tiempo. De hecho, mi hermana y yo (caerse / nosotros) todos los días.   **7.** Recuerdo que cuando (andar / yo) en Europa, mis amigos y yo (andar) sin parar.   **8.** Teníamos que escondernos, pero no pudimos hacerlo en la misma caja: yo (caber) pero no (caber / nosotros) los dos.   **9.** Cuando yo (tener) hambre, no podía comer de inmediato. En mi familia (tener / nosotros) que esperar la hora exacta de la siguiente comida.   **10.** Nunca (hacer / yo) las tortillas sola: mi mamá y yo las (hacer) juntas.   **11.** Recuerdo que si yo le (dar) la espalda a mi amiguito Luis, él se enojaba, y eventualmente nos (dar) de golpes hasta agotarnos. **12.** Cuando estaba en la playa, yo siempre (dormir) a gusto. Todos (dormir / nosotros) en hamacas.   **13.** Cada vez que (reírse / yo), me sentía mejor; a veces (reírse / nosotros) horas sin parar.   **14.** Cuando vivía en ese apartamento, yo (oír) todas las discusiones de mis vecinos. A veces mi mejor amiga y yo (oír) peleas horribles, y no sabíamos si llamar a la policía o no.

Ejercicio 5.11   *Conjugue el verbo en el imperfecto del indicativo de la persona indicada.*

> **Vocabulario: a pesar de todo** *in spite of it all;* **alumno** *student;* **avergonzar** *to embarrass;* **avergonzarse** *to be embarrassed;* **castigar** *to punish;* **chillón** *shrill;* **competencia** *competition;* **darse por vencido** *to give up;* **en vez** *instead;* **enterarse** *to find out;* **enviar** *to send;* **fingir** *to pretend;* **ganarle** *to beat her;* **gritar** *to scream;* **lograr** *to manage to;* **mandar** *to send;* **odiar** *to hate;* **platicar** *to chat;* **portarse** *to behave;* **quedarse** *to stay;* **regañar** *to scold;* **soportar** *to tolerate;* **travesura** *mischief, prank*

En la escuela, yo (**1.** tener) maestros muy severos, que siempre (**2.** insistir) en que mis compañeros y yo nos portáramos° muy bien. Recuerdo que cada día cuando yo (**3.** caminar) a la escuela, me (**4.** preguntar) si ese día algún maestro me regañaría° o me castigaría°. Yo siempre (**5.** avergonzarse°) fácilmente, especialmente cuando mis maestros me (**6.** sorprender) hablando con un compañero, y me (**7.** regañar°) frente a todos. Al final de cada año ellos (**8.** evaluar) nuestro trabajo y nuestra conducta, y cada año nosotros (**9.** adquirir) nuevas estrategias para esconder nuestras travesuras°.

Cuando (**10.** ponerse / nosotros) a platicar° y a jugar y pasarnos notitas, la maestra de castellano nos (**11.** interrogar) en su voz chillona°: "¡¿Qué (**12.** hacer / vosotros)?! ¡¿De qué (**13.** hablar / vosotros)?!" Y nosotros le (**14.** contestar) que no (**15.** hacer) nada, que sólo (**16.** hablar) de la tarea. Ella nos (**17.** creer), o (**18.** darse) por vencida° y nosotros (**19.** salir) ganando: eso (**20.** pensar / nosotros) entonces al menos.

A veces pienso que (**21.** aprender / nosotros) muy poco, justo lo suficiente para sobrevivir en la escuela. (**22.** Buscar / nosotros) siempre la manera de no concentrarnos en lo que el maestro (**23.** querer) que hiciéramos, y por lo general (**24.** lograr° / nosotros) divertirnos a pesar de todo.

Mi maestro de historia (**25.** ser) el peor de todos: cada vez que (**26.** poder / él), nos (**27.** avergonzar° / él). A veces nos (**28.** decir / él) que si no (**29.** portarse° / nosotros) bien, nos mandaría° a la oficina del director. Y casi cada semana, (**30.** enviar° / él) a uno a hablar con el director. Pero no (**31.** ser) grave: el alumno° que (**32.** deber) ir a la oficina del director no (**33.** ir): en vez, (**34.** salir) al corredor y (**35.** tomar) agua, luego (**36.** meterse) en el baño y (**37.** quedarse°) allí hasta el final de la hora. Y el maestro nunca (**38.** enterarse°) de nada.

Recuerdo la travesura° favorita de los chicos más traviesos de la clase: les (**39.** gustar) poner una silla defectuosa en el escritorio de las maestras nuevas: ellas (**40.** llegar) muy serias y nerviosas con sus libros muy apretados contra su pecho, y a la hora de sentarse, (**41.** caerse). Casi siempre (**42.** gritar° / ellas), y siempre (**43.** ponerse / ellas) rojas. A veces hasta (**44.** llorar / ellas). Nosotros (**45.** reírse). ¡Qué vergüenza me da ahora!

(**46.** Tener / yo) una maestra de matemáticas que me (**47.** detestar) porque yo siempre (**48.** terminar) los ejercicios de práctica antes que ella. Cuando le (**49.** llevar / yo) mi respuesta, ella (**50.** ponerse) furiosa y me (**51.** preguntar / ella) por qué no (**52.** esperar / yo) a que ella terminara primero. No sé por qué (**53.** insistir) yo en ganarle: me imagino que (**54.** existir) un tipo de competencia° con los maestros.

Nosotros (**55.** creer) que (**56.** ser) invencibles. (**57.** Sentirse / nosotros) superiores a los maestros, los (**58.** contradecir), y (**59.** rehusarse) a aprender las cosas como ellos (**60.** querer). Nosotros los (**61.** odiar°) a ellos, y ellos nos (**62.** odiar) a nosotros, o al menos, eso es lo que (**63.** fingir° / nosotros). Porque en realidad, bajo la superficie de competencia, (**64.** saber / nosotros) muy bien que (**65.** ser) importante estudiar, y (**66.** reconocer / nosotros) el valor de los conocimientos. Lo que no (**67.** soportar° / nosotros) era la disciplina excesiva, los uniformes, la uniformidad reglamentaria de todo. Y por eso (**68.** rebelarse / nosotros).

Ejercicio 5.12   Temas de ensayo.

Prestando atención a las formas verbales, escriba un párrafo sobre un día típico en su vida en la escuela primaria o secundaria; use el imperfecto del indicativo como base para su redacción, pero no es necesariamente el único tiempo verbal que puede necesitar: use su sentido común.

ATAJO

Phrases: Talking about daily routines
Vocabulary: Upbringing; School
Grammar: Verbs: Imperfect

Indicative Mood (Past Tenses of the Indicative: Preterite)

[Chapter 5.A.2.b, pages 154–157]

Ejercicio 5.13   *Conjugue el verbo en el pretérito de la persona indicada.*

1. ¿(Hablar / tú) con tus padres anoche?   **2.** Ayer (comer / nosotros) pescado.   **3.** Mis tíos (vivir) veinte años en Guadalajara.   **4.** Esta mañana (caminar / yo) cinco kilómetros.   **5.** ¿Por dónde (andar / tú)?   **6.** El niño trató de meterse en la caja, pero no (caber / él).   **7.** Este verano (estar / nosotros) en el campo.   **8.** Ayer (arrestar / nosotros) al sospechoso.   **9.** El año pasado (haber) menos crimen que el anterior.   **10.** Yo no (saber / yo) la respuesta.   **11.** ¿(Poder / tú) terminar tu trabajo?   **12.** Mi mamá (poner) la mesa.   **13.** ¿A qué hora (salir / vosotros)?   **14.** Mis vecinos (tener) que mudarse.   **15.** Este fin de semana no (hacer / yo) nada porque hacía muchísimo calor.   **16.** ¿Qué (querer / tú) decir con eso?   **17.** Ese gran autor (venir) a nuestra clase para hablar con nosotros.

Ejercicio 5.14   *Conjugue el verbo en el pretérito de la persona indicada.*

1. Le (dar / nosotros) flores a mi mamá para su cumpleaños.   **2.** Blanca (hacer) las paces *(made up)* con su novio.   **3.** Anoche (ir / yo) al cine.   **4.** Nunca (ser / yo) tan atlético como mi hermano.   **5.** ¿Qué (decir / vosotros)?   **6.** Me sorprende lo mucho que (producir / tú) en tan poco tiempo.   **7.** Mis primas (traer / ellas) las tortillas.

Ejercicio 5.15   *Conjugue el verbo en el pretérito de **yo** y **él**.*

1. (sentir) Después de comer, yo me _____ mal, pero él no _____ nada.   **2.** (pedir) Para la cena, yo _____ mejillones, y el _____ camarones.   **3.** (reír) Yo me _____ mucho durante esa película, pero el resto del público no se _____ casi para nada. **4.** (dormir) Yo _____ bien anoche, pero mi compañero de cuarto no _____ para nada. **5.** (caer) Creo que le _____ bien a tu novio, pero no estoy segura de si él le _____ bien mi mamá.   **6.** (creer) Yo no le _____ nada a la gitana *(gypsy),* pero mi hermana sí le _____.   **7.** (leer) _____ ese libro el año pasado; el profesor lo _____ cuando tenía nuestra edad.   **8.** (oír) Yo no _____ nada, pero mi compañera de cuarto dice que _____ gritos *(screams).*   **9.** (concluir) Yo _____ algo muy diferente de lo que _____ él.   **10.** (buscar) Yo _____ mi anillo *(ring)* en todos lados, y mi mejor amigo también _____, pero no lo encontramos.   **11.** (llegar) Yo _____ ayer, pero mi hermano mayor _____ hace una semana.   **12.** (alcanzar [*to reach*]) Yo no _____ la guayaba en esa rama *(branch),* pero Juanito sí la _____.   **13.** (explicar) Yo le _____ mis razones y él me _____ las suyas.   **14.** (almorzar) Yo _____ más de lo que _____ el resto de la gente.   **15.** (apagar [*to turn off*]) A las diez, yo _____ todas las luces excepto la de la cocina; mi compañera de casa _____ ésa antes de acostarse, a eso de la una de la mañana.   **16.** (sacar [*to take out*]) Yo _____ la basura *(garbage)* esta semana porque él la _____ la semana pasada.   **17.** (comenzar) Yo _____ a trabajar a las seis, y ella _____ a las diez.   **18.** (colgar [*to hang*]) Yo _____ ese cuadro *(painting)* en la sala, luego mi mamá lo _____ en el comedor.   **19.** (tocar) Yo _____ el piano para Navidades; mi primo _____ la guitarra para el día de Reyes.   **20.** (empezar) Yo _____ a hablar español a los cinco años, pero mi papá no _____ hasta los treinta.   **21.** (entregar [*to deliver*]) Yo le _____ el paquete al señor Ruiz, y él se lo _____ a la señora Gómez.   **22.** (pagar) Yo _____ las cuentas *(bills)* el mes pasado, y mi compañero de casa las _____ el mes anterior.

Ejercicio 5.16 *Conjugue el verbo en el pretérito de la persona indicada. Si no hay persona indicada, use el contexto para determinar cuál es el sujeto: puede ser impersonal, o tener el sujeto ya mencionado.*

> Vocabulario: **a la vez** *at the same time;* **acercarse** *to come near;* **agotado** *exhausted;* **alquilar** *to rent;* **apodo** *nickname;* **arena** *sand;* **averiguar** *to find out;* **de hecho** *as a matter of fact;* **en fin de cuentas** *all in all;* **encerrarse** *to lock oneself up;* **estadía** *stay;* **estrella** *star;* **fijarse** *to notice;* **grito** *scream;* **impresionadísima** *very impressed;* **inolvidable** *unforgettable;* **médico** *doctor;* **pegar un grito** *to scream;* **pelando** *peeling;* **por detrás** *from behind;* **quedar impresionado** *to be impressed;* **quemarse** *to get burned;* **regresar** *to return;* **seguir** *to continue;* **sitio** *place;* **sombra** *shade;* **tipo** *character*

El año pasado (**1.** ir / yo) a Cancún por primera vez: (**2.** ser) una experiencia inolvidable°, y a la vez°, (**3.** haber) algunos incidentes que quisiera olvidar. Mi mejor amiga (**4.** ir) conmigo. El primer día (**5.** quedar° / yo) impresionadísima° cuando (**6.** ver / yo) la blancura de la arena° y la transparencia azul del agua; (**7.** acostarse / nosotros) al sol un ratito, y luego (**8.** entrar / nosotros) al hotel a bañarnos. (**9.** Cenar / nosotros), acompañadas de la música de los mariachis, y luego (**10.** salir / nosotros) a pasear en la noche llena de estrellas°.

De repente mi amiga (**11.** sentirse) muy mal, y (**12.** regresar° / nosotros) al hotel. (**13.** Tener / yo) que preguntar en la recepción si había un médico°. Por fin (**14.** venir) uno, la (**15.** ver / él), y le (**16.** decir / él) que tenía gastroenteritis, causada por el cambio de bacterias en el agua o la comida. Nos (**17.** contar / él) que esta enfermedad era tan común que tenía un apodo°: le decían "la venganza de Moctezuma", o "el turista". Le (**18.** traer / él) un té caliente que habían inventado en el hotel para curar este mal, y le (**19.** recomendar / él) un medicamento que luego yo le (**20.** poder) comprar en la farmacia del hotel. (**21.** Fijarse° / yo) que era el producto que más se vendía.

Mi amiga (**22.** sufrir) con esta enfermedad por dos días enteros: no (**23.** volver / ella) a ver el sol ni la playa, (**24.** encerrarse° / ella) en el cuarto con las cortinas cerradas, y no (**25.** hacer / ella) nada más que dormir. Yo (**26.** estar) sola todo este tiempo, y (**27.** pasarse / yo) el rato leyendo con la luz de una lámpara, y también (**28.** escribir / yo) unas veinte tarjetas postales: no quería dejar a mi amiga sola, por si necesitaba algo. Además, ese primer día de sol (**29.** quemarse° / yo) por completo: la mañana siguiente, cuando (**30.** ir / yo) a bañarme, y (**31.** mirarse / yo), (**32.** pegar / yo) un grito° de horror al ver que toda la piel de la cara, y del cuerpo, se me estaba pelando°. Por dos días más, (**33.** pedir / yo) que me trajeran la comida al cuarto.

El cuarto día de nuestra estadía° en Cancún, como no podíamos ir a la playa, (**34.** decidir / nosotros) hacer un poco de turismo. (**35.** Ir / nosotros) a ver las ruinas de los antiguos mayas; para llegar allá, (**36.** alquilar° / nosotros) un coche. Yo (**37.** tener) que manejar porque mi amiga estaba un poco débil. (**38.** Estar / nosotros) manejando como una hora, en un cochecito sin aire acondicionado, bajo un sol implacable, y para cuando (**39.** llegar / nosotros), estábamos ya agotadas° por el calor sofocante. Nunca se nos (**40.** ocurrir) que haría tanto calor. (**41.** Sentarse / nosotros) en la sombra° de un árbol y (**42.** beber / nosotros) un refresco. De lejos (**43.** mirar / nosotros) las ruinas, inertes. Un tipo° (**44.** acercarse° / él) a nosotros por detrás° y nos (**45.** ofrecer / él) ayuda. Yo (**46.** hablar) un poco con él y (**47.** averiguar° / yo) todo lo que (**48.** poder / yo) sobre las ruinas: en primer lugar, el hombre me (**49.** corregir / él) con un tono muy severo: me (**50.** decir / él) que no les dicen "ruinas", sino "edificios". Francamente, me (**51.** caer) bastante mal su actitud; el tipo (**52.** ofenderse / él) con mi ignorancia, lo cual me (**53.** parecer) un poco absurdo. Le (**54.** dar / yo) las gracias por su oferta de ayuda, pero no la (**55.** aceptar / nosotros). De hecho°, (**56.** irse / nosotros) rápidamente de allí, (**57.** ver / nosotros) superficialmente lo que (**58.** poder / nosotros) del sitio°, y (**59.** conducir / nosotros) de vuelta al hotel. En el coche, de repente, mi amiga (**60.** reírse / ella), luego (**61.** reírse / yo) yo, y (**62.** seguir° / nosotros) riendo todo el camino por lo ridículo de la situación.

En fin de cuentas°, nuestra visita a Cancún (**63.** ser) una experiencia que nunca olvidaremos.

Ejercicio 5.17 Temas de ensayo.

Prestando atención a las formas verbales, escriba un párrafo sobre su primer día o su primera noche en algún lugar especial (una casa nueva, una ciudad nueva, la escuela secundaria, la universidad, etc.). Use el pretérito del indicativo como base para su redacción, pero no es necesariamente el único tiempo verbal que puede necesitar: use su sentido común.

ATAJO

Phrases:	Describing places; Talking about past events
Grammar:	Verbs: Preterite

Indicative Mood (Past Tenses of the Indicative: Present Perfect)

[Chapter 5.A.2.c, page 157]

Ejercicio 5.18 *Conjugue el verbo en el presente perfecto del indicativo de la persona indicada.*

1. Nunca _____ (caminar / yo) por ahí.   **2.** ¿_____ (hacer / tú) algo hoy?   **3.** Todavía no me _____ (devolver / él) todas las cosas que le presté. *(He has still not returned to me all of the things I lent him.)*   **4.** _____ (andar / nosotros) casi tres kilómetros.

5. ¿Qué _____ (aprender / vosotros) en vuestro viaje?   **6.** Creo que no _____ (tomar / ellos) agua en horas.   **7.** Nunca _____ (traer / yo) tanto.   **8.** ¿_____ (averiguar / tú) algo sobre los horarios nuevos? *(Have you found out anything about the new schedules?)*   **9.** Todavía no _____ (buscar / ella) alojamiento *(lodging)* en ese barrio.
10. Nunca _____ (caber [*to fit*] / nosotros) todos en este coche.   **11.** ¿_____ (cerrar / vosotros) la puerta con llave? *(Did you lock the door?)*   **12.** Ya _____ (recoger / ellas) las hojas tres veces. *(They already picked up the leaves three times.)*

Indicative Mood (Past Tenses of the Indicative: Pluperfect)

[Chapter 5.A.2.d, page 158]

Ejercicio 5.19 *Conjugue el verbo en el pluscuamperfecto del indicativo de la persona indicada.*

1. Estaba agotada *(exhausted)* porque _____ (correr / yo) por una hora para llegar.
2. Me dijiste que nunca te _____ (graduar / tú) de la escuela secundaria.   **3.** Cuando yo llegué, él ya *(already)* se _____ (ir).   **4.** No les _____ (decir / nosotros) a nuestros padres que nos queríamos casar.   **5.** ¿_____ (ver / vosotros) esa película antes?
6. Ellos ya *(already)* _____ (volver) de su viaje a España.   **7.** Yo te _____ (escribir / yo) seis cartas antes que tú me contestaras.   **8.** Yo creía que ya *(already)* le _____ (poner / tú) baterías nuevas al reloj.   **9.** Cuando por fin llegó la policía, ella ya _____ (resolver / ella) el crimen.   **10.** Nunca _____ (abrir / nosotros) esa puerta antes.
11. ¿_____ (cerrar / vosotros) las ventanas antes de que empezara a llover?   **12.** No vieron nada porque _____ (taparse / ellas) los ojos *(they had covered their eyes)*.

Indicative Mood (Future: Simple Future)

[Chapter 5.A.3.a, pages 158–159]

Ejercicio 5.20 *Conjugue el verbo en el futuro para la persona indicada.*

1. Te _____ (amar / yo) para siempre.   **2.** ¿Dónde _____ (vivir / tú) cuando estés allá?   **3.** Sé que _____ (entender / él) el problema cuando yo se lo explique.   **4.** ¿A qué hora _____ (comer / nosotros) allá?   **5.** ¿En qué año os _____ (graduar / vosotros)?   **6.** _____ (tomar / ellos) el autobús para llegar a la ciudad.   **7.** Me _____ (despedir / yo) pronto porque ya me voy. *(I'll say good-bye, because I'm leaving now.)*   **8.** ¿Cómo _____ (averiguar [*to find out*] / tú) lo que necesitas si no preguntas?
9. Estoy seguro que ella _____ (buscar / ella) en este lugar.   **10.** Esta noche _____ (cantar / nosotros) juntos.   **11.** Con este sol, os _____ (calentar / vosotros) pronto.
12. Sé que ellas _____ (escoger [*to choose*] / ellas) lo mejor.

Ejercicio 5.21 *Conjugue el verbo en el futuro para la persona indicada.*

1. Si sigo comiendo tanto, no _____ (caber / yo) dentro de mi ropa. *(If I continue to eat so much, I will not fit in my clothes.)* **2.** ¡Tú _____ (decir / tú)! *(It's up to you!)* **3.** ¿Cuántos estudiantes _____ (haber) en esta universidad? **4.** Nosotros _____ (hacer) lo posible por ayudar. **5.** Vosotros _____ (poder) venir también. **6.** Sé que ellos se _____ (poner) furiosos cuando oigan la noticia. **7.** Esta noche no _____ (querer / yo) nada para cenar. **8.** ¿Cuándo _____ (saber / tú) si te van a aceptar? **9.** Su vuelo _____ (salir) mañana por la noche. **10.** _____ (tener / nosotros) muchas horas libres. **11.** ¿Cuánto _____ (valer) esa camisa? *(I wonder how much that shirt costs.)* **12.** ¿ _____ (venir / vosotros) con nosotros?

Ejercicio 5.22 Temas de ensayo.

Prestando atención a las formas verbales, escriba un párrafo sobre sus planes para mañana. Use el futuro como base para su redacción, pero no es necesariamente el único tiempo verbal que puede necesitar: use su sentido común.

ATAJO 💿

Grammar: Verbs: Future

Indicative Mood (Future: Future Perfect)

[Chapter 5.A.3.b, page 159]

Ejercicio 5.23 *Conjugue el verbo en el futuro perfecto para la persona indicada.*

1. _____ (decir / yo) lo mismo veinte veces. **2.** ¿Cuántas veces _____ (ver / tú) la misma película? **3.** Supongo que él se _____ (cubrir / él) la cabeza. **4.** Nosotros _____ (volver / nosotros) para entonces. **5.** Me imagino que vosotros _____ (hacer / vosotros) este ejercicio antes. **6.** _____ (tomar / ellos) agua sucia. **7.** No sé dónde _____ (poner / yo) mis lentes. **8.** _____ (experimentar / tú) con esto antes. **9.** _____ (buscar / ella) por todos lados antes de darse por vencida. **10.** Antes de que se acabe la noche, _____ (cantar / nosotros) todo nuestro repertorio. **11.** ¿ _____ (envejecer / vosotros) tanto? **12.** Ellas _____ (escribir) primero. **13.** Yo me _____ (ir) antes de que tú llegues. **14.** ¿Cuánto dinero _____ (gastar / tú)? **15.** Mi prima se _____ (graduar) antes que yo. **16.** _____ (salir / nosotros) antes de que ustedes lleguen. **17.** Supongo que _____ (estudiar / vosotros) varias lenguas. **18.** _____ (tener / ellos) otra de sus peleas. **19.** _____ (terminar / ellas) antes que nadie. **20.** Yo ya _____ (llegar) para esa hora.

Conditional Mood (Present Conditional)

[Chapter 5.B.1, page 160]

Ejercicio 5.24 *Conjugue el verbo en el condicional presente para la persona indicada.*

1. Si pudiera, _____ (secar [*to dry*] / yo) mi ropa en el sol.   **2.** Pensé que no te _____ (preocupar / tú) tanto esta vez.   **3.** Él no _____ (vivir / él) aquí si no fuera por ella.
4. Me pregunto si _____ (llover) anoche.   **5.** ¿Cómo _____ (pronunciar / vosotros) esto?   **6.** Estoy segura que ellas _____ (pagar) si pudieran.   **7.** Si fuera yo, me _____ (organizar / yo) primero.   **8.** Si te lo pidieran, _____ (atestiguar [*to testify*] / tú), ¿verdad?   **9.** ¿_____ (Leer / ella) el libro antes de ver la película?   **10.** No nos _____ (quejar [*to complain*] / nosotros) si no hicieran tanto ruido.   **11.** Vosotros _____ (sonreír) también con ese chiste *(joke)*.   **12.** Allá todo el mundo nos _____ (tutear). (*Over there, everyone would address us with* tú.)

Ejercicio 5.25 *Conjugue el verbo en el condicional presente para la persona indicada.*

1. Yo no _____ (caber [*to fit*]) por esa ventana aunque quisiera.   **2.** ¿Qué _____ (decir / tú) tú en mi lugar?   **3.** ¿Cuánta gente _____ (haber) en el público *(audience)*?   **4.** Nosotros lo _____ (hacer) de manera diferente.   **5.** ¿_____ (Poder / vosotros) venir a eso de las nueve?   **6.** ¿Dónde _____ (poner / ellos) las llaves *(keys)*?   **7.** ¿Qué _____ (querer) ese vagabundo?   **8.** Si te ocurriera a ti, estoy seguro que _____ (saber / tú) cómo reaccionar.   **9.** ¿Cuánto les _____ (costar) el viaje?
10. ¿_____ (Tener) usted tiempo para ayudarme, por favor?   **11.** ¿Cuánto _____ (valer) eso?   **12.** Si las invitáramos, _____ (venir / ellas).

Conditional Mood (Conditional Perfect)

[Chapter 5.B.2, page 161]

Ejercicio 5.26 *Conjugue el verbo en el condicional perfecto para la persona indicada.*

1. Si no me hubieran llevado a México, yo no _____ (hablar / yo) el español desde los cinco años *(since I was five years old)*.   **2.** Nunca _____ (comer / tú) eso si hubieras sabido lo que era.   **3.** Él _____ (vivir / él) muchos años más si no se hubiera enfermado.   **4.** Si hubiéramos sabido lo que había en ese cuarto, no _____ (abrir / nosotros) la puerta.   **5.** De haber sabido que había cucarachas allí, _____ (cubrir / vosotros) mejor la comida.   **6.** Si no les hubiéramos preguntado, no _____ (decir / ellos) nada.   **7.** Te _____ (escribir / yo) más si hubiera podido.   **8.** Sé que no lo _____ (hacer / tú) solo.   **9.** Sin medicamentos, _____ (morir / ella) antes.

10. ¿Dónde _____ (poner / nosotros) el paraguas?   **11.** Nunca _____ (resolver / vosotros) el caso sin la ayuda de la policía.   **12.** Usted _____ (volver) en taxi si no lo hubiéramos llevado.

Ejercicio 5.27   Temas de ensayo.

Si no estuviera ahora en la universidad (o en la escuela secundaria), ¿en qué sería diferente su vida? ¿Le gustaría a usted este cambio? ¿Por qué? Prestando atención a las formas verbales, escriba un párrafo sobre este tema; use el condicional para indicar los cambios hipotéticos en su vida.

Phrases:	Hypothesizing
Grammar:	Verbs: Conditional

 # Subjunctive Mood (Present Subjunctive)

[Chapter 5.C.1, pages 161–164]

Ejercicio 5.28   *Conjugue el verbo en el presente del subjuntivo para la persona indicada.*

1. Es posible que yo _____ (caminar) hoy.   **2.** Te prohíben que _____ (hablar / tú).
3. Me sorprende que él _____ (estudiar) tanto.   **4.** Nos gusta que ella _____ (cantar).
5. Se nos quitará el frío cuando _____ (bailar / nosotros).   **6.** Dudo que vosotros _____ (remar [*to row*]) tan rápido como ellos.   **7.** Algunos hacen locuras (*do foolish things*) para que los _____ (amar / ellos).   **8.** Tan pronto _____ (preparar / ellos) la cena, comeremos.   **9.** Es imperativo que usted _____ (tolerar) las diferencias de los demás.   **10.** Si no pueden cantar, les digo que _____ (tararear [*to hum*] / ustedes) la canción.

Ejercicio 5.29   *Conjugue el verbo en el presente del subjuntivo para la persona indicada.*

1. Es imposible que yo _____ (comer) tanto.   **2.** Te traigo esto para que lo _____ (leer / tú).   **3.** ¿Crees que él _____ (ver) la diferencia?   **4.** Cuando ella _____ (vivir) allá, se acostumbrará (*she will get used to it*).   **5.** Espero que no _____ (toser [*to cough*] / nosotros) durante la obra.   **6.** No se va a ver bien a menos que lo _____ (coser [*to sew*] / vosotros) con hilo del mismo color.   **7.** Dales ánimo (*Encourage them*) para que

_____ (correr / ellos) más rápido.   **8.** Es esencial que _____ (compartir [*to share*] / ellos) su comida con sus compañeros.   **9.** Le recomiendo que no _____ (beber / usted) ninguna bebida alcohólica con esta medicina.   **10.** Es admirable que _____ (escribirse / ustedes) tan frecuentemente.

Ejercicio 5.30   *Conjugue el verbo en el presente del subjuntivo para **yo** y **nosotros**.*

1. (cerrar) Primero me dice a mí que _____ al salir, y luego nos dice a los dos que _____: ¿creerá que soy irresponsable?   **2.** (perder) Para que yo me _____, es necesario que _____ el mapa primero.   **3.** (contar) No importa que yo _____ el cuento sola o que lo _____ juntos.   **4.** (volver) Es imposible que yo _____ y que no _____ los dos.   **5.** (sentir) Cuando yo _____ frío, ya será de noche. Entonces es probable que los dos _____ frío.   **6.** (dormir) Es una lástima que yo no _____ bien cuando hay visita. De hecho, dudo que _____ lo suficiente cuando hay gente en la casa. **7.** (enviar) Es esencial que _____ este paquete hoy. Espero que lo _____ con el resto del correo al mediodía.   **8.** (evaluar) Me dicen que _____ a mis compañeros; es obligatorio que todos _____ a los demás.

Ejercicio 5.31   *Conjugue el verbo en la tercera personal singular del presente del subjuntivo.*

1. Me encanta que usted me _____ (pedir) favores.   **2.** Dudo que Germán les _____ (decir) a sus padres.   **3.** Espero que mi hermano no _____ (oír) esta música. **4.** Cuando Rosita _____ (tener) quince años, la dejarán salir con él.   **5.** Ojalá que esto _____ (concluir) todos los debates sobre el asunto.   **6.** ¿Se podrá arreglar sin que _____ (parecer) un remiendo?   **7.** Le prohíben ir a menos que _____ (conducir) su hermano mayor.   **8.** No creo que eso me _____ (caber).   **9.** Ojalá que Carlos le _____ (caer) bien a esa gente.   **10.** Es increíble que _____ (hacer) tanto calor. **11.** No dejes que _____ (ponerse) esos zapatos.   **12.** Espero que todo _____ (salir) bien.   **13.** ¿Quieres que Yolanda _____ (traer) algo?   **14.** Ojalá que este trabajo _____ (valer) la pena.   **15.** Me gusta que Paco _____ (venir) a visitar a su papá.

Ejercicio 5.32   *Conjugue el verbo en el presente del subjuntivo.*

1. Es necesario que yo _____ (dar) dinero para esta causa.   **2.** No es que _____ (estar / tú) gordo: es que la ropa se encogió.   **3.** Tengo miedo de que no _____ (haber) suficiente tiempo.   **4.** Le molesta que _____ (irse / nosotros) tan pronto. **5.** No importa que no _____ (saber / vosotros) la respuesta.   **6.** Conviene que _____ (ser / ellas) tolerantes.   **7.** Más vale que yo _____ (escoger) el número ganador. **8.** No significa que tú no los _____ (dirigir) bien: son ellos los que no te hacen caso. **9.** Es una lástima que no _____ (distinguir) esos colores.   **10.** No irán a menos que los _____ (convencer / nosotros) de que no hay peligro.   **11.** Es necesario que lo _____ (buscar) vosotros mismos.   **12.** No abran la puerta hasta que _____ (llegar / yo). **13.** Te presto mi auto para que _____ (alcanzar / tú) el tren en la próxima estación.

Ejercicio 5.33 *Repaso del subjuntivo presente.*

1. Ojalá que _____ (dominar / yo) el idioma para entonces.   **2.** Es increíble que él les _____ (temer / él) a los demás.   **3.** Te ruego que te _____ (defender / tú).   **4.** Es mejor que les _____ (dar / nosotros) nuestro número de teléfono ahora.   **5.** Espero que _____ (estar / vosotros) cómodos.   **6.** No creo que _____ (haber) más de cien personas en el público.   **7.** Es importante que yo _____ (ir / yo) a la biblioteca hoy. **8.** Aunque _____ (saber / tú) la verdad, no la digas.   **9.** Para que la fiesta _____ (ser) perfecta, vamos a poner música de salsa.   **10.** A menos que _____ (recoger / nosotros) a los niños, no van a llegar a tiempo.   **11.** Es curioso que no _____ (corregir / tú) errores tan graves.   **12.** Ojalá que _____ (seguir / vosotros) gozando de vuestro viaje.   **13.** Espero que pronto _____ (vencer / ella) esa enfermedad.   **14.** Me dice que no me _____ (rascar / yo).   **15.** Lo hará sin que le _____ (rogar / tú).   **16.** Más vale que _____ (rezar / él).   **17.** No puedo creer que realmente _____ (entender / ella).   **18.** Espero que usted _____ (encontrar) lo que busca.   **19.** Se lo presto con tal de que me lo _____ (devolver / ellos) mañana.   **20.** Espero que no lleguen antes de que _____ (envolver / nosotros) los regalos.   **21.** Es imposible que yo _____ (confiar) en esa gente.   **22.** Es deseable que _____ (criar / nosotros) a nuestros hijos de una manera responsable.   **23.** Te dejo para que _____ (continuar / tú) con tu ensayo. **24.** No nos darán nada hasta que nos _____ (graduar / nosotros).   **25.** Parece imposible que ellas _____ (creer) semejantes mentiras.   **26.** Ojalá que _____ (ver / yo) a mis amigos allá.   **27.** Le daremos la mano para que _____ (subir / ella).   **28.** Me sorprende que ellas lo _____ (hacer) todo tan bien.   **29.** No les ganarán a menos que los _____ (dividir / ellos).   **30.** Es importante que usted _____ (investigar) este asunto con cuidado.   **31.** A veces me molesta que ustedes lo _____ (analizar) todo de esa manera.   **32.** Prefiero que no _____ (discutir / tú) tanto.   **33.** Insiste en que su hijo no _____ (pelear) con sus amigos.   **34.** Ojalá que ella _____ (llegar) tarde hoy: no estoy listo aún.   **35.** Vendrán con sus amigos aunque no lo _____ (querer / nosotros).   **36.** Insisto en que vosotros _____ (entrar) primero.   **37.** No se irán hasta que ellas _____ (salir).   **38.** La profesora se empeña en que ellos lo _____ (repetir) todo. **39.** Lamentamos que usted no _____ (oír) la música.   **40.** Esperaremos hasta que ustedes _____ (volver).

Subjunctive Mood (Imperfect Subjunctive)

[Chapter 5.C.2, pages 164–165]

Ejercicio 5.34 *Conjugue el verbo en el imperfecto del subjuntivo.*

1. El doctor me recomendó que _____ (caminar / yo) todos los días un poco.
2. Preferiría que _____ (hablar / tú) conmigo primero.   **3.** Quería darle un libro que _____ (estudiar / él) con gusto.   **4.** Ojalá que ella _____ (cantar) esta vez.   **5.** Nos pusieron esa música para que _____ (bailar / nosotros).   **6.** No significa que no

_____ (escuchar / vosotros).   **7.** Era imposible que ellas los _____ (amar / ellas).
8. Pedí que me _____ (preparar / ellos) una paella.   **9.** Le dieron esa droga para que
_____ (tolerar / usted) mejor el dolor.   **10.** Sólo les pedía que _____ (tararear /
ustedes) la canción una vez.   **11.** No podían encontrar nada que yo _____ (comer)
sin enfermarme.   **12.** Me sorprendió que _____ (leer / tú) su diario.   **13.** Esperaba
que él _____ (ver) lo que yo había visto.   **14.** Tenía miedo que ella no _____ (vivir)
en esa dirección.   **15.** Se avergonzaban de que nosotros _____ (toser) durante toda la
obra.   **16.** Si vosotros _____ (coser) vuestra propia ropa, no tendríais este problema.
17. Teníamos que apurarnos en caso de que ellas _____ (correr).   **18.** Se lo dimos a
condición de que lo _____ (compartir / ellos) entre ellos.   **19.** Escondimos todas las
bebidas alcohólicas para que no _____ (beber / él).   **20.** Antes de que ustedes nos
_____ (escribir), nosotros ya les habíamos escrito.   **21.** No dejaría de mojarse hasta
que yo _____ (cerrar) las ventanas.   **22.** Era imposible que yo ganara sin que tú
_____ (perder) como consecuencia.   **23.** Le pedimos que nos _____ (contar / ella) de
su viaje.   **24.** Nos enteraríamos en cuanto _____ (volver / nosotros).   **25.** No nos
creerían hasta que ellos mismos _____ (sentir) el temblor.   **26.** Les había conseguido
este cuarto de atrás para que _____ (dormir / ustedes) mejor.   **27.** Nunca llegaría a
menos que él lo _____ (enviar) por correo aéreo.   **28.** Me dijo que te daría un auto
cuando te _____ (graduar / tú).

Ejercicio 5.35 _Conjugue el verbo en el imperfecto del subjuntivo._

1. Se sorprendieron de que yo _____ (andar) por esos lares.   **2.** Nadie pudo creer que
tú _____ (caber) por esa ventana.   **3.** No lo aceptaría a menos que les _____ (caer /
él) bien a sus padres.   **4.** Si ella no _____ (concluir) lo mismo que nosotros, tendríamos que cambiar el plan.   **5.** No irían a menos que usted _____ (conducir).   **6.** Nos
pidieron que _____ (dar / nosotros) una presentación.   **7.** Si vosotros les _____
(decir) eso, no lo creerían.   **8.** Les dieron café para que no _____ (dormirse / ellos).
9. Hablaban como si _____ (estar / ellas) de acuerdo.   **10.** No podía creer que _____
(haber) tantos problemas en ese pueblito.   **11.** Resolvieron el caso antes de que yo
_____ (irse).   **12.** Te lo di a fin de que _____ (leer / tú) algo interesante.   **13.** Entré
sin que nadie me _____ (oír).   **14.** Ojalá que mi mamá no _____ (pedir / ella) tanto
de mí.   **15.** Si usted _____ (poder) ayudarme, se lo agradecería.   **16.** Era esencial
que _____ (poner / nosotros) el despertador.   **17.** No podíamos creer que vosotros
_____ (poseer) esos poderes.   **18.** Queríamos encontrar una playa que ellos _____
(preferir).   **19.** No trabajaría en la película a menos que ellas la _____ (dirigir).
20. Traje el auto en caso de que ustedes _____ (querer) salir hoy.   **21.** Por suerte se
calló antes de que yo _____ (reírse).   **22.** Si tú _____ (saber) lo que siento, no
hablarías de esa manera.   **23.** Cambió su número para que él no la _____ (seguir)
llamando.   **24.** Me encantó que ella _____ (sentir) lo mismo que yo.   **25.** No podíamos encontrar una casa que _____ (ser) tan barata como queríamos.   **26.** Dudo que
nosotros _____ (ser) tan inocentes como ellos a su edad.   **27.** Os comportáis como si

no _____ (tener / vosotros) nada que hacer. **28.** Les pedimos que _____ (traer / ellos) pan. **29.** No empezaríamos hasta que ellas _____ (venir) a ayudarnos.

Subjunctive Mood (Present Perfect Subjunctive)

[Chapter 5.C.3, page 166]

Ejercicio 5.36 *Conjugue el verbo en el presente perfecto del subjuntivo.*

1. Ojalá que él _____ (ganar). **2.** Tan pronto como _____ (graduarse / tú) iremos a Europa. **3.** Haremos la sopa con tal de que él _____ (conseguir) los ingredientes. **4.** No pueden creer que _____ (andar / nosotros) tanto. **5.** Espero que _____ (aprender / vosotros) algo nuevo. **6.** Esperamos que ellos no _____ (tomar) el agua. **7.** Es posible que yo los _____ (avergonzar) sin darme cuenta. **8.** Parece imposible que tú _____ (averiguar) tanto en tan poco tiempo. **9.** Me alegro de que no _____ (buscar / ella) aquí. **10.** Ahora les sorprende que nosotros _____ (cantar) esa canción. **11.** Les dio coraje que vosotros _____ (cerrar) la puerta con llave. **12.** Ojalá que ellas _____ (recoger) el correo hoy. **13.** Todavía les sorprende que no me _____ (caber) esa camisa. **14.** Lamentamos que no _____ (poder / tú) venir a la fiesta. **15.** Puede ser que ella ya _____ (vender) el coche. **16.** No importa que no _____ (viajar / nosotros) a ese país antes. **17.** No creen que vosotros _____ (salir) anoche. **18.** Basta que ellos _____ (tener) razón una vez. **19.** No puedo creer que esos aretes _____ (costar) tanto. **20.** ¡Qué bueno que yo _____ (venir) a tiempo!

Subjunctive Mood (Pluperfect Subjunctive)

[Chapter 5.C.4, page 166]

Ejercicio 5.37 *Conjugue el verbo en el pluscuamperfecto del subjuntivo.*

1. No podían creer que yo les _____ (escribir) tantas veces. **2.** Si no me _____ (decir / ellos) eso ellos, no lo habría creído. **3.** Lo decían como si lo _____ (ver / ellos) en persona. **4.** Me parecía raro que no _____ (llegar / nosotros) todavía. **5.** No nos gustó que nos _____ (tratar / ellos) de esa manera. **6.** Era probable que nadie lo _____ (oír) antes. **7.** Dudaban que yo _____ (hacer) el trabajo en sólo un mes. **8.** Nos bastaba que nuestros vecinos _____ (limpiar) su patio. **9.** Si me _____ (llamar / tú), no me habría preocupado tanto. **10.** Habría sido preferible que mis padres _____ (enterarse) desde un principio. **11.** Le molestó que tú no lo _____ (considerar). **12.** Ojalá que nunca _____ (lavar / vosotros) esa ropa en cloro. **13.** Si no _____ (volver / ellos) antes de la medianoche, habríamos llamado a la policía. **14.** Era imposible que _____ (resolver / él) el caso tan rápidamente. **15.** Estarías más cómoda si _____ (ponerse / tú) ropa de algodón. **16.** A veces me pregunto cómo sería mi vida si mi padre no _____ (morirse). **17.** Si _____ (abrir / nosotros) las ventanas, no haría tanto calor ahora. **18.** Ojalá que no _____ (comer / yo) tanto para la cena. **19.** Nos lo iban a decir tan pronto como _____ (confesar / nosotros) lo del robo. **20.** Les quitó el plato antes de que _____ (terminar / ellos) de comer.

Subjunctive Mood (Review)

Ejercicio 5.38   Temas de ensayo.

Prestando atención a las formas verbales, describa su relación con sus padres; piense en lo que ellos le dicen que haga o no haga, le piden que haga o no haga; en lo que usted les pide que hagan o no hagan. Use el subjuntivo cuando el contexto lo requiera.

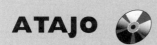

ATAJO

Phrases: Expressing a wish or desire
Grammar: Verbs: Subjunctive

Imperative Mood (Direct Commands: *Tú*)

[Chapter 5.D.1.a, pages 167–168]

Ejercicio 5.39   *Conjugue en el imperativo de tú.*

1. (Hablar) más alto, por favor. **2.** (Comer) todo lo que tienes en el plato. **3.** (Vivir) como se debe. **4.** (Cerrar) las puertas con llave al salir. **5.** (Abrir) esa ventana, por favor. **6.** (Saltar) un poco. **7.** (Escuchar) lo que te dicen tus padres. **8.** (Volver) antes de las diez. **9.** (Pedir) lo que tú quieras. **10.** (Conseguir) este libro en la biblioteca. **11.** (Repetir) varias veces el mismo ejercicio, hasta memorizarlo. **12.** (Mentir) sólo si al mentir puedes hacer bien. **13.** (Comenzar) ahora. **14.** (Comentar) sobre el libro que leíste. **15.** (Defender) a tus amigos. **16.** (Seguir) trabajando. **17.** (Pensar) en mí. **18.** (Servir) la sopa, por favor. **19.** (Elegir) el color que tú prefieras. **20.** (Votar) por el mejor candidato. **21.** (Envolver) los regalos antes de que lleguen los niños. **22.** (Contar) conmigo. **23.** (Cortar) el césped mientras yo barro. **24.** (Apostar) poco dinero cada vez. **25.** (Podar) los rosales con cuidado. **26.** (Llorar) y te desahogarás. **27.** (Recordar) lo que te digo. **28.** (Recortar) los anuncios que te interesen. **29.** (Oler) esta rosa. **30.** (Jugar) con nosotros. **31.** (Jurar) decir la verdad. **32.** (Proteger) a los animalitos indefensos. **33.** (Seguir)

caminando.   **34.** (Obedecer) a tus padres.   **35.** (Traducir) este documento.
36. (Producir) más si quieres ganar más.   **37.** (Enviar) el paquete por correo aéreo.
38. (Continuar) con el trabajo.   **39.** (Confiar) en mí.   **40.** (Reunir) a todos tus compañeros aquí esta tarde.   **41.** (Criar) a tus hijos como yo te crié a ti.   **42.** (Evaluar) este ensayo usando los mismos criterios.   **43.** (Concluir) tu trabajo.   **44.** ¡(Huir)!
45. (Callar) a esos niños ruidosos.   **46.** (Traer) una ensalada, si quieres.   **47.** (Dar) dos pasos para adelante.   **48.** (Oír), ¿vienes a la fiesta?

Ejercicio 5.40   *Conjugue en el imperativo de **tú**.*

1. (Decir) la verdad siempre.   **2.** (Hacer) lo mejor que puedas.   **3.** (Ir) a la tienda a comprar pan.   **4.** (Poner) la mesa.   **5.** (Salir) ahora a regar las matas.   **6.** (Ser) bueno.
7. (Tener) valor.   **8.** (Venir) conmigo.

Ejercicio 5.41   *Conjugue en el imperativo de **tú**.*

1. (cantar), pero (no bailar)   **2.** (estudiar), pero (no hablar) en voz alta   **3.** (beber) mucho jugo, y (no comer) nada artificial   **4.** (leer) el artículo, pero (no creer) todo lo que dice   **5.** (volver) a casa, pero (no correr)   **6.** (descoser) el bolsillo, y (no coser) la bastilla   **7.** (escribir) una carta, pero (no describir) lo que pasó   **8.** (contar) lo que debes, y (no descontar) nada   **9.** (dormir) al bebé, pero (no dormirse) tú   **10.** (pedir) favores, y (no impedir) que te ayuden   **11.** (regalar) tu amistad, y (no prestar) nada
12. (buscar) el ungüento, y (no te rascar) la picada   **13.** (escoger) la película que quieras ver, pero por favor (no escoger) una en inglés

Ejercicio 5.42   *Conjugue en el imperativo de **tú**.*

1. (decir) la verdad, y (no decir) mentiras   **2.** (hacer) la lectura para mañana, pero (no hacer) la tarea   **3.** (ir a la tienda, pero (no ir) al correo   **4.** (poner) tu abrigo aquí, y (no poner) tus zapatos en la mesa   **5.** (salir) a recoger el periódico, pero (no salir) por esa puerta   **6.** (ser) bueno, pero (no ser) tonto   **7.** (tener) hijos, pero (no tener) tantos como ella   **8.** (venir) a casa, pero (no venir) temprano

Imperative Mood (Direct Commands: *Usted / Ustedes*)

[Chapter 5.D.1.b, pages 168–169]

Ejercicio 5.43   *Conjugue en el imperativo de **usted**.*

1. (Caminar) una cuadra más.   **2.** (No hablar) tan alto.   **3.** (Estudiar) solo.   **4.** (No cantar) ahora, por favor.   **5.** (Bailar) con nosotros.   **6.** (Tararear) la canción, a ver si la reconocemos.   **7.** (Comer) un poco para ver si le gusta.   **8.** (No leer) ese periódico.   **9.** (Vivir) feliz.   **10.** (No toser) durante la obra, por favor.   **11.** ¡(Correr)! ¡Se le va a ir el tren!   **12.** (No beber) agua de la llave.   **13.** (Escribir) tarjetas postales.

14. (Cerrar) la ventana, por favor.   **15.** (No perder) su mapa.   **16.** (Contar) el vuelto que le dan.   **17.** (No volver) a ese restaurante.   **18.** (Dormir) con la ventana abierta. **19.** (No pedir) favores.   **20.** ¿(Decir)?   **21.** (Oír), ¿sabe qué hora es?   **22.** (No tener) miedo.   **23.** (Conducir) con cuidado.   **24.** (No caer) en la trampa.   **25.** (Hacer) la tarea.   **26.** (Poner) la mesa, por favor.   **27.** (No salir) después de la medianoche. **28.** (Traer) el dinero mañana.   **29.** (Venir) pronto.   **30.** (No dar) nada.   **31.** (Ir) con ellos.   **32.** (No ser) ridículo.   **33.** (Dirigir) al grupo.   **34.** (Buscar) el tesoro.   **35.** (No llegar) tarde.

Imperative Mood (Direct Commands: *Vosotros*)

[Chapter 5.D.1.c, page 170]

Ejercicio 5.44 *Conjugue en el imperativo de **vosotros**.*

1. (Hablar) más claramente, por favor.   **2.** (Comer) un poco de todo.   **3.** (Exprimir) el jugo de los limones.   **4.** (Cerrar) las puertas.   **5.** (Abrir) los ojos.   **6.** (Saltar) por encima de los charcos.   **7.** (Escuchar) con cuidado.   **8.** (Volver) a tiempo.   **9.** (Pedir) lo que queráis.   **10.** (Conseguir) el mapa antes del viaje.   **11.** (Repetir) conmigo. **12.** (Mentir) si es necesario.   **13.** (Comenzar) ahora.   **14.** (Comentar) sobre el artículo.   **15.** (Defender) a vuestra familia.   **16.** (Seguir) tratando.   **17.** (Pensar) en lo positivo.   **18.** (Servir) primero a los invitados.   **19.** (Elegir) el que prefiráis. **20.** (Votar) hoy.   **21.** (Decir) sólo lo necesario.   **22.** (Hacer) el trabajo.   **23.** (Ir) a visitar a vuestros abuelos.   **24.** (Poner) esas cosas aquí.   **25.** (Salir) temprano. **26.** (Ser) discretos.   **27.** (Tener) paciencia.   **28.** (Venir) a verme.

Ejercicio 5.45 *Conjugue en el imperativo de **vosotros**.*

1. ¡(Despertarse)! ¡Ya es tarde!   **2.** (Levantarse) más temprano.   **3.** (Lavarse) las manos antes de comer.   **4.** (Marcharse) con los demás.   **5.** (Acostarse) temprano. **6.** ¡(Dormirse) ya!   **7.** (Irse) con ellos.   **8.** (Despedirse) de la visita.   **9.** ¡(Callarse)!

Ejercicio 5.46 *Conjugue en el imperativo de **vosotros**.*

1. (cantar), pero (no bailar)   **2.** (estudiar), pero (no hablar) en voz alta   **3.** (beber) mucho jugo, y (no comer) nada artificial   **4.** (leer) el artículo, pero (no creer) todo lo que dice   **5.** (volver) a casa, pero (no correr)   **6.** (descoser) el bolsillo, y (no coser) la bastilla   **7.** (escribir) una carta, pero (no describir) lo que pasó   **8.** (contar) lo que debéis, y (no descontar) nada   **9.** (dormir) al bebé, pero (no dormirse) vosotros **10.** (pedir) favores, y (no impedir) que os ayuden   **11.** (regalar) vuestra amistad, y (no prestar) nada   **12.** (buscar) el ungüento, y (no os rascar) la picada   **13.** (escoger) la película que quieras ver, pero por favor (no escoger) una en inglés

Ejercicio 5.47 *Conjugue en el imperativo de **vosotros**.*

1. (decir) la verdad, y (no decir) mentiras **2.** (hacer) la lectura para mañana, pero (no hacer) la tarea **3.** (ir) a la tienda, pero (no ir) al correo **4.** (poner) vuestro abrigo aquí, y (no poner) vuestros zapatos en la mesa **5.** (salir) a recoger el periódico, pero (no salir) por esa puerta **6.** (ser) buenos, pero (no ser) tontos **7.** (tener) hijos, pero (no tener) tantos como ellos **8.** (venir) a casa, pero (no venir) temprano

Imperative Mood (Direct Commands: *Nosotros*)

[Chapter 5.D.1.d, page 171]

Ejercicio 5.48 *Conjugue en el imperativo de **nosotros**.*

1. (Caminar) por esta calle. **2.** (No hablar) para que no nos oiga nadie. **3.** (Estudiar) un poco antes de ir. **4.** (No cantar) por favor. **5.** (Bailar), ¿quieres? **6.** (Tararear) la canción a ver si la reconocen. **7.** (Comer) aquí. **8.** (No leer) más. **9.** (Vivir) en la Costa del Sol. **10.** (No toser) sin taparnos la boca. **11.** ¡(Correr)! **12.** (No beber) tequila esta noche. **13.** (Escribir) unas cartas antes de salir hoy. **14.** (Cerrar) las ventanas antes de prender el aire acondicionado. **15.** (No perder) de vista lo esencial. **16.** (Contar) nuestro dinero antes de salir. **17.** (No volver) a entrar aquí. **18.** (Dormir) afuera hoy. **19.** (No pedir) favores. **20.** (Decir) que sí entendemos. **21.** (Oír) su respuesta primero. **22.** (No tener) miedo. **23.** (Conducir) con cuidado. **24.** (No caer) en la trampa. **25.** (Hacer) la tarea. **26.** (Poner) las flores aquí. **27.** (No salir) esta noche. **28.** (No dar) nada. **29.** (Ir) con ellos. **30.** (No ser) tontos. **31.** (Dirigir) al grupo. **32.** (Buscar) su dirección. **33.** (No llegar) tarde esta vez.

Ejercicio 5.49 *Conjugue en el imperativo de **nosotros**.*

1. (Despertarlas) antes de que sea muy tarde. **2.** (No levantarse) tan temprano hoy. **3.** (Lavarlo) con cloro. **4.** (Marcharse) ya. **5.** (No acostarse) en la arena esta vez. **6.** ¡(Dormirse) ya! **7.** (Irse) de aquí. **8.** (No irse) hasta que nos traigan la cuenta.

Imperative Mood (Indirect Commands)

[Chapter 5.D.2, page 172]

Ejercicio 5.50 *Traduzca usando mandatos indirectos.*

1. I do not want to cook; let them cook today. **2.** Have the manager call me. **3.** If you do not have the money, let Mirta pay. **4.** Have them send it to me.

Imperative Mood (Review)

Conteste las preguntas de los siguientes ejercicios (5.51–5.54) usando el imperativo en la persona indicada y transformando los nombres en pronombres cada vez que se pueda.

Ejercicio 5.51 *Use el **imperativo familiar (tú)** en el afirmativo y en el negativo.*

1. ¿Les digo el secreto?   **2.** ¿Hago los mandados?   **3.** ¿Le vendo los libros?   **4.** ¿Voy al mercado?   **5.** ¿Le pongo los zapatos al niño?

Ejercicio 5.52 *Use el **imperativo formal (Ud. o Uds.)** en el afirmativo y en el negativo.*

1. ¿Cantamos la canción?   **2.** ¿Le digo lo que pasó?   **3.** ¿Les enviamos las cartas?   **4.** ¿Vamos al cine?   **5.** ¿Me quito los zapatos?

Ejercicio 5.53 *Use el **imperativo de nosotros** en el afirmativo y en el negativo.*

1. ¿Cantamos las canciones juntos?   **2.** ¿Vamos al cine?   **3.** ¿Le damos el dinero?   **4.** ¿Nos vamos ahora?   **5.** ¿Nos ponemos el abrigo?

Ejercicio 5.54 *Traduzca la parte en negrilla usando el mandato indirecto (**Que** + subjunctivo).*

1. Have them prepare it.   **2.** I don't want to do it. **Let Guillermo do it.**   **3. Have her come see me.**   **4. Have them call me.**   **5.** If they're hungry, **let them eat.**

Ejercicio 5.55 Temas de ensayo.

Prestando atención a las formas verbales, escriba un diálogo usando el imperativo al máximo para la siguiente situación: es de noche, y de repente Luisito huele humo (smoke): va corriendo a despertar a su padre y a su madre.

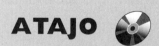

ATAJO

Phrases: Attracting attention
Grammar: Verbs: Imperative

Participle (Present Participle)

[Chapter 5.F.1, page 173]

Ejercicio 5.56 *Llene el espacio en blanco con el participio presente del verbo indicado.*

1. Yo estaba _____ (hablar) por teléfono. **2.** Estábamos _____ (comer) cuando llamaste. **3.** En esa época estábais _____ (vivir) con vuestros abuelos. **4.** Mi papá se estaba _____ (sentir) mejor. **5.** No te estoy _____ (pedir) nada. **6.** ¿Estás _____ (dormirse)? **7.** Siempre estaban _____ (concluir) lo mismo. **8.** Los niños estaban _____ (caer). **9.** Estabas _____ (leer) el libro. **10.** ¿Usted me está _____ (oír)? **11.** Estaba _____ (decir) la verdad. **12.** Nos fuimos _____ (ir) poco a poco. **13.** _____ (Venir) por este camino se llega más rápido. **14.** Creo que estaba _____ (poder).

Ejercicio 5.57 *Llene el espacio en blanco con el participio presente del verbo indicado.*

1. Llegué _____ (caminar). **2.** Estaba _____ (actuar). **3.** Se fueron _____ (andar). **4.** Habíamos estado _____ (aprender) el idioma desde hacía tiempo. **5.** No sabía qué estaban _____ (decir). **6.** Andaban _____ (buscar) a su tío. **7.** _____ (Ser) extranjero, no sentía que tuviera los mismos derechos. **8.** La vi _____ (cerrar) el portón. **9.** Estaban _____ (construir) un puente. **10.** Iba _____ (conducir) a paso de tortuga. **11.** Ese año estaban _____ (producir) más que nunca. **12.** Me venía _____ (contar) sus aventuras. **13.** Iban _____ (recordar) poco a poco su pasado. **14.** _____ (Creer) en su fuerza, lograrán más. **15.** Estábamos _____ (almorzar). **16.** Les iban _____ (dar) las respuestas una tras otra. **17.** Se la pasaban _____ (elegir) a los candidatos más improbables. **18.** Ellos iban _____ (seguir) el tren. **19.** No sé qué estaban _____ (hacer). **20.** _____ (Jugar) se aprende.

Ejercicio 5.58 *Llene el espacio en blanco con el participio presente del verbo indicado.*

1. Venían _____ (llegar) poco a poco. **2.** Estaban _____ (morirse) todas las plantas. **3.** Lo iban _____ (mover) muy lentamente. **4.** Nadie les estaba _____ (negar) nada. **5.** ¿Por qué estabais _____ (sonreírse)? **6.** El perro estaba _____ (oler) la flor. **7.** Los andaban _____ (despedir) uno tras otro. **8.** ¿Quién estaba _____ (poner) esas cartas allí? **9.** Los iban _____ (reunir) poco a poco. **10.** _____ (Tener) el dinero, se podría hacer. **11.** Los están _____ (traer) ahora mismo. **12.** Siempre se la pasan _____ (intervenir) en los asuntos de otros. **13.** Los estamos _____ (ver). **14.** La estás _____ (volver) loca.

Participle (Past Participle)

[Chapter 5.F.2, pages 173–174]

Ejercicio 5.59 *Llene el espacio en blanco con el participio pasado del verbo indicado.*

1. Había _____ (hablar) con tu papá. **2.** Nunca hemos _____ (comer) aquí. **3.** Su tía ha _____ (vivir) en Argentina. **4.** He _____ (caminar) cuatro cuadras. **5.** Juan: te has _____ (sentar) en mi silla. **6.** ¿Habéis _____ (aprender) a bailar el merengue? **7.** Ojalá que no haya _____ (conducir) el abuelo. **8.** Hemos _____ (almorzar) ya. **9.** No habían _____ (dar) las tres todavía. **10.** No te has _____ (mover) en horas. **11.** Nunca había _____ (oler) ese perfume antes. **12.** Los Gómez han _____ (venir) a nuestra casa varias veces.

Ejercicio 5.60 *Llene el espacio en blanco con el participio pasado del verbo indicado.*

1. Esa ventana nunca se ha _____ (abrir). **2.** El pasto estaba _____ (cubrir) de granizo. **3.** Nadie me había _____ (decir) eso antes. **4.** ¿Les has _____ (escribir) a tus padres? **5.** ¿Has _____ (hacer) tu cama? **6.** No han _____ (morirse) los peces. **7.** Ya habíamos _____ (ponerse) el traje de baño. **8.** Si hubieran _____ (resolver) el caso, todos estarían satisfechos. **9.** Ojalá que ya haya _____ (volver) Jorge. **10.** ¿Qué pasaría si nunca hubieran _____ (descubrir) América? **11.** Nunca había _____ (devolver) ese libro a la biblioteca. **12.** Era imposible que hubieran _____ (suponer) eso.

Ejercicio 5.61 *Traduzca.*

1. This is holy water. **2.** They have blessed the food. **3.** I want fried potatoes. **4.** He had fried the potatoes. **5.** Cursed luck! **6.** I have never cursed anyone. **7.** She wore her hair loose. **8.** They have released the bulls. **9.** The printed word is very important. **10.** Have you printed your paper?

Chapter 6   Verbs: Usage

 Present Indicative

[Chapter 6.A, pages 176–177]

(For practice of the forms of the present indicative, see Exercises 5.1–5.8. We recommend that you do those exercises before these.)

Ejercicio 6.1   *Usando sus conocimientos de los usos del presente del indicativo, traduzca los verbos de las oraciones siguientes.*

1. Los Gómez *(live)* aquí.   **2.** Profesora, ¿cuántos idiomas *(do you speak)*?   **3.** Mi auto está muy viejo. ¿Lo *(should I sell it)* para poder comprarme uno nuevo?   **4.** Si *(it rains)*, no *(we don't have to)* regar.   **5.** ¿Me *(Would you bring me)* un vaso de agua, por favor?   **6.** ¿Tienes sueño? Sí, _____ de despertarme *(I just...)*.   **7.** Mañana *(we are leaving* [salir]) temprano.

Ejercicio 6.2   Temas de ensayo.

Prestando atención al uso del presente del indicativo, y usando una variedad de verbos, escriba una cartita informal:

a. de un amigo(a) a otro(a) que ya no vive en el mismo lugar, describiendo su vida estos días, lo que hace como rutina solo(a) y con sus amigos, y lo que hace con su tiempo libre, solo(a) y con sus amigos. Compare y contraste lo que prefieren hacer sus amigos y las actividades que usted prefiere. Haga preguntas sobre el otro amigo (o amiga).

b. respuesta a la carta en parte **a.**

ATAJO

Phrases: Writing a letter (informal)
Grammar: Verbs: Present

c. de un(a) novio(a) a otro(a) que vive lejos, contándole de su amor y describiendo su vida en su ausencia. No tenga miedo de ser melodramático(a). Haga preguntas sobre la vida del otro o la otra.

d. respuesta a la carta en parte **c.**

e. de un(a) ex-novio(a) a otro(a) que le hace mucha falta y que quiere que vuelva. Use su imaginación para dramatizar la situación. Haga promesas sobre cómo va a cambiar su comportamiento si regresa ("Sólo pienso en ti. No como. No duermo. Mis amigos no sabe cómo consolarme...").

f. respuesta a la carta en parte **e.**

g. de un(a) amigo(a) "electrónico(a)" a otro(a) conocidos por la red mundial; prepare preguntas sobre la vida presente del individuo y de su familia, y haga lo posible por hacer preguntas detalladas, personales pero no indiscretas. Prepare un mínimo de diez preguntas.

h. la respuesta a la carta en parte **g.**

Ejercicio 6.3   Temas de ensayo.

Diario. En su diario personal, escriba un párrafo sobre uno de los temas que siguen, prestando atención al uso del presente del indicativo. Use un máximo de verbos diferentes.

a. Describa una costumbre que tiene usted o alguien que conoce y que le causa frustración.

Phrases: Saying how often you do things; Self-approaching
Vocabulary: Emotions: Negative
Grammar: Verbs: Present

b. Describa una virtud que usted admira en otra persona y que usted quisiera tener.

Phrases: Describing people
Vocabulary: Emotions: Positive
Grammar: Verbs: Present

c. Describa en detalle un objeto nuevo que acaba de obtener y que le gusta mucho.

Phrases: Describing objects
Grammar: Verbs: Present

d. Describa en detalle un lugar donde usted se encuentra muy cómodo.

Phrases: Describing places
Grammar: Verbs: Present

Past Indicative Tenses (Preterite vs. Imperfect vs. Pluperfect)

[Chapter 6.B, pages 177–189]

(See the corresponding exercises in Chapter 5 for practice of the forms of the imperfect indicative [5.9–5.12] and the preterite [5.13–5.17]. We recommend that you do those exercises before these.)

Ejercicio 6.4 *Uno de los criterios para decidir si va a usar el imperfecto o el pretérito es el tipo de verbo del que se trata: de acción o de estado* [Chapter 6.B.2, pages 177–184]. *En las frases que siguen, marque los verbos que son de acción con la letra (A). Indique si son de acto único (AU), acto habitual (AH), acto interrumpido (AI), acto fotográfico o simultáneo (AS), acto futuro (AF) o acto repetido (AR). Luego seleccione los verbos que no son de acción, o que son de estado (E). Identifique los que son de estado cambiado (EC), de estado durante un tiempo limitado (ET), de reacción (R). Luego conjugue el verbo en el tiempo correcto (pretérito o imperfecto); para los verbos reflexivos, recuerde usar el pronombre apropiado.*

1. Esta mañana Paco (levantarse) temprano, (bañarse) y (bajar) a la cocina a desayunar.   **2.** Ese hombre (ser) un cantante muy famoso, (tener) unos cincuenta años y (estar) casado con una modelo.   **3.** Todos los días mi padre (salir) para el trabajo a las cinco de la mañana y (volver) a la hora de la cena.   **4.** Yo (ver) esa película cuatro veces y cada vez me (gustar) por razones diferentes.   **5.** Mis amigos y yo (estar) en el parque cuando de repente (empezar) a caer granizo: todos juntos (correr) al árbol más cercano y (sentarse) a esperar a que pasara la tormenta; durante media hora *vendría* (estar) ahí sin poder escaparnos.   **6.** Esta mañana Juanita me (decir) que (venir) a verme a las seis.   **7.** Cuando yo (ser) niño, (creer) en Santa Claus; luego cuando (tener) seis años, (descubrir) que (ser) un mito creado por la sociedad; me (molestar) mucho descubrir este engaño, y la vida no (ser) igual para mí de ese momento en adelante.   **8.** Cuando yo (entrar) al salón, (ver) que algunos de los estudiantes *to seem* (comer), otros (hablar) y algunos (tratar) de estudiar.   **9.** La vida (parecer) más fácil *hacía* *decían* en mi niñez: mis padres lo (decidir) todo por mí, y yo sólo (hacer) lo que me (decir *querían* ellos) o lo que (querer).   **10.** Nadie (poder) creerlo: un boxeador le (morder) la oreja al otro dos veces, primero le (arrancar) un pedazo de la oreja izquierda, y luego le (enterrar) los dientes en la oreja derecha; el público (ponerse) furioso porque el árbitro (interrumpir) la pelea.

Ejercicio 6.5 *Transforme el párrafo siguiente al pasado, empezando con "En esa época,..."*.
tenía *encantaba*
Vivo bien. Tengo tres gatos y dos perros, y una casa que me encanta. A mi esposa y a
aba
mí nos gusta lo mismo, y nos hacemos compañía en todo. Ganamos suficiente dinero
hacíamos

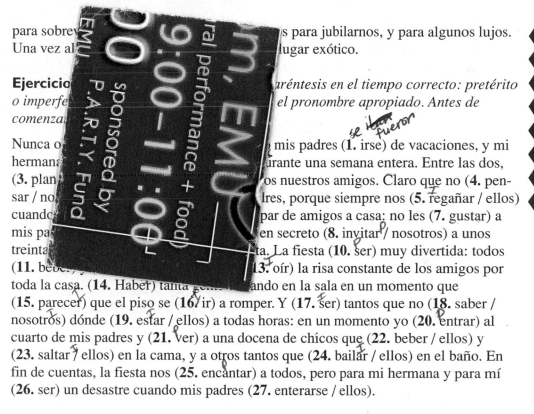

para sobre... ...s para jubilarnos, y para algunos lujos.
Una vez al... ...lugar exótico.

Ejercicio ...aréntesis en el tiempo correcto: pretérito
o imperfe... ...el pronombre apropiado. Antes de
comenza...

Nunca o... mis padres (**1.** irse) de vacaciones, y mi
herman... ...urante una semana entera. Entre las dos,
(**3.** plan... ...os nuestros amigos. Claro que no (**4.** pensar / no... ...res, porque siempre nos (**5.** regañar / ellos)
cuando... ...par de amigos a casa: no les (**7.** gustar) a
mis pa... ...en secreto (**8.** invitar / nosotros) a unos
treinta... ...ta. La fiesta (**10.** ser) muy divertida: todos
(**11.** beb... ...(**13.** oír) la risa constante de los amigos por
toda la casa. (**14.** Haber) tanta g... ...ando en la sala en un momento que
(**15.** parecer) que el piso se (**16.** ir) a romper. Y (**17.** ser) tantos que no (**18.** saber /
nosotros) dónde (**19.** estar / ellos) a todas horas: en un momento yo (**20.** entrar) al
cuarto de mis padres y (**21.** ver) a una docena de chicos que (**22.** beber / ellos) y
(**23.** saltar / ellos) en la cama, y a otros tantos que (**24.** bailar / ellos) en el baño. En
fin de cuentas, la fiesta nos (**25.** encantar) a todos, pero para mi hermana y para mí
(**26.** ser) un desastre cuando mis padres (**27.** enterarse / ellos).

Ejercicio 6.7 Temas de ensayo.

*Actos simultáneos, interrumpidos y fotográficos. Escriba un párrafo en el pasado
para cada una de las situaciones que siguen. Elabore usando su imaginación.*

1. Después de estudiar hasta las diez de la noche en la biblioteca, llegó usted a su
cuarto esa noche, y al abrir la puerta vio que su compañero(a) de cuarto tenía
varios amigos que estaban haciendo cosas diferentes: describa la escena.

2. Describa la escena que vio un viajero al entrar a un avión que lo iba a llevar a una
isla del Caribe para las vacaciones de Navidad: cada uno de los pasajeros del
avión estaba haciendo algo diferente.

3. Encuentre entre sus fotos de familia y de amigos algunas que tengan acciones en
proceso. Fotocopie cada foto en una hoja aparte, y en la misma hoja, describa la
escena, usando el pasado (¿cuándo se tomó esta foto? ¿quién tomó la foto? ¿qué
estaba haciendo usted cuando se tomó esa foto? Y su hermana o amigo, ¿qué
estaban haciendo?).

Ejercicio 6.8 *Futuro. La semana pasada, yo estaba con mi amiga Luisa en una discoteca, y ella me dijo muchas cosas. Ayer, Gregorio me pidió que le dijera lo que Luisa me había dicho. Como Gregorio está enamorado de Luisa, decidí contestar su pregunta: ¿Qué dijo? Aquí siguen las frases de Luisa. Dígale a Gregorio lo que dijo Luisa, empezando cada frase con: "Luisa dijo que...".*

1. "Mañana comemos en el restaurante mexicano." **2.** "Esta noche bailo tango."
3. "Después de esta canción, bailo." **4.** "El mes entrante mi familia va a Argentina."
5. "Mis vecinos se mudan pronto." **6.** "Mañana llueve." **7.** "Esta noche termino de leer mi novela."

Ejercicio 6.9 *¿Actos consecutivos o simultáneos? Indique para los actos entre paréntesis cuáles son los actos consecutivos [AC] (uno después de otro) y cuáles son los simultáneos [AS] (al mismo tiempo). Luego escriba oraciones en el pasado usando los elementos dados.*

> **Vocabulario: becerrito** *little calf;* **brillar** *to shine;* **brisa** *breeze;* **cola** *tail;* **menearse** *to move;* **monte** *hill;* **oler** *to smell;* **pájaro** *bird;* **rama** *branch;* **sol** *sun;* **vaca** *cow*

1. Esta mañana yo (despertarse), (levantarse), (bañarse) y (vestirse). **2.** Esta mañana cuando me desperté, los pájaros° (cantar), el sol° (brillar°), y yo (oler°) el pan tostado que (preparar / ellos) en la cocina. **3.** El espectáculo era hermoso: las vacas° (comer) pacíficamente en el monte°, los becerritos° (correr) para todos lados con la cola° en el aire, las ramas° de los árboles (menearse°) suavemente con la brisa° y hasta los insectos (cantar) de manera melodiosa. **4.** El profesor (entrar) al salón y les (anunciar) a los estudiantes la tarea para la semana siguiente. Luego (empezar) a hablarles del tema del día.

Ejercicio 6.10 *Conjugue los verbos entre paréntesis en el tiempo más lógico del pasado. Luego explique la diferencia entre los actos de las frases siguientes: 1 y 2; 3, 4 y 5; 6 y 7.*

1. Cuando yo estaba en la escuela primaria, (sentarse) en una silla del frente.
2. Ayer (sentarse / yo) por accidente en un chicle. **3.** Esta mañana (ir / yo) a mi primera clase cuando vi un accidente. **4.** Anoche (ir / yo) al cine. **5.** En esa época, (ir / yo) todos los días a visitar a mi abuelo que estaba en el hospital. **6.** Abrí la puerta de mi cuarto y vi el desastre: las ardillas *(squirrels)* se habían metido; una de ellas (comer) cacahuates *(peanuts)* en mi escritorio, otra (buscar) algo entre las colchas *(blankets)* de mi cama y una tercera (correr) como loca por las paredes.
7. Esta mañana me levanté tarde porque mi <u>despertador</u> no funcionó. (Comer / yo) rápidamente, (buscar / yo) mis llaves a toda velocidad y (correr / yo) al trabajo.

Ejercicio 6.11 *Traduzca las palabras en negrilla de las oraciones siguientes, prestando atención a los usos diferentes de "would."* [See "Special Note on 'Would'," page 180.]

1. I avoided the presence of my sister, because she **would say** the most embarrassing things about me.   **2.** If my mother were here, she **would say** she had told you so.   **3.** I know you **would not say** a word against me even if you were paid.   **4.** I insisted, but the boy **would not say** who had given him the money.   **5.** My mother **would not say** anything to anyone about our family's difficulties: she was that way.

[handwritten: aunque te pagaran]
[handwritten: diría]
[handwritten: no decía]
[handwritten: insistí]
[handwritten: le había dado]
[handwritten: se puso así]

Ejercicio 6.12 *Traduzca el verbo en negrilla, usando el verbo entre paréntesis.* (you = **tú**)

1. Yesterday I **met** your brother. *(conocer)*   **2.** We **met** at a party. *(conocer)*   **3.** I **knew** everyone there. *(conocer)*   **4.** When you were an adolescent, **could** you go to parties? *(poder)*   **5.** The prisoner **wanted** to get out, but he **knew** it was impossible so he did not even try. *(querer / saber)*   **6.** I **wanted** to tear the curtain (and tried), but I **was unable to.** *(querer / poder)*   **7.** My sister **did not want** to go with us (refused to), in spite of our insistence. *(querer)*   **8.** My sister **did not want** to go with us, but my father made her go. *(querer)*   **9.** When **did** you **find out** about the accident? *(saber)*

[handwritten: quiso que fuera]

Ejercicio 6.13 *Pluscuamperfecto. Conjugue los verbos en el imperfecto, el pretérito o el pluscuamperfecto.*

1. Los indígenas les (tener) terror a los conquistadores porque nunca (ver) caballos antes.   **2.** No (comer / yo) nada en el cine porque (cenar) antes de ir.   **3.** Esta mañana me (doler) las piernas porque (bailar / yo) toda la noche.

Ejercicio 6.14 *¿Pretérito, imperfecto o pluscuamperfecto? Complete con la forma apropiada del verbo indicado.*

> **Vocabulario: alumbrar** *to light;* **balde** *bucket;* **caballo** *horse;* **ensillar** *to saddle;* **ganado** *cattle;* **guiándose por el sonido** *being led just by sound;* **leña** *fire wood;* **madrugada** *early morning hours;* **ojo de agua** *water hole;* **vela** *candle*

El rancho de mi padre

Nunca olvidaré las semanas que (**1.** pasar / nosotros) en el rancho de mi padre. En esa época yo (**2.** tener) unos doce o trece años, y mi hermana unos catorce. En el rancho no (**3.** haber) ni electricidad ni agua corriente: todo se (**4.** alumbrar°) con velas o linternas, y mi hermana y yo (**5.** ir) a buscar agua en baldes° al ojo de agua° cerca de la casa. (**6.** Cocinar / nosotros) las tortillas y los frijoles con leña°. La rutina (**7.** ser) la siguiente: (**8.** levantar / nosotros) a las cuatro de la mañana, y mientras una de nosotras (**9.** salir) a la oscuridad de la madrugada° a buscar los caballos°, guiándose por el sonido° nada más, la otra (**10.** preparar) el desayuno. (**11.** Terminar / nosotros) de desayunar, (**12.** ensillar° / nosotros) los caballos y (**13.** irse / nosotros) antes de que saliera el sol. Para cuando (**14.** llegar / nosotros) adonde (**15.** estar) el ganado°, ya el sol (**16.** salir) con todo su poder.

[handwritten: había salido]

Ejercicio 6.15 *¿Pretérito, imperfecto o pluscuamperfecto? Complete con la forma apropiada del verbo indicado.*

> **Vocabulario: a la carrera** *in a hurry;* **agarrar** *to grab;* **alumbrado** *lit up;* **apagar** *to put out;* **azotar** *to beat, whip;* **de repente** *suddenly;* **durar** *to last;* **fuego** *fire;* **golpes** *loud knock-ing or blows;* **gritos** *yelling, screams;* **impedir** *to prevent;* **incendio** *fire;* **llama** *flame;* **lograr** *to succeed;* **monte** *hill;* **rama** *branch*

Fuego° en el monte°

Recuerdo la noche del incendio° en el rancho. (**1.** Estar / nosotros) todos dormidos cuando de repente° se (**2.** oír) golpes° y gritos° en la puerta. Eran los hombres que (**3.** venir) a decirle a mi padre que (**4.** haber) fuego en el monte. (**5.** Vestirse / noso-tros) a la carrera° y (**6.** ir / nosotros) corriendo al monte que se (**7.** ver) alumbrado° desde la casa. Una vez que llegamos allí, (**8.** formar / nosotros) entre todos una línea y así (**9.** empezar) una batalla que (**10.** durar°) hasta el día siguiente. (**11.** Agarrar° / nosotros) constantemente ramas° verdes de los árboles más cercanos para azotar° las llamas° y así impedir° que avanzaran. (**12.** Lograr° / nosotros) apagar° el fuego, y salvar el ganado. Luego nos (**13.** contar / ellos) los hombres que ellos mismos (**14.** provocar) el incendio accidentalmente con un cigarrillo.

Ejercicio 6.16 *¿Pretérito o imperfecto? Complete con la forma apropiada del verbo indicado.*

> **Vocabulario: acostumbrarse** *to get used to;* **chiquitito** *tiny;* **escalones** *steps;* **herido** *injured;* **leche** *milk;* **maullido** *meowing;* **platito** *little plate;* **por todos lados** *everywhere;* **tener terror** *to be terrified*

Gato

En mi casa, (**1.** ser / nosotros) gente de perros y no de gatos; de hecho, los gatos nos (**2.** caer) mal, quizá porque les (**3.** tener / nosotros) algo de miedo y no nos (**4.** respetar / ellos) como los perros. Pero un día el verano pasado todo eso (**5.** cambiar). (**6.** Estar / nosotros) sentados en la terraza tomando café cuando de repente (**7.** empezar / nosotros) a oír los maullidos° insistentes de un gatito perdido. Los maullidos eran tan fuertes que nos (**8.** imaginar / nosotros) que el gatito estaría atrapado en algún lugar, herido°. Lo (**9.** buscar / nosotros) por todos lados°, y por fin lo (**10.** encontrar / nosotros), debajo de los escalones° del frente de la casa. (**11.** Ser) un gato tan chiquitito° que no (**12.** parecer) posible que esos maullidos salieran de él. (**13.** Ser) una cría, y nos (**14.** tener / él) terror°. (**15.** Estar / él) debajo de los escalo-nes, pero (**16.** poder / él) salir. (**17.** Parecer) que su mamá lo (**18.** abandonar) y que no (**19.** saber) adónde ir. Nos (**20.** tomar) toda la mañana lograr que saliera de debajo de los escalones para tomar el platito° de leche° que le (**21.** ofrecer / nosotros). Muy lentamente (**22.** acostumbrarse / él) a nosotros y nos (**23.** adoptar / él). Desde enton-ces, somos gente de perros y de gatos.

Ejercicio 6.17   Temas de ensayo.

Escriba un párrafo describiendo una costumbre cultural o una fiesta típica en su infancia.

ATAJO 💿

Phrases: Describing the past; Talking about habitual events
Vocabulary: Holiday greetings; Religious holidays
Grammar: Verbs: Preterite and imperfect

Ejercicio 6.18   Temas de ensayo.

Imagínese que usted tiene un hermanito, y que éste le pide que le cuente un cuento. Cuéntele en el pasado uno de los cuentos siguientes, prestando atención al uso correcto del pretérito y del imperfecto: La Cenicienta *(Cinderella);* Caperucita Roja *(Little Red Riding Hood);* Los Tres Cerditos *(The Three Little Pigs);* Romeo y Julieta.

> **Vocabulario:** *ashes* **ceniza;** *balcony* **balcón;** *ball* **baile;** *basket* **canasta;** *brick* **ladrillo;** *carriage* **carroza;** *enemy* **enemigo;** *fairy godmother* **hada madrina;** *friar* **fraile;** *glass, crystal* **cristal;** *granny, grandmother* **abuelita;** *horse* **caballo;** *little pig* **cerdito;** *lumberjack* **leñador;** *masked ball* **baile de disfraces;** *mouse* **ratón;** *palace* **palacio;** *pig* **cerdo;** *poison* **veneno;** *prince* **príncipe;** *pumpkin* **calabaza;** *rival* **rival;** *stepmother* **madrastra;** *stepsister* **hermanastra;** *straw* **paja;** *the big bad wolf* **el lobo malo;** *to blow* **soplar;** *to exile* **exiliar;** *to make something fall down* **tumbar;** *to see you better* **para verte mejor;** *to seem dead* **parecer muerto;** *What big eyes you have!* **¡Qué ojos más grandes tienes!;** *wolf* **lobo;** *wood* **madera;** *woods* **bosque**

ATAJO 💿

Vocabulary: Fairy tales and legends
Grammar: Verbs: Preterite and imperfect

Ejercicio 6.19   Temas de ensayo.

Cuente en el pasado uno de sus recuerdos de infancia favoritos.

 # Compound Tenses

[Chapter 6.C, pages 190–197]

(For practice of the forms of compound tenses, and of the present and past participle, see Exercises 5.18–5.19; 5.23; 5.26; 5.36–5.37; 5.56–5.61. We recommend that you do those exercises before these.)

Ejercicio 6.20   *Traduzca.* (you = **tú**)

1. I am writing a letter.   **2.** They have been working there since last week.   **3.** I was eating when you arrived.   **4.** He had been in the sun for three hours.   **5.** She had been calling for two days.   **6.** We have eaten.   **7.** We will have eaten by then *(para entonces).*   **8.** I was working on the computer all day yesterday.   **9.** He said he would have finished.   **10.** I thought it would be raining by now *(para ahora).*

Ejercicio 6.21   Temas de ensayo.

Escriba el cuento de "Rizos de Oro" (Goldilocks) *en el pasado, usando el progresivo y el pluscuamperfecto cada vez que lo necesite.*

> **Vocabulario:** *bear* **oso;** *bed* **cama;** *chair* **silla;** *mama bear* **la mamá osa;** *papa bear* **el papá oso;** *porridge* **avena;** *somebody* **alguien;** *soup* **sopa;** *the little bear* **el osito;** *to be lying down* [position] **estar acostado;** *to be sitting* [position] **estar sentado;** *to fall asleep* **dormirse;** *to lie down* [change position from standing or sitting to lying down] **acostarse;** *to sit down* [change position from standing to sitting] **sentarse;** *to sleep* **dormir;** *woods* **bosque**

D Ways of Expressing the Future

[Chapter 6.D, pages 197–198]

(For practice of the forms of the future, see the corresponding exercises for Chapter 5. We recommend that you do those exercises before these.)

Ejercicio 6.22 *Traduzca de tres formas distintas.* (you = **tú**)

1. Tomorrow we will eat at a restaurant.   **2.** This evening we are going to the movies.
3. I will call you this afternoon.   **4.** What are you doing tonight?

Ejercicio 6.23 Temas de ensayo.

Usando el futuro cada vez que pueda, prepare una lista de diez promesas para mejorarse o para mejorar su vida; use verbos diferentes para cada promesa. (Por ejemplo: Me levantaré temprano. Haré mi cama cada mañana. No le gritaré a mi hermano aunque él me provoque.)

ATAJO

Grammar: Verbs: Future

E Conditional

[Chapter 6.E, pages 198–200]

(For practice of the forms of the conditional, see Exercises 5.24–5.27. We recommend that you do those exercises before these.)

Ejercicio 6.24 *Cambie las oraciones siguientes para que sean más corteses.*

1. ¿Puedes ayudarme con esto?   **2.** ¿Tienes tiempo para ayudarme?   **3.** No debes hacer eso.   **4.** Quiero que vengas.

Ejercicio 6.25 *Cambie las oraciones al pasado.*

1. Pienso que llegarán a tiempo.   **2.** Creo que lo terminarán pronto.   **3.** Dice que lo hará.   **4.** Sé que cumplirá con su promesa.

Ejercicio 6.26 Temas de ensayo.

Escriba un diálogo entre un mesero en un restaurante y un par de clientes difíciles, uno porque no quiere aumentar de peso, y el otro porque no tiene mucho dinero.

Probability

[Chapter 6.F, pages 200–201]

(For practice of the forms of the future and the conditional, see Exercises 5.20–5.27. We recommend that you do those exercises before these.)

Ejercicio 6.27 *Conteste las preguntas expresando conjetura y usando la información entre paréntesis.*

1. ¿Por qué salgo mal en todas las pruebas? (no estudiar lo suficiente) **2.** ¿Por qué se veía verde ese hombre? (ser marciano) (estar enfermo) (algo asustarlo) **3.** ¿Dónde está tu hermano? (estar en el sótano) (ir a la tienda)

Ejercicio 6.28 Temas de ensayo.

Usted es detective, y debe escribir un informe de lo que cree que pasó basándose en los hechos (facts) *que observa en un crimen: se encuentra el cadáver* (corpse) *de un hombre flotando boca abajo en la piscina* (swimming pool) *de la casa de su vecino; no hay ninguna evidencia de violencia física. El cadáver está casi completamente desnudo* (naked): *sólo tiene puesto un reloj* (watch) *que paró a las tres y media. La autopsia revela que no murió ahogado* (drowned), *sino envenenado* (poisoned). *Escriba dos probables maneras en que pudo haber terminado así, usando un máximo de detalle descriptivo. Esto lo hace sin saber de seguro nada de nada* (without knowing anything at all for certain). *(Por ejemplo: El hombre sería rico, y su esposa por alguna razón lo odiaría y querría deshacerse de él; lo habrá envenenado y luego, una vez que había muerto, ella habrá empujado el cadáver dentro de la piscina, con la ayuda de alguien.)*

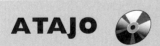

ATAJO

Phrases: Weighing the evidence; Hypothesizing
Grammar: Verbs: Preterite and perfect; Verbs: Conditional; Verbs: Future

Subjunctive (Nominal Clauses)

[Chapter 6.G.2, pages 202–210]

(For practice of the forms of the subjunctive, see Exercises 5.28–5.38. We recommend that you do those exercises before these.)

Ejercicio 6.29 *Conjugue el verbo entre paréntesis en el **presente del subjuntivo o del indicativo** según lo requiera el contexto.*

1. Sus padres lo obligan a que (trabajar / él). **2.** Creo que (tener / tú) razón. **3.** Basta que (pagar / tú) la mitad. **4.** Conviene que (salir / nosotros) temprano. **5.** ¿Desea usted que le (servir / nosotros) en su habitación? **6.** Mi padre se empeña en que yo no (ir) sola. **7.** Es bueno que ellos (aprender) a nadar. **8.** Es cierto que nosotros lo (ver). **9.** Es evidente que tú (comer) demasiado temprano. **10.** Es importante que yo la (llevar). **11.** Es triste que ellos no (poder) salir de allí. **12.** Es una lástima que tus vecinos no te (caer bien). **13.** Eso no significa que tu novia no te (querer). **14.** Veo que el pájaro no (poder) volar. **15.** Insisto en que me (dejar / ustedes) pagar a mí. **16.** Lamento que (ser) así. **17.** Mi madre siempre me aconseja que (llevar / yo) más dinero del que necesito. **18.** Nos encanta que nuestros amigos nos (sorprender) con sus visitas. **19.** Te ruego que me (escuchar). **20.** Ella siempre lo convence de que (quedarse) tarde.

Ejercicio 6.30 *Conjugue el verbo entre paréntesis en el **presente del subjuntivo o del indicativo** según lo requiera el contexto.*

1. Piensan que les (deber / nosotros) dinero. **2.** Más vale que ustedes (levantarse) temprano. **3.** Le enoja que su hermano siempre (ganar). **4.** ¿Necesitas que te (llevar / yo)? **5.** El testigo niega que su hijo (ser) culpable. **6.** No es que (llover) demasiado—al contrario. **7.** No importa que no (querer / ellos); tienen que hacerlo. **8.** Sé que me (querer / ella). **9.** Los vecinos se quejan de que los niños (gritar) tanto. **10.** Puede ser que ella (llegar) temprano. **11.** Los adolescentes se avergüenzan de que sus padres los (controlar) en público. **12.** Me opongo a que él lo (ver). **13.** Estamos seguras de que mañana (ir) a llover. **14.** Su hermana la persuade a que (hacer / ella) lo que ella quiere. **15.** Mi mamá me manda que le (llevar) sus cartas al correo. **16.** Les advierto que (callarse / ustedes). **17.** Me prohíben que (salir) tarde. **18.** Tienen miedo que yo los (denunciar) a la policía. **19.** Dice que no (saber / él) nada. **20.** Tenemos que impedir que él (pagar) esta vez.

Ejercicio 6.31 *Conjugue el verbo entre paréntesis en el **presente del subjuntivo o un tiempo** (tense) **del indicativo** según lo requiera el contexto.*

1. Ella cree que él no la (querer). **2.** Ella no cree que él la (querer). **3.** Su padre le dice que él (levantarse) temprano de niño. [*He used to get up early.*] **4.** Su padre le dice que (levantarse) temprano. [*He tells her to get up early.*] **5.** Te recomiendo que (dormir / tú) más. **6.** ¿Te pide que (ir / tú) con él? **7.** Espero que (poder / ellos) venir a la fiesta. **8.** Me molesta que no me (hacer / tú) caso. **9.** Me alegro que (ser / tú) feliz. **10.** No me gusta que me (gritar / ellos). **11.** Parece que (estar / él) triste. **12.** No parece que (estar / él) triste. **13.** Parece increíble que ellos no lo (saber). **14.** Me sorprende que no me (llamar / él). **15.** Te sugiero que (tomar / tú) vitaminas.

Ejercicio 6.32 *Traduzca.* (you = **tú**)

1. She lets me drive. **2.** I hope I can do it. **3.** I hope you can do it. **4.** I feel it is going to rain. **5.** I am sorry it is going to rain. **6.** I am sorry I cannot do it.

Ejercicio 6.33 Temas de ensayo.

Usando varias de las expresiones en la lista del capítulo 6.G.2.b ("Subjunctive After Expressions of Emotion"), páginas 203–205, escriba diez frases describiendo sus esperanzas, sus temores, lo que lamenta, lo que lo (la) emociona a usted.

ATAJO

Grammar: Verbs: Subjunctive

Ejercicio 6.34 Temas de ensayo.

Usando varias de las expresiones en la lista del capítulo 6.G.2.c ("Subjunctive After Expressions of Volition and Influence"), páginas 205–207, escriba diez frases describiendo lo que sus padres le aconsejan, le prohíben, le recomiendan, etc.

ATAJO

Grammar: Verbs: Subjunctive

Ejercicio 6.35 Temas de ensayo.

Usando varias de las expresiones en la lista del capítulo 6.G.2.d ("Subjunctive After Expressions of Doubt and Negation of Reality"), página 208, escriba diez frases describiendo una de sus dudas más importantes, como por ejemplo sobre el origen del mundo, la existencia de Dios, la vida en Marte (Mars), el racismo, etc.

ATAJO

Grammar: Verbs: Subjunctive

Ejercicio 6.36   Temas de ensayo.

Usando varias de las expresiones en la lista del capítulo 6.G.2.e ("Subjunctive After Impersonal Expressions with Ser"), páginas 209–210, escriba diez consejos e ideas que usted le da a un amigo sobre un viaje a un país hispano.

ATAJO

Grammar: Verbs: Subjunctive

Ejercicio 6.37   Temas de ensayo.

Usando el mayor número posible de verbos de la lista de abajo para introducir cláusulas nominales, escriba un párrafo sobre el tema del amor en el mundo de hoy: piense en términos de establecer una pareja, la opción entre la soltería (no casarse) y el matrimonio (casarse), tener hijos o no y el divorcio. Si lo desea, puede usar su vida personal para expresar su opinión. Preste atención al uso del subjuntivo, del infinitivo o del indicativo, dependiendo del contexto. Mire las páginas sobre las cláusulas nominales para ver ejemplos de usos de estos verbos.

querer, parecer, dudar, gustar, esperar, tener miedo de, alegrarse, enojar, molestar, sorprender, necesitar, preferir, oponerse a, dejar, obligar a, convencer, impedir, mandar, pedir, permitir, recomendar, sugerir, bastar, convenir, no creer, no ser, no significar, ser bueno (malo, raro, triste, importante, necesario, difícil, imposible, una lástima) que

ATAJO

Phrases: Persuading; Weighing the evidence; Hypothesizing
Grammar: Verbs: Subjunctive

Subjunctive (Adjectival Clauses)

[Chapter 6.G.3, pages 211–212]

Ejercicio 6.38 *Complete con el presente del subjuntivo o algún tiempo del indicativo del verbo entre paréntesis, según lo requiera el contexto.*

1. Estamos esperando a la mujer que (calcular) nuestros impuestos. **2.** Quiero encontrar a una mujer que (saber) hacerlo. **3.** ¿Conoces a un hombre que (poder) hacerlo? **4.** Yo conozco a un hombre que (poder) hacerlo. **5.** No hay nadie que (poder) hacerlo como tú. **6.** Hay alguien que (poder) hacerlo. **7.** Haz lo que te (decir / yo) ayer. **8.** Siempre hace lo que le (decir / ellos), sea lo que sea. **9.** Digan lo que (decir / ellos), nunca te abandonaré.

Ejercicio 6.39 Temas de ensayo.

Haga una lista de diez deseos en su vida, usando cláusulas adjetivales. (Por ejemplo: Quiero conseguir un trabajo que me pague bien.)

Subjunctive (Adverbial Clauses)

[Chapter 6.G.4, pages 212–217]

Ejercicio 6.40 *Conjugue el verbo entre paréntesis en el **presente del subjuntivo o un tiempo del indicativo** según lo requiera el contexto.*

1. Ellos llegaron después de que nosotros (salir). **2.** Lo hago para que tú no (tener) que hacerlo. **3.** Ven a visitarnos tan pronto como (poder / tú). **4.** Mañana iremos al parque aunque (llover). **5.** Quiero hablar con ella por teléfono antes de que (irse / ella). **6.** Me lo dará, a no ser que (arrepentirse / él) primero. **7.** Comerá después de que los niños (acostarse). **8.** Caminó hasta que no (poder) más. **9.** Caminará hasta que no (poder) más. **10.** Tendrá el dinero, a menos que no le (pagar / ellos) hoy. **11.** Lo haremos cuando (querer / tú). **12.** Comí aunque no (tener) hambre. **13.** Me gusta mirar por la ventana cuando (llover). **14.** Los vemos a ellos sin que ellos nos (ver) a nosotros. **15.** Lo haré con tal que no se lo (decir / tú) a los vecinos.

Ejercicio 6.41 *Traduzca.* (you = **tú**)

1. She will not go unless we go. **2.** I will do it as long as (or provided) you do not tell anyone. **3.** We will leave as soon as you get dressed. **4.** He will insist until she accepts. **5.** I do not know anyone who can do that without your explaining how.

Ejercicio 6.42 Temas de ensayo.

Usando el mayor número posible de conjunciones de la lista de abajo para introducir cláusulas adverbiales, escriba un diálogo entre dos compañeros de casa que están preparándose para una fiesta en su casa.

para que, a menos que, antes de que, con tal de que, sin que, en caso de que, cuando, en cuanto, aunque, a pesar de que, después de que, mientras, hasta que

Subjunctive (Sequence of Tenses)

[Chapter 6.G.5, pages 217–226]

Ejercicio 6.43 *Combine las dos oraciones, usando la que está entre paréntesis como cláusula principal. Haga las transformaciones necesarias.*

1. Mañana llegarán nuestros amigos. (No creo que...) **2.** Raúl vive en Suiza. (Parece increíble que...) **3.** Los vecinos ya han visto esa película. (Me sorprende que...)
4. Ayer hacía calor. (Dudo que...) **5.** Se levantó a las cinco. (Me sorprende que...)
6. Ya habrán terminado a esa hora. (Parece dudoso que...) **7.** Mi abuelo ya había muerto cuando llegué. (Lamento que...) **8.** Pronto estará lista la cena. (Mi padre dudaba que...) **9.** Siempre hace frío en el monte. (Mi tía se quejaba de que...)
10. Tú bailabas el tango a los cinco años. (Era imposible que...) **11.** Los perros se escaparon. (Temían que...) **12.** Luisa nunca les ha dicho el secreto a sus hijos. (A Roberto le molestaba que...) **13.** Habrán regresado para la medianoche. (Me sorprendería mucho que...) **14.** Miguel ya había leído esa novela. (Yo tenía miedo que...)

Ejercicio 6.44 *Transforme el verbo de la cláusula subordinada (en negrilla) para concordar en el nuevo contexto con el verbo principal en el pasado (entre paréntesis).*

1. No creo que **puedan** venir. (No creía que...) **2.** Parece posible que **haga** calor hoy. (Parecía posible que... ese día.) **3.** Lamento que no les **guste.** (Lamentaba que...) **4.** ¿Conoces a alguien que **sea** de allí? (¿Conocías a alguien que... ?)
5. Queremos encontrar una casa que **tenga** piscina. (Queríamos...) **6.** Haremos lo que tú **quieras.** (Te dije que haríamos lo que...) **7.** Te doy las llaves a fin de que tú **abras.** (Te di las llaves...) **8.** Llama antes de que **sea** muy tarde. (Quería llamar antes de que...)

Ejercicio 6.45 *Forme una frase usando la primera como subordinada.*

1. Cantaban bien. (Me parecía increíble que...) **2.** Ellos caminaron. (Dudo que...)
3. Yo había caminado. (Ellos no creyeron que...) **4.** Perdí las llaves. (Ella se quejó de que yo...) **5.** Por fin pudimos ver la película. (Me alegro de que...) **6.** Los perros no habían ladrado en toda la noche. (A él le sorprendió que...)

Ejercicio 6.46 *Conjugue el verbo entre paréntesis en la forma correcta.*

1. Nosotros queríamos que ellos nos (llamar) primero.   **2.** A ella le gustaría que ustedes (ser) más directos.   **3.** El profesor dijo que no sabía si existía un texto que (explicar) más claramente ese punto.   **4.** ¿Había alguien que (poder) hacerlo?   **5.** Nos encantaría que las vacaciones (ser) más largas.   **6.** Me prometiste que me llamarías tan pronto (poder).   **7.** Les pedía que (callarse) a fin de que no (despertar) a los niños.   **8.** Yo no podía creer que ella (cortarse) el pelo la semana anterior.

Ejercicio 6.47 Temas de ensayo.

Deseos cambiados. Piense en su vida, y en los sueños y deseos que ha tenido desde la infancia. Algunos de sus deseos y sueños habrán cambiado a través de los años. Escriba un párrafo describiendo cuatro o cinco de sus sueños y deseos en su infancia, cómo se lograron o no, y cómo cambiaron. Use al máximo las expresiones en la lista del capítulo 6.G.2.b ("Subjunctive After Expressions of Emotion"), *páginas 203–205.*

ATAJO

Phrases: Expressing a wish or desire; Expressing hopes and aspirations
Vocabulary: Dreams and aspirations
Grammar: Verbs: Subjunctive

Ejercicio 6.48 Temas de ensayo.

Entreviste a alguien de una generación anterior a la suya, sobre la disciplina en la vida cuando era joven. Usando varias de las expresiones en la lista del capítulo 6.G.2.c ("Subjunctive After Expressions of Volition and Influence"), *páginas 205–207, escriba diez frases describiendo lo que sus padres le aconsejaban, le prohibían, le recomendaban, etc. a este individuo.*

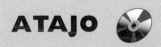

ATAJO

Grammar: Verbs: Subjunctive; Verbs: Imperfect

Ejercicio 6.49 Temas de ensayo.

Entreviste a uno de sus padres, o a alguien de una generación anterior a la suya, sobre lo que pensaban de la guerra y de la política cuando tenían la edad que usted tiene ahora. Usando varias de las expresiones en la lista del capítulo 6.G.2.d ("Subjunctive After Expressions of Doubt and Negation of Reality"), *página 208, escriba unas diez frases.*

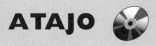

ATAJO

Grammar: Verbs: Subjunctive

Ejercicio 6.50 Temas de ensayo.

Usando varias de las expresiones en la lista del capítulo 6.G.2.e ("Subjunctive After Impersonal Expressions with Ser"), *páginas 209–210, escriba diez consejos e ideas que usted le dio a un amigo antes de que éste viajara a un país hispano. Por ejemplo: Le dije que era mejor que llevara ropa ligera; que era malo que no tratara de hablar español; etc.*

ATAJO

Grammar: Verbs: Subjunctive

Ejercicio 6.51 Temas de ensayo.

Entreviste a alguien que pertenezca a una generación anterior a la suya sobre el tema del amor cuando era adolescente, y sus sueños o sus ideales para el amor en su vida; averigüe si los padres de esta persona afectaron de alguna manera su punto de vista o su comportamiento. Usando el mayor número posible de verbos de la lista de abajo para introducir cláusulas nominales, escriba un párrafo sobre lo que pensaba esta persona. Preste atención al uso del subjuntivo, del infinitivo o del indicativo, dependiendo del contexto. Mire las páginas sobre las cláusulas nominales para ver ejemplos de usos de estos verbos.

querer, parecer, dudar, gustar, esperar, tener miedo de, alegrarse, enojar, molestar, sorprender, necesitar, preferir, oponerse a, dejar, obligar a, convencer, impedir, mandar, pedir, permitir, recomendar, sugerir, bastar, convenir, no creer, no ser, no significar, ser bueno (malo, raro, triste, importante, necesario, difícil, imposible, una lástima) que

Subjunctive (If [*Si*] Clauses)

[Chapter 6.G.6, pages 226–227]

Ejercicio 6.52   *Conjugue el verbo entre paréntesis en la forma correcta.*

1. Ella habría llegado a tiempo si no (haber) una tormenta.   **2.** Si él tuviera dinero, (comprarse) todos los coches antiguos del mundo.   **3.** Iría al supermercado si (ser) absolutamente necesario.   **4.** Si hubiéramos estudiado más, no (tener) tantas dificultades en el examen de ayer.   **5.** Si tuviera tiempo, te (ayudar / yo).   **6.** Se abrazaron como si no (verse) en años.   **7.** Lo trata como si (ser) adulto.

Ejercicio 6.53   Temas de ensayo.

Describa en un párrafo lo que pasaría si pudiera cambiar algún aspecto de su vida futura.

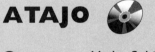
Ejercicio 6.54   Temas de ensayo.

Describa en un párrafo cómo habría sido diferente su vida si algún elemento hubiera sido diferente desde el principio.

Subjunctive *(Ojalá)*

[Chapter 6.G.7, page 228]

Ejercicio 6.55 *Traduzca usando **Ojalá**.* (you = **tú**)

1. I wish we had not gone. **2.** I wish you had listened to me. **3.** I hope you eat today. **4.** I wish he could see me now. **5.** I hope they did not do it. **6.** I hope we get there on time. **7.** I hope they finished. **8.** I hope she likes it. **9.** I hope they bought it. **10.** I wish she could hear me.

ATAJO

Grammar: Verbs: Subjunctive with *Ojalá*

Ejercicio 6.56 *Haga una lista de deseos para usted usando **Ojalá**.*

1. un deseo posible para el futuro **2.** un deseo posible para el presente **3.** un deseo posible para el pasado **4.** un deseo contrario a la realidad presente **5.** un deseo contrario a la realidad pasada

Subjunctive (Expressions Of Leave-Taking)

[Chapter 6.G.8, pages 229–230]

Ejercicio 6.57 *Traduzca estas expresiones usando la persona indicada.*

1. Get well. *(tú)* **2.** Have a good weekend. *(tú)* **3.** Have a good day. *(ustedes)* **4.** Have fun. *(usted)*

Ejercicio 6.58 *Despídase de las siguientes personas usando **irle bien a uno**.*

1. de un amigo **2.** de un profesor **3.** de unos amigos (en Latinoamérica) **4.** de unos amigos (en España)

Ejercicio 6.59 *Despídase de las mismas personas usando **pasarlo bien**.*

1. de un amigo **2.** de un profesor **3.** de unos amigos (en Latinoamérica) **4.** de unos amigos (en España)

Ejercicio 6.60 *Escriba dialoguitos de despedida para cada situación.*

1. despedida de un amigo en cualquier momento **2.** despedida de un profesor un viernes antes de un fin de semana normal **3.** despedida de una pareja de amigos antes de un viaje que va a hacer la pareja **4.** despedida de varios amigos antes de una fiesta **5.** despedida de un amigo enfermo **6.** despedida de unos amigos antes de una experiencia placentera

Infinitives and Present Participles

[Chapter 6.H, pages 231–235]

(For practice of the forms of the present participle, see Exercises 5.56–5.58. We recommend that you do those exercises before these.)

Ejercicio 6.61 *Escoja la forma correcta entre paréntesis.*

1. (Beber / Bebiendo) agua es muy saludable. **2.** No les gusta (cantar / cantando). **3.** Pensaban (viajar / viajando) al Caribe este invierno. **4.** Se fueron sin (decir / diciendo) nada. **5.** Eso es lo que te pasa por (hablar / hablando) tanto. **6.** Estoy cansado de (correr / corriendo). **7.** Al (salir / saliendo), no se les olvide llevarse el paraguas. **8.** El anuncio decía: "No (fumar / fumando)".

Ejercicio 6.62 *Traduzca las oraciones siguientes.*

1. That language is difficult to learn. **2.** It is difficult to learn that language. **3.** That recipe is easy to prepare. **4.** It is easy to say the truth. **5.** It is possible to live more than ninety years. **6.** Some things are impossible to change.

Ejercicio 6.63 *Las frases siguientes tienen participios presentes en inglés. ¿Cuáles usarían un participio presente en español también?*

1. That is one of the world's **increasing** problems. **2.** What an **interesting** person! **3.** She is one of the **leading** experts in that subject. **4.** I need to buy some **writing** paper. **5.** That psychologist says that all of the problems of adolescence are caused by **growing** pains. **6.** They have **running** water. **7.** Take a photo of the pitcher **containing** the blue liquid. **8.** The court wanted a number of items **belonging** to her. **9.** There he was, **standing** in the middle of the room. **10.** The movie was **boring.** **11.** That is an **amusing** game. **12.** I found the cat **lying** on the bed. **13.** She was **sitting** in front of me at the movies. **14.** This exercise is **entertaining.** **15.** Do you have any **drinking** water?

Ejercicio 6.64 *Traduzca al español las frases del ejercicio anterior.*

Ejercicio 6.65 *Traduzca las oraciones siguientes.*

1. Look: they are **increasing** the weight.   **2.** They were **directing** the traffic to the side.   **3.** They left **running**.   **4.** The speaker was **boring** us all.   **5.** They were just **sitting** down (in the process of taking their seats) when the movie ended.   **6.** We were **entertaining** the guests.

Ejercicio 6.66 *Identifique la diferencia gramatical entre las palabras idénticas en cada par de frases; luego traduzca al español.*

1.a. I am concerned about my **increasing** weight.   **1.b.** They are **increasing** our taxes.   **2.a.** That class is **boring.**   **2.b.** Am I **boring** you?   **3.a.** I was just **sitting** down (in the process) when the phone rang.   **3.b.** I have serious news: are you **sitting** down?

Ejercicio 6.67 *Traduzca usando el infinitivo o el participio presente.* (you = **tú**)

1. They must have eaten.   **2.** She has to eat more.   **3.** They were planning on going to the beach.   **4.** I do not have anything to wear.   **5.** Put on your coat before leaving. **6.** To see those effects, it is necessary to wear special glasses.   **7.** He was glad to see her.   **8.** Upon entering, they took off their shoes.   **9.** My brother had the veterinarian come.   **10.** Those seeds are hard to plant.   **11.** That book is easy to read.   **12.** It is easy to read that book.   **13.** Seeing is believing.   **14.** He forbids me to drive. **15.** The children love playing in the water.   **16.** He left without saying a thing. **17.** They were sorry after hanging up the phone.   **18.** They separated without really having gotten to know each other.   **19.** Do not stop me from moving.   **20.** My back hurts from having worked so much in the garden.

Ejercicio 6.68 Temas de ensayo.

*Usted es un médico muy concienzudo y debe indicarle a un paciente las actividades que son buenas o malas para la salud. Use una variedad de formatos: infinitivo como sujeto, como objeto directo, como objeto de preposición, con **hay que** o **tiene que**, **nada que** y **poco que**, con **fácil de** y **difícil de**, con **al**.*

ATAJO

Vocabulary: Body; Health: Disease and illnesses
Grammar: Verbs: Infinitive

Ejercicio 6.69   Temas de ensayo.

Escriba un párrafo sobre las acciones simultáneas de un individuo que está buscando como loco sus llaves perdidas (lost keys). *Haga lo posible por incorporar el equivalente correcto en español de las siguientes expresiones:* interesting, growing, existing, writing paper, containing, belonging, standing, sitting, lying down, boring, amusing, entertaining.

Verbs Like *Gustar*

[Chapter 6.I, pages 236–240]

Ejercicio 6.70   *Traduzca usando la expresión **caer bien**.* (you = **tú**)

1. He likes you.   **2.** I like them.   **3.** She likes us.   **4.** They like her.   **5.** We like him.
6. You like them.

Ejercicio 6.71   *Traduzca las oraciones siguientes, usando los pronombres necesarios para enfatizar lo que está en negrilla. (Siga usando la expresión **caer bien**.)*

1. Nobody likes you. **He** likes me.   **2.** Yes, but **she** does not like you.   **3.** **You** like **her,** but **she** does not like **you.**

Ejercicio 6.72   *Conteste las siguientes preguntas con **a mí** o **yo**; luego traduzca la pregunta y la respuesta al inglés.*

1. ¿A quién le interesa la magia?   **2.** ¿A quién le toca pagar la cuenta?   **3.** ¿A quién le gustó la cena?   **4.** ¿Quién comió más?

Ejercicio 6.73   *Traduzca usando **caer bien, gustar, encantar** o **querer**.*

1. I love him.   **2.** I love my classes.   **3.** I like your house.   **4.** I like my neighbors.

Ejercicio 6.74   *Traduzca usando **faltar, hacer falta, quedar** o **sobrar**.*

1. They need food.   **2.** They have two days left.   **3.** We had time to spare (left over).
4. I miss you.   **5.** She is lacking twenty cents.

Ejercicio 6.75   Temas de ensayo.

Escriba un párrafo describiendo sus gustos en general; indique lo que le gusta y lo que no le gusta, el tipo de gente que le cae bien, y quiénes le caen mal, a quién quiere, lo que le encanta, qué o quién le hace falta, lo que le importa, le interesa, le parece bien o mal o increíble.

ATAJO

Grammar: Verbs: Use of *gustar*

J Reflexive Verbs

[Chapter 6.J, pages 241–249]

(For practice of the reflexive pronouns, see Exercises 3.18–3.20. We recommend that you do those exercises before these.)

Ejercicio 6.76 *Traduzca usando verbos reflexivos.* (you = **tú**)

1. We got bored at the party. **2.** Did you remember the keys? **3.** She got used to him very soon. **4.** I am glad to see you. **5.** He was ashamed of his lie. **6.** I got off the bus at the third stop. **7.** The other children always made fun of me. **8.** You are going to have to confront that problem some day. **9.** She realized that she had to say good-bye to me. **10.** We must all make an effort to keep the environment clean. **11.** How did he find out about that? **12.** Do not trust anyone. **13.** Notice their eyes when they dance. **14.** Where are we going to meet him for lunch? **15.** Why did your parents move? **16.** What is his name? **17.** Please do not leave now. **18.** You must not interfere with those children. **19.** They stayed with us for the summer. **20.** He fought with his father. **21.** You look like me. **22.** Now he is going to start barking. **23.** I feel sad today. **24.** I sit here. **25.** I felt sad yesterday. **26.** I sat here yesterday. **27.** I used to feel sad when I heard that song. **28.** I used to sit here. **29.** He kept my book. **30.** Dry yourself well.

Ejercicio 6.77 *Llene el espacio en blanco con la preposición correcta, o con Ø si no se necesita preposición.*

1. Me enamoré _____ ella hace mucho tiempo. **2.** Se casó _____ él en junio. **3.** Ella se reía _____ mí. **4.** Se quejan _____ todo. **5.** No te preocupes _____ mí. **6.** Nos parecemos _____ nuestro padre. **7.** Se interesa _____ las carreras de caballo. **8.** No te fijes _____ los demás. **9.** Él se fiaba _____ todos. **10.** Nos esforzábamos _____ hablar bajo. **11.** Mi madre se empeñaba _____ que limpiara el cuarto todos los días. **12.** Por fin se decidieron _____ salir. **13.** Se atrevió _____ dirigirse _____ él después de unos minutos. **14.** El vino se convirtió _____ vinagre. **15.** Él no puede deshacerse _____ nada. **16.** ¿Te das cuenta _____ la hora que es? **17.** Se curaron _____ los enfermos. **18.** Me citaré _____ el dentista mañana. **19.** Se arrepintieron _____ haber dicho eso. **20.** ¡Aléjate _____ la calle!

Ejercicio 6.78   Temas de ensayo.

Usando al máximo los verbos reflexivos de las listas del capítulo 6.J, páginas 244–249, escriba el resumen de una telenovela (soap opera) *imaginaria y melodramática.*

ATAJO

Phrases: Writing about characters; Writing about theme, plot or scene
Grammar: Verbs: Reflexives

K Indirect Discourse

[Chapter 6.K, pages 249–255]

Ejercicio 6.79   *Reescriba la frase original usando las segundas como nuevo principio. Haga todos los cambios necesarios.*

MODELO: Compró la casa. **a.** Dice que... **b.** Dijo que...

   a. *Dice que compró la casa.* **b.** *Dijo que había comprado la casa.*

1. Iremos al cine esta noche. **a.** Dice que... **b.** Ayer dijo que... **c.** Esta mañana dijo que...   2. Yo sé hacerlo. **a.** Ella supone que... **b.** Ella suponía que... **c.** Ella supuso que...   3. Yo hice tu trabajo. **a.** Te digo que... **b.** Le dije que... **c.** Me dijo que...   4. Levántate. **a.** Te pido que... **b.** Me pidió que... **c.** Le pedí que...   5. Si pudiera ir ahora, lo haría. **a.** Dice que... **b.** Dijo que...   6. ¿Quieres que vayamos la semana entrante? **a.** Me preguntó esta mañana... **b.** Me preguntó el mes pasado... **c.** Sé que me preguntará...   7. Si quieres comer, come. **a.** Me respondió... **b.** Te estoy diciendo...   8. Vete. **a.** Te ruego... **b.** Me suplicó... **c.** Insistieron...   9. —¿Sabes qué hora es? —No. **a.** Siempre me pregunta... y yo siempre le contesto... **b.** Me preguntó... y yo le contesté...   10. —¿Les gustaría salir a cenar? —¡Sí! **a.** El domingo por la tarde siempre nos pregunta... y nosotros siempre le gritamos... **b.** Nos preguntó... y nosotros le gritamos...

Ejercicio 6.80   Temas de ensayo.

Escriba uno de los diálogos siguientes usando lo más posible el discurso indirecto.

a. entre un testigo *(witness)* y un abogado *(lawyer),* en que el abogado trata de demostrar que el testigo está mintiendo. (Por ejemplo: —Pero ayer usted dijo que...; —No, yo dije que...). Pueden ser personajes verdaderos o ficticios.

b. entre un padre y su hijo, en que el padre le recrimina al hijo algo que ha hecho en contra de las reglas que el padre le había dado y que el hijo dice que malentendió, o que contradicen otras cosas que dijo el padre

c. entre dos compañeros de casa que tuvieron un malentendido *(misunderstood each other)* sobre quién iba a encargarse de qué *(who was going to take care of what)* en cuanto a las responsabilidades de la casa. Se acusan entre ellos de haber dicho que iban a hacer algo que luego no hicieron.

d. entre dos niños traviesos *(naughty)* que habían planeado alguna travesura *(naughty act, trick, practical joke)* y que fueron descubiertos por culpa de un error que cada uno de los niños cree que fue la culpa del otro.

Chapter 6 Review

Ejercicio 6.81 *Conjugue cada verbo en el tiempo y modo más lógico para el contexto. Lea todo el contexto antes de comenzar.*

a caballo *on horseback;* **aficionado** *fan;* **arena** *sand;* **asunto** *matter;* **banderilla** *bullfighting term, "banderilla";* **bravo** *fierce;* **caballo** *horse;* **como si nada** *as if nothing were going on;* **corrida** *bullfight;* **criar** *to breed;* **daño (hacer)** *to injure;* **desequilibrio** *imbalance;* **desfilar** *to parade;* **estado de ánimo** *state of mind;* **estocada** *thrust of the sword;* **estoque** *sword of the bullfighter;* **grabado** *engraved;* **herir** *to injure;* **lanzar** *to toss;* **lidia** *bullfighting;* **lidia (toro de)** *bull bred for bullfighting;* **lidiar** *to fight (bulls);* **luchar** *to struggle;* **maltrato** *abuse;* **matador** *bullfighter of the highest rank, so named because he is to kill the bull;* **mezclar** *to mix;* **molestar** *to bother;* **oreja** *ear;* **pasodoble** *type of music;* **pena (dar)** *to be sorry;* **picador** *bullfighting term, "picador";* **plaza de toros** *bullring;* **por mi cuenta** *on my own;* **presenciar** *to witness;* **público** *audience;* **recuerdos** *memories;* **reverencia** *bow (bending at the waist);* **rito** *ritual;* **sangre** *blood;* **sangrienta** *bloody;* **temporada** *season;* **torero** *bullfighter;* **toro** *bull;* **traje de luces** *suit of lights, bullfighter's suit;* **valiente** *courageous;* **vencer** *to vanquish, beat;* **verónica** *cape pass*

Mi padre era un aficionado° de las corridas° de toros°: para él (**1.** ser) una necesidad cultural asistir a todas las corridas de toros durante la temporada°, no sólo para él sino para toda la familia. Por eso cada domingo por la tarde (**2.** ir) todos juntos a la plaza de toros°, y (**3.** presenciar°) este espectáculo de música y de vida hispana. En esa época yo (**4.** ser) niña: hoy en día (**5.** recordar) muy poco de esas tardes; todas las corridas que (**6.** ver) se han (**7.** mezclar°) en una masa sin forma. Sólo (**8.** quedar) grabados° en mi memoria los recuerdos° de los momentos que marcan el transcurso de la corrida: la música de pasodoble° que (**9.** tocar / ellos) al principio, la entrada de los toreros° y todos los ayudantes que (**10.** desfilar°) muy valientes° y elegantes en sus trajes de luces° y capas de colores vivos, el torero que (**11.** presentarse) con una reverencia° frente al presidente y que a veces le (**12.** lanzar°) su sombrero a alguien del público°, generalmente a una mujer; la entrada de cada toro que (**13.** salir) corriendo y (**14.** parecer) muy bravo, el público° que (**15.** gritar) "Olé" con cada pase de capa, el picador° a caballo°, las banderillas°, la llegada del matador° con su capa roja que (**16.** indicar) el final que se (**17.** acercar), y la estocada° final, que (**18.** dejar) al toro muerto o casi muerto. A veces le (**19.** cortar / ellos) una o ambas orejas° al toro para dárselas al torero, y éste se (**20.** dar) la vuelta a la plaza con su premio, como héroe victorioso. Luego (**21.** limpiar / ellos) la arena° sangrienta° para que el próximo toro (**22.** entrar).

Sólo hay una corrida que me (**23.** dejar) recuerdos más claros, y (**24.** ser) la vez que (**25.** venir) El Cordobés, que (**26.** ser) un torero español, de Córdoba, que (**27.** hacerse) famoso por su pelo largo y su personalidad; además, las mujeres (**28.** pensar) que (**29.** ser) muy guapo. Recuerdo que cuando él (**30.** ir) a empezar a lidiar°, (**31.** ir) al lugar de siempre frente al presidente, y cuando (**32.** quitarse) el sombrero, todo el público (**33.** gritar) y (**34.** reírse) por su pelo. En realidad no (**35.** tener) el pelo tan largo: hoy en día no (**36.** ser) nada sorprendente ver a alguien con el pelo así; pero en esa época (**37.** acabar) de hacerse famosos los Beatles por su pelo largo, y a cualquier hombre que (**38.** tener) pelo que le (**39.** tapar) las orejas se le (**40.** considerar) un rebelde o una anomalía.

La única otra imagen que tengo de ese día (**41.** ser) cuando El Cordobés, después de una verónica° que (**42.** dejar) al toro parado como hipnotizado, (**43.** pararse) de espaldas al toro y (**44.** sacar) de no sé dónde un enorme peine°, y (**45.** peinarse) tranquilamente, como si nada°. El público (**46.** morirse) de la risa.

En ningún momento pensé en la moralidad de lo que (**47.** pasar) en las corridas, y no (**48.** ser) sino hasta que (**49.** llegar) a ser adulta y que (**50.** mudarse) a los Estados Unidos que se me (**51.** ocurrir) que estos ritos° culturales (**52.** contener) elementos de injusticia. Debo confesar que en realidad no (**53.** ser) yo la que (**54.** pensar) en esto por mi cuenta°. (**55.** Ser) las preguntas de otros que me (**56.** hacer) ver el maltrato° hacia los toros. Yo no (**57.** saber) nada de lo que (**58.** pasar) antes de que el toro (**59.** entrar) a la plaza. Y nunca (**60.** pensar) en el toro. Para mí (**61.** tratarse) de un evento en que el torero (**62.** tener) que luchar° para que el toro no lo (**63.** matar) o (**64.** herir°). En realidad no me (**65.** gustar) que le (**66.** hacer / ellos) daño° al toro, y francamente me (**67.** molestar°) ver tanta sangre°, pero nunca (**68.** dejar) que eso (**69.** afectar) mi estado de ánimo°, o al menos la superficie. En mi familia, si yo (**70.** reaccionar) de alguna manera negativa en contra de las corridas, (**71.** haber) un escándalo. Para mi padre, una crítica (**72.** ser) una afrenta a la cultura.

Me da mucha pena° ahora que mi padre ya (**73.** morirse), porque si no, yo (**74.** poder) tener una conversación con él sobre el asunto°. Me (**75.** interesar) saber qué importancia le (**76.** dar) él al desequilibrio° de la batalla entre el hombre y el toro. Después de todo, es fácil (**77.** matar) a un toro si se considera todo el arsenal que se usa contra él. Yo (**78.** dudar) que un torero solo, con una capa y un estoque°, sin la ayuda de nadie, ni de banderillas ni de picadores, (**79.** poder) vencer° a un toro de lidia, sin que el toro lo (**80.** lastimar) mucho.

A pesar de todo, (**81.** tener / yo) que admitir que no (**82.** avergonzarse) de (**83.** asistir) a tantas corridas sin nunca (**84.** pensar) en el toro. Al contrario: si (**85.** tener / yo) la opción ahora de formar mi pasado, (**86.** preferir) haber tenido la experiencia, y no habérmela perdido. Las corridas de toros (**87.** representar) un aspecto importante de la cultura hispana, y (**88.** pensar / yo) que (**89.** ser) esencial que (**90.** reconocer / nosotros) este hecho y que (**91.** ser / nosotros) tolerantes de otros puntos de vista y sistemas de valores. Uno de los argumentos a favor de esta ceremonia (**92.** ser) que los toros de lidia se (**93.** criar°) con el único propósito de (**94.** participar) en las corridas. Pero (**95.** estar / yo) segura de que el debate (**96.** seguir) hasta que los críticos (**97.** lograr) que se (**98.** prohibir) las corridas, y cuando eso (**99.** ocurrir), (**100.** ser) el final de una gran tradición hispana.

Ejercicio 6.82   Temas de ensayo.

Prestando atención a la selección de tiempos y modos verbales, escriba un ensayo sobre uno de los temas siguientes. Narre su propia experiencia en el pasado con el tema, o sus observaciones de las experiencias de otros, y exprese su opinión, elaborando con cuidado los argumentos que se pueden hacer para cada lado del debate.

a. el uso de animales para experimentos en laboratorios

ATAJO

Phrases: Writing an essay; Weighing the evidence; Expressing indecision
Vocabulary: Animals; Body; Health
Grammar: Verbs: Preterite and imperfect

b. la legalización de la mariguana para propósitos medicinales

ATAJO

Phrases: Weighing the evidence
Vocabulary: Health: Diseases and illnesses

c. las ventajas y las desventajas de la estadidad *(statehood)* o independencia de Puerto Rico

Phrases: Weighing the evidence
Grammar: Verbs: Conditional

d. la libertad de palabra *(freedom of speech)* para los grupos que odian *(hate)* a otros

Phrases: Linking ideas; Expressing an opinion

e. los perros o los gatos: ¿cuáles son mejores como animales domésticos?

Phrases: Expressing an opinion

f. la eficiencia del sistema legal (escoja uno o dos casos específicos)

g. los deportes como espectáculo o diversión por un lado y como profesión por otro

Vocabulary: Leisure

Chapter 7 *Ser, Estar, Haber, Hacer, and Tener*

◆B◆ *Ser* vs. *Estar*

[Chapter 7.B.1–3, pages 259–267]

Ejercicio 7.1 *¿Es o está? Si los dos son posibles, explique por qué.*

Esa película _____ ...
1. mi favorita **2.** la que quiero ver **3.** la mejor **4.** mía **5.** de horror **6.** aburrida
7. buena **8.** dañada **9.** interesante **10.** de Argentina **11.** lista para mostrarse
12. de Almodóvar **13.** a las ocho esta noche **14.** en la mesa **15.** mostrándose ahora
mismo

Ejercicio 7.2 *¿Soy o Estoy? Si los dos son posibles, explique por qué.*

1. _____ tu amiga. **2.** No _____ lo que crees. **3.** _____ de pie. **4.** _____ donde
quiero. **5.** _____ alto y moreno. **6.** _____ aburrido. **7.** _____ bueno. **8.** _____
bien. **9.** _____ enfermo. **10.** _____ de Argentina. **11.** _____ lista para salir.
12. _____ tuyo. **13.** _____ harto de tanto trabajo. **14.** _____ contento con la vida.
15. _____ llamando para pedir un favor. **16.** _____ emocionado.

Ejercicio 7.3 *Traduzca de la manera más natural en español. Si hay más de una
traducción posible, explique la diferencia, si la hay.*

1. I am back. **2.** I am blind. **3.** I am bored. **4.** I am boring. **5.** I am clever.
6. I am hot. **7.** I am comfortable. **8.** I am done. **9.** I am excited. **10.** I am fat.
11. I am fed up. **12.** I am finished. **13.** I am from Ithaca. **14.** I am glad. **15.** I am
good (virtuous). **16.** I am happy. **17.** I am here. **18.** I am dead (figuratively).
19. I am hungry. **20.** I am at the university. **21.** I am interested. **22.** I am late.
23. I am mature. **24.** I am okay. **25.** I am quiet. **26.** I am ready. **27.** I am rich.
28. I am sad to hear that. **29.** I am sick (ill). **30.** I am sitting. **31.** I am sorry. **32.** I
am standing. **33.** I am short. **34.** I am the one who gave you the flowers. **35.** I am
working. **36.** I was born.

Ejercicio 7.4 *Traduzca de la manera más natural en español. Si hay más de una
traducción posible, explique la diferencia, si la hay. Convendría repasar el uso del
infinitivo y del subjuntivo.*

1. It is okay for you to be early. **2.** It was good to be there. **3.** "To be or not to be,"
that is the question. **4.** It is time to leave. **5.** We were comfortable because we were

sitting.   **6.** It was interesting to see that they were always late.   **7.** It was clear that it wasn't working properly *(bien).*   **8.** He was happy that I was done.   **9.** I am sorry but I am not hungry.   **10.** I am glad you agree with me.

Ejercicio 7.5   *¿Ser o estar? Llene el espacio en blanco con el verbo correcto.*

1. Ese hombre _____ profesor.   **2.** _____ importante llegar temprano.   **3.** Martina _____ de vacaciones.   **4.** _____ bien que estudien esta noche.   **5.** Luisa _____ de Guadalajara.   **6.** ¿Qué hora _____?   **7.** _____ la una de la tarde.   **8.** _____ las siete de la mañana.   **9.** ¿ _____ claro lo que tienen que hacer?   **10.** Los pisos en esa casa _____ de madera.   **11.** Mis padres _____ de acuerdo con nosotros.   **12.** Esa mujer _____ de gerente esta semana, hasta que regrese la gerente oficial.   **13.** ¿Para cuándo _____ la próxima composición?   **14.** Este libro _____ de Mario.   **15.** La ceremonia de la graduación siempre _____ en el gimnasio.   **16.** Mis libros _____ en mi casillero.   **17.** Su hermano _____ en Madrid.   **18.** Nosotros _____ en Sevilla.   **19.** Tu mochila _____ en el escritorio.   **20.** La conferencia _____ a las nueve de la mañana.   **21.** Esta carta _____ para mi papá.   **22.** El vuelo _____ por salir.   **23.** Ese puente _____ construido por un ingeniero famoso.   **24.** Las ventanas _____ cerradas. ¿Quieres que las abra?   **25.** Bertita _____ aprendiendo a caminar.

Ejercicio 7.6   *¿Ser o estar? Llene el espacio en blanco con la forma correcta para el contexto.*

1. Ese actor _____ muerto.   **2.** Los cuellos de las jirafas _____ largos.   **3.** El café de Colombia _____ bueno.   **4.** Madonna _____ atlética.   **5.** ¡Qué rico _____ el café esta mañana!   **6.** Oprah _____ más delgada que hace un año.   **7.** Mi coche _____ averiado.   **8.** Su cuarto _____ desordenado hoy. ¿Qué pasaría?   **9.** La esposa _____ harta de tener que aguantar sus engaños.   **10.** El presidente _____ contento con los resultados.   **11.** —Hola, Quique. ¿_____ bien? (tú) —No, _____ enfermo. (yo) Pero ya _____ mejor que hace una semana. (yo)   **12.** Esa película _____ aburrida.   **13.** Mi compañero de cuarto, que por lo general _____ muy platicador, ahora _____ callado.   **14.** Mi hija _____ más lista que sus amiguitos.   **15.** Ya _____ hora de irnos. ¿_____ listos? ¡Vámonos!

Ejercicio 7.7   *Conteste las preguntas siguientes prestando atención a la elección de verbos. Elabore cada respuesta, y dé como mínimo cinco elementos en su respuesta.*

1. ¿Quién es usted?   **2.** ¿Cómo es usted? *(What are you like?)*   **3.** ¿Cómo está usted? *(How are you?)*   **4.** ¿Quién es su mejor amigo o amiga?   **5.** ¿Cómo es su mejor amigo o amiga?   **6.** ¿Por qué es su mejor amigo o amiga?   **7.** ¿Quién es Antonio Banderas?   **8.** ¿Cómo es Antonio Banderas?   **9.** ¿Quién era Evita Perón?   **10.** ¿Cómo era Evita?

Ser vs. *Estar* (With Past Participles: Passive Voice and Resultant Condition)

[Chapter 7.B.4.b, pages 268–270]

Ejercicio 7.8 *¿Activo, pasivo o **se** impersonal? Repase los usos del **se** impersonal (Chapter 3.B.4, pages 76–79), y luego traduzca las oraciones siguientes usando la estructura que sería **más natural** en español. Puede haber más de una posibilidad, dependiendo del contexto adicional que se visualice. Explique su razonamiento para cada traducción si da más de una.*

1. She was given the car.   **2.** The house was built by the owner.   **3.** Books are sold there.   **4.** Why wasn't I told?   **5.** She was not invited.   **6.** I was awakened by the light.   **7.** He was taken to the airport.   **8.** The hunter was attacked by the lion, and was killed.   **9.** It is forbidden to smoke here.   **10.** The man was not read his rights.

C *Estar* vs. *Haber*

[Chapter 7.C, page 271]

Ejercicio 7.9 *¿Están o hay? Llene el espacio en blanco.*

1. _____ veinte estudiantes en esta clase.   **2.** Los estudiantes _____ sentados cerca de la ventana.   **3.** _____ muchas cosas que hacer.   **4.** Los libros _____ en la biblioteca.   **5.** _____ libros en la biblioteca.   **6.** No _____ suficientes fondos para cubrir su cheque.   **7.** ¿Dónde _____ taxis?   **8.** Los taxis _____ a dos cuadras de aquí.   **9.** Ya no _____ tantos árboles como antes.   **10.** Las leyes que _____ no bastan para controlar el crimen.

D Expressions with *Estar* and *Tener*

[Chapter 7.D, pages 272–273]

Ejercicio 7.10 *Llene el espacio en blanco con la forma correcta de **estar** o **tener**.*

1. Cuando entré, vi que el hombre _____ de pie frente al altar, y la mujer _____ de rodillas. Se veía que los dos _____ calor, y parecía que _____ contentos de poder pasar un rato en la iglesia.   **2.** Yo _____ hambre, y decidí ir a la panadería porque _____ ganas de comer un pan dulce.   **3.** Mi madre _____ a favor de la pena de muerte, pero mi padre dice que hay que _____ en cuenta que a veces se cometen errores, y se condena a uno que no _____ la culpa por el crimen.   **4.** Ayer _____ ausente porque _____ tanto sueño que no me levanté cuando sonó el despertador.

Ahora _____ vergüenza. **5.** Nosotros _____ de visita ahora. _____ de vacaciones hasta septiembre, pero _____ de vuelta la semana entrante. **6.** Tú _____ razón: me quejo mucho. Pero _____ (yo) de mal humor porque (yo) _____ frío, _____ sueño, _____ sed y _____ miedo de no pasar este examen. **7.** Los obreros _____ de huelga porque sus salarios son muy bajos. Espero que (ellos) _____ éxito en conseguir lo que quieren. **8.** Los vecinos _____ de viaje, y no _____ de regreso hasta la semana entrante.

Ejercicio 7.11 *Traduzca las oraciones siguientes usando la mejor estructura en español.*

1. It seems they are in a hurry. **2.** Jimmy, hurry up! **3.** I am sorry for being late.
4. I am glad. **5.** I was standing and you were sitting. **6.** Luisita, sit down! **7.** You are right and I am wrong. **8.** I was sleepy, I fell asleep and had a very strange dream.

Ser, Estar, Tener, Haber, and Hacer (Review)

[Chapter 7.A–D, pages 258–273]

Ejercicio 7.12 *Traduzca estas frases usando **ser, estar, tener, haber** o **hacer.***

1. I have been on my knees too long. **2.** Is it cold in winter here? **3.** The children were thirsty. **4.** I do not know why I am sad. **5.** It is not that the party is boring, it is that the people are bored. **6.** Was it raining? **7.** How many rooms are there in that building? **8.** Where are you from? **9.** Is the conference in this building?

Ejercicio 7.13 *Complete con el presente de **ser, estar, haber** o **tener**.*

1. El pan _____ cortado. ¿Tú comiste? **2.** Las cuentas _____ pagadas por el banco.
3. Yo ya _____ visto esa película cuatro veces. **4.** Lo _____ todo preparado para los invitados.

Ejercicio 7.14 Temas de ensayo.

*Usando al máximo las expresiones con **estar** y **tener**, escriba un párrafo sobre un amigo.*

ATAJO

Phrases: Describing people
Grammar: Verbs: Uses of *estar*; Verbs: Uses of *tener*

Time Expressions

[Chapter 7.E, pages 273–276]

Ejercicio 7.15 *Traduzca estas frases de dos formas si se puede, usando **hacer** y **llevar**.*

1. I have been here for an hour. **2.** They had been working for twenty minutes when she came in. **3.** We called him a week ago. **4.** She had not cut her hair for many years. **5.** My niece has been learning ballet for three years. **6.** She came to visit us two months ago. **7.** How long have we been waiting?

Ejercicio 7.16 Temas de ensayo.

*Usando las expresiones **hace que** y **llevar**, haga una lista de los momentos más importantes de su vida pasada. (Hace diecinueve años que nací; ...).*

Chapter 7 Review

Ejercicio 7.17 *Llene el espacio en blanco con el verbo más lógico y en la forma correcta para el contexto.*

Querida Luisa,

Te escribo desde Madrid donde Jorge y yo **(1)** _____ de visita por unos días. **(2)** _____ extraño porque **(3)** _____ más turistas que madrileños en la ciudad: todos **(4)** _____ de vacaciones en agosto. Pero **(5)** _____ bien, me mezclo con los demás turistas. En realidad, lo que yo **(6)** _____ ganas de hacer era de conocer Madrid porque dicen que **(7)** _____ una ciudad fascinante. Y los que dicen esto **(8)** _____ razón: esta ciudad **(9)** _____ un centro cultural impresionante. Siempre **(10)** _____ algo nuevo que hacer cada día.

(11) _____ (nosotros) muy contentos con el hotel, aunque **(12)** _____ mucho calor y parece que no **(13)** _____ aire acondicionado que pueda ser suficiente para dominar este calor. Casi siempre **(14)** _____ cansados por el calor, y no podemos hacer tanto como quisié-ramos cada día. Tenemos que **(15)** _____ cuidado y tomar la siesta cada día, como lo hacen los demás. Pero en fin, ya sabes cómo **(16)** _____ nosotros: nos quejamos de todo pero en fin de cuentas terminamos contentos.

¿Cómo **(17)** _____ ustedes? Espero que no **(18)** _____ lloviendo mucho allá. Creo que ayer **(19)** _____ el cumpleaños de Martita, ¿verdad? ¿Cuántos años **(20)** _____ ya? Salúdala de nuestra parte, y dile que pronto **(21)** _____ de regreso con un regalito para ella.

Bueno, me despido por ahora: **(22)** _____ sueño, y mañana **(23)** _____ un día de muchos planes.

Un fuerte abrazo para ti y para David,

Victoria

Ejercicio 7.18 Temas de ensayo.

Prestando atención a la selección del verbo correcto para indicar to be, *escriba un párrafo sobre uno de los temas siguientes:*

a. Describa a alguien a quien usted admira.

ATAJO

Phrases: Describing people
Vocabulary: Personality
Grammar: Verbs: Uses of *ser* and *estar*

b. Escriba su autorretrato. Describa sus rasgos físicos y de personalidad, y los cambios por los que ha pasado.

ATAJO

Phrases: Describing people
Vocabulary: Personality
Grammar: Verbs: Uses of *ser* and *estar*

Chapter 8 Lexical Variations

 Terms and Expressions

1. ACABAR

[Chapter 8.B.1, pages 278–279]

Ejercicio 8.1 *Llene el espacio en blanco con* **acabé, acabé de, acababa, acababa de, acabo, acabo de** *o* **se me acabó.**

1. No tengo hambre ahora porque _____ comer. **2.** Cuando yo era niña tenía una manía: siempre _____ ponerme los dos calcetines antes de ponerme los zapatos. **3.** Estoy celebrando porque por fin _____ pintar el cuarto. **4.** Tengo que ir a la tienda porque _____ la leche. **5.** Anoche por fin _____ mi trabajo escrito para la clase de historia. **6.** Cuando era joven, a la hora de comer siempre _____ primero y salía corriendo a jugar; ahora encuentro que como más despacio que los demás, y _____ último.

Ejercicio 8.2 *Traduzca.*

1. I finished my work. **2.** They finished repairing the bridge in October. **3.** He will be finished with the construction by three in the afternoon. **4.** I just got up. **5.** When I got there, they had just eaten. **6.** The exam ended at ten. **7.** We finished the bread. **8.** We ran out of bread.

2. APPLY

[Chapter 8.B.2, pages 279–280]

Ejercicio 8.3 *Llene el espacio en blanco con la expresión correcta:* **aplicar, aplicación, solicitar, solicitud.**

1. Como no tenía suficiente dinero, tuve que _____ una beca. **2.** Cuando el doctor me recetó este ungüento, me dijo que se debía _____ con cuidado. **3.** Voy a _____ admisión a cuatro universidades. **4.** El trabajo que iba a _____ para el verano ya no existe. **5.** La _____ con la que estudia ese alumno es admirable. **6.** Recibieron mi _____ para el préstamo, pero no han decidido todavía si me lo van a otorgar.

Ejercicio 8.4 *Traduzca.*

1. She applied for a scholarship. **2.** The doctor applied pressure to the wound to stop the bleeding. **3.** Apply this ointment three times a day. **4.** We will apply for a loan at the bank. **5.** The job you applied for no longer exists. **6.** I sent my application for the job yesterday.

3. ASK

[Chapter 8.B.3, page 280]

Ejercicio 8.5 *Llene el espacio en blanco con la expresión correcta: **pedir, preguntar, hacer, pregunta, pedido, cuestión.** Si se trata de un verbo, conjúguelo en el pretérito.*

1. Luis me _____ si tenía tiempo. **2.** Yo le _____ a María que me ayudara. **3.** Les _____ un favor a mis amigos. **4.** Roberto _____: —¿Cuándo nos vamos? **5.** Los niños _____ mil preguntas antes de acostarse anoche. **6.** No se trata de dinero: es una _____ de principios. **7.** Tengo una _____ para ti: ¿dónde conseguiste ese libro? **8.** Necesito hacer otro _____ de papel de color: se nos está acabando.

Ejercicio 8.6 *Traduzca.*

1. I want to ask you a favor. **2.** I asked him a question. **3.** She asked me to take her to town. **4.** He asked me, "Are you really sixteen?" **5.** We asked him if he had eaten. **6.** They asked us why we had called. **7.** Do not ask me so many questions. **8.** I thought it was a question of ethics.

4. AT

[Chapter 8.B.4, page 281]

Ejercicio 8.7 *Llene el espacio en blanco con **a** o **en.***

1. Los niños se quedaron _____ casa. **2.** Ellos están _____ Nueva York. **3.** La clase es _____ las diez, _____ el edificio de Morrill. **4.** Me siento mejor _____ este momento. **5.** No sé qué decir _____ veces. **6.** Me parece que oí pasos. Creo que hay alguien _____ la puerta. **7.** Hay alguien _____ la puerta preguntando por ti. **8.** Le gusta tener a su amiga _____ su lado.

Ejercicio 8.8 *Traduzca.*

1. At this moment, I can't go. **2.** My first class is at eight. **3.** We are at the university. **4.** They were not at home. **5.** We are going to sit at the table. **6.** In Mexico I used to stay at my uncle's house at times.

5. ATTEND

[Chapter 8.B.5, pages 281–282]

Ejercicio 8.9 *Llene el espacio en blanco con la expresión correcta: **asistir, atender, asistencia, atento.***

1. La maestra, impaciente con la distracción de los alumnos, les dijo: —¡_____me!
2. El dependiente de la tienda se me acercó y me preguntó: —¿En qué puedo _____la hoy, señora?   3. Ayer yo no _____ a clase porque estaba enfermo.   4. La mesera nos _____ tan pronto entramos, y nos trajo el menú.   5. Toda la familia _____ al funeral ayer.   6. La _____ a clase cuenta más que los exámenes.   7. Tu hermano siempre me abre la puerta: ¿por qué no puedes ser tan _____ como él?
8. Los servicios de _____ social son esenciales para mucha gente.

Ejercicio 8.10 *Traduzca.*

1. We attended the lecture in the afternoon.   2. She did not attend class because she was ill.   3. May I assist you?   4. Tend to the guests, please.   5. Did you have a good audience?   6. Some politicians want to eliminate welfare.   7. Young people today are more polite with their elders than in the previous generation.

6. BECAUSE

[Chapter 8.B.6, pages 282–283]

Ejercicio 8.11 *Llene el espacio en blanco con la expresión correcta: **por, a causa de, porque, gracias a.** A veces se puede usar más de una: incluya todas las posibles.*

1. Es _____ tus dudas que no ganamos la lotería.   2. Me voy a poner un suéter _____ tengo frío.   3. Cerré las ventanas _____ el frío.   4. No pude cerrar la puerta _____ la humedad: la madera está hinchada.   5. Sé que me curaré pronto _____ todo el apoyo y la ayuda de mis amigos.   6. Me dio dolor de cabeza _____ leer tanto.
7. _____ la tormenta no voy a poder ir al cine.

Ejercicio 8.12 *Traduzca.*

1. I went home because of my brother's illness.   2. They had to cancel the trial because of the news.   3. They had to let him leave because of that.   4. She lost her voice because she screamed so much.   5. They did not go out because it was snowing.   6. It's because of your friendship that I managed to get where I am.

7. Become or Get

[Chapter 8.B.7, pages 283–285]

Ejercicio 8.13 *Llene el espacio en blanco con la expresión correcta para significar* became.

1. De joven _____ médico, y eventualmente _____ millonario. **2.** Mi padre _____ muy contento cuando le dije que me había ganado la lotería. **3.** Esa noche, el conde _____ vampiro. **4.** Al ver el fantasma, la mujer _____ pálida. **5.** Tenía muchas ambiciones, y eventualmente _____ para todos un símbolo del éxito.

Ejercicio 8.14 *Traduzca.*

1. I am glad it's Friday. **2.** The children became quiet. **3.** He calmed down after that. **4.** They got tired of walking. **5.** I got sick during the vacation. **6.** They got mad because I did not write. **7.** You get old fast in this job. **8.** The horse calmed down after the shot *(inyección)*. **9.** I noticed she had become pale. **10.** He became a doctor. **11.** She wanted to become a respected citizen. **12.** The flower had become a fruit.

Review: *Acabar*, Apply, Ask, At, Attend, Because, Become

[Chapter 8.1–8.7, pages 278–285]

Ejercicio 8.15 Temas de ensayo.

Prestando atención al uso correcto en español del léxico indicado, escriba un párrafo sobre uno de los temas que siguen. Refiérase a las páginas apropiadas del capítulo 8 para usar al máximo las expresiones que se deben practicar.

1. (Si está en la universidad.) Describa sus planes para venir a la universidad, y el proceso por el que pasó para llegar aquí.

2. (Si tiene planes de ir a la universidad.) Describa sus planes para ir a la universidad, y el proceso por el que está pasando para llegar allá.

3. Describa un trabajo que tenga o que haya tenido, y el proceso por el que pasó para conseguirlo.

8. But

[Chapter 8.B.8, pages 285–286]

Ejercicio 8.16 *Llene el espacio en blanco con la expresión correcta para significar* but.

1. Estudié el idioma, _____ no me atrevo a hablar.   **2.** Ese hombre no es mi tío, _____ mi cuñado.   **3.** No fueron a Puerto Rico, _____ a México.   **4.** Esta clase es interesante, _____ difícil.   **5.** No lo compró, _____ se lo regaló su hermana.   **6.** No hablo el idioma, _____ voy a viajar al país.

9. COME AND GO

[Chapter 8.B.9, page 286]

Ejercicio 8.17   *Llene el espacio en blanco con la expresión correcta:* ***ven, voy, llegar, ir, vine.***

(La mamá de Beto acaba de llegar del supermercado, y al entrar a la cocina, lo llama.)

—Beto, **(1)** _____ acá, necesito tu ayuda.
—Ya **(2)** _____, Mami.

(Pasa un rato, la mamá sigue metiendo bolsas, pero Beto no se aparece.)

—Apúrate, m'ijo, o **(3)** _____ a buscarte yo.

(Beto llega por fin.)

—¿Dónde estabas? ¿Por qué tardaste tanto en **(4)** _____?
—Pero Mami, **(5)** _____ tan pronto como me llamaste.
—No, en lo que te esperaba, tuve tiempo de **(6)** _____ al coche dos veces.
—Lo siento, Mami. No me di cuenta.

Ejercicio 8.18   *Traduzca.*

1. When are your parents coming to see us?   **2.** He went to the movies.   **3.** I am going to the movies.   **4.** Can I come with you?   **5.** "Come here, Juanita!" "I'm coming!"   **6.** They are always late.   **7.** Do not be late.   **8.** I am sorry I am late.
9. When did you get here?

10. *DESPEDIR*

[Chapter 8.B.10, page 287]

Ejercicio 8.19   *Llene el espacio en blanco con la expresión correcta:* ***despidieron, se despidieron, nos despidieron, los despedimos.***

1. Como no teníamos en ese trabajo la antigüedad que tenían los demás, _____.
2. Se formó una protesta cuando _____ a todos los empleados de esa empresa.
3. Cuando fue hora de separarnos, mi novia y yo _____ con un abrazo.   **4.** A los empleados que son menos productivos _____ cuando el mercado lo requiere.

Ejercicio 8.20 *Traduzca.*

1. They fired me yesterday.   **2.** I said good-bye to my friends.   **3.** I fired him.
4. I said good-bye to her.   **5.** We said good-bye at the door.

11. Exit and Success

[Chapter 8.B.11, page 287]

Ejercicio 8.21 *Llene el espacio en blanco con la expresión correcta:* ***éxitos,
salidas, sucesos.***

1. Para el periódico local, sólo hay espacio para reportar los _____ de mayor importancia.   **2.** ¿Dónde están las _____ de emergencia?   **3.** Mis fracasos son mucho más
frecuentes que mis _____.

Ejercicio 8.22 *Traduzca.*

1. If we work hard, we shall be successful.   **2.** Our success depends upon our effort.
3. The exit is to the right.   **4.** My grandmother liked to talk about the terrible events
of World War I.

12. Go and Leave

[Chapter 8.B.12, pages 288–289]

Ejercicio 8.23 *Llene el espacio en blanco con la expresión correcta:* ***ir, irse, salir,
dejar, dejar de.***

Los turistas **(1)** _____ de su hotel temprano para **(2)** _____ al aeropuerto porque su
vuelo iba a **(3)** _____ esa mañana: habían estado en Madrid dos semanas, y ya era
hora de **(4)** _____. El viaje les había encantado: **(5)** _____ a muchos lugares turísti-
cos, y todas las noches **(6)** _____ a restaurantes y bares. Tenían muchos recuerdos:
uno de ellos se enfermó el tercer día, pero aun así no **(7)** _____ acompañar a los
demás en todas sus aventuras. Otro **(8)** _____ sus tarjetas de crédito en casa en los
Estados Unidos, y tuvo que tomar dinero prestado de los demás. Y todos peleaban
con Doña Lupe, que quería comprarse objetos muy frágiles: por fin no la **(9)** _____
comprar más que uno o dos platos. El taxista los **(10)** _____ en el aeropuerto, y todos
estaban tristes de que se terminara el viaje.

Ejercicio 8.24 *Traduzca.*

1. We are going to school.   **2.** She left an hour ago.   **3.** The cat went outside.
4. They are going out tonight.   **5.** The nurse went out to lunch.   **6.** We were playing
out in the park, and Luisito got mad and left.   **7.** At what time does your flight leave?

8. Could you leave me at the corner, please?   **9.** You will not let me do anything.
10. They stopped screaming.

13. GUIDE

[Chapter 8.B.13, page 289]

Ejercicio 8.25   *Llene el espacio en blanco con **el** o **la**.*

Estábamos en el museo del Prado, y **(1)** _____ guía nos estaba llevando de un cuarto
al otro, hablándonos de la historia de cada obra, cuando de repente se cayó: uno de
sus tacones se había atorado en un escalón. La pobre se hizo daño y no pudo seguir.
De ahí en adelante, tuvimos que consultar **(2)** _____ guía que nos habían dado al
entrar para averiguar lo que no sabíamos: era un librito bastante gordo. Después de
un rato, nos unimos a otro grupo: **(3)** _____ guía que tenían ellos era un joven que
parecía saber mucho de Goya.

Ejercicio 8.26   *Traduzca.*

1. Our guide at the museum was an old man.   **2.** The tour guide was from Venezuela.
3. You will find the rules in the guide book.

REVIEW: BUT, COME AND GO, *DESPEDIR*, EXIT AND SUCCESS, GO AND LEAVE, GUIDE

[Chapter 8.8–8.13, pages 285–289]

Ejercicio 8.27   Temas de ensayo.

*Prestando atención al uso correcto en español del léxico indicado, escriba un párrafo
sobre uno de los temas que siguen. Refiérase a las páginas apropiadas del capítulo 8
para usar al máximo las expresiones que se deben practicar.*

1. Describa las aventuras de unos turistas en un país hispano.
2. Describa una experiencia que usted haya tenido en un viaje.
3. Describa sus planes para su vida profesional.

14. KNOW

[Chapter 8.B.14, page 290]

Ejercicio 8.28   *Llene el espacio en blanco con la expresión correcta para significar* know.

Yo **(1)** _____ que ellos **(2)** _____ la ciudad mejor que yo, y que **(3)** _____ (ellos)
exactamente dónde está la casa de su amigo. Hace muchos años que **(4)** _____ (ellos)

a este amigo. Es un individuo que **(5)** _____ que lo andamos buscando, y **(6)** _____ esconderse bien. Me han dicho que **(7)** _____ disfrazarse. No **(8)** _____ (yo) qué vamos a hacer para **(9)** _____ dónde está.

Ejercicio 8.29 *Traduzca.*

1. I know you. **2.** He met his new wife in Mexico. **3.** He does not know the area. **4.** He knows my phone number. **5.** They know how to skate. **6.** We knew it was cold. **7.** They did not know what to say. **8.** Do you know what time it is? **9.** Do you know that hotel? **10.** He did not know how to swim.

15. LEARN

[Chapter 8.B.15, pages 290–291]

Ejercicio 8.30 *Llene el espacio en blanco con la expresión correcta:* **aprender, enterarse de, averiguar, saber.** *Si existe más de una opción, explique la diferencia.*

1. Me gustaría _____ a bailar la salsa. **2.** Los jóvenes pensaban que nadie iba a _____ nada de lo que estaban haciendo. **3.** Usando sus poderes de análisis, el detective _____ quiénes eran los ladrones. **4.** Nunca _____ (yo) por qué no me habían invitado a su boda, pero verdaderamente no me importa.

Ejercicio 8.31 *Traduzca.*

1. She learned to dance. **2.** They found out about our secret. **3.** When I found out that you were here, I came immediately.

16. MEET

[Chapter 8.B.16, page 291]

Ejercicio 8.32 *Llene el espacio en blanco con la expresión correcta:* **conocer, encontrar, encontrarse, encontrarse con, toparse con, tropezar con.**

1. Ayer _____ al nuevo director del programa: me lo presentó el profesor López. **2.** Voy a salir a almorzar con mi mejor amiga: vamos a _____ en el centro. **3.** Me gustaría _____ a tus padres: si son como tú han de ser muy interesantes. **4.** No tengo ganas de _____ ningún conocido hoy. **5.** Esta tarde voy a _____ mis amigos para repasar para el examen. **6.** Ando buscando mis llaves, y no las _____.

Ejercicio 8.33 *Traduzca.*

1. She met her in the office. (first acquaintance) **2.** Then they decided to meet in the afternoon to discuss the job. **3.** Guess whom I met on my way to the library.

17. ORDER

[Chapter 8.B.17, page 292]

Ejercicio 8.34 *Llene el espacio en blanco con **el** o **la**.*

1. Mi tía es una mujer obsesiva: para ella no hay nada más importante que _____ orden. **2.** Los soldados dispararon cuando el general les dio _____ orden. **3.** ¿Cuál es _____ orden que siguieron para organizar estas fichas? **4.** —Estoy a _____ orden del cliente —dijo el mesero.

Ejercicio 8.35 *Traduzca.*

1. Everything had to be placed in a specific order. **2.** I did it because I received the order from above. **3.** "Hello, my name is Julia Ruiz." "Hello, Victoria Vargas, at your service."

18. PENSAR

[Chapter 8.B.18, pages 292–293]

Ejercicio 8.36 *Llene el espacio en blanco con **en, de** o **Ø** (nada).*

1. Cuando pienso _____ mi niñez, no recuerdo nada que sea triste. **2.** Este verano pienso _____ viajar a Europa. **3.** Cada vez que veo a ese actor, pienso _____ mi padre. **4.** ¿Qué pensarán _____ mí? **5.** Pienso _____ que vamos a tener bastante tiempo. **6.** A él nunca le importó lo que pensaban _____ sus películas.

Ejercicio 8.37 *Traduzca.*

1. I cannot stop thinking of you. **2.** What were you thinking of? **3.** What do you think of me? **4.** She refused to tell me what she thought of the workshop. **5.** We are planning on visiting our friends next week.

19. PEOPLE VS. MACHINES

[Chapter 8.B.19, pages 293–295]

Ejercicio 8.38 *Subraye la expresión correcta para el contexto.*

1. Mi reloj no (trabaja / funciona). **2.** Jorge (apagó / salió) la luz. **3.** El auto no (empieza / arranca). **4.** Cuando primero compré este coche, (corría / andaba) muy bien. **5.** Tuvimos que entregar el examen incompleto porque (corrimos fuera de / se nos acabó el) tiempo.

Ejercicio 8.39 *Traduzca.*

1. The children were running. **2.** That motor stopped running. **3.** They work from nine to five. **4.** It does not work like that. **5.** When did the movie start? **6.** I am going to start the car so it will get warm. **7.** The lights went out after ten. **8.** He works out every day. **9.** We can work it out. **10.** I ran out. **11.** He ran across his cousin at the museum. **12.** The batteries ran down. **13.** My watch ran down. **14.** He ran down the stairs. **15.** They ran into their friends at the bar. **16.** He ran into the wall. **17.** Turn out the lights. **18.** Everything turned out okay.

20. PLAY

[Chapter 8.B.20, page 295]

Ejercicio 8.40 *Llene el espacio en blanco con la expresión correcta:* **jugar, tocar, obra, juego, jugada, partido, partida.**

1. No tenían mucho tiempo, así que decidieron limitarse a una sola _____ de ajedrez. **2.** Con esa _____ ganó el _____ de damas *(checkers)*. **3.** Me encanta _____ el piano y _____ al tenis. **4.** Cuando fuimos a Madrid asistimos a una _____ de teatro y a un _____ de futbol. **5.** La canasta es un _____ de cartas. **6.** Yo _____ varios instrumentos musicales.

Ejercicio 8.41 *Traduzca.*

1. They played tennis all afternoon. **2.** What are you playing? **3.** Do you play the guitar? **4.** Don't play with your sister's violin. **5.** She will be playing the violin tonight.

REVIEW: KNOW, LEARN, MEET, ORDER, *PENSAR*, PEOPLE VS. MACHINES, PLAY

[Chapter 8.B.14–20, pages 290–295]

Ejercicio 8.42 Temas de ensayo.

Prestando atención al uso correcto en español del léxico indicado, escriba un párrafo sobre uno de los temas que siguen. Refiérase a las páginas apropiadas del capítulo 8 para usar al máximo las expresiones que se deben practicar.

a. Describa una experiencia que haya tenido con problemas de automóvil.

ATAJO

Phrases: Describing the past
Vocabulary: Automobile

b. Describa un día en que alguien nuevo entró en su vida.

c. Describa una aventura de un deportista o músico famoso con problemas mecánicos, eléctricos o electrónicos.

21. Put

[Chapter 8.B.21, page 296]

Ejercicio 8.43 *Llene el espacio en blanco con la expresión correcta:* **aguantar, ahorrar, apoyar, mantener, poner, ponerse, soportar.**

Don José se levantó esa mañana y **(1)** _____ la ropa del día anterior porque no tenía nada limpio. Ya no **(2)** _____ más: su esposa no tenía tiempo de lavarle la ropa ahora que ella también trabajaba, y él no podía exigirle lo mismo que antes. El mundo moderno no era para él: no podía **(3)** _____ el hecho de que los hombres y las mujeres fueran iguales. Él quería ser el único en **(4)** _____ a su familia, y por eso no **(5)** _____ a su esposa cuando ésta le pidió permiso para conseguir empleo. A pesar de todo, ella había encontrado un trabajo, y ganaba lo suficiente para **(6)** _____ algo de dinero cada mes.

Ejercicio 8.44 *Traduzca.*

1. She put her hand on my shoulder. **2.** I put on my boots. **3.** He put his hand in his jacket. **4.** Help me set the table, please. **5.** His face became green. **6.** Do not put your finger in your brother's eye. **7.** I can't stand your attitude. **8.** My mother supports the family with two jobs. **9.** My brother supports me no matter what I want to do. **10.** Why do you put up with such stupidity?

22. Realize

[Chapter 8.B.22, page 297]

Ejercicio 8.45 *Llene el espacio en blanco con la expresión correcta:* **darse cuenta de, realizar.**

1. Este es un ideal que nunca podré _____. **2.** A veces es difícil _____ los sentimientos de los demás. **3.** Si puedo _____ este proyecto de manera eficiente, estoy seguro que me darán el trabajo.

Ejercicio 8.46 *Traduzca.*

1. I realize that I cannot realize your dreams in an instant. **2.** If you carry out all your duties with responsibility, you can stay. **3.** She realized that he was unhappy. **4.** He realized his dreams were impossible.

23. SERVE

[Chapter 8.B.23, page 297]

Ejercicio 8.47 *Llene el espacio en blanco con **lo(s), la(s), le(s)** o **Ø** (nada).*

(Dos meseras hablan en un restaurante.)

—Llegaron unos clientes nuevos a la mesa número 4. Te toca servir **(1)** _____.
—No, yo **(2)** _____ serví a los de la mesa 3 y 2.
—Sí, pero tienes tres mesas.
—Bueno, pues, si insistes.

(En la mesa)

—Buenas tardes, señores, ¿en qué puedo **(3)** servir_____?
—¿Podemos cenar a esta hora?
—Claro. La cena **(4)** _____ servimos a partir de las seis.
—¿Nos trae una botella de Marqués de Riscal, por favor?
—Bueno.

(Trae el vino.)

—Si le parece bien, abro ahora el vino y **(5)** _____ sirvo luego.
—No, no, **(6)** sírva_____ de inmediato.

Ejercicio 8.48 *Traduzca.*

1. Do not serve me so much rice, please. **2.** How can I help you? **3.** Dinner is usually served at eight. Tonight we will serve it at seven thirty.

24. SPEND

[Chapter 8.B.24, page 298]

Ejercicio 8.49 *Llene el espacio en blanco con la expresión correcta: **desperdiciar, gastar, pasar.***

1. Me encanta _____ *(spend)* tiempo con mi abuela en el campo. **2.** No quiero _____ *(spend)* mucho dinero esta vez. **3.** ¿Quieres _____ *(spend)* un rato conmigo?

4. Me molesta _____ *(waste)* el agua.   **5.** Sólo _____ *(I only spent)* unos minutos en la cocina.   **6.** No hay que _____ *(waste)* dinero: sólo se debe _____ *(spend)* para lo que se necesita.

Ejercicio 8.50   *Traduzca.*

1. You spend more money on your children than you do on yourself.   **2.** I spent three hours on this paper yesterday.   **3.** She spent some time in jail.   **4.** It is terrible to waste time and money.

25. TAKE

[Chapter 8.B.25, pages 298–299]

Ejercicio 8.51   *Llene el espacio en blanco con la expresión más natural para el contexto. Use cada uno sólo una vez: apuntar, bajar, llevar, llevarse, quitarse, sacar, subir, tener, tomar, traer.*

1. Tenemos que _____ la basura hoy.   **2.** Voy a _____ tu número de teléfono en este papelito.   **3.** No quiero _____ esta caja al sótano porque tengo miedo que se moje.
4. ¿Me puede _____ un vaso de agua, por favor?   **5.** Los hombres deben _____ el sombrero al entrar a la iglesia.   **6.** ¿Podrían _____ a mi hermanita cuando se vayan?
7. Durante el desayuno, el niño le dijo a su mamá: —La maestra nos dijo que teníamos que _____ el libro a clase todos los días.   **8.** En clase, la maestra le dijo a un niño al que se le había olvidado el libro: —¿No les dije que debían _____ su libro a clase todos los días?   **9.** El mensajero tenía que _____ el paquete hasta el quinto piso.   **10.** No sabemos cuándo va a _____ lugar ese evento.

Ejercicio 8.52   *Traduzca.*

1. What would you like to drink?   **2.** He took his beer to the table.   **3.** She took the pencil and left.   **4.** "Can we take you?" "No, thanks, I will take the bus."   **5.** This is taking too long.   **6.** Here. This is yours.   **7.** We took the camera to the store.
8. They took away our towels.   **9.** Let me take this down. (write)   **10.** Do you want me to take your books down?   **11.** They took the food up to the room.   **12.** We have to take the garbage out.   **13.** Do not take off your socks.   **14.** The exam will take place here.   **15.** Can I bring a friend to your party?   **16.** BYOB.

26. TIME

[Chapter 8.B.26, page 300]

Ejercicio 8.53   *Llene el espacio en blanco con la expresión correcta: tiempo, vez, hora, rato.*

1. ¿Qué _____ hace allá en invierno?   **2.** ¿Cuánto _____ nos queda?   **3.** Esta _____ no les voy a contar el final de la película.   **4.** Es _____ de cerrar la tienda.   **5.** Nos iremos dentro de un _____.   **6.** Es la primera _____ que oigo esa canción.

Ejercicio 8.54   *Traduzca.*

1. Do you have time to talk to me?   **2.** What was the weather like?   **3.** How many times do I have to tell you?   **4.** That time it was different.   **5.** He would not tell me what time it was.   **6.** I knew it was time to get up.   **7.** She will be here in a little while.   **8.** We had a good time.   **9.** We had good weather.

27. WHAT

[Chapter 8.B.27, pages 300–301]

Ejercicio 8.55   *Llene el espacio en blanco con la expresión correcta:* **qué, lo que, cuál, cómo.**

1. No le importaba _____ yo pensaba de la situación.   **2.** —¿_____ es? —Es el de piedra.   **3.** —¿_____ es? —Es un animal.   **4.** El niño, que no había oído lo que su papá le había dicho, preguntó: —¿_____? Su padre rápidamente lo corrigió: —La gente bien educada no dice ¿_____? sino ¿ _____?

Ejercicio 8.56   *Traduzca.* (you = **tú**)

1. What is *cucurucho*?   **2.** Which one is yours?   **3.** What countries did you visit?   **4.** Excuse me? (*polite* "What?")   **5.** What you do not know will not hurt you.

REVIEW: PUT, REALIZE, SERVE, SPEND, TAKE, TIME, WHAT

[Chapter 8.B.21–8.27, pages 296–301]

Ejercicio 8.57   Temas de ensayo.

Prestando atención al uso correcto en español del léxico indicado, escriba un párrafo sobre uno de los temas que siguen. Refiérase a las páginas apropiadas del capítulo 8 para usar al máximo las expresiones que se deben practicar.

1. Describa las aventuras de verano de un joven que trabaja de mesero en un restaurante.
2. Describa un día en su vida, usando las expresiones indicadas.
3. Describa una lección cultural que usted haya aprendido en su vida.

Verb Tables

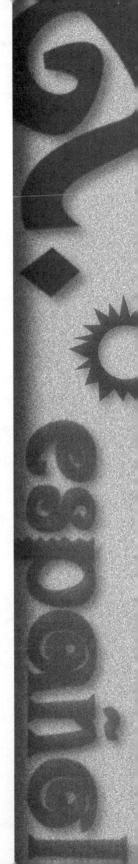

Lista de verbos conjugados

1. actuar	15. concluir	29. estar	43. pedir	57. sentir
2. adquirir	16. conducir	30. forzar	44. perder	58. ser
3. andar	17. contar	31. haber	45. poder	59. soler
4. aprender	18. creer	32. hacer	46. podrir	60. tener
5. avergonzar	19. cruzar	33. ir	47. poner	61. teñir
6. averiguar	20. dar	34. jugar	48. prohibir	62. traer
7. buscar	21. decir	35. llegar	49. querer	63. valer
8. caber	22. dirigir	36. lucir	50. regir	64. vencer
9. caer	23. discernir	37. morir	51. reír	65. venir
10. caminar	24. distinguir	38. mover	52. reunir	66. ver
11. cerrar	25. dormir	39. negar	53. rogar	67. vivir
12. cocer	26. enviar	40. oír	54. saber	68. volcar
13. coger	27. errar	41. oler	55. salir	69. volver
14. comenzar	28. esparcir	42. parecer	56. seguir	

Mini-índice de verbos

(El número de la derecha de cada verbo es el que corresponde al verbo modelo de conjugación. Vea la "Lista de verbos conjugados" para la referencia. NOTE: Los verbos con -se al final son reflexivos. Es necesario usarlos con los pronombres reflexivos: "yo me abstengo", por ejemplo.)

abandonar 10	abortar 10	acallar 10	achocar 7	acorralar 10
abanicar 7	abotonar 10	acalorar 10	acinturar 10	acorrer 4
abaratar 10	abrasar 10	acampar 10	aclamar 10	acortar 10
abarcar 7	abrazar 19	acaparar 10	aclarar 10	acosar 10
abarrotar 10	abreviar 10	acaramelar 10	aclimatar 10	acostar 17
abastecer 42	abrigar 35	acariciar 10	acobardar 10	acostumbrar 10
abatir 67	abrillantar 10	acarrear 10	acobijar 10	acrecentar 11
abdicar 7	abrir 67	acceder 4	acodar 10	acreditar 10
aberrar 27	abrochar 10	accidentar 10	acoger 13	acribillar 10
abjurar 10	abrogar 35	acechar 10	acojinar 10	activar 10
ablandar 10	abrumar 10	aceitar 10	acolchonar 10	actualizar 19
ablandecer 42	absolver 69	acelerar 10	acomedirse 43	actuar 1
abnegar 39	absorber 4	acentuar 1	acometer 4	acuchillar 10
abobar 10	abstenerse 60	acepillar 10	acomodar 10	acuclillarse 10
abocar 7	abstraer 62	aceptar 10	acompañar 10	acudir 67
abochornar 10	abultar 10	acequiar 10	acompasar 10	acurrucarse 7
abofetear 10	abundar 10	acercar 7	acomplejar 10	acusar 10
abogar 35	aburguesarse 10	acertar 11	aconchabarse 10	adaptar 10
abombar 10	aburrir 67	achacar 10	acondicionar 10	adelantar 10
abominar 10	abusar 10	achaparrarse 10	acongojar 10	adelgazar 19
abonar 10	acabar 10	achatar 10	aconsejar 10	adentrar 10
abordar 10	acaecer 42	achicar 7	acontecer 42	aderezar 19
aborrecer 42	acalambrarse 10	achicharrar 10	acordar 17	adeudar 10

adherir 57	agonizar 19	allegar 35	anestesiar 10	aplaudir 67
adicionar 10	agraciar 10	almacenar 10	anexar 10	aplazar 19
adiestrar 10	agradar 10	almidonar 10	anexionar 10	aplicar 7
adivinar 10	agradecer 42	almorzar 30	angostar 10	apocar 7
adjetivar 10	agrandar 10	alojar 10	angustiar 10	apocopar 10
adjudicar 7	agravar 10	aloquecerse 42	anhelar 10	apodar 10
adjuntar 10	agregar 35	alquilar 10	anidar 10	apoderar 10
administrar 10	agriar 10	alterar 10	anihilar 10	apolillar 10
admirar 10	agrietar 10	altercar 7	animalizar 19	aporrear 10
admitir 67	agringarse 35	alternar 10	animar 10	aportar 10
adobar 10	agrumar 10	alucinar 10	aniñarse 10	apostar 17
adoctrinar 10	agrupar 10	aludir 67	aniquilar 10	apostrofar 10
adoptar 10	aguantar 10	alumbrar 10	anivelar 10	apoyar 10
adorar 10	aguar 6	alzar 19	anochecer 42	apreciar 10
adormecer 42	aguardar 10	amadrinar 10	anonadar 10	aprehender 4
adornar 10	agudizar 19	amaestrar 10	anotar 10	apremiar 10
adosar 10	aguijonear 10	amalgamar 10	anquilosar 10	aprender 4
adquirir 2	agujerear 10	amamantar 10	ansiar 26	aprestar 10
adscribir 67	aguzar 19	amanecer 42	anteceder 4	apresurar 10
adular 10	aherrumbrar 10	amanerarse 10	antedatar 10	apretar 11
adulterar 10	ahogar 35	amansar 10	anteponer 47	apretujar 10
adverbializar 19	ahorcar 7	amar 10	anticipar 10	aprisionar 10
advertir 57	ahorrar 10	amargar 35	antojarse 10	aprobar 17
afanar 10	ahuecar 7	amarillar 10	antorchar 10	aprontar 10
afectar 10	ahuyentar 10	amarillecer 42	anular 10	apropiar 10
afeitar 10	airear 10	amarrar 10	anunciar 10	aprovechar 10
afeminar 10	ajetrear 10	amasar 10	añadir 67	aprovisionar 10
aferrar 11	ajorar 17	ambicionar 10	añejar 10	aproximar 10
afianzar 19	ajustar 10	ambientar 10	añorar 10	apuntar 10
aficionar 10	alabar 10	ambular 10	apabilar 10	apuntillar 10
afilar 10	alagar 35	amedrentar 10	apacentar 11	apuñalar 10
afiliar 10	alargar 35	amelcochar 10	apachurrar 10	apurar 10
afinar 10	albergar 35	amenazar 19	apaciguar 6	arar 10
afincar 7	alborotar 10	amenizar 19	apadrinar 10	arbitrar 10
afirmar 10	alcahuetear 10	amenorar 10	apagar 35	arbolecer 42
afligir 22	alcanzar 19	americanizar 19	apalear............... 10	archivar 10
aflojar 10	alegar 35	ametrallar 10	aparcar 7	arder 4
aflorar 10	alegorizar 19	aminorar 10	aparear 10	argentinizar 19
afluir 15	alegrar 10	amodorrarse 10	aparecer............. 42	argüir 15
afrancesar 10	alejar 10	amolar 17	aparentar 10	argumentar 10
afrentar 10	alentar 11	amoldar 10	apartar 10	aridecer 42
africanizar 19	alertar 10	amonestar 10	apasionar 10	aristocratizar 19
afrontar 10	alfabetizar 19	amontonar 10	apear 10	armar 10
agachar 10	alfombrar 10	amortiguar 6	apedrear 10	armonizar 19
agarrar 10	alforzar 19	amortizar 19	apegar 35	aromatizar 19
agasajar 10	aligerar 10	amparar 10	apellidar 10	arquear 10
agazapar 10	alijar 10	ampliar 26	apestar 10	arraigar 35
agermanarse 10	alimentar 10	amplificar 7	apetecer 42	arrancar 7
agilizar 19	alinear 10	ampollar 10	apiadar 10	arrasar 10
agitanar 10	alisar 10	amputar 10	apilar 10	arrastrar 10
agitar 10	alistar 10	analizar 19	apiñar 10	arrear 10
aglomerar 10	alivianar 10	anclar 10	aplacar 7	arrebatar 10
agobiar 10	aliviar 10	andar 3	aplanar 10	arreglar 10
agolpar 10	allanar 10	anegar 35	aplastar.............. 10	arrellanarse 10

arremangar	35	atarear	10	azuzar	19	cabrear	10	cazar	19
arremedar	10	atascar	7			cacarear	10	cazcalear	10
arremeter	4	atemorizar	19	babear	10	cachetear	10	cebar	10
arremolinar	10	atender	44	babosear	10	caducar	7	cecear	10
arrempujar	10	atenerse	60	bailar	10	caer	9	ceder	4
arrendar	11	atentar	10	bajar	10	cagar	35	cegar	39
arrepentirse	57	atenuar	1	balancear	10	calar	10	cejar	10
arrestar	10	aterrar	11	balbucear	10	calcar	7	celar	10
arriar	26	aterrizar	19	barnizar	19	calcificar	7	celebrar	10
arribar	10	aterrorizar	19	barrenar	10	calcinar	10	cementar	10
arriesgar	35	atesorar	10	barrer	4	calcografiar	26	cenar	10
arrimar	10	atestar	10	basar	10	calcular	10	censurar	10
arrinconar	10	atestiguar	6	bastar	10	calentar	11	centralizar	19
arrojar	10	atinar	10	batallar	10	calibrar	10	centrar	10
arropar	10	atolondrar	10	batir	67	calificar	7	ceñir	61
arrugar	35	atomizar	19	bautizar	19	caligrafiar	26	cepillar	10
arruinar	10	atontar	10	beatificar	7	callar	10	cercar	7
arrullar	10	atorar	10	beber	4	calmar	10	cerciorar	10
articular	10	atormentar	10	beneficiar	10	calumniar	10	cernir	23
asaltar	10	atornillar	10	berrear	10	calzar	19	cerrar	11
asar	10	atraer	62	besar	10	cambiar	10	certificar	7
asaselar	10	atragantarse	10	bienquerer	49	caminar	10	cesar	10
ascender	44	atrancar	7	bifurcarse	7	camuflar	10	chantajear	10
asear	10	atrapar	10	blanquear	10	canalizar	19	chapotear	10
asechar	10	atrasar	10	blanquecer	42	cancelar	10	charlar	10
asediar	10	atravesar	11	blindar	10	canjear	10	chequear	10
asegurar	10	atribuir	15	bloquear	10	canonizar	19	chicanear	10
asemejar	10	atrofiar	10	bofetear	10	cansar	10	chiflar	10
asentar	11	atronar	17	boicotear	10	cantar	10	chillar	10
asentir	57	atropellar	10	bombardear	10	capacitar	10	chinear	10
aserrar	11	aturdir	67	bordear	10	capar	10	chingar	35
asesinar	10	augurar	10	borrar	10	capitalizar	19	chirriar	26
asesorar	10	aumentar	10	borronear	10	capitular	10	chismear	10
asestar	10	auscultar	10	bosquejar	10	captar	10	chismorrear	10
asfaltar	10	ausentar	10	bostezar	19	capturar	10	chismotear	10
asfixiar	10	auspiciar	10	botar	10	caracolear	10	chispear	10
asignar	10	autenticar	7	boxear	10	caracterizar	19	chistar	10
asimilar	10	autentificar	7	bramar	10	caramelizar	19	chocar	7
asistir	67	autografiar	26	bregar	35	carbonizar	19	chocarrear	10
asociar	10	automatizar	19	brillar	10	carcomer	4	chorrear	10
asolear	10	autorizar	19	brincar	7	cardar	10	chotear	10
asomar	10	avanzar	19	brindar	10	carecer	42	chupar	10
asombrar	10	aventajar	10	bromear	10	cargar	35	chutear	10
aspirar	10	aventar	11	broncear	10	caricaturizar	19	cicatrizar	19
asquear	10	aventurar	10	brotar	10	casar	10	cimentar	11
astillar	10	avergonzar	5	brutalizar	19	castigar	35	circular	10
asumir	67	averiguar	6	bucear	10	castrar	10	circundar	10
asustar	10	avisar	10	burocratizar	19	catalogar	35	circunferir	57
atacar	7	avivar	10	buscar	7	catapultar	10	circunscribir	67
atajar	10	ayudar	10			catar	10	circunvenir	65
atapuzar	19	ayunar	10	cabalgar	35	causar	10	circunvolar	17
atar	10	azorar	10	cabecear	10	cauterizar	19	citar	10
atarantar	10	azotar	10	caber	8	cautivar	10	civilizar	19
atardecer	42	azucarar	10	cablegrafiar	26	cavar	10	clamar	10

clamorear 10	compartir 67	configurar 10	contorsionarse ... 10	cubrir 67
clarear 10	compasar 10	confinar 10	contraer 62	cucar 7
clarecer 42	compeler 4	confirmar 10	contraponer 47	cucharear 10
clarificar 7	compendiar 10	confiscar 7	contraproponer .. 47	cuchichear 10
clasificar 7	compendizar 19	conformar 10	contrariar 26	cuestionar 10
claudicar 7	compenetrarse ... 10	confortar 10	contrarrestar 10	cuidar 10
clausurar 10	compensar 10	confrontar 10	contrastar 10	culminar 10
clavar 10	competir 43	confundir 67	contratar 10	culpar 10
clavetear 10	compilar 10	congelar 10	contribuir 15	cultivar 10
climatizar 19	complementar ... 10	congestionar 10	controlar 10	cumplir 67
coadquirir 2	completar 10	conglomerar 10	controvertir 57	curar 10
coagular 10	complicar 7	congregar 35	convalecer 42	curiosear 10
coarrendar 11	complotar 10	conjeturar 10	convencer 64	cursar 10
cobijar 10	componer 47	conjugar 35	convenir 65	curtir 67
cobrar 10	comportarse 10	conllevar 10	conversar 10	curvear 10
cocer 12	comprar 10	conmemorar 10	convertir 57	
cocinar 10	comprender 4	conmocionar 10	convidar 10	dactilografiar 26
codear 10	comprimir 67	conmover 38	convivir 67	danzar 19
codiciar 10	comprobar 17	conmutar 10	convocar 7	dañar 10
codificar 7	comprometer 4	connotar 10	cooperar 10	dar 20
coercer 64	computadorizar...19	conocer 42	coordinar 10	deambular 10
coexistir 67	computar 10	conquistar 10	copiar 10	debatir 67
coger 13	computarizar 19	consagrar 10	coquetear 10	deber 4
cohabitar 10	comulgar 35	conseguir 56	corregir 50	debilitar 10
cohibir 48	comunicar 7	consentir 57	correr 4	decaer 9
coincidir 67	concatenar 10	conservar 10	corresponder 4	decampar 10
cojear 10	concebir 43	considerar 10	corretear 10	decantar 10
colaborar 10	conceder 4	consignar 10	corroborar 10	decapitar 10
colar 10	concentrar 10	consistir 67	cortar 10	decepcionar 10
coleccionar 10	conceptuar 1	consolar 17	cortejar 10	decidir 67
colegir 50	concernir 23	consolidar 10	coscorronear 10	decir 21
colgar 53	concertar 11	consonantizar 19	cosechar 10	declamar 10
colindar 10	concienciar 10	conspirar 10	coser 4	declarar 10
colmar 10	concientizar 19	constar 10	costar 17	declinar 10
colocar 7	conciliar 10	constatar 10	costear 10	decolorar 10
colonizar 19	concluir 15	consternar 10	cotizar 19	decorar 10
colorear 10	concomitar 10	constipar 10	cotorrear 10	decrecer 42
columpiar 10	concordar 17	constitucionalizar19	crear 10	decretar 10
comadrear 10	concretar 10	constituir 15	crecer 42	decuplar 10
combatir 67	concurrir 67	construir 15	creer 18	dedicar 7
combinar 10	concursar 10	consultar 10	crepitar 10	deducir 16
comedirse 43	condecorar 10	consumar 10	criar 26	defender 44
comentar 10	condenar 10	consumir 67	criminalizar 19	deferir 57
comenzar........... 14	condensar 10	contactar 10	cristalizar 19	definir 67
comer 4	condescender 44	contagiar 10	criticar 7	deforestar 10
comercializar 19	condicionar 10	contaminar 10	croar 10	deformar 10
cometer 4	condimentar 10	contar 17	cronometrar 10	defraudar 10
comisionar 10	condolecerse 42	contemplar 10	crucificar 7	degenerar 10
compactar 10	condonar 10	contender 44	crujir 67	deglutir 67
compadecer 42	conducir 16	contener 60	cruzar 19	degollar 17
compadrear 10	conectar 10	contentar 10	cuadrar 10	degradar 10
compaginar 10	conferir 57	contestar........... 10	cuajar 10	degustar............ 10
comparar 10	confesar............ 11	continuar 1	cualificar 7	deificar 7
comparecer 42	confiar 26	contonearse 10	cuantificar 7	dejar 10

delatar 10	desafinar 10	desconfiar 26	desenmarañar 10	desmentir 57
delegar 35	desagradar 10	descongelar 10	desenmascarar ... 10	desmenuzar 19
deleitar 10	desagradecer 42	descongestionar 10	desenmohecer ... 42	desmitificar 7
deletrear 10	desaguar 6	desconocer 42	desenredar 10	desmontar 10
deliberar 10	desahogar 35	descontaminar ... 10	desenrollar 10	desmoralizar 19
delimitar 10	desajustar 10	descontar 17	desenroscar 7	desmoronar 10
delinear 10	desalentar 11	descontinuar 1	desensamblar 10	desnivelar 10
delirar 10	desalojar 10	descoser 4	desensartar 10	desnudar 10
deludir 67	desamarrar 10	descotar 10	desensillar 10	desobedecer 42
demandar 10	desamontonar 10	descoyuntar 10	desenterrar 11	desocupar 10
demarcar 7	desamparar 10	descrecer 42	desentonar 10	desodorizar 19
democratizar 19	desanimar 10	descreer 18	desentrenar 10	desorbitar 10
demorar 10	desaparecer 42	describir 67	desentumecer 42	desordenar 10
demostrar 17	desapegar 35	descruzar 19	desentumir 67	desorganizar 19
denegar 39	desapreciar 10	descuartizar 19	desenvainar 10	desorientar 10
denigrar 10	desapretar 11	descubrir 67	desenvolver 69	despabilar 10
denominar 10	desaprobar 17	descuidar 10	desequilibrar 10	despachar 10
denotar 10	desapropiar 10	desdentar 11	desertar 10	desparramar 10
densificar 7	desarmar 10	desdeñar 10	desesperar 10	despedazar 19
dentar 11	desarmonizar 19	desdibujar 10	desestabilizar 19	despedir 43
denunciar 10	desarreglar 10	desdoblar 10	desestancar 7	despegar 35
deparar 10	desarrollar 10	desdorar 10	desfallecer 42	despeinar 10
departir 67	desarropar 10	desear 10	desfavorecer 42	despejar 10
depender 4	desarrugar 35	desecar 7	desfigurar 10	despellejar 10
depilar 10	desatar 10	desechar 10	desfilar 10	desperdiciar 10
deplorar 10	desatinar 10	desembalar 10	desfondar 10	despertar 11
deponer 47	desatornillar 10	desembarazar 19	desgajar 10	despilfarrar 10
deportar 10	desayunar 10	desembarcar 7	desgarrar 10	despintar 10
depositar 10	desbarajustar 10	desembarrar 10	desgastar 10	despiojar 10
depravar 10	desbaratar 10	desembocar 7	desgraciar 10	despistar 10
deprecar 7	desbordar 10	desemejar 10	desgreñar 10	desplegar 39
depreciar 10	desboronar 10	desempacar 7	deshacer 32	desplomar 10
deprimir 67	desbridar 10	desempañar 10	deshebrar 10	despoblar 17
depurar 10	descalcar 7	desempaquetar .. 10	deshelar 11	despojar 10
derivar 10	descalificar 7	desemparejar 10	desheredar 10	despreciar 10
derogar 35	descansar 10	desempatar 10	deshidratar 10	desprender 4
derramar 10	descargar 35	desempeñar 10	deshilachar 10	despreocuparse... 10
derrengar 39	descarrillar 10	desemperezar 19	deshinchar 10	desprestigiar 10
derretir 43	descartar 10	desempolvar 10	deshojar 10	desquiciar 10
derribar 10	descender 44	desencadenar 10	deshonrar 10	desquitar 10
derrocar 7	descentralizar 19	desencajar 10	deshuesar 10	destacar 7
derrochar 10	descentrar 10	desencarcelar 10	deshumanizar 19	destapar 10
derrotar 10	descifrar 10	desencerrar 11	designar 10	desteñir 61
derrumbar 10	desclasificar 7	desenchufar 10	desigualar 10	desterrar 11
desabotonar 10	descoagular 10	desenfadar 10	desilusionar 10	destetar 10
desabrigar 35	descobijar 10	desenfilar 10	desinfectar 10	destilar 10
desabrochar 10	descocar 7	desenfocar 7	desinflar 10	destinar 10
desacomodar 10	descocer 12	desenfrenar 10	desintegrar 10	destituir 15
desacordar 17	descolgar 53	desenfundar 10	desintoxicar 7	destorcer 12
desacreditar 10	descompaginar .. 10	desenfurecer 42	desistir 67	destornillar 10
desactivar 10	descomponer 47	desenganchar 10	desmaquillar 10	destrabar 10
desaferrar 11	desconcertar 11	desengañar 10	desmarañar 10	destrenzar 19
desafiar 26	desconchinflar... 10	desenlazar 19	desmayar 10	destripar 10
desafilar 10	desconectar 10	desenlodar 10	desmejorar 10	destrizar 19

destrozar 19	disciplinar 10	dosificar 7	embromar 10	enchilar 10
destruir 15	discordar 17	dotar 10	embrujar 10	enchinar 10
desunir 67	discriminar 10	dramatizar ...., 19	embrutecer 42	enchuecar 7
desvalijar 10	disculpar 10	duchar 10	emburujar 10	enchufar 10
desvalorar 10	discurrir 67	dudar 10	embustir 67	encoger 13
desvalorizar 19	discursar 10	dulcificar 7	emerger 13	encomendar 11
desvaluar 1	discutir 67	duplicar 7	emigrar 10	encontrar 17
desvanecer 42	disecar 7	durar 10	emitir 67	encorvar 10
desvariar 26	diseminar 10		emocionar 10	encuadernar 10
desvelar 10	disentir 57	echar 10	empacar 7	encuerar 10
desvencijar 10	diseñar 10	eclipsar 10	empachar 10	enderezar 19
desvergonzarse 5	disertar 10	economizar 19	empadronar 10	endeudarse 10
desvestir 43	disfrazar 19	edificar 7	empalagar 35	endiablar 10
desviar 26	disfrutar 10	editar 10	empalidecer 42	endomingarse 35
desvivirse 67	disgustar 10	educar 7	empañar 10	endosar 10
desyerbar 10	disimular 10	efectuar 1	empapar 10	endulzar 19
detallar 10	disipar 10	egresar 10	empapelar 10	endurecer 42
detectar 10	dislocar 7	ejecutar 10	empaquetar 10	enfadar 10
detener 60	disminuir 15	ejemplarizar 19	emparedar 10	enfangar 35
deteriorar 10	disolver 69	ejemplificar 7	emparejar 10	enfatizar 19
determinar 10	disparar 10	ejercer 64	empedrar 11	enfermar 10
detestar 10	dispensar 10	ejercitar 10	empelotarse 10	enfilar 10
detractar 10	dispersar 10	elaborar 10	empeñar 10	enflacar 7
detraer 62	disponer 47	electrificar 7	empeorar 10	enfocar 7
devaluar 1	disputar 10	electrocutar 10	empequeñecer ... 42	enfrentar 10
devastar 10	distanciar 10	electrolizar 19	empezar 14	enfriar 26
devengar 35	distar 10	elegir 50	empilar 10	enfurecer 42
devolver 69	distinguir 24	elevar 10	empinar 10	enganchar 10
devorar 10	distorsionar 10	elidir 67	emplear 10	engañar 10
devotar 10	distraer 62	eliminar 10	empobrecer 42	engendrar 10
diagnosticar 7	distribuir 15	elogiar 10	empolvar 10	engordar 10
dialogar 35	disuadir 67	elucidar 10	emprender 4	engrasar 10
dibujar 10	divagar 35	eludir 67	empujar 10	enharinar 10
dictar 10	divergir 22	emanar 10	emular 10	enjabonar 10
difamar 10	diversificar 7	emancipar 10	emulsionar 10	enjaular 10
diferenciar 10	divertir 57	emascular 10	enamorar 10	enjuagar 35
diferir 57	dividir 67	embabucar 7	encabezar 19	enlatar 10
dificultar 10	divisar 10	embadurnar 10	encadenar 10	enlazar 19
difundir 67	divorciar 10	embalar 10	encajar 10	enlodar 10
digerir 57	divulgar 35	embanderar 10	encaminar 10	enloquecer 42
dignarse 10	doblar 10	embarazar 19	encandilar 10	enlutar 10
dignificar 7	doblegar 35	embarcar 7	encantar 10	enmarcar 7
dilapidar 10	doctrinar 10	embargar 35	encapricharse 10	enmascarar 10
dilatar 10	documentar 10	embarrar 10	encaramar 10	enmendar 11
dilucidar 10	dogmatizar 19	embellecer 42	encarar 10	enmudecer 42
diluir 15	doler 38	embestir 43	encarcelar 10	enmugrar 10
diminuir 15	domar 10	embobar 10	encargar 35	ennegrecer 42
dimitir 67	domesticar 7	embocar 7	encariñar 10	enojar 10
dinamitar 10	dominar 10	embolsar 10	encarnar 10	enorgullecer 42
diplomar 10	donar 10	emborrachar 10	encebollar 10	enredar 10
diptongar 35	dopar 10	emboscar 7	encender 44	enriquecer 42
diputar 10	dorar 10	embotellar 10	encerar 10	enrojecer 42
dirigir 22	dormir 25	embriagar 35	encerrar 11	enrollar 10
discernir 23	dormitar 10	embrollar 10	encestar 10	enroscar 7

ensamblar 10	erradicar 7	estipular 10	expiar 26	fomentar 10
ensanchar 10	errar 27	estirar 10	explicar 7	forjar 10
ensangrentar 11	eructar 10	estorbar 10	explorar 10	formalizar 19
ensayar 10	escalar 10	estornudar 10	explotar 10	formar 10
enseñar 10	escalofriar 26	estrangular 10	exponer 47	formular 10
ensillar 10	escandalizar 19	estratificar 7	expresar 10	forrar 10
ensimismarse 10	escapar 10	estrellar 10	exprimir 67	forzar 30
ensordecer 42	escarbar 10	estremecer 42	expulsar 10	fosilizarse 19
ensuciar 10	escasear 10	estrenar 10	expurgar 35	fotocopiar 10
entablar 10	escavar 10	estreñir 61	extasiarse 26	fotografiar 26
entender 44	escenificar 7	estribar 10	extender 44	fracasar 10
enterar 10	esclavizar 19	estropear 10	extenuar 1	fracturar 10
enternecer 42	escoger 13	estructurar 10	exteriorizar 19	fragmentar 10
enterrar 11	esconder 4	estrujar 10	exterminar 10	fraternizar 19
entibiar 10	escribir 67	estudiar 10	extinguir 24	frecuentar 10
entiesar 10	escuchar 10	eternizar 19	extirpar 10	fregar 39
entiznar 10	escudriñar 10	etiquetar 10	extraer 62	freír 51
entonar 10	esculcar 7	evacuar 10	extrañar 10	frenar 10
entornar 10	esculpir 67	evadir 67	extrapolar 10	frotar 10
entorpecer 42	escupir 67	evaluar 1	extraviar 26	fruncir 28
entrar 10	escurrir 67	evaporar 10		frustrar 10
entreabrir 67	esforzar 30	evitar 10	fabricar 7	fugarse 35
entrecerrar 11	esfumar 10	evocar 7	facilitar 10	fumar 10
entregar 35	esmaltar 10	evolucionar 10	facturar 10	fumigar 35
entrenar 10	esmerar 10	exacerbar 10	fallar 10	funcionar 10
entretejer 4	espandir 67	exagerar 10	fallecer 42	fundar 10
entretener 60	espantar 10	exaltar 10	falsificar 7	fundir 67
entrever 66	esparcir 28	examinar 10	faltar 10	fusilar 10
entrevistar 10	esparramar 10	exasperar 10	familiarizar 19	fusionar 10
entristecer 42	espatarrarse 10	excarcelar 10	fascinar 10	
entrometer 4	especializar 19	excavar 10	fastidiar 10	galantear 10
entumecer 42	especificar 7	exceder 4	favorecer 42	galardonar 10
entumirse 67	especular 10	excepcionar 10	fechar 10	galopear 10
entusiasmar 10	esperar 10	exceptuar 1	felicitar 10	ganar 10
enumerar 10	espesar 10	excitar 10	fermentar 10	garabatear 10
enunciar 10	espiar 26	exclamar 10	festejar 10	garantizar 19
envasar 10	espolvorear 10	excluir 15	fiar 26	gargarizar 19
envejecer 42	espulgar 35	excomulgar 35	fichar 10	gastar 10
envenenar 10	esquiar 26	excretar 10	figurar 10	gatear 10
enverdecer 42	esquivar 10	exculpar 10	fijar 10	gemir 43
enviar 26	estabilizar 19	excusar 10	filar 10	generalizar 19
envidiar 10	establecer 42	exentar 10	filmar 10	generar 10
envigorizar 19	estacionar 10	exhalar 10	filtrar 10	germinar 10
enviudar 10	estafar 10	exhibir 67	finalizar 19	gestar 10
envolver 69	estallar 10	exigir 22	financiar 10	gesticular 10
enyesar 10	estancar 7	exiliar 10	fincar 7	gestionar 10
equilibrar 10	estandardizar 19	eximir 67	fingir 22	girar 10
equipar 10	estandarizar 19	existir 67	firmar 10	glorificar 7
equiparar 10	estar 29	exonerar 10	fiscalizar 19	gobernar 11
equivaler 63	estereotipar 10	exorcizar 19	florear 10	golpear 10
equivocar 7	esterilizar 19	expandir 67	florecer 42	gotear 10
erigir 22	estigmatizar 19	expatriarse 26	flotar 10	gozar 19
erizar 19	estimar 10	expectorar 10	fluctuar 1	grabar 10
erosionar 10	estimular 10	experimentar 10	fluir 15	graduar 1

granizar 19	huir 15	individualizar 19	interesar 10	juguetear 10
gratificar 7	humanizar 19	inducir 16	interferir 57	juntar 10
gravitar 10	humectar 10	indultar 10	interiorizar 19	jurar 10
gritar 10	humedecer 42	industrializar 19	intermediar 10	justiciar 10
guardar 10	humillar 10	infectar 10	internacionalizar 19	justificar 7
guarnecer 42	hundir 67	inferir 57	internar 10	juzgar 35
guerrear 10	hurgar 35	infestar 10	interpelar 10	
guerrillear 10	hurgonear 10	infiltrar 10	interpolar 10	kilometrar 10
guiar 26	husmear 10	inflamar 10	interponer 47	
guindar 10		inflar 10	interpretar 10	labrar 10
guiñar 10	idealizar 19	infligir 22	interrogar 35	lacerar 10
guisar 10	identificar 7	influir 15	interrumpir 67	lactar 10
guisotear 10	idiotizar 19	informar 10	intersecarse 7	ladear 10
guitarrear.......... 10	idolatrar 10	infringir 22	intervenir 65	ladrar 10
gustar 10	ignorar 10	infundir 67	intervertir 57	lagrimear 10
	igualar 10	ingerir 57	intimar 10	lamentar 10
haber 31	iluminar 10	ingresar 10	intimidar 10	lamer 4
habilitar 10	ilustrar 10	inhalar 10	intoxicar 7	laminar 10
habitar 10	imaginar 10	inhibir 67	intricar 7	lancear 10
habituar 1	imitar 10	iniciar 10	intrigar 35	languidecer 42
hablar 10	impacientar 10	injuriar 10	intrincar 7	lanzar 19
hacer 32	impedir 43	inmigrar 10	introducir 16	laquear 10
hachear 10	impersonalizar .. 19	inmiscuir 15	intuir 15	largar 35
halagar 35	implantar 10	inmovilizar 19	inundar 10	lastimar 10
halar 10	implicar 7	inmunizar 19	invadir 67	lateralizar 19
hallar 10	implorar 10	inmutar 10	invalidar 10	latinizar 19
harmonizar 19	imponer 47	innovar 10	inventar 10	latir 67
hechizar 19	imposibilitar 10	inocular 10	inventariar 26	laudar 10
heder 44	impresionar 10	inquietar 10	invernar 11	lavar 10
helar 11	imprimir 67	inquirir 2	invertir 57	leer 18
heredar 10	improvisar 10	inscribir 67	investigar 35	legalizar 19
herir 57	impulsar 10	insensibilizar 19	invitar 10	legar 35
herrar.............. 11	imputar 10	insinuar 1	invocar 7	legislar 10
hervir 57	inaugurar 10	insistir 67	involucrar 10	legitimar 10
hilar 10	incapacitar 10	inspeccionar 10	inyectar 10	lesionar 10
hilvanar 10	incendiar 10	inspirar 10	ionizar 19	levantar 10
hincar 7	incitar 10	instalar 10	ir 33	liar 26
hinchar 10	inclinar 10	instar 10	irradiar 10	liberalizar 19
hipnotizar 19	incluir 15	instaurar 10	irrigar 35	liberar 10
hipotecar 7	incomodar 10	instigar 35	irritar 10	libertar 10
hispanizar 19	incorporar 10	instilar 10	irrumpir 67	librar 10
hojear 10	incrementar 10	institucionalizar 19	italianizar 19	licenciar 10
homenajear 10	incriminar 10	instituir 15	iterar 10	licuar 1
homogeneizar ... 19	incrustar 10	instruir 15	izar 19	lidiar 10
homologar 35	inculcar 7	insubordinar 10		ligar 35
honrar 10	incumbir 67	insultar 10	jactarse 10	lijar 10
hormiguear........ 10	incurrir 67	integrar 10	jadear 10	limar 10
hornear 10	indagar 35	intelectualizar ... 19	jalar 10	limitar 10
horrificar 7	indemnizar 19	intensificar 7	jalear 10	limosnear 10
horripilar 10	independizar 19	intentar 10	jaspear 10	limpiar 10
horrorizar 19	indicar 7	intercalar 10	jerarquizar 19	lindar 10
hospedar 10	indignar 10	intercambiar 10	jorobar 10	liquidar 10
hospitalizar 19	indisciplinarse ... 10	interceder 4	jubilar 10	lisiar 10
hostigar 35	indisponer 47	interceptar 10	jugar 34	lisonjear 10

litigar	35	marcar	7	militar	10	naufragar	35	ofrecer	42
lividecer	42	marchar	10	militarizar	19	nausear	10	ofuscar	7
llamar	10	marchitar	10	mimar	10	navegar	35	oír	40
llegar	35	marear	10	mimeografiar	26	necesitar	10	ojear	10
llenar	10	marginar	10	minar	10	negar	39	oler	41
llevar	10	martillear	10	mineralizar	19	negociar	10	olfatear	10
llorar	10	martirizar	19	miniaturizar	19	neutralizar	19	olvidar	10
lloriquear	10	mascar	7	minimizar	19	nevar	11	omitir	67
llover	38	masculinizar	19	mirar	10	neviscar	7	ondear	10
lloviznar	10	mascullar	10	mistificar	7	nidificar	7	ondular	10
loar	10	masticar	7	mitigar	35	nivelar	10	opacar	7
localizar	19	matar	10	mitotear	10	noctambular	10	opalizar	19
lograr	10	materializar	19	mochar	10	nombrar	10	operar	10
lubricar	7	matizar	19	modelar	10	nominar	10	opinar	10
lubrificar	7	matraquear	10	moderar	10	noquear	10	oponer	47
luchar	10	matricular	10	modernizar	19	normalizar	19	oprimir	67
lucir	36	maximizar	19	modificar	7	normar	10	optar	10
lucrar	10	mecanizar	19	mofar	10	notar	10	optimar	10
lucubrar	10	mecanografiar	26	mojar	10	notificar	7	optimizar	19
lustrar	10	mecer	64	moldear	10	nublar	10	orar	10
		mediar	10	moler	38	numerar	10	ordenar	10
macanear	10	medicamentar	10	molestar	10	nutrir	67	ordeñar	10
macerar	10	medir	43	molificar	7			organizar	19
machacar	7	meditar	10	mondar	10	ñangotarse	10	orientalizar	19
machetear	10	mejicanizar	19	monologar	35			orientar	10
machucar	7	mejorar	10	monopolizar	19	obedecer	42	originalizarse	19
macizar	19	melancolizar	19	montar	10	objetar	10	originar	10
madrugar	35	melcochar	10	moralizar	19	objetivar	10	orillar	10
madurar	10	mellar	10	morar	10	obligar	35	orinar	10
madurecer	42	memorar	10	morder	38	obliterar	10	ornamentar	10
magnetizar	19	memorizar	19	mordisquear	10	obrar	10	ornar	10
magnificar	7	mencionar	10	morir	37	obscurecer	42	ornear	10
magullar	10	mendigar	35	mortificar	7	obseder	4	orquestar	10
majar	10	menear	10	mostrar	17	obsequiar	10	ortografiar	26
malcriar	26	menguar	6	motivar	10	observar	10	osar	10
malentender	44	menospreciar	10	motorizar	19	obsesionar	10	oscilar	10
malgastar	10	menstruar	1	mover	38	obstaculizar	19	oscurecer	42
maliciar	10	mensualizar	19	movilizar	19	obstar	10	osificar	7
mallugar	35	mentar	11	mudar	10	obstinarse	10	ostentar	10
malograr	10	mentir	57	mugir	22	obstruir	15	otorgar	35
maltratar	10	mercantilizar	19	multar	10	obtemperar	10	ovalar	10
mamar	10	mercerizar	19	multicopiar	10	obtener	60	oxidar	10
manar	10	merecer	42	multiplicar	7	obturar	10	oxigenar	10
manchar	10	merendar	11	municipalizar	19	obviar	10		
mandar	10	mermar	10	murmurar	10	ocasionar	10	pacer	42
manejar	10	merodear	10	musitar	10	occidentalizar	19	pacificar	7
manifestar	11	mestizar	19	mutilar	10	ocluir	15	pactar	10
maniobrar	10	metaforizar	19			ocultar	10	padecer	42
manipular	10	metalizar	19	nacer	42	ocupar	10	paganizar	19
manosear	10	metamorfosear	10	nacionalizar	19	ocurrir	67	pagar	35
mantener	60	meter	4	nadar	10	odiar	10	paginar	10
manufacturar	10	metodizar	19	narrar	10	ofender	4	palear	10
maquinar	10	mexicanizar	19	nasalizar	19	oficializar	19	palidecer	42
maravillar	10	mezclar	10	naturalizar	19	oficiar	10	palmear	10

palpar 10	penetrar 10	pintar 10	predeterminar 10	profesar 10
palpitar 10	penitenciar 10	piropear 10	predicar 7	profesionalizar .. 19
parafrasear 10	pensar 11	pisar 10	predisponer 47	profetizar 19
paralelar 10	pensionar 10	pisotear 10	predominar 10	profundar 10
paralizar 19	percatar 10	pitar 10	preestablecer 42	profundizar 19
parapetar 10	perchonar 10	pizcar 7	preexistir 67	programar 10
parar 10	percibir 67	plagar 35	prefabricar 7	progresar 10
parcelar 10	percudir 67	plagiar 10	preferir 57	prohibir 48
parchear 10	percutir 67	planchar 10	prefigurar 10	proletarizar 19
parcializar 19	perder 44	planear 10	prefijar 10	proliferar 10
parear 10	perdonar 10	planificar 7	pregonar 10	prologar 35
parecer 42	perdurar 10	plantar 10	preguntar 10	prolongar 35
parir 67	perecer 42	plantear 10	premeditar 10	promediar 10
parodiar 10	peregrinar 10	plantificar 7	premiar 10	prometer 4
parpadear 10	perfeccionar 10	plasmar 10	prender 4	promover 38
parquear 10	perfilar 10	plastificar 7	prensar 10	promulgar 35
parrafear 10	perforar 10	platicar 7	preñar 10	pronosticar 7
parrandear 10	perfumar 10	plebiscitar 10	preocupar 10	pronunciar 10
partear 10	perjudicar 7	plisar 10	preparar 10	propagar 35
participar 10	permanecer 42	pluralizar 19	preponer 47	propasar 10
particularizar 19	permitir 67	poblar 17	presagiar 10	propiciar 10
partir 67	permutar 10	podar 10	prescindir 67	proponer 47
pasar 10	pernoctar 10	poder 45	prescribir 67	proporcionar 10
pasear 10	perorar 10	podrir 46	presenciar 10	propulsar 10
pasmar 10	perpetrar 10	poetizar 19	presentar 10	prorrogar 35
pastar 10	perpetuar 1	polarizar 19	presentir 57	prorrumpir 67
pasteurizar 19	perquirir 2	polemizar 19	preservar 10	proscribir 67
pastorear 10	perseguir 56	politizar 19	presidiar 10	proseguir 56
patalear 10	perseverar 10	ponderar 10	presidir 67	prosificar 7
patear 10	persignar 10	poner 47	presionar 10	prospectar 10
patentar 10	persistir 67	pontificar 7	prestar 10	prosperar 10
patentizar 19	personalizar 19	popularizar 19	presumir 67	prosternarse 10
patinar 10	personificar 7	pordiosear 10	presuponer 47	prostituir 15
patrocinar 10	perspirar 10	porfiar 26	presupuestar 10	protagonizar 19
patrullar 10	persuadir 67	portar 10	pretender 4	proteger 13
pausar 10	pervertir 57	posar 10	pretextar 10	protestar 10
pautar 10	pesar 10	poseer 18	prevalecer 42	proveer 18
pavonear 10	pescar 7	posesionar 10	prevaler 63	provenir 65
payasear 10	pespuntar 10	posfechar 10	prevaricar 7	provocar 7
pealar 10	pespuntear 10	posibilitar 10	prevenir 65	proyectar 10
pecar 7	pestañear 10	posponer 47	prever 66	publicar 7
pedalear 10	petardear 10	postergar 35	privar 10	pujar 10
pedir 43	petrificar 7	postrar 10	privilegiar 10	pulsar 10
pedorrear 10	piafar 10	postular 10	probar 17	pulular 10
pegar 35	pialar 10	potenciar 10	proceder 4	pulverizar 19
peinar 10	piar 26	practicar 7	procesar 10	puntualizar 19
pelar 10	picanear 10	precaver 4	proclamar 10	puntuar 1
pelear 10	picar 7	preceder 4	procrastinar 10	punzar 19
peligrar 10	picardear 10	preciar 10	procrear 10	puñalear 10
pellizcar 7	picotear 10	precipitar 10	procurar 10	purgar 35
pelotear 10	pigmentar 10	precisar 10	prodigar 35	purificar 7
penalizar 19	pimentar 10	preconcebir 43	producir 16	
penar 10	pincelar 10	preconizar 19	profanar 10	quebrajar 10
pender 4	pinchar 10	predefinir 67	proferir 57	quebrantar 10

quebrar 11	reapretar 11	recostar 17	regatear 10	remojar 10
quedar 10	reasegurar 10	recrear 10	regenerar 10	remolcar 7
quejar 10	reasumir 67	recriminar 10	regentar 10	remontar 10
quejumbrar 10	reavivar 10	rectificar 7	regimentar 11	remorder 38
quemar 10	rebajar 10	recubrir 67	regionalizar 19	remover 38
querer 49	rebanar 10	recuperar 10	regir 50	remplazar 19
quijotear 10	rebasar 10	recurrir 67	registrar 10	rempujar 10
quimerizar 19	rebautizar 19	recusar 10	reglamentar 10	remunerar 10
quintuplicar 7	rebelarse 10	redactar 10	regocijar 10	renacer 42
quitar 10	rebosar 10	redimir 67	regresar 10	rendir 43
	rebotar 10	redituar 1	reguardarse 10	renegar 39
rabiar 10	rebozar 19	redoblar 10	regular 10	renovar 17
raciocinar 10	rebuscar 7	redoblegar 35	regularizar 19	renquear 10
racionalizar 19	rebuznar 10	redolar 10	regurgitar 10	rentabilizar 19
racionar 10	recaer 9	redondear 10	rehabilitar 10	rentar 10
radicalizar 19	recalcitrar 10	reducir 16	rehacer 32	renunciar 10
radicar 7	recalentar 11	redundar 10	rehogar 35	reñir 61
radiodifundir 67	recapacitar 10	reduplicar 7	rehuir 15	reordenar 10
radiografiar 26	recapitular 10	reedificar 7	rehumedecer 42	reorganizar 19
radioguiar 26	recargar 35	reeditar 10	reimprimir 67	repagar 35
radiotelegrafiar .. 26	recatar 10	reeducar 7	reinar 10	reparar 10
rajar 10	recaudar 10	reelegir 50	reincidir 67	repasar 10
rallar 10	recavar 10	reembarcar 7	reincorporar 10	repatriar 26
ramificar 7	recetar 10	reembolsar 10	reingresar 10	repeinar 10
ranciar 10	rechazar 19	reemplazar 19	reinscribir 67	repensar 11
rapar 10	rechinar 10	reemprender 4	reinstalar 10	repercutir 67
raptar 10	recibir 67	reengendrar 10	reintegrar 10	repetir 43
rarificar 7	reciclar 10	reensayar 10	reír 51	repicar 7
rasar 10	reciprocar 7	reentrar 10	reiterar 10	replegar 39
rascar 7	recitar 10	reestructurar 10	reivindicar 7	repletar 10
rasgar 35	reclamar 10	reexaminar 10	rejonear 10	replicar 7
rasguear 10	reclinar 10	reexpedir 43	rejuntar 10	repoblar 17
rasguñar 10	reclutar 10	refaccionar 10	rejuvenecer 42	repodar 10
raspar 10	recobrar 10	referir 57	relacionar 10	reponer 47
rastrar 10	recodar 10	refilar 10	relajar 10	reportar 10
rastrear 10	recoger 13	refinar 10	relamer 4	reposar 10
rastrillar 10	recolectar 10	refirmar 10	relampaguear 10	reprender 4
rasurar 10	recomendar 11	reflejar 10	relatar 10	representar 10
ratificar 7	recomenzar 14	reflexionar 10	releer 18	reprimir 67
rayar 10	recompensar 10	reflorecer 42	relegar 35	reprobar 17
razonar 10	recomponer 47	reforestar 10	relinchar 10	reprochar 10
reabrir 67	reconcentrar 10	reformar 10	relingar 35	reproducir 16
reabsorber 4	reconciliar 10	reforzar 30	rellenar 10	reptar 10
reaccionar 10	reconfirmar 10	refregar 39	relucir 36	republicanizar ... 19
reactivar 10	reconocer 42	refreír 51	remachar 10	repudiar 10
readmitir 67	reconquistar 10	refrenar 10	remar 10	repugnar 10
reafirmar 10	reconsiderar 10	refrescar 7	rematar 10	repulsar 10
reagrupar 10	reconstituir 15	refrigerar 10	rembolsar 10	requebrar 11
reajustar 10	reconstruir 15	refugiar 10	remedar 10	requerir 57
realizar 19	reconvenir 65	refunfuñar 10	remediar 10	resaltar 10
realzar 19	recopilar 10	refutar 10	rememorar 10	resbalar 10
reanimar 10	recordar 17	regalar 10	remendar 11	rescatar 10
reanudar 10	recorrer 4	regañar 10	remilitarizar 19	rescindir 67
reaparecer 42	recoser 4	regar 39	remitir 67	rescribir 67

suponer 47	titubear 10	trastear 10	valuar 1	vomitar 10
suprimir 67	titular 10	trastornar 10	vanagloriarse 10	vosear 10
supurar 10	tiznar 10	tratar 10	vaporizar 19	votar 10
surcar 7	tocar 7	traumatizar 19	variar 26	vulgarizar 19
surgir 22	tolerar 10	trazar 19	vaticinar 10	
suscitar 10	tomar 10	trenzar 19	vedar 10	xerocopiar 10
suscribir 67	tonsurar 10	trepar 10	vegetar 10	
suspender 4	topar 10	trepidar 10	velar 10	yuxtaponer 47
suspirar 10	torcer 12	triar 26	vencer 64	
sustanciar 10	torear 10	trillar 10	vendar 10	zabordar 10
sustantivar 10	tormentar 10	trinar 10	vender 4	zafar 10
sustentar 10	tornar 10	trincar 7	vendimiar 10	zangolotear 10
sustituir 15	tornear 10	trinchar 10	venerar 10	zapatear 10
sustraer 62	torpedear 10	triplicar 7	vengar 35	zarandear 10
susurrar 10	tostar 17	triturar 10	venir 65	zarpar 10
suturar 10	tostar 17	triunfar 10	ventilar 10	zigzaguear 10
	totalizar 19	trocar 68	ver 66	zonificar 7
tachar 10	trabajar 10	trompetear 10	veranear 10	zozobrar 10
taconear 10	trabar 10	tronar 17	verdecer 42	zumbar 10
tajar 10	traducir 16	tropezar 14	verificar 7	zurcir 28
taladrar 10	traer 62	trotar 10	versificar 7	zurrar 10
talar 10	traficar 7	tumbar 10	verter 44	
tallar 10	tragar 35	turbar 10	vestir 43	
tambalear 10	traicionar 10	tutear 10	vetar 10	
tamizar 19	trajinar 10		viajar 10	
tantear 10	tramar 10		vibrar 10	
tapar 10	tramitar 10	ubicar 7	viciar 10	
tapizar 19	trancar 7	ufanarse 10	victimar 10	
tararear 10	tranquilizar 19	ulcerar 10	vigilar 10	
tardar 10	transcender 44	ultrajar 10	vigorizar 19	
tarifar 10	transcribir 67	ulular 10	vincular 10	
tartamudear 10	transcurrir 67	uncir 28	vindicar 7	
tatuar 1	transferir 57	undular 10	violar 10	
tejer 4	transformar 10	unificar 7	violentar 10	
telefonear 10	transitar 10	uniformar 10	virar 10	
telegrafiar 26	translucirse 36	uniformizar 19	virilizar 19	
televisar 10	transmitir 67	unir 67	visar 10	
temblar 11	transparentarse .. 10	universalizar 19	visitar 10	
temer 4	transpirar 10	untar 10	vislumbrar 10	
templar 10	transplantar 10	urbanizar 19	visualizar 19	
tender 44	traquetear 10	urgir 22	vitalizar 19	
tener 60	trascender 44	usar 10	vivaquear 10	
tentar 11	trascribir 67	usurpar 10	vivificar 7	
teñir 61	trascurrir 67	utilizar 19	vivir 67	
teorizar 19	trasladar 10		vocalizar 19	
terminar 10	traslucir 36	vaciar 26	vocear 10	
testificar 7	traslumbrar 10	vacilar 10	vociferar 10	
tintinear 10	trasmitir 67	vacunar 10	volar 17	
tipificar 7	trasnochar 10	vagabundear 10	volatilizar 19	
tiranizar 19	traspasar 10	vagar 35	volatizar 19	
tirar 10	traspirar 10	vaguear 10	volcanizar 19	
tiritar 10	trasplantar 10	valer 63	volcar 68	
tironear 10	trasponer 47	validar 10	voltear 10	
tirotear 10	trasquilar 10	valorar 10	volver 69	
		valorizar 19		

1. ACTUAR
(to act)

Verbo en -AR con cambio de *u → ú*
(Como **acentuar, continuar, evaluar, graduar, insinuar**)

Participio presente: actuando | **Participio pasado:** actuado

Imperativo: actúa (no actúes), actúe Ud., actuemos, actuad (no actuéis), actúen Uds.

Indicativo				Condicional	Subjuntivo	
Presente	**Imperfecto**	**Pretérito**	**Futuro**	**Presente**	**Presente**	**Imperfecto**
actúo	actuaba	actué	actuaré	actuaría	actúe	actuara
actúas	actuabas	actuaste	actuarás	actuarías	actúes	actuaras
actúa	actuaba	actuó	actuará	actuaría	actúe	actuara
actuamos	actuábamos	actuamos	actuaremos	actuaríamos	actuemos	actuáramos
actuáis	actuabais	actuasteis	actuaréis	actuaríais	actuéis	actuarais
actúan	actuaban	actuaron	actuarán	actuarían	actúen	actuaran
Pres. perfecto	**Pluscuamperf.**		**Futuro perfecto**	**Perfecto**	**Pres. perfecto**	**Pluscuamperf.**
he actuado	había actuado		habré actuado	habría actuado	haya actuado	hubiera actuado

2. ADQUIRIR
(to acquire)

Verbo en -IR con cambio de *i → ie*
(Como **coadquirir, inquirir, perquirir**)

Participio presente: adquiriendo | **Participio pasado:** adquirido

Imperativo: adquiere (no adquieras), adquiera Ud., adquiramos, adquirid (no adquiráis), adquieran Uds.

Indicativo				Condicional	Subjuntivo	
Presente	**Imperfecto**	**Pretérito**	**Futuro**	**Presente**	**Presente**	**Imperfecto**
adquiero	adquiría	adquirí	adquiriré	adquiriría	adquiera	adquiriera
adquieres	adquirías	adquiriste	adquirirás	adquirirías	adquieras	adquirieras
adquiere	adquiría	adquirió	adquirirá	adquiriría	adquiera	adquiriera
adquirimos	adquiríamos	adquirimos	adquiriremos	adquiriríamos	adquiramos	adquiriéramos
adquirís	adquiríais	adquiristeis	adquiriréis	adquiriríais	adquiráis	adquirierais
adquieren	adquirían	adquirieron	adquirirán	adquirirían	adquieran	adquirieran
Pres. perfecto	**Pluscuamperf.**		**Futuro perfecto**	**Perfecto**	**Pres. perfecto**	**Pluscuamperf.**
he adquirido	había adquirido		habré adquirido	habría adquirido	haya adquirido	hubiera adquirido

3. ANDAR
(to go)

Verbo irregular

Participio presente: andando | **Participio pasado:** andado

Imperativo: anda (no andes), ande Ud., andemos, andad (no andéis), anden Uds.

Indicativo				Condicional	Subjuntivo	
Presente	**Imperfecto**	**Pretérito**	**Futuro**	**Presente**	**Presente**	**Imperfecto**
ando	andaba	anduve	andaré	andaría	ande	anduviera
andas	andabas	anduviste	andarás	andarías	andes	anduvieras
anda	andaba	anduvo	andará	andaría	ande	anduviera
andamos	andábamos	anduvimos	andaremos	andaríamos	andemos	anduviéramos
andáis	andabais	anduvisteis	andaréis	andaríais	andéis	anduvierais
andan	andaban	anduvieron	andarán	andarían	anden	anduvieran
Pres. perfecto	**Pluscuamperf.**		**Futuro perfecto**	**Perfecto**	**Pres. perfecto**	**Pluscuamperf.**
he andado	había andado		habré andado	habría andado	haya andado	hubiera andado

4. APRENDER
(to learn)

Verbo regular 2ª conjugación

(Como **depender, emprender, meter, prender, responder**)

Participio presente: aprendiendo | **Participio pasado:** aprendido

Imperativo: aprende (no aprendas), aprenda Ud., aprendamos, aprended (no aprendáis), aprendan Uds.

Indicativo				Condicional	Subjuntivo	
Presente	**Imperfecto**	**Pretérito**	**Futuro**	**Presente**	**Presente**	**Imperfecto**
aprendo	aprendía	aprendí	aprenderé	aprendería	aprenda	aprendiera
aprendes	aprendías	aprendiste	aprenderás	aprenderías	aprendas	aprendieras
aprende	aprendía	aprendió	aprenderá	aprendería	aprenda	aprendiera
aprendemos	aprendíamos	aprendimos	aprenderemos	aprenderíamos	aprendamos	aprendiéramos
aprendéis	aprendíais	aprendisteis	aprenderéis	aprenderíais	aprendáis	aprendierais
aprenden	aprendían	aprendieron	aprenderán	aprenderían	aprendan	aprendieran
Pres. perfecto	**Pluscuamperf.**		**Futuro perfecto**	**Perfecto**	**Pres. perfecto**	**Pluscuamperf.**
he aprendido	había aprendido		habré aprendido	habría aprendido	haya aprendido	hubiera aprendido

5. AVERGONZAR
(to shame)

Verbo en -AR con cambio de *u* → *ü* frente a E; *z* → *c* frente a E

(Como **desvergonzarse**)

Participio presente: avergonzando | **Participio pasado:** avergonzado

Imperativo: avergüenza (no avergüences), avergüence Ud., avergoncemos, avergonzad (no avergoncéis), avergüencen Uds.

Indicativo				Condicional	Subjuntivo	
Presente	**Imperfecto**	**Pretérito**	**Futuro**	**Presente**	**Presente**	**Imperfecto**
avergüenzo	avergonzaba	avergoncé	avergonzaré	avergonzaría	avergüence	avergonzara
avergüenzas	avergonzabas	avergonzaste	avergonzarás	avergonzarías	avergüences	avergonzaras
avergüenza	avergonzaba	avergonzó	avergonzará	avergonzaría	avergüence	avergonzara
avergonzamos	avergonzábamos	avergonzamos	avergonzaremos	avergonzaríamos	avergoncemos	avergonzáramos
avergonzáis	avergonzabais	avergonzasteis	avergonzaréis	avergonzaríais	avergoncéis	avergonzarais
avergüenzan	avergonzaban	avergonzaron	avergonzarán	avergonzarían	avergüencen	avergonzaran
Pres. perfecto	**Pluscuamperf.**		**Futuro perfecto**	**Perfecto**	**Pres. perfecto**	**Pluscuamperf.**
he avergonzado	había avergonzado		habré avergonzado	habría avergonzado	haya avergonzado	hubiera avergonzado

6. AVERIGUAR
(to ascertain)

Verbo en -AR con cambio de *u* → *ü* frente a E

(Como **aguar, amortiguar, apaciguar, atestiguar, santiguar**)

Participio presente: averiguando | **Participio pasado:** averiguado

Imperativo: averigua (no averigües), averigüe Ud., averigüemos, averiguad (no averigüéis), averigüen Uds.

Indicativo				Condicional	Subjuntivo	
Presente	**Imperfecto**	**Pretérito**	**Futuro**	**Presente**	**Presente**	**Imperfecto**
averiguo	averiguaba	averigüé	averiguaré	averiguaría	averigüe	averiguara
averiguas	averiguabas	averiguaste	averiguarás	averiguarías	averigües	averiguaras
averigua	averiguaba	averiguó	averiguará	averiguaría	averigüe	averiguara
averiguamos	averiguábamos	averiguamos	averiguaremos	averiguaríamos	averigüemos	averiguáramos
averiguáis	averiguabais	averiguasteis	averiguaréis	averiguaríais	averigüéis	averiguarais
averiguan	averiguaban	averiguaron	averiguarán	averiguarían	averigüen	averiguaran
Pres. perfecto	**Pluscuamperf.**		**Futuro perfecto**	**Perfecto**	**Pres. perfecto**	**Pluscuamperf.**
he averiguado	había averiguado		habré averiguado	habría averiguado	haya averiguado	hubiera averiguado

7. BUSCAR
(to look for)

Verbo en -AR con cambio de *c* → *qu* frente a E
(Como **acercar, explicar, justificar, sacar, significar**)

Participio presente: buscando | **Participio pasado:** buscado

Imperativo: busca (no bus**ques**), bus**que** Ud., bus**quemos**, buscad (no bus**quéis**), bus**quen** Uds.

Indicativo				Condicional	Subjuntivo	
Presente	Imperfecto	Pretérito	Futuro	Presente	Presente	Imperfecto
busco	buscaba	bus**qué**	buscaré	buscaría	bus**que**	buscara
buscas	buscabas	buscaste	buscarás	buscarías	bus**ques**	buscaras
busca	buscaba	buscó	buscará	buscaría	bus**que**	buscara
buscamos	buscábamos	buscamos	buscaremos	buscaríamos	bus**quemos**	buscáramos
buscáis	buscabais	buscasteis	buscaréis	buscaríais	bus**quéis**	buscarais
buscan	buscaban	buscaron	buscarán	buscarían	bus**quen**	buscaran

Pres. perfecto	Pluscuamperf.		Futuro perfecto	Perfecto	Pres. perfecto	Pluscuamperf.
he buscado	había buscado		habré buscado	habría buscado	haya buscado	hubiera buscado

8. CABER
(to fit)

Verbo irregular

Participio presente: cabiendo | **Participio pasado:** cabido

Imperativo: cabe (no **quepas**), **quepa** Ud., **quepamos**, cabed (no **quepáis**), **quepan** Uds.

Indicativo				Condicional	Subjuntivo	
Presente	Imperfecto	Pretérito	Futuro	Presente	Presente	Imperfecto
quepo	cabía	**cupe**	cabré	cabría	**quepa**	**cupiera**
cabes	cabías	**cupiste**	cabrás	cabrías	**quepas**	**cupieras**
cabe	cabía	**cupo**	cabrá	cabría	**quepa**	**cupiera**
cabemos	cabíamos	**cupimos**	cabremos	cabríamos	**quepamos**	**cupiéramos**
cabéis	cabíais	**cupisteis**	cabréis	cabríais	**quepáis**	**cupierais**
caben	cabían	**cupieron**	cabrán	cabrían	**quepan**	**cupieran**

Pres. perfecto	Pluscuamperf.		Futuro perfecto	Perfecto	Pres. perfecto	Pluscuamperf.
he cabido	había cabido		habré cabido	habría cabido	haya cabido	hubiera cabido

9. CAER
(to fall)

Verbo irregular
(Como **decaer, recaer**)

Participio presente: cayendo | **Participio pasado:** caído

Imperativo: cae (no ca**igas**), ca**iga** Ud., ca**igamos**, caed (no ca**igáis**), ca**igan** Uds.

Indicativo				Condicional	Subjuntivo	
Presente	Imperfecto	Pretérito	Futuro	Presente	Presente	Imperfecto
ca**igo**	caía	caí	caeré	caería	caiga	cayera
caes	caías	caíste	caerás	caerías	caigas	cayeras
cae	caía	ca**yó**	caerá	caería	caiga	cayera
caemos	caíamos	caímos	caeremos	caeríamos	caigamos	cayéramos
caéis	caíais	caísteis	caeréis	caeríais	caigáis	cayerais
caen	caían	ca**yeron**	caerán	caerían	caigan	cayeran

Pres. perfecto	Pluscuamperf.		Futuro perfecto	Perfecto	Pres. perfecto	Pluscuamperf.
he caído	había caído		habré caído	habría caído	haya caído	hubiera caído

10. CAMINAR
(to walk)

Verbo regular 1ª conjugación

(Como **acabar, comentar, enamorar, interesar, tardar**)

Participio presente: caminando | **Participio pasado:** caminado

Imperativo: camina (no camines), camine Ud., caminemos, caminad (no caminéis), caminen Uds.

Indicativo				Condicional	Subjuntivo	
Presente	**Imperfecto**	**Pretérito**	**Futuro**	**Presente**	**Presente**	**Imperfecto**
camino	caminaba	caminé	caminaré	caminaría	camine	caminara
caminas	caminabas	caminaste	caminarás	caminarías	camines	caminaras
camina	caminaba	caminó	caminará	caminaría	camine	caminara
caminamos	caminábamos	caminamos	caminaremos	caminaríamos	caminemos	camináramos
camináis	caminabais	caminasteis	caminaréis	caminaríais	caminéis	caminarais
caminan	caminaban	caminaron	caminarán	caminarían	caminen	caminaran
Pres. perfecto	**Pluscuamperf.**		**Futuro perfecto**	**Perfecto**	**Pres. perfecto**	**Pluscuamperf.**
he caminado	había caminado		habré caminado	habría caminado	haya caminado	hubiera caminado

11. CERRAR
(to close)

Verbo en -AR con cambio de e → ie

(Como **acertar, calentar, despertar, quebrar, sentar**)

Participio presente: cerrando | **Participio pasado:** cerrado

Imperativo: cierra (no cierres), cierre Ud., cerremos, cerrad (no cerréis), cierren Uds.

Indicativo				Condicional	Subjuntivo	
Presente	**Imperfecto**	**Pretérito**	**Futuro**	**Presente**	**Presente**	**Imperfecto**
cierro	cerraba	cerré	cerraré	cerraría	cierre	cerrara
cierras	cerrabas	cerraste	cerrarás	cerrarías	cierres	cerraras
cierra	cerraba	cerró	cerrará	cerraría	cierre	cerrara
cerramos	cerrábamos	cerramos	cerraremos	cerraríamos	cerremos	cerráramos
cerráis	cerrabais	cerrasteis	cerraréis	cerraríais	cerréis	cerrarais
cierran	cerraban	cerraron	cerrarán	cerrarían	cierren	cerraran
Pres. perfecto	**Pluscuamperf.**		**Futuro perfecto**	**Perfecto**	**Pres. perfecto**	**Pluscuamperf.**
he cerrado	había cerrado		habré cerrado	habría cerrado	haya cerrado	hubiera cerrado

12. COCER
(to cook)

Verbo en -ER con cambio de o → ue; c → z frente a A y O

(Como **descocer, destorcer, retorcer, torcer**)

Participio presente: cociendo | **Participio pasado:** cocido

Imperativo: cuece (no cuezas), cueza Ud., cozamos, coced (no cozáis), cuezan Uds.

Indicativo				Condicional	Subjuntivo	
Presente	**Imperfecto**	**Pretérito**	**Futuro**	**Presente**	**Presente**	**Imperfecto**
cuezo	cocía	cocí	coceré	cocería	cueza	cociera
cueces	cocías	cociste	cocerás	cocerías	cuezas	cocieras
cuece	cocía	coció	cocerá	cocería	cueza	cociera
cocemos	cocíamos	cocimos	coceremos	coceríamos	cozamos	cociéramos
cocéis	cocíais	cocisteis	coceréis	coceríais	cozáis	cocierais
cuecen	cocían	cocieron	cocerán	cocerían	cuezan	cocieran
Pres. perfecto	**Pluscuamperf.**		**Futuro perfecto**	**Perfecto**	**Pres. perfecto**	**Pluscuamperf.**
he cocido	había cocido		habré cocido	habría cocido	haya cocido	hubiera cocido

13. COGER
(to take hold of)

Verbo en -ER con cambio de $g \rightarrow j$ frente a A y O
(Como **acoger, encoger, escoger, proteger, recoger**)

Participio presente: cogiendo	**Participio pasado:** cogido

Imperativo: coge (no cojas), coja Ud., cojamos, coged (no cojáis), cojan Uds.

Indicativo				Condicional	Subjuntivo	
Presente	**Imperfecto**	**Pretérito**	**Futuro**	**Presente**	**Presente**	**Imperfecto**
cojo	cogía	cogí	cogeré	cogería	coja	cogiera
coges	cogías	cogiste	cogerás	cogerías	cojas	cogieras
coge	cogía	cogió	cogerá	cogería	coja	cogiera
cogemos	cogíamos	cogimos	cogeremos	cogeríamos	cojamos	cogiéramos
cogéis	cogíais	cogisteis	cogeréis	cogeríais	cojáis	cogierais
cogen	cogían	cogieron	cogerán	cogerían	cojan	cogieran
Pres. perfecto	**Pluscuamperf.**		**Futuro perfecto**	**Perfecto**	**Pres. perfecto**	**Pluscuamperf.**
he cogido	había cogido		habré cogido	habría cogido	haya cogido	hubiera cogido

14. COMENZAR
(to begin)

Verbo en -AR con cambio de $e \rightarrow ie$; $z \rightarrow c$ frente a E
(Como **empezar, recomenzar, tropezar**)

Participio presente: comenzando	**Participio pasado:** comenzado

Imperativo: comienza (no comiences), comience Ud., comencemos, comenzad (no comencéis), comiencen Uds.

Indicativo				Condicional	Subjuntivo	
Presente	**Imperfecto**	**Pretérito**	**Futuro**	**Presente**	**Presente**	**Imperfecto**
comienzo	comenzaba	comencé	comenzaré	comenzaría	comience	comenzara
comienzas	comenzabas	comenzaste	comenzarás	comenzarías	comiences	comenzaras
comienza	comenzaba	comenzó	comenzará	comenzaría	comience	comenzara
comenzamos	comenzábamos	comenzamos	comenzaremos	comenzaríamos	comencemos	comenzáramos
comenzáis	comenzabais	comenzasteis	comenzaréis	comenzaríais	comencéis	comenzarais
comienzan	comenzaban	comenzaron	comenzarán	comenzarían	comiencen	comenzaran
Pres. perfecto	**Pluscuamperf.**		**Futuro perfecto**	**Perfecto**	**Pres. perfecto**	**Pluscuamperf.**
he comenzado	había comenzado		habré comenzado	habría comenzado	haya comenzado	hubiera comenzado

15. CONCLUIR
(to conclude)

Verbo en -IR con cambio de $i \rightarrow y$
(Como **atribuir, construir, distribuir, excluir, huir**)

Participio presente: concluyendo	**Participio pasado:** concluido

Imperativo: concluye (no concluyas), concluya Ud., concluyamos, concluid (no concluyáis), concluyan Uds.

Indicativo				Condicional	Subjuntivo	
Presente	**Imperfecto**	**Pretérito**	**Futuro**	**Presente**	**Presente**	**Imperfecto**
concluyo	concluía	concluí	concluiré	concluiría	concluya	concluyera
concluyes	concluías	concluiste	concluirás	concluirías	concluyas	concluyeras
concluye	concluía	concluyó	concluirá	concluiría	concluya	concluyera
concluimos	concluíamos	concluimos	concluiremos	concluiríamos	concluyamos	concluyéramos
concluís	concluíais	concluisteis	concluiréis	concluiríais	concluyáis	concluyerais
concluyen	concluían	concluyeron	concluirán	concluirían	concluyan	concluyeran
Pres. perfecto	**Pluscuamperf.**		**Futuro perfecto**	**Perfecto**	**Pres. perfecto**	**Pluscuamperf.**
he concluido	había concluido		habré concluido	habría concluido	haya concluido	hubiera concluido

16. CONDUCIR
(to conduct)

Verbo en -IR con cambio de $c \rightarrow zc$ frente a A y O; $c \rightarrow j$

(Como **deducir, introducir, producir, reducir, traducir**)

Participio presente: conduciendo | **Participio pasado:** conducido

Imperativo: conduce (no conduzcas), conduzca Ud., conduzcamos, conducid (no conduzcáis), conduzcan Uds.

Indicativo				Condicional	Subjuntivo	
Presente	**Imperfecto**	**Pretérito**	**Futuro**	**Presente**	**Presente**	**Imperfecto**
conduzco	conducía	conduje	conduciré	conduciría	conduzca	condujera
conduces	conducías	condujiste	conducirás	conducirías	conduzcas	condujeras
conduce	conducía	condujo	conducirá	conduciría	conduzca	condujera
conducimos	conducíamos	condujimos	conduciremos	conduciríamos	conduzcamos	condujéramos
conducís	conducíais	condujisteis	conduciréis	conduciríais	conduzcáis	condujerais
conducen	conducían	condujeron	conducirán	conducirían	conduzcan	condujeran
Pres. perfecto	**Pluscuamperf.**		**Futuro perfecto**	**Perfecto**	**Pres. perfecto**	**Pluscuamperf.**
he conducido	había conducido		habré conducido	habría conducido	haya conducido	hubiera conducido

17. CONTAR
(to tell, to count)

Verbo en -AR con cambio de $o \rightarrow ue$

(Como **acostar, costar, encontrar, mostrar, probar**)

Participio presente: contando | **Participio pasado:** contado

Imperativo: cuenta (no cuentes), cuente Ud., contemos, contad (no contéis), cuenten Uds.

Indicativo				Condicional	Subjuntivo	
Presente	**Imperfecto**	**Pretérito**	**Futuro**	**Presente**	**Presente**	**Imperfecto**
cuento	contaba	conté	contaré	contaría	cuente	contara
cuentas	contabas	contaste	contarás	contarías	cuentes	contaras
cuenta	contaba	contó	contará	contaría	cuente	contara
contamos	contábamos	contamos	contaremos	contaríamos	contemos	contáramos
contáis	contabais	contasteis	contaréis	contaríais	contéis	contarais
cuentan	contaban	contaron	contarán	contarían	cuenten	contaran
Pres. perfecto	**Pluscuamperf.**		**Futuro perfecto**	**Perfecto**	**Pres. perfecto**	**Pluscuamperf.**
he contado	había contado		habré contado	habría contado	haya contado	hubiera contado

18. CREER
(to believe)

Verbo irregular

(Como **descreer, leer, poseer, proveer, releer**)

Participio presente: creyendo | **Participio pasado:** creído

Imperativo: cree (no creas), crea Ud., creamos, creed (no creáis), crean Uds.

Indicativo				Condicional	Subjuntivo	
Presente	**Imperfecto**	**Pretérito**	**Futuro**	**Presente**	**Presente**	**Imperfecto**
creo	creía	creí	creeré	creería	crea	creyera
crees	creías	creíste	creerás	creerías	creas	creyeras
cree	creía	creyó	creerá	creería	crea	creyera
creemos	creíamos	creímos	creeremos	creeríamos	creamos	creyéramos
creéis	creíais	creísteis	creeréis	creeríais	creáis	creyerais
creen	creían	creyeron	creerán	creerían	crean	creyeran
Pres. perfecto	**Pluscuamperf.**		**Futuro perfecto**	**Perfecto**	**Pres. perfecto**	**Pluscuamperf.**
he creído	había creído		habré creído	habría creído	haya creído	hubiera creído

19. CRUZAR
(to cross)

Verbo en -AR con cambio de z → c frente a E

(Como **abrazar, bostezar, especializar, lanzar, reemplazar**)

Participio presente: cruzando

Participio pasado: cruzado

Imperativo: cruza (no cru**c**es), cru**c**e Ud., cru**c**emos, cruzad (no cru**c**éis), cru**c**en Uds.

Indicativo				Condicional	Subjuntivo	
Presente	**Imperfecto**	**Pretérito**	**Futuro**	**Presente**	**Presente**	**Imperfecto**
cruzo	cruzaba	crucé	cruzaré	cruzaría	cruce	cruzara
cruzas	cruzabas	cruzaste	cruzarás	cruzarías	cruces	cruzaras
cruza	cruzaba	cruzó	cruzará	cruzaría	cruce	cruzara
cruzamos	cruzábamos	cruzamos	cruzaremos	cruzaríamos	crucemos	cruzáramos
cruzáis	cruzabais	cruzasteis	cruzaréis	cruzaríais	crucéis	cruzarais
cruzan	cruzaban	cruzaron	cruzarán	cruzarían	crucen	cruzaran
Pres. perfecto	**Pluscuamperf.**		**Futuro perfecto**	**Perfecto**	**Pres. perfecto**	**Pluscuamperf.**
he cruzado	había cruzado		habré cruzado	habría cruzado	haya cruzado	hubiera cruzado

20. DAR
(to give)

Verbo irregular

Participio presente: dando

Participio pasado: dado

Imperativo: da (no des), **dé** Ud., demos, dad (no deis), den Uds.

Indicativo				Condicional	Subjuntivo	
Presente	**Imperfecto**	**Pretérito**	**Futuro**	**Presente**	**Presente**	**Imperfecto**
doy	daba	**di**	daré	daría	dé	diera
das	dabas	diste	darás	darías	des	dieras
da	daba	dio	dará	daría	dé	diera
damos	dábamos	dimos	daremos	daríamos	demos	diéramos
dais	dabais	disteis	daréis	daríais	deis	dierais
dan	daban	dieron	darán	darían	den	dieran
Pres. perfecto	**Pluscuamperf.**		**Futuro perfecto**	**Perfecto**	**Pres. perfecto**	**Pluscuamperf.**
he dado	había dado		habré dado	habría dado	haya dado	hubiera dado

21. DECIR
(to say)

Verbo irregular

Participio presente: diciendo

Participio pasado: dicho

Imperativo: **di** (no di**g**as), di**g**a Ud., di**g**amos, decid (no di**g**áis), di**g**an Uds.

Indicativo				Condicional	Subjuntivo	
Presente	**Imperfecto**	**Pretérito**	**Futuro**	**Presente**	**Presente**	**Imperfecto**
di**g**o	decía	di**j**e	diré	diría	diga	di**j**era
dices	decías	di**j**iste	dirás	dirías	digas	di**j**eras
dice	decía	di**j**o	dirá	diría	diga	di**j**era
decimos	decíamos	di**j**imos	diremos	diríamos	digamos	di**j**éramos
decís	decíais	di**j**isteis	diréis	diríais	digáis	di**j**erais
dicen	decían	di**j**eron	dirán	dirían	digan	di**j**eran
Pres. perfecto	**Pluscuamperf.**		**Futuro perfecto**	**Perfecto**	**Pres. perfecto**	**Pluscuamperf.**
he **dicho**	había **dicho**		habré **dicho**	habría **dicho**	haya **dicho**	hubiera **dicho**

22. DIRIGIR
(to direct)

Verbo en -IR con cambio de g → j frente a A y O
(Como **afligir, exigir, fingir, surgir, urgir**)

Participio presente: dirigiendo | **Participio pasado:** dirigido

Imperativo: dirige (no dirijas), dirija Ud., dirijamos, dirigid (no dirijáis), dirijan Uds.

Indicativo				Condicional	Subjuntivo	
Presente	**Imperfecto**	**Pretérito**	**Futuro**	**Presente**	**Presente**	**Imperfecto**
dirijo	dirigía	dirigí	dirigiré	dirigiría	dirija	dirigiera
diriges	dirigías	dirigiste	dirigirás	dirigirías	dirijas	dirigieras
dirige	dirigía	dirigió	dirigirá	dirigiría	dirija	dirigiera
dirigimos	dirigíamos	dirigimos	dirigiremos	dirigiríamos	dirijamos	dirigiéramos
dirigís	dirigíais	dirigisteis	dirigiréis	dirigiríais	dirijáis	dirigierais
dirigen	dirigían	dirigieron	dirigirán	dirigirían	dirijan	dirigieran
Pres. perfecto	**Pluscuamperf.**		**Futuro perfecto**	**Perfecto**	**Pres. perfecto**	**Pluscuamperf.**
he dirigido	había dirigido		habré dirigido	habría dirigido	haya dirigido	hubiera dirigido

23. DISCERNIR
(to discern)

Verbo en -IR con cambio de e → ie
(Como **cernir, concernir**)

Participio presente: discerniendo | **Participio pasado:** discernido

Imperativo: discierne (no disciernas), discierna Ud., discernamos, discernid (no discernáis), disciernan Uds.

Indicativo				Condicional	Subjuntivo	
Presente	**Imperfecto**	**Pretérito**	**Futuro**	**Presente**	**Presente**	**Imperfecto**
discierno	discernía	discerní	discerniré	discerniría	discierna	discerniera
disciernes	discernías	discerniste	discernirás	discernirías	disciernas	discernieras
discierne	discernía	discernió	discernirá	discerniría	discierna	discerniera
discernimos	discerníamos	discernimos	discerniremos	discerniríamos	discernamos	discerniéramos
discernís	discerníais	discernisteis	discerniréis	discerniríais	discernáis	discernierais
disciernen	discernían	discernieron	discernirán	discernirían	disciernan	discernieran
Pres. perfecto	**Pluscuamperf.**		**Futuro perfecto**	**Perfecto**	**Pres. perfecto**	**Pluscuamperf.**
he discernido	había discernido		habré discernido	habría discernido	haya discernido	hubiera discernido

24. DISTINGUIR
(to distinguish)

Verbo en -IR con cambio de gu → g frente a A y O
(Como **extinguir**)

Participio presente: distinguiendo | **Participio pasado:** distinguido

Imperativo: distingue (no distingas), distinga Ud., distingamos, distinguid (no distingáis), distingan Uds.

Indicativo				Condicional	Subjuntivo	
Presente	**Imperfecto**	**Pretérito**	**Futuro**	**Presente**	**Presente**	**Imperfecto**
distingo	distinguía	distinguí	distinguiré	distinguiría	distinga	distinguiera
distingues	distinguías	distinguiste	distinguirás	distinguirías	distingas	distinguieras
distingue	distinguía	distinguió	distinguirá	distinguiría	distinga	distinguiera
distinguimos	distinguíamos	distinguimos	distinguiremos	distinguiríamos	distingamos	distinguiéramos
distinguís	distinguíais	distinguisteis	distinguiréis	distinguiríais	distingáis	distinguierais
distinguen	distinguían	distinguieron	distinguirán	distinguirían	distingan	distinguieran
Pres. perfecto	**Pluscuamperf.**		**Futuro perfecto**	**Perfecto**	**Pres. perfecto**	**Pluscuamperf.**
he distinguido	había distinguido		habré distinguido	habría distinguido	haya distinguido	hubiera distinguido

25. DORMIR
(to sleep)

Verbo en -IR con cambio de *o → ue* y *o → u*

Participio presente: durmiendo

Participio pasado: dormido

Imperativo: duerme (no duermas), duerma Ud., durmamos, dormid (no durmáis), duerman Uds.

Indicativo				Condicional	Subjuntivo	
Presente	**Imperfecto**	**Pretérito**	**Futuro**	**Presente**	**Presente**	**Imperfecto**
duermo	dormía	dormí	dormiré	dormiría	duerma	durmiera
duermes	dormías	dormiste	dormirás	dormirías	duermas	durmieras
duerme	dormía	durmió	dormirá	dormiría	duerma	durmiera
dormimos	dormíamos	dormimos	dormiremos	dormiríamos	durmamos	durmiéramos
dormís	dormíais	dormisteis	dormiréis	dormiríais	durmáis	durmierais
duermen	dormían	durmieron	dormirán	dormirían	duerman	durmieran
Pres. perfecto	**Pluscuamperf.**		**Futuro perfecto**	**Perfecto**	**Pres. perfecto**	**Pluscuamperf.**
he dormido	había dormido		habré dormido	habría dormido	haya dormido	hubiera dormido

26. ENVIAR
(to send)

Verbo en -AR con cambio de *i → í*

(Como **ampliar, confiar, enfriar, rociar, vaciar, variar**)

Participio presente: enviando

Participio pasado: enviado

Imperativo: envía (no envíes), envíe Ud., enviemos, enviad (no enviéis), envíen Uds.

Indicativo				Condicional	Subjuntivo	
Presente	**Imperfecto**	**Pretérito**	**Futuro**	**Presente**	**Presente**	**Imperfecto**
envío	enviaba	envié	enviaré	enviaría	envíe	enviara
envías	enviabas	enviaste	enviarás	enviarías	envíes	enviaras
envía	enviaba	envió	enviará	enviaría	envíe	enviara
enviamos	enviábamos	enviamos	enviaremos	enviaríamos	enviemos	enviáramos
enviáis	enviabais	enviasteis	enviaréis	enviaríais	enviéis	enviarais
envían	enviaban	enviaron	enviarán	enviarían	envíen	enviaran
Pres. perfecto	**Pluscuamperf.**		**Futuro perfecto**	**Perfecto**	**Pres. perfecto**	**Pluscuamperf.**
he enviado	había enviado		habré enviado	habría enviado	haya enviado	hubiera enviado

27. ERRAR
(to wander)

Verbo en -AR con cambio de *e → ye*

(Como **aberrar**)

Participio presente: errando

Participio pasado: errado

Imperativo: yerra (no yerres), yerre Ud., erremos, errad (no erréis), yerren Uds.

Indicativo				Condicional	Subjuntivo	
Presente	**Imperfecto**	**Pretérito**	**Futuro**	**Presente**	**Presente**	**Imperfecto**
yerro	erraba	erré	erraré	erraría	yerre	errara
yerras	errabas	erraste	errarás	errarías	yerres	erraras
yerra	erraba	erró	errará	erraría	yerre	errara
erramos	errábamos	erramos	erraremos	erraríamos	erremos	erráramos
erráis	errabais	errasteis	erraréis	erraríais	erréis	errarais
yerran	erraban	erraron	errarán	errarían	yerren	erraran
Pres. perfecto	**Pluscuamperf.**		**Futuro perfecto**	**Perfecto**	**Pres. perfecto**	**Pluscuamperf.**
he errado	había errado		habré errado	habría errado	haya errado	hubiera errado

28. ESPARCIR
(to scatter)

Verbo en -IR con cambio de *c* → *z* **frente a A y O**
(Como fruncir, uncir, zurcir)

Participio presente: esparciendo | **Participio pasado:** esparcido

Imperativo: esparce (no esparzas), esparza Ud., esparzamos, esparcid (no esparzáis), esparzan Uds.

Indicativo				Condicional	Subjuntivo	
Presente	**Imperfecto**	**Pretérito**	**Futuro**	**Presente**	**Presente**	**Imperfecto**
esparzo	esparcía	esparcí	esparciré	esparciría	esparza	esparciera
esparces	esparcías	esparciste	esparcirás	esparcirías	esparzas	esparcieras
esparce	esparcía	esparció	esparcirá	esparciría	esparza	esparciera
esparcimos	esparcíamos	esparcimos	esparciremos	esparciríamos	esparzamos	esparciéramos
esparcís	esparcíais	esparcisteis	esparciréis	esparciríais	esparzáis	esparcierais
esparcen	esparcían	esparcieron	esparcirán	esparcirían	esparzan	esparcieran
Pres. perfecto	**Pluscuamperf.**		**Futuro perfecto**	**Perfecto**	**Pres. perfecto**	**Pluscuamperf.**
he esparcido	había esparcido		habré esparcido	habría esparcido	haya esparcido	hubiera esparcido

29. ESTAR
(to be)

Verbo irregular

Participio presente: estando | **Participio pasado:** estado

Imperativo: está (no estés), esté Ud., estemos, estad (no estéis), estén Uds.

Indicativo				Condicional	Subjuntivo	
Presente	**Imperfecto**	**Pretérito**	**Futuro**	**Presente**	**Presente**	**Imperfecto**
estoy	estaba	estuve	estaré	estaría	esté	estuviera
estás	estabas	estuviste	estarás	estarías	estés	estuvieras
está	estaba	estuvo	estará	estaría	esté	estuviera
estamos	estábamos	estuvimos	estaremos	estaríamos	estemos	estuviéramos
estáis	estabais	estuvisteis	estaréis	estaríais	estéis	estuvierais
están	estaban	estuvieron	estarán	estarían	estén	estuvieran
Pres. perfecto	**Pluscuamperf.**		**Futuro perfecto**	**Perfecto**	**Pres. perfecto**	**Pluscuamperf.**
he estado	había estado		habré estado	habría estado	haya estado	hubiera estado

30. FORZAR
(to force)

Verbo en -AR con cambio de *o* → *ue; z* → *c* **frente a E**
(Como almorzar, esforzar, reforzar)

Participio presente: forzando | **Participio pasado:** forzado

Imperativo: fuerza (no fuerces), fuerce Ud., forcemos, forzad (no forcéis), fuercen Uds.

Indicativo				Condicional	Subjuntivo	
Presente	**Imperfecto**	**Pretérito**	**Futuro**	**Presente**	**Presente**	**Imperfecto**
fuerzo	forzaba	forcé	forzaré	forzaría	fuerce	forzara
fuerzas	forzabas	forzaste	forzarás	forzarías	fuerces	forzaras
fuerza	forzaba	forzó	forzará	forzaría	fuerce	forzara
forzamos	forzábamos	forzamos	forzaremos	forzaríamos	forcemos	forzáramos
forzáis	forzabais	forzasteis	forzaréis	forzaríais	forcéis	forzarais
fuerzan	forzaban	forzaron	forzarán	forzarían	fuercen	forzaran
Pres. perfecto	**Pluscuamperf.**		**Futuro perfecto**	**Perfecto**	**Pres. perfecto**	**Pluscuamperf.**
he forzado	había forzado		habré forzado	habría forzado	haya forzado	hubiera forzado

31. HABER
(to have)

Verbo irregular (*Para la conjugación del uso impersonal, vea la 3ª persona de cada tiempo excepto el presente del indicativo, que es "hay".)

Participio presente: habiendo | **Participio pasado:** habido

Imperativo: he (no hayas), haya Ud., hayamos, habed (no hayáis), hayan Uds.

Indicativo				Condicional	Subjuntivo	
Presente	**Imperfecto**	**Pretérito**	**Futuro**	**Presente**	**Presente**	**Imperfecto**
he	había	hube	habré	habría	haya	hubiera
has	habías	hubiste	habrás	habrías	hayas	hubieras
ha (hay*)	había*	hubo*	habrá*	habría*	haya*	hubiera*
hemos	habíamos	hubimos	habremos	habríamos	hayamos	hubiéramos
habéis	habíais	hubisteis	habréis	habríais	hayáis	hubierais
han	habían	hubieron	habrán	habrían	hayan	hubieran
Pres. perfecto	**Pluscuamperf.**		**Futuro perfecto**	**Perfecto**	**Pres. perfecto**	**Pluscuamperf.**
he habido	había habido		habré habido	habría habido	haya habido	hubiera habido

32. HACER
(to do)

Verbo irregular

(Como **deshacer, rehacer, satisfacer**)

Participio presente: haciendo | **Participio pasado:** hecho

Imperativo: haz (no hagas), haga Ud., hagamos, haced (no hagáis), hagan Uds.

Indicativo				Condicional	Subjuntivo	
Presente	**Imperfecto**	**Pretérito**	**Futuro**	**Presente**	**Presente**	**Imperfecto**
hago	hacía	hice	haré	haría	haga	hiciera
haces	hacías	hiciste	harás	harías	hagas	hicieras
hace	hacía	hizo	hará	haría	haga	hiciera
hacemos	hacíamos	hicimos	haremos	haríamos	hagamos	hiciéramos
hacéis	hacíais	hicisteis	haréis	haríais	hagáis	hicierais
hacen	hacían	hicieron	harán	harían	hagan	hicieran
Pres. perfecto	**Pluscuamperf.**		**Futuro perfecto**	**Perfecto**	**Pres. perfecto**	**Pluscuamperf.**
he hecho	había hecho		habré hecho	habría hecho	haya hecho	hubiera hecho

33. IR
(to go)

Verbo irregular

Participio presente: yendo | **Participio pasado:** ido

Imperativo: ve (no vayas), vaya Ud., vamos (no vayamos), id (no vayáis), vayan Uds.

Indicativo				Condicional	Subjuntivo	
Presente	**Imperfecto**	**Pretérito**	**Futuro**	**Presente**	**Presente**	**Imperfecto**
voy	iba	fui	iré	iría	vaya	fuera
vas	ibas	fuiste	irás	irías	vayas	fueras
va	iba	fue	irá	iría	vaya	fuera
vamos	íbamos	fuimos	iremos	iríamos	vayamos	fuéramos
vais	ibais	fuisteis	iréis	iríais	vayáis	fuerais
van	iban	fueron	irán	irían	vayan	fueran
Pres. perfecto	**Pluscuamperf.**		**Futuro perfecto**	**Perfecto**	**Pres. perfecto**	**Pluscuamperf.**
he ido	había ido		habré ido	habría ido	haya ido	hubiera ido

34. JUGAR
(to play)
Verbo en -AR con cambio de *u* → *ue*; *g* → *gu* frente a E

Participio presente: jugando	**Participio pasado:** jugado

Imperativo: ju**e**ga (no ju**e**gues), ju**e**gue Ud., juguemos, jugad (no jugu**é**is), ju**e**guen Uds.

Indicativo				Condicional	Subjuntivo	
Presente	Imperfecto	Pretérito	Futuro	Presente	Presente	Imperfecto
ju**e**go	jugaba	jugu**é**	jugaré	jugaría	ju**e**gue	jugara
ju**e**gas	jugabas	jugaste	jugarás	jugarías	ju**e**gues	jugaras
ju**e**ga	jugaba	jugó	jugará	jugaría	ju**e**gue	jugara
jugamos	jugábamos	jugamos	jugaremos	jugaríamos	juguemos	jugáramos
jugáis	jugabais	jugasteis	jugaréis	jugaríais	jugu**é**is	jugarais
ju**e**gan	jugaban	jugaron	jugarán	jugarían	ju**e**guen	jugaran
Pres. perfecto	**Pluscuamperf.**		**Futuro perfecto**	**Perfecto**	**Pres. perfecto**	**Pluscuamperf.**
he jugado	había jugado		habré jugado	habría jugado	haya jugado	hubiera jugado

35. LLEGAR
(to arrive)
Verbo en -AR con cambio de *g* → *gu* frente a E
(Como abrigar, cargar, entregar, obligar, pagar)

Participio presente: llegando	**Participio pasado:** llegado

Imperativo: llega (no llegues), llegue Ud., lleguemos, llegad (no llegu**é**is), lleguen Uds.

Indicativo				Condicional	Subjuntivo	
Presente	Imperfecto	Pretérito	Futuro	Presente	Presente	Imperfecto
llego	llegaba	llegu**é**	llegaré	llegaría	llegue	llegara
llegas	llegabas	llegaste	llegarás	llegarías	llegues	llegaras
llega	llegaba	llegó	llegará	llegaría	llegue	llegara
llegamos	llegábamos	llegamos	llegaremos	llegaríamos	lleguemos	llegáramos
llegáis	llegabais	llegasteis	llegaréis	llegaríais	llegu**é**is	llegarais
llegan	llegaban	llegaron	llegarán	llegarían	lleguen	llegaran
Pres. perfecto	**Pluscuamperf.**		**Futuro perfecto**	**Perfecto**	**Pres. perfecto**	**Pluscuamperf.**
he llegado	había llegado		habré llegado	habría llegado	haya llegado	hubiera llegado

36. LUCIR
(to shine)
Verbo en -IR con cambio de *c* → *zc* frente a A y O
(Como relucir, translucirse, traslucir)

Participio presente: luciendo	**Participio pasado:** lucido

Imperativo: luce (no lu**zc**as), lu**zc**a Ud., lu**zc**amos, lucid (no lu**zc**áis), lu**zc**an Uds.

Indicativo				Condicional	Subjuntivo	
Presente	Imperfecto	Pretérito	Futuro	Presente	Presente	Imperfecto
lu**zc**o	lucía	lucí	luciré	luciría	lu**zc**a	luciera
luces	lucías	luciste	lucirás	lucirías	lu**zc**as	lucieras
luce	lucía	lució	lucirá	luciría	lu**zc**a	luciera
lucimos	lucíamos	lucimos	luciremos	luciríamos	lu**zc**amos	luciéramos
lucís	lucíais	lucisteis	luciréis	luciríais	lu**zc**áis	lucierais
lucen	lucían	lucieron	lucirán	lucirían	lu**zc**an	lucieran
Pres. perfecto	**Pluscuamperf.**		**Futuro perfecto**	**Perfecto**	**Pres. perfecto**	**Pluscuamperf.**
he lucido	había lucido		habré lucido	habría lucido	haya lucido	hubiera lucido

37. MORIR
(to die)

Verbo en -IR con cambio de *o* → *ue*; participio pasado irregular

Participio presente: muriendo	**Participio pasado:** muerto

Imperativo: muere (no mueras), muera Ud., muramos, morid (no muráis), mueran Uds.

Indicativo				Condicional	Subjuntivo	
Presente	**Imperfecto**	**Pretérito**	**Futuro**	**Presente**	**Presente**	**Imperfecto**
muero	moría	morí	moriré	moriría	muera	muriera
mueres	morías	moriste	morirás	morirías	mueras	murieras
muere	moría	murió	morirá	moriría	muera	muriera
morimos	moríamos	morimos	moriremos	moriríamos	muramos	muriéramos
morís	moríais	moristeis	moriréis	moriríais	muráis	murierais
mueren	morían	murieron	morirán	morirían	mueran	murieran
Pres. perfecto	**Pluscuamperf.**		**Futuro perfecto**	**Perfecto**	**Pres. perfecto**	**Pluscuamperf.**
he muerto	había muerto		habré muerto	habría muerto	haya muerto	hubiera muerto

38. MOVER
(to move)

Verbo en -ER con cambio de *o* → *ue*

(Como **doler, llover, morder, promover, remorder**)

Participio presente: moviendo	**Participio pasado:** movido

Imperativo: mueve (no muevas), mueva Ud., movamos, moved (no mováis), muevan Uds.

Indicativo				Condicional	Subjuntivo	
Presente	**Imperfecto**	**Pretérito**	**Futuro**	**Presente**	**Presente**	**Imperfecto**
muevo	movía	moví	moveré	movería	mueva	moviera
mueves	movías	moviste	moverás	moverías	muevas	movieras
mueve	movía	movió	moverá	movería	mueva	moviera
movemos	movíamos	movimos	moveremos	moveríamos	movamos	moviéramos
movéis	movíais	movisteis	moveréis	moveríais	mováis	movierais
mueven	movían	movieron	moverán	moverían	muevan	movieran
Pres. perfecto	**Pluscuamperf.**		**Futuro perfecto**	**Perfecto**	**Pres. perfecto**	**Pluscuamperf.**
he movido	había movido		habré movido	habría movido	haya movido	hubiera movido

39. NEGAR
(to deny)

Verbo en -AR con cambio de *e* → *ie*; *g* → *gu* frente a E

(Como **cegar, fregar, regar, renegar, restregar**)

Participio presente: negando	**Participio pasado:** negado

Imperativo: niega (no niegues), niegue Ud., neguemos, negad (no neguéis), nieguen Uds.

Indicativo				Condicional	Subjuntivo	
Presente	**Imperfecto**	**Pretérito**	**Futuro**	**Presente**	**Presente**	**Imperfecto**
niego	negaba	negué	negaré	negaría	niegue	negara
niegas	negabas	negaste	negarás	negarías	niegues	negaras
niega	negaba	negó	negará	negaría	niegue	negara
negamos	negábamos	negamos	negaremos	negaríamos	neguemos	negáramos
negáis	negabais	negasteis	negaréis	negaríais	neguéis	negarais
niegan	negaban	negaron	negarán	negarían	nieguen	negaran
Pres. perfecto	**Pluscuamperf.**		**Futuro perfecto**	**Perfecto**	**Pres. perfecto**	**Pluscuamperf.**
he negado	había negado		habré negado	habría negado	haya negado	hubiera negado

40. OÍR
(to hear)

Verbo irregular

Participio presente: oyendo | **Participio pasado:** oído

Imperativo: oye (no **oig**as), **oig**a Ud., **oig**amos, oíd (no **oig**áis), **oig**an Uds.

Indicativo				Condicional	Subjuntivo	
Presente	**Imperfecto**	**Pretérito**	**Futuro**	**Presente**	**Presente**	**Imperfecto**
oigo	oía	oí	oiré	oiría	oiga	oyera
oyes	oías	oíste	oirás	oirías	oigas	oyeras
oye	oía	oyó	oirá	oiría	oiga	oyera
oímos	oíamos	oímos	oiremos	oiríamos	oigamos	oyéramos
oís	oíais	oísteis	oiréis	oiríais	oigáis	oyerais
oyen	oían	oyeron	oirán	oirían	oigan	oyeran

Pres. perfecto	**Pluscuamperf.**		**Futuro perfecto**	**Perfecto**	**Pres. perfecto**	**Pluscuamperf.**
he oído	había oído		habré oído	habría oído	haya oído	hubiera oído

41. OLER
(to smell)

Verbo en -ER con cambio de *o → hue*

Participio presente: oliendo | **Participio pasado:** olido

Imperativo: **hue**le (no **hue**las), **hue**la Ud., olamos, oled (no oláis), **hue**lan Uds.

Indicativo				Condicional	Subjuntivo	
Presente	**Imperfecto**	**Pretérito**	**Futuro**	**Presente**	**Presente**	**Imperfecto**
huelo	olía	olí	oleré	olería	**hue**la	oliera
hueles	olías	oliste	olerás	olerías	**hue**las	olieras
huele	olía	olió	olerá	olería	**hue**la	oliera
olemos	olíamos	olimos	oleremos	oleríamos	olamos	oliéramos
oléis	olíais	olisteis	oleréis	oleríais	oláis	olierais
huelen	olían	olieron	olerán	olerían	**hue**lan	olieran

Pres. perfecto	**Pluscuamperf.**		**Futuro perfecto**	**Perfecto**	**Pres. perfecto**	**Pluscuamperf.**
he olido	había olido		habré olido	habría olido	haya olido	hubiera olido

42. PARECER
(to seem)

Verbo en -ER con cambio de *c → zc* frente a A y O
(Como **agradecer, conocer, crecer, merecer, nacer**)

Participio presente: pareciendo | **Participio pasado:** parecido

Imperativo: parece (no pare**zc**as), pare**zc**a Ud., pare**zc**amos, pareced (no pare**zc**áis), pare**zc**an Uds.

Indicativo				Condicional	Subjuntivo	
Presente	**Imperfecto**	**Pretérito**	**Futuro**	**Presente**	**Presente**	**Imperfecto**
pare**zc**o	parecía	parecí	pareceré	parecería	pare**zc**a	pareciera
pareces	parecías	pareciste	parecerás	parecerías	pare**zc**as	parecieras
parece	parecía	pareció	parecerá	parecería	pare**zc**a	pareciera
parecemos	parecíamos	parecimos	pareceremos	pareceríamos	pare**zc**amos	pareciéramos
parecéis	parecíais	parecisteis	pareceréis	pareceríais	pare**zc**áis	parecierais
parecen	parecían	parecieron	parecerán	parecerían	pare**zc**an	parecieran

Pres. perfecto	**Pluscuamperf.**		**Futuro perfecto**	**Perfecto**	**Pres. perfecto**	**Pluscuamperf.**
he parecido	había parecido		habré parecido	habría parecido	haya parecido	hubiera parecido

43. PEDIR
(to ask for)

Verbo en -IR con cambio de e → i

(Como **competir, despedir, medir, repetir, servir**)

Participio presente: pidiendo | **Participio pasado:** pedido

Imperativo: pide (no pidas), pida Ud., pidamos, pedid (no pidáis), pidan Uds.

Indicativo				Condicional	Subjuntivo	
Presente	**Imperfecto**	**Pretérito**	**Futuro**	**Presente**	**Presente**	**Imperfecto**
pido	pedía	pedí	pediré	pediría	pida	pidiera
pides	pedías	pediste	pedirás	pedirías	pidas	pidieras
pide	pedía	pidió	pedirá	pediría	pida	pidiera
pedimos	pedíamos	pedimos	pediremos	pediríamos	pidamos	pidiéramos
pedís	pedíais	pedisteis	pediréis	pediríais	pidáis	pidierais
piden	pedían	pidieron	pedirán	pedirían	pidan	pidieran
Pres. perfecto	**Pluscuamperf.**		**Futuro perfecto**	**Perfecto**	**Pres. perfecto**	**Pluscuamperf.**
he pedido	había pedido		habré pedido	habría pedido	haya pedido	hubiera pedido

44. PERDER
(to lose)

Verbo en -ER con cambio de e → ie

(Como **atender, defender, encender, entender, tender**)

Participio presente: perdiendo | **Participio pasado:** perdido

Imperativo: pierde (no pierdas), pierda Ud., perdamos, perded (no perdáis), pierdan Uds.

Indicativo				Condicional	Subjuntivo	
Presente	**Imperfecto**	**Pretérito**	**Futuro**	**Presente**	**Presente**	**Imperfecto**
pierdo	perdía	perdí	perderé	perdería	pierda	perdiera
pierdes	perdías	perdiste	perderás	perderías	pierdas	perdieras
pierde	perdía	perdió	perderá	perdería	pierda	perdiera
perdemos	perdíamos	perdimos	perderemos	perderíamos	perdamos	perdiéramos
perdéis	perdíais	perdisteis	perderéis	perderíais	perdáis	perdierais
pierden	perdían	perdieron	perderán	perderían	pierdan	perdieran
Pres. perfecto	**Pluscuamperf.**		**Futuro perfecto**	**Perfecto**	**Pres. perfecto**	**Pluscuamperf.**
he perdido	había perdido		habré perdido	habría perdido	haya perdido	hubiera perdido

45. PODER
(to be able)

Verbo irregular

Participio presente: pudiendo | **Participio pasado:** podido

Imperativo: puede (no puedas), pueda Ud., podamos, poded (no podáis), puedan Uds.

Indicativo				Condicional	Subjuntivo	
Presente	**Imperfecto**	**Pretérito**	**Futuro**	**Presente**	**Presente**	**Imperfecto**
puedo	podía	pude	podré	podría	pueda	pudiera
puedes	podías	pudiste	podrás	podrías	puedas	pudieras
puede	podía	pudo	podrá	podría	pueda	pudiera
podemos	podíamos	pudimos	podremos	podríamos	podamos	pudiéramos
podéis	podíais	pudisteis	podréis	podríais	podáis	pudierais
pueden	podían	pudieron	podrán	podrían	puedan	pudieran
Pres. perfecto	**Pluscuamperf.**		**Futuro perfecto**	**Perfecto**	**Pres. perfecto**	**Pluscuamperf.**
he podido	había podido		habré podido	habría podido	haya podido	hubiera podido

46. PODRIR o PUDRIR   Verbo irregular
(to rot)

| **Participio presente:** pudriendo | | | | **Participio pasado:** podrido | | |

Imperativo: pudre (no pudras), pudra Ud., pudramos, pudrid (no pudráis), pudran Uds.

Indicativo				Condicional	Subjuntivo	
Presente	**Imperfecto**	**Pretérito**	**Futuro**	**Presente**	**Presente**	**Imperfecto**
pudro	pudría	pudrí; podrí	pudriré; podriré	pudriría	pudra	pudriera
pudres	pudrías	pudriste	pudrirás	pudrirías	pudras	pudrieras
pudre	pudría	pudrió	pudrirá	pudriría	pudra	pudriera
pudrimos	pudríamos	pudrimos	pudriremos	pudriríamos	pudramos	pudriéramos
pudrís	pudríais	pudristeis	pudriréis	pudriríais	pudráis	pudrierais
pudren	pudrían	pudrieron	pudrirán	pudrirían	pudran	pudrieran
Pres. perfecto	**Pluscuamperf.**		**Futuro perfecto**	**Perfecto**	**Pres. perfecto**	**Pluscuamperf.**
he podrido	había podrido		habré podrido	habría podrido	haya podrido	hubiera podrido

47. PONER   Verbo irregular
(to put)   (Como **componer, disponer, oponer, proponer, suponer**)

| **Participio presente:** poniendo | | | | **Participio pasado:** puesto | | |

Imperativo: pon (no pongas), ponga Ud., pongamos, poned (no pongáis), pongan Uds.

Indicativo				Condicional	Subjuntivo	
Presente	**Imperfecto**	**Pretérito**	**Futuro**	**Presente**	**Presente**	**Imperfecto**
pongo	ponía	puse	pondré	pondría	ponga	pusiera
pones	ponías	pusiste	pondrás	pondrías	pongas	pusieras
pone	ponía	puso	pondrá	pondría	ponga	pusiera
ponemos	poníamos	pusimos	pondremos	pondríamos	pongamos	pusiéramos
ponéis	poníais	pusisteis	pondréis	pondríais	pongáis	pusierais
ponen	ponían	pusieron	pondrán	pondrían	pongan	pusieran
Pres. perfecto	**Pluscuamperf.**		**Futuro perfecto**	**Perfecto**	**Pres. perfecto**	**Pluscuamperf.**
he puesto	había puesto		habré puesto	habría puesto	haya puesto	hubiera puesto

48. PROHIBIR   Verbo en -IR con cambio de *i* → *í*
(to prohibit)   (Como **cohibir**)

| **Participio presente:** prohibiendo | | | | **Participio pasado:** prohibido | | |

Imperativo: prohíbe (no prohíbas), prohíba Ud., prohibamos, prohibid (no prohibáis), prohíban Uds.

Indicativo				Condicional	Subjuntivo	
Presente	**Imperfecto**	**Pretérito**	**Futuro**	**Presente**	**Presente**	**Imperfecto**
prohíbo	prohibía	prohibí	prohibiré	prohibiría	prohíba	prohibiera
prohíbes	prohibías	prohibiste	prohibirás	prohibirías	prohíbas	prohibieras
prohíbe	prohibía	prohibió	prohibirá	prohibiría	prohíba	prohibiera
prohibimos	prohibíamos	prohibimos	prohibiremos	prohibiríamos	prohibamos	prohibiéramos
prohibís	prohibíais	prohibisteis	prohibiréis	prohibiríais	prohibáis	prohibierais
prohíben	prohibían	prohibieron	prohibirán	prohibirían	prohíban	prohibieran
Pres. perfecto	**Pluscuamperf.**		**Futuro perfecto**	**Perfecto**	**Pres. perfecto**	**Pluscuamperf.**
he prohibido	había prohibido		habré prohibido	habría prohibido	haya prohibido	hubiera prohibido

49. QUERER
(to want)

Verbo irregular
(Como **bienquerer**)

Participio presente: queriendo | **Participio pasado:** querido

Imperativo: quiere (no quieras), quiera Ud., queramos, quered (no queráis), quieran Uds.

Indicativo				Condicional	Subjuntivo	
Presente	Imperfecto	Pretérito	Futuro	Presente	Presente	Imperfecto
quiero	quería	quise	querré	querría	quiera	quisiera
quieres	querías	quisiste	querrás	querrías	quieras	quisieras
quiere	quería	quiso	querrá	querría	quiera	quisiera
queremos	queríamos	quisimos	querremos	querríamos	queramos	quisiéramos
queréis	queríais	quisisteis	querréis	querríais	queráis	quisierais
quieren	querían	quisieron	querrán	querrían	quieran	quisieran
Pres. perfecto	**Pluscuamperf.**		**Futuro perfecto**	**Perfecto**	**Pres. perfecto**	**Pluscuamperf.**
he querido	había querido		habré querido	habría querido	haya querido	hubiera querido

50. REGIR
(to rule)

Verbo en -IR con cambio de e → i; g → j frente a A y O
(Como **colegir, corregir, elegir, reelegir**)

Participio presente: rigiendo | **Participio pasado:** regido

Imperativo: rige (no rijas), rija Ud., rijamos, regid (no rijáis), rijan Uds.

Indicativo				Condicional	Subjuntivo	
Presente	Imperfecto	Pretérito	Futuro	Presente	Presente	Imperfecto
rijo	regía	regí	regiré	regiría	rija	rigiera
riges	regías	registe	regirás	regirías	rijas	rigieras
rige	regía	rigió	regirá	regiría	rija	rigiera
regimos	regíamos	regimos	regiremos	regiríamos	rijamos	rigiéramos
regís	regíais	registeis	regiréis	regiríais	rijáis	rigierais
rigen	regían	rigieron	regirán	regirían	rijan	rigieran
Pres. perfecto	**Pluscuamperf.**		**Futuro perfecto**	**Perfecto**	**Pres. perfecto**	**Pluscuamperf.**
he regido	había regido		habré regido	habría regido	haya regido	hubiera regido

51. REÍR
(to laugh)

Verbo irregular
(Como **freír, refreír, sofreír, sonreír**)

Participio presente: riendo | **Participio pasado:** reído

Imperativo: ríe (no rías), ría Ud., riamos, reíd (no riáis), rían Uds.

Indicativo				Condicional	Subjuntivo	
Presente	Imperfecto	Pretérito	Futuro	Presente	Presente	Imperfecto
río	reía	reí	reiré	reiría	ría	riera
ríes	reías	reíste	reirás	reirías	rías	rieras
ríe	reía	rió	reirá	reiría	ría	riera
reímos	reíamos	reímos	reiremos	reiríamos	riamos	riéramos
reís	reíais	reísteis	reiréis	reiríais	riáis	rierais
ríen	reían	rieron	reirán	reirían	rían	rieran
Pres. perfecto	**Pluscuamperf.**		**Futuro perfecto**	**Perfecto**	**Pres. perfecto**	**Pluscuamperf.**
he reído	había reído		habré reído	habría reído	haya reído	hubiera reído

52. REUNIR
(to assemble)
Verbo en -IR con cambio de *u* → *ú*

Participio presente: reuniendo | **Participio pasado:** reunido

Imperativo: reúne (no reúnas), reúna Ud., reunamos, reunid (no reunáis), reúnan Uds.

Indicativo				Condicional	Subjuntivo	
Presente	**Imperfecto**	**Pretérito**	**Futuro**	**Presente**	**Presente**	**Imperfecto**
reúno	reunía	reuní	reuniré	reuniría	reúna	reuniera
reúnes	reunías	reuniste	reunirás	reunirías	reúnas	reunieras
reúne	reunía	reunió	reunirá	reuniría	reúna	reuniera
reunimos	reuníamos	reunimos	reuniremos	reuniríamos	reunamos	reuniéramos
reunís	reuníais	reunisteis	reuniréis	reuniríais	reunáis	reunierais
reúnen	reunían	reunieron	reunirán	reunirían	reúnan	reunieran
Pres. perfecto	**Pluscuamperf.**		**Futuro perfecto**	**Perfecto**	**Pres. perfecto**	**Pluscuamperf.**
he reunido	había reunido		habré reunido	habría reunido	haya reunido	hubiera reunido

53. ROGAR
(to beg)
Verbo en -AR con cambio de *o* → *ue*; *g* → *gu* frente a E
(Como **colgar, descolgar**)

Participio presente: rogando | **Participio pasado:** rogado

Imperativo: r**ue**ga (no r**ue**gues), r**ue**gue Ud., roguemos, rogad (no roguéis), r**ue**guen Uds.

Indicativo				Condicional	Subjuntivo	
Presente	**Imperfecto**	**Pretérito**	**Futuro**	**Presente**	**Presente**	**Imperfecto**
r**ue**go	rogaba	rogué	rogaré	rogaría	r**ue**gue	rogara
r**ue**gas	rogabas	rogaste	rogarás	rogarías	r**ue**gues	rogaras
r**ue**ga	rogaba	rogó	rogará	rogaría	r**ue**gue	rogara
rogamos	rogábamos	rogamos	rogaremos	rogaríamos	roguemos	rogáramos
rogáis	rogabais	rogasteis	rogaréis	rogaríais	roguéis	rogarais
r**ue**gan	rogaban	rogaron	rogarán	rogarían	r**ue**guen	rogaran
Pres. perfecto	**Pluscuamperf.**		**Futuro perfecto**	**Perfecto**	**Pres. perfecto**	**Pluscuamperf.**
he rogado	había rogado		habré rogado	habría rogado	haya rogado	hubiera rogado

54. SABER
(to know)
Verbo irregular

Participio presente: sabiendo | **Participio pasado:** sabido

Imperativo: sabe (no s**e**pas), s**e**pa Ud., s**e**pamos, sabed (no s**e**páis), s**e**pan Uds.

Indicativo				Condicional	Subjuntivo	
Presente	**Imperfecto**	**Pretérito**	**Futuro**	**Presente**	**Presente**	**Imperfecto**
sé	sabía	supe	sabré	sabría	sepa	supiera
sabes	sabías	supiste	sabrás	sabrías	sepas	supieras
sabe	sabía	supo	sabrá	sabría	sepa	supiera
sabemos	sabíamos	supimos	sabremos	sabríamos	sepamos	supiéramos
sabéis	sabíais	supisteis	sabréis	sabríais	sepáis	supierais
saben	sabían	supieron	sabrán	sabrían	sepan	supieran
Pres. perfecto	**Pluscuamperf.**		**Futuro perfecto**	**Perfecto**	**Pres. perfecto**	**Pluscuamperf.**
he sabido	había sabido		habré sabido	habría sabido	haya sabido	hubiera sabido

55. SALIR
(to go out)

Verbo irregular
(Como **sobresalir**)

Participio presente: saliendo   **Participio pasado:** salido

Imperativo: sal (no sal**gas**), sal**ga** Ud., sal**gamos**, salid (no sal**gáis**), sal**gan** Uds.

Indicativo				Condicional	Subjuntivo	
Presente	**Imperfecto**	**Pretérito**	**Futuro**	**Presente**	**Presente**	**Imperfecto**
salgo	salía	salí	saldré	saldría	salga	saliera
sales	salías	saliste	saldrás	saldrías	salgas	salieras
sale	salía	salió	saldrá	saldría	salga	saliera
salimos	salíamos	salimos	saldremos	saldríamos	salgamos	saliéramos
salís	salíais	salisteis	saldréis	saldríais	salgáis	salierais
salen	salían	salieron	saldrán	saldrían	salgan	salieran
Pres. perfecto	**Pluscuamperf.**		**Futuro perfecto**	**Perfecto**	**Pres. perfecto**	**Pluscuamperf.**
he salido	había salido		habré salido	habría salido	haya salido	hubiera salido

56. SEGUIR
(to follow)

Verbo en -IR con cambio de *gu → g* frente a A y O; *e → i*
(Como **conseguir, perseguir, proseguir**)

Participio presente: siguiendo   **Participio pasado:** seguido

Imperativo: sigue (no si**gas**), si**ga** Ud., si**gamos**, seguid (no si**gáis**), si**gan** Uds.

Indicativo				Condicional	Subjuntivo	
Presente	**Imperfecto**	**Pretérito**	**Futuro**	**Presente**	**Presente**	**Imperfecto**
sigo	seguía	seguí	seguiré	seguiría	siga	siguiera
sigues	seguías	seguiste	seguirás	seguirías	sigas	siguieras
sigue	seguía	siguió	seguirá	seguiría	siga	siguiera
seguimos	seguíamos	seguimos	seguiremos	seguiríamos	sigamos	siguiéramos
seguís	seguíais	seguisteis	seguiréis	seguiríais	sigáis	siguierais
siguen	seguían	siguieron	seguirán	seguirían	sigan	siguieran
Pres. perfecto	**Pluscuamperf.**		**Futuro perfecto**	**Perfecto**	**Pres. perfecto**	**Pluscuamperf.**
he seguido	había seguido		habré seguido	habría seguido	haya seguido	hubiera seguido

57. SENTIR
(to feel)

Verbo en -IR con cambio de *e → ie; e → i*
(Como **arrepentirse, divertir, mentir, preferir, sugerir**)

Participio presente: sintiendo   **Participio pasado:** sentido

Imperativo: si**e**nte (no si**e**ntas), si**e**nta Ud., si**n**tamos, sentid (no si**n**táis), si**e**ntan Uds.

Indicativo				Condicional	Subjuntivo	
Presente	**Imperfecto**	**Pretérito**	**Futuro**	**Presente**	**Presente**	**Imperfecto**
siento	sentía	sentí	sentiré	sentiría	sienta	sintiera
sientes	sentías	sentiste	sentirás	sentirías	sientas	sintieras
siente	sentía	sintió	sentirá	sentiría	sienta	sintiera
sentimos	sentíamos	sentimos	sentiremos	sentiríamos	sintamos	sintiéramos
sentís	sentíais	sentisteis	sentiréis	sentiríais	sintáis	sintierais
sienten	sentían	sintieron	sentirán	sentirían	sientan	sintieran
Pres. perfecto	**Pluscuamperf.**		**Futuro perfecto**	**Perfecto**	**Pres. perfecto**	**Pluscuamperf.**
he sentido	había sentido		habré sentido	habría sentido	haya sentido	hubiera sentido

58. SER

Verbo irregular

(to be)

Participio presente: siendo | **Participio pasado:** sido

Imperativo: sé (no seas), sea Ud., seamos, sed (no seáis), sean Uds.

Indicativo				Condicional	Subjuntivo	
Presente	**Imperfecto**	**Pretérito**	**Futuro**	**Presente**	**Presente**	**Imperfecto**
soy	era	fui	seré	sería	sea	fuera
eres	eras	fuiste	serás	serías	seas	fueras
es	era	fue	será	sería	sea	fuera
somos	éramos	fuimos	seremos	seríamos	seamos	fuéramos
sois	erais	fuisteis	seréis	seríais	seáis	fuerais
son	eran	fueron	serán	serían	sean	fueran
Pres. perfecto	**Pluscuamperf.**		**Futuro perfecto**	**Perfecto**	**Pres. perfecto**	**Pluscuamperf.**
he sido	había sido		habré sido	habría sido	haya sido	hubiera sido

59. SOLER

Verbo irregular (defectivo—*this means some tenses are not used*)

(to accustom)

Participio presente: soliendo | **Participio pasado:** solido

Imperativo:

Indicativo				Condicional	Subjuntivo	
Presente	**Imperfecto**	**Pretérito**	**Futuro**	**Presente**	**Presente**	**Imperfecto**
suelo	solía	solí			suela	soliera
sueles	solías	soliste			suelas	solieras
suele	solía	solió			suela	soliera
solemos	solíamos	solimos			solamos	soliéramos
soléis	solíais	solisteis			soláis	solierais
suelen	solían	solieron			suelan	solieran
Pres. perfecto	**Pluscuamperf.**		**Futuro perfecto**	**Perfecto**	**Pres. perfecto**	**Pluscuamperf.**

60. TENER

Verbo irregular

(to have)

(Como atenerse, contener, mantener, obtener, sostener)

Participio presente: teniendo | **Participio pasado:** tenido

Imperativo: ten (no tengas), tenga Ud., tengamos, tened (no tengáis), tengan Uds.

Indicativo				Condicional	Subjuntivo	
Presente	**Imperfecto**	**Pretérito**	**Futuro**	**Presente**	**Presente**	**Imperfecto**
tengo	tenía	tuve	tendré	tendría	tenga	tuviera
tienes	tenías	tuviste	tendrás	tendrías	tengas	tuvieras
tiene	tenía	tuvo	tendrá	tendría	tenga	tuviera
tenemos	teníamos	tuvimos	tendremos	tendríamos	tengamos	tuviéramos
tenéis	teníais	tuvisteis	tendréis	tendríais	tengáis	tuvierais
tienen	tenían	tuvieron	tendrán	tendrían	tengan	tuvieran
Pres. perfecto	**Pluscuamperf.**		**Futuro perfecto**	**Perfecto**	**Pres. perfecto**	**Pluscuamperf.**
he tenido	había tenido		habré tenido	habría tenido	haya tenido	hubiera tenido

61. TEÑIR
(to dye)

Verbo en -IR con cambio de e → i; pierde la *i* átona de la terminación
(Como **ceñir, desteñir, estreñir, reñir**)

Participio presente: tiñendo | **Participio pasado:** teñido

Imperativo: tiñe (no tiñas), tiña Ud., tiñamos, teñid (no tiñáis), tiñan Uds.

Indicativo				Condicional	Subjuntivo	
Presente	**Imperfecto**	**Pretérito**	**Futuro**	**Presente**	**Presente**	**Imperfecto**
tiño	teñía	teñí	teñiré	teñiría	tiña	tiñera
tiñes	teñías	teñiste	teñirás	teñirías	tiñas	tiñeras
tiñe	teñía	tiñó	teñirá	teñiría	tiña	tiñera
teñimos	teñíamos	teñimos	teñiremos	teñiríamos	tiñamos	tiñéramos
teñís	teñíais	teñisteis	teñiréis	teñiríais	tiñáis	tiñerais
tiñen	teñían	tiñeron	teñirán	teñirían	tiñan	tiñeran
Pres. perfecto	**Pluscuamperf.**		**Futuro perfecto**	**Perfecto**	**Pres. perfecto**	**Pluscuamperf.**
he teñido	había teñido		habré teñido	habría teñido	haya teñido	hubiera teñido

62. TRAER
(to bring)

Verbo irregular
(Como **atraer, contraer, detraer, distraer, extraer**)

Participio presente: trayendo | **Participio pasado:** traído

Imperativo: trae (no traigas), traiga Ud., traigamos, traed (no traigáis), traigan Uds.

Indicativo				Condicional	Subjuntivo	
Presente	**Imperfecto**	**Pretérito**	**Futuro**	**Presente**	**Presente**	**Imperfecto**
traigo	traía	traje	traeré	traería	traiga	trajera
traes	traías	trajiste	traerás	traerías	traigas	trajeras
trae	traía	trajo	traerá	traería	traiga	trajera
traemos	traíamos	trajimos	traeremos	traeríamos	traigamos	trajéramos
traéis	traíais	trajisteis	traeréis	traeríais	traigáis	trajerais
traen	traían	trajeron	traerán	traerían	traigan	trajeran
Pres. perfecto	**Pluscuamperf.**		**Futuro perfecto**	**Perfecto**	**Pres. perfecto**	**Pluscuamperf.**
he traído	había traído		habré traído	habría traído	haya traído	hubiera traído

63. VALER
(to be worth)

Verbo irregular
(Como **equivaler, prevaler**)

Participio presente: valiendo | **Participio pasado:** valido

Imperativo: vale (no valgas), valga Ud., valgamos, valed (no valgáis), valgan Uds.

Indicativo				Condicional	Subjuntivo	
Presente	**Imperfecto**	**Pretérito**	**Futuro**	**Presente**	**Presente**	**Imperfecto**
valgo	valía	valí	valdré	valdría	valga	valiera
vales	valías	valiste	valdrás	valdrías	valgas	valieras
vale	valía	valió	valdrá	valdría	valga	valiera
valemos	valíamos	valimos	valdremos	valdríamos	valgamos	valiéramos
valéis	valíais	valisteis	valdréis	valdríais	valgáis	valierais
valen	valían	valieron	valdrán	valdrían	valgan	valieran
Pres. perfecto	**Pluscuamperf.**		**Futuro perfecto**	**Perfecto**	**Pres. perfecto**	**Pluscuamperf.**
he valido	había valido		habré valido	habría valido	haya valido	hubiera valido

64. VENCER
(to conquer)

Verbo en -ER con cambio de c → z frente a A y O
(Como **coercer, convencer, ejercer, mecer**)

Participio presente: venciendo | **Participio pasado:** vencido

Imperativo: vence (no venzas), venza Ud., venzamos, venced (no venzáis), venzan Uds.

Indicativo				Condicional	Subjuntivo	
Presente	**Imperfecto**	**Pretérito**	**Futuro**	**Presente**	**Presente**	**Imperfecto**
venzo	vencía	vencí	venceré	vencería	venza	venciera
vences	vencías	venciste	vencerás	vencerías	venzas	vencieras
vence	vencía	venció	vencerá	vencería	venza	venciera
vencemos	vencíamos	vencimos	venceremos	venceríamos	venzamos	venciéramos
vencéis	vencíais	vencisteis	venceréis	venceríais	venzáis	vencierais
vencen	vencían	vencieron	vencerán	vencerían	venzan	vencieran
Pres. perfecto	**Pluscuamperf.**		**Futuro perfecto**	**Perfecto**	**Pres. perfecto**	**Pluscuamperf.**
he vencido	había vencido		habré vencido	habría vencido	haya vencido	hubiera vencido

65. VENIR
(to come)

Verbo irregular
(Como **convenir, intervenir, prevenir, provenir, reconvenir**)

Participio presente: viniendo | **Participio pasado:** venido

Imperativo: ven (no vengas), venga Ud., vengamos, venid (no vengáis), vengan Uds.

Indicativo				Condicional	Subjuntivo	
Presente	**Imperfecto**	**Pretérito**	**Futuro**	**Presente**	**Presente**	**Imperfecto**
vengo	venía	vine	vendré	vendría	venga	viniera
vienes	venías	viniste	vendrás	vendrías	vengas	vinieras
viene	venía	vino	vendrá	vendría	venga	viniera
venimos	veníamos	vinimos	vendremos	vendríamos	vengamos	viniéramos
venís	veníais	vinisteis	vendréis	vendríais	vengáis	vinierais
vienen	venían	vinieron	vendrán	vendrían	vengan	vinieran
Pres. perfecto	**Pluscuamperf.**		**Futuro perfecto**	**Perfecto**	**Pres. perfecto**	**Pluscuamperf.**
he venido	había venido		habré venido	habría venido	haya venido	hubiera venido

66. VER
(to see)

Verbo irregular (Como **entrever, prever**; Note: 3ª pers. sing. pres. y el
imperativo de **entrever** y **prever** tienen acento: **entrevé, prevé,** etc.)

Participio presente: viendo | **Participio pasado:** visto

Imperativo: ve (no veas), vea Ud., veamos, ved (no veáis), vean Uds.

Indicativo				Condicional	Subjuntivo	
Presente	**Imperfecto**	**Pretérito**	**Futuro**	**Presente**	**Presente**	**Imperfecto**
veo	veía	vi	veré	vería	vea	viera
ves	veías	viste	verás	verías	veas	vieras
ve	veía	vio	verá	vería	vea	viera
vemos	veíamos	vimos	veremos	veríamos	veamos	viéramos
veis	veíais	visteis	veréis	veríais	veáis	vierais
ven	veían	vieron	verán	verían	vean	vieran
Pres. perfecto	**Pluscuamperf.**		**Futuro perfecto**	**Perfecto**	**Pres. perfecto**	**Pluscuamperf.**
he visto	había visto		habré visto	habría visto	haya visto	hubiera visto

67. VIVIR
(to live)

Verbo regular 3ª conjugación

(Como **compartir, decidir, emitir, permitir, resumir**)

Participio presente: viviendo **Participio pasado:** vivido

Imperativo: vive (no vivas), viva Ud., vivamos, vivid (no viváis), vivan Uds.

Indicativo				Condicional	Subjuntivo	
Presente	**Imperfecto**	**Pretérito**	**Futuro**	**Presente**	**Presente**	**Imperfecto**
vivo	vivía	viví	viviré	viviría	viva	viviera
vives	vivías	viviste	vivirás	vivirías	vivas	vivieras
vive	vivía	vivió	vivirá	viviría	viva	viviera
vivimos	vivíamos	vivimos	viviremos	viviríamos	vivamos	viviéramos
vivís	vivíais	vivisteis	viviréis	viviríais	viváis	vivierais
viven	vivían	vivieron	vivirán	vivirían	vivan	vivieran
Pres. perfecto	**Pluscuamperf.**		**Futuro perfecto**	**Perfecto**	**Pres. perfecto**	**Pluscuamperf.**
he vivido	había vivido		habré vivido	habría vivido	haya vivido	hubiera vivido

68. VOLCAR
(to tip over)

Verbo en -AR con cambio de o → ue; c → qu frente a E

(Como **revolcar, trocar**)

Participio presente: volcando **Participio pasado:** volcado

Imperativo: vuelca (no **vuelques**), **vuelque** Ud., volquemos, volcad (no volquéis), **vuelquen** Uds.

Indicativo				Condicional	Subjuntivo	
Presente	**Imperfecto**	**Pretérito**	**Futuro**	**Presente**	**Presente**	**Imperfecto**
vuelco	volcaba	volqué	volcaré	volcaría	**vuelque**	volcara
vuelcas	volcabas	volcaste	volcarás	volcarías	**vuelques**	volcaras
vuelca	volcaba	volcó	volcará	volcaría	**vuelque**	volcara
volcamos	volcábamos	volcamos	volcaremos	volcaríamos	volquemos	volcáramos
volcáis	volcabais	volcasteis	volcaréis	volcaríais	volquéis	volcarais
vuelcan	volcaban	volcaron	volcarán	volcarían	**vuelquen**	volcaran
Pres. perfecto	**Pluscuamperf.**		**Futuro perfecto**	**Perfecto**	**Pres. perfecto**	**Pluscuamperf.**
he volcado	había volcado		habré volcado	habría volcado	haya volcado	hubiera volcado

69. VOLVER
(to return)

Verbo en -ER con cambio de o → ue; participio pasado irregular

(Como **devolver, disolver, envolver, resolver, revolver**)

Participio presente: volviendo **Participio pasado:** **vuelto**

Imperativo: **vuelve** (no **vuelvas**), **vuelva** Ud., volvamos, volved (no volváis), **vuelvan** Uds.

Indicativo				Condicional	Subjuntivo	
Presente	**Imperfecto**	**Pretérito**	**Futuro**	**Presente**	**Presente**	**Imperfecto**
vuelvo	volvía	volví	volveré	volvería	**vuelva**	volviera
vuelves	volvías	volviste	volverás	volverías	**vuelvas**	volvieras
vuelve	volvía	volvió	volverá	volvería	**vuelva**	volviera
volvemos	volvíamos	volvimos	volveremos	volveríamos	volvamos	volviéramos
volvéis	volvíais	volvisteis	volveréis	volveríais	volváis	volvierais
vuelven	volvían	volvieron	volverán	volverían	**vuelvan**	volvieran
Pres. perfecto	**Pluscuamperf.**		**Futuro perfecto**	**Perfecto**	**Pres. perfecto**	**Pluscuamperf.**
he **vuelto**	había **vuelto**		habré **vuelto**	habría **vuelto**	haya **vuelto**	hubiera **vuelto**

VERB TABLES

Index

INDEX

I
N
D
E
X

Answer Key

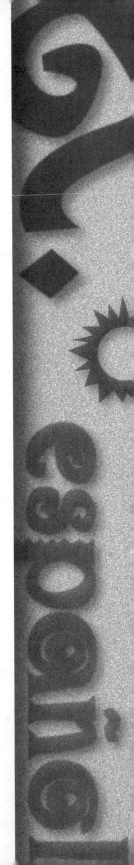

Chapter 1 Overview

A Sentence Components

Ejercicio 1.1

1. **de:** preposición; **en:** preposición; **se:** pronombre personal reflexivo 2. **Cuando:** adverbio; **clásica:** adjetivo calificativo 3. **Ayer:** adverbio de tiempo; **a:** preposición; **amigos:** sustantivo o nombre 4. **Mi:** adjetivo posesivo; **por:** preposición; **las:** artículo definido 5. **Este:** adjetivo demostrativo; **ése:** pronombre demostrativo 6. **tus:** adjetivo posesivo; **míos:** pronombre posesivo 7. **Algunos:** adjetivo indefinido; **otros:** pronombre indefinido 8. **que:** pronombre relativo; **mucho:** adjetivo cuantitativo 9. **que:** conjunción de subordinación; **un:** artículo indefinido 10. **y:** conjunción de coordinación; **pero:** conjunción de coordinación

Ejercicio 1.2

1. **Los:** art. def., masc. pl., acompaña el sustantivo "niños"; **niños:** sustantivo común, masc. pl., sujeto del verbo "cantaron"; **cantaron:** verbo "cantar", 3ª pers. plural del pretérito del indicativo; **una:** art. indef., fem. sing., acompaña el sustantivo "canción"; **canción:** sustantivo común, fem. sing., objeto directo de "cantaron" 2. **Marta:** sustantivo propio, sujeto del verbo "regaló"; **me:** pronombre personal, 1ª pers. sing., objeto indirecto del verbo "regaló"; **regaló:** verbo "regalar", 3ª pers. sing. del pretérito del indicativo; **este:** adjetivo demostrativo, masc. sing., modifica el sustantivo "libro"; **libro:** sustantivo común, masc. sing., objeto directo de "regaló" 3. **Estos:** adjetivo demostrativo, masc. pl., modifica el sustantivo "ejercicios"; **ejercicios:** sustantivo común, masc. pl., sujeto del verbo "son"; **son:** verbo "ser", 3ª pers. pl. del presente del indicativo; **fáciles:** adjetivo calificativo, masc. pl., modifica el sustantivo "ejercicios"

B Verb Structure

Ejercicio 1.3

Estábamos: INDICATIVO imperfecto; **preparando:** PARTICIPIO presente; **anunció:** INDICATIVO pretérito; **se había ganado:** INDICATIVO pluscuamperfecto; **pensara:** SUBJUNTIVO imperfecto; **hacer:** INFINITIVO presente; **gastaría:** CONDICIONAL presente; **preocupes:** IMPERATIVO; **daré:** INDICATIVO futuro; **pongan:** SUBJUNTIVO presente; **necesito:** INDICATIVO presente

C Sentence Structure

Ejercicio 1.4

Para las vacaciones de Navidad, mi papá, mi hermana y yo <u>íbamos</u> a San Blas, y nos <u>quedábamos</u> en un hotel en la playa. La noche de Navidad, cuando todos los demás <u>estaban</u> celebrando en el hotel, nosotros nos <u>íbamos</u> a un lugar ya seleccionado en la playa oscura y <u>hacíamos</u> un fuego con leña que <u>habíamos recogido</u> el día anterior. <u>Llevábamos</u> comida para cocinar en el fuego, y <u>pasábamos</u> la noche allí, oyendo las olas del mar y mirando las estrellas.

Ejercicio 1.5

Necesito / que me ayudes a preparar la cena. (2)   Tendremos cinco invitados a cenar / y quiero / que todo esté perfecto. (3)   ¿Podrías poner la mesa, por favor? (1) Y cuando acabes con eso, / ven a la cocina para ayudarme con la comida. (2) Las verduras para la ensalada están lavadas; / sólo hay que cortarlas y ponerlas en la ensaladera. (2)   Quiero prepararles la receta de pollo / que les gustó tanto la última vez / que vinieron. (3)

Ejercicio 1.6

<u>El invierno está casi terminado.</u> <u>Ya no hace frío</u>, y <u>la nieve se ha transformado en lluvia</u>. Pronto tendremos que empezar a preparar el jardín para que podamos plantar las hortalizas. Estoy tan contento de que la primavera esté en camino porque me gusta el calor. <u>El invierno aquí es tan triste y gris</u>, y me canso de la ropa pesada que tengo que ponerme.

Ejercicio 1.7

El invierno está casi terminado. Ya no hace frío, y la nieve se ha transformado en lluvia. Pronto <u>tendremos que empezar a preparar el jardín</u> para que podamos plantar las hortalizas. <u>Estoy tan contento de</u> que la primavera esté en camino porque me gusta el calor. El invierno aquí es tan triste y gris, y <u>me canso de la ropa pesada</u> que tengo que ponerme.

Ejercicio 1.8

El invierno está casi terminado. Ya no hace frío, y la nieve se ha transformado en lluvia. Pronto tendremos que empezar a preparar el jardín <u>para que podamos plantar las hortalizas</u>. Estoy tan contento de <u>que la primavera esté en camino porque me gusta el calor</u>. El invierno aquí es tan triste y gris, y me canso de la ropa pesada <u>que tengo que ponerme</u>.

Ejercicio 1.9

1. Necesito un libro: cláusula principal; **que describa la revolución mexicana:** cláusula subordinada adjetiva, modifica el sustantivo "libro"   **2. Te prestaré dinero:** cláusula principal; **a condición de que me pagues mañana:** cláusula subordinada adverbial, modifica el verbo "prestaré"   **3. Sé:** cláusula principal; **que no puedes hablar ahora:** cláusula subordinada nominal, objeto directo del verbo "sé"

Ejercicio 1.10

Diagramas:

1. Quiero que veas el libro que conseguí sobre la revolución mexicana.

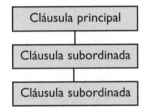

2. Es necesario que los norteamericanos comprendan que estas tierras les pertenecían a los mexicanos originalmente, y que antes eran de los indios que vivieron en ellas por siglos.

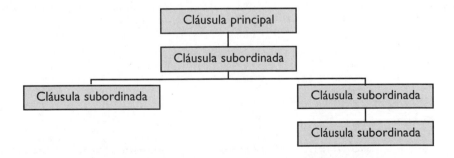

3. Me pidió que le comprara pan y le contesté que no tenía dinero.

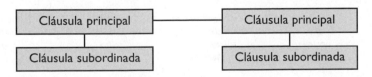

D Accents (Syllabification: Consonants)

Ejercicio 1.11

ra/za	me/ta	vi/sa	ca/llo	se/rra/no
fe/cha	ce/rro	ca/ba/llo	me/ti/che	

Ejercicio 1.12

cam/po	pan/te/ra	án/gu/lo	mus/go	re/fres/co
fan/to/che	man/ti/lla	mer/ca/do	sin/ce/ro	cen/ce/rro
vi/bra	ha/blo	au/to/gra/fiar	re/tra/to	a/dre/na/li/na
re/flo/re/cer	a/glo/me/rar	ne/gro	a/plas/tar	re/pri/mir
de/cli/ve				

Ejercicio 1.13

an/glo/sa/jón	em/pre/sa/rio	cons/tan/te	es/tre/cho	es/plén/di/do
ins/ti/tu/to	ins/pec/ción	ins/tru/men/to	em/bro/llo	trans/mi/tir
res/plan/dor	trans/cri/bir			

Accents (Syllabification: Vowels)

Ejercicio 1.14

re/ca/er	cre/ar	cre/er	ve/o	se/a
ca/os	bo/a	co/ac/tar	co/e/xis/tir	gen/tí/o
frí/o	re/í	ves/tí/a	e/tí/o/pe	a/ta/úd
ra/íz	ví/a	mí/o	re/ú/nan	con/ti/nú/a
re/hú/sa				

Ejercicio 1.15

a/via/dor	ai/re	bie/nes/tar	de/lei/te	mio/pe
oi/ga	res/guar/do	cau/sa	fue/ron	en/deu/dar/se
fui/mos	diur/no	duo/de/no	/Dios/	hue/so
ca/riá/ti/de	re/cién	co/mió	a/guán/ta/te	a/cuér/den/se
can/táis	vol/véis	ói/gan/los	en/jáu/la/lo	

Ejercicio 1.16

ve/í/an	se/áis	ca/í/a/mos	es/quiáis	vi/ví/ais
tra/í/an	ca/e/rí/ais	o/í/ais	en/viéis	cre/í/as
ac/tuéis	ad/qui/rie/rais			

Ejercicio 1.17

a/ho/ra	re/ha/go	a/hí	re/hí/ce	pro/hí/ben
re/hú/sa	a/ho/gar	de/sa/ho/gar	ahu/ma/do	ca/ca/hua/te
al/ca/hue/te	co/he/te	re/hú/yen	so/bre/hu/ma/no	za/he/rir

Ejercicio 1.18

di/vi/da	/las/	si/guien/tes	pa/la/bras	/en/
sí/la/bas	lue/go	ve/a	cuan/do	ne/ce/si/tan
a/cen/tos	por/que	/rey/	rei/na	/voy/
boi/na	bue/no	/bien/		

Accents (Stress)

Ejercicio 1.19

1. camino **(llana)** 2. caminó **(aguda)** 3. caminaba **(llana)** 4. caminábamos **(esdrújula)** 5. caminad **(aguda)** 6. compra **(llana)** 7. compró **(aguda)** 8. compraba **(llana)** 9. comprábamos **(esdrújula)** 10. cómpralo **(esdrújula)** 11. cómpramelo **(sobresdrújula)** 12. español **(aguda)** 13. españoles **(llana)** 14. francés **(aguda)** 15. trances **(llana)** 16. encéstalo **(esdrújula)**

Ejercicio 1.20

1. prestó 2. enterrar 3. preparad 4. desperté 5. dividir 6. farol 7. piedad 8. pedí 9. peor 10. caimán 11. cocinar 12. imparcial 13. cajón 14. finlandés 15. trajín 16. temblor 17. cristal 18. riñón

Ejercicio 1.21

1. lápiz 2. llamas 3. llaman 4. pluma 5. hablaron 6. españoles 7. dioses 8. día 9. deme 10. españolita 11. peruano 12. consigo 13. traje 14. examen 15. carácter 16. lunes 17. labio 18. infértil

Ejercicio 1.22

1. mátalo 2. regálamelo 3. cállense 4. estúpido 5. párpado 6. capítulo 7. prójimo 8. bájame 9. ánimo 10. cáscara 11. década 12. éxito 13. pájaro 14. áspero 15. húngaro 16. vínculo 17. máquina 18. píldora

Ejercicio 1.23

1. rápidamente 2. fácilmente 3. lentamente 4. difícilmente 5. piadosamente 6. brillantemente 7. fríamente 8. despiadadamente 9. secamente 10. felizmente 11. fijamente 12. cálidamente 13. científicamente 14. misericordiosamente 15. solamente *(Notice that the adverb* solamente *is formed with the adjective* sola, *which has no accent. There is another adverb,* sólo *[only], synonymous with* solamente, *and not to be confused with the adjective* solo *[alone].)* 16. finalmente 17. gravemente 18. próximamente

Ejercicio 1.24

1. A él le va bien. 2. Di que el rey te lo dio. 3. Vio a Dios. 4. El **té** no me da tos. 5. No sé si se fue. 6. **Tú** no le des. 7. Tu voz se te va. 8. Sin ti no se lo da. 9. No le **dé** la fe. 10. Yo **sí** se la di. 11. A ti te doy lo que hay. 12. No hay más miel por **mí**.

Ejercicio 1.25

1. Aun los ricos necesitan amor. 2. Los niños aún no han comido. 3. Estoy solo. 4. Sólo me siento solo cuando ando mal acompañado. 5. Pásame esa llave, por favor. 6. No quiero esta fruta, prefiero ésa. (The accent on *ésa* is optional.) 7. Por eso no quiso ir con nosotros. 8. Me gustaría comprarme ese terreno. 9. ¡Qué buena suerte tienes! 10. ¡Cómo canta!

Ejercicio 1.26

1. Prefiero **que** no llueva. 2. ¿**Qué** dijiste? 3. No sé **qué** dije. 4. Creo **que** dije **que** preferiría **que** no lloviera. 5. ¡**Qué** locura! 6. [2 posibilidades] Dime **qué** crees. *(Tell me what you believe.)* Dime **que** crees. *(Tell me that you believe.)* 7. El día **que** no llueva aquí, no sabremos **qué** hacer. 8. Haremos lo **que** ustedes quieran. 9. La última vez **que** vinieron, nos costó mucho decidir **qué** cuarto darles. 10. ¡**Que** duerman en el piso!

Ejercicio 1.27

1. Te llamé **porque** tengo noticias. 2. ¿**Por qué** no me llamaste antes? 3. No te puedo decir **por qué**: ¡es un secreto! 4. El asesino no pudo explicar **por qué** había matado al policía. *(The murderer was not able to explain **why** he had killed the policeman.)* 5. El asesino no lo pudo explicar **porque** había matado al policía. *(The murderer was not able to explain it **because** he had killed the policeman.)* 6. Yo creo que lo hizo **porque** tenía miedo. 7. ¿**Tú** matarías a alguien simplemente **porque** tienes miedo? 8. ¿**Por qué** no? 9. ¡**Porque** no se debe matar a nadie! 10. No sé **por qué** se fue. 11. Se fue **porque** no le hacías caso.

Ejercicio 1.28

1. Como no tengo hambre, no **como**. **2.** ¿**Cómo** puedes decir eso? **3.** Necesitas pensar **como** yo para comprenderme. **4.** Muéstrame **cómo** comes con palillos. *(Show me how you eat with chopsticks.)* **5.** ¡**Cómo** comes! *(How you eat! Boy, do you ever eat!)* **6.** ¿**Cómo como** ? *(How do I eat?)* **7. Como como como**. *(I eat the way I eat.)* **8.** Ella se viste **como** yo. **9.** Es un libro **como** los demás. **10.** Si baila **como** canta, ha de ser una maravilla.

Ejercicio 1.29

1. ¿**Cuánto** cuesta este cuarto? **2.** No sé **cuánto** cuesta. **3.** ¿**Cuántos** hermanos tienes? **4.** Me pregunto **cuántos** años tiene esa mujer. **5.** Nadie sabe **cuántas** veces se repetirá. **6.** Le di **cuanto** dinero tenía al ladrón. **7.** No sabe **cuánto** me arrepentí de darle mi dinero. **8.** La profesora le dará **cuanta** información tenga.

Ejercicio 1.30

1. ¿**Dónde** vives? **2.** Vivo **donde** viven mis padres. **3.** No sé **dónde** vive mi amiga. **4.** Me dijo **dónde** vivía, pero se me olvidó. **5.** Apunté su dirección en la libreta **donde** tengo todas las direcciones. **6.** No sé **dónde** puse la libreta. **7.** ¿No estará **donde** siempre la pones?

Ejercicio 1.31

1. Llegarán **cuando** estemos en la finca. **2.** ¿**Cuándo** llegas? **3.** No me dijo **cuándo** iban a llegar. **4. Cuando** lleguen, les serviremos cerveza. **5.** ¿Nos escondemos **cuando** los veamos llegar? **6. Cuando** me gradúe, iré al Caribe. **7.** ¿ **...cuando** te gradúes? *(... when you graduate?)* **8.** ¿**Cuándo** te gradúas? *(When do you graduate?)*

Ejercicio 1.32

1. ¿**Quién** se llevó mi paraguas? **2.** No sé **quién** se lo llevó. **3.** El amigo con **quien** vino Marieta tenía paraguas. **4.** ¿Te dijo **quién** era el chico con **quien** estaba? **5.** No me dijo con **quién** había venido. **6.** Dime con **quién** andas y te diré **quién** eres.

Accents (Review)

Ejercicio 1.33

ARMANDO: ¿Está Juan?

MIGUEL: Creo que fue al cine, y no s**é** cuándo va a regresar. ¿Para qu**é** lo quieres?

ARMANDO: Quiero pedirle prestado un libro para mi clase de español.

MIGUEL: ¿Sabes qu**é** libro es?

ARMANDO: Sí. Es uno que tiene la portada negra.

MIGUEL: Yo s**é** d**ó**nde lo tiene, pero no estoy seguro si te lo podría prestar.

ARMANDO: A m**í** me dijo que no lo necesitaba este semestre.

MIGUEL: Si t**ú** te lo llevas, y **é**l lo necesita, yo voy a sentirme muy mal. ¿Por qu**é** no te tomas una taza de t**é**, y esperas a que regrese Juan?

ARMANDO: Bueno. Mientras espero, pr**é**stame el libro para mirarlo, por favor.

MIGUEL: Voy a buscarlo. [...] ¿Es **é**ste*, verdad?

ARMANDO: No, **é**se* no. Es el otro, el de gramática. Tiene casi la misma portada, pero un t**í**tulo diferente.

MIGUEL: A ver si lo encuentro; esp**é**rame. [...] Aquí lo tienes.

ARMANDO: Gracias.

*The accents on these demonstrative pronouns are optional.

Ejercicio 1.34

Temas de ensayo.

Chapter 2 Nouns and Noun Determiners

A Nouns and Their Equivalents (Introduction)

Ejercicio 2.1

A noun is a part of a sentence (a word) which can be the subject of a verb. It can also be a direct or an indirect object, or an object of a preposition. Other words which behave this way are pronouns, infinitives, and any nominalized word. A nominalized word is one which is used as if it were a noun. For example, "red" is an adjective, but in the sentence, "The red of those flowers was astonishing," "red" is being used as a noun. In other words, it has been converted from an adjective to a noun, or nominalized.

Ejercicio 2.2

1. —¿Cuál de estos libros es el mío? —Ése es el tuyo. 2. Prefiero caminar en la mañana. 3. Los altos y los rubios siempre sobresalen aquí. 4. En el mundo hispano, los mayores viven con su familia. 5. Los decentes pierden a menudo. 6. El bueno y el malo en esta película se parecen. 7. Lo bueno y lo malo son enemigos. 8. Lo extraño es el color. 9. Ese extranjero habla español. 10. A veces lo extranjero asusta porque es diferente. 11. En esta foto, el del traje gris es mi padre, el del sombrero es mi hermano, y los de arriba son mis primos. (o: las de arriba/primas)

Nouns and Their Equivalents (Nouns: Gender and Number)

Ejercicio 2.3

el amanecer; el amor; la vida; la cena; la sal; la miel; el arroz; el poema; el metal; del barandal; el auto; el barro; el ataúd; los días; la cama; la casa; la mañana; el periódico; el crucigrama; los problemas; la capital; el carril; la catedral; la cárcel; el césped; las ramas; la costumbre; la propiedad; la televisión; los dramas; las tramas; las telenovelas; los programas; el hotel; los huéspedes; el español; el idioma; la foto; la cara; del juez; la libertad; al asesino; la mano; el papel; la imagen; la luz; la piel; la rabia; el lunes; la corte; el lápiz; del ruido; la señal; del radar; la corrupción; el sistema; la moto; el tranvía; el mapa; la ciudad; la distancia; el poder; del mal; la imposibilidad; la moral; la justicia; el viaje; los Pirineos

Ejercicio 2.4

el hombre—la mujer; el estudiante—la estudiante; el joven—la joven; el actor—la actriz; el modelo—la modelo; el turista—la turista; el rey—la reina; el policía—la policía, el comunista—la comunista; el toro—la vaca

Ejercicio 2.5

1. el policía / la policía: el masculino es el hombre o el individuo; el femenino es el departamento, o una mujer 2. el papa / la papa: el masculino es el de Roma; el femenino es lo que se come 3. el guía / la guía: el masculino es el hombre que lleva a los turistas de un lugar a otro y les habla de lo que ven; el femenino es un libro con información, o una mujer que hace el papel de dirigir e instruir a los turistas 4. el cura / la cura: el masculino es el de la iglesia; el femenino es la solución a una enfermedad

Nouns and Their Equivalents (Personal A)

Ejercicio 2.6

1. [Ø] 2. a 3. a 4. A 5. [Ø] 6. [Ø] 7. [Ø] 8. a 9. [Ø] 10. a 11. A 12. a 13. a 14. [Ø]

Ejercicio 2.7

1. Miro el libro, el jardín, a mi hermanito, tus ojos, la pizarra, la película, a los vecinos, el periódico, el espejo. 2. No oye el teléfono, a Juan, a mi gato, a nadie, la tarea, al profesor, la explosión, tu voz, a los niños en la calle, nada. 3. Jorge tiene un apartamento, un hermano, una computadora, dos coches, a su abuelo en un asilo de ancianos. 4. Quiero dinero, amigos, felicidad, amor, comida, a mis padres, a mi familia, vivir bien. 5. Espera mi llamada, la alarma, a Luis, su respuesta, a tus hermanos, a tu padre, a alguien, ¿A quién espera? ¿Qué espera? 6. Vio una casa, a una amiga, la pantalla, el reloj, a mi

perro, la carta, **a** la gente que quería, gente. **7.** Buscaban respuestas, el banco, una receta, **a** sus hijos, empleados, algo, **a** sus gatitos, **a** alguien, ¿**A** quién buscaban?, ¿Qué buscaban?

Ejercicio 2.8

(Los objetos directos están en bastardilla.)

Miró *el espejo* y luego miró *a su novio* afuera en el jardín. Luego verificó *su maquillaje* y *su peinado*, y admiró *su vestido*. Tenía *dos hermanas* que se habían casado antes que ella. Tenía *a su madre* esperando afuera mientras pasaba *un último momento* sola. Quería *a Rodolfo*. Nunca había conocido *a nadie* como él. Quería *esta boda*, pero tenía miedo. No quería perder *su juventud*. No quería perder *a su familia*. De repente, oyó *su nombre*. Oyó *a su madre*. Y recordó *a su madre* y *a su padre* y *su felicidad*. Y se sintió lista.

Noun Determiners (Articles: Definite Articles)

Ejercicio 2.9

la avioneta, la atracción, la avenida, el agua, la alarma, el alma, el ama, el águila, la aguja, la autonomía, el aula, la avicultura, el ave, la habitación, la habichuela, el hacha, la hamburguesa, el hambre, la hartura, las aguas, las alarmas, las almas, las hambres

Ejercicio 2.10

1. La vida debe disfrutarse. **2. El** señor Ruiz dice que **el** chocolate es malo para **la** salud, pero **[Ø]** doña Luisa sabe que él come **[Ø]** chocolate todos los días. **3.** —**[Ø]** Señorita Guzmán, ¿le gusta **el** chocolate? **4.** Ayer compramos **[Ø]** verduras, pero no tenían **las** verduras que tú pediste. **5. El** inglés es más difícil que **el** español. **6.** Hablo **[Ø]** español, pero sueño en **[Ø]** inglés. **7.** Mi clase de **[Ø]** español es la más divertida de todas. **8.** Aprendí **[Ø] el** español cuando tenía seis años. **9.** A mi padre le costó trabajo aprender **el** español. **10.** Salieron temprano de **la** escuela y, como su padre había salido de **la** cárcel ese día, fueron a **la** iglesia a dar gracias. **11.** Salimos de **[Ø]** clase y fuimos directamente a **[Ø]** casa porque teníamos que vestirnos para llegar a **[Ø]** misa a tiempo. **12. El** miércoles vamos a tener una prueba. **13.** ¡Hasta **el** jueves! **14.** Hoy es **[Ø]** viernes.

Ejercicio 2.11

1. La felicidad se encuentra en el amor. **2.** La familia y los amigos son la base de una buena vida. **3.** Hablo español. Leo fácilmente el francés. **4.** Vamos a casa. **5.** ¡Hasta el lunes! **6.** La gente que necesita a la gente tiene suerte. **7.** Llegaba gente constantemente. **8.** Las noticias en los periódicos son sobre todo malas noticias. **9.** Profesor López, hoy llegaron noticias de su colega el profesor Gómez. **10.** Me lavé las manos. **11.** Alzó la mano. **12.** Lo metieron en la cárcel. **13.** El viernes no hay clase. **14.** El pollo es para el martes.

Noun Determiners (Articles: Indefinite Articles)

Ejercicio 2.12

1. Jorge es **[Ø]** arquitecto. **2.** Carlitos es **[Ø]** argentino. **3.** Rafael es **un** hombre interesante. **4.** Es **un** cantante mexicano. **5.** Georgina es **una** protestante muy severa. **6.** ¡Qué **[Ø]** dilema! **7.** ¡Qué **[Ø]** lindo día! **8.** Esa viejita acaba de cumplir **[Ø]** cien años. **9.** Vamos a discutir **[Ø]** otro tema ahora. **10.** Tomaría **[Ø]** mil años corregir el daño que se ha hecho. Lo dudo—yo creo que tomaría **un** millón. **11.** Dentro de **[Ø]** media hora nos iremos. **12.** No tengo **[Ø]** bicicleta. **13.** Ese pobre chico no tiene ni **un** amigo. **14.** Se fue sin **[Ø]** chaqueta.

Ejercicio 2.13

Margarita era puertorriqueña. Era estudiante en la Universidad de Puerto Rico. Era una estudiante aplicada, y tenía cierto estilo en su manera de expresarse que sus profesores consideraban original. Una vez ganó un premio de cien dólares por un ensayo analítico. Escribió cien palabras sobre un tema y con tres páginas y media de referencias. Escribía sin computadora, ni siquiera tenía máquina de escribir. ¡Qué escritora! Nadie había visto tal cosa antes. No ha habido otro escritor de su calidad desde que se graduó.

Noun Determiners (Adjectives: Demonstrative Adjectives)

Ejercicio 2.14

1. ¿De quién es **este / ese / aquel** automóvil?   2. ¿Para quién son **estos / esos / aquellos** mensajes?   3. ¿Por qué viajan por **estas / esas / aquellas** carreteras?   4. ¿Te acuerdas de **esta / esa / aquella** mañana?   5. ¿Por qué no paramos en **esta / esa / aquella** gasolinera?   6. **Este / Ese / Aquel** mapa no nos sirve para nada.   7. ¿Ves **esas / aquellas** montañas? No paremos hasta llegar allá.

Ejercicio 2.15

1. ¿Son nuevos esos libros?   2. Estas manzanas son para ti.   3. Esa clase no cubre estos temas.   4. Estos estudiantes son buenísimos.   5. Ese hombre es un amigo.   6. Aquellos días son inolvidables.

Noun Determiners (Adjectives: Possessive Adjectives)

Ejercicio 2.16

1. Ésa es **mi / tu / su / nuestra / vuestra** casa.   2. **Tu / Su / Nuestro / Vuestro** coche es más económico que el mío.   3. **Mis / Tus / Sus / Nuestros / Vuestros** problemas no se pueden resolver en un día.   4. **Tus / Sus / Nuestras / Vuestras** manos son más grandes que las mías.   5. ¿Tienes las llaves **mías / tuyas / suyas / nuestras / vuestras** ahí?   6. ¿Cuántos amigos **míos / tuyos / suyos / nuestros / vuestros** vienen?   7. Espero que **mi / tu / su / nuestra / vuestra** familia haya pasado un fin de semana fantástico.

Ejercicio 2.17

1. Hoy vienen mis primos.   2. ¿Llamó tu hermano hoy?   3. Su brazo está hinchado.   4. Sus libros están mojados.   5. Me dio su anillo.   6. Es una amiga mía.   7. Esta pluma es mía.

Noun Determiners (Adjectives: Forms of Descriptive Adjectives)

Ejercicio 2.18

1. la casa **verde**   2. la casa **blanca**   3. la casa **azul**   4. el político **respetable**   5. el político **izquierdista**   6. el político **prometedor**   7. la profesora **severa**   8. la maestra **comunista**   9. los niños **felices**   10. los vecinos **gritones**

Noun Determiners (Adjectives: Position of Descriptive Adjectives)

Ejercicio 2.19

1. La **primera** vez que fui a Madrid fue en 1992.   2. ¡**Muchas** gracias!   3. Luisito no tiene **tanto** dinero.   4. Somos **medios** hermanos.   5. Tráeme **otro** cuchillo, por favor. (Fíjese en la omisión obligatoria del artículo indefinido "un" por el uso de "otro".)

1. The first time I went to Madrid was in 1992.   2. Thank you very much!   3. Luis doesn't have that much money.   4. We are half brothers.   5. Bring me another knife, please.

Ejercicio 2.20

1. Ese hombre vende muebles **antiguos**. [*old, not previous*]   2. La gente **pobre** no siempre es infeliz. [*penniless, not unfortunate—the context says so*]   3. A esa **pobre** millonaria la persiguen los periodistas. [*unfortunate; she could not be penniless by definition*]   4. Te presento a Guzmán, un **viejo** amigo; hoy es su cumpleaños—cumple dieciocho años. [*long-time friend; he couldn't be old at 18*]   5. Desde que construyeron el **nuevo** garaje / garaje **nuevo**, ya no usan el viejo. [*before the noun: recent, latest; after the noun, just constructed. In this sentence, either one could be accurate.*]   6. Te presento a mi **nuevo** vecino. [*newest, latest*]   7. Mi **linda** esposa está de viaje. [*only one wife: no contrast*]   8. Cornell es una **gran** universidad / universidad **grande**. [*before: great; after: large*]   9. Charlie Chaplin fue un **gran** actor. [*great, not large*]   10. En esta tina, el agua **caliente** se abre aquí. [*contrast with the cold water*]   11. Subimos a la **alta** torre / torre **alta** de la biblioteca. [*before: there is only one tower, and it is high—no contrast. after: there is more than one, and one of them is higher*

than the rest—contrast]   **12.** Está enamorado de tu **bella** hermana / hermana **bella.** [before: there is only one sister, and she is beautiful—no contrast; after: there are other sisters, but only one beautiful one—contrast]   **13.** Cruzaron el **ancho** río Amazonas. [there is only one, and it is wide—no contrast]   **14.** Visitaron la **impresionante** catedral de Gaudí. [only one—no contrast]   **15.** Ésta es la **única** oportunidad que tendremos. [only, not unique]   **16.** Me gustan las casas **blancas.** [contrast with the rest, restrictive]   **17.** Las **blancas** nubes flotaban como algodón por el valle. [no contrast; merely painting an inherent characteristic]   **18.** Era un cielo extraño: abajo había nubes **blancas,** y arriba nubes **negras.** [contrast]   **19.** Esa película es de un director **español.** [nationality always follows its noun]   **20.** Se le veía un **cierto** aire de inseguridad. [indeterminate]   **21.** Sabían que eran acusaciones **ciertas.** [true]   **22.** Tenía la **rara** capacidad de hacer que todos se sintieran a gusto. [rare]   **23.** Era un sonido **raro** que nadie podía identificar. [strange]   **24.** Te voy a decir la **pura** verdad. [fixed order]   **25.** Es un disco de **alta** fidelidad. [fixed order]   **26.** Querían estar en Sevilla para la Semana **Santa.** [fixed order]   **27.** La mejor solución es usar nuestro sentido **común.** [fixed order]

Ejercicio 2.21

1. We went to different (several) places. We went to places which were different (original).   **2.** He is a good politician (professionally). He is an ethical politician.   **3.** That car caused me nothing but problems. He looks for the pure life (virtuous, unsoiled).   **4.** We have rare (few and far between) moments of satisfaction. It's a strange dish.   **5.** It took me half an hour. That used to be done in the Middle Ages.   **6.** It's the only problem. It's a unique problem.

Noun Determiners (Adjectives: Comparisons)

Ejercicio 2.22

1. Beto come más ruidosamente **que** nadie.   **2.** Sabina es más lista **que** Raúl.   **3.** Elsa gana menos dinero **que** tú.   **4.** Hay más **de** veinte árboles aquí.   **5.** Me diste menos **de** la mitad.   **6.** Mi bicicleta es mejor **que** la tuya.   **7.** Hace más frío **de lo que** esperaba.   **8.** Llovió menos **de lo que** creíamos.   **9.** Nunca ganaré tanto dinero **como** Héctor.   **10.** Ese coche es **tan** bello como éste.   **11.** Esa niña grita más **que** las demás.   **12.** Había menos **de** cinco jugadores en la cancha.   **13.** Ese examen no fue tan fácil **como** los otros.   **14.** Compré más servilletas **de las que** necesitábamos.   **15.** Hay más servilletas **que** invitados.   **16.** Tengo menos trabajo **del que** esperaba.   **17.** Elvira trabaja **tanto** como su hermano, pero no gana **tanto** dinero como él. Y a mí me parece que él no es **tan** listo como ella.

Ejercicio 2.23

(Este ejercicio tiene una infinidad de respuestas posibles. Aquí les ofrecemos unos modelos.)

1. España y México. España queda más lejos que México. Hay menos mexicanos en España que en México. En España se come tan bien como en México.
2. Los Estados Unidos e Hispanoamérica. Los Estados Unidos son más poderosos que Hispanoamérica. Hay menos gente en los Estados Unidos que en Hispanoamérica. Hay tanto patriotismo en los Estados Unidos como en Hispanoamérica.
3. Las culturas hispanas y las culturas anglosajonas. Las culturas hispanas son más expresivas que las anglosajonas. Hay menos fiestas en las culturas anglosajonas que en las hispanas. Hay tantas tradiciones en las culturas hispanas como en las anglosajonas.
4. El amor y el odio. Si hubiera más amor que odio en el mundo tendríamos paz mundial. El amor puede durar menos que el odio. El amor es una emoción tan fuerte como el odio.
5. La televisión y el cine. La televisión es más accesible que el cine. La televisión cuesta menos que el cine. Me gusta tanto la televisión como el cine.
6. La escuela y la universidad. La escuela fue más fácil que la universidad. En la universidad tengo menos clases que en la escuela. Tengo tantos amigos en la universidad como en la escuela.
7. Los niños y los adultos. Los niños pueden ser más listos que los adultos. Los adultos son menos flexibles que los niños. Los niños tienen tantos intereses como los adultos.

Chapter 2 Review

Ejercicio 2.24

Hace como veinte años yo fui a estudiar a **los** Estados Unidos para obtener **un** bachillerato en **una** universidad allá. **El** primer año lo pasé con muchísimos contratiempos causados por **el** inglés, idioma que en **aquel** entonces yo casi no hablaba y mucho menos comprendía. Tuve que tomar **un** examen para demostrar cuánto inglés sabía, y qué clases necesitaba tomar para poder comprender **las** conferencias y hacer todos **los** trabajos escritos durante **mis** futuros estudios en **esa / aquella** universidad. Se me hizo muy difícil comprender **aquellas** conferencias de biología, dadas en **un** enorme salón con otros cientos de estudiantes que, al igual que yo, estaban en **su** primer año. Recuerdo que casi no podíamos ver **al** profesor si no teníamos **la** suerte de sentarnos hacia **el** frente del salón, cosa que yo siempre trataba de hacer pues se me facilitaba así entender mejor lo que él decía.

Algunos de mis recuerdos más gratos de **ese primer año** fueron de **mis nuevos amigos** allá, por medio de los cuales pude comprender y aprender un poco sobre **la cultura de ese país** donde iba a vivir durante **tanto tiempo.** No es por nada, pero de verdad que la mía fue **una experiencia única** comparada con **la** de muchos que **estaban mejor preparados que yo.** Imagínate **ese tipo** de estudiante que se la pasa perdiendo el tiempo, yendo a fiestas cada semana, y dejando **su** trabajo para último minuto, **ese** mismo que se queja **más fuertemente que nadie.** En realidad puedo decir que aproveché **mi** tiempo en Estados Unidos. El último año ya **el inglés** era parte de **mi vida diaria,** podía hacer todos los trabajos **sin problema** y salí **tan bien como mis amigos** en todas las clases que tomé.

¿Qué fue **lo mejor** de haber estudiado allá? Creo que fue el haber conocido **otra cultura** y el haber compartido **la mía** con **muchos otros estudiantes extranjeros** cuyos intereses y experiencias eran a veces diferentes y otras similares a los míos. **Lo** bueno fue haber visto en persona **el gran crisol** de razas y culturas en un ámbito estudiantil y con todos nosotros llenos de esperanzas para **un mejor futuro internacional.** Por eso, hija mía, yo estoy contentísima de **tu** interés en estudiar **en el extranjero** y apoyo tu decisión.

Ejercicio 2.25

Temas de ensayo.

Chapter 3 Pronouns

Personal Pronouns (Definitions)

Ejercicio 3.1

A pronoun is a word that replaces a noun and has the same function as a noun (subject, direct object, object of preposition, indirect object). Its relationship to the noun is that it replaces it, usually to avoid repetition. There are different pronouns: personal, demonstrative, possessive, interrogative, indefinite, negative, and relative.

Personal Pronouns (Subject Pronouns)

Ejercicio 3.2

1. —¿Cuándo salieron? —Salimos a las siete.   2. —¿Quién está ahí? —Soy yo.   3. —¿Qué hacen? —Están comiendo.
4. Mis vecinos sacaron la basura, pero yo no me acordé.   5. ¿Tendrías tiempo de ayudarme?   6. —¿Por qué no está Luis?
—Está enfermo.

Ejercicio 3.3

1. Compré un libro.   2. Está en el cuarto de José.   3. Vamos a estudiar juntos esta tarde.   4. Tienes que empezar tus tareas para mañana.   5. Son largas.   6. Sé que tú estudiaste, pero yo no he terminado todavía.   7. María está aquí; quiere hablar contigo.

Ejercicio 3.4

Mike y Luisa han sido novios desde hace ya cinco años. ~~Ellos~~ se quieren mucho y ~~ellos~~ se van a casar. **Él** tiene seis años más que ella, pero **ella** parece más madura que él. Desde niña **ella** había soñado en una boda maravillosa, con toda su familia y sus amigos presentes. Pero **él** no quiere lo mismo que ella: prefiere una boda muy privada, en que sólo estén ellos dos, y dos testigos.

Personal Pronouns (Direct Object Pronouns)

Ejercicio 3.5

1. Tráigan**la**. 2. Quiero guardar**la**. **La** quiero guardar. 3. **La** he guardado. 4. Están cocinándo**la**. **La** están cocinando. 5. **La** compramos. 6. No **la** toques.

Ejercicio 3.6

1. **La** veo por esta ventana. 2. **Las** llevé al banco. 3. No **la** conocen. 4. Josefina es un poco extraña; nadie **la** entiende. 5. Los vecinos **la** miraban mientras barría la calle. 6. El vendedor **la** llamó. 7. **La** oían cantar. 8. **La** oían cantar**la**. 9. **La** buscaron. 10. **La** encontraron. 11. **La** invitaron al baile. 12. **La** extraño.

Ejercicio 3.7

*(The **lo** and **los** forms have been used only for direct objects; note that in **leísta** dialects in Spain, **le** would be used for human masculine direct objects.)*

1. **Lo** veo por esta ventana. 2. **Los** llevé al banco. 3. No **lo** conocen. 4. Roberto es un poco extraño; nadie **lo** entiende. 5. Los vecinos **lo** miraban mientras barría la calle. 6. El vendedor **lo** llamó. 7. **Lo** oían cantar. 8. **Lo** oían cantar**la**. 9. **Lo** buscaron. 10. **Lo** encontraron. 11. **Lo** invitaron al baile. 12. **Lo** extraño.

Ejercicio 3.8

Tengo la costumbre de observar a mis vecinos. Ayer **los** vi ~~a mis vecinos~~ llegar en su coche: habían comprado plantas nuevas; **las** sacaron ~~las plantas~~ del coche y **las** dejaron ~~las plantas~~ en la tierra cerca de la casa porque no podían ponerse de acuerdo sobre dónde poner**las** ~~las plantas~~. Ella quería meter**las** ~~las plantas~~ en la casa. Él le dijo que **las** prefería ~~las plantas~~ afuera. Ella dijo que el frío de la noche iba a matar**las** ~~las plantas~~, y él le contestó que era necesario acostumbrar**las** ~~las plantas~~ a los cambios de temperatura. La situación era típica, y terminó como siempre: ella **lo** miró mal ~~a su marido~~ y se fue, y él se encogió de hombros y siguió con lo que hacía como si nada. Después de una hora ella **lo** llamó ~~a su marido~~ para que entrara a cenar. Yo podía oír sus risas mientras platicaban durante la cena.

Personal Pronouns (Direct and Indirect Object Pronouns)

Ejercicio 3.9

1. Los turistas **los** miraban. 2. El policía **le** dijo que se tenía que ir. 3. **Se los** regaló. 4. **Se lo** mandaron. 5. El abuelo **se lo** contó. 6. **Se la** hicieron. 7. El padre **se la** quitó. 8. Mi amigo **se lo** pidió.

Ejercicio 3.10

1. **Le** gané. 2. **Lo** gané. 3. **Le** robaron. 4. **Lo** robaron. 5. **Le** creemos. 6. **Lo** creemos. 7. **Le** pegaron. 8. **Lo** pegaron. 9. **Le** pagué. 10. **La** pagué.

Ejercicio 3.11

1. Luisa es una amiga mía que va a estudiar a España durante un año. **La** conozco desde hace cuatro años. **La** vi ayer y **le** hablé de su año en el extranjero; **le** prometí que **le** escribiría durante su ausencia.
2. El hijo de la señora Ruiz no llegó a su casa en toda la noche. La señora Ruiz **lo** llamó a su teléfono celular y **le** preguntó por qué no **le** había hablado de sus planes; **lo** regañó por su irresponsabilidad; él **le** pidió que **lo** perdonara.
3. Su adorado perrito nuevo había desaparecido. Habían estado buscándo**lo** desde hacía varias horas cuando por fin **lo** oyeron llorando, y **lo** encontraron medio enterrado en el barro; **lo** sacaron y **lo** llevaron a casa donde **le** dieron un baño.

Ejercicio 3.12

Conocí a Elena el primer día que llegué a la universidad, cuando **la** vi en el cuarto que íbamos a compartir como compañeras de cuarto. **La** saludé y **le** dije que estaba contenta de conocer**la**. Ella **me** abrazó y **me** contó con mucho entusiasmo sus planes para la universidad. Poco a poco llegué a conocer**la** y cada vez **la** encontraba más simpática. Le gustaban las mismas cosas que **a mí**, teníamos el mismo horario para todo, y nunca nos peleamos. Hasta el día en que entró en nuestra vida Julio. Yo **lo** vi primero, un día de frío intenso, en la cafetería, y me enamoré a primera vista. **Le** conté **a ella** de mi experiencia, y lo único que ella quería era conocer**lo**, supuestamente por mi bien, para animarme más. Pues no fue así: cuando ella **lo** vio por primera vez, ella **lo** quiso también, y él parecía querer**la a ella** de la misma manera. Yo me quedé congelada, mirándo**la a ella** primero, luego **a él**, en unos segundos que parecieron durar una eternidad. Después, **le** dije **a ella** que yo **lo** había visto primero, y que ella no tenía el derecho de quitár**me**lo. Como yo nunca **le** había dicho **a él** lo que sentía, sin embargo, y ellos dos evidentemente compartían el mismo sentimiento de amor, yo ya había perdido. Y lo sabía. Ahora, después de muchos años, **los** quiero a los dos, y **los** visito **a ellos** y a su familia cada vez que puedo: están casados y tienen cuatro hijos. Yo nunca me casé, y así me gusta.

Personal Pronouns (Required Repetitive Object Pronouns)

Ejercicio 3.13

1. Ø 2. lo 3. Ø 4. lo 5. Ø 6. Ø 7. Ø 8. lo 9. Ø 10. los 11. le 12. le 13. se lo 14. nos 15. Ø

Personal Pronouns (Order of Object Pronouns When Combined)

Ejercicio 3.14

1. Sí, **me los** dio. 2. Sí, **se la** enseñé. 3. Sí, **me la** contó. 4. Sí, **se lo** dije. 5. Sí, **nos las** limpiamos. 6. Sí, **nos la** enviaron.

Personal Pronouns (Position of Object Pronouns)

Ejercicio 3.15

1. Sí, **la** están preparando. OR: Sí, están preparándo**la**. 2. Sí, **se la** pudieron vender. OR: Sí, pudieron vendér**sela**. 3. Sí, **se los** va a hacer. OR: Sí, va a hacér**selos**. 4. Sí, **se lo** he mandado. 5. Sí, está pintada. OR: Sí, **lo** está. 6. Sí, me gustó. 7. Sí, **se las** dio. 8. Sí, se habla.

Personal Pronouns (Prepositional Object Pronouns)

Ejercicio 3.16

1. Esto es para ti. 2. Según ella, estaba mal. 3. Lo estaban mirando. OR: Estaban mirándolo. 4. Lo estaban buscando. OR: Estaban buscándolo. 5. Esto es entre él y yo. 6. Sus hijos son como ella. 7. Estoy hablando de ti. 8. Canta conmigo. 9. Cantaré con él. 10. Se lo llevó consigo.

Personal Pronouns (Review 1)

Ejercicio 3.17

(Los pronombres excesivos están tachados, y los opcionales están entre paréntesis.)

Para Navidad (yo) siempre he querido ir a la playa, porque desde niña mi padre me acostumbró ~~a mí~~ a celebrar este día lejos de la sociedad materialista, en un rito de comunión con la naturaleza y el universo. Mi hermana, mi padre y yo, ~~nosotros~~ íbamos a quedarnos una semana en la playa, y desde el día en que ~~nosotros~~ llegábamos, ~~nosotros~~ empezábamos a juntar leña en un lugar que mi padre escogía en la playa, donde hubiera un enorme tronco para descansar. ~~Nosotros~~ Juntábamos leña por toda la playa cada día antes de la Nochebuena, y esa noche, cuando el resto de la gente en el hotel estaba celebrando con grandes banquetes y bailes, nosotros salíamos a escondidas por detrás, ~~nosotros~~ íbamos en la oscuridad a encontrar nuestro sitio escogido, y allí ~~nosotros~~ nos instalábamos para pasar la noche en la playa. ~~Nosotros~~ Encendíamos la hoguera con la leña que ~~nosotros~~ habíamos juntado, y ~~nosotros~~ nos recargábamos contra el tronco a mirar el cielo y el mar. En el cielo brillaban las estrellas, y en el mar se veían las luces que echaban unos pececitos minúsculos. Era un espectáculo realmente impresionante. Las olas producían un ritmo que nos calmaba ~~a nosotros~~. De vez en cuando mi padre rompía el silencio, y ~~él~~ nos contaba ~~a nosotros~~ de sus experiencias como vaquero, o ~~él~~ nos recitaba a nosotros uno de sus poemas, o él nos cantaba a nosotros una canción y él nos pedía a nosotros que nosotros cantára-mos también. Son momentos que (yo) jamás olvidaré. Y por eso ahora que ya yo soy mayor y que mi padre ha muerto, cada vez que llega la época de Navidad, yo me dirijo hacia una playa.

Se (Reflexive Pronouns)

Ejercicio 3.18

1. Nos fijamos en su sonrisa. 2. Se enamoró de ella. 3. Nos preocupamos por ti. 4. Se enteraron del accidente el día siguiente. 5. Me quité la ropa. 6. Se quedó allí (ahí). 7. Nos quejamos (quejábamos) de la hora. 8. Se despidió de su familia. 9. Se dieron cuenta (de) que era tarde. 10. Nunca se acostumbraron al clima. 11. No se atreve a tocar a la puerta. 12. Se parecen a su madre.

Ejercicio 3.19

1. La conocemos a ella pero nos conocemos a nosotros mismos mejor. 2. Los oyes a ellos, y te oyes a ti mismo al mismo tiempo. 3. Roberto los respeta a ellos y se respeta a sí mismo también.

Ejercicio 3.20

1. Ø 2. estirarse 3. se 4. se 5. se 6. se 7. Ø 8. se 9. se 10. Ø 11. Se 12. Ø 13. asegurarse 14. se 15. Se 16. Ø 17. Ø 18. la 19. la 20. Ø 21. se 22. Ø 23. Ø 24. desilusionarla 25. se 26. se 27. la una a la otra.

Se (*Se Me* Construction: Accidental or Irresponsible *Se*)

Ejercicio 3.21

1. Se nos olvidó la cita. 2. Se me quemaron los plátanos. 3. Se nos perdieron las llaves. 4. Se les / le mojó el pelo.
5. Se te rompió la taza.

Ejercicio 3.22

1. Se le quedó el libro. 2. Se nos mojó la ropa. 3. Se me acabó el café. 4. Se te cayeron los papeles. 5. Se le olvidaron los apuntes. 6. Se les rompieron los platos.

Ejercicio 3.23

1. le 2. nos 3. me 4. te 5. les

Ejercicio 3.24

1. olvidaron 2. olvidaron 3. bajaron 4. rompió 5. fue

Ejercicio 3.25

1. Se nos olvidó la cita. 2. Se te rompió el plato. 3. Se le quemó la cena. 4. Se me fue la luz. 5. Se te ensuciaron los zapatos. 6. Se nos quedaron los guantes en casa.

Personal Pronouns (Review 2)

Ejercicio 3.26

(Yo) fui estudiante de intercambio hace unos años en México, y cuando yo estuve allá, yo viví con los Rodríguez, una familia muy simpática y generosa que yo nunca olvidaré. Un día cuando yo estaba viviendo con ellos, ellos (se) ganaron la lotería, y la vida se puso de repente más compleja. Cada uno de ellos quería algo diferente.

Don Carlos, el padre, él quería jubilarse porque él quería poder pasar más tiempo con la familia; a él se le había ocurrido también comprar un yate para que todos pudieran divertirse paseándose por el mundo.

Doña Julia, la madre, ~~ella~~ nunca había trabajado más que para su familia, y en realidad ~~ella~~ no tenía ambiciones. ~~Ella~~ deseaba que no <u>le</u> faltara nada a ninguno de sus hijos, y ~~ella~~ esperaba que el dinero sirviera ese propósito. ~~Ella~~ prefería no gastar<u>lo</u> en nada, sino más bien depositar<u>lo</u> en el banco. En realidad, ~~a ella~~ no <u>le</u> gustaba el dinero, ~~el dinero~~ representaba para <u>ella</u> una maldición, y ~~ella~~ hasta <u>le</u> tenía un poco de miedo ~~al dinero~~.

Los hijos, Carlitos, Matilde y Rosita, ~~ellos~~ tenían cada uno de ellos un plan distinto.

Carlitos, el mayor, ~~él~~ ya <u>se</u> había graduado de la universidad, y ~~él~~ estaba buscando trabajo en diferentes bufetes de abogados, pero ~~él~~ no había conseguido nada aún. Él seguía viviendo con la familia, y esto <u>le</u> daba ~~a él~~ algo de vergüenza porque ~~él~~ tenía novia, ~~él~~ estaba comprometido ya, pero si ~~él~~ no tenía trabajo, ~~él~~ no podía formar su propia familia. Él se imaginaba que el dinero <u>le</u> podría servir ~~a él~~ para abrir su propio bufete, y así ~~él~~ podría empezar a trabajar solo y ganar suficiente dinero para poder casar<u>se</u>.

Matilde estaba todavía en la universidad: ~~ella~~ estudiaba medicina. ~~Ella~~ era modesta, y ~~ella~~ no tenía ningún plan personal para el dinero, sino que <u>lo</u> veía ~~el dinero~~ como un premio para sus padres . ~~Ella~~ esperaba que con <u>él</u> ~~ellos~~ pudieran vivir más a gusto. <u>Ellos</u> habían sacrificado tanto para <u>ella</u> y sus hermanos, que ahora ~~ellos~~ <u>se</u> merecían un descanso. ~~Ella~~ siempre había sido muy generosa, y ~~ella~~ pensaba en los problemas de otros en vez de los suyos. Por ejemplo, una vez, cuando ~~ella~~ trabajaba de voluntaria en una escuela de niños pobres, un niño no tenía bastante dinero para comprar<u>se</u> ~~a sí mismo~~ los zapatos del uniforme de la escuela, y entonces ~~ella~~ usó su propio dinero para comprár<u>selos</u>.

Rosita era la más ambiciosa de todos: para <u>ella</u> este dinero representaba la liberación posible de toda dependencia. <u>(Ella)</u> quería su parte del dinero para conseguir<u>se</u> ~~a sí misma~~ un apartamento y vivir lejos de la familia, independiente y libre. <u>Yo</u> conocía mejor <u>a Rosita</u> que a los demás, porque ~~ella~~ era compañera mía en el colegio y ~~nosotros~~ compartíamos la misma habitación en su casa. <u>Ella</u> <u>me</u> contaba ~~a mí~~ sus planes de manera muy emocional. Cuando <u>yo</u> <u>la</u> escuchaba ~~a ella~~, <u>yo</u> podía ver la pasión que <u>la</u> impulsaba.

Se (Impersonal *Se*)

Ejercicio 3.27

1. Se vendió la casa. ¿Cuándo se vendió? 2. Uno se broncea fácilmente en el Caribe. 3. Se despidió a los empleados. ¿Por qué se les despidió? 4. No se les avisó. 5. Eso no se dice en público.

Ejercicio 3.28

1. toma 2. habla 3. dijo 4. mataba 5. recibió 6. mandó 7. anunciaron 8. venden 9. aceptan 10. dieron

Ejercicio 3.29

1. El ruido lo despertó. 2. Se toma la siesta al mediodía. *(The singular of* siesta *is used because it is perceived as an activity that takes place once a day, like breakfast or dinner.)* 3. Nos crió nuestra madre. 4. Te rescató el salvavidas. 5. El discurso me conmovió. 6. La mandaron al hospital. 7. El pan se hacía en casa en aquel entonces. 8. El pasivo casi nunca se usa en español. 9. Acaban de entregar la pizza. 10. Alguien dejó un mensaje en la puerta.

Ejercicio 3.30

Temas de ensayo.

◆ Demonstrative and Possessive Pronouns

Ejercicio 3.31

1. Esa casa era más cara que ésta*. 2. —¿Qué casa prefieres? —Me gustó más ésa* (OR: aquélla*). 3. —Dame eso. —¿Qué? ¿Esto? 4. Mi hermana es tan valiente como la tuya. 5. —Mis padres vienen para la graduación. ¿Y los tuyos? —Los míos no vienen. 6. Esa medicina es suya. (OR: de él) 7. —¿Cuál es tu toalla? —Ésta* es la mía, y ésa* es la tuya. 8. —¿De quién son estas llaves? —Éstas* son de usted, éstas* son de él y éstas* son de ella.

*All of these accentuated pronouns can also be written without the accent.

D Interrogatives

Ejercicio 3.32

1. ¿Cómo llegaron? 2. ¿Cuánta azúcar usas? 3. ¿Qué color te gusta? 4. ¿Cuál quieres? 5. ¿A qué distancia queda la tienda de aquí? 6. ¿Cuál es tu nombre? 7. ¿Cómo te llamas? 8. ¿Cuántos libros compraste? 9. ¿Con qué frecuencia vas?

Ejercicio 3.33

1. ¿Qué es? 2. ¿Quién lo hizo? 3. ¿Cuántos años tienes? 4. ¿Dónde vives? 5. ¿De dónde eres? 6. ¿Por qué cerraste la ventana? 7. ¿A qué hora llegaron? 8. ¿Cuál es el tuyo? 9. ¿Cuál es la diferencia entre las dos películas? 10. ¿Cómo estás?

Ejercicio 3.34

1. Quieren saber de dónde son los aztecas. 2. Me pregunto cuál es la religión. 3. Les interesa saber dónde vivían los incas. 4. Quieren averiguar cuánto dinero gana un arqueólogo. 5. Se le olvidó cómo conoció Romeo a Julieta. 6. No recordaba quién era el actor.

E Exclamatives

Ejercicio 3.35

1. ¡Qué trabajo! 2. ¡Qué lindo(a)(os)(as)! *(Instead of* lindo, *other possibilities could be* bonito, precioso, hermoso, *etc.)* 3. ¡Qué juego más (tan) divertido! 4. ¡Qué buen café! (OR: ¡Qué café más [tan] bueno, rico, sabroso...!) 5. ¡Qué rápido corres! 6. ¡Cómo cantan los pájaros! 7. ¡Cuánto la queríamos! 8. ¡Cuánta hambre tengo! (OR: ¡Qué hambre tengo!) 9. ¡Cuántos primos visitamos! 10. ¡Quién pudiera volar como ellos!

Ejercicio 3.36

1. Qué 2. Cómo (OR: Cuánto) 3. Qué 4. Qué 5. Cuánto 6. Cuántos 7. Qué 8. Qué 9. Cómo (OR: Cuánto) 10. Qué

F Indefinites and Negatives

Ejercicio 3.37

1. Algo se cayó. 2. Alguien habló. 3. No veo a nadie. 4. ¿Necesitas algo? 5. No quiero nada. 6. —Quizá alguno (OR: uno) de los vecinos lo haya visto. —No, ninguno (de ellos) lo vio. 7. —Ayer fui al cine. —Yo también. 8. —Juan no podía ver. —Nosotros tampoco. 9. —¿Has ido a Chile alguna vez? —No, nunca he ido. Algún día iré. Mi hermana fue una vez y le gustó. 10. No puedo encontrar mis llaves en ninguna parte. Sé que están en alguna parte en este cuarto.

G Relative Pronouns

Ejercicio 3.38

1. que 2. que 3. que 4. Lo que 5. la que 6. que (OR: la que, la cual) 7. que 8. que / lo que (OR: lo cual) 9. que 10. la cual (OR: la que) 11. la cual 12. cuyas 13. Quien *(proverbio)* 14. El que 15. la que (OR: lo que)

Ejercicio 3.39

1. La persona que llamó preguntó por ti. (OR: El / La que llamó preguntó por ti). 2. Lo que te dio era robado. 3. No me gusta lo que hacen. 4. Ése* es el autobús que esperaba. 5. La que cantaba esa canción era Rose. (OR: La que cantó esa canción...)

*optional accent

Ejercicio 3.40

Un amigo mío que se llama Ernesto me llamó de Florida. Me contó de su perrito que había comprado hacía tres semanas y que estaba dormido a su lado. Ernesto me contó que Chico, el nombre que le dio al perrito, estaba destruyendo el apartamento que Ernesto había conseguido con tanta dificultad y en que había gastado todo su dinero. Pero Ernesto no quería deshacerse de este perrito que ahora era su mejor amigo. Por eso Ernesto me pidió que le mandara el dinero que él me había prestado hacía más de un año.

Chapter 3 Review

Ejercicio 3.41

1. verlos 2. recibirlos 3. les 4. Ø 5. les 6. los 7. les 8. los 9. les 10. se 11. que 12. Ø 13. éstos les
14. que 15. que 16. que 17. Los 18. nada 19. les 20. que 21. que 22. la suya 23. dominarlos 24. que
25. suyo 26. que 27. se 28. que 29. que 30. cuyo 31. los 32. que 33. al que 34. se 35. que 36. las que
37. qué / quiénes 38. algunos 39. algunos 40. que 41. que

*optional accent

Ejercicio 3.42

Temas de ensayo.

Chapter 4 Prepositions, Adverbs, and Conjunctions

Ⓐ Prepositions (Function of Prepositions)

Ejercicio 4.1

A preposition is a word that introduces a noun or its equivalent. Its name is derived from the Latin—pre- *(before)* position—and explains its function in a sentence: a preposition goes before a noun, thus introducing it. A conjunction joins two parts of speech. Its name is also derived from the Latin—con- *(with)* -junction *(to join),* or to join together. Conjunctions of coordination join two equal parts of speech (and, or…), whereas conjunctions of subordination join a subordinate (or dependent) clause to its main clause.

Prepositions (Individual Prepositions)

Ejercicio 4.2

1. a, en 2. a 3. a, con, en 4. en, a 5. en 6. a 7. en, de 8. a, de 9. a, en, a 10. a, en, de, con

Ejercicio 4.3

1. a 2. del, de 3. de, en, de 4. a, con 5. a 6. a, con 7. a 8. con, a 9. a, de 10. a, en / a, en

Ejercicio 4.4

1. en, de 2. a, en 3. a, con 4. a, del, en 5. a 6. a 7. de, de 8. En, a 9. en 10. con, a

Ejercicio 4.5

1. de, a 2. a 3. con, de 4. de, con, con 5. con 6. Ø, Ø 7. a, con 8. a, de 9. a, de 10. a, en

Ejercicio 4.6

1. a 2. A 3. De, a 4. De, a 5. Con 6. a 7. Ø, de 8. a 9. a, de 10. en

Ejercicio 4.7

1. con 2. De 3. a 4. en, a 5. de 6. de 7. de 8. a 9. en 10. A 11. de 12. a 13. a 14. en

Ejercicio 4.8

1. para 2. por 3. para 4. por 5. por 6. para 7. por 8. por 9. para, porque 10. Por

Ejercicio 4.9

1. Ø 2. para 3. para 4. por 5. por 6. para 7. Ø 8. por 9. por 10. para

Ejercicio 4.10

1. Por 2. para 3. Por 4. Por 5. por 6. por 7. por 8. Para, por 9. por 10. por

Ejercicio 4.11

1. Se preocupan por ti. 2. Se enamoró de ella. 3. Consiste en dos secciones. 4. La decisión depende de ti. 5. Se rieron de él. 6. Sueño contigo todas las noches. 7. Se despidieron de mí. 8. No quiero que mis ideas influyan en tu decisión. 9. Se casó con mi hermano. 10. Dejó de beber.

Ejercicio 4.12

1. Llegamos a Madrid a las dos. 2. Se opone a todo lo que digo. 3. Trato de ayudar. 4. Me di cuenta de mi error. 5. Me agradeció el favor. 6. Nos subimos al autobús. 7. Su casa está a cinco millas. 8. Me encontré con mis amigos en el restaurante. 9. Estudia en la universidad. 10. Serán los primeros en irse.

Ejercicio 4.13

1. Pienso en mis padres todos los días. 2. El libro de Luisa es interesante. 3. Me fijé en el cambio. 4. No puedo ayudarte en este momento. 5. Se enojaron conmigo por mi error. 6. Miramos el reloj. 7. Vio a su hermana. 8. Te pedí dinero, no consejo. 9. Acabo de comer. 10. Trabajan para mí.

Ejercicio 4.14

1. Lo envié por correo aéreo. 2. Fueron a la tienda por pan. 3. Me quedan dos trabajos por escribir. 4. Habremos terminado para las diez. 5. Para un niño, sabe mucho. 6. Salieron para Guatemala ayer. 7. Están buscando sus llaves. 8. Hablaron por tres horas. 9. Se preocupa por ti. 10. ¿Para qué es esto?

Ejercicio 4.15

1. a 2. en 3. a 4. de 5. de 6. de 7. en 8. para 9. Por 10. a 11. Ø 12. a 13. a 14. para 15. a 16. con 17. De 18. a 19. de

Ejercicio 4.16

1. por lo general 2. a veces 3. a pie 4. a pesar de 5. en cambio 6. a caballo 7. A eso de 8. a la vez 9. en seguida 10. Al menos 11. de pie

Ejercicio 4.17

1. Con respecto a 2. con tal de que 3. de mala gana 4. de esta manera 5. de veras 6. De vez en cuando 7. de nuevo 8. de modo que

Ejercicio 4.18

1. Por poco 2. En vez de 3. por eso 4. Por otra parte 5. por más que 6. En cuanto a 7. por supuesto 8. en cuanto 9. Por fin 10. a tiempo 11. en frente de 12. por lo menos 13. para siempre

Ejercicio 4.19

1. de 2. de 3. a 4. Ø 5. de 6. a 7. de 8. de 9. de 10. de 11. a 12. con 13. en 14. en 15. a 16. Ø 17. a 18. Ø 19. a

Ejercicio 4.20

I. de 2. con 3. de 4. de 5. a 6. de 7. con 8. en 9. con 10. a 11. de 12. a 13. Ø 14. por 15. en 16. en 17. en 18. Ø 19. a 20. con 21. a 22. Ø 23. por 24. a 25. en

Ejercicio 4.21

I. de 2. a 3. de 4. por 5. por 6. de 7. a 8. con 9. de 10. por 11. Ø 12. de 13. de 14. a 15. Ø 16. para 17. de

Adverbs (Adverbs Ending in -mente, Word Order, Multiple-Function Words)

Ejercicio 4.22

Antes me llevaba bien con mis vecinos, pero el otro día cambió nuestra relación. Vi que su hijo no estaba jugando limpio: cada vez que mi hija ganaba, él le pegaba, y le pegaba duro. Después de ver eso dos veces, decidí que tenía que hacer algo rápido. Fui derecho a la casa de mis vecinos, y le dije a la madre lo que había visto. Ella respiró hondo, y me miró raro. Me dijo que sabía esto: su hijo era bajo, pero altamente competitivo. No podía jugar igual que el resto: tenía que jugar distinto. Era natural.

Adverbs (Adverbs of Place)

Ejercicio 4.23

I. abajo 2. arriba 3. adelante 4. atrás 5. Afuera 6. Dónde 7. aquí 8. adentro 9. Allí / Ahí 10. acá 11. allá 12. Adónde 13. lejos

Adverbs (Adverbs of Time)

Ejercicio 4.24

I. Siempre 2. anteayer 3. cuando 4. cuándo 5. ahora 6. todavía no / aún no 7. Entonces 8. ya 9. Ayer 10. Mientras 11. (nunca) jamás 12. Pronto 13. Anoche 14. hoy 15. ya 16. Todavía no 17. recién 18. mañana 19. luego / entonces 20. ya no 21. Tarde o temprano

Ejercicio 4.25

I. Todavía 2. ya 3. ya no 4. todavía no

Adverbs (Adverbs of Manner)

Ejercicio 4.26

I. así 2. bien 3. bien 4. cómo 5. mal 6. como 7. Según 8. bien 9. bien

Adverbs (Adverbs of Quantity)

Ejercicio 4.27

I. bastante 2. apenas 3. bastante 4. Casi 5. mucho (OR: demasiado) 6. tanto 7. algo (OR: un poco) 8. poco 9. sólo 10. medio 11. más 12. muy 13. demasiado 14. tanto 15. Cuánto 16. nada

Adverbs (Adverbs of Confirmation, Doubt, or Negation)

Ejercicio 4.28

—Tú vas a pagar nuestros boletos, ¿no?
—Sí, pero me falta un dólar. Beto, ¿acaso tienes un dólar que me puedas prestar?
—No, no tengo un dólar, pero sí tengo 75 centavos. ¿Los quieres?
—Bueno. Quizá Quique o Marisol tengan los otros 25 centavos. Quique, ¿tienes 25 centavos?
—No.
—¿Marisol?
—No, yo tampoco.
—Bueno, pues, tal vez no vayamos al cine después de todo. ¿Quieren pasearse por el parque?
—Ah, no, ¡eso sí que no!

Adverbs (Adverbial Phrases)

Ejercicio 4.29

1. a menudo (OR: por momentos, a cada rato) 2. a gusto 3. por poco 4. a medias 5. por cierto 6. al final 7. hasta 8. En fin 9. por fin 10. en resumen (OR: al fin y al cabo) 11. alguna vez 12. en algún lugar

Adverbs (Related Adverbs and Prepositions)

Ejercicio 4.30

1. abajo 2. delante de 3. afuera 4. detrás de 5. frente a 6. dentro del 7. debajo del 8. tras 9. bajo 10. adentro

Conjunctions (Usage, Conjunctions of Coordination)

Ejercicio 4.31

1. e 2. y 3. o 4. sino también 5. y 6. u 7. pero 8. y/o 9. sino 10. ni 11. sino 12. ni 13. ni 14. sino

Ejercicio 4.32

1. Tenía miedo **pero** lo hice. 2. No era azul, **sino** rojo. 3. No era azul, **pero** lo compré de todas formas. 4. No compré un coche rojo, **sino** azul. 5. No quería un coche rojo, **pero** compré uno de todas maneras. 6. Quería un coche rojo, **pero** en vez me compré uno azul. 7. No compré el carro, **sino que** lo vendí.

Ejercicio 4.33

Norberto me llamó **y** me contó de su viaje a México y a Puerto Rico. Le gustó mucho México, **pero** se enfermó con la comida, **y** le encantó Puerto Rico, **pero** sufrió del calor. El país que más le gustó no fue México **sino** Puerto Rico, no sólo porque tiene muchas playas, **sino** también porque es una isla **y** pudo conocerla mejor en el poco tiempo que tenía.

Conjunctions (Conjunctions of Subordination)

Ejercicio 4.34

1. que 2. Ø 3. que 4. que 5. Ø 6. que 7. que 8. Ø 9. que 10. que 11. Ø 12. que

Ejercicio 4.35

Dijiste que ibas a la tienda a comprar leche. Te dije que no sólo necesitábamos leche, sino también pan. Veo que no compraste ni pan ni leche, sino que alquilaste un vídeo.

D Transitions

Ejercicio 4.36

1. Por lo general 2. En primer lugar 3. porque 4. en segundo lugar 5. Sin embargo 6. De hecho 7. en realidad 8. quizá / tal vez / a lo mejor 9. Acaso 10. por desgracia 11. como consecuencia 12. a pesar de 13. tal vez / quizá / a lo mejor 14. Por otro lado 15. por suerte 16. sin embargo 17. Por lo que se refiere a / Con respecto a / En cuanto a / En lo tocante a 18. en gran parte 19. cada vez más 20. en todo caso 21. casi nunca 22. En fin de cuentas 23. En resumidas cuentas / En resumen 24. actualmente / hoy en día

Ejercicio 4.37

1. por eso 2. a pesar de 3. Según 4. porque 5. Por consiguiente 6. por lo tanto 7. Con respecto al 8. De hecho 9. por ejemplo 10. Además 11. ya que 12. Por otro lado 13. casi siempre 14. En fin de cuentas

Chapter 4 Review

Ejercicio 4.38

(Algunas respuestas tienen más de una posibilidad.)

1. y 2. a 3. de 4. en primer lugar 5. en segundo lugar 6. Con respecto a 7. Según 8. u 9. o 10. Sin embargo 11. en realidad sí 12. pero 13. para 14. por 15. para 16. de hecho 17. En lo tocante a 18. ya 19. en 20. pero 21. muy 22. que 23. a 24. en 25. de 26. entonces 27. en realidad 28. ya 29. sino que 30. a la vez 31. también 32. por 33. a pesar de 34. ya 35. aún 36. En resumen 37. porque 38. sí 39. después de todo

Ejercicio 4.39

Temas de ensayo.

Chapter 5 Verbs: Formation

A Indicative Mood (Present Indicative)

Ejercicio 5.1

1. amo 2. canto 3. como 4. vivo 5. hablo 6. camino 7. coso 8. bebo 9. abro 10. imprimo

Ejercicio 5.2

1. miento 2. sigo 3. pido 4. repito 5. comento 6. mezclo 7. impido 8. me defiendo 9. quiero 10. elijo 11. consigo 12. revelo 13. sirvo 14. me canso 15. cierro 16. siento 17. comienzo 18. pienso 19. me pierdo

Ejercicio 5.3

1. piensa 2. quiere 3. hace 4. recuerda 5. corta 6. poda 7. duele 8. vota 9. es 10. vuelve 11. huele 12. se acuesta 13. va 14. juega 15. se levanta 16. mira 17. ve 18. llueve 19. domina 20. cuenta 21. interrumpe 22. llora 23. puede 24. sale 25. siente 26. jura

Ejercicio 5.4

1. protejo 2. sigo 3. obedezco 4. traduzco 5. tuerzo 6. recojo 7. consigo 8. agradezco 9. produzco 10. convenzo

Ejercicio 5.5

1. envías 2. continúas 3. confías 4. reúnes 5. crías 6. te gradúas 7. guías 8. actúas 9. concluyes 10. huyes

Ejercicio 5.6

1. me caigo / se cae / nos caemos 2. hago / hace / hacemos 3. me pongo / se pone / nos ponemos 4. salgo / sale / salimos 5. traigo / trae / traemos 6. valgo / vale / valemos 7. vengo / viene / venimos 8. digo / dice / decimos 9. tengo / tiene / tenemos 10. doy / da / damos 11. voy / va / vamos 12. soy / es / somos 13. estoy / está / estamos 14. he / ha / hemos 15. oigo / oye / oímos 16. sé / sabe / sabemos 17. veo / ve / vemos

Ejercicio 5.7

1. camino 2. actúas 3. actuamos 4. adquiero 5. adquirimos 6. andáis 7. aprendemos 8. toma 9. avergüenzan 10. avergonzamos 11. averiguo 12. digo 13. dice 14. decimos 15. buscan 16. quepo 17. cabe 18. me caigo 19. cae 20. cierras 21. cerráis 22. escojo 23. escogen 24. comienzo 25. comenzamos 26. contribuye 27. construimos 28. conduzco 29. produces 30. cuenta 31. me sueno 32. recordamos 33. creo 34. poseen 35. leemos 36. cruzo 37. almuerzas 38. doy 39. digo 40. me contradigo 41. elijo 42. exiges 43. sigo 44. consigue 45. perseguimos 46. duermo 47. dormís 48. envían 49. enviamos 50. escribo 51. estoy 52. fuerzan 53. hago 54. satisfacen 55. voy 56. van 57. juega 58. llegan 59. muere 60. mueves 61. niegan 62. oigo 63. oyes 64. oímos 65. huelo 66. huelen 67. me parezco 68. pido 69. pide 70. pierdes 71. pueden 72. pongo 73. quieren 74. me río 75. se sonríe 76. reúnen 77. ruega 78. tengo 79. tienes 80. tuerzo 81. se retuerce 82. traigo 83. valgo 84. convenzo 85. vengo 86. intervienen 87. vemos 88. vive 89. vuelve

Ejercicio 5.8

Temas de ensayo.

Indicative Mood (Past Tenses of the Indicative: Imperfect)

Ejercicio 5.9

1. hablaba 2. comías 3. vivía 4. caminábamos 5. corríais 6. tomaban 7. comenzaba 8. decías 9. veía 10. concluíamos

Ejercicio 5.10

1. iba / íbamos 2. era / éramos 3. veía / veíamos 4. pedía / pedíamos 5. cerraba / cerrábamos 6. me caía / nos caíamos 7. andaba / andábamos 8. cabía / cabíamos 9. tenía / teníamos 10. hacía / hacíamos 11. daba / dábamos 12. dormía / dormíamos 13. me reía / nos reíamos 14. oía / oíamos

Ejercicio 5.11

1. tenía 2. insistían 3. caminaba 4. preguntaba 5. me avergonzaba 6. sorprendían 7. regañaban 8. evaluaban 9. adquiríamos 10. nos poníamos 11. interrogaba 12. hacíais 13. hablabais 14. contestábamos 15. hacíamos 16. hablábamos 17. creía 18. se daba 19. salíamos 20. pensábamos 21. aprendíamos 22. Buscábamos 23. quería 24. lográbamos 25. era 26. podía 27. avergonzaba 28. decía 29. nos portábamos 30. enviaba 31. era 32. debía 33. iba 34. salía 35. tomaba 36. se metía 37. se quedaba 38. se enteraba 39. gustaba 40. llegaban 41. se caían 42. gritaban 43. se ponían 44. lloraban 45. nos reíamos 46. Tenía 47. detestaba 48. terminaba 49. llevaba 50. se ponía 51. preguntaba 52. esperaba 53. insistía 54. existía 55. creíamos 56. éramos 57. Nos sentíamos 58. contradecíamos 59. nos rehusábamos 60. querían 61. odiábamos 62. odiaban 63. fingíamos 64. sabíamos 65. era 66. reconocíamos 67. soportábamos 68. nos rebelábamos

Ejercicio 5.12

Temas de ensayo.

Indicative Mood (Past Tenses of the Indicative: Preterite)

Ejercicio 5.13

1. hablaste 2. comimos 3. vivieron 4. caminé 5. anduviste 6. cupo 7. estuvimos 8. arrestamos 9. hubo 10. supe 11. pudiste 12. puso 13. salisteis 14. tuvieron 15. hice 16. quisiste 17. vino

Ejercicio 5.14

1. dimos 2. hizo 3. fui 4. fui 5. dijisteis 6. produjiste 7. trajeron

Ejercicio 5.15

1. sentí / sintió 2. pedí / pidió 3. reí / rió 4. dormí / durmió 5. caí / cayó 6. creí / creyó 7. leí / leyó 8. oí / oyó
9. concluí / concluyó 10. busqué / buscó 11. llegué / llegó 12. alcancé / alcanzó 13. expliqué / explicó 14. almorcé /
almorzó 15. apagué / apagó 16. saqué / sacó 17. comencé / comenzó 18. colgué / colgó 19. toqué / tocó
20. empecé / empezó 21. entregué / entregó 22. pagué / pagó

Ejercicio 5.16

1. fui 2. fue 3. hubo 4. fue 5. quedé 6. vi 7. nos acostamos 8. entramos 9. Cenamos 10. salimos 11. se sintió
12. regresamos 13. Tuve 14. vino 15. vio 16. dijo 17. contó 18. trajo 19. recomendó 20. pude 21. Me fijé
22. sufrió 23. volvió 24. se encerró 25. hizo 26. estuve 27. me pasé 28. escribí 29. me quemé 30. fui 31. me
miré 32. pegué 33. pedí 34. decidimos 35. Fuimos 36. alquilamos 37. tuve 38. Estuvimos 39. llegamos
40. ocurrió 41. Nos sentamos 42. bebimos 43. miramos 44. se acercó 45. ofreció 46. hablé 47. averigüé
48. pude 49. corrigió 50. dijo 51. cayó 52. se ofendió 53. pareció 54. di 55. aceptamos 56. nos fuimos
57. vimos 58. pudimos 59. condujimos 60. se rió 61. me reí 62. seguimos 63. fue

Ejercicio 5.17

Temas de ensayo.

Indicative Mood (Past Tenses of the Indicative: Present Perfect)

Ejercicio 5.18

1. he caminado 2. has hecho 3. ha devuelto 4. hemos andado 5. habéis aprendido 6. han tomado 7. he traído
8. has averiguado 9. ha buscado 10. hemos cabido 11. habéis cerrado 12. han recogido

Indicative Mood (Past Tenses of the Indicative: Pluperfect)

Ejercicio 5.19

1. había corrido 2. habías graduado 3. había ido 4. habíamos dicho 5. habíais visto 6. habían vuelto 7. había
escrito 8. habías puesto 9. había resuelto 10. habíamos abierto 11. habíais cerrado 12. habían tapado

Indicative Mood (Future: Simple Future)

Ejercicio 5.20

1. amaré 2. vivirás 3. entenderá 4. comeremos 5. graduaréis 6. tomarán 7. despediré 8. averiguarás 9. buscará
10. cantaremos 11. calentaréis 12. escogerán

Ejercicio 5.21

1. cabré 2. dirás 3. habrá 4. haremos 5. podréis 6. pondrán 7. querré 8. sabrás 9. saldrá 10. tendremos
11. valdrá 12. vendréis

Ejercicio 5.22

Temas de ensayo.

Indicative Mood (Future: Future Perfect)

Ejercicio 5.23

1. habré dicho 2. habrás visto 3. habrá cubierto 4. habremos vuelto 5. habréis hecho 6. habrán tomado 7. habré puesto 8. habrás experimentado 9. habrá buscado 10. habremos cantado 11. habréis envejecido 12. habrán escrito 13. habré ido 14. habrás gastado 15. habrá graduado 16. habremos salido 17. habréis estudiado 18. habrán tenido 19. habrán terminado 20. habré llegado

Conditional Mood (Present Conditional)

Ejercicio 5.24

1. secaría 2. preocuparías 3. viviría 4. llovería 5. pronunciaríais 6. pagarían 7. organizaría 8. atestiguarías 9. leería 10. quejaríamos 11. sonreiríais 12. tutearía

Ejercicio 5.25

1. cabría 2. dirías 3. habría 4. haríamos 5. podríais 6. pondrían 7. querría 8. sabrías 9. costaría 10. tendría 11. valdría 12. vendrían

Conditional Mood (Conditional Perfect)

Ejercicio 5.26

1. habría hablado 2. habrías comido 3. habría vivido 4. habríamos abierto 5. habríais cubierto 6. habrían dicho 7. habría escrito 8. habrías hecho 9. habría muerto 10. habríamos puesto 11. habríais resuelto 12. habría vuelto

Ejercicio 5.27

Temas de ensayo.

Subjunctive Mood (Present Subjunctive)

Ejercicio 5.28

1. camine 2. hables 3. estudie 4. cante 5. bailemos 6. reméis 7. amen 8. preparen 9. tolere 10. tararen

Ejercicio 5.29

1. coma 2. leas 3. vea 4. viva 5. tosamos 6. cosáis 7. corran 8. compartan 9. beba 10. se escriban

Ejercicio 5.30

1. cierre / cerremos 2. pierda / perdamos 3. cuente / contemos 4. vuelva / volvamos 5. sienta / sintamos 6. duerma / durmamos 7. envíe / enviemos 8. evalúe / evaluemos

Ejercicio 5.31

1. pida 2. diga 3. oiga 4. tenga 5. concluya 6. parezca 7. conduzca 8. quepa 9. caiga 10. haga 11. se ponga 12. salga 13. traiga 14. valga 15. venga

Ejercicio 5.32

1. dé 2. estés 3. haya 4. nos vayamos 5. sepáis 6. sean 7. escoja 8. dirijas 9. distingan 10. convenzamos 11. busquéis 12. llegue 13. alcances

Ejercicio 5.33

1. domine 2. tema 3. defiendas 4. demos 5. estéis 6. haya 7. vaya 8. sepas 9. sea 10. recojamos 11. corrijas
12. sigáis 13. venza 14. rasque 15. ruegues 16. rece 17. entienda 18. encuentre 19. devuelvan 20. envolvamos
21. confíe 22. criemos 23. continúes 24. graduemos 25. crean 26. vea 27. suba 28. hagan 29. dividan
30. investigue 31. analicen 32. discutas 33. pelee 34. llegue 35. queramos 36. entréis 37. salgan 38. repitan
39. oiga 40. vuelvan

Subjunctive Mood (Imperfect Subjunctive)

Ejercicio 5.34

1. caminara 2. hablaras 3. estudiara 4. cantara 5. bailáramos 6. escucharais 7. amaran 8. prepararan 9. tolerara
10. tararearan 11. comiera 12. leyeras 13. viera 14. viviera 15. tosiéramos 16. cosierais 17. corrieran
18. compartieran 19. bebiera 20. escribieran 21. cerrara 22. perdieras 23. contara 24. volviéramos
25. sintieran 26. durmieran 27. enviara 28. graduaras

Ejercicio 5.35

1. anduviera 2. cupieras 3. cayera 4. concluyera 5. condujera 6. diéramos 7. dijerais 8. se durmieran 9. estuvieran 10. hubiera 11. me fuera 12. leyeras 13. oyera 14. pidiera 15. pudiera 16. pusiéramos 17. poseyerais
18. prefirieran 19. dirigieran 20. quisieran 21. me riera 22. supieras 23. siguiera 24. sintiera 25. fuera
26. fuéramos 27. tuvierais 28. trajeran 29. vinieran

Subjunctive Mood (Present Perfect Subjunctive)

Ejercicio 5.36

1. haya ganado 2. te hayas graduado 3. haya conseguido 4. hayamos andado 5. hayáis aprendido 6. hayan tomado
7. haya avergonzado 8. hayas averiguado 9. haya buscado 10. hayamos cantado 11. hayáis cerrado 12. hayan
recogido 13. haya cabido 14. hayas podido 15. haya vendido 16. hayamos viajado 17. hayáis salido 18. hayan
tenido 19. hayan costado 20. haya venido

Subjunctive Mood (Pluperfect Subjunctive)

Ejercicio 5.37

1. hubiera escrito 2. hubieran dicho 3. hubieran visto 4. hubiéramos llegado 5. hubieran tratado 6. hubiera oído
7. hubiera hecho 8. hubieran limpiado 9. hubieras llamado 10. se hubieran enterado 11. hubieras considerado
12. hubierais lavado 13. hubieran vuelto 14. hubiera resuelto 15. hubieras puesto 16. se hubiera muerto
17. hubiéramos abierto 18. hubiera comido 19. hubiéramos confesado 20. hubieran terminado

Ejercicio 5.38

Temas de ensayo.

Imperative Mood (Direct Commands: *Tú*)

Ejercicio 5.39

1. Habla 2. Come 3. Vive 4. Cierra 5. Abre 6. Salta 7. Escucha 8. Vuelve 9. Pide 10. Consigue 11. Repite
12. Miente 13. Comienza 14. Comenta 15. Defiende 16. Sigue 17. Piensa 18. Sirve 19. Elige 20. Vota
21. Envuelve 22. Cuenta 23. Corta 24. Apuesta 25. Poda 26. Llora 27. Recuerda 28. Recorta 29. Huele
30. Juega 31. Jura 32. Protege 33. Sigue 34. Obedece 35. Traduce 36. Produce 37. Envía 38. Continúa
39. Confía 40. Reúne 41. Cría 42. Evalúa 43. Concluye 44. Huye 45. Calla 46. Trae 47. Da 48. Oye

Ejercicio 5.40

1. Di 2. Haz 3. Ve 4. Pon 5. Sal 6. Sé 7. Ten 8. Ven

Ejercicio 5.41

1. **Canta,** pero **no bailes.** 2. **Estudia,** pero **no hables** en voz alta. 3. **Bebe** mucho jugo, y **no comas** nada artificial. 4. **Lee** el artículo, pero **no creas** todo lo que dice. 5. **Vuelve** a casa, pero **no corras.** 6. **Descose** el bolsillo, y **no cosas** la bastilla. 7. **Escribe** una carta, pero **no describas** lo que pasó. 8. **Cuenta** lo que debes, y **no descuentes** nada. 9. **Duerme** al bebé, pero **no te duermas** tú. 10. **Pide** favores, y **no impidas** que te ayuden. 11. **Regala** tu amistad, y **no prestes** nada. 12. **Busca** el ungüento, y **no te rasques** la picada. 13. **Escoge** la película que quieras ver, pero por favor **no escojas** una en inglés.

Ejercicio 5.42

1. **Di** la verdad, y **no digas** mentiras. 2. **Haz** la lectura para mañana, pero **no hagas** la tarea. 3. **Ve** a la tienda, pero **no vayas** al correo. 4. **Pon** tu abrigo aquí, y **no pongas** tus zapatos en la mesa. 5. **Sal** a recoger el periódico, pero **no salgas** por esa puerta. 6. **Sé** bueno, pero **no seas** tonto. 7. **Ten** hijos, pero **no tengas** tantos como ella. 8. **Ven** a casa, pero **no vengas** temprano.

Imperative Mood (Direct Commands: *Usted / Ustedes*)

Ejercicio 5.43

1. Camine 2. No hable 3. Estudie 4. No cante 5. Baile 6. Tararee 7. Coma 8. No lea 9. Viva 10. No tosa 11. Corra 12. No beba 13. Escriba 14. Cierre 15. No pierda 16. Cuente 17. No vuelva 18. Duerma 19. No pida 20. Diga 21. Oiga 22. No tenga 23. Conduzca 24. No caiga 25. Haga 26. Ponga 27. No salga 28. Traiga 29. Venga 30. No dé 31. Vaya 32. No sea 33. Dirija 34. Busque 35. No llegue

Imperative Mood (Direct Commands: *Vosotros*)

Ejercicio 5.44

1. Hablad 2. Comed 3. Exprimid 4. Cerrad 5. Abrid 6. Saltad 7. Escuchad 8. Volved 9. Pedid 10. Conseguid 11. Repetid 12. Mentid 13. Comenzad 14. Comentad 15. Defended 16. Seguid 17. Pensad 18. Servid 19. Elegid 20. Votad 21. Decid 22. Haced 23. Id 24. Poned 25. Salid 26. Sed 27. Tened 28. Venid

Ejercicio 5.45

1. Despertaos 2. Levantaos 3. Lavaos 4. Marchaos 5. Acostaos 6. Dormíos 7. Idos 8. Despedíos 9. Callaos

Ejercicio 5.46

1. **Cantad,** pero **no bailéis.** 2. **Estudiad,** pero **no habléis** en voz alta. 3. **Bebed** mucho jugo, y **no comáis** nada artificial. 4. **Leed** el artículo, pero **no creáis** todo lo que dice. 5. **Volved** a casa, pero **no corráis.** 6. **Descosed** el bolsillo, y **no cosáis** la bastilla. 7. **Escribid** una carta, pero **no describáis** lo que pasó. 8. **Contad** lo que debéis, y **no descontéis** nada. 9. **Dormid** al bebé, pero **no os durmáis** vosotros. 10. **Pedid** favores, y **no impidáis** que os ayuden. 11. **Regalad** vuestra amistad, y **no prestéis** nada. 12. **Buscad** el ungüento, y **no os rasquéis** la picada. 13. **Escoged** la película que queréis ver, pero por favor **no escojáis** una en inglés.

Ejercicio 5.47

1. **Decid** la verdad, y **no digáis** mentiras. 2. **Haced** la lectura para mañana, pero **no hagáis** la tarea. 3. **Id** a la tienda, pero **no vayáis** al correo. 4. **Poned** vuestro abrigo aquí, y **no pongáis** vuestros zapatos en la mesa. 5. **Salid** a recoger el periódico, pero **no salgáis** por esa puerta. 6. **Sed** buenos, pero **no seáis** tontos. 7. **Tened** hijos, pero **no tengáis** tantos como ellos. 8. **Venid** a casa, pero **no vengáis** temprano.

Imperative Mood (Direct Commands: *Nosotros*)

Ejercicio 5.48

1. caminemos 2. no hablemos 3. estudiemos 4. no cantemos 5. bailemos 6. tarareemos 7. comamos 8. no leamos 9. vivamos 10. no tosamos 11. corramos 12. no bebamos 13. escribamos 14. cerremos 15. no perdamos 16. contemos 17. no volvamos 18. durmamos 19. no pidamos 20. digamos 21. oigamos 22. no tengamos 23. conduzcamos 24. no caigamos 25. hagamos 26. pongamos 27. no salgamos 28. no demos 29. vamos 30. no seamos 31. dirijamos 32. busquemos 33. no lleguemos

Ejercicio 5.49

1. despertémoslas 2. no nos levantemos 3. lavémoslo 4. marchémonos 5. no nos acostemos 6. durmámonos 7. vámonos 8. no nos vayamos

Imperative Mood (Indirect Commands)

Ejercicio 5.50

1. No quiero cocinar; que cocinen ellos hoy. 2. Que me llame el gerente. 3. Si no tienes el dinero, que pague Mirta. 4. Que me lo manden.

Imperative Mood (Review)

Ejercicio 5.51

1. Sí, díselo. No, no se lo digas. (OR: dínoslo, no nos lo digas) 2. Sí, hazlos. No, no los hagas. 3. Sí, véndeselos. No, no se los vendas. (OR: véndemelos, no me los vendas) 4. Sí, ve. No, no vayas. 5. Sí, pónselos. No, no se los pongas.

Ejercicio 5.52

1. Sí, cántenla. No, no la canten. 2. Sí, dígaselo. No, no se lo diga. (OR: dígamelo, no me lo diga) 3. Sí, envíenselas. No, no se las envíen. (OR: envíennoslas, no nos las envíen) 4. Sí, vayan. No, no vayan. 5. Sí, quíteselos. No, no se los quite.

Ejercicio 5.53

1. Sí, cantémoslas juntos. No, no las cantemos juntos. 2. Sí, vamos. No, no vayamos. 3. Sí, démoselo. No, no se lo demos. 4. Sí, vámonos ahora. No, no nos vayamos ahora. 5. Sí, pongámonoslo. No, no nos lo pongamos.

Ejercicio 5.54

1. **Que lo preparen.** 2. Yo no quiero hacerlo. **Que lo haga Guillermo.** 3. **Que venga a verme.** 4. **Que me llamen.** 5. Si tienen hambre, **que coman.**

Ejercicio 5.55

Temas de ensayo.

Participle (Present Participle)

Ejercicio 5.56

1. hablando 2. comiendo 3. viviendo 4. sintiendo 5. pidiendo 6. durmiéndote (OR: te estás durmiendo) 7. concluyendo 8. cayendo 9. leyendo 10. oyendo 11. diciendo 12. yendo 13. viniendo 14. pudiendo

Ejercicio 5.57

1. caminando 2. actuando 3. andando 4. aprendiendo 5. diciendo 6. buscando 7. siendo 8. cerrando 9. construyendo 10. conduciendo 11. produciendo 12. contando 13. recordando 14. creyendo 15. almorzando 16. dando 17. eligiendo 18. siguiendo 19. haciendo 20. jugando

Ejercicio 5.58

1. llegando 2. muriéndose (OR: se estaban muriendo) 3. moviendo 4. negando 5. sonriéndoos (OR: os estabais sonriendo) 6. oliendo 7. despidiendo 8. poniendo 9. reuniendo 10. teniendo 11. trayendo 12. interviniendo 13. viendo 14. volviendo

Participle (Past Participle)

Ejercicio 5.59

1. hablado 2. comido 3. vivido 4. caminado 5. sentado 6. aprendido 7. conducido 8. almorzado 9. dado 10. movido 11. olido 12. venido

Ejercicio 5.60

1. abierto 2. cubierto 3. dicho 4. escrito 5. hecho 6. se han muerto 7. nos habíamos puesto 8. resuelto 9. vuelto 10. descubierto 11. devuelto 12. supuesto

Ejercicio 5.61

1. Ésta* es agua bendita. 2. Habían bendecido la comida. 3. Quiero papas fritas. (OR: patatas [in Spain]) 4. Él había freído las papas. 5. ¡Maldita suerte! 6. Nunca he maldecido a nadie. 7. Llevaba el pelo suelto. 8. Han soltado a los toros. 9. La palabra impresa es muy importante. 10. ¿Has imprimido tu trabajo?

*optional accent

Chapter 6 Verbs: Usage

A Present Indicative

Ejercicio 6.1

1. viven 2. habla (OR: habla usted) 3. vendo 4. llueve / tenemos 5. trae / traes 6. acabo 7. salimos

Ejercicio 6.2

Temas de ensayo.

Ejercicio 6.3

Temas de ensayo.

B Past Indicative Tenses (Preterite vs. Imperfect vs. Pluperfect)

Ejercicio 6.4

1. (A) se levantó, se bañó, bajó 2. (E) era, tenía, estaba 3. (AH) salía, volvía 4. (A) vi; (R) gustó 5. (E) estábamos; (A) empezó; corrimos, nos sentamos; (ET) estuvimos. 6. (A) dijo; (AF) venía 7. (E) era, creía, tenía; (A) descubrí; (E) era; (R) molestó; (EC) fue 8. (A) entré, vi; (AS) comían, hablaban, trataban 9. (E) parecía; (AH) decidían, hacía, decían; (E) quería 10. (E) podía; (A) mordió, arrancó, enterró; (R) se puso; (A) interrumpió

Ejercicio 6.5

Vivía, Tenía, encantaba, gustaba, hacíamos, Ganábamos, ahorrábamos, íbamos

Ejercicio 6.6

1. se fueron 2. nos quedamos 3. planeamos 4. pensábamos 5. regañaban 6. invitábamos 7. gustaba 8. invitamos
9. vinieron 10. fue 11. bebían 12. bailaban 13. oía 14. Había 15. parecía 16. iba 17. eran 18. sabíamos
19. estaban 20. entré 21. vi 22. bebían 23. saltaban 24. bailaban 25. encantó 26. fue 27. se enteraron

Ejercicio 6.7

Temas de ensayo.

Ejercicio 6.8

1. "Luisa dijo que el día siguiente comíamos en el restaurante mexicano". 2. "Luisa dijo que esa noche bailaba tango."
3. "Luisa dijo que después de esa canción, bailaba." 4. "Luisa dijo que el mes entrante su familia iba a Argentina."
5. "Luisa dijo que sus vecinos se mudaban pronto." 6. "Luisa dijo que el día siguiente llovía." 7. "Luisa dijo que esa noche terminaba de leer su novela."

Ejercicio 6.9

1. [AC] me desperté, me levanté, me bañé, me vestí 2. [AS] cantaban, brillaba, olía, preparaban 3. [AS] comían, corrían, se meneaban, cantaban 4. [AC] entró, anunció, empezó

Ejercicio 6.10

1. me sentaba [acto habitual] 2. me senté [acto único] 3. iba [acto interrumpido] 4. fui [acto único] 5. iba [acto habitual] 6. comía, buscaba, corría [actos simultáneos, fotográficos] 7. comí, busqué, corrí [actos consecutivos]

Ejercicio 6.11

1. decía 2. diría 3. no dirías 4. no quiso decir 5. no decía

Ejercicio 6.12

1. conocí 2. nos conocimos 3. conocía 4. podías 5. quería, sabía 6. quise, no pude 7. no quiso 8. no quería
9. supiste

Ejercicio 6.13

1. tenían, habían visto 2. comí, había cenado 3. dolían, había bailado

Ejercicio 6.14

1. pasábamos o pasamos 2. tenía 3. había 4. alumbraba 5. íbamos 6. Cocinábamos 7. era 8. nos levantábamos
9. salía 10. preparaba 11. Terminábamos 12. ensillábamos 13. nos íbamos 14. llegábamos 15. estaba 16. había salido

Ejercicio 6.15

1. Estábamos 2. oyeron 3. venían 4. había 5. Nos vestimos 6. fuimos 7. veía 8. formamos 9. empezó
10. duró 11. Agarrábamos 12. Logramos 13. contaron 14. habían provocado

Ejercicio 6.16

1. éramos 2. caían 3. teníamos 4. respetaban 5. cambió 6. Estábamos 7. empezamos 8. imaginamos (OR: imaginábamos) 9. buscamos 10. encontramos 11. Era 12. parecía 13. Era 14. tenía 15. Estaba 16. podía 17. Parecía 18. había abandonado 19. sabía 20. tomó 21. ofrecíamos 22. se acostumbró 23. adoptó

Ejercicio 6.17–6.19

Temas de ensayo.

Compound Tenses

Ejercicio 6.20

1. Estoy escribiendo una carta. 2. Han estado trabajando allí desde la semana pasada. 3. Estaba comiendo cuando llegaste. 4. Había estado en el sol por tres horas. 5. Había estado llamando por dos días. 6. Hemos comido. 7. Habremos comido para entonces. 8. Ayer estuve trabajando en la computadora todo el día. 9. Dijo que habría terminado. 10. Pensé que estaría lloviendo para ahora.

Ejercicio 6.21

Temas de ensayo.

Ways of Expressing the Future

Ejercicio 6.22

1. Mañana comeremos (vamos a comer / comemos) en un restaurante. 2. Esta noche iremos (vamos a ir / vamos) al cine. 3. Te llamaré (voy a llamar / llamo) esta tarde. 4. ¿Qué harás (vas a hacer / haces) esta noche?

Ejercicio 6.23

Temas de ensayo.

Conditional

Ejercicio 6.24

1. ¿Podrías ayudarme con esto? 2. ¿Tendrías tiempo para ayudarme? 3. No deberías hacer eso. 4. Quisiera que vinieras. [NOTE: Quisiera is **not** the conditional. Why not?]

Ejercicio 6.25

1. Pensaba que llegarían a tiempo. 2. Creía que lo terminarían pronto. 3. Dijo que lo haría. 4. Sabía que cumpliría con su promesa.

Ejercicio 6.26

Temas de ensayo.

Probability

Ejercicio 6.27

1. No estudiarás lo suficiente. 2. Sería marciano. Estaría enfermo. Algo lo habría asustado. 3. Estará en el sótano. Habrá ido a la tienda.

Ejercicio 6.28

Temas de ensayo.

Subjunctive (Nominal Clauses)

Ejercicio 6.29

1. trabaje 2. tienes 3. pagues 4. salgamos 5. sirvamos 6. vaya 7. aprendan 8. vemos 9. comes 10. lleve
11. puedan 12. caigan bien 13. quiera 14. puede 15. dejen 16. sea 17. lleve 18. sorprendan 19. escuches
20. se quede

Ejercicio 6.30

1. debemos 2. se levanten 3. gane 4. lleve 5. sea 6. llueva 7. quieran 8. quiere 9. griten 10. llegue 11. contro-
len 12. vea 13. va 14. haga 15. lleve 16. se callen 17. salga 18. denuncie 19. sabe 20. pague

Ejercicio 6.31

1. quiere 2. quiera 3. se levantaba 4. se levante 5. duermas 6. vayas 7. puedan 8. hagas 9. seas 10. griten
11. está 12. esté 13. sepan 14. llame 15. tomes

Ejercicio 6.32

1. (Ella) me deja manejar. 2. Espero poder hacerlo. (OR: Ojalá que pueda hacerlo.) 3. Espero que puedas hacerlo. (OR:
Ojalá que puedas hacerlo.) 4. Siento que va a llover. 5. Siento que vaya a llover. (OR: Lamento que vaya a llover.)
6. Siento no poder hacerlo. (OR: Lamento no poder hacerlo.)

Ejercicio 6.33–6.37

Temas de ensayo.

Subjunctive (Adjectival Clauses)

Ejercicio 6.38

1. calcula 2. sepa 3. pueda 4. puede 5. pueda 6. puede 7. dije 8. digan 9. digan

Ejercicio 6.39

Temas de ensayo.

Subjunctive (Adverbial Clauses)

Ejercicio 6.40

1. salimos 2. tengas 3. puedas 4. llueva 5. se vaya 6. se arrepienta 7. se acuesten 8. pudo 9. pueda
10. paguen 11. quieras 12. tenía 13. llueve 14. vean 15. digas

Ejercicio 6.41

1. Ella no irá a menos que vayamos nosotros. 2. Lo haré con tal (de) que no se lo digas a nadie. 3. Nos iremos tan
pronto como te vistas. 4. Él insistirá hasta que ella acepte. 5. No conozco a nadie que pueda hacer eso sin que tú le
expliques cómo.

Ejercicio 6.42

Temas de ensayo.

Subjunctive (Sequence of Tenses)

Ejercicio 6.43

1. No creo que nuestros amigos lleguen mañana. **2.** Parece increíble que Raúl viva en Suiza. **3.** Me sorprende que los vecinos ya hayan visto esa película. **4.** Dudo que ayer hiciera calor. **5.** Me sorprende que se haya levantado (OR: se levantara) a las cinco. **6.** Parece dudoso que ya hayan terminado a esa hora. **7.** Lamento que mi abuelo ya hubiera muerto cuando llegué. **8.** Mi padre dudaba que pronto estuviera lista la cena. **9.** Mi tía se quejaba de que siempre hiciera frío en el monte. **10.** Era imposible que tú bailaras el tango a los cinco años. **11.** Temían que los perros se hubieran escapado. **12.** A Roberto le molestaba que Luisa nunca les hubiera dicho el secreto a sus hijos. **13.** Me sorprendería mucho que hubieran regresado para la medianoche. **14.** Yo tenía miedo que Miguel ya hubiera leído esa novela.

Ejercicio 6.44

1. pudieran **2.** hiciera **3.** gustara **4.** fuera **5.** tuviera **6.** quisieras **7.** abrieras **8.** fuera

Ejercicio 6.45

1. Me parecía increíble que cantaran bien. **2.** Dudo que ellos caminaran. (OR: hayan caminado; hubieran caminado) **3.** Ellos no creyeron que yo hubiera caminado. **4.** Ella se quejó de que yo perdiera las llaves. (OR: hubiera perdido) **5.** Me alegro de que por fin pudiéramos ver la película. (OR: hayamos podido) **6.** A él le sorprendió que los perros no hubieran ladrado en toda la noche.

Ejercicio 6.46

1. llamaran **2.** fueran **3.** explicara **4.** pudiera **5.** fueran **6.** pudieras **7.** se callaran / despertaran **8.** se hubiera cortado

Ejercicio 6.47–6.51

Temas de ensayo.

Subjunctive (If [Si] Clauses)

Ejercicio 6.52

1. hubiera habido (OR: hubiera) **2.** se compraría **3.** fuera **4.** habríamos tenido **5.** ayudaría **6.** se hubieran visto **7.** fuera

Ejercicio 6.53–6.54

Temas de ensayo.

Subjunctive (Ojalá)

Ejercicio 6.55

1. Ojalá que no hubiéramos ido. **2.** Ojalá que me hubieras escuchado. **3.** Ojalá que comas hoy. **4.** Ojalá que me pudiera ver ahora. **5.** Ojalá que no lo hayan hecho. **6.** Ojalá que lleguemos allá a tiempo. **7.** Ojalá que hayan terminado. **8.** Ojalá que le guste. **9.** Ojalá que lo hayan comprado. **10.** Ojalá que me pudiera oír.

Ejercicio 6.56

Respuestas personales.

Subjunctive (Expressions of Leave-Taking)

Ejercicio 6.57

1. Que te mejores. (OR: Que te alivies.) **2.** Que tengas un buen fin de semana. **3.** Que pasen buen día. **4.** Que se divierta.

Ejercicio 6.58

1. Que te vaya bien. **2.** Que le vaya bien. **3.** Que les vaya bien. **4.** Que os vaya bien.

Ejercicio 6.59

1. Que lo pases bien. **2.** Que lo pase bien. **3.** Que lo pasen bien. **4.** Que lo paséis bien.

Ejercicio 6.60

Respuestas individualizadas.

Infinitives and Present Participles

Ejercicio 6.61

1. Beber **2.** cantar **3.** viajar **4.** decir **5.** hablar **6.** correr **7.** salir **8.** fumar

Ejercicio 6.62

1. Ese idioma es difícil de aprender. **2.** Es difícil aprender ese idioma. **3.** Esa receta es fácil de preparar. **4.** Es fácil decir la verdad. **5.** Es posible vivir más de noventa años. **6.** Algunas cosas son imposibles de cambiar.

Ejercicio 6.63

Ninguna de las frases del 6.63 usaría el participio presente en español.

Ejercicio 6.64

(Puede haber variación.)

1. Ése es uno de los problemas mundiales **que está aumentando.** **2.** ¡Qué persona más **interesante!** **3.** Es una de las expertas **más importantes** en esa materia. **4.** Necesito comprar papel **para escribir.** **5.** Ese sicólogo dice que todos los problemas de la adolescencia surgen de los dolores **de crecimiento.** **6.** Tienen agua **corriente.** **7.** Toma una foto del jarro **con** líquido azul. **8.** La corte quería una cantidad de objetos **de ella** (OR: **que le pertenecían a ella, que le pertenecieran a ella**) **9.** Ahí estaba, **parado** en medio del cuarto. **10.** La película fue **aburrida.** **11.** Es un juego **divertido.** **12.** Encontré al gato **acostado** en la cama. **13.** Estaba **sentada** frente a mí en el cine. **14.** Este ejercicio es **entretenido.** **15.** ¿Tiene agua **potable?**

Ejercicio 6.65

(Todas las frases del 6.65 podrían usar el participio presente, porque se trata de verbos en el progresivo y de adverbios.)

1. Mira: están **aumentando** el peso. **2.** Estaban **dirigiendo** el tráfico para el lado. **3.** Se fueron **corriendo.**
4. El conferenciante nos estaba **aburriendo** a todos. **5.** Estaban apenas **sentándose** cuando se acabó la película.
6. Estábamos **entreteniendo** a los invitados.

Ejercicio 6.66

1.a. *Increasing* es un adjetivo. **1.b.** *Increasing* es parte del verbo progresivo. **2.a.** *Boring* es un adjetivo. **2.b.** *Boring* es parte del verbo progresivo. **3.a.** *Sitting* es parte del verbo progresivo. **3.b.** *Sitting* es un adjetivo.

1.a. Me preocupa mi peso que aumenta. **1.b.** Nos van a aumentar los impuestos. (NOTE: *This progressive in English indicates future, which cannot be translated with the progressive in Spanish.*) **2.a.** Esa clase es aburrida. **2.b.** ¿Te estoy aburriendo? **3.a.** Me estaba sentando cuando sonó el teléfono. **3.b.** Tengo noticias graves: estás sentado (o sentada)?

Ejercicio 6.67

1. Deben de haber comido.   2. Tiene que comer más.   3. Pensaban ir a la playa.   4. No tengo nada que ponerme.
5. Ponte el abrigo antes de salir.   6. Para ver esos efectos, hay que ponerse lentes especiales.   7. Estaba contento de verla.   8. Al entrar, se quitaron los zapatos.   9. Mi hermano hizo venir al veterinario.   10. Esas semillas son difíciles de plantar.   11. Ese libro es fácil de leer.   12. Es fácil leer ese libro.   13. Ver es creer. (OR: Ver para creer.)   14. Me prohíbe manejar.   15. A los niños les encanta jugar en el agua.   16. Se fue sin decir nada.   17. Se arrepintieron después de colgar el teléfono.   18. Se separaron sin realmente haber llegado a conocerse.   19. No me impidas moverme (OR: mudarme).
20. Me duele la espalda de haber trabajado tanto en el jardín.

Ejercicio 6.68–6.69

Temas de ensayo.

Verbs Like *Gustar*

Ejercicio 6.70

(Lo que está entre paréntesis no es obligatorio, pero no es incorrecto.)

1. (Tú) le caes bien (a él).   2. (Ellos) me caen bien (a mí).   3. (Nosotros) le caemos bien (a ella).   4. (Ella) les cae bien (a ellos).   5. (Él) nos cae bien (a nosotros).   6. (Ellos) te caen bien (a ti).

Ejercicio 6.71

1. No le caes bien a nadie. Le caigo bien **a él.**   2. Sí, pero no le caes bien **a ella.**   3. **Ella** te cae bien **a ti,** pero **tú** no le caes bien **a ella.**

Ejercicio 6.72

1. A mí. (Who is interested in magic? Me. OR: I am.)   2. A mí. (Whose turn is it to pay the bill? Mine.)   3. A mí. (Who liked dinner? Me. OR: I did.)   4. Yo. (Who ate more? Me. OR: I did.)

Ejercicio 6.73

1. Lo quiero.   2. Me encantan mis clases.   3. Me gusta tu casa.   4. Me caen bien mis vecinos.

Ejercicio 6.74

1. Les hace falta comida.   2. Les quedan dos días.   3. Nos sobró tiempo.   4. Me haces falta.   5. Le faltan veinte centavos.

Ejercicio 6.75

Temas de ensayo.

Reflexive Verbs

Ejercicio 6.76

1. Nos aburrimos en la fiesta.   2. ¿Te acordaste de las llaves?   3. Se acostumbró a él muy pronto.   4. Me alegro de verte.
5. Se avergonzó de su mentira.   6. Me bajé del autobús (camión, guagua, bus, ómnibus...) en la tercera parada.   7. Los otros niños siempre se burlaban de mí.   8. Vas a tener que enfrentarte (OR: encararte) a ese problema algún día.   9. Se dio cuenta de que tenía que despedirse de mí.   10. Todos debemos esforzarnos por mantener limpio el medio ambiente.
11. ¿Cómo se enteró de eso?   12. No te fíes de nadie.   13. Fíjate en sus ojos cuando bailan.   14. ¿Dónde nos vamos a encontrar con él para almorzar?   15. ¿Por qué se mudaron tus padres?   16. ¿Cómo se llama?   17. Por favor no te vayas ahora.   18. No debes meterte con esos niños.   19. Se quedaron con nosotros durante el verano.   20. Se peleó con su padre.   21. Te pareces a mí.   22. Ahora va a ponerse a ladrar.   23. Me siento triste hoy.   24. Me siento aquí.   25. Me sentí triste ayer.   26. Me senté aquí ayer.   27. Me sentía triste cuando oía esa canción.   28. Me sentaba aquí.   29. Se quedó con mi libro.   30. Sécate bien.

Ejercicio 6.77

1. de 2. con 3. de 4. de 5. por 6. a 7. por 8. en 9. de 10. por 11. en 12. a 13. a / a 14. en 15. de 16. de 17. Ø 18. con 19. de 20. de

Ejercicio 6.78

Temas de ensayo.

Indirect Discourse

Ejercicio 6.79

1.a. Dice que iremos al cine esta noche. **1.b.** Ayer dijo que iríamos al cine anoche. **1.c.** Esta mañana dijo que iríamos al cine esta noche. **2.a.** Ella supone que yo sé hacerlo. **2.b.** Ella suponía que yo sabía hacerlo. **2.c.** Ella supuso que yo sabía hacerlo. **3.a.** Te digo que yo hice tu trabajo. **3.b.** Le dije que yo había hecho su trabajo. **3.c.** Me dijo que él (ella) había hecho mi trabajo. **4.a.** Te pido que te levantes. **4.b.** Me pidió que me levantara. **4.c.** Le pedí que se levantara. **5.a.** Dice que si pudiera ir ahora, lo haría. **5.b.** Dijo que si pudiera ir entonces, lo haría. **6.a.** Me preguntó esta mañana si quería que fuéramos la semana entrante. **6.b.** Me preguntó el mes pasado si quería que fuéramos la próxima semana. **6.c.** Sé que me preguntará si quiero que vayamos la semana entrante. **7.b.** Te estoy diciendo que si quieres comer, que comas. **7.a.** Me respondió que si quería comer, que comiera. **8.a.** Te ruego que te vayas. **8.b.** Me suplicó que me fuera. **8.c.** Insistieron en que me fuera. **9.a.** Siempre me pregunta si sé qué hora es, y yo siempre le contesto que no. **9.b.** Me preguntó si sabía qué hora era, y yo le contesté que no. **10.a.** El domingo por la tarde siempre nos pregunta si nos gustaría salir a cenar, y nosotros siempre le gritamos que sí. **10.b.** Nos preguntó si nos gustaría salir a cenar, y nosotros le gritamos que sí.

Ejercicio 6.80

Temas de ensayo.

Chapter 6 Review

Ejercicio 6.81

1. era 2. íbamos 3. presenciábamos 4. era 5. recuerdo 6. he visto 7. mezclado 8. quedan 9. tocaban 10. desfilaban 11. se presentaba 12. lanzaba 13. salía 14. parecía 15. gritaba 16. indicaba 17. acercaba 18. dejaba 19. cortaban 20. daba 21. limpiaban 22. entrara 23. dejó (OR: ha dejado) 24. fue 25. vino 26. era 27. se había hecho 28. pensaban 29. era 30. iba 31. fue 32. se quitó 33. gritó 34. se rió 35. tenía 36. sería 37. acababan 38. tuviera 39. tapara 40. hubiera considerado o consideraba 41. fue 42. dejó 43. se paró 44. sacó 45. se peinó 46. se moría 47. pasaba 48. fue 49. llegué 50. me mudé 51. ocurrió 52. contenían 53. fui 54. pensé 55. Fueron 56. hicieron 57. sabía 58. pasaba 59. entrara 60. había pensado 61. se trataba 62. tenía 63. matara 64. hiriera 65. gustaba 66. hicieran 67. molestaba 68. dejé 69. afectara 70. hubiera reaccionado 71. hubiera habido 72. hubiera sido 73. se haya muerto 74. podría 75. interesaría 76. daría 77. matar 78. dudo 79. pueda 80. lastime 81. tengo 82. me avergüenzo 83. haber asistido 84. haber pensado 85. tuviera 86. preferiría 87. representan 88. pienso 89. es 90. reconozcamos 91. seamos 92. es 93. crían 94. participar 95. estoy 96. seguirá 97. logren 98. prohíban 99. ocurra 100. será

Ejercicio 6.82

Temas de ensayo.

Chapter 7 *Ser, Estar, Haber, Hacer,* and *Tener*

Ⓑ *Ser* vs. *Estar*

Ejercicio 7.1

1. es 2. es 3. es 4. es 5. es 6. es 7. es 8. está 9. es 10. es 11. está 12. es 13. es 14. está 15. está

Ejercicio 7.2

1. Soy 2. soy 3. Estoy 4. Estoy 5. Soy 6. Soy *(boring)* OR: Estoy *(bored)* 7. Soy *(good)* OR: Estoy [*best avoided because of its sexual implications in some dialects; but it can mean "in good health" in some dialects*] 8. Estoy 9. Estoy *(I am sick)* OR: Soy *(I am a sick person or a patient* [*For example, if someone in a hospital thinks mistakenly that a patient is a nurse, she might say: No soy enfermera, soy enferma.*]) 10. Soy 11. Estoy 12. Soy 13. Estoy 14. Estoy 15. Estoy 16. Estoy

Ejercicio 7.3

1. Estoy de regreso. OR: Estoy de vuelta. OR: Regresé. 2. Soy ciego(a). [*permanent*] Estoy ciego(a). [*as in "blinded" by something temporarily*] 3. Estoy aburrido(a). *(I am bored.)* 4. Soy aburrido(a). *(I am a boring person.)* 5. Soy listo(a). 6. Tengo calor. OR: Estoy caliente. [*The second would be used if I touch my skin and it feels hot to the touch, but I am not necessarily feeling hot at the time: actually I could feel cold.*] 7. Estoy cómodo(a). 8. Terminé. OR: He terminado. OR: Ya acabé. 9. Estoy emocionado(a). 10. Soy gordo(a). [*by nature*] Estoy gordo(a). [*current condition*] 11. Estoy harto(a). 12. Terminé. OR: He terminado. OR: Ya acabé. 13. Soy de Ithaca. 14. Me alegro. 15. Soy bueno(a). 16. Estoy contento(a). [*reaction to something*] Soy feliz. [*My life is perfect.*] 17. Estoy aquí. 18. Estoy muerto(a). OR: Estoy agotado(a). 19. Tengo hambre. 20. Estoy en la universidad. 21. Me interesa. 22. Llegué tarde. 23. Soy maduro(a). 24. Estoy bien. 25. Soy callado(a). [*by nature*] Estoy callado(a). [*I am not speaking now.*] 26. Estoy listo(a). 27. Soy rico(a). 28. Me apena oír eso. OR: Me da pena oír eso. 29. Estoy enfermo(a). 30. Estoy sentado(a). 31. Lo siento. 32. Estoy de pie. 33. Soy bajo(a). [*not tall*] No tengo suficiente dinero. [*short of funds*] 34. Soy yo el (la) que te di las flores. 35. Estoy trabajando. 36. Nací.

Ejercicio 7.4

1. Está bien que llegues temprano. 2. Era (Fue) bueno estar allí. 3. "Ser o no ser", he ahí el problema (OR: ése es el problema / el dilema OR: ésa es la cuestión, etc.). 4. Es hora de irse. 5. Estábamos cómodos porque estábamos sentados. 6. Era (Fue) interesante ver que siempre llegaban tarde. 7. Estaba claro que no estaba funcionando bien. 8. Estaba contento que yo hubiera terminado. 9. Lo siento pero no tengo hambre. 10. Me alegro de que estés de acuerdo conmigo.

Ejercicio 7.5

1. es 2. Es 3. está 4. Está 5. es 6. es 7. Es 8. Son 9. Está 10. son 11. están 12. está 13. es 14. es 15. es 16. están 17. está 18. estamos 19. está 20. es 21. es 22. está 23. fue 24. están 25. está

Ejercicio 7.6

1. está 2. son 3. es 4. es 5. está 6. está 7. está 8. está 9. está 10. está 11. Estás, estoy, estoy 12. es 13. es, está 14. es 15. es, Están

Ejercicio 7.7

Preguntas de respuesta variada.

Ser vs. *Estar* (With Past Participles: Passive Voice and Resultant Condition)

Ejercicio 7.8

1. Le dieron el coche. [*sujeto tácito: sus padres*] Se le dio el coche. 2. El dueño construyó la casa. 3. Se venden libros allí. 4. ¿Por qué no me dijeron? [*ustedes o ellos—sujeto tácito*] ¿Por qué no se me dijo? 5. A ella no la invitaron. [*sujeto*

tácito: los que dieron la fiesta] No se le invitó.   **6.** La luz me despertó.   **7.** Lo llevaron al aeropuerto. [sujeto tácito: sus amigos, sus padres, etc.] Se le llevó al aeropuerto.   **8.** El león atacó al cazador y lo mató.   **9.** Se prohíbe fumar aquí. **10.** Al hombre no le leyeron sus derechos. (OR: Al hombre no se le leyeron sus derechos.)

◆C *Estar* vs. *Haber*

Ejercicio 7.9

1. Hay   **2.** están   **3.** Hay   **4.** están   **5.** Hay   **6.** hay   **7.** hay   **8.** están   **9.** hay   **10.** hay

◆D Expressions with *Estar* and *Tener*

Ejercicio 7.10

1. estaba, estaba, tenían, estaban   **2.** tenía, tenía   **3.** está, tener, tiene   **4.** estuve, tenía, tengo   **5.** estamos, Estamos, estaremos   **6.** tienes, estoy, tengo, tengo, tengo, tengo   **7.** están, tengan   **8.** están, estarán

Ejercicio 7.11

1. Parecen estar de prisa.   **2.** ¡Apúrate, Jimmy!   **3.** Lo siento por llegar tarde.   **4.** Estoy contento(a).   **5.** Yo estaba de pie y tú estabas sentado.   **6.** ¡Siéntate, Luisita!   **7.** Tú tienes razón y yo estoy equivocado(a).   **8.** Tenía sueño, me dormí y tuve un sueño rarísimo.

Ser, Estar, Tener, Haber, and *Hacer* (Review)

Ejercicio 7.12

1. He estado de rodillas demasiado tiempo.   **2.** ¿Hace frío en el invierno aquí?   **3.** Los niños tenían sed.   **4.** No sé por qué estoy triste.   **5.** No es que la fiesta sea aburrida, es que la gente está aburrida.   **6.** ¿Estaba lloviendo?   **7.** ¿Cuántos cuartos hay en ese edificio?   **8.** ¿De dónde eres?   **9.** ¿La conferencia es en este edificio?

Ejercicio 7.13

1. está   **2.** son   **3.** he   **4.** tengo

Ejercicio 7.14

Temas de ensayo.

◆E Time Expressions

Ejercicio 7.15

1. Hace una hora que estoy aquí. Llevo una hora aquí.   **2.** Hacía veinte minutos que trabajaban cuando ella entró. Llevaban veinte minutos trabajando cuando ella entró.   **3.** Hace una semana que lo llamamos. [No se puede usar **llevar** aquí.] **4.** Hacía muchos años que no se cortaba el pelo. Llevaba muchos años sin cortarse el pelo.   **5.** Hace tres años que mi sobrina aprende el ballet. Mi sobrina lleva tres años aprendiendo ballet.   **6.** Hace dos meses que vino a visitarnos. [No se puede usar **llevar** aquí.]   **7.** ¿Cuánto tiempo hace que esperamos? ¿Cuánto tiempo llevamos esperando?

Ejercicio 7.16

Temas de ensayo.

Chapter 7 Review

Ejercicio 7.17

1. estamos 2. Es 3. hay 4. están 5. está 6. tenía 7. es 8. tienen 9. es 10. hay 11. Estamos 12. hace 13. hay 14. estamos 15. tener 16. somos 17. están 18. esté 19. fue 20. tiene 21. estaremos 22. tengo 23. es

Ejercicio 7.18

Temas de ensayo.

Chapter 8   Lexical Variations

Ⓑ Terms and Expressions

1. *Acabar*

Ejercicio 8.1

1. acabo de 2. acababa de 3. acabé de 4. se me acabó 5. acabé 6. acababa, acabo

Ejercicio 8.2

1. Acabé mi trabajo. 2. Acabaron de reparar el puente en octubre. 3. Habrá acabado con la construcción para las tres de la tarde. 4. Acabo de levantarme. 5. Cuando llegué, acababan de comer. 6. El examen se acabó a las diez. 7. Nos acabamos el pan. 8. Se nos acabó el pan.

2. Apply

Ejercicio 8.3

1. solicitar 2. aplicar 3. solicitar 4. solicitar 5. aplicación 6. solicitud

Ejercicio 8.4

1. Solicitó una beca. 2. El doctor aplicó presión a la herida para parar el sangrado. 3. Aplique este ungüento tres veces al día. 4. Solicitaremos un préstamo en el banco. 5. El puesto que solicitaste ya no existe. 6. Envié mi solicitud para el empleo (trabajo, puesto) ayer.

3. Ask

Ejercicio 8.5

1. preguntó 2. pedí 3. pedí 4. preguntó 5. hicieron 6. cuestión 7. pregunta 8. pedido

Ejercicio 8.6

1. Te quiero pedir un favor. 2. Le hice una pregunta. 3. Me pidió que la llevara al pueblo. 4. Me preguntó: —De veras tienes dieciséis años? 5. Le preguntamos si había comido. 6. Nos preguntaron por qué habíamos llamado. 7. No me hagas tantas preguntas. 8. Pensé que era una cuestión de ética.

4. At

Ejercicio 8.7

1. en 2. en 3. a, en 4. en 5. a 6. a 7. en 8. a

Ejercicio 8.8

1. En este momento, no puedo ir.   2. Mi primera clase es a las ocho.   3. Estamos en la universidad.   4. No estaban en casa.   5. Vamos a sentarnos a la mesa.   6. En México me quedaba en la casa de mi tío a veces.

5. ATTEND

Ejercicio 8.9

1. atiéndanme   2. atenderla   3. asistí   4. atendió   5. asistió   6. asistencia   7. atento   8. asistencia

Ejercicio 8.10

1. Asistimos a la conferencia por la tarde.   2. No asistió a clase porque estaba enferma.   3. ¿Puedo atenderlo? (OR: ¿Puedo atenderte?, ¿Puedo atenderlos?, ¿Puedo atenderos?)   4. Atiende a los invitados, por favor.   5. ¿Tuviste buena asistencia?   6. Algunos políticos quieren eliminar la asistencia social.   7. Los jóvenes hoy en día son más atentos con sus mayores que en la generación anterior.

6. BECAUSE

Ejercicio 8.11

1. por, a causa de   2. porque   3. por, a causa del frío   4. por, a causa de   5. gracias a, por, a causa de   6. por   7. Por, A causa de (Gracias a—*only if the speaker did not want to go to the movies*)

Ejercicio 8.12

1. Fui a casa a causa de (por) la enfermedad de mi hermano.   2. Tuvieron que cancelar el proceso por las noticias. 3. Tuvieron que dejarlo ir por eso.   4. Perdió la voz por gritar tanto.   5. No salieron porque estaba nevando.   6. Es gracias a tu amistad que logré llegar donde estoy.

7. BECOME OR GET

Ejercicio 8.13

1. se hizo / llegó a ser   2. se puso   3. se convirtió en   4. se puso   5. llegó a ser

Ejercicio 8.14

1. Me alegro de que sea viernes.   2. Los niños se callaron.   3. Se calmó después de eso.   4. Se cansaron de caminar. 5. Me enfermé durante las vacaciones.   6. Se enojaron porque no escribí.   7. Se envejece rápido en este trabajo.   8. El caballo se tranquilizó después de la inyección.   9. Me fijé que se había puesto pálida.   10. Se hizo médico.   11. Quería llegar a ser una ciudadana respetada.   12. La flor se había convertido en fruta.

REVIEW: *ACABAR,* APPLY, ASK, AT, ATTEND, BECAUSE, BECOME

Ejercicio 8.15

Temas de ensayo.

8. BUT

Ejercicio 8.16

1. pero   2. sino   3. sino   4. pero   5. sino que   6. pero

9. COME AND GO

Ejercicio 8.17

1. ven 2. voy 3. voy 4. llegar (OR: venir) 5. vine 6. ir

Ejercicio 8.18

1. ¿Cuándo vienen a vernos tus padres? 2. Fue al cine. 3. Voy al cine. 4. ¿Puedo ir contigo? 5. —¡Ven acá, Juanita! —¡Voy! 6. Siempre llegan tarde. 7. No llegues tarde. 8. Lo siento por llegar tarde. 9. ¿Cuándo llegaste?

10. *DESPEDIR*

Ejercicio 8.19

1. nos despidieron 2. despidieron 3. nos despedimos 4. los despedimos

Ejercicio 8.20

1. Me despidieron ayer. 2. Me despedí de mis amigos. 3. Lo despedí. 4. Me despedí de ella. 5. Nos despedimos en la puerta.

11. EXIT AND SUCCESS

Ejercicio 8.21

1. sucesos 2. salidas 3. éxitos

Ejercicio 8.22

1. Si trabajamos mucho, tendremos éxito. 2. Nuestro éxito depende de nuestro esfuerzo. 3. La salida está a la derecha. 4. A mi abuela le gustaba hablar de los terribles sucesos de La Primera Guerra Mundial.

12. GO AND LEAVE

Ejercicio 8.23

1. salieron 2. ir 3. salir 4. irse 5. habían ido 6. habían salido 7. dejó de 8. dejó 9. dejaron 10. dejó

Ejercicio 8.24

1. Vamos a la escuela. 2. Se fue hace una hora. 3. El gato salió. 4. Van a salir esta noche. 5. La enfermera salió a almorzar. 6. Estábamos jugando afuera en el parque, y Luisito se enojó y se fue. 7. ¿A qué hora sale tu vuelo? 8. ¿Podría dejarme en la esquina, por favor? 9. No me dejas hacer nada. 10. Dejaron de gritar.

13. GUIDE

Ejercicio 8.25

1. la 2. la 3. el

Ejercicio 8.26

1. Nuestro guía en el museo era un anciano. 2. El guía / La guía era de Venezuela. 3. Encontrará las reglas en la guía.

Review: But, Come and Go, *Despedir*, Exit and Success, Go and Leave, Guide

Ejercicio 8.27

Temas de ensayo.

14. Know

Ejercicio 8.28

1. sé 2. conocen 3. saben 4. conocen 5. sabe 6. sabe 7. sabe 8. sé 9. saber

Ejercicio 8.29

1. Te conozco. 2. Conoció a su nueva esposa en México. 3. No conoce la región. 4. Sabe mi número de teléfono. 5. Saben patinar. 6. Sabíamos que hacía frío. 7. No sabían qué decir. 8. ¿Sabes qué hora es? 9. ¿Conoces ese hotel? 10. No sabía nadar.

15. Learn

Ejercicio 8.30

1. aprender 2. averiguar, enterarse de *(find out)*; saber *(know)*; aprender *(learn)* 3. averiguó 4. supe

Ejercicio 8.31

1. Aprendió a bailar. 2. Se enteraron de nuestro secreto. (OR: Averiguaron nuestro secreto.) 3. Cuando supe (OR: me enteré) que estabas aquí, vine en seguida.

16. Meet

Ejercicio 8.32

1. conocí 2. encontrarnos 3. conocer 4. tropezar con (OR: toparme con, encontrarme con) 5. encontrarme con 6. encuentro

Ejercicio 8.33

1. La conoció en la oficina. 2. Entonces decidieron encontrarse por la tarde para discutir el trabajo. 3. Adivina con quién me topé *(ran into)* en camino a la biblioteca. (OR: Advina a quién conocí [*was introduced to*] en camino a la biblioteca.)

17. Order

Ejercicio 8.34

1. el 2. la 3. el 4. la

Ejercicio 8.35

1. Todo se tenía que colocar en un orden específico (OR: tenía que colocarse). 2. Lo hice porque recibí la orden de arriba. 3. —Hola, me llamo Julia Ruiz. —Hola, Victoria Vargas, a tus órdenes (OR: a sus órdenes).

18. *Pensar*

Ejercicio 8.36

1. en 2. Ø 3. en 4. de 5. Ø 6. de

Ejercicio 8.37

1. No puedo dejar de pensar en ti.   2. ¿En qué pensabas?   3. ¿Qué piensas de mí?   4. No quiso decirme lo que pensó del taller.   5. Pensamos visitar a nuestros amigos la semana que viene.

19. PEOPLE VS. MACHINES

Ejercicio 8.38

1. funciona   2. apagó   3. arranca   4. andaba   5. se nos acabó

Ejercicio 8.39

1. Los niños corrían.   2. Ese motor dejó de andar (OR: funcionar).   3. Trabajan de nueve a cinco.   4. No funciona así. 5. ¿Cuándo empezó la película?   6. Voy a arrancar el coche para que se caliente.   7. Las luces se apagaron después de las diez.   8. Hace ejercicio todos los días.   9. Podemos resolverlo.   10. Salí corriendo.   11. Se tropezó con su primo en el museo.   12. Las baterías se descargaron.   13. A mi reloj se le acabó la cuerda (OR: la batería).   14. Bajó las escaleras corriendo.   15. Se encontraron con sus amigos en el bar.   16. Chocó con la pared.   17. Apaga las luces.   18. Todo salió bien.

20. PLAY

Ejercicio 8.40

1. partida   2. jugada, partido (OR: juego)   3. tocar, jugar   4. obra, partido   5. juego   6. toco

Ejercicio 8.41

1. Jugaron al tenis toda la tarde.   2. ¿A qué juegas?   3. ¿Tocas la guitarra?   4. No juegues con el violín de tu hermana. 5. Esta noche va a tocar el violín.

REVIEW: KNOW, LEARN, MEET, ORDER, *PENSAR*, PEOPLE VS. MACHINES, PLAY

Ejercicio 8.42

Temas de ensayo.

21. PUT

Ejercicio 8.43

1. se puso   2. aguantaba   3. soportar   4. mantener   5. apoyó (OR: había apoyado)   6. ahorrar

Ejercicio 8.44

1. Me puso la mano en el hombro.   2. Me puse las botas.   3. Metió la mano en su chaqueta.   4. Ayúdame a poner la mesa, por favor.   5. La cara se le puso verde.   6. No le metas el dedo en el ojo a tu hermano.   7. No soporto tu actitud. 8. Mi madre mantiene a la familia con dos trabajos (OR: empleos, puestos).   9. Mi hermano me apoya en lo que sea que yo quiera hacer.   10. ¿Por qué aguantas semejante estupidez?

22. REALIZE

Ejercicio 8.45

1. realizar   2. darse cuenta de   3. realizar

Ejercicio 8.46

1. Me doy cuenta de que no puedo realizar tus sueños en un instante.   2. Si realizas todos tus deberes con responsabilidad, te puedes quedar.   3. Se dio cuenta de que era infeliz.   4. Se dio cuenta de que sus sueños eran imposibles.

23. SERVE

Ejercicio 8.47

1. les 2. les 3. les 4. la 5. lo 6. sírvalo

Ejercicio 8.48

1. No me sirvas (OR: No me sirva [usted]) tanto arroz, por favor. 2. ¿Cómo puedo servirle? 3. La cena se sirve por lo general a las ocho. Esta noche la serviremos a las siete y media.

24. SPEND

Ejercicio 8.49

1. pasar 2. gastar 3. pasar 4. desperdiciar 5. pasé 6. desperdiciar, gastar

Ejercicio 8.50

1. Gastas más dinero en tus hijos que en ti. 2. Pasé tres horas en (OR: Me pasé tres horas con) este trabajo ayer. 3. Pasó un tiempo en la cárcel. 4. Es terrible desperdiciar el tiempo y el dinero.

25. TAKE

Ejercicio 8.51

1. sacar 2. apuntar 3. bajar 4. traer 5. quitarse 6. llevarse 7. llevar 8. traer 9. subir 10. tener

Ejercicio 8.52

1. ¿Qué te gustaría tomar? 2. Llevó su cerveza a la mesa. 3. Tomó el lápiz y se fue. 4. —¿Te podemos llevar? —No, gracias, tomaré el autobús. 5. Esto está tomando demasiado tiempo. 6. Toma. Esto es tuyo. 7. Llevamos la cámara a la tienda. 8. Se llevaron nuestras toallas. 9. Déjame apuntar esto. 10. ¿Quieres que te baje los libros? 11. Subieron la comida al cuarto. 12. Tenemos que sacar la basura. 13. No te quites los calcetines. 14. El examen tendrá lugar aquí. 15. ¿Puedo llevar a un amigo a tu fiesta? 16. Trae tu propia bebida.

26. TIME

Ejercicio 8.53

1. tiempo 2. tiempo 3. vez 4. hora 5. rato 6. vez

Ejercicio 8.54

1. ¿Tienes tiempo para hablar conmigo? 2. ¿Qué tiempo hacía? (OR: ¿Cómo estuvo el tiempo?) 3. ¿Cuántas veces te lo tengo que decir? 4. Esa vez fue diferente. 5. No me quiso decir qué hora era. 6. Sabía (OR: Supe) que era hora de levantarme. 7. Estará aquí dentro de un ratito. 8. Nos divertimos. 9. Tuvimos buen tiempo.

27. WHAT

Ejercicio 8.55

1. lo que (*To use* que, *you would have to invert the verb and the subject:* No le importaba qué pensaba yo...) 2. Cuál 3. Qué 4. Qué, Qué, Cómo

Ejercicio 8.56

1. ¿Qué es un "cucurucho"? 2. ¿Cuál es el tuyo? 3. ¿Qué países visitaste? 4. ¿Cómo? 5. Lo que no sabes no te hará daño.

Review: Put, Realize, Serve, Spend, Take, Time, What

Ejercicio 8.57

Temas de ensayo.